Introduction to Organizational Behavior

The Goodyear Series in
Administration and Business Management

Lyman W. Porter
Joseph W. McGuire
Series Editors

MICHAEL BEER, *Organization Change and Development: A Systems View*
(1980)
Y. N. CHANG, FILEMON CAMPO-FLORES, *Business Policy and Strategy:
Text and Cases* (1980)
  Business Policy and Strategy (soft-cover version—text only) (1980)
G. JAMES FRANCIS, GENE MILBOURN, JR., *Human Behavior in the Work
Environment* (1980)
ROBERT H. MILES, *Macro Organizational Behavior* (1980)
  Resourcebook in Macro Organizational Behavior (1980)
BRIAN HAWKINS and PAUL PRESTON, *Managerial Communications* (1981)
ANDREW D. SZILAGYI, JR., *Management and Performance* (1981)

Introduction to Organizational Behavior

Richard M. Steers
University of Oregon

Goodyear Publishing Company, Inc.
Santa Monica, California

Library of Congress Cataloging in Publication Data

STEERS, RICHARD M.
  Introduction to organizational behavior
  (The Goodyear series in administration and business management)
  Includes bibliographical references and indexes.
  1. Organizational behavior.   2. Industrial management.
3. Psychology, Industrial.
I. Title.   II. Series: Goodyear series in
administration and business management.
HD58.7.S74   658.3'001'9   80-23138
ISBN 0-8302-4459-X

© 1981 by Goodyear Publishing Company, Inc.
Santa Monica, California

Current printing
10 9 8 7 6 5 4 3 2 1

Cover and Interior Design: Kenny Beck

Printed in the United States of America

Dedicated with sincere appreciation to Dorothy Wynkoop

contents

14. Employee Attachment to Organizations

15. Work and Stress

16. Work Design

preface

Five years ago, Richard K. Irish wrote a book called *If Things Don't Improve Soon I May Ask You to Fire Me* (Anchor Books, 1976). Dedicated to all those who labor in the vineyards, whether they "press the grapes or work in top management," the book was a comical—if accurate—expose on life in contemporary work organizations. The major conclusion was that organizations are more often than not mismanaged, leading to an employee work climate that is not only inefficient but also stressful, dissatisfying, and just plain no fun. Although Irish may have overstated the problem slightly, the fact remains that significant improvements could be made in contemporary organizational life, if only managers knew what to do.

The problems of contemporary work organizations include problems of low morale, poor motivation, high job stress, high turnover and absenteeism, poor product quality, distrust and conflict between groups and levels in the organizational hierarchy, and poor decision making. Problems such as these—and how managers can attempt to solve them—constitute the major focus of this book. We introduce the student to the topic of organizational behavior by examining in some detail the nature of people at work, and by exploring the nature of individual differences, group dynamics, work environment, and individual and collective behaviors. In this way, we can develop an appreciation for work-related problems and managerial solutions.

The primary emphasis of this book is on what has become known as the more "micro" aspects of organizational behavior. That is, we will focus primarily on the study of individual and group processes in work situations. We will highlight the events and activities that take place inside an organization, not those that occur between organizations, as would be the case in the more "macro" approach. Even so, a general overview of these macro conditions is given in Chapter 3 to provide a useful frame of reference as we explore the topic of individuals and groups at work.

At least two additional unique features of this book should be noted. First, each chapter contains boxed summaries of either classic studies or practical examples from work organzations that illustrate the conceptual materials presented in the text. Second, both cases and exercises have been included in the Appendices to allow for greater application of the materials presented. These cases and exercises are designed to further students' analytical abilities and to provide opportunities for students to learn something about themselves as potential managers.

Throughout this book, an attempt has been made to integrate theory, research, and application. This has been done in the belief that effective managerial action can only follow from an understanding and appreciation of human behavior. Based on this knowledge, managers can develop the strategies necessary to facilitate collective action toward organizational goals and effectiveness.

Many individuals have contributed to the realization of this project. Initially, I must recognize a special debt to my colleagues and doctoral students at the University of Oregon who have provided the challenging intellectual atmosphere necessary to stimulate new ideas and ways of thinking about organizational behavior. Many of the ideas expressed in this book are the result of prolonged discussions with colleagues and students on various subjects germane to the study of people at work.

In addition, I should like to express my sincere appreciation to Lyman W. Porter of the University of California, Irvine, for his assistance and patience as academic editor for Goodyear Publishing Company during the lengthy writing and rewriting process. Special thanks is also in order to some very special people who reviewed various portions of the manuscript or the entire book. These people include Robert H. Miles, Harvard University; Richard T. Mowday, University of Oregon; Douglas T. Hall, Boston University; Benjamin Schneider, Michigan State University; Ricky Griffin, University of Missouri, Columbia; and William H. Mobley, Texas A & M University. The final product benefited considerably from their comments and suggestions.

A special note of appreciation is also due my wife, Sheila, for her patience and support during the rather lengthy periods of cloistering while the manuscript took shape. Finally, I should like to acknowledge a debt of gratitude to Dorothy Wynkoop, my secretary, to whom this book is dedicated, for her enthusiastic support of the project and her continuing dedication to management education. Without people such as these, a project of this magnitude could never have become a reality.

Richard M. Steers

part one
Introduction

chapter 1

People at Work:
An Introduction

Being a manager is no simple task. In fact, the manager's job is often cited as an example of a high stress position because of the many conflicting demands and pressures placed on managers in our contemporary society. The problems managers face are multi-faceted and include dealing with people, production, finances, marketing, accounting, and so forth. Of particular concern to us in this book are people problems: the nature of employees, the work environment, and the interaction between the two. To the extent that we can learn more about the nature of people at work—how employees see, perform, and react to their jobs—we can perhaps make the job of manager a bit easier to perform. It is with this goal that we begin our exploration of employee behavior in organizations.

When we ask managers to discuss human problems in the workplace, we usually hear questions such as the following:

- Why don't my employees work harder?
- Why is absenteeism and turnover so high? What can I do to reduce it?
- Why do we have so many communication problems?
- What kinds of characteristics should I look for in hiring people?
- How can I improve job satisfaction among my employees?

- How can I reduce—or at least cope with—job-related stress?
- How do I evaluate and reward employee performance?
- How can I become a more effective leader?

Questions such as these point to a general frustration among many managers who seek to deal effectively with individuals and groups on the job. These questions also point to an inadequacy among managers in understanding the nature of people at work. It is the goal of this volume to increase this understanding and minimize the effect of future frustrations by reviewing what we have learned from the behavioral and social sciences about organizational behavior and people at work. It is hoped that this knowledge will help managers answer questions such as those above and improve both productivity and the quality of working life in contemporary organizations.

Throughout this book, we shall be concerned with four central topics: people, the work people perform, the work environment or organizations where the work is performed, and the role of management in coordinating people, work, and work environment. Our intention is to facilitate a better understanding of how these four variables interact and how they relate to employee need satisfaction and organizational effectiveness. Before discussing these relationships, it will be useful to consider what we mean by the term work, as well as its role in modern society. Based on this understanding, we can begin assembling the building blocks that are necessary for an understanding and appreciation of organizational behavior.

Nature of Work

Meaning of Work

What is work and how do people feel about the work they do? This question could be answered in several ways. Perhaps one of the best ways to understand how people feel about their jobs is simply to ask them. This has been done in an interesting book, *Working,* by Studs Turkel (1972). Turkel interviewed scores of people in a wide variety of jobs. How do these people feel about their jobs? Listen.*

> I'm a dying breed. . . . A laborer. Strictly muscle work . . . pick it up, put it down, pick it up, put it down. . . . You can't take pride any more. You remember when a guy could point to a house he built, how many logs he stacked. He built it and he was proud of it (p. 1).
>
> Steelworker

*Working: People Talk About What They Do All Day and How They Feel About What They Do © 1972, 1974 by Studs Terkel. Reprinted by permission of Pantheon Books, a division of Random House, Inc., and Wildwood House, Ltd., London.

I changed my opinion of receptionists because now I'm one. It wasn't the dumb broad at the front desk who took telephone messages. She had to be something else because I thought I was something else. I was fine until there was a press party. We were having a fairly intelligent conversation. Then they asked me what I did. When I told them, they turned around to find other people with name tags. I wasn't worth bothering with. I wasn't being rejected because of what I said or the way I talked, but simply because of my function (p. 57).

Receptionist

I think switchboard operators are the most underpaid, 'cause we are the hub of everything. When you call somebody, you want immediate service. Of course, I chose the job. If you choose the job, it's your responsibility. Just because I feel I'm not paid enough doesn't mean I'm not gonna give 'em good work (p. 63).

Switchboard operator

People ask me what I do, I say, "I drive a garbage truck for the city." . . . I have nothing to be ashamed of. I put in my eight hours. We make a pretty good salary. I feel I earn my money. . . . My wife is happy; this is the big thing. She doesn't look down at me. I think that's more important than the white-collar guy looking down at me (p. 149).

Sanitation truck driver

I'm human. I make mistakes like everybody else. If you want a robot, build machines. If you want human beings, that's what I am (p. 186).

Policeman

The almighty dollar is not the only thing in my estimation. There's more to it—how I'm treated. What I have to say about what I do, how I do it. It's more important than the almighty dollar (p. 259–260).

President, Lordstown Local, UAW

I usually say I'm an accountant. Most people think it's somebody who sits there with a green eyeshade and his sleeves rolled up with a garter, poring over books, adding things—with glasses. I suppose a certified public accountant has status. It doesn't mean much to me. Do I like the job or don't I. That's important (p. 351).

Accountant

These other people, they work, work, work, work and nothing comes of it. They're the ones that catch hell. The ones that come in every day on time, do the job, and try to keep up with everybody else. A timekeeper . . . she's a fanatic about time. She would argue with you if you were late or something. She's been working for the government twenty-five years and she hasn't gotten a promotion, 'cause she's not a fighter. . . .

The boss whose typing I messed up lost his secretary. She got promoted. They told this old timekeeper she's to be his secretary-assistant. Oh, she's in her glory. No more money or anything and she's doing two jobs all day long. She's rushin' and runnin' all the time, all day. She's a nervous wreck. And when she asked him to write her up for an award, he refused. That's her reward for being so faithful, obedient (p. 461).

Process clerk

Examples such as these—and there are many, many more—explain how some employees view their jobs and the work they perform. Obviously, some jobs are more meaningful than others and some individuals are more easily satisfied with their jobs than others. In any case, people clearly have strong feelings about what they do on the job and about the people they work with. We shall examine what people do, what causes them to do it, and how they feel about what they do. As a prelude to this analysis, however, we should first consider the basic unit of analysis in this study: work itself. What is work and what functions does it serve in today's society?

Work has a variety of meanings in contemporary society. Oftentimes we think of work as paid employment, the exchange of services for money. While this definition may suffice in a technical sense, it does not adequately describe why work is necessary. Hence, perhaps a more meaningful definition of *work* is to view it as "an activity that produces something of value for other people" (Dept. of Health, Education & Welfare, 1973, p. 3).

This definition broadens the scope of work and emphasizes the social context in which the wage-effort bargain transpires. Moreover, it clearly recognizes that work has purpose; it is productive. This is not to say that work is necessarily interesting or rewarding or satisfying. On the contrary, we know that many jobs are dull, repetitive, and stressful. Even so, the activities performed do have utility for society at large. One of the challenges of management (discussed in Chapter 16) is to discover ways of transforming necessary yet distasteful jobs into more meaningful situations that are more satisfying and rewarding for individuals and which still contribute to organizational productivity and effectiveness.

Functions of Work

We know why work activities are important from an organization's viewpoint. Without work there is no product or service to provide. But why is work important to individuals? What functions does it serve? Work fulfills several useful functions for individuals.

First, work serves a rather obvious *economic* function. In exchange for labor, individuals receive necessary income with which to support themselves and their families. But people work for many reasons beyond simple economic necessity.

Work also serves several *social* functions. The workplace provides many opportunities for meeting new people and developing friendships. Many people spend more time at work with their co-workers than they spend at home with their own families.

Work also provides a source of social *status* in the community. It is a clue to how an individual is regarded based on standards of importance prescribed by the community. For instance, in the United States a corporate president is generally accorded greater status than a janitor in the same corporation. In China, on the other hand, great status is held by peasants and people from the working class, whereas managers are not so significantly differentiated from those they manage. It is important to note here that the status associated with the work we perform often transcends the boundaries of our organization. A corporate president or a university president may have a great deal of status in the community at large because of his or her position in the organization. Hence, the work we do can simultaneously represent a source of social differentiation as well as a source of social integration.

Work can be an important source of *identity, self-esteem, and self-actualization*. It provides a sense of purpose for individuals and clarifies their value or contribution to society. As Freud (1930, p. 34) noted long ago, "work has a greater effect than any other technique of living in binding the individual more closely to reality; in his work he is at least securely attached to a part of reality, the human community." Work contributes to self-esteem in at least two ways. First, it provides individuals with an opportunity to demonstrate competence or mastery over both themselves and their environment. Individuals discover that they can actually *do* something. Second, work reassures individuals that they are carrying out activities that produce something of value to others. It reassures them that they have something significant to offer. Without this, the individual feels he or she has little to contribute and is, hence, of little value to society.

We clearly see, then, that work serves several useful purposes from an individual's standpoint. It provides a degree of economic self-sufficiency, social interchange, social status, self-esteem, and identity. Without this, individuals often experience sensations of powerlessness, meaninglessness, and normlessness. This condition is called *alienation*. In work, individuals have the possibility of finding some meaning in their day-to-day activities, providing, of course, that their work is sufficiently challenging. When work is not sufficiently challenging and when employees are not involved in their jobs, organizations run the risk of jeopardizing productivity and organizational effectiveness by creating situations where employees simply see no reason to contribute or to maximize their efforts on the job. This situation has given rise to a general concern by managers with declining productivity and work values. In fact, concern with this crisis has caused many managers to take a renewed interest in learning how the behavioral sciences can help them solve many of the problems of people at work.

The Crisis of Productivity and Work Values

During the past several years, it has become apparent that the U. S. economy is not as vigorous as it was in the twenty years following World War II. As inflation increases, unemployment rises, and other industrialized nations surpass our previously unchallenged rates of productivity and output, concerns are often expressed that today's managers and workers are simply not doing enough to compete successfully in the economy of the 1980s.

A search for the root causes of this problem yields a variety of possible answers. As Yankelovich (1979, p. 61) notes:

> Our productivity is slowing for many reasons: the cost of energy, the crippling effects of government regulations, the distortions of inflation, environmental costs, a slackening of investment, a shift to services, and so on. But careful studies show that, collectively, all these factors can account for only a fraction of the present slippage.
>
> If you look at changing American attitudes toward work, you catch a glimpse of what is a major factor contributing to the decline. People who work at all levels of enterprise . . . are no longer motivated to work as hard and as effectively as in the past.

As proof, Yankelovich cites the following statistics. In the 1960s approximately 50 percent of employed Americans considered their work a source of personal fulfillment; now the total is fewer than 25 percent. Moreover, in the 1960s, 58 percent believed that "hard work always pays off;" now only 43 percent hold this belief. Finally, today only 13 percent of working Americans find their work truly meaningful and more important to them than their leisure-time activities.

Based on this survey of employees, Yankelovich estimated that the workforce can be divided into five categories. He further estimated the number and type of employees in each category as follows:

Go-getters (15% of the workforce)   Young, ambitious, predominantly in sales, motivated by money and getting ahead.

Work before pleasure (19%)   Older, dedicated, hard-working, want to make a contribution.

Habitual workers (22%)   Older, poorer, mostly blue-collar or clerical, want job security, structure, and guidance.

Middle-management (17%)   Young, highly educated, managers and professionals, hungry for responsibility and challenge, seek interesting and vital work.

Turned off (27%)   Poorly educated, low income, largely blue-collar, least motivated, living for today.

Although one may argue with the classification or the estimated percentages in each category, this analysis serves to highlight the fact that today's workforce is highly diversified, characterized by different educations, skills, age groups, responsibilities, and job challenges. Perhaps most important are the different levels of motivation and drive.

This issue is further highlighted when we consider the current debate over the relative motivation levels of younger and older workers. We frequently hear comments about the lack of dedication and hard work among younger employees. The image is that younger workers are lazy, lack direction and purpose, and are untrustworthy. Available evidence fails to support this image. Rather, while younger employees (or prospective employees) still appear to value hard work, there has been an apparent shift in their expectations of their jobs.

Several recent studies have shown that younger employees have higher job expectations than they did in the past. A survey by the American Institutes for Research (1971), for instance, surveyed over 400,000 high school sudents in 1960 and a comparable sample again in 1970. It was found that while the 1960 sample valued job security and opportunity for promotion, the 1970 group placed a higher value on "freedom to make my own decisions" and "work that seems important to me." Job security or promotional opportunities have either become less important or else more recent students have come to assume such things as given and demand more from a job. In either case, younger employees have apparently come to expect more meaningful input and responsibility from the jobs they select instead of "waiting in line" to move up the hierarchy.

In a more recent survey, Taylor and Thompson (1976) found similar results. In their study of a large sample of workers, they found no generation gap between younger and older employees. Differences were noted, however, between the two age groups. Younger workers were found to value self-expression through work to a greater extent than did older workers. Younger workers attached particular significance to opportunities to learn and chances to make responsible decisions. Workers of all ages, especially more educated workers, showed a strong sense of pride and valued both intrinsic (job based) and extrinsic (economic) rewards.

Based on their findings, Taylor and Thompson (1976, p. 534) conclude:

> The study suggests that managers, union leaders, and public policymakers will face new challenges in the years to come. Young workers will be demanding both with job satisfaction and higher income. At the same time, more educated persons entering the labor force are less likely to trust existing institutions to meet their needs. Young managers may have as much difficulty as their older superiors in relating to young workers.

In summary, it appears that younger workers have not lowered the value they place on hard work. Instead, they generally want to contribute to organizations in meaningful ways and get frustrated by what they perceive as bureaucratic or needless hurdles to their effective job performance. Hence, the challenge for management is how to design a work environment and provide the necessary leadership so that employees are motivated to perform on the job.

Social Problems of Work

In addition to the general problem of work values, it is possible to identify a series of other social problems associated with work. These problems result largely from either an individual's reactions to the work itself or to the work environment (Argyle, 1972). Examples of these problems include the following:

Alienation and low job satisfaction   Many employees today are unable to identify with the work they do or with their employer. They work on jobs that have little meaning and under conditions over which they have little control. As such, it is not surprising to find workers who are alienated and dissatisfied.

Lack of employee motivation   Contemporary managers are finding that employees—at all levels—are simply not motivated to perform. Turnover and absenteeism remain high and, even among those workers who are present, many seem less than enthusiastic about carrying out their assigned tasks.

Difficulties of communication   As organizations grow in size and complexity, patterns of communication (the lifeblood of organizations) become more structured and formal. Delays and distortions of information increase, leading to misunderstandings and to decisions being made with information of poor quality.

Conflicts within and between groups   Conflict is a fact of life in contemporary work organizations. Different individuals and interest groups expect, demand, and work for their specific objectives in spite of the fact that many of these objectives create problems for others. Such conflict creates a permanent source of stress at work as each group lobbies to have its own way.

Problems of technological change   Contemporary organizations must find ways of adapting to environmental pressures and market opportunities. Such changes occur and recur with alarming frequency, creating anxiety among members of the workforce who don't know how such changes will affect them. Will a change put them out of work? Reduce their job security? Job status? Will the job be less enjoyable? More stressful? Change and its accompanying anxieties and frustrations must be faced by managers interested in keeping their organization in a balance with or ahead of environmental, technological, and societal pressures and demands.

Other problems could be mentioned. The point here is that managers have a responsibility to recognize the existence of such social problems and also to recognize the extent to which the influence of these problems inhibits productivity and the quality of working life. Many of the topics discussed throughout this book focus both on these work-related problems and on what managers can do to alleviate such problems. Throughout, we shall attempt to develop a conceptual appreciation of the nature of the problems as well as analyze the theoretical underpinnings of the solutions themselves. Hence, an attempt will be made to bridge theory and application in the belief that appropriate applications can only follow from a solid understanding of the theory behind them.

People at Work: A Framework for Analysis

In view of these problems and in view of management's responsibility to help solve them, how then do we proceed to study people at work? The model advanced here is taken from the socio-technical systems school of thought that advocates that work behavior is best understood in terms of the interaction of the social system (individuals and groups) with the technical system (the nature of jobs). Hence, throughout this book, we will consider how people relate to and react to work activities.

As we proceed we will make use of the following building blocks in a study of employee behavior in work organizations: 1) individuals; 2) groups; 3) people at work; 4) the role of management (see Exhibit 1-1).

Individual Behavior

We begin our examination in Part II with the study of individual behavior in organizations. The focus here is on gaining a detailed awareness of how people view themselves and others, why they behave as they do, and how they learn from prior experiences and from their environment. Specifically, we shall examine the following topics: individual needs and basic motivational processes, in Chapter 4; individual abilities and traits, in Chapter 5; perceptual processes at work, in Chapter 6; learning processes and behavior modification, in Chapter 7; and complex cognitive models of employee motivation and performance, in Chapter 8. Throughout we shall be building a portrait of individuals in the workplace, observing how such individuals are similar and how they are different.

Group Behavior

Next, in Part III, individuals are studied as they come together in the workplace to form groups. Our discussion of group dynamics will include both

Exhibit 1–1   A framework for analyzing people at work

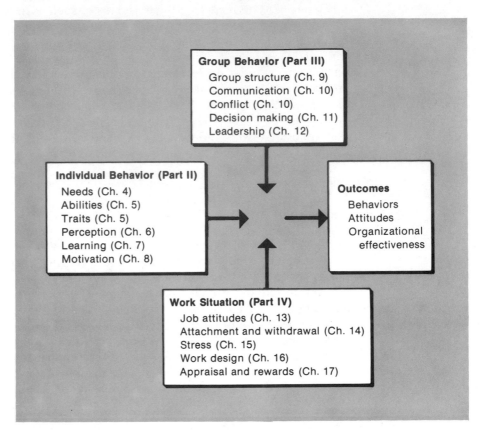

consideration of group structure and of group processes. That is, in Chapter 9 we will review various aspects of group structure and consider variations among different types of groups. Why do groups form and what are the stages of group development? How do structural variations influence behavior? In the next several chapters, four group processes will be discussed. In Chapter 10, we examine the two related processes of communication and conflict. In Chapter 11, we focus on decision-making processes. Finally, in Chapter 12, we review leadership processes as they influence group effectiveness.

People at Work

Based on an awareness of individuals and groups, we will then be in a position to consider how people react within the workplace. In Part IV, we put people together with jobs. We will consider the nature of job attitudes, how they are formed, and how they are changed (Chapter 13). We also consider how people join organizations, become attached to them, and leave them (Chapter 14). Work-related stress is introduced and discussed in Chapter 15, and work design and job enrichment are covered in Chapter 16. Finally, the concepts of performance appraisals and reward systems are reviewed in Chapter 17. We want to present a comprehensive portrait of the dynamics of the workplace, emphasizing the simultaneous study of both people and their work activities, so as to better grasp the dualistic nature of organizational behavior.

Role of Management

Finally, throughout our discussions, we will examine the role of managers in facilitating both employee development and satisfaction and organizational effectiveness. In fact, each chapter will begin by highlighting several of the reasons why the topic of the chapter has relevance for contemporary managers. Specific lessons for management can be found throughout the various chapters. By doing this, it is hoped the sometimes esoteric topic of organizational behavior can be presented at a practical level and help answer the question, ''How can I manage better?''

Before we launch into this discussion, however, it is necessary to set the stage by reviewing two important topics. First, how do we learn about human behavior in organizations? This is done in Chapter 2. Second, in Chapter 3 we will consider the larger issue of the work setting; the nature of organizations and their external environment. These two topics will provide a useful background for our exploration of people at work.

Summary

It should be clear that the major focus of this book is on the role of managers in facilitating organizational effectiveness by working through people. The nature of work is discussed, as well as several of the functions served by work in our contemporary society. In addition, the crisis in productivity and work values is reviewed, as are social problems relating to the work place. Throughout this discussion, it is hoped that the student of management will gain a clear picture of some of the problems facing contemporary managers in work organzations.

Key Words

work	alienation
social status	self-actualization
self-esteem	work values

Questions for Discussion

1. Define what is meant by work.
2. What functions does work serve in modern society?
3. Describe the nature of the crisis of productivity and personal work values. What can be done about this crisis?
4. Do younger workers have less commitment to work than older workers? Explain.
5. Discuss several major social problems associated with work today.

chapter 2

Scientific Method in Organizational Research

It is very common for students of management to make pleas against following "theoretical" or "abstract" approaches to a subject and to argue in favor of "relevant" and "applied" approaches. The feeling is that there usually exist two distinct ways to study a topic and, from a managerial standpoint, a focus on application is the preferred way. Serious reflection about this problem may suggest a somewhat different approach, however. Consider the following situation:

As a personnel manager for a medium-sized firm, you have been asked to discover why employee turnover in the firm is so high. Your boss has told you that it is your responsibility to arrive at a well-documented assessment of this problem, as well as to offer suggestions aimed at reducing turnover. What would you do? Several possible strategies come to mind. You may decide to:

- talk with those who have quit the organization
- talk with those who remain
- talk to the employees' supervisors

- consult with personnel managers in other companies
- measure job satisfaction
- examine company policies and practices
- examine the jobs where most turnover occurs

In fact, none of these actions will likely be very successful in helping you arrive at sound conclusions. Talking with those who have left usually yields a variety of biased responses by those who either want to ''get back at'' the company, or who fear criticism will negatively affect their chances for future recommendations. Talking with those still employed has similar problems: why should they be candid and jeopardize their jobs? Talking with supevisors will help little if they themselves are the problem. Asking other personnel managers, while comforting, ignores major differences between organizations that may be part of the problem. Measuring job satisfaction, examining company policies, or examining the jobs themselves may help if you are fortunate enough to hit upon the right problem. But the probability of doing so is minimal. In short, many of the most obvious ways a manager may choose to solve a problem may yield biased results at best and possibly no results at all.

A sounder approach to solving the problem would be to view it as a research problem and to use widely accepted methods of scientific inquiry to arrive at a solution that minimizes potentially biased results. For most of what we know about organizational behavior results from people's efforts to apply such methods in the solution of organizationally relevant problems (e.g., How do we motivate employees? How do we develop effective leaders? How do we reduce stress at work?). Since an awareness of the nature of scientific inquiry is useful both for understanding how we learned what we know about organizations and in facilitating manager's efforts to solve behavioral problems at work, we shall devote this chapter to an examination of this process. Such knowledge will make the student of management an intelligent consumer of behavioral data and, as a result, a more informed and analytical manager.

Importance of Topic for Managers

As implied in the previous discussion, a knowledge of the nature of research methods in organizations is important for several reasons:

1. It provides an understanding of how behavioral scientists discover new information about people at work.

2. It assists managers in solving their own problems at work. In fact, research methodology is simply another name for problem solving. Both researchers and managers have a responsibility to solve problems (although the nature of the problems may differ) and each hopes to arrive at the most accurate and useful conclusions. Hence, words like *theory* and *research* should not be seen as irrelevant but rather should be interpreted as mechanisms for understanding the world of work.

3. An understanding of research methods also protects managers from those who would sell them panaceas for managerial problems. If a consultant offers a manager a test that purports to measure employee motivation or management potential, an informed manager can ask intelligent questions about the validity and reliability of the test. Are we getting our money's worth? Is it a sham or a useful tool? The uninformed manager is at the mercy of the consultant, while the informed manager can make a reasoned assessment.

4. A knowledge of research methods also assists managers in designing and carrying out their own studies. If questionnaires need to be developed to measure some unique aspect of the company (e.g., a particular organizational climate), an informed manager can do it. We want to emphasize that our approach includes problem-solving as well as research, for management is often defined as a problem-solving function.

5. Finally, a knowledge of research methodology allows the manager to remain current in his or her field by reading journals and periodicals and evaluating the accuracy and utility of the information presented. In this way, the manager does not have to rely on others to interpret (or possibly misinterpret) new developments in the field.

Throughout this chapter, we will continually make reference to the utility or application of research methods in the practice of management. Then, with such knowledge as a backdrop, we will be ready to launch our investigation into the behavior of people at work.

Theory-Building in Organizations

Theory Defined

Briefly stated, a *theory* is a set of statements which serve to amplify the manner in which certain concepts or variables are interrelated. These statements result both from our present level of knowledge on the topic and from our assumptions about the variables themselves. These statements allow us to deduce logical propositions, or hypotheses, which can then be tested in the field or laboratory. In short, a theory is simply a technique or model that allows us to better understand how different variables fit together. Their use in research and in management is invaluable (see Dubin, 1976).

Uses of a Theory

Why do we have theories in the study of organizational behavior? Hamner and Organ (1978) suggest at least three reasons. First, theories help us *organize* our knowledge about a given subject into a pattern of relationships that lends meaning to a series of observed events. They provide a structure for understanding. For instance, rather than struggling with a lengthy list of factors found to relate to employee turnover, a theory of turnover might suggest how such factors fit together and are related.

Second, theories help us to *summarize* diverse findings so that we can focus on the major relationships and not get bogged down in details. A theory "permits us to handle large amounts of empirical data with relatively few propositions" (Shaw and Costanzo, 1970, p. 9).

Finally, theories are useful in that they *point the way* to future research efforts. They raise new questions and suggest where answers may lie. In this sense, they serve a useful heuristic value in helping us differentiate between important and trivial questions for future research. Theories are useful both for the study and management of organizations. As Kurt Lewin often said, "There is nothing so practical as a good theory."

What is a Good Theory?

Abraham Kaplan (1964) discusses in detail the criteria for evaluating the utility or soundness of a theory. At least five such criteria can be mentioned:

Internal consistency   Are the propositions inherent in the theory free from contradiction? Are they logical?

External consistency   Are the propositions of a theory consistent with observations from real life?

Scientific parsimony   Does the theory contain only those concepts that are necessary to account for findings or explain relationships? Simplicity of presentation is preferred unless added complexity furthers our understanding or clarifies additional research findings.

Generalizability   In order for a theory to have much utility, it must apply to a wide range of situations or organizations. A theory of employee motivation that applies only to one company hardly helps us understand motivational processes or apply such knowledge elsewhere.

Verification   A good theory presents propositions that can be tested. Without an ability to operationalize the variables and subject the theory to field or laboratory testing, we are unable to determine its accuracy or utility.

To the extent that a theory satisfies these requirements, its usefulness both to researchers and managers is enhanced and we can learn more about the nature of people at work. However, a theory is only a starting point. Based on theory, researchers and problem solvers can proceed to design studies aimed at verifying and refining the theories themselves. These studies must proceed according to commonly accepted principles of scientific method.

Scientific Method in Organizational Behavior Research

Many years ago, Cohen and Nagel (1934) suggested that there were four basic "ways of knowing." These are: tenacity, intuition, authority, and science. Managers and researchers use all four techniques. Managers use *tenacity* when they form a belief (e.g., a happy worker is a productive worker) and continue to hold that belief out of habit and often in spite of contradictory information. They use *intuition* when they feel the answer is self-evident or when they have a hunch how to solve a problem. They use *authority* when they seek an answer to a problem from an expert or consultant who supposedly has experience in the area. Finally, they use *science* perhaps all too seldom—when they are convinced that the three previous methods allow for too much subjectivity in interpretation.

In contrast to tenacity, intuition, and authority, the scientific method of inquiry "aims at knowledge that is *objective* in the sense of being intrasubjectively certifiable, independent of individual opinion or preference, on the basis of data obtainable by suitable experiments or observations" (Hempel, 1965, p. 141). In other words, the scientific approach to problem solving sets some fairly rigorous standards in an attempt to substitute objectivity for subjectivity.

The scientific method in organizational behavior consists of four stages: 1) observation of the phenomena (facts) in the real world; 2) formulation of explanations for such phenomena using the inductive process; 3) generation of predictions or hypotheses about the phenomena using the deductive process; and 4) verification of the predictions or hypotheses using systematic, controlled observation (Stone, 1978). This process is shown in Exhibit 2–1.

When this rather abstract description of the steps of scientific inquiry is shown within the framework of an actual research study, the process becomes much clearer. A basic research paradigm is shown in Exhibit 2–2. In essence, a scientific approach to research requires that the investigator or manager first recognize clearly what research questions are being posed. To paraphrase Lewis Carroll, if you don't know where you're going, any road will take you there. Many managers identify what they think is a problem (e.g., turnover) only to later discover that their turnover rate is much lower than comparable industries. Or, some managers look for the solution to poor employee morale and performance and ignore what may be the real problem (e.g., poor leadership).

Based on the research questions, specific hypotheses are identified. These hypotheses represent our best guesses about what we expect to find.

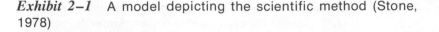

Exhibit 2–1 A model depicting the scientific method (Stone, 1978)

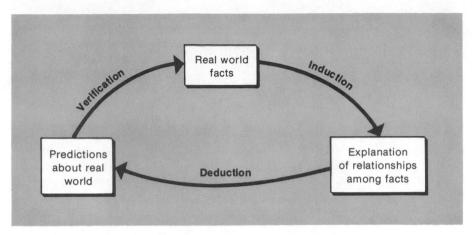

We set forth hypotheses to determine if we can predict the right answer so we can select a study design that allows for a suitable testing. Based on the study design (to be discussed shortly), we observe or measure the variables under study, analyze the data we collect, and draw relevant conclusions and management implications. By following this process, the risks of being guided by our own opinions or prejudices are minimized and we arrive at useful answers to our original research questions.

Basic Research Designs

While a detailed discussion of the various research designs is beyond the scope of this book (see Stone, 1978; Mowday and Steers, 1979; Dunnette, 1976), we can review several of the more common research designs that have been used to collect data in the study of people at work. Specifically, we will examine five different research designs that are commonly used to study behavior at work. These are: 1) naturalistic observation; 2) survey research; 3) field study; 4) field experiment; and 5) laboratory experiment. In general, the level of rigor of the design increases as we move from naturalistic observation toward laboratory study. Unfortunately, so do the costs in many cases.

Criteria for Evaluating Research Designs

Before examining the five designs, it will be helpful to consider how a researcher or manager selects from among the various designs. Clearly, no one

Exhibit 2–2 A model of the empirical research process (Stone, 1978)

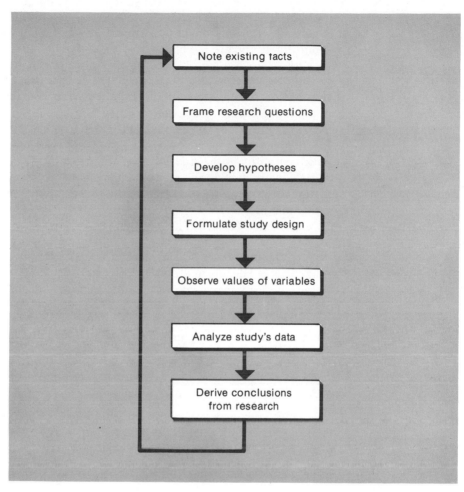

strategy or design is superior in all cases. Each has its place depending upon the research goals and the constraints placed on the research.

However, when choosing among the potential designs, researchers generally look for several things:

Specification of hypotheses in advance Does the design require that you specify *a priori* hypotheses? If you specify such hypotheses and are able to confirm them, then you can predict behavior in organizations. As a manager, being able to predict behavior in advance allows you to intervene in the system and make necessary changes to remedy problem situations. The ability to accurately predict behavior is clearly superior to simply being able to explain behavior after the fact.

Measures   Does the method use qualitative or quantitative measures? While qualitative measures may be useful for generating future hypotheses, it is generally felt that quantitative measures add more rigor to results.

Control   If you are interested in demonstrating causal relationships, it is necessary to have a high degree of control over the study variables. You must be able to manipulate the primary study variable to determine the results of this manipulation, while at the same time keeping other potentially contaminating variables constant so they do not interfere in the results.

External validity   To what extent can you generalize the results from your study to apply to other organizations or situations? Results that are situation-specific are of little use to managers.

Cost   In practical terms, how much is it going to cost you to carry out the study and discover a solution? Cost can be measured in many ways, including time and money.

Overall level of rigor   The analysis of the previous five criteria provides insight to the manager concerning the extent to which the research design is rigorous. The more rigorous the design, the more confidence one has in the results. This is because more rigorous designs typically employ more accurate measures or interventions and attempt to control for contaminating influences on study results.

With these six criteria in mind, we are now in a position to consider various research designs.

Naturalistic Observation

Naturalistic observations represent the most primitive (least rigorous) method of research in organizations. Simply put, *naturalistic observations* represent conclusions drawn from observing events around us. At least two forms of such research can be identified: authoritative opinions and case studies.

In essence, *authoritative opinions* are concerned with the opinions of experts in the field. When Henri Fayol wrote his early works on management, for example, he was offering his advice as a former industrial manager. Based on his experience in real work situations, Fayol and others suggest that what they have learned can be applied to a variety of work organizations with relative ease. Other examples of authoritative opinions can be found in Barnard's *The Functions of the Executive,* Sloan's *My Years with General Motors,* and Townsend's *Up the Organization.* Throughout their works, these writers attempt to draw lessons from their own practical experience that can help other managers assess their problems.

The second use of naturalistic observation can be seen in the *case study.* Case studies attempt to take one situation in one organization and to analyze it in detail with regard to the interpersonal dynamics between the various members. For instance, we may have a case of one middle manager who appears to have burned out on the job; his performance seems to have reached a plateau. The case would then review the cast of characters in the situation and how each one related to this manager's problem. Moreover, the case would review any actions that were taken to remedy the problem. Throughout, emphasis would be placed on what managers could learn from this one real life problem that can possibly relate to other situations.

Survey Research

Many times, managers wish to know something about the extent to which employees are satisfied with their jobs, are loyal to the organization, or experience stress on the job. In such cases, the managers (or the researchers) are interested mainly in considering how high or how low the responses are. Questionnaires designed to measure such variables are an example of *survey research*. Here we are not attempting to relate the results to subsequent events. We simply wish to assess the general feelings and attitudes of employees.

These surveys are particularly popular with managers today as a method of assessing relative job attitudes (see Chapter 13). Hence, we may make an annual attitude survey and track changes in attitudes over time. If attitudes begin to decline, management is alerted to the problem and can take steps to remedy the situation.

Field Study

In a *field study*, the manager or researcher is interested in the relationship between a *predictor* variable (e.g., job satisfaction) and a subsequent *criterion* variable (e.g., employee turnover or performance). Measures of each variable are taken (satisfaction, perhaps through a questionnaire, and turnover from company records) and are compared to determine the extent of correlation. No attempt is made to intervene in the system or to manipulate any of the variables, as is the case with experimental approaches.

To continue the simple example we began with, a manager may have an hypothesis that says that satisfaction is a primary indicator of employee turnover. After measuring both, it is found that there is a moderate relationship between the two variables. Hence, the manager may conclude that the two are probably related. Even so, due to the moderate nature of the relationship, it is clear that other factors also influence turnover; otherwise, there would be a much stronger relationship. Hence, the manager concludes that, while efforts to improve job satisfaction may help solve the problem, other influences on turnover must also be looked at, such as salary level and supervisory style.

Field Experiment

A *field experiment* is much like a field study with one important exception. Instead of simply measuring job satisfaction, the manager or researcher makes efforts to actually change satisfaction levels. In an experiment, we attempt to manipulate the predictor variable. This is most often done by dividing the sample into two groups: an experimental group and a control group. In the experimental group, we intervene and introduce a major change. Perhaps we alter the compensation program or give supervisors some human relations training. The control group receives no such treatment. After a period of time, we compare turnover rates in the two groups. If we have identified the correct treatment (that is, a true influence on turnover), turnover rates would be reduced in the experimental group but not in the control group.

In other words, in a field experiment, as opposed to a field study, we intentionally change one aspect of the work environment in the experimental group and compare the impact of the change with the untreated control group. In this way, we can be relatively assured that the solution we have identified is in fact a true predictor variable and is of use to management.

Laboratory Experiment

Up to this point, we have considered a variety of research designs that all make use of the actual work environment, the *field*. In this last design, *laboratory experiments,* we employ the same level of rigor as that of the field experiment and actually manipulate the predictor variable, but we do so in an artificial environment instead of a real one.

We might, for instance, wish to study the effects of various compensation programs (hourly rate vs. piece-rate) on performance. To do this, we might employ two groups of business students and have both groups work on a simulated work exercise. In doing so, we are *simulating* a real work situation. Each group would then be paid differently. After the experiment, an assessment would be made on the impact of the two compensation plans on productivity.

Comparing Research Designs

Now that we have reviewed various research designs, the obvious question that remains is which are best? This question is not easily answered. All designs have been used by managers and researchers in studying problems of people at work. Perhaps this question can best be answered by considering the relative strengths and weaknesses of each of the designs. We should then have a better idea of when one design or designs would be appropriate for a particular problem or situation.

Exhibit 2–3   A comparison of various research designs

Research Design	*A priori* hypotheses	Qualitative vs. quantitative measures	Control	External validity	Costs	Overall level of rigor
Naturalistic observation	No	Qualitative	Low	Low	Low	Low
Survey research	No	Qualitative and quantitative	Low	High	Low	Medium
Field study	Yes	Quantitative	Medium	High	Medium	Medium
Field experiment	Yes	Quantitative	High	High	High	High
Laboratory experiment	Yes	Quantitative	High	Low	High	High

Note: This table represents general trends and exceptions can clearly be identified.

Following the criteria for evaluating research designs set forth at the beginning of this section, we can conclude the following (see Exhibit 2–3).

Specification of hypotheses in advance   It was noted earlier that the ability to specify *a priori* hypotheses adds rigor to the study. In general, hypotheses are not set forth for naturalistic observations or survey research. These two techniques are used commonly for exploratory analyses and for identifying pertinent research questions for future, more rigorous study. On the other hand, the remaining three designs (field study, field experiment, and laboratory experiment) do allow explicitly for *a priori* hypotheses. Hence, they are superior in this sense.

Qualitative vs. quantitative measures   Naturalistic observations typically involve qualitative data, while field studies and both forms of experiments typically involve quantitative data. Survey research most often provides for both. Hence, if it is important to provide hard data to one's superior concerning a problem (e.g., what is the magnitude of the relationship between satisfaction and turnover?), quantitative designs would clearly be preferred. On the other hand, if one's superior is more concerned about identifying major reasons for turnover and little prior knowledge about the problem exists, qualitative data may be preferred and survey research may be a better research strategy. The selection of an appropriate design hinges in part on the uses to which the information is to be put.

Control   As noted earlier, control represents the extent to which potentially contaminating influences can be minimized in a study. Clearly, experimental procedures allow for better control than do non-experimental ones. The researcher or manager can systematically structure the desired work environment and minimize irrelevant or contaminating influences. As a result, conclusions concerning causal relations between variables can be made with some degree of certainty. Where it is not possible to secure such high control, however—perhaps because the organization does not wish to make a major structural change simply for purposes of the experiment—a field study represents a compromise design. It allows for some degree of control but does not require changing the organization.

External validity   The question of external validity is crucial to any study. If the results of a study in one setting cannot be applied with confidence to other settings, the utility of the results for managers is limited. In this regard, survey research, field studies, and field experiments have higher levels of external validity than naturalistic observations or laboratory experiments. Naturalistic observations are typically based on non-random samples and such samples typically exhibit unique characteristics that may not allow for transfers of learning from one organization to another. A clear example can be seen in the case of a small company in which the president implemented a unique compensation plan that proved successful. Whether such a plan would work in a major, multinational corporation would be highly doubtful because of the radically different nature of the organizations. Similarly, there is some question about how realistic a work environment is actually created in a laboratory situation. If managers are to learn from the lessons of other organizations, they should first learn the extent to which the findings from one kind of organization are applicable elsewhere.

Cost   As one would expect, the quality of information and its price covary. The more rigorous the design (and thus the more accurate the information), the higher the cost. Costs can be incurred in a variety of ways and include such things as actual out-of-pocket expenses, time invested, and residue costs. The organization is left with the aftermath of an experiment, which could mean raised employee expectations and anxieties, as well as the possibility of disillusionment if the experiment fails. Here, it should be noted that in survey research, a large amount of general information can be gathered rather quickly and cheaply.

Overall level of rigor   In summary, then, the real answer to our question concerning which strategy is best lies in the degrees of freedom a manager has in selecting the design. If an experiment is clearly out of the question (perhaps because one's superior doesn't want anything altered), a field study may be the best possible strategy given the constraints. In fact, field studies are often considered a good compromise strategy in that they have a medium amount of rigor but are also fairly quick and inexpensive. On the other hand, if one simply wishes to take an attitude survey, survey research is clearly in order. If one is not allowed to do anything, authoritative opinions from others may be the only information available. However, if constraints are not severe, experimental methods are clearly superior in that they allow for greater certainty concerning major influences on the criterion variable and on the problem itself.

Summary

We have attempted in this chapter to provide a brief overview of how research is done in organizational settings. The notion of theory was introduced as a useful way to model employee behavior. The basic research paradigm was discussed to guide in the development of applied research designs. Finally, various research designs are reviewed and advantages and disadvantages of each were noted. Throughout, it was argued that a knowledge of scientific method and research design was essential in order to help managers act as intelligent consumers of behavioral data.

Key Words

theory	naturalistic observation
internal consistency	survey research
external consistency	field study
external validity	field experiment
scientific approach	laboratory experiment
control	scientific rigor

Questions for Discussion

1. To what use can theories be put in studying organizational behavior?
2. What factors contribute toward the development of a good or useful theory?
3. Kurt Lewin once observed that "there is nothing so practical as a good theory." Explain.
4. As discussed by Cohen and Nagel, what are the four ways of knowing?
5. Describe the general research paradigm.
6. What criteria should be used in evaluating the various research designs that are available for investigating the behavior of people at work?
7. Define the major characteristics of each of the research designs.
8. What are the major advantages and drawbacks of experimental designs in contrast to non-experimental designs?
9. Why has a field study been described as a compromise design?
10. What are the major uses of naturalistic observation?

chapter 3

Organizations: The Work Setting

This book is about people at work. We will focus our attention primarily at the individual and group level of analyses, that is, on characteristics of employees and on determinants of their behavior on the job. As a prelude to this analysis, however, it is necessary to gain a firm grasp of the nature of the larger work setting; that is, organizations. Organizations are the vehicles by which people coordinate their efforts for task accomplishment. Because of this, we should understand something about the nature of organizations— and their diversity—before pursuing our analysis of the people who work there. We shall do so in this chapter.

First, we will examine just what is meant by organization. Following this, we will consider the nature of organization structure and technology and the external environment in which organizations operate. Finally, we will say a few words about organizational effectiveness and the role managers play therein. Before we begin this discussion, however, we should consider why it is important for managers to have an understanding of the nature of organizations.

Importance of Topic for Managers

A thorough understanding of the dynamics of organizations is important to managers for several reasons:

1. To begin with, as noted above, people work in organizations. It is difficult to understand employee behavior on the job without understanding the social and technological milieu in which such behavior occurs. In fact, structure and technology can place considerable constraints on such behavior.

2. In later chapters we shall consider such topics as job redesign, stress, turnover, and absenteeism. It is not possible for a manager to gain a thorough grasp of such variables without also knowing something about how the larger work setting—the organization—influences them.

3. Many decisions that affect people at work result from changes in the external environment. Such issues as how people do their jobs, job security, salary levels, and so forth are greatly influenced by outside competitive factors. Because of this, it is important for managers to be familiar with these external forces.

4. Finally, if the primary function of management is to facilitate an effective level of operations, it is important to have at least a rudimentary understanding of the related concepts of organizational effectiveness and efficiency. Such knowledge can help managers in an assessment of their own performance and the performance of others.

Nature of Organizations

Definition of Organization

In the literature on organizations, a wide variety of definitions can be found for *organizations*. One of the earliest definitions was advanced by Barnard (1938, p. 73), who viewed an organization as "a system of consciously coordinated activities of two or more persons." Organizations are considered to have stated purposes, communications systems and other coordinating processes, and a network of individuals who willingly cooperate on tasks that are necessary for specific goal attainment. Similarly, Etzioni (1964, p. 4) describes organizations as "planned units, deliberately structured for the purpose of attaining specific goals." Finally, Porter, Lawler, and Hackman (1975) argue that organizations are typically characterized by five basic factors: 1) social composition; 2) goal orientation; 3) differentiated functions; 4) intended rational coordination; and 5) continuity through time.

Several common themes run through these different definitions of organizations. First, organizations are seen as collectivities of people working together for common goals. They are goal-seeking systems in which individuals join together and coordinate their efforts (through differentiated functions, rational coordination, etc.) to create a viable system capable of accomplishing common objectives. Each member of an organization may not value all objectives similarly. Instead, individuals might possibly pursue less valued goals (goals valued by the organization) in exchange for securing the efforts of others for those goals that are more highly valued by the individual. Hence, through coalition and cooperation, individual members of an organization try to satisfy their own diverse needs and goals as much as possible commensurate with available resources.

Open Systems Theory

Our definition of organization includes the notion of a goal-seeking system. As such, it will be useful, then, to briefly review the concept of open systems. This concept will emerge frequently throughout our analysis of people at work. Briefly defined, an *open system* is "a set of elements standing in interrelation among themselves and with the environment" (von Bertalanffy, 1972, p. 417). Attention is directed toward "problems of relationships, of structure, and of interdependence rather than the constant attributes of objects" (Katz and Kahn, 1966, p. 18). This notion is basic to the study of organizational behavior since, in a very real sense, all behavior is influenced by the interaction between individuals and their surrounding environments.

The principle underlying open systems theory is straightforward and consists of three components: inputs, throughputs, and outputs (see Exhibit 3–1). *Inputs* represent all those factors that are invested in an organization by the external environment. These inputs can include money, new employees, raw materials, new machines, etc. These inputs are then transformed (that is, acted upon) in the *throughput* stage into a variety of *outputs* that are returned to the environment. Outputs may include finished products, profits on return on investment or retiring or terminating employees. Hence, the organization is seen as continually interacting with its environment in a series of exchange relationships aimed at furthering the well-being of the organization and its members.

Two social psychologists who have made substantial contributions to the development of open systems theory are Daniel Katz and Robert Kahn (1978). They have built upon the three basic characteristics of open systems and suggested nine properties that are common to all open systems. These properties are:

- *Importation of energy*   (Inputs) from the external environment.
- *Transformation of energy*   (Throughputs) by means of work activities.

- *Exportation of transformed energy*   (Outputs) to the external environment.
- *Cyclic character of the transformation processes*   Throughput activities produce outputs that alternately become new sources for inputs.
- *Negative entropy*   Organizations import more energy than they export. That is, systems use up energy in the transformation process and store energy for future needs.
- *Information control mechanisms*   Systems receive information from the environment, employ coding procedures that screen out certain information, and receive feedback from the environment in response to system activities. Systems are directed and redirected based on information.
- *Steady state behavior*   Systems tend to maintain, or at least attempt to maintain, their basic character by controlling or neutralizing threatening external forces for change.
- *Role differentiation and specialization*   As systems grow and develop, there is an increasing tendency toward the elaboration of roles and the specialization of function.
- *Equifinality*   Systems can often reach the same ends by different means. This concept emphasizes the flexibility and adaptability inherent in most organizations.

These nine characteristics of open systems together emphasize the dynamic interrelationships that exist between various components of an organizational system. Not only are most components related to and affected by other components of the system, in addition, the precise nature of such relationships can be expected to change over time in response to en-

Exhibit 3–1   A basic paradigm for an open systems model

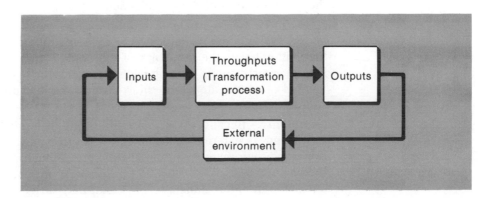

vironmental changes. As long as this dynamic perspective is kept in mind, our analysis of the role people play in work activity and organizational effectiveness can benefit significantly. That is, not only does organizational membership change over time, but the goals, needs, and abilities of those who remain with the organization also change over time. These differences among employees will be seen throughout our subsequent discussions of individual and group behavior.

Requirements of Organizations

In order to survive and maintain a certain amount of stability and predictability amidst the surrounding external environment, organizations must meet a series of *organizational requirements* for survival. The extent to which organizations can successfully satisfy these requirements will largely determine their ability to persist in the pursuit of their goals and objectives. If an organization cannot fulfill these requirements, severe threats to its stability can occur which jeopardize its chances for survival. These threats can take the form of loss of resources, loss of legitimacy from the supporting environment or organizational stagnation. Such losses have obvious implications for the people who work for the organization.

Organizational requirements include the following (Etzioni, 1975; Gross, 1965):

- *Resource acquisition*   Organizations must be able to compete successfully for scarce and necessary resources to serve as inputs for organizational work activities.
- *Efficiency*   Organizations must strive to secure the most advantageous ratio of inputs to outputs in the transformation process.
- *Production or output*   It is necessary for organizations to produce and deliver their goods and services in a steady and predictable fashion.
- *Rational coordination*   The activities of the organization must be integrated and coordinated in a logical, predictable fashion consistent with the ultimate goals of the organization.
- *Organizational renewal and adaptation*   In most organizations, it is necessary for some resources to be set aside and invested in activities that will enhance the net worth of the organization in the future (e.g., R & D investments). Without such renewal efforts, organizational survival is often threatened by short-term shifts in market demands, resources, etc.
- *Conformity*   Because of the close interrelationship between an organization and its external environment, it is often necessary for organizations (and their members) to follow the prevailing dictates and norms of the environment. Wide deviation from social norms, laws, regulations, and shifts in moral standards can result in a variety of sanctions being

levied against the organization that can reduce its sources of legitimacy and threaten its survival.

• *Constituency satisfaction* Finally, organizations are composed of a variety of constituencies, including employees, investors, and consumers. For system effectiveness, it is necessary to satisfy—or at least partially satisfy—these various constituencies to achieve their necessary support and cooperation. In view of the often conflicting demands made by these various constituents (e.g., employees want more money, while investors want more profits and consumers want lower prices), a major function of managers is to somehow achieve a workable balance so that all parties are at least marginally satisfied and willing to continue participating in the venture.

Generic Subsystems

In order to accomplish their goals, organizations must obviously divide and distribute the various tasks and engage in some form of specialization. When we view organizations as open systems, these various areas of specialization can be categorized into five *generic subsystems* (Katz and Kahn, 1978):*

• The *productive* subsystem, where concern is focused on the major functions or work of the system (e.g., a manufacturing department).

• The *supportive* subsystem, which acquires necessary raw materials for the productive subsystem and distributes the system's finished products (e.g., a purchasing or marketing department).

• The *maintenance* subsystem, which maintains and protects the organization's structural integrity and character (e.g., training programs, compensation plans, company newspapers).

• The *adaptive* subsystem, which focuses on the adaptation and long range survival of the organization in a changing environment (e.g., an R & D department, long-range planning functions).

• The *managerial* subsystem, which coordinates, controls, and directs the other four subsystems so that maximum effort can be directed toward goal attainment.

All five subsystems, when taken together, represent the concept we call an organization. As we shall see throughout this book, the study of people at work is colored by all five of these subsystems since people in various roles and capacities operate all five subsystems.

It is important to note that the characteristics of each of these subsystems can vary considerably across organizations. In fact, a major problem that

*Adapted from *The Social Psychology of Organizations, Second Edition,* D. Katz and R. Kahn, copyright 1978. Reprinted by permission of John Wiley & Sons, Inc.

continues to complicate the study of organizational behavior is the heterogeneity of organizations. That is, organizations differ not only in their size and shape (tall vs. flat), but also in the technologies they employ, the external environments in which they function, the work climates they create, and the types of goals and objectives they pursue. It is this property of uniqueness—that is, every organization is an original—that complicates attempts to draw meaningful generalizations concerning what managers can do to improve their effectiveness of operations. Such a fact cautions against the search for hard and fast *principles* of management and instead suggests a contingency approach to the study of organizations and the people who work within them.

Structure and Technology

When we discuss the notion of organization, it is of central importance to examine the related concepts of structure and technology, for these two concepts largely define the organization. While a detailed examination of this topic is more appropriately addressed in a book on organization theory, it is useful to introduce and discuss the concepts here since they have clear importance for the study of people at work.

Organization Structure

Simply put, *organization structure* refers to the way in which an organization organizes (or structures) its human resources for goal-directed activities. It is the way the human parts of an organization are fitted together into relatively fixed relationships that largely define patterns of social interaction, coordination, and task-oriented behavior. The role of structure in the success and functioning of an enterprise has long been a topic of concern among organizational analysts (Blau, 1955; Dubin, 1958; Worthy, 1950).

The concept of structure can, in turn, be broken down into various dimensions of structure. At least six such dimensions have relevance for the study of organizational behavior and will be referred to throughout this book. These are as follows:

Decentralization   This refers to the extent to which power and authority are extended (that is, decentralized) throughout the organization hierarchy. Decentralization is strongly related to the concept of employee participation in decision-making. The greater the decentralization, the greater the extent to which rank and file employees can participate in (and accept responsibility for) decisions concerning their jobs and the future of the organization.

Specialization   Specialization refers to the number of divisions within an organization and the number of specialties within each division (R. Hall, 1977). Since the time of Adam Smith and the classical economists, it has been believed that specialization leads to increased effectiveness of operation. It allows each employee to develop expertise in one particular area and thereby maximize his or her contribution to overall goal attachment. It is only recently that attention has focused on the human consequences of such organizational efforts.

Formalization   This refers to the extent to which employee work activities are specified or regulated by official rules and standard operating procedures (R. Hall, 1977). The greater the rules, regulations, codified job duties, etc., the greater the formalization.

Span of control   Span of control refers to the average number of subordinates per supervisor. Classical management theorists (like Fayol and Graicunas) attempted to identify an ideal span of control that maximized the effectiveness of supervision. More recently, however, attention has simply focused on the attitudinal and behavioral consequences of varying degrees of closeness of supervision.

Organization size   In the study of organizations, a good deal has been written concerning the impact on employees of large vs. small organizations (Porter and Lawler, 1965; Porter and Steers, 1973; Cummings and Berger, 1976). Large organizations tend to structure themselves differently, often using different technologies and different management systems. These differences are obviously influential on employee reactions.

Work-unit size   Finally, in studying the effects of structure on employee attitudes and behavior, it is important to recognize variations in the size of the work group. For instance, increases in work unit size are consistently related to decreases in job satisfaction, lower attendance and retention rates, and increased labor disputes. (Porter and Lawler, 1965). We shall examine such relationships more fully in Chapter 9.

Technology

Although organizational analysts have long recognized the centrality of technology in the study of organizations, they have yet to agree on what exactly is meant by the term. (See Lynch, 1974, for a review). In recent studies, *technology* has been variously defined with regard to the extent of task interdependence, automation of equipment, uniformity or complexity of materials used, the degree of uncertainty in the task environment, and the degree of routineness of work.

If we examine this diversity of definitions for some uniformity of opinion, two conclusions emerge. First, there is general agreement that the technology dimension involves either mechanical or intellectual processes by which an organization transforms inputs, or raw materials, into outputs. It deals with "who does what with whom, when, where, and how often" (Chapple and Sayles, 1961, p. 34).

Second, we must be careful to identify the level of analysis we wish to employ in any discussion of technology. That is, we can look at a large organization (like General Motors) and observe that its technology is largely the manufacture of automobiles using assembly lines. Or, conversely, we can examine technology on an individual or group level and differentiate between the various functional areas within General Motors (production, R & D, accounting, personnel, marketing), all of which may employ different technologies.

Several attempts have been made to identify classification schemes, or typologies, of technology in order to study the effects of such variations in human behavior and organizational effectiveness (Woodward, 1958; Thompson, 1967; Hickson et al., 1969). Since the role of technology will be discussed in detail in the chapter on job design (Chapter 16), it should be useful here to summarize briefly two different approaches to classifying technologies.

First, Woodward's (1958) scheme attempts to classify industrial firms. Three categories are suggested:

Small batch, or unit production Here the product is custom made on a small scale to customer specifications (e.g., airplanes or trains). The operations performed on each unit are typically nonrepetitive in nature.

Mass production In this case, the product is manufactured in an assemblyline fashion (e.g., automobiles), and the operations performed are repetitious, routine, and predictable.

Continuous process production Here the product is transformed from raw material to finished good using a series of machine, or processing, transformations (e.g., chemicals, oil refining).

While Woodward addressed herself specifically to industrial organizations, Hickson and associates (1969) broadened their typology to include organizations differing considerably in size, shape, and purpose. Moreover, Hickson identified categories that are not mutually exclusive. That is, an organization may exhibit some form of all three technologies at the same time. More specifically, Hickson and associates suggested the following three categories:

Operations technology This focuses on the techniques used in the work flow activities of an organization (e.g., handcrafting *vs*. mass production).

Materials technology Here the concern is with the type of materials used in the work flow.

Knowledge technology This aspect of technology focuses on the amount, quality, level of sophistication, and dispersion of information relevant to decision making and production in an organization.

Perhaps an example will serve to highlight the differences between these three types of technology. In a particular organization, managers may employ a highly advanced manufacturing process (operations technology) on a relatively simple raw material (materials technology). Moreover, such a process may require highly skilled and well-educated employees with a high degree of interdepartmental cooperation and communication (knowledge technology). In other words, the technological typology advanced by Hickson et al. really emphasizes the need to talk about *technologies* instead of a single technology when attempting to understand the transformation processes in organizations.

In a wide variety of studies, variations in technology have been found to influence the way in which an organization is structured. For instance, Woodward (1958) found that increases in the complexity of the technology used were associated with an increased ratio of administrators to workers, an increased ratio of supporting staff and specialists to workers, increased levels of authority, increased span of control, and decreased relative labor costs. In other words, Woodward concluded that there appeared to be an optimal level for a number of structural characteristics used by the more successful firms in each of her three technological categories. Less successful firms in each category employed structural ratios that were either too large or too small. In summarizing the findings from her own studies, Woodward (1958, pp. 69–71) concluded that "the fact that organizational characteristics, technology, and success were linked together in this way suggested that not only was the system of production (that is, technology) an important variable in the determination of organization structure, but also that one particular form of organization was most appropriate to each system of production."

Clearly, technology represents an important variable in the study of how people perform and behave on the job, as well as how they react to the work situation. This point will emerge continually throughout this book as we examine various aspects of the workplace and the people who are asked to contribute their efforts toward organizational goal attainment.

External Environment

Organizations obviously do not exist in a vacuum. They must interact with the outside world. This outside world is referred to as the *external environment* of organizations. The external environment consists of several aspects that have relevance for goal-directed activities. In particular, it includes customers, suppliers, competitors, government, and certain aspects of technology (see Exhibit 3–2).

As can be seen from this list, the external environment significantly influences the shape and nature of an organization. All inputs used by the organization come from the environment (e.g., availability of raw materials). Moreover, outputs must find a market in the environment (e.g., availability of customers). Finally, many aspects of the transformation process are lim-

Exhibit 3–2 Components of the external task environment for a typical industrial firm

---

Customer Component
  Distributors of product or service
  Actual users of product or service

Suppliers Component
  New materials suppliers
  Equipment suppliers
  Product parts suppliers
  Labor supply

Competitor Component
  Competitors for suppliers
  Competitors for customers

Socio-political Component
  Government regulatory control over the industry
  Public political attitude towards industry and its particular product
  Relationship with trade unions with jurisdiction in the organization

Technological Component
  Meeting new technological requirements of own industry and related industries in production of product or service
  Improving and developing new products by implementing new technological advances in the industry

---

Source: Reprinted from "Characteristics of Organizational Environments and Perceived Environmental Uncertainty" by Robert B. Duncan, published in *Administrative Science Quarterly,* Vol. 17 #3 (September 1972), p. 315, by permission of *The Administrative Science Quarterly,* ©1972 Cornell University.

ited or regulated by factors in the environment (e.g., legal or governmental regulations). Such factors can have a significant impact upon the lives of people at work.

Dimensions of Environment

If changes in the external environment can affect employees within a given organization, it is important for managers to know something about basic differences in the nature of environments. In an effort to simplify the multitude of environmental characteristics, Thompson (1967) and Duncan (1972) have identified three major dimensions by which environments can be measured. These are simple-complex, static-dynamic, and environmental uncertainty.

The *simple-complex* dimension focuses on the complexity and qualitative nature of the environment. A simple, or placid, environment is one in which the external factors with which an organization must deal are relatively few in number and are relatively homogeneous. For example, a company that manufactures spark plugs produces a product that is limited in terms of product line, uses simple and stable technologies, and has a predictable, relatively constant market. Contrast this to the manufacture of a Boeing 747 or Douglas DC-10, where various components of the airplane are subcontracted to other companies, where technologies change rapidly, and where the market (often measured five to ten years beyond the drawing board) is anything but constant.

The *static-dynamic* dimension focuses on the relative degree of stability in organization-environmental relations. For example, compare the stability of the automotive parts company mentioned above that manufactures spark plugs year after year, to an aerospace firm that may receive a contract to build satellites one year and modular houses the next. Clearly, such differences require organizations that can develop different structures to respond adequately to environmental demands.

The third dimension, the relative degree of *environmental uncertainty,* is really a result of the first two dimensions. That is, the relative complexity and the relative stability of the environment jointly determine the amount of certainty and predictability (or, conversely, uncertainty) in dealing with the environment. More specifically, environmental uncertainty is a result of three conditions (Duncan, 1972): 1) a lack of information concerning the environmental factors associated with a particular organizational decision-making situation; 2) an inability to accurately assign probabilities with regard to how environmental factors will affect the success or failure of a decision unit in peforming its functions; and 3) a lack of information regarding the costs associated with an incorrect decision or action.

When we put all three of these dimensions together, it is possible to develop generalized portraits of various task environments (see Exhibit 3-3). As can be seen in this exhibit, static-simple environments contain the lowest amount of environmental uncertainty for organizational planners and decision-makers. On the other hand, dynamic-complex environments contain the highest amount of uncertainty. Based on such information, managers can make more informed decisions concerning how best to structure their organization for goal-directed activities that take advantage of, instead of opposing, environmental demands.

Environment and Structure

The next logical question concerns how environmental variations influence structure. Many theories can be identified which attempt to address this issue (Lawrence and Lorsch, 1967; Chandler, 1962; Burns and Stalker, 1961). For our purposes here—that is, for the purpose of studying human behavior in organizations—perhaps the most useful framework has been

Exhibit 3–3   Characteristics of various environmental states

	Simple	Complex
Static	CELL 1: *Low Perceived Uncertainty* 1. Small number of factors and components in the environment 2. Factors and components are somewhat similar to one another 3. Factors and components remain basically the same and are not changing	CELL 2: *Moderately Low Perceived Uncertainty* 1. Large number of factors and components in the environment 2. Factors and components are not similar to one another 3. Factors and components remain basically the same
Dynamic	CELL 3: *Moderately High Perceived Uncertainty* 1. Small number of factors and components in the environment 2. Factors and components are somewhat similar to one another 3. Factors and components of the environment are in continual process of change	CELL 4: *High Perceived Uncertainty* 1. Large number of factors and components in the environment 2. Factors and components are not similar to one another 3. Factors and components of environment are in a continual process of change

Source: Reprinted from "Characteristics of Organizational Environments and Perceived Environmental Uncertainty," by Robert B. Duncan, published in *Administrative Science Quarterly,* Vol. 17 #3 (September 1972), p. 322, by permission of *The Administrative Science Quarterly,* © 1972 Cornell University.

presented by Burns and Stalker (1961). These investigators surveyed various British firms in an attempt to uncover the basic relationship between the nature of the environment and subsequent structural arrangements and management practices. As a result of their analysis, they concluded that there exist two relatively distinct approaches to management and that each is largely influenced by the relative degree of stability in the environment.

These two styles are labeled *mechanistic* and *organic.* As shown in Exhibit 3–4, the characteristics of these two styles are quite different. Mechanistic systems are typically characterized by centralization of control and authority, a high degree of task specialization, and primarily vertical (and particularly downward) lines of communication. On the other hand, organic systems tend to exhibit a higher degree of task interdependence, greater decentralization of control and authority, and more horizontal (that is, between departments) communication. In addition, mechanistic systems are relatively fixed and inflexible, while organic systems are generally more flexible and adaptable over time.

Exhibit 3–4 Comparison of mechanistic and organic systems
in organizations

Mechanistic	Organic
1. Tasks are highly fractionated and specialized; little regard paid to clarifying relationship between tasks and organizational objectives.	1. Tasks are more interdependent; emphasis on relevance of tasks and organizational objectives.
2. Tasks tend to remain rigidly defined unless altered formally by top management.	2. Tasks are continually adjusted and redefined through interaction of organizational members.
3. Specific role definition (rights, obligations, and technical methods prescribed for each member).	3. Generalized role definition (members accept general responsibility for task accomplishment beyond individual role definition).
4. Hierarchic structure of control, authority, and communication. Sanctions derive from employment contract between employee and organization.	4. Network structure of control, authority, and communication. Sanctions derive more from community of interest than from contractual relationship.
5. Information relevant to situation and operations of the organization formally assumed to rest with chief executive.	5. Leader not assumed to be omniscient; knowledge centers identified where located throughout organization.
6. Communication is primarily vertical between superior and subordinate.	6. Communication is both vertical and horizontal, depending upon where needed information resides.
7. Communications primarily take form of instructions and decisions issued by superiors, of information and requests for decisions supplied by interiors.	7. Communications primarily take form of information and advice.
8. Insistence on loyalty to organization and obedience to superiors.	8. Commitment to organization's tasks and goals more highly valued than loyalty or obedience.
9. Importance and prestige attached to identification with organization and its members.	9. Importance and prestige attached to affiliations and expertise in external environment.

Source: Adapted from T. Burns and G. M. Stalker, *The Management of Innovation* (London: Tavistock Publications, Ltd., 1961), pp. 119–22. Used by permission.

The important point here is that Burns and Stalker are not arguing that
one system is superior to another. Rather, each has its place depending upon
the nature of the environment. That is, in highly stable and predictable

environments, where market and technology remain largely unchanged over time (e.g., the automotive industry), a mechanistic system of organization is generally more effective. Since the environment is highly predictable, it is possible to routinize tasks and centralize directions in order to maximize effectiveness and efficiency (if not satisfaction). However, when the environment is in a constant state of flux and when the organization has to adapt quickly to such changes (e.g., the aerospace industry), organic systems provide the needed flexibility and are generally more appropriate.

In short, managers must be aware of variations in the environment and structure their utilization of human resources in such a way as to facilitate goal-attainment. Such structuring will obviously take different forms based on the environment and available resources. Significantly, the important role of the manager is highlighted as the person most responsible for determining how best to utilize the limited resources available.

Organizational Effectiveness

Definition of Effectiveness

The term organizational effectiveness has been used and misused in a variety of ways in the literature on organizations. Some people equate the term with profit or productivity, while others view it with regard to job satisfaction and still others see it in light of societal good. Such simplistic definitions tend to be far too narrow to be of much use; they are situation specific and value laden. Instead, as noted earlier, organizations are quite diverse in their nature and mission. As such, a more comprehensive approach to defining *organizational effectiveness* is to follow Talcott Parsons and Amitai Etzioni and define it in terms of an organization's ability to acquire and efficiently use available resources to achieve specific goals.

This definition requires elaboration. To begin with, we are focusing on operative goals, not official goals, meaning our concern is with what the organization is really trying to do, not with public relations statements concerning what it says it is doing. For many years, a major company used to say ''progress is our most important product;'' obviously this was not the case. Second, inherent in this definition is the realization that effectiveness is best judged against an organization's ability to compete in a turbulent environment and successfully acquire and utilize its resources. This emphasizes the fact that managers must deal effectively with their external environments to secure needed resources. Finally, this approach clearly recognizes that the concept of efficiency is a necessary yet insufficient ingredient of effectiveness.

Effectiveness and Efficiency

Many managers equate the terms effectiveness and efficiency. Treating these two related but distinct concepts as interchangeable only serves to confuse the assessment process. Hence, we need to clearly distinguish between the two. While effectiveness is the extent to which operative goals can be attained, *efficiency* is the cost/benefit ratio incurred in the pursuit of those goals.

It is easy to see how decreased efficiency would have a detrimental effect on organizational effectiveness. The more costly goal effort becomes, the less likely the organization is able to survive. For instance, consider the results of recent job enrichment experiments by such automobile manufacturers as Volvo and Saab-Scania. Such efforts were undertaken to improve the quality of working life. However, as noted by several prominent investigators, while job enrichment may have highly desirable social consequences, the costs associated with such efforts may be so high that they increase the price of the product beyond what customers are willing to pay, resulting in decreased sales. This is obviously self-defeating for both the auto firm and its employees.

Influences on Organizational Effectiveness

It has often been argued that the true test of good management is the ability to organize and utilize available resources to achieve and maintain an effective level of operations. If managerial success is defined in terms of organizational performance, it is necessary to ask what managers can do to facilitate this effectiveness. Based on recent work in the area (Goodman and Pennings, 1977; Steers, 1975, 1977), it would appear that organizational effectiveness is influenced by four major categories of variables over which managers have some degree of control (see Exhibit 3–5). These four categories are: 1) organizational characteristics, such as structure and technology; 2) environmental characteristics, such as economic and market conditions; 3) employee characteristics, such as job performance and job attachment; and 4) managerial policies and practices. Examples of organizations that were unable to coordinate these four major influences are discussed in Box 3–1.

The first two characteristics—organizational and environmental characteristics—have been reviewed in this chapter. The second two characteristics—employee characteristics and managerial actions—are the subject of the remainder of this book. Based on this brief review of the organizational setting, we are now in a position to examine how people fit into the organizational effectiveness equation. What causes employee behavior and job attitudes? How do variations in the work environment affect such behavior and attitudes? What is the role of the work group in such

Exhibit 3–5   Major influences on organizational effectiveness

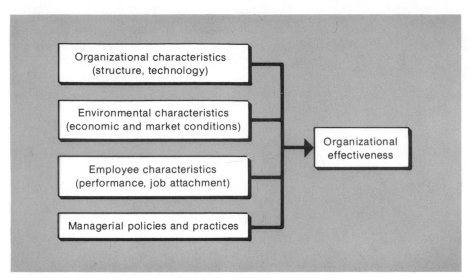

Organizational characteristics
(structure, technology)

Environmental characteristics
(economic and market conditions)

Employee characteristics
(performance, job attachment)

Managerial policies and practices

Organizational
effectiveness

outcomes? Finally, what can managers do to facilitate employee perfor-mance and job satisfaction? It is hoped that the information presented here will help answer these questions and provide managers and prospective managers with useful knowledge that can be applied in a wide variety of organizations in attempting to achieve an effective level of operations.

Two general conclusions result from this discussion of organizational effectiveness. First, the concept of organizational effectiveness is perhaps best understood in terms of a continuous process rather than an end state. Marshaling an organization's resources for goal-directed activities is a never-ending task for most contemporary managers. Because of the chang-ing nature of the goals pursued in most organizations, managers must con-tinually be sensitive to environmental changes, restructure available re-sources where necessary, modify technologies, and train and retrain employees so maximum use is made of available talent and resources. In this way, the organization is in its most advantageous position for pursuing goals.

Second, the central role of contingencies must be clearly recognized in any discussion of organizational effectiveness. It is incumbent upon manag-ers to recognize the unique qualities that define their organization (e.g., its goals, structure, technology, people, etc.) and to respond in a manner sensi-tive to this uniqueness. As a result, we must caution against the arbitrary use of rules or principles for achieving success. Such principles may be of little

---

Box 3–1 Effective and Ineffective Organizations

What differentiates an effective organization from an ineffective one? In many cases, a major factor is the extent to which an organization's managers can successfully balance and integrate organizational, environmental, and employee characteristics with managerial policies and practices. One of the best ways to understand this interaction is to examine instances of organizational *in*effectiveness.* Consider the following two examples:

Farm tractors Here we have an example of a company that correctly identified a problem and set relevant goals but then employed a less than optimal strategy for attaining those goals. Specifically, during the depression of the 1930s, Ford Motor Company decided to use its production facilities (underutilized because of sagging auto sales) to produce farm tractors. Within a short period of time, Ford designed and built a versatile yet inexpensive tractor. Unfortunately, however, Ford attempted to market its new product through the company's existing automobile distribution channels, primarily located in the cities and not attuned to the needs of farms. Hence, the product never reached the intended market and sales were minimal until Ford realized the mistake and developed a separate distribution system that was suited to market realities.

Slide rules If the above example represents an attempt to apply the wrong strategy to the right goal, this next example may be described as an attempt to apply the right strategy to the wrong goal. Specifically, for many years, this organization had a strong reputation for producing and selling high quality slide rules for a variety of applications. However, with the advent and widespread dissemination of inexpensive electronic calculators, sophisticated calculations could now be made more quickly and accurately than ever before. As a result, demand for slide rules decreased almost immediately and product sales dropped by 75% in just two years. The company had either failed to predict environmental changes accurately or was unable to adapt to such changes in order to achieve its profit goal.

Examples such as these highlight the importance for managers to accurately diagnose environmental changes and to structure their organization and its people in such a way that a satisfactory response can be made to environmental demands.

Source: R. M. Steers. *Organizational Effectiveness: A Behavioral View.* Santa Monica, Ca.: Goodyear Publishing Co., 1977.

---

use when viewed against the background of organizational diversity. Instead, responsibility must fall to management to develop employees who can most successfully recognize and understand the nature of a particular situation and respond accordingly. When viewed in this manner, organizational effectiveness is largely the extent to which managers and employees can join together and pool their knowledge and efforts to overcome obstacles that inhibit the attainment of the organization's goals.

Summary

This chapter has focused on several of the more important "macro" concerns in organizational behavior. First, we considered various approaches to defining just what we mean by organizations. This was followed by a look at the concept of open systems theory and the requirements of organizations. Major aspects of organization design were then reviewed, particularly organization structure and technology. Next, consideration was given to the relationship between the organization and the external environment and it was noted that a major influence on structure was the character of the external environment. Finally, the concept of organizational effectiveness was introduced and discussed. Efficiency was contrasted with effectiveness and major influences on effectiveness were identified. Throughout, emphasis was placed on developing a clear portrait of this macro environment in which individual employees behave and perform.

Since this book focuses primarily on individuals and groups at work, this chapter must of necessity be a brief overview. However, many lessons can be learned. In particular, it was noted that all organizations are not alike and that differences between organizations often represent important influences on behavior. For example, employees working for a major automotive company may be affected by environmental changes and pressures since such changes could allow a competitor to increase its market share if corrective action does not forestall this. Employees in a federal bureaucracy, however, may not be influenced by environmental changes and pressures since there is no competition for their service.

In addition, various aspects of an organization's structure and technology can often constrain both human behavior and attempts to improve the quality of work. For instance, despite a recognition that some jobs (e.g., keypunch operator) are less than satisfying for many employees, the technology of the job makes major enrichment efforts difficult or impossible.

Finally, it should be noted that decisions concerning the facilitation of organizational effectiveness largely depend upon how effectiveness is defined. If management wishes to improve the quality of work for some employees but does so at the expense of profits, stockholders may move to change the management. Hence, there are very real constraints on managers in their efforts to improve worklife and simultaneously increase performance.

Key Words

organization	organizational effectiveness
open systems theory	organizational efficiency
transformation processes	generic subsystems

negative entropy
steady state behavior
equifinality
constituency satisfaction
rational coordination
technology
external environment
environmental uncertainty

organization structure
decentralization
specialization
formalization
span of control
mechanistic
organic

Questions for Discussion

1. Discuss the various approaches to defining organizations.
2. What is meant by open systems theory? How can this approach help us to better understand organizational dynamics?
3. What are the properties of open systems?
4. Describe some of the requirements of organizations.
5. Identify the five generic subsystems.
6. What is meant by organization structure? Identify various dimensions of structure.
7. Discuss the role of technology in organizations.
8. How can we classify organizations according to technology? Compare and contrast methods of classification.
9. What is meant by an organization's external environment?
10. Identify the various dimensions of the external environment.
11. What is the relationship between environment and organization structure?
12. Discuss the major differences between mechanistic and organic organizations.
13. What is meant by organizational effectiveness? How does it compare to the concept of efficiency?
14. What are the major influences on organizational effectiveness?

part two

Individual Behavior

chapter 4

Individual Needs and Motivation

Many years ago, Kurt Lewin (1937) proposed that a useful way to study human behavior was to consider behavior (B) as a function of the interaction between a person (P) and his or her environment (E). Hence, Lewin proposed that $B = f(P,E)$. It is clear from this simple formula that an understanding of the person is central to mastering organizational behavior and managerial effectiveness. Because of this, we shall devote this chapter and the next to the study of the person or, more specifically, the study of individual differences. In this chapter, we shall consider employee needs and basic motivational processes. Then, in Chapter 5, we shall examine employee abilities and traits. Overall, it is hoped that these two chapters will help develop an appreciation for the differences that exist between employees in work organizations.

Importance of Topic for Managers

The concept of individual differences and, more specifically, employee need strengths, and the related concept of motivation are important for several reasons:

1. Managers must recognize that employees are not the same and do not react in the same way to similar situations. A knowledge of how employees differ can help the manager better understand his or her employees and, as a result, to take actions aimed at facilitating (and not inhibiting) employee need satisfaction.

2. An awareness of the concept of employee needs has clear implications for employee selection and placement. For instance, as we shall see, certain types of employees are likely to be more successful in sales positions, while others are likely to excel in staff positions (like personnel administration). Understanding these differences can therefore facilitate decisions concerning who is placed in which positions.

3. The concept of needs also has clear implications for reward practices. Since employees respond differently to different rewards, an awareness of differences in needs can help the manager design reward systems appropriate to employee needs.

4. The recognition that employees pursue different needs also helps the manager understand to some extent why different employees behave as they do. For instance, an employee with a high need for achievement is likely to pursue task-related activities with vigor, while an employee with a high need for affiliation may devote more attention to developing social relationships on the job.

5. Finally, on a general level, a thorough knowledge of basic motivational processes (including the concept of needs) is essential to an awareness of organizational dynamics. Why do people behave as they do? What causes good or bad performance? Why is absenteeism or turnover high? The answers to questions such as these rest very squarely on understanding what motivates the employee.

In this chapter, then, we shall consider employee needs and basic motivational processes. In Chapter 5, we shall continue our discussion of individual differences by examining employee abilities and traits. Then, in Chapter 6, we consider perceptual processes in organizations, followed by a review of learning processes and behavior modification in Chapter 7. Finally, Chapter 8 attempts to integrate these various materials as we consider more complex models of employee motivation. These models attempt to draw upon our cumulative knowledge of the topic and to point the way for managers to develop motivating and rewarding environments.

Nature of Motivation

Motivation Defined

The word *motivation* derives from the ancient Latin *movere,* which means to move. As used in the study of employee motivation in work settings, however, this definition is clearly inadequate. A more comprehensive approach defines motivation as that which energizes, directs, and sustains human behavior.

This more complete definition emphasizes three distinct aspects of motivation that are important. First, motivation represents an energetic force which *drives* people to behave in particular ways. Second, this drive is directed *toward* something. In other words, motivation has strong goal orientation. Third, the idea of motivation is best understood within a *systems* perspective. That is, to understand human motivation, it is necessary to examine the forces within individuals and their environments that provide them with feedback and reinforce their intensity and direction.

Basic Motivational Processes

Before considering the various models of employee motivation that are currently in use, we will first examine the nature of the underlying motivational process. While the models of motivation may sometimes differ in certain aspects, they all tend to share basic assumptions about how behavior is energized, directed, and sustained through time.

A generalized model of basic motivational processes is shown in Exhibit 4–1. As can be seen in this exhibit, there are four basic components of the process (Dunnette and Kirchner, 1965): 1) needs or expectations; 2) behavior; 3) goals; and 4) feedback. At any point in time, individuals are seen as having a constellation of needs, desires, and expectations. For instance, one employee may have a strong need for achievement, a desire for monetary gain, and an expectation that doing his job well will, in fact, lead to the receipt of desired rewards. When such needs, desires, and expectations are

Exhibit 4–1   A model of basic motivational processes

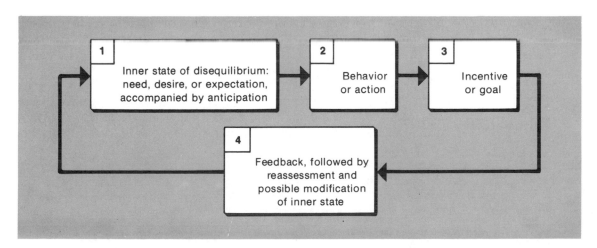

present, individuals experience a state of inner disequilibrium. This disequilibrium, in turn, may cause behavior that is motivated toward specific goals. Having these goals facilitates a return to a state of homeostasis or balance. The resulting behavior activates a series of cues (either within the individuals or from the external environment) that feed messages back to the individuals concerning the impact of their behavior. This feedback may serve to reassure individuals that the behavior is correct (that is, it satisfies their needs) or it may tell them that their present course of action is incorrect and should be modified.

Consider the following example. A young salesperson has a high need for personal achievement. As such, she experiences an inner state of disequilibrium; a need exists that has not been met (box 1 in Exhibit 4–1). Based on the strength or potency of this need, the salesperson attempts to engage in behavior (box 2) which she feels will lead to feelings of personal accomplishment (box 3). For instance, she may attempt to outsell her colleagues, thereby receiving recognition for a job well done. Based on this goal-directed behavior, she receives feedback both from her own assessment of her behavior and from others (box 4) which may tell her that she has indeed accomplished something important or worthwhile. This feeling should serve to return her (at least temporarily) to a state of homeostasis with respect to this particular need.

While this simple model of motivation obviously does not take into account all influences on human motivation, it is illustrative of the basic nature of the process. Moreover, it emphasizes the cyclical nature of motivation. It shows that people are in a continual state of disequilibrium, constantly striving to satisfy a variety of needs. Once one need has been adequately met, another need or desire emerges to stimulate further action. In this way, people direct and redirect their energies as they attempt to adapt to changing needs and a changing environment.

Early Theories of Motivation

The topic of motivation has long been of concern to both managers and psychologists. However, until recently, the emphasis and approach of these two divergent groups differed sharply. Hence, in order to gain a clearer understanding of how today's contemporary models evolved, it is necessary first to examine briefly the developmental sequence of both managerial and psychological models of motivation.

Managerial Approaches to Motivation

The evolution of management thought concerning employee motivation passed through three relatively distinct stages: 1) traditional; 2) human relations; and 3) human resources (Miles, Porter, and Craft, 1966).

Traditional model (1900–1930). With the emergence of the industrial revolution in the late 1800s, it became necessary to redefine both our conception of the nature of work and the social relationships between people in various levels in organizations. A need existed for a new philosophy of management that was consistent with the prevailing managerial beliefs of the times. These beliefs held that the average worker was basically lazy and was motivated almost entirely by money. Moreover, it was felt that few workers wanted (or could handle) a high degree of autonomy or self-direction on their jobs. (These assumptions are summarized in Exhibit 4–2).

Based on these assumptions, it was felt that the best way to motivate employees was to pay them using a piece-rate system and then redesign their jobs so the average worker could maximize his or her output. This job redesign, which was at the heart of the *scientific management* movement, was aimed not at enrichment but at increased job simplification and fractionization. The simpler the task, it was reasoned, the greater the output. Far from being exploitative in nature, the original advocates of scientific management (like Frederick Taylor) saw this approach as being in the best interest of the worker since workers' pay increased with output. It was felt that, in exchange for increased income, workers would tolerate the fractionated and routinized jobs of the factory.

Human relations model (1930–1960). As the scientific management movement gained momentum, several problems began to emerge. First, it became increasingly apparent that factors other than money had motivating potential. This is not to say that money was unimportant, only that it was not the sole influence on employee effort. Second, managers became aware that many employees were self-starters; and did not need to be closely supervised and controlled. Finally, some managers attempted to use the job simplification techniques of scientific management without tying resulting output to pay increases. This practice quickly led to employee distrust of management as wages fell behind productivity and as more workers were laid off because of increased efficiency. The result was often reduced effort by workers, accompanied by drives for unionization. Thus, managers learned that the human factor had to be taken into account if long term productivity was to be maintained.

This emphasis on the human factor in employee performance, beginning around 1930, became known as the *human relations movement.* With this added perspective, the basic assumptions about the nature of people at work changed. It was now known that people wanted to feel useful and important at work; they wanted to be recognized as individuals. Such needs were seen to be as important as money (see Exhibit 4–2). Hence, managerial approaches to motivation were characterized by a strong *social* emphasis. Attention shifted away from the study of man–machine relations and toward a better understanding of the nature of interpersonal and group relations on the job. The clearest example of this new emphasis was the Hawthorne

Exhibit 4–2. General patterns of managerial approaches to motivation (*after Miles, Porter, and Craft, 1966*)

Traditional model	Human relations model	Human resources model
Assumptions 1. Work is inherently distasteful to most people. 2. What they do is less important than what they earn for doing it. 3. Few want or can handle work which requires creativity, self-direction, or self-control.	**Assumptions** 1. People want to feel useful and important. 2. People desire to belong and to be recognized as individuals. 3. These needs are more important than money in motivating people to work.	**Assumptions** 1. Work is not inherently distasteful. People want to contribute to meaningful goals which they have helped establish. 2. Most people can exercise far more creative, responsible self-direction and self-control than their present jobs demand.
Policies 1. The manager's basic task is to closely supervise and control subordinates. 2. He or she must break tasks down into simple, repetitive, easily learned operations. 3. He or she must establish detailed work routines and procedures, and enforce these firmly but fairly.	**Policies** 1. The manager's basic task is to make each worker feel useful and important. 2. He or she should keep subordinates informed and listen to their objections to his plans. 3. The manager should allow subordinates to exercise some self-direction and self-control on routine matters.	**Policies** 1. The manager's basic task is to make use of "untapped" human resources. 2. He or she must create an environment in which all members may contribute to the limits of their ability. 3. He or she must encourage full participation on important matters, continually broadening subordinate self-direction and control.
Expectations 1. People can tolerate work if the pay is decent and the boss is fair. 2. If tasks are simple enough and people are closely controlled, they will produce up to standard.	**Expectations** 1. Sharing information with subordinates and involving them in routine decisions will satisfy their basic needs to belong and to feel important. 2. Satisfying these needs will improve morale and reduce resistance to formal authority—subordinates will "willingly cooperate."	**Expectations** 1. Expanding subordinate influence, self-direction, and self-control will lead to direct improvements in operating efficiency. 2. Work satisfaction may improve as a "by-product" of subordinates making full use of their resources.

Source: Adapted from Miles, Porter, and Craft, 1966, *56*, 1990–2005 *Leadership Attitudes Among Public Health Officials.*

studies (Roethlisberger and Dickson, 1939), where it was concluded that the failure to treat employees as human beings was largely responsible for the existence of problems such as low morale and poor performance.

In order to overcome these problems, managers were told to make employees feel important and involved. Morale surveys emerged as a popular index of employee discontent. Moreover, increased efforts were directed at opening new communication channels within organizations. Departmental meetings, company newspapers, and seminars on improving communications effectiveness all emerged to insure that employees felt they were involved and were important to the organization. Finally, supervisory training programs were begun to train managers to understand the nature of group dynamics and how the forces that operate within them could be used for the benefit of the organization.

Two features carried through from the traditional theories of motivation. First, the basic goal of management under human relations was still to secure employee compliance with managerial authority. Changed were the strategies for accomplishing this. Second, throughout the human relations movement, almost no attention was given to changing the nature of the job itself. Instead, emphasis was placed on making employees more satisfied (and, it was hoped, more productive) primarily through interpersonal strategies.

Human resources model (1960–present). Recently, it has become increasingly apparent that the assumptions underlying the human relations model represent an incomplete statement of human behavior at work. More contemporary models (to be discussed in this and the following chapters) view motivation in more complex terms, assuming that *many* factors are capable of influencing behavior. These factors may include the nature of the incentive system, social influences, the nature of the job, supervisory style, employees' needs and values, and one's perceptions of the work environment.

These newer models also assume that different employees want different rewards from their jobs, that many employees sincerely want to truly contribute, and that employees by and large have the capacity to exercise a great deal of self-direction and self-control at work (see Exhibit 4–2). In short, many contemporary managerial views of motivation focus on employees as potential human *resources*. Given this assumption, it becomes management's responsibility to find ways to tap these resources in such a way that both the employees' and the organization's needs and goals are facilitated.

The utilization of an organization's human resources can be accomplished in a variety of ways. First, attempts can be made to fit the person to the job so employees can most fully use their talents. Efforts can be made to integrate personal goals with organizational goals so employees can satisfy their own needs while working for organizational objectives. The popular practice of paying sales representatives a commission or bonus based on level of sales is a good example of such goal integration. In addition, some organizations have increasingly turned to the various forms of participative decision making to better utilize the talents, ideas, and suggestions of their employees in solving organizational problems (Vroom and Yetton, 1973). Contemporary managerial approaches to employee motivation stress the importance of managers understanding basic motivational processes so as to better deal with their employees and their work environment and to facilitate the achievement of both high levels of performance and high levels of job satisfaction.

Psychological Approaches to Motivation

Just as there has been an evolutionary process in managerial approaches to motivation, so too has there been a similar developmental trend among psychologists interested in motivation. This trend passed through an evolution of four stages: 1) hedonism; 2) instinct theories; 3) reinforcement theories; 4) cognitive theories. As we shall see, while psychologists originally approached the topic of motivation from a quite different perspective than did management theorists, the contemporary positions of both groups have apparently converged to a considerable extent. This convergence is shown in Exhibit 4–3).

Hedonism. The first coherent documentation of the principle of *hedonism* dates from the time of the early Greeks. It later reemerged in the eighteenth and nineteenth centuries as a popular explanation of behavior among such philosophers as Locke, Bentham, and Mill. Briefly, the principle of hedonism implies that individuals will tend to seek pleasure and avoid pain. It is assumed that individuals are likely to do those things that bring them some kind of satisfaction and to avoid those that are less satisfying.

While the concept of hedonism is still pervasive throughout our current models of motivation, it is far too simplistic to represent a comprehensive explanation of motivated behavior. Moreover, it fails to account for those instances when people engage in various activities even though they may be unpleasant. Hence, more complete explanations of behavior were needed. The first such theory that evolved chronologically was instinct theory.

Instinct theory (1890–1920). The first psychological *theory* of motivation emerged late in the last century as a result of the work of James, Freud, and McDougall. These theorists argued that a large portion of human behavior was not conscious and rational, as suggested by hedonism. Instead, behavior was thought to be largely influenced by instincts. An *instinct* was defined as an inherited biological tendency toward certain objects or actions (McDougall, 1908). Included in the list of instincts were locomotion, curiosity, love, fear, jealousy, and sympathy. These instincts were thought to be the primary determinants of behavior.

Exhibit 4–3 Historical development of approaches to motivation

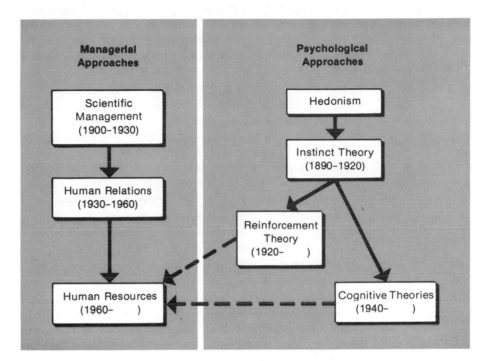

While instinct theory was fairly widely accepted during the first quarter of this century, it came under increasing attack beginning in the 1920s on several grounds (Hilgard and Atkinson, 1967). The list of instincts continued to grow, ultimately reaching almost 6,000. With so many variables, it became exceedingly difficult to develop a cogent explanation of human behavior. There was no acceptable explanation concerning which of the many instincts would be stronger influences on performance. So, in the absence of a solid conceptual framework, it was difficult to predict behavior. Also, it was found in various research studies that only a very weak relationship existed between an instinct and subsequent behavior. Hence, other factors were apparently also influencing behavior in addition to the instincts under study. Finally, it was argued by some psychologists that instincts were not, in fact, inherited but rather represented *learned* behavior. This last criticism was advanced by those who subsequently suggested a quite different theory of motivation: reinforcement theory.

Reinforcement theory (1920–present). Beginning with the early work of Thorndike, Woodworth, and Hull, reinforcement theory (also known as drive theory) emerged as a widely accepted, systematic explanation of behavior. Reinforcement theory assumes that people make decisions about their current behavior based on the consequences or rewards of past behavior. When past actions lead to positive consequences or rewards, individuals are likely to repeat such actions. On the other hand, when past actions lead to negative consequences or punishment, individuals are likely to avoid repeating them. This contention, known as the *law of effect* (Thorndike, 1911), emphasizes the role of learning on human behavior. Past learning and previous *stimulus-response* connections are viewed as the major cause of behavior.

Today, reinforcement still remains a popular explanation of human behavior. This is discussed in the chapter on behavior modification, an application of reinforcement theory.

Cognitive theory (1940–present).   The most recent psychological approach to understanding motivation is cognitive theory. In contrast to reinforcement theory, where emphasis is placed on the influence of past rewards and reinforcements, cognitive models emphasize future expectations and beliefs. That is, individuals are viewed as thinking, rational beings who make conscious decisions about their present and future behavior based on what they believe will happen (Lewin, 1938; Tolman, 1959). Past behavior influences these decisions only to the extent that the individual believes that past cause-effect relationships affect future events. Behavior is therefore seen as purposeful, goal-directed, and based on the conscious behavioral intentions of individuals. Significantly, it is this emphasis on reasoning and anticipation that sets cognitive models apart from other models of motivation.

The influence of the cognitive approach to understanding motivation is pervasive and can be seen in several models of employee effort and performance that are discussed in Chapter 8. In particular, equity theory, goal-setting teory, and expectancy/valence theory all draw heavily from the basic cognitive model.

Before examining these complex models of employee motivation, it will be useful to review two somewhat simpler approaches to motivation. These two models, advanced by Maslow (1954) and Murray (1938) focus primarily on the interrelationship between individual motives or needs and subsequent behavior. Both of these *need theories* provide a useful foundation for understanding the more complex models that follow.

Maslow's Need Hierarchy Theory

Perhaps the most widely known theory of individual needs and motivation is the one embodied in the need hierarchy model proposed by Abraham Maslow. Maslow was a clinical psychologist who did his early developmental work on this theory, starting in the 1940s among children with mental or emotional problems. Based on his observations, he attempted to develop a model of how the healthy personality grows and develops over time and how personality manifests itself in terms of motivated behavior. Somewhat later, during the 1960s, the theory was popularized among managers and organization analysts, primarily by the work of Douglas McGregor (1960).

Basic Premises of the Need Hierarchy Model

The need hierarchy model consists of two basic premises. First, people are seen as being motivated by a desire to simultaneously satisfy several types of specific needs. Second, it is postulated that these needs are arranged in a hierarchical form and that people work their way through this hierarchy as their needs are satisfied.

Maslow (1968) argues that there are two basic kinds of needs: deficiency needs and growth needs. *Deficiency needs* are needs which must be satisfied if the individual is to be healthy and secure. "Needs for safety, the feeling of belonging, love and respect (from others) are all clearly deficits." (Maslow, 1954, p. 10). To the extent that these needs are not met, the individual will fail to develop a healthy personalty. *Growth needs,* on the other hand, refer to those needs which relate to the development and achievement of one's potential. Maslow notes that the concept of growth needs is a vague one: "growth, individuation, autonomy, self-actualization, self-development, productiveness, self-realization, are all crudely synonymous, designating a vaguely perceived area rather than a sharply defined concept" (Maslow, 1968, p. 24).

Maslow goes further to suggest that people are motivated by five rather general needs and that these needs are arranged in a hierarchy. In their order of ascendance they are:

Deficiency Needs

- *Physiological needs* These needs are thought to be the most basic needs and include the needs for food, water, and sex.
- *Safety needs* The second level of needs centers around the need to provide a safe and secure physical and emotional environment, one that is free from threats to continued existence.
- *Belongingness needs* The third level consists of those needs relating to one's desire to be accepted by one's peers, to have friendships, and to be loved.

Growth Needs

- *Esteem needs* These needs focus on one's desire to have a worthy self image and to receive recognition, attention, and appreciation from others for one's contributions.

• *Self-actualization needs* The highest need category is the need for self-fulfillment. Here the individual is concerned with developing his or her full potential as an individual and of becoming all that it is possible to become.

Individuals move up the hierarchy by a process of *deprivation* and *gratification*. That is, when a particular need is unfulfilled (i.e., deprived), this need will emerge to dominate the individual's consciousness. Hence, a person concerned about physical safety will ignore other higher-order needs and devote all of his or her efforts to securing a safer environment. Once this need is gratified, however, that need submerges in importance and the next need up the hierarchy is activated (in this case, belongingness needs). This dynamic cycle of alternating deprivation, domination, gratification and activation continues throughout the various need levels until the individual reaches the self-actualization level.

Maslow in his later writings suggested that, unlike the other needs, gratification of the need for self-actualization tended to cause an *increase* in the potency of this need instead of a decline. In other words, self-actualization is a process of *becoming* and this process is intensified, as well as sustained, as one gradually approaches self fulfillment.

While Maslow did not feel that growth needs could be defined precisely, he did suggest some characteristics exhibited by individuals manifesting such needs based on his clinical observations. These include (1968, p. 25):

1. Superior perception of reality.
2. Increased acceptance of self, of others, and of nature.
3. Increased spontaneity.
4. Increase in problem-centering.
5. Increased detachment and desire for privacy.
6. Increased autonomy, and resistance to enculturation.
7. Greater freshness of appreciation; and richness of emotional reaction.
8. Higher frequency of peak experiences.
9. Increased identification with the human species.
10. Changed (the clinician would say, improved) interpersonal relations.
11. More democratic character structure.
12. Greatly increased creativeness.
13. Certain changes in the value system.

Parenthetically, it should also be noted that Maslow (1954) also discussed two other needs in his early work: These needs are thought to transcend the notion of the hierarchy and, as such, are not included in the hierarchy itself. The two needs are cognitive needs and aesthetic needs. *Cognitive* needs refer to the desire to know and understand one's environment. Examples include the need to satisfy one's curiosity and the desire to learn. *Aesthetic* needs include the desire for beauty, harmony, and order in nature. While the notion of aesthetic needs may have little relevance for the study of organizational behavior, such is not the case for cognitive needs. The importance of cognitive needs in organizations can be seen in attempts by employees to understand and relate to the tasks they perform and to be able to master tasks that are meaningful for them. In this sense, Maslow's cognitive needs are similar to Robert White's (1959) notion of the *competence motive*. White, like Maslow, argued that individuals have a strong need to develop mastery over their environment. The importance of such a need becomes apparent in the recent efforts to redesign employees' jobs so they are more challenging and meaningful. It is hoped by job redesign experts that such job redesign efforts will facilitate the feeling of mastery necessary to satisfy the cognitive and competence motives.

Implications for Management

Maslow's need hierarchy theory has proved to be particularly popular among managers, probably because of its simplicity as a conceptual framework in the discussion of motivation. When it is applied to organizations, clear recommendations for management emerge. The theory suggests that managers have a responsibility to create a work climate in which employees can satisfy their needs. Assuming that most employees have largely met their deficiency needs (i.e., they are free from hunger and threat and have established sufficient social relationships), managers can focus on creating a work climate that is aimed at satisfying growth needs. For instance, the proper climate may include opportunities for greater variety, autonomy, and responsibility so that employees can more fully realize their potential. Failure to provide such a climate would logically lead to increased employee frustration, poorer performance, lower job satisfaction, and increased withdrawal from work activities.

Research Evidence on Need Hierarchy Theory

Maslow's work has prompted a good deal of research into the utility of the theory in organizational settings. For instance, it has been found that managers in higher echelons of organizations are generally more able to satisfy their growth needs than lower level managers (Porter, 1961). Such a finding follows from the fact that upper level managers tend to have more challenging, autonomous jobs where it is possible to seriously pursue growth needs. Lower level managers, on the other hand, tend to have more routine jobs, thus making it more difficult to satisfy these needs.

However, while it is possible to differentiate between jobs that facilitate growth need satisfaction and those that inhibit it, it is much more difficult to establish the validity of the need hierarchy itself. In fact, after an extensive review of the research findings on the need hierarchy concept, Wahba and Bridwell (1976, p. 212) conclude: ''Maslow's need hierarchy theory presents the student of work motivation with an interesting paradox: The theory is widely accepted, but there is little research evidence to support it.''

Wahba and Bridwell examined three aspects of Maslow's model: 1) the existence of the hierarchy itself; 2) the proposition that deprivation of a need leads to domination of the individual by that need; and 3) the proposition that gratification of one need activates the next higher need. To examine the first issue, whether or not there is a five level hierarchy of needs, 17 studies were reviewed. These studies used either a factor analytic approach or a ranking approach to test the hypothesis. Based on this review, Wahba and Bridwell (1976, p. 224) conclude:

> Taken together, the results of the factor analytic studies and the ranking studies provide no consistent support for Maslow's need classification as a whole. There is no clear evidence that human needs are classified in five distinct categories, or that these categories are structured in a special hierarchy. There is some evidence for the existence of possibly two types of needs, deficiency and growth needs, although this categorization is not always operative.

The second of Maslow's propositions that was examined by Wahba and Bridwell was the deprivation/domination proposition. This proposition states that the higher the deprivation or deficiency of a given need, the higher will be its importance to the individual. Thus, if an employee feels highly deficient in his belongingness or social needs, these needs will become paramount in his motivated behavior to the exclusion of other needs. Only mixed results were found concerning this proposition, with some studies supporting the proposition and some failing to support it.

The final proposition is the gratification/activation proposition. Maslow's theory states that as one need is gratified it diminishes as a motivator and the next need up the hierarchy is activated. Hence, once an individual has sufficiently satisfied his esteem needs, he will focus his total energies toward self-actualization. Again, after reviewing the available evidence, Wahba and Bridwell (1976, p. 227) note that the progression from one need to another does not always follow the same pattern and that the trends in these patterns ''are not in agreement with those proposed by Maslow as far as the progression of satisfaction.''

These findings, when taken together, are not generally supportive of the need hierarchy theory as proposed by Maslow. However, in fairness, several limitations of the various studies reviewed above must be acknowledged. First, most tests of Maslow's theory were carried out among samples of working adults at one (or only a few) point(s) in time. In contrast, Maslow saw his theory as operating throughout one's lifetime. Hence, many of the studies purporting to examine Maslow's hypotheses are highly restrictive;

they used only adults and they measured the needs at only one point in time (or at several points in time but across only a few years). Hence, a true test of Maslow may only be possible by following people as they grow from childhood through adulthood—no easy task for any researcher.

Second, there are a variety of problems encountered when one attempts to measure needs. In fact, the imprecision of the need concept has led some to suggest that Maslow's theory is basically non-testable because of the difficulty of operationalizing the study variables.

Even so, the fairly consistent negative findings that have emerged raise doubts about the validity of the model as it now stands. The one conclusion that did appear to stand empirical testing is the notion of two distinct need levels, deficiency needs and growth needs. That is, people generally attempt to satisfy deficiency needs before attending to growth needs. Ultimately, Maslow's need hierarchy model has proved useful in generating ideas about the basic nature of human motives and in providing a conceptual framework for understanding the diverse research findings about people at work (Miner and Dachler, 1973).

ERG Theory: A Reformulation

A modification of Maslow's original theory has been proposed by Clayton P. Alderfer (1969, 1972). Alderfer's reformulation was suggested largely in response to the failure of Maslow's five-level hierarchy to hold up to empirical validation. Instead of Maslow's five need levels, Alderfer reformulates them into three more general need levels:

Existence needs Those needs required to sustain human existence, including both physiological and safety needs.

Relatedness needs Those needs concerning how people relate to their surrounding social environment, including the need for meaningful social and interpersonal relationships.

Growth needs Those needs relating to the development of human potential, including the needs for self-esteem and self-actualization. Growth needs are thought to be the highest need category.

Alderfer's model is similar to Maslow's earlier formulation in that both models posit that individuals move up the hierarchy one step at a time. The model differs from Maslow's, however, in two important regards. First, according to Maslow, individuals progress up the hierarchy as a result of the satisfaction of the lower-order needs. In contrast, Alderfer's ERG theory suggests that in addition to this satisfaction-progression process, there is also a frustration-regression process. (see Exhibit 4–4). Hence, when an individual is continually frustrated in his or her attempts to satisfy growth

Exhibit 4–4 Satisfaction-progression, frustration-regression components of ERG theory

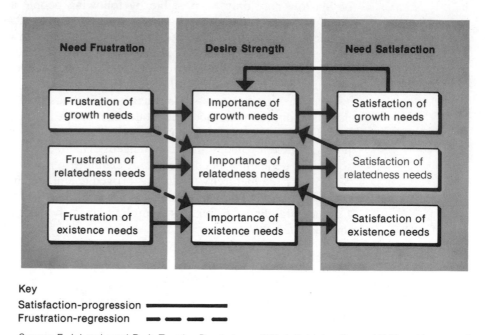

Key

Satisfaction-progression ▬▬▬▬▬▬

Frustration-regression ▬ ▬ ▬ ▬

Source: F. J. Landy and D. A. Trumbo *Psychology of Work Behavior, Second Edition,* Homewood Illinois: Dorsey Press, 1980. Reprinted by permission.

needs, relatedness needs will reemerge as a primary motivating force and the individual is likely to redirect his or her efforts toward lower level needs.

Second, while Maslow's model has individuals focusing on one need at a time, Alderfer's model suggests that more than one need may be operative (or activated) at the same time. As such, Alderfer's model is less rigid, allowing for greater flexibility in describing human behavior.

Murray's Manifest Needs Theory

The second need theory of motivation was developed by Henry A. Murray (1938) and is called the *manifest needs theory* (or the need-press model). While the initial formulations were developed by Murray in the 1930s and 1940s, the model has been considerably developed and extended by David McClelland and John Atkinson (Atkinson, 1964; McClelland et al., 1953).

Basic Premises of the Manifest Needs Model

Like Maslow, Murray felt that individuals could be classified according to the strengths of various needs. People were thought to possess at any one time a variety of divergent—and often conflicting—needs which influence behavior. A *need* was defined as a "recurrent concern for a goal state" (McClelland, 1971, p. 13). Each need was believed to be composed of two components: 1) a qualitative, or directional, component which includes the object toward which the need is directed; and 2) a quantitative, or energetic, component which consists of the strength or intensity of the need toward the object. Needs were thus viewed as the central motivating force for people in terms of both direction and intensity.

Overall, Murray posited that individuals possess about two dozen needs, including the needs for achievement, affiliation, power, and so forth. These needs and their definitions are shown in Exhibit 4–5. Murray believed that needs are mostly learned, rather than inherited, and are activated (or manifested) by cues from the external environment. For example, an employee who had a high need for achievement would only be expected to pursue that need (that is, to try to achieve something) when the environmental conditions were appropriate (e.g., when he was given a challenging task). Only then would the need become *manifest*. When the need was not cued, the need was said to be *latent*, or not activated.

Maslow vs. Murray

The manifest needs theory resembles Maslow's model in that both theories identify a set of needs and goals toward which behavior is directed. The two models differ, however, in two important respects. First, Murray does not suggest that needs are arranged in an hierarchical form as does Maslow. And, second, Murray's model allows for more flexibility in describing people. Maslow's need hierarchy model places individuals on one level at a time in the hierarchy (e.g., esteem needs). Using Murray's manifest needs model, on the other hand, we can describe an individual as having high needs for achievement and autonomy and low needs for affiliation and power—all at the same time. Hence, we are able to be more specific in describing people, instead of merely claiming they have "higher-order need strengths" as is the case with Maslow.

While the manifest needs model encompasses an entire set of needs, most research in organizational settings has focused on the four needs of achievement, affiliation, autonomy, and power. These four needs seem to be particularly important for understanding people at work. Therefore, we shall consider each of these needs as they relate to work settings.

Exhibit 4–5   Murray's needs

Need	Characteristics
Achievement	Aspires to accomplish difficult tasks; maintains high standards and is willing to work toward distant goals; responds positively to competition; willing to put forth effort to attain excellence.
Affiliation	Enjoys being with friends and people in general; accepts people readily; makes efforts to win friendships and maintain associations with people.
Aggression	Enjoys combat and argument; easily annoyed; sometimes willing to hurt people to get his or her way; may seek to "get even" with people perceived as having harmed him or her.
Autonomy	Tries to break away from restraints, confinement, or restrictions of any kind; enjoys being unattached, free, not tied to people, places, or obligations; may be rebellious when faced with restraints.
Endurance	Willing to work long hours; doesn't give up quickly on a problem; persevering, even in the face of great difficulty; patient and unrelenting in his work habits.
Exhibition	Wants to be the center of attention; enjoys having an audience; engages in behavior which wins the notice of others; may enjoy being dramatic or witty.
Harmavoidance	Does not enjoy exciting activities, especially if danger is involved; avoids risk of bodily harm; seeks to maximize personal safety.

Need for Achievement

Basic concepts.   By far the most prominent need from the standpoint of studying organizational behavior is the need for achievement (also known as *n Ach* or n Achievement). Need for achievement is defined as "behavior toward competition with a standard of excellence" (McClelland et al., 1953). High need for achievement is characterized by: 1) a strong desire to assume personal responsibility for finding solutions to problems; 2) a tendency to set moderately difficult achievements goals and take calculated risks; 3) a strong desire for concrete feedback on task performance; and 4) a single-minded preoccupation with task and task accomplishment. Low need for achievement, on the other hand, is typically characterized by a preference for low risk levels on tasks and for shared responsibility on tasks.

Need for achievement is an important motive in organizations because many managerial and entrepreneurial positions require such drive in order to

Exhibit 4–5 Murray's needs (continued)

Need	Characteristics
Impulsivity	Tends to act on the "spur of the moment" and without deliberation; gives vent readily to feelings and wishes; speaks freely; may be volatile in emotional expression.
Nurturance	Gives sympathy and comfort; assists others whenever possible, interested in caring for children, the disabled, or the infirm; offers a "helping hand" to those in need; readily performs favors for others.
Order	Concerned with keeping personal effects and surroundings neat and organized; dislikes clutter, confusion, lack of organization; interested in developing methods for keeping materials methodically organized.
Power	Attempts to control the environment and to influence or direct other people; expresses opinions forcefully; enjoys the role of leader and may assume it spontaneously.
Succorance	Frequently seeks the sympathy, protection, love, advice, and reassurance of other people; may feel insecure or helpless without such support; confides difficulties readily to a receptive person.
Understanding	Wants to understand many areas of knowledge; values synthesis of ideas, verifiable generalization, logical thought, particularly when directed at satisfying intellectual curiosity.

Source: Adapted from the Personality Research Form Manual, published by Research Psychologists Press, Inc., P.O. Box 984, Port Huron, MI 48060. Copyright © 1967, 1974, by Douglas N. Jackson.

be successful. Thus, when a manager who has a high *n Ach* is placed on a difficult job, the challenging nature of the task serves to cue the achievement motive which, in turn, activates achievement-oriented behavior. However, it is important to point out that when high need achievers are placed on routine or non-challenging jobs, the achievement motive will probably not be activated. Hence, there would be little reason to expect them to perform in a superior fashion under such conditions (McClelland, 1961; Steers and Spencer, 1977).

The concept of need for achievement is important, not only for understanding human behavior in its own right, but also for understanding how people respond to the work environment. As such, the concept has important implications for job design. Enriching an employee's job by providing greater amounts of variety, autonomy, and responsibility would probably enhance performance only for those employees who were challenged by such a job (that is, high need achievers). Low need achievers, on the other hand, may be frustrated by the increased personal responsibility for task accomplishment and, as such, may perform poorly or may even withdraw from the situation. We shall examine this phenomenon more in Chapter 16 when we explore job design.

Need for achievement and economic development.　McClelland (1961) has applied the notion of n Achievement to the study of economic development in underdeveloped countries. These studies are described in an interesting book entitled *The Achieving Society.*

As a result of several years of study, two general findings emerged. First, according to McClelland, there is a fairly consistent correlation between a country's current state of economic development and measurable mean levels of n Achievement in that country. Higher mean levels of *n Ach* are found in more prosperous nations, while lower levels are found in the less prosperous. Second, when McClelland examined the literature of ancient cultures for references to achievement-oriented aspirations and behaviors, he found some evidence that increases in the achievement motive preceded subsequent economic development in those civilizations.

Based on these findings, McClelland argues that economic development and prosperity at a national level can be influenced to some extent by the achievement strivings of a nation's people. Such findings have important implications for current efforts to assist underdeveloped nations in that they suggest a need to instill the achievement motive in the population (in addition to economic aid) in order to facilitate development.

Developing n Achievement.　Need for achievement, like other needs, is apparently learned at an early age and is influenced largely by the independence training given children by their parents. As Sanford and Wrightsman (1970, p. 212) point out, ''the relatively demanding parent who clearly instigates self-reliance in the child and who then rewards independent behavior is teaching the child a need for achievement.''

Since it is estimated that only about 10 percent of the population are high need achievers, questions are logically raised concerning how one becomes a high need achiever. McClelland's (1965) answer to this question is that achievement motivation can be taught to adults with moderate success. Achievement motivation training consists of four steps:

1. Teach participants how to think, talk, and act like a person with high need achievement.

2. Stimulate participants to set higher, but carefully planned and realistic, work goals for themselves.

3. Give the participants knowledge about themselves.

4. Create a group *esprit de corps* from learning about each others' hopes and fears, successes and failures, and from going through an emotional experience together.

To date, the evidence appears to support the usefulness of such training programs for increasing *n Ach*. With few exceptions, managers in various countries who attended such programs received more rapid promotions, made more money, and expanded their businesses more quickly after completing the course than did control groups. It is important to note here, however, that such managers were consistently chosen from entrepreneurial-type jobs thought to be most suited for high need achievers. The success of such programs on employees who perform routine, clerical, or automated tasks remains very doubtful because such jobs are not designed to activate the achievement motive.

Need for Affiliation

In contrast to the need for achievement, relatively little is known about the behavioral consequences of the need for affiliation, despite the fact that this need has been widely recognized since early in this century (Trotter, 1916). The need for affiliation *(n Aff)* may be defined as an "attraction to another organism in order to feel reassured from the other that the self is acceptable" (Birch and Veroff, 1966, p. 65). This need should not be confused with being sociable or popular; instead, it is the need for human companionship and reassurance.

People with a high need for affiliation are typified by the following: 1) a strong desire for approval and reassurance from others; 2) a tendency to conform to the wishes and norms of others when pressured by people whose friendship they value; and 3) a sincere interest in the feelings of others. High *n Aff* individuals tend to take jobs characterized by a high amount of interpersonal contact, like sales, teaching, public relations, and counseling.

How does *n Aff* influence employee behavior? Some evidence suggests that individuals with a high need for affiliation have better attendance records than those with a low *n Aff* (Steers and Braunstein, 1976). Moreover, some research suggests that high *n Aff* employees perform somewhat better in situations where personal support and approval is tied to performance. Support for this position comes from French (1958) who found in a laboratory experiment that, while high *n Ach* individuals performed better when given *task-related* feedback, high *n Aff* individuals performed better when given *supportive* feedback. Effort and performance for those high in *n Aff* can also be enhanced somewhat under a cooperative work norm where pressure for increased output is exerted by one's *friends* only (French, 1955; Atkinson and Raphelson, 1956; DeCharms, 1957). The implications of such findings for leadership or supervisory behavior are fairly clear. To the extent that supervisors can create a cooperative, supportive work environment where positive feedback is tied to task performance, we would expect high *n Aff* employees to be more productive. The reason for this is simple: Working harder in such an environment would lead to the kinds of need satisfaction desired by those high in *n Aff*.

Need for Autonomy

Need for autonomy *(n Aut)* is a desire for independence and for freedom from any kind of constraint. Individuals with a high need for autonomy prefer situations where they: 1) work alone; 2) control their own work pace; and 3) are not hampered by excessive rules or procedures governing their work behavior (Birch and Veroff, 1966).

The effects of a high need for autonomy on employee behavior can be significant. For instance, it has been found that high *n Aut* individuals: 1) tend not to react to external pressures for conformity to group norms (Kasl, Sampson, and French, 1964); 2) tend to be poor performers unless they are allowed to participate in the determination of their tasks (Vroom, 1959); 3) are not committed to the goals and objectives of the organization; and 4) are typically found among craft and tradespeople and lower-echelon employees, not managers (Vroom, 1959). This last finding may be explained by the fact that managerial success is in large measure determined by a manager's ability to interact successfully with others, to cooperate, and compromise. Individuals with a high need for autonomy typically refuse to do this.

Need for Power

A final need that has proved important for understanding organizational behavior is an individual's need for power (or dominance). Need for power represents a desire to influence others and to control one's environment. It has a strong social connotation, in contrast to n Autonomy, in that a high *n Pow* employee will try to control (or lead) those around him.

Interest in the power motive dates from the early work of Alfred Adler (1930), who believed that power was the major goal of all human activity. Adler saw human development as a process by which people learn to exert control over the forces that have power over them. Hence, a person's ultimate satisfaction comes with his or her ability to have influence over the environment. While the subsequent work of Murray (1938), McClelland (1975), and others do not see power as an all-consuming drive as Adler did, they nevertheless view it as an important need.

In summarizing the research on need for power, here's how Litwin and Stringer (1968, p. 18) describe individuals high in *n Pow:*

> . . . They usually attempt to influence others directly—by making suggestions, by giving their opinions and evaluations, and by trying to talk others into things. They seek positions of leadership in group activities; whether they become leaders or are seen only as "dominating individuals" depends on other attributes such as ability and sociability. They are usually verbally fluent, often talkative, sometimes argumentative.

Additional recent research demonstrates that employees with high needs for power or dominance tend to be superior performers, have above average attendance records, and tend to be in supervisory positions (Steers and

Braunstein, 1976). Moreover, such individuals were rated by others as having good leadership abilities.

Two faces of power. McClelland (1976) notes that n Power can take two forms among managers: personal power and institutionalized power. Employees with a *personal-power* orientation strive for dominance almost for the sake of dominance. Personal conquest is very important to them. Moreover, such individuals tend to reject institutional responsibilities. McClelland likens personal-power types to conquistadors or feudal chieftains; that is, they attempt to inspire their subordinates to heroic performance but want their subordinates to be responsible to their leader, not to the organization.

The *institutionalized-power* manager, on the other hand, is far more concerned with problems of the organization and what he or she can do to facilitate goal attainment. McClelland (1976) describes institutionalized-power types as follows: 1) they are organization-minded and feel personal responsibility for building up the organization; 2) they enjoy work and getting things done in an orderly fashion; 3) they seem quite willing to sacrifice some of their own self-interest for the welfare of the organization; 4) they have a strong sense of justice or equity; and 5) they are more mature (i.e., they are less defensive and more willing to seek expert advice when necessary).

A recent study of managers and their motives has been carried out by Maccoby (1976) which leads to the same conclusions as did McClelland's work. The results are summarized in Box 4–1. Although Maccoby uses different terms (e.g., the gamesman), his work rests largely on managers' need for power.

Manifest Needs and Managerial Effectiveness

Based on the foregoing discussion of the various needs, questions are logically raised concerning the influence various manifest needs have on managerial behavior and effectiveness. Is it possible to build a profile of a successful manager based on these needs? Recent research by McClelland (1975, 1976) suggests that such a profile is possible on a very general level.

McClelland's (1976, p. 102) argument begins by asking what we mean by managerial success:

> Almost by definition, a good manager is one who, among other things, helps subordinates feel strong and responsible, who rewards them properly for good performance, and who sees that things are organized in such a way that subordinates feel they know what they should be doing. Above all, managers should foster among subordinates a strong sense of team spirit, of pride in working as part of a particular team. If a manager creates and encourages this spirit, his subordinates certainly should perform better.

Box 4–1 The Gamesman

In the past 20 years, we have witnessed significant changes in the way organizations are managed.* There are fewer autocratic managers, teamwork has often replaced the individual star, experiments in job satisfaction and the quality of working life are rampant, and flexible approaches to both working hours and division of labor are commonplace. As a result, organizations and their managers have had to adapt to a changing work environment and, all too often, the past keys to managerial success no longer work. New patterns of managerial behavior must be found.

A recent study made by Michael Maccoby focused on this problem by observing 250 middle and top managers from 12 major corporations. Maccoby began with the proposition that any strategy for social change must account for the personal characteristics of those responsible for change. "What mix of motives—ambition, greed, fascination with technology, scientific interest, security-seeking, or idealism—determined their actions?" (p. 1). As a result of his study, Maccoby identified four relatively distinct "corporate personalities" based on the motives of the individuals involved. These four types are:

• *The craftsman* The goal of a craftsman is to perfect the work at hand. As such, the individual identifies only with his or her own job and often ignores larger corporate objectives. The craftsman's narrowness of view and obsession with perfection at the expense of production usually limits him or her to middle management.

• *The company man or woman.* This person identifies only with corporate goals and, in a real sense, the company is his or her life. This individual questions little and follows blindly. He or she is loyal, has limited vision, and often ends up as second in command.

• *The jungle fighter.* These managers are often useful in a crisis when strong and decisive (if autocratic) leadership is necessary in the short run. Maccoby differentiates here between lions, who have both strength and ability and lead naturally but ruthlessly, and foxes, who scheme and manipulate. Both are often dispensed with by the organization when the crisis is over and members want a return to normalcy.

• *The gamesman* The gamesman is the ultimate careerist who recognizes both personal goals and those of the corporation and who devotes his or her life to reconciling the two. The gamesman's main interest is in competitive activity, where he or she can prove to be a winner by taking moderate risks and motivating others to push themselves beyond their normal pace. The gamesman responds to work as a game. The contest energizes the individual and this energy is communicated to others. Emphasis is on new ideas, new techniques, and shortcuts. The main goal of such people is to be a winner, and talking about themselves invariably leads to a discussion of their tactics and strategies in the corporate contest.

*Source: M. Maccoby, *The Gamesman*. New York: Simon & Schuster, 1976.

Maccoby argues, based on his clinical observations, that the new corporate top executives combine many gamesman traits with aspects of the company man or woman. That is, successful top executives are team players who are committed to the organization and who feel personally responsible for its success. Career goals have merged with corporate goals and one's focus is on what is good for the company without separating that from what is good for the individual. Such individuals tend to be worriers and see people in terms of their use to the organization. Moreover, they generally succeed in submerging their own egos and gain strength from this exercise in self-control.

As Maccoby (p. 42) notes, "to function, the corporations need craftsmen, scientists, and company men (many could do without jungle fighters), but their future depends most of all on the gamesman's capacity for mature development."

Based on this description, what type of manager is most suited to the tasks of managing? A manager with a high need for achievement? need for affiliation? need for power? McClelland argues persuasively that the best manager is one who has a high need for power! Let's examine why.

Managers who have a high need for *achievement* concentrate their efforts on personal accomplishment and improvement. They tend to be highly independent individuals who want to assume responsibility (and credit) for task accomplishment and who want short-term concrete feedback on their performance so they know how well they are doing. These characteristics are often closely associated with *entrepreneurial* success (such as an independent business person). However, these same characteristics can be detrimental where the individual has to manage others. In complex organizations, managers obviously cannot perform all the tasks necessary for success; teamwork is necessary. Moreover, feedback on the group's effort and performance is often vague and delayed. Hence, the managerial environment is not totally suitable to stimulate the achievement motive in managers.

Managers who have a high need for *affiliation* fare no better. Affiliative managers have a high need for group acceptance and, partly as a result of this, they often tend to be indecisive in decision-making for fear of alienating one faction or another. Moreover, this concern for maintaining good interpersonal relationships often results in their attention being focused on keeping subordinates happy instead of on work group performance. McClelland (1976, p. 104) summed up his research findings on the affiliative manager by noting:

The manager who is concerned about being liked by people tends to have subordinates who feel that they have very little personal responsibility, that organizational procedures are not clear, and that they have little pride in their work groups.

In contrast, managers with a high need for *institutionalized* power were found in McClelland's (1976) study to supervise work groups that were both more productive and more satisfied than other managers. (McClelland also found that managers high in need for *personal* power were far less successful managers than those with a need for institutionalized power.) Several reasons exist for the success of the n Power manager. One explanation is suggested by Zaleznik (1970, p. 47):

> Whatever else organizations may be (problem-solving instruments, sociotechnical systems, reward systems, and so on), they are political structures. This means that organizations operate by distributing authority and setting a stage for the exercise of power. It is no wonder, therefore, that individuals who are highly motivated to secure and use power find a familiar and hospitable environment in business.

In other words, power-oriented managers, when truly concerned about the organization as a whole (instead of themselves) provide the structure, drive, and support necessary to facilitate goal-oriented group behavior. In this sense, they fit very nicely into the definition of managerial success noted above. However, as noted by McClelland (1976), a power-oriented manager pays a price in terms of personal health. He measured need for power among a group of Harvard graduates over twenty years ago. Twenty years later in a follow-up study, McClelland found that 58% of those rated high in power in the earlier study either had high blood pressure or had died of heart failure!

One final point needs to be discussed before leaving the topic of needs and managerial success. This concerns the *interactive* effects of the various needs on performance. In particular, a study by Andrews (1967) looked at both n Power and n Achievement in two Mexican companies. Company A was a dynamic and rapidly growing organization characterized by high employee morale and enthusiasm. Company B, on the other hand, had shown almost no growth despite large initial investments and a favorable market; moreover, Company B had serious problems of employee dissatisfaction and turnover. An assessment of the various need strengths among managers in both companies revealed several interesting findings. To begin with, the upper management of Company A (the more dynamic firm) were much higher on n Achievement than managers in Company B. The presidents of both companies were extremely high in n Power. However, in Company A, the president's n Power was combined with a moderately high n Achievement. This was not the case in the less successful Company B. Hence, based on these findings, it would appear that the most successful managers may be those who combine a power-orientation *with* an achievement-orientation.

Summary

This chapter has introduced the concept of motivation as it relates to individual employee needs. Motivation was defined as that which energizes, directs, and sustains human behavior. Based on this, a basic model of the motivational process was presented.

Next, the development of management thought on employee motivation was reviewed and was compared to various developments in the study of motivation by psychologists.

Based on this discussion, two need theories of motivation were presented. The first, by Maslow, suggests that individual needs are arranged in a hierarchy and that people move from one level in the hierarchy to the next. The second, by Murray and McClelland, on the other hand, does not recognize the existence of such a hierarchy. Instead, focus is on describing various human needs, such as achievement, affiliation, and power. The implications for managerial effectiveness with regard to the various needs are discussed.

Key Words

motivation	law of effect
need	cognitive theory
scientific management	need hierarchy theory
human relations	manifest needs theory
human resources	n Achievement
hedonism	n Affiliation
instinct theory	n Autonomy
reinforcement theory	n Power

Questions for Discussion

1. Define motivation.
2. Describe the basic motivational process.
3. Review the development of management thought concerning approaches to motivation. How does this compare to the development of psychological approaches to motivation?
4. What is the basic difference between the human relations approach to management and motivation and the human resources approach?
5. What is the law of effect?

6. Compare and contrast the reinforcement theory and the cognitive theory of motivation.
7. Compare and contrast Maslow's need hierarchy theory and Murray's manifest needs theory. What model do you prefer as a manager?
8. Describe Maslow's deprivation/gratification cycle.
9. What changes did Alderfer's ERG theory make in Maslow's original formulation of the need hierarchy theory?
10. Review the research evidence on Maslow's need hierarchy theory.
11. Discuss the role of achievement motivation in economic development.
12. How is need for achievement developed?
13. What impact does need for affiliation have on employee performance?
14. Describe the two faces of power and how each impacts on organizational performance.
15. What are the basic characteristics of Maccoby's "gamesman"?
16. What kind of need set combination makes the best manager?

chapter 5

Individual
Abilities
and Traits

In this chapter, we continue our discussion of individual differences among employees and the role such differences can play in job attitudes and behavior. In the last chapter, we examined employee needs as they relate to basic motivational processes. Here, we consider two additional factors: employee abilities and personal traits. Based on the information provided in these two chapters, we will then proceed to discuss how people behave in work situations and how behavior can differ as a result of variations among individuals.

Importance of Topic for Managers

A knowledge of employee abilities and traits is important for several reasons:

1. Employee abilities and traits represent those individual characteristics that determine an employee's *capacity* to contribute to the organization, in contrast to motivation, which determines an employee's *will* to contri-

bute. If we expect actual performance to be a joint function of motivation *and* abilities and traits, a knowledge of these latter variables is certainly important.

2. A clear recognition of differences in employee abilities and traits allows managers to do a better job of selection and placement. People can be placed in jobs most suited to their individual talents and skills. This matching process will enhance the utilization of an organization's human resources.

3. In this chapter we discuss the fact that individual characteristics and needs often conflict with organizational requirements. The nature of this conflict—as well as modes of conflict resolution—should be clearly understood by managers interested in optimizing both employee commitment and employee performance.

4. Finally, a good deal of research has been conducted over the years on the subject of employee differences and how they affect work behavior. It is an advantage for managers to have a familiarity with this literature. While these findings do not always provide clear answers to all personnel problems, an awareness of their scope can at least help managers better understand human behavior so personnel decisions can be made with as much available information as possible.

Employee Abilities

Employee *abilities* are generally defined as those physical and intellectual characteristics of individuals that are relatively stable over time. Although such characteristics can in some instances change (e.g., through training or physical maturation), we generally expect them to be stable attributes of the individual. Our concern in this section is not so much with a detailed examination of the range of human abilities or their measurement. Rather we will attempt to develop an appreciation of these abilities as they influence job attitudes and performance.

Abilities are an important aspect of understanding organizational behavior since they determine the extent to which an employee can perform adequately on the job. For instance, if a clerk typist simply cannot master typing skills, his or her performance would clearly be limited no matter how much compensation was offered. Organizational effectiveness is enhanced to the extent that managers can hire and train individuals with sufficient job-related abilities.

There are many ways to categorize human abilities. Perhaps one of the most useful is to divide abilities into three areas (McCormick & Tiffin, 1974):

Mental abilities These abilities deal with one's intellectual capacities and are closely related to how people make decisions. Research has shown, for example, that managerial success is closely related to the level of one's intellectual capabilities (e.g., verbal comprehension, inductive reasoning, and memory). In fact, some have argued that the higher one reaches in the organizational hierarchy, the more important intellectual abilities are for managerial performance (Ghiselli, 1966).

Mechanical abilities   These abilities focus on one's capacity to comprehend relationships between objects and to adequately perceive and manipulate spatial relations (the ability to visualize how parts fit together). Mechanical abilities are of central importance when considering an employee's capacity to respond.

Psychomotor abilities   This category includes a wide range of abilities, including manual dexterity, eye-hand coordination, and motor and manipulative ability. Psychomotor abilities describe various aspects of skilled muscular performance typically involving some degree of visual control.

All three of these abilities are important for understanding the nature of people at work and how they are better managed. The recognition of such abilities—and the recognition that people have *different* abilities—has clear implications in recruitment and selection decisions and emphasizes the importance of matching people to jobs. There are also clear implications for overly skilled personnel. Hiring highly skilled employees and then placing them on dull, repetitive jobs would not only stifle their performance potential but could also hasten their withdrawal from the organization. As we examine people at work, therefore, consideration should be given to the role played by human abilities in daily performance and behavior.

Personal Traits

The third individual difference characteristic we wish to consider (after employee needs and abilities) is personal traits. When taken together, these three factors help us considerably in developing portraits of various individuals in the workplace. Information about these characteristics will prove useful as we consider a variety of topics throughout this book, including employee reactions to work design, stress, reward systems, and group dynamics. A major lesson to be learned here is that all individuals do not react similarly to the same stimuli or events. The information provided here can help us understand and predict employee behavior and attitudes on the job.

We shall use the term personal traits instead of personality because of the various and often conflicting definitions of the concept of personality. Instead of engaging in debate over definitions, we feel it is preferable to focus exclusively on identifying measurable traits that describe individuals and which are relevant to workplace considerations. Specifically, a *personal trait* may be defined as a consistent predisposition or tendency to behave in a particular way (Brody, 1972). The primary focus in this definition is on observed and measurable behaviors (or predispositions to behave). We shall be concerned with traits such as interpersonal style, emotional stability, and cognitive style rather than on the more esoteric self-concept or psychoanalytic processes. First, we will consider how personal traits are measured, followed by a consideration of major influences in their development. In the next section, we will examine several important work-related personal traits. Finally, we will examine a particular model that focuses on the interaction of the person and the organization.

The Measurement of Personal Traits

Personal traits can be assessed in organizations in at least three different ways: 1) inventories; 2) experimental procedures; and 3) independent ratings. (For a detailed discussion of the various techniques as well as a critique of each method, see Maier, 1973).

By far the most popular technique used by industry is the self-report inventory. In this approach, individuals are asked a series of standardized questions and their responses are recorded using either a true-false format or a Likert-type scale (that is, a scale where the respondent answers on a continuum from strongly agree to strongly disagree). Some of the more popular personality inventories include the California Psychological Inventory, the Minnesota Multiphasic Personality Inventory, and the Personality Research Form. These inventories are structured to provide percentile scores on a variety of personal traits or characteristics (e.g., dogmatism, aggressiveness, and cognitive complexity). A major benefit of such inventories is that a large number of traits can be measured with little time or effort.

A second approach that is receiving increased attention in organizations is the use of experimental procedures. Individuals are placed in artificially created situations which attempt to simulate real life. The clearest industrial application of this procedure is the use of the assessment center, where personal characteristics are appraised through a series of simulated management exercises like role playing, in-basket techniques, or stress interviews.

The third technique, independent ratings, makes use of either trained experts or peers to evaluate individuals on a set of pre-determined traits. The most frequent use of independent ratings in industry are the recommendation forms many companies use for personnel selection and placement.

Major Influences on Individual Development

Early research on personality development focused largely on the issue of whether heredity or environment determined an individual's personality.

While a few researchers are still concerned with this issue, most contemporary psychologists now feel this debate is fruitless. As noted long ago by Kluckhohn and Murray (1953):

> the two sets of determinants can rarely be completely disentangled once the environment has begun to operate. The only pertinent questions therefore are: (1) which of the various genetic potentialities will be actualized as a consequence of a particular series of life-events in a given physical, social, and cultural environment? and (2) what limits to the development of this personality are set by genetic constitution?

In other words, if the individual is viewed from the whole person perspective, the search for the determinants of personal traits focuses on both heredity and environment, as well as the interaction between the two over time. In this regard, five major categories of determinants of personal traits may be identified:

Physiological determinants Factors such as stature, health, and sex often act as constraints on personal growth and development. For instance, tall people often tend to become more domineering and self-confident than shorter people. Traditional sex role stereotyping has served to channel males and females into different developmental patterns (e.g., males were trained to be more assertive, females more passive).

Cultural determinants Because of the central role of culture in the survival of a society, there is great emphasis on instilling cultural norms and values in children as they grow up. For instance, in capitalist societies, where individual responsibility is highly prized, emphasis is placed on developing achievement-oriented, independent, self-reliant people, while in socialistic societies, emphasis is placed on developing cooperative, group-oriented individuals who place the welfare of the whole of society ahead of individual needs. As Mussen (1963, p. 62) notes, "the child's cultural group defines the range of experiments and situations he is likely to encounter and the values and personality characteristics that will be reinforced and hence learned."

Family and social group determinants Perhaps the most important influence on personal development is one's immediate family and social group. For instance, it has been found that children who grow up in democratic homes tend to be more stable, less argumentative, more socially successful, and more sensitive to praise or blame than those who grow up in authoritarian homes (Mussen, 1963). One's family and immediate peers also contribute significantly to the socialization process, influencing how we think and behave through an intricate system of rewards and penalties.

Role determinants People are assigned to various roles very early in life, based on factors such as sex, socio-economic background, and race. As one grows older, other factors like age and occupation influence the roles we are expected to play. The roles we are channeled into often limit our personal growth and development as individuals and significantly control acceptable behavior patterns.

Situational determinants   Finally, personal development can be influenced by unique factors that are often unpredictable, such as a divorce or death in the family. For instance, Abegglen (1958) studied twenty successful male executives who had risen from lower-class childhoods and discovered that in three-fourths of the cases these executives had experienced some form of severe separation trauma from their fathers. Their fathers (and role models) had either died, been seriously ill, or had serious financial setbacks. Abegglen hypothesized that the sons' negative identification with their fathers' plights represented a major motivational force for achievement and success.

Personal Traits and Work Behavior

The concept of personal traits (and theories based on personal traits) has proven to be popular among investigators of employee behavior in organizations. There are several reasons for this. To begin with, trait theories focus largely on the normal or healthy adult, in contrast to psychoanalytic and other personality theories which focus largely on abnormal behavior. Trait theories identify several specific characteristics that describe people. Allport (1961) insisted that our understanding of individual behavior could progress only by breaking behavior patterns down into a series of elements (traits). "The only thing you can do about a *total* personality is to send flowers to it," he once said. Hence, in the study of people at work, we may discuss an employee's dependability, or emotional stability, or cognitive complexity. These traits, when taken together, form a large mosaic that provides much insight into individuals. Finally, a third reason for the popularity of trait theories in the study of organizational behavior is that the traits that are identified tend to remain relatively stable over time and are measurable. These tangible qualities make comparisons among employees much easier than either the somewhat mystical psychoanalytic theories or the highly abstract and volatile self theories.

The number of traits people exhibit varies depending upon which theory one wishes to use. In an exhaustive search, Allport and Odbert (1936) were able to identify over 17,000 traits that describe people. However, such a large list makes it impossible to develop a parsimonious model of human behavior. Efforts to reduce or cluster such traits have been welcome (see, e.g., Cattell, 1965; Shaw, 1976). Building upon these earlier works, we will assess six relatively discreet clusters of personal traits (see Exhibit 5–1). They are: 1) interpersonal style; 2) social sensitivity; 3) ascendant tendencies; 4) dependability; 5) emotional stability; and 6) cognitive style. While no cluster of traits is ideal, these six identify important variables that have been shown to relate to organizational behavior.

Interpersonal Style

In the study of people at work, a major facet of individual characteristics is interpersonal style, or the way in which people typically behave in group settings. This variable is particularly important in the study of supervisory behavior and of people's reactions to the exercise of authority. Personal characteristics which fall into the interpersonal style cluster include the general tendency to trust (or not to trust) others, openness (or social distance), and one's orientation toward authority.

Exhibit 5–1   Major clusters of personal traits

Personal Trait Cluster	Emphasis	Examples
Interpersonal style	The way individuals interact with others; how they behave in groups.	Trust, openness, authoritarian-orientation
Social sensitivity	The way individuals perceive and respond to the needs, emotions, and preferences of others.	Empathy, social judgment, insight
Ascendant tendencies	Focuses on the extent to which individuals attempt to dominate or control others.	Assertiveness, dominance, prominence
Dependability	The level of consistency, responsibility, and predictability of individuals in group situations.	Self reliance, responsibility, integrity
Emotional stability	Reflects the emotional and mental well being of individuals.	Emotional control, defensiveness, anxiety, neuroticism
Cognitive style	Focuses on the way individuals process information and the judgments made based on these observations.	Dogmatism, risk taking, cognitive complexity

In particular, a great deal has been written about individual orientations towards authority. Early work by Adorno and his associates (Adorno et al., 1950) found that this trait varies widely with people. An *authoritarian-orientation* (or authoritatian personality) is characterized by several features all reflecting the notion that it is right and proper for there to be clear status and power differences between people. A high authoritarian is typically: 1) demanding, directive, and controlling of subordinates; 2) submissive and deferential to superiors; 3) intellectually rigid; 4) fearful of social change; 5) highly judgmental and categorical in reactions to others; 6) distrustful; and 7) hostile in response to restraint. Non-authoritarians, on the other hand, believe more firmly that status and power differences should be minimized, that social change can be constructive, and that people should be more accepting and less judgmental of others.

Studies of authoritarian personalities in groups and organizations are widespread. For instance, Vroom (1959) found that employees rated high in authoritarianism were more productive under autocratic supervision, while employees rated low in authoritarianism were more productive under participative or democratic supervisors. Shaw (1976) notes that high authoritarians strongly adhere to the rules and norms of groups to which they belong. They show greater conformity behavior in the face of group consensus than do nonauthoritarians.

One particularly harmful effect of such submissive conformity can be seen in the classic Milgram (1973) study. In this study (see Box 5–1), subjects persisted at tasks they knew to be harmful to others because of their belief that an authority figure had a right to so instruct them in such behavior. The implications for management of this study are clear.

Social Sensitivity

A second set of personal traits clusters around the extent to which individuals perceive and respond to the needs, emotions, and preferences of others. These traits include empathy, social judgment, and insight. Research studies have consistently shown a moderate relationship between these social skills and acceptance by group members, successful leadership attempts, amount of participation, and group performance effectiveness (Shaw, 1976). The lack of these skills is inversely related to friendliness and social interaction, as would be expected.

Ascendant Tendencies

People in any organization vary considerably in the extent to which they desire and attempt to be prominent, assertive, and domineering. Such an orientation reflects a strong desire by an individual to stand apart from the group, to be different or unique in a superior sort of way. People with

Box 5–1 Milgram's Study of Obedience

Obedience to authority is a basic element in the social structure of any organization. The issue here for managers is the extent to which managers or employees should follow rules or directives that conflict with their own moral values. A classic series of experiments assessing the extent to which people would obey authority was carried out by Stanley Milgram.*

Research design. In these experiments, subjects were brought into a laboratory under the impression that they were going to participate in a study of the effects of electrical shocks on learning and memory. Each time a fellow subject (who was actually a "confederate," that is, who knew the real purpose of the study) erred in a word-pair test, the real subject was instructed to administer an electrical shock of increasingly higher voltage. The shock machine (which was actually harmless) showed calibrations of 15–volt increments up to 450 volts. The calibrations were also labeled "extremely intense," "dangerous," and "XXX" as they approached the upper voltage limits. The research question was: At what point would the person refuse to continue administering ever-increasing (and "dangerous") shocks when the confederate missed the correct answer?

Results. Because no base line data were available, Milgram asked a group of psychiatrists to estimate the proportion of subjects who would follow orders and administer shocks to a fellow subject up to the highest voltage level. Their estimate was one in 1,000. In actuality, Milgram found that a full 60% of the subjects

proceeded to administer the highest possible shocks. Milgram later confessed that it was a brutal and depressing scene "seeing ordinary people administering presumably torturous pain to the confederates, even despite the confederate's screams and protests that he no longer wanted to participate in the experiment." Milgram concluded that almost anything can be done by someone if the command to do so comes from a legitimate authority and is backed up by sufficient definitions of the situation.

Implications. Milgram's findings in the laboratory can be seen repeatedly in real life (e.g., the Nazis in World War II, the My Lai massacre, corporate payoffs, the Watergate break-in). In every case, people willingly broke the law because they had been ordered to do so by a higher authority. This higher authority relieved them of personal responsibility and made their job easier. Managers consistently face similar dilemmas in balancing their own moral values against direct orders. Results indicate that in a large number of cases, the managers will sacrifice what they think is right and follow authority.

As Milgram (1963, p. 376) notes, however, such subservience is not without cost: "I observed a mature and initially poised businessman enter the laboratory smiling and confident. Within 20 minutes he was reduced to a twitching, stuttering wreck, who was rapidly approaching a point of nervous collapse. . . . and yet he continued to respond to every word of the experimenter, and obeyed to the end."

Source: S. Milgram, "Behavioral study of obedience." *Journal of Abnormal and Social Psychology,* 1963, 67, 371–378. See also: S. Milgram, *Obedience to Authority: An Experimental Inquiry.* New York: Harper & Row, 1973.

ascendant tendencies are often self-assertive, creative, and popular. They often emerge as leaders and tend to be quite dissatisfied with the performance of *other* leaders (Shaw, 1976).

Dependability

People can also be differentiated with respect to their behavioral consistency and personal integrity. Individuals who are seen as self-reliant, consistent, and dependable are typically viewed by others as desirable colleagues or group members who will cooperate and work steadfastly toward group goals (Stogdill, 1948; Greer, 1955). Unconventional people, on the other hand, are often thought to lack dependability and commitment to group goals. As such, they are often disrespected and rejected by other group members (Schachter, 1959). Consider the implications of these perceptions on hiring and promotion decisions.

Emotional Stability

Emotional stability refers to a class of personal traits that relate to the emotional and mental well-being of the individual. It includes the positive traits of emotional control and adjustment, as well as the negative traits of anxiety, defensiveness, depressive tendencies, and neuroticism.

Studies have revealed that one of the most important personal traits is *anxiety.* Anxiety, discussed in detail in Chapter 15, is a general uneasiness or concern about some uncertain or future event. Anxious individuals experience a vague and uneasy feeling that is psychologically unpleasant and interferes with their responses to everyday life events. People who are highly anxious consistently have problems in developing rewarding interpersonal relationships, generally have low aspirations on task performance, conform easily to group norms, alter their judgments and opinions when confronted by differing opinions, and are highly dependent on others for clues to acceptable behavior (Shaw, 1976). Many recent attempts in organizations to open communication and develop more interpersonal trust are intended to create a work climate where employees will experience less threat and anxiety and hence become more productive members of the organization.

Cognitive Style

Cognitive style refers to the way in which people process and organize information and arrive at judgments or conclusions based on their observations of situations. Three aspects of cognitive style are of particular importance for the study of people at work: 1) dogmatism; 2) risk-taking propensity; and 3) cognitive complexity.

Dogmatism.   Dogmatism refers to a particular cognitive style that is characterized by closed-mindedness and inflexibility (Rokeach, 1960). This trait has received special attention in the area of managerial decision-making. In particular, highly dogmatic managers tend to reach decisions quickly following only a limited search for information, but are highly confident about the accuracy of the resulting decisions (Taylor and Dunnette, 1974).

There is also evidence that dogmatism interferes with efficient performance of duties. For instance, Esposito and Richards (1974) found that highly dogmatic individuals report large discrepancies between how they actually spent their time on the job and how they would ideally spend their time. Apparently, their inflexibility and rigidity of cognitive style interferes with their handling of work-related problems.

Risk-taking propensity.   Individuals also vary in their willingness to take risks in decision-making (Kogan and Wallach, 1967). Research by Taylor and Dunnette (1974) among managers indicates that high risk takers, like those high in dogmatism, tend to make decisions more rapidly (with limited searching for relevant information) than do low risk takers. Such differences can be important for organizations depending upon what type of jobs high and low risk takers are placed in. For instance, a high risk taking propensity may be desirable for a sales representative who must act quickly to make a sale. On the other hand, such a propensity (accompanied by little search behavior) could be financially disastrous for a personnel manager negotiating a new labor contract.

Cognitive complexity.   This trait describes the ability of an individual to differentiate and integrate various aspects of a cognitive domain. That is, it outlines a person's capacity to acquire and sort through various pieces of information from the environment and organize them in such a way that they make sense. People with a high cognitive complexity tend to use more information   and to see the relationships between this information—than people with low cognitive complexity. For example, if a manager was assigned a particular problem, would he have the capacity to break the problem down into its various facets and understand how these various facets relate to one another? A manager with low cognitive complexity would tend to see only one or two salient aspects of the problem, while a manager with a higher cognitive complexity would understand more of the nuances and subtleties of the problem as they relate to each other and to other problems.

People with *low* cognitive complexity typically exhibit the following characteristics (Ebert and Mitchell, 1975, p. 81):

1. They tend to be categorical and stereotypic. Cognitive structures that depend upon simple fixed rules of integration tend to reduce the possibility of thinking in terms of degrees.

2. Internal conflict appears to be minimized with simple structures. Since few alternative relationships are generated, closure is quick.
3. Behavior is apparently anchored in external conditions. There is less personal contribution in simple structures.
4. Fewer rules cover a wider range of phenomena. There is less distinction between separate situations.

On the other hand, people with *high* levels of cognitive complexity are typically characterized by the following (Ebert and Mitchell, 1975, p. 81):

1. Their cognitive system is less deterministic. Numerous alternative relationships are generated and considered.
2. The environment is tracked in numerous ways. There is less compartmentalization of the environment.
3. The individual utilizes more internal processes. The self as an individual operates on the process.

Research on cognitive complexity has focused on two important areas from a managerial standpoint: leadership style and decision-making. In the area of leadership, it has been found that managers rated high on cognitive complexity are better able to handle complex situations, such as rapid changes in the external environment. Moreover, such managers also tend to use more resources and information when solving a problem and tend to be somewhat more considerate and consultative in their approach to managing their subordinates (Mitchell, 1970).

In the area of decision-making, fairly consistent findings show that individuals with high cognitive complexity: 1) seek out more information for a decision; 2) actually process or use more information; 3) are better able to integrate discrepant information; 4) consider a greater number of possible solutions to the problem; and 5) employ more complex decision strategies than individuals with low cognitive complexity. (Schroder, Driver, and Streufert, 1967)

It should be noted, however, that high cognitive complexity is not always an asset, particularly when it is combined in one individual with other traits such as dogmatism, lack of social sensitivity, or ascendant tendencies. In these cases, the highly capable and analytical (that is, cognitively complex) person may become impatient with his less intelligent co-workers, resulting in what has been called an abrasive personality. This abrasive personality, and the problems it creates for management, are discussed in Box 5–2.

Personality and Organization: A Basic Conflict?

Most theories of personality stress that an individual's personality becomes complete only when it interacts with other people; growth and development

Box 5–2 The Abrasive Personality at the Office

A particularly annoying yet frequently encountered problem in work organizations is the abrasive personality.* As described by Levinson, some men and women of high achievement work hard and contribute a great deal to the organization, yet in doing so rub people the wrong way. These people are often characterized by self-centeredness, isolation, perfectionism, condescending contempt, and a tendency to attack others. Yet at the same time, they demonstrate a keen analytical capability necessary in management circles. Levinson (p. 78) describes one case:

A couple of years ago, when Henry Weigl was abruptly relieved of all his operating responsibilites as chairman of Standard Brands, *Forbes* magazine carried this account: "Weigl's abrasive, authoritarian style drove potential successors from the company, even while he was building Standard Brands in the market place. Says a person close to the company: "There isn't a company in American industry with an executive turnover rate like that of Standard Brands." Another observer states: "Weigl had a way of publicly humiliating men at the executive level that no self-respecting person could stand."

Hence the problem: a high level of contribution to the company combined with a personality or interpersonal style unacceptable to others. Levinson notes that such people are relatively common in business firms and are not limited to the executive level.

The abrasive individual places considerable emphasis on control of himself and others. He is, to all appearances, emphatically right, self-confident, and self-assured. He stubbornly adheres to a position and considers compromise a lowering of standards. As a result, such individuals are often held back from promotions—or fired—despite the considerable expertise they can bring to problem solving.

Levinson suggests several useful strategies for dealing with abrasive personalities aimed at curbing such tendencies while simultaneously utilizing the individual's capabilities. He suggests that the supervisor should: 1) recognize the origins of such behavior—the vulnerable self-image, the hunger for affection, and the eagerness for perfection—and not become angry or provocative; 2) report observations concerning the individual's behavior uncritically and ask how he or she felt others would respond; 3) acknowledge his or her desire to achieve but emphasize that the individual must take others into account if success is to be attained; 4) emphasize that goal attainment is usually a step-by-step process, that compromise is not necessarily second best, and that an all–or–nothing approach usually leads to failure; and 5) if all else fails, confront the individual's arrogance and point out clearly that such behavior is unsatisfactory.

Levinson notes that these techniques are not always successful but that they often work. He further notes that many managers are reluctant to address the problem squarely and develop internal hostilities toward the individual themselves as they suppress the problem. Such behavior by the supervisor only compounds the problem and often delays a satisfactory solution to the point where one party has to leave.

Source: H. Levinson, "The abrasive personality at the office". *Psychology Today,* 1978, *11,* (12), 78–84.

do not occur in a vacuum. Or, as noted by Frank (in Argyris, 1957), human personalities are the individual expressions of our culture, and our culture and social order are the group expressions of individual personalities. This being the case, it is important to understand how work organizations influence the growth and development of the adult employee.

A model of person-organization relationships has been proposed by Chris Argyris (1957, 1973). This model, called the *basic incongruity thesis,* consists of three parts: what individuals want from organizations, what organizations want from individuals, and how these two potentially conflicting sets of desires are harmonized.

Argyris begins by examining how healthy individuals change as they mature. Based on previous work, Argyris suggests that as people grow to maturity, seven basic changes of needs and interests occur:

- People develop from a state of passivity as infants to a state of increasing activity as adults.

- People develop from a state of dependence upon others to a state of relative independence.

- People develop from having only a few ways of behaving to having many diverse ways of behaving.

- People develop from having shallow, casual, and erratic interests to having fewer but deeper interests.

- People develop from having a short time perspective (i.e., behavior is determined by present events) to having a longer time perspective (behavior is determined by a combination of past, present, and future events).

- People develop from being in subordinate positions (from child to parent or from trainee to manager).

- People develop from a low understanding or awareness of themselves to a greater understanding of and control over themselves as adults.

While Argyris acknowledges that these developments may differ between individuals, the general tendencies from childhood to adulthood are believed to be fairly common.

Next, Argyris turns his attention to the defining characteristics of more traditional work organizations. In particular, he argues that in the pursuit of efficiency and effectiveness, organizations create work situations aimed more at getting the job done than at satisfying employees' personal goals. Examples include increased task specialization, unity of command, a rules orientation, and other things aimed at turning out a standardized product with standardized people. In the pursuit of this standardization, Argyris argues, organizations often create work situations characterized by the following:

- Employees are allowed minimal control over their work; control is often shifted to machines.
- They are expected to be passive, dependent, and subordinate.
- They are allowed only a short-term horizon in their work.
- They are placed on repetitive jobs that require only minimal skills and abilities.
- Based on the first four items, people are expected to produce under conditions leading to psychological failure.

Hence, Argyris (1957) argues persuasively that many jobs in our technological society are structured in such a way that they conflict with the basic growth needs of a healthy personality. This conflict is represented in Exhibit 5–2. The magnitude of this conflict between personality and organization is a function of several factors. The strongest conflict can be expected

Exhibit 5–2   Basic conflict between employees and organizations

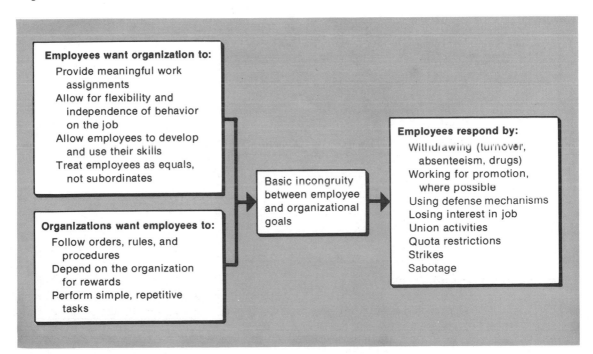

Employees want organization to:
Provide meaningful work assignments
Allow for flexibility and independence of behavior on the job
Allow employees to develop and use their skills
Treat employees as equals, not subordinates

Organizations want employees to:
Follow orders, rules, and procedures
Depend on the organization for rewards
Perform simple, repetitive tasks

Basic incongruity between employee and organizational goals

Employees respond by:
Withdrawing (turnover, absenteeism, drugs)
Working for promotion, where possible
Using defense mechanisms
Losing interest in job
Union activities
Quota restrictions
Strikes
Sabotage

under conditions where: 1) employees are of high maturity; 2) organizations are highly structured and rules and procedures are highly formalized; and 3) jobs are highly fractionated and mechanized. Hence, we would expect the strongest conflict to be at the lower levels of the organization, among blue-collar and clerical workers. Managers tend to have jobs that are less mechanized and tend to be less subject to formalized rules and procedures.

Where strong conflicts between personalities and organizations exist or, more precisely, where strong conflicts exist between what employees and organizations want from each other, employees are faced with difficult choices. Several methods or combinations of adaptation mechanisms may be pursued:

- Employees may leave the organization.
- They may work hard to climb the ladder into the upper echelons of management.
- They may defend their self concepts and adapt through the use of defense mechanisms.
- They may adapt by disassociating themselves psychologically from the organization (e.g., losing interest in their work, lowering their work standards, etc.) and instead concentrate on the material rewards available from the organization.
- They may find allies in their fellow workers and, in concert, may further adapt *as a group* by such activities as quota restrictions, unionizing efforts, strikes, and sabotage.

Unfortunately, while such activities may help employees feel that they are getting back at the organization, they do not alleviate the basic situation that is causing the problem. To do this, one has to examine the nature of the job and the work climate. This we do in Chapter 16. Personality represents a powerful force in the determination of work behavior and must be recognized before meaningful change can be implemented by managers to improve the effectiveness of their organizations.

Summary

In this chapter we continued our discussion of employee characteristics as they relate to work. The role of human abilities was discussed. Various aspects of personal traits (also called personality) were examined. Included in this examination was a consideration of measuring such traits, major influences on trait development, and a discussion of the traits themselves as they affect work behavior.

Following this discussion, Argyris' basic incongruity thesis was introduced as it relates to people at work. Finally, two studies were presented dealing with various aspects of personal traits. The first, by Milgram, examined the effects of authoritarian orientation on obedience under stress. The second, by Levinson, examined the effects of the abrasive personality in the office.

Together, this chapter and the previous one have attempted to present a well-rounded introduction to the nature of individual differences in organizations. It has been emphasized that people differ on several dimensions and that these differences can have a substantial impact on how people view their jobs and can vary the extent to which they are capable of performing satisfactorily on the job. Such differences caution us against the traditional machine theory of employee behavior that assumes people are relatively homogeneous and therefore can be treated as interchangeable parts in the workplace. People are not the same and managers who ignore the differences risk creating a work environment that jeopardizes both performance and satisfaction.

Individual differences will continue to emerge as we discuss various aspects of organizational behavior in the chapters to come. For instance, it will be seen in the next chapter, on perception, that our perceptual processes are modified by personal characteristics. When we examine complex models of employee motivation the role of personal characteristics will be seen as prominent. Hence, it appears that a major lesson for managers is the importance of recognizing these differences and making attempts to accommodate them in their management practices.

Key Words

abilities	anxiety
personal traits	cognitive style
authoritarian-orientation	dogmatism
social sensitivity	cognitive complexity
ascendant tendencies	basic incogruity thesis
dependability	

Questions for Discussion

1. Discuss the role of human abilities in employee behavior and performance.
2. How do we measure personal traits?
3. Discuss some major influences on the development of personal traits.

4. Allport once remarked that "the only thing you can do about a total personality is to send flowers to it." What did he mean by this comment?

5. What is meant by an authoritarian orientation and what relation does it have to the workplace?

6. What are the major conclusions of Milgram's study?

7. What is meant by ascendant tendencies? Social sensitivity? Emotional stability?

8. What is the influence of emotional stability on employee behavior and performance?

9. What is meant by cognitive style? Describe the various aspects of cognitive style.

10. Discuss the major differences between high and low cognitive complexity in terms of their implications for work.

11. What is the basic incongruity thesis? Do you agree with this thesis? Why or why not?

12. Discuss the impact of the abrasive personality in the workplace.

chapter 6

Perceptual Processes

People are constantly being subjected to stimuli, or cues from their environment, all of which compete for their attention. In the work place, these stimuli include such things as supervisors' instructions, co-worker's comments, machine noises, people walking by, and posted signs and notices. Given the very large number of these stimuli, individuals are faced with the problem of how to make sense out of so many variables, how to organize and interpret the more relevant stimuli, and how to respond to them. The process by which this is done is *perception*.

In this chapter we will examine various aspects of the perceptual process as they relate to organizational behavior. Topics covered include: 1) basic perceptual processes; 2) perceptual selectivity; 3) social perception at work; 4) attribution theory; 5) perceptual differences between superiors and subordinates; and 6) barriers to accurate perception of others. First, though, we should say a few words about why the general topic area is pertinent to the management process.

Importance of Topic for Managers

The nature of employee perception and the perceptual process is relevant for managers in the following ways:

1. First of all, as noted by Lewin (1935) and others, people behave based on how they see the environment, and views of the world differ considerably between individuals. For instance, a management directive to work harder may be seen by an aspiring young manager as a way of moving up in the organization. This same directive, however, may be interpreted by a factory worker as another attempt by management to exploit the worker. It is important for managers to recognize that people perceive things differently and attempt to understand how perceptual processes work.

2. Perceptual processes also play an important role in the decisions managers make concerning employee selection, placement, and promotion. Most people have subtle biases that affect their decisions. In view of the significance of managerial decisions, both for the individuals involved and for the organization, it is important to understand as clearly as possible how these biases are formed and how they affect our attitudes and behavior.

3. Perception also plays a large part in the performance appraisal process. One of the most popular methods of evaluating employees is with the use of rating forms. These forms are subject to a wide variety of potential errors, many of which can be attributed to poor or inaccurate perception. An understanding of perceptual processes can therefore facilitate more accurate appraisal systems which, in turn, have the capability of more accurately tying rewards to behavior.

4. A knowledge of perception can improve a manager's ability to communicate—orally or in writing—with employees. The notion of perceptual selectivity, discussed in this chapter, acts to screen out or allow in various messages from the environment. A knowledge of what gets attention can aid us in getting our messages across to those we work with.

5. Finally, an understanding of the basic nature of perceptual processes can also help us better understand ourselves and our reactions to our surroundings. For instance, many students of management—as well as many managers—perceive blue-collar workers as being basically lazy. Such generalizations about any occupational grouping are seldom accurate and hardly serve to improve the capacity to manage.

Basic Perceptual Processes

By *perception* we mean the process by which an individual screens, selects, organizes, and interprets stimuli so that they have meaning to the individual.

It is a process of making sense out of one's environment so an appropriate behavioral response can be made. Perception does not necessarily lead to an accurate portrait of the environment, but rather, to a unique portrait, influenced by the needs, desires, values, and disposition of the perceiver. As described by Krech et al. (1962, p. 20), an individual's perception of a given situation:

> is not, then, a photographic representation of the physical world; it is, rather, a partial, personal construction in which certain objects, selected out by the individual for a major role, are perceived in an individual manner. Every perceiver is, as it were, to some degree a nonrepresentational artist, painting a picture of the world that expresses his individual view of reality.

The multitude of objects that vie for attention are first selected or screened by individuals. This process is called *perceptual selectivity*. Certain of these objects catch our attention, while others do not. For example, once individuals notice a particular object, they then attempt to make sense out of it by organizing or categorizing it according to their own unique frame of reference and their needs. This second process is termed *perceptual organization*. Once meaning has been attached to an object, individuals are in a position to determine an appropriate response or reaction to it. Hence, if we clearly recognize and understand we are in danger from a falling rock or a car we can quickly move out of the way.

Because of the importance of perceptual selectivity for an understanding of the perceptual process in work situations, we will examine this concept in some detail before considering the topic of social perception.

Perceptual Selectivity

As noted above, *perceptual selectivity* refers to the process by which certain objects in the environment are selected by individuals for attention. Without this ability to focus on one or a few stimuli instead of the hundreds of stimuli constantly surrounding us, individuals would be unable to process all the relevant information necessary to initiate behavior.

Perceptual selectivity is enhanced by two related processes: 1) absolute thresholds of activation and 2) sensory adaptation. First, it is believed that all sense organs have *absolute thresholds of activation;* thus, many stimuli go unnoticed by individuals because they are not strong, bright, or loud enough to activate our senses. The use of camouflage by the military is an example of intentionally attempting to reduce the chance of sense (in this case, optical) activation. Choosing neutral colors like grey or beige for clothing is another example. *Sensory adaptation,* on the other hand, is a process by which individuals tune out certain objects or stimuli after continued exposure. The ticking of a clock, for instance, may appear to be very loud for an individual who has focused on this sound, but another individual may not even hear the ticking because the senses have adapted to it and nullified its impact on perception.

Hence, many objects or stimuli are removed from the perceptual field by the above two processes. Beyond this, all other stimuli must compete for our attention. A variety of factors influence which stimuli we notice and which we ignore. These various influences on perceptual selectivity can be divided into external influences and internal influences (see Exhibit 6–1).

External Influences on Perceptual Sensitivity

External influences consist of the characteristics of the observed object or person that activate the senses. Most external influences affect perceptual selectivity either because of their physical properties or their dynamic properties.

Physical properties. The physical properties of the objects themselves often affect which objects receive attention by the perceiver. Emphasis here is on the unique; what is different, out of the ordinary. Important physical properties include the following:

1. Size Generally, larger objects receive more attention than smaller ones. Advertising companies use the largest signs and billboards allowed to capture the perceiver's attention. The reverse of this idea is evidenced when most of the surrounding objects are also large. In this case, a small object

Exhibit 6–1 Major influences on perceptual selectivity

I. *External Influences*

  Physical Properties
    Size
    Intensity
    Contrast
    Novelty or familiarity

  Dynamic Properties
    Motion
    Repetition
    Ordering

II. *Personal Influences*

  Response salience
  Response disposition
  Attitudes and feelings toward object or person

against a field of large objects may receive more attention. In either case, size represents an important variable in perception.

2. Intensity   Brighter, louder, more colorful objects tend to attract more attention than objects of less intensity. For example, when a factory foreman yells an order at his or her subordinates, it will probably receive more notice (although it may not receive the desired response by workers). It must be remembered here, however, that intensity heightens activation only when compared to other comparable stimuli. Hence, if the foreman always yells, sensory adaptation may tune out the message.

3. Contrast   Objects that contrast strongly with the background against which they are observed tend to receive more attention than less contrasting objects. An example of the contrast principle can be seen in the use of plant and highway safety signs. A terse message like DANGER is lettered in black against a yellow or orange background.

4. Novelty or familiarity   A final physical characteristic that can heighten perceptual awareness is the novelty or unfamiliarity of the object. Specifically, the unique or unexpected seen in a familiar setting (an executive of a conservative company who comes to work in burmudas) or the familiar seen in an incongruous setting (someone in church holding a can of beer) will receive attention.

Dynamic properties.   The second set of external influences on perceptual selectivity concerns those properties which either change over time or derive their uniqueness from the order in which they are presented. Several organizationally relevant examples can be identified:

1. Motion   The most obvious dynamic property is motion. We tend to pay attention to objects that move against a relatively static background. This principle has long been recognized by advertisers who often use signs with moving lights or moving objects to attract attention. In an organizational setting, a clear example is a rate-buster, who works substantially faster than his or her colleagues, attracting more attention.

2. Repetition   Another principle basic to advertising is repetition of a message or image. As noted by Morgan and King (1966, p. 343), ''A stimulus that is repeated has a better chance of catching us during one of the periods when our attention to a task is waning. In addition, repetition increases our sensitivity or alertness to the stimulus.'' Work instructions that are repeated tend to be received better, particularly on a dull or boring task on which it is difficult to concentrate. This process is particularly effective in the area of plant safety. Most industrial accidents occur because of careless mistakes during monotonous activities. Repeating safety rules and procedures can often help keep workers alert to the possibilities of accidents.

3. Ordering   A final external influence on perceptual selectivity is the order in which the objects or stimuli are presented (Secord and Backman,

1964). This principle is particularly important in interpersonal communications in organizational settings. Generally, research has shown that the order in which objects are presented to individuals can have a dramatic impact on what is noticed and what is not.

Two kinds of ordering effects have been found; primacy effects and recency effects. *Primacy effects* occur when the first stimulus or piece of information received from an object receives the greatest weight and colors subsequent information. *Recency effects,* on the other hand, occur when the last, or most recent, stimulus receives the greatest attention. Recency effects are often employed in both written and oral communications where the writer or speaker intentionally builds up to a major point by proceeding through several smaller, less important points. The initial points thus build and set the stage for the final (most recent) message. For instance, in a sales meeting the general sales manager may plod through sales statistics from the past ten years and finally, perhaps enthusiastically, present the present year's target. If this final stimulus is presented with enthusiasm and vigor, it may override earlier stimuli and create a heightened awareness of the need to increase sales *this* year.

Personal Influences on Perceptual Selectivity

In addition to a variety of external factors, several important personal factors are also capable of influencing the extent to which an individual pays attention to a particular stimuli or object in the environment. The three most important personal influences on perceptual readiness are: 1) response salience; 2) response disposition; and 3) attitudes and feelings toward an object or person.

Response salience.   This is a tendency to focus on objects that relate to our *immediate* needs or wants. Secord and Backman (1964, p. 14) describe response salience as the influence of ''the contemporary factors prevailing at the moment of perception. Certain current conditions, such as hunger, fatigue, or anxiety may affect what is perceived.'' As examples, a very nervous person may react intensely to sudden, loud noises, or a person who is hungry may miss a stop light in the haste to find a restaurant.

Response salience in the work environment is easily identified. A worker who is tired from many hours of work may be acutely sensitive to the number of hours (or minutes) until quitting time. Employees negotiating a new contract may know to the penny the hourly wage of workers doing similar jobs across town. Managers with a high need to achieve may be sensitive to opportunities for work achievement, success, and promotion. Finally, female managers may be more sensitive than many male managers to condescending male attitudes toward women.

Response salience, in turn, can distort the view of our surroundings. For example, as noted by Ruch (1967, p. 323):

> Time spent on monotonous work is usually overestimated. Time spent in interesting work is usually underestimated. . . . Judgment of time is related to feelings of success or failure. Subjects who are experiencing failure judge a given interval as longer than do subjects who are experiencing success. A given interval of time is also estimated as longer by subjects trying to get through a task in order to reach a desired goal than by subjects working without such motivation.

Response disposition. Whereas response salience deals with immediate needs and concerns, *response disposition* is the tendency to recognize familiar objects more quickly than unfamiliar ones. The notion of response disposition carries with it a clear recognition of the importance of past learning on what we perceive in the present. For instance, in an early study, Bruner and Postman (1949) presented a group of individuals with a set of playing cards with the colors and symbols reversed. That is, hearts and diamonds were printed in black and spades and clubs in red. Surprisingly, when subjects were presented with these cards for brief time periods, individuals consistently described the cards as they expected them to be (red hearts and diamonds, black spades and clubs) instead of how they really were. They were predisposed to see things as they always had been in the past.

Attitudes and feelings toward an object or person. The way people feel toward a particular object or person can also have a marked influence on how (or whether) the object or person is perceived. In general, research has found that objects about which we have strong feelings are more readily perceived than more neutral objects (Secord and Backman, 1964). For instance, in one experiment, subjects were given a questionnaire designed to identify which values were more important to them. Six categories of values were used: political, aesthetic, theoretical, economic, religious, and social. Words were then chosen from these various categories and shown briefly to the subjects on a screen. The experiment found that the greater the interest a person had in a particular value area, the more rapidly he or she recognized the words relevant to that area. For instance, words like money and bank were more readily perceived by those with strong economic interests, even though the words were presented so rapidly that many were below the threshold of recognition. Attitudes and values sensitize us so we more readily recognize stimuli or objects related to our strongest feelings.

The basic perceptual process is in reality a fairly complicated process. Several factors, including our own personal make-up and the environment, influence how we interpret and respond to the events we focus on. While the process itself may seem somewhat complicated, it in fact represents a shorthand to guide us in our everyday behavior. That is, without perceptual selectivity we would be immobilized by the millions of stimuli competing for our attention and action. The perceptual process allows us to focus our attention on the more salient events or objects and, in addition, allows us to categorize such events or objects so that they fit into our own conceptual map of the environment. The importance of perception should not be overlooked by managers interested in the study of people at work.

Social Perception at Work

Up to this point, we have focused on an examination of basic perceptual processes; how we see objects or attend to various stimuli. Based on this discussion, we are now ready to examine a special case of the perceptual process, namely, social perception as it relates to the work place. Social perception consists of those processes by which we perceive other *people*. Particular emphasis in the study of social perception is placed on how we interpret other people, how we categorize them, and how we form impressions of them.

Clearly, the process of social perception is far more complex than the perception of inanimate objects, like tables, chairs, signs, and buildings. This is true for at least two reasons. First, people are obviously far more complex and dynamic than tables and chairs. More careful attention must be paid in perceiving them so as not to miss important details. Second, an accurate perception of others is usually far more important to us personally than are our perceptions of inanimate objects. The consequences of misperceiving people are great. Failure to accurately perceive the location of a desk in a large room may mean we bump into it by mistake. Failure to accurately perceive a social situation (e.g., power relationships, status symbols, the attitudes of others) can have severe consequences in work situations. Social perception deserves special attention as it relates to the work situation.

We will concentrate now on the major influences on social perception. There are three basic categories of influence in the way we perceive other people: 1) the characteristics of the person being perceived; 2) the characteristics of the particular situation; and 3) the characteristics of the perceiver. When taken together, these three major influences are the dimensions of the environment in which we view other people. As such, it is important for students of management to understand the way in which these sets of influences interact if perceptual accuracy is to be facilitated at work (see Exhibit 6–2).

Characteristics of the Person Perceived

The way in which people are perceived in social situations is greatly influenced by their characteristics. That is, our dress, talk, and gestures deter-

Exhibit 6–2 Major influences on social perception at work

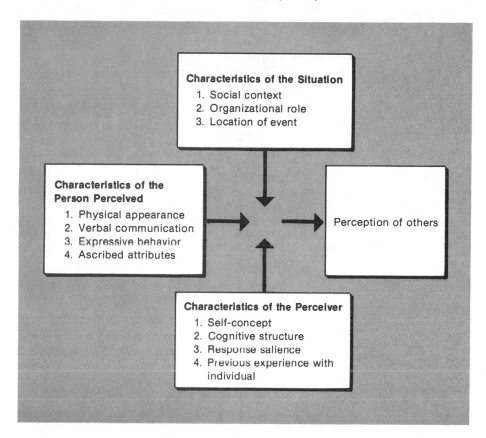

mine the kind of impressions people form of us. In particular, four characteristics of our selves can be identified: 1) physical appearance, 2) verbal communication, 3) expressive behavior, and 4) ascribed attributes.

Physical appearance.   A variety of physical attributes influence how we are seen by others. These include many of the obvious demographic characteristics like age, sex, race, height, and weight. A study by Mason (1957) found that most people agree on the physical attributes of a leader (i.e., what leaders *should* look like), even though these attributes were not found to be consistently held by actual leaders. However, when we see a person who appears to be assertive, goal oriented, confident, and articulate, we infer that this person is a natural leader.

Another example of the potency of physical appearance in influencing perception is in the clothing we wear. People dressed in business suits are generally thought to be professionals, while people dressed in work clothes are assumed to be lower level employees. The importance of these distinctions is that physical appearance, like clothing, influences how we respond to individuals; whether we are assertive or deferent, polite or gruff.

Verbal communications. What we *say* to others—as well as how we say it—can influence the impressions others form of us. Several aspects of verbal communication can be noted. First, the *precision* with which one uses language can influence impressions about cultural sophistication or education. An *accent* provides clues about a person's geographic background. The *tone of voice* used provides clues about whether people are happy, angry, or sad. Finally, the *topics* people choose to converse about provides clues about them.

Expressive behavior. Impressions are also influenced by how people behave. For instance, facial expressions often provide good clues in forming impressions of others. People who consistently smile are often thought to have positive attitudes (Secord, 1958). A whole field of study has recently emerged in *body language,* or the way in which we express our inner feelings subconsciously through physical actions; sitting up straight vs. being relaxed; looking people straight in the eye vs. looking away from people. Such forms of expressive behavior provide information to the perceiver concerning such things as how approachable others are, how self-confident they are, or how sociable they are.

Ascribed attributes. Finally, certain attributes are often ascribed before or at the beginning of an encounter and these attributes can influence how we perceive others. Three such ascribed attributes are status, occupation, and personal characteristics. *Status* is ascribed to someone when we are told that he or she is an executive, holds the greatest sales record, or has in some way achieved unusual fame or wealth. Research has consistently shown that people infer different motives to people they believe to be high or low in status, even though they may behave in an identical fashion (Thibaut and Riecker, 1955). For instance, high status people are seen as having greater control over their behavior, as being more self-confident, and competent and are given greater influence in group decisions than low status people. Moreover, high status people are generally better liked than low status people.

Occupations also play an important part in how we perceive people. Describing people as salespersons, accountants, teamsters, or research scientists conjures up distinct pictures of these various people before any first hand encounters. In fact, these pictures may even determine whether there *can be* an encounter.

Other ascribed attributes involve presumed *personal characteristics*. For instance, research by Kelley (1950) found that when a man others were about to meet was described as warm, people made different judgments about him and behaved more cordially than when he was described as cold—even though this was the same person! Strickland (1958) found that supervisors who thought certain employees were more trustworthy than others (based on prior information) felt these employees needed less supervision, even though both sets of employees had similar performance records.

Characteristics of the Situation

The second major influence on how we perceive others is the situation in which the perceptual process occurs. Three such situational influences can be identified: 1) the social context, 2) the organization and the employee's place in it; and 3) the location of the event (Zalkind and Costello, 1962).

Social context. A great deal of research has focused on social influences on perception. Relating these findings to organizational behavior, several conclusions can be drawn. First, when people are given an opportunity to interact in a friendly and sociable work situation, they tend to see one another as similar to themselves (Rosenbaum, 1959). This environment is felt to be less threatening, allowing people to be more open and trusting and more willing to be open in their perceptions of others. Findings suggest that cooperative (rather than competitive) work situations are colored by less defensiveness and more trust (Cherrington, 1973). This environment would be particularly well-suited for a research laboratory, where creativity requires the right to be wrong.

In addition, findings by Exline (1960) suggest that when members of a group or committee are congenial, they tend to be more accurate in assessing the work motives and goals of their colleagues, although they are less accurate in assessing personal (as opposed to work-related) goals. These findings imply that committees or work groups composed of adversaries may devote more time and energy to personal clashes at the expense of group goals. The implications of this for personnel selection and placement are clear.

Organizational role. An employee's place in the organizational hierarchy can also influence his or her perceptions. A classic study of managers by Dearborn and Simon (1958) emphasizes this point. In this study, executives from various departments (accounting, sales, production) were asked to read a detailed and factual case about a steel company. Next, each executive was asked to identify the major problem a new president of the company should address. The findings showed clearly that the executives' perceptions of the most important problems in the company were influenced by the departments in which they worked. Sales executives saw sales as the biggest problem, while production executives cited production issues. Industrial relations and public relations executives identified human relations as the primary problem in need of attention.

In addition to perceptual differences emerging horizontally across departments, such differences can also be found when we move vertically up or down the hierarchy. The most obvious difference here is seen between managers and union, where the former sees profits, production, and sales as vital areas of concern for the company, while the latter places much greater emphasis on wages, working conditions, and job security. Indeed, our views of managers and workers are clearly influenced by the group to which we belong. Hence, the positions we occupy in organizations can easily color how we view our work world and those in it.

Location of event.   Finally, how we interpret events is also influenced by the location of the event. Behaviors that may be appropriate at home, like taking off one's shoes, may be unacceptable in the office. Acceptable customs vary from country to country. For instance, assertiveness may be a desirable trait for a sales representative in the United States, but may be seen as being brash or coarse in Japan or China.

Characteristics of the Perceiver

The third major influence on social perception is the perceiver. Several characteristics unique to our personalities can affect how we see others. These include: 1) the self concept; 2) cognitive structure; 3) response salience, and 4) previous experience with the individual.

Self concept.   Our self-concept represents a major influence on how we perceive others. This influence is manifested in several ways (Zalkind and Costello, 1962). First, when we understand ourselves (i.e., can accurately describe our own personal characteristics), we are better able to perceive others accurately (Norman, 1953). Second, when we accept ourselves (i.e., have a positive self-image), we are more likely to see favorable characteristics in others. Studies have shown that if we accept ourselves as we are, we broaden our view of others and are more likely to view people uncritically. Conversely, less secure people often find faults in others (Omwake, 1954). Third, our own personal characteristics influence the characteristics we are likely to see in others. For instance, people with authoritarian tendencies (see Chapter 5) tend to view others in terms of power, while secure people tend to see others as warm rather than cold (Bossom & Maslow, 1957). From a management standpoint, these findings emphasize the importance for administrators to understand themselves. They also provide an argument for the kind of human relations training programs that are popular in many organizations today.

Cognitive structure.   Our cognitive structures (described in Chapter 5) also influence how we view people. People describe each other differently

(Scott and Mitchell, 1976). Some use physical characteristics like tall or short, while others use central traits like deceitful, forceful, or meek. Still others have more complex cognitive structures and use multiple traits in their descriptions of others; hence, a person may be described as being aggressive, honest, friendly, *and* hardworking.

Ostensibly, the greater our cognitive complexity (i.e., our ability to differentiate between people using multiple criteria), the more accurate is our perception of others. People who tend to make more complex assessments of others also tend to be more positive in their appraisals (Frauenfelder, 1974). Research in this area highlights the importance of selecting managers who exhibit high degrees of cognitive complexity. These individuals should form more accurate perceptions of the strengths and weaknesses of their subordinates and be able to capitalize on their strengths while ignoring or working to overcome their weaknesses.

Response salience.   Response salience refers to our sensitivity to objects in the environment as influenced by our particular needs or desires. Response salience can play an important role in social perception because we have a tendency to see what we *want* to see. A company personnel manager who has a bias against women, minorities, or "handicapped persons" would tend to be adversely sensitive to them during an employment interview. This focus may cause the manager to look for other potentially negative traits in the candidate to confirm his biases. The influence of these arbitrary biases is an example of the halo effect. Another personnel manager without these biases would be much less inclined to be influenced by these characteristics when viewing prospective job candidates.

Previous experience with individual.   Our previous experiences with others often will influence the way in which we view their current behavior. When an employee has consistently received poor performance evaluations, a marked improvement in performance may go unnoticed because the supervisor continues to think of the individual as a poor performer. Similarly employees who begin their career with several successes develop a reputation as fast-track individuals and may continue to rise in the organization long after their performance has leveled off or even declined. The impact of previous experience on present perceptions should be respected and studied by students of management. For instance, when a previously poor performer earnestly tries to perform better, it is important for this improvement to be recognized early and properly rewarded. Otherwise, employees may feel that nothing they do will make any difference and give up.

Together, these three sets of factors—characteristics of the person perceived, the situation, and the perceiver—jointly determine the impressions we form of others (see Exhibit 6–2). With these impressions, we make conscious and unconscious decisions about how we intend to behave toward people. Our behavior toward others, in turn, influences the way they regard us. Consequently, the importance of understanding the perceptual process, as well as factors that contribute to it, is apparent for managers. A better understanding of ourselves and careful attention to others and to our particular situations leads to more accurate perceptions and, as a result, more appropriate actions.

Perception and Behavior: An Attributional Approach

Attribution Theory

A major influence on how people behave is the way they interpret the events around them. People who feel they have control over what happens to them are more likely to accept responsibility for their actions than those who feel control of events is out of their hands. The cognitive process by which people interpret the reasons or causes for their behavior is an area of study known as *attribution theory* (Kelley, 1967; Heider, 1958; Weiner, 1974). Specifically, ''attribution theory concerns the process by which an individual interprets events as being caused by a particular part of a relatively stable environment'' (Kelley, 1967, p. 193).

Attribution theory is based largely on the work of Fritz Heider (1958). Heider argues that behavior is determined by a combination of internal forces (e.g., abilities or effort) and external forces (e.g., task difficulty or luck). Following the cognitive approach of Lewin and Tolman, he emphasizes that it is the *perceived* determinants, not the actual ones, that influence behavior. Hence, if employees perceive that their success is a function of their own abilities and efforts, they can be expected to behave differently than they would if they believed job success was due to chance.

The underlying assumption of attribution theory is that people are motivated to understand their environment and the *causes* of particular events. If individuals can understand the causes of events, they will then be in a better position to influence or control the sequence of future events. This process is diagrammed in Exhibit 6–3.

Specifically, attribution theory suggests that particuar behavioral events (e.g., the receipt of a promotion) are analyzed by individuals to determine their causes. This cognitive interpretation process may lead to the conclusion that the promotion resulted from the individual's own effort or, alternatively, from some other cause, maybe luck. Based on cognitive interpretations of events, individuals revise their cognitive (or causal) structures, and rethink their assumptions about causal relationships. For instance, an individual may infer that performance does indeed lead to promotion. Based on this new structure, the individual makes choices about future behavior. In

Exhibit 6–3 Schematic representation of the attribution process (Korman, 1977, p. 273)

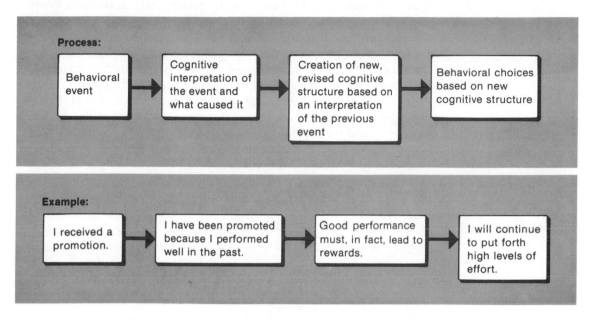

some cases, the individual may decide to continue exerting high levels of effort in the hope that it will lead to further promotions.

On the other hand, if an individual concludes that the promotion resulted primarily from chance and was largely unrelated to peformance, a different cognitive structure might be created and there might be little reason to continue exerting high levels of effort. In other words, the way in which we perceive and interpret events around us significantly affects our future behaviors.

Locus of Control

Attributions in psychological research are typically measured by the concept of *locus of control* (Rotter, 1966). An *internal* locus of control is a feeling by employees that they can personally influence their own outcomes and behavior through their abilities, skills, and effort. An *external* locus of control, on the other hand, is a feeling by employees that their outcomes or behavior is largely beyond their own control.

Research on attribution processes and locus of control has led to several interesting results. For example, in a series of experiments, Weiner (1974) consistently found that when individuals perceive a high internal locus of control, and seem to have control over their own behavior, successful performance on previous tasks leads to increased expectations of success on future tasks. Unsuccessful previous performance leads to reduced expectations for success on future tasks. As shown in Exhibit 6–4, success in one task for internals causes individuals to attribute the success to their own efforts, which augments the pride in accomplishment. This augmented pride in accomplishment, in turn, leads to increased expectations of success in future events. Failure on previous tasks for internals, in contrast, leads to frustration, lack of confidence, and reduced future expectations. For persons perceiving an external locus of control, on the other hand, neither success nor failure on previous tasks would influence subsequent expectations (see Exhibit 6–4). This is because individuals feel that behavior and

Exhibit 6–4   The influence of locus of control on performance expectations

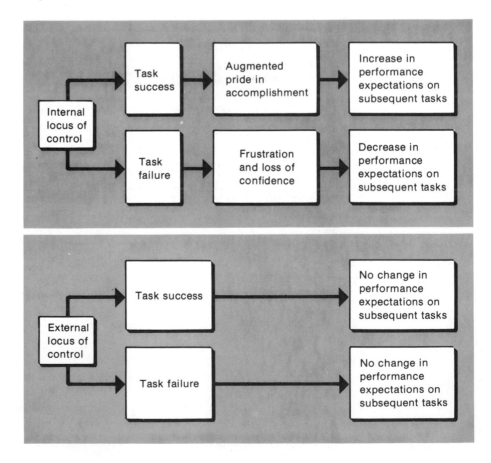

performance are largely influenced by other people or events. Consequently, people feel there is little reason to try.

More research on locus of control has been summarized by Mitchell, Smyser, and Weed (1975). They found that people with a high internal locus of control (internals) were more satisfied with their work and were happier working under a participative-style manager. Externals, on the contrary, preferred a more directive style of management. Internals were more successful in their careers and were more often found in managerial positions (Valecha, 1972).

Perceptual Differences Between Superiors and Subordinates

Most of our discussion so far on social perception in organizations has focused on person-to-person perception without much regard to rank or position in the hierarchy. Realistically, it is impossible to ignore the influence of position when examining major influences on social perception. It has been consistently found that superiors and subordinates tend to view situations somewhat differently and these varying viewpoints influence how everyone behaves.

It was noted earlier that managers and union leaders tend to have distorted views of each others' competence and motives (Haire, 1955). It has also been shown that employees systematically distort their perceptions of the salaries earned by those above and below them in the organizational hierarchy (Lawler, 1971). The question we wish to pose here is what influence, if any, does position have in the perceived behavior of others? Several studies address this issue.

In one of the earliest studies of major importance, Likert (1961) examined the perceptions of superiors and subordinates in an attempt to determine the amounts and types of recognition subordinates received for good performance. Both superiors and subordinates were asked how often superiors gave rewards for good work. Results are shown in Exhibit 6–5.

As can be seen in this exhibit, superiors saw themselves as giving a wide variety of rewards for good performance fairly frequently. Subordinates, on the other hand, felt they received rewards from these same superiors much less frequently. In fact, the average percentage of time superiors felt they were giving such rewards was 63%, compared to 11% for subordinates. Hence, marked differences occur between superior and subordinate perceptions of the superiors' behavior.

Similar findings have been reported by Webber (1970) in superior-subordinate communications. Both superiors and subordinates in work organizations were asked how much time was spent by the superiors in initiating verbal communications with the subordinates. Superiors responded that

Exhibit 6–5 Differences in perception between supervisors and subordinates

Types of Recognition	Frequency with which *supervisors* say they give various types of recognition for good performance	Frequency with which *subordinates* say supervisors give various types of recognition for good performance
Gives privileges	52%	14%
Gives more responsibility	48%	10%
Gives a pat on the back	82%	13%
Gives sincere and thorough praise	80%	14%
Trains for better jobs	64%	9%
Gives more interesting work	51%	5%

Source: Adapted from R. Likert, *New Patterns in Management.* New York: McGraw-Hill, 1961, p. 91.

they spent on the average of 2.8 hours per week initiating such communications, while subordinates held that their superiors spent only about 1.6 hours. Again, superiors and subordinates looking at the same situation saw them differently.

Such discrepant findings raise questions about the accuracy of perceptions in work situations. Whose perception are we to believe? Haire (1976) argues persuasively that superiors probably are somewhat more accurate in their perceptions of situations than subordinates for at least two reasons: 1) superiors tend to be more at the center of the communication network and hence have more information on which to base their judgements; and 2) superiors often achieve their leadership positions because of their ability to see situations clearly and act accordingly.

Barriers to Accurate Perception of Others

In the perceptual process, at least seven barriers can be identified that inhibit our accuracy of perception. These barriers are: 1) stereotyping; 2) halo effects; 3) implicit personality theory; 4) selective perception; 5) projection; 6) temporal extension; and 7) perceptual defense. Each of these will be briefly considered as they relate to social perception in work situations (see Exhibit 6–6).

Exhibit 6–6   Barriers to accurate perception of others

Barrier	Definition
Stereotyping	A tendency to assign attributes to people solely on the basis of their class or category.
Halo effects	A tendency to allow the traits exhibited by people to influence our impressions of their other traits.
Implicit personality theory	A tendency to have an *a priori* picture of what other people are like that colors how we see them.
Selective perception	A process by which we systematically screen or discredit information we don't wish to hear and focus instead on more salient information.
Projection	A tendency to ascribe to others those negative characteristics or feelings we have about ourselves.
Temporal extension	A tendency to consider the first impressions we have of others to be their enduring characteristics.
Perceptual defense	A tendency to distort or ignore information which is either personally threatening or culturally unacceptable.

Stereotyping

One of the most common barriers in perceiving others at work is *stereotyping*. Stereotyping is a process in which attributes are assigned to people solely on the basis of their class or category. Stereotyping can be particularly critical when meeting new people, since we know very little about them then. Based on a few prominent characteristics like sex, race, or age we tend to categorize them into a few general categories. We ascribe a series of traits to them *based* upon the attributes of the category we have put them in. We assume that an older person is old-fashioned, conservative, obstinate, and perhaps senile. Or, professors may be misjudged as absent-minded, impractical, idealistic, or eccentric.

One explanation for the existence of stereotypes has been suggested by Triandis (1971). He argues that stereotypes may be to some extent based upon fact. People tend to compare other groups with their own group. In so doing, minor differences between groups become accentuated to form a stereotype. For example, older people as a group may indeed be more conservative or more old-fashioned. These traits then become accentuated and attributed to *all* older people.

Stereotypes are not always dysfunctional for people. In fact, in many instances they can be quite helpful. In unfamiliar social situations, we need general guidelines to assist us in interpreting our environment. Stereotypes provide us with simple and quick ways of classifying people and reducing the ambiguity of our situations. They often protect us from making embarrassing social mistakes. Even so, while stereotypes have certain positive effects for the perceiver, they more often have detrimental effects for the person being perceived.

The power of stereotypes in organizational settings has been demonstrated in a variety of studies. Two particularly important studies (Box 6–1 and 6–2) found that managers and union leaders have clear stereotypes concerning the characteristics and motives of each other (Haire, 1955), and also that men and women managers both tend to view a managerial career as predominantly male. (Schein, 1973, 1975).

Several other relevant findings about sex role stereotypes in work situations are worthy of note. In one study of business students, Bartol and Butterfield (1976) found that a manager's sex influenced the way in which people responded to variations in leadership style. Specifically, female managers were rated as being more effective when they emphasized interpersonal relations on the job, while male managers were seen as more effective when they emphasized task accomplishment.

Cohen and Bunker (1975) studied company recruiters and found that in the initial screening interview, female applicants were more often slotted into traditionally female jobs, while male applicants were more often directed into traditionally male jobs. Apparently, recruiters tended to type-cast people according to sex and attribute certain work related skills to them depending upon whether they were male or female. Finally, Rosen and Jerdee (1974) found that sex-role stereotypes influenced the behavior of bank supervisors toward their subordinates. Supervisors tended to discriminate against women employees in personnel decisions involving promotion and development and against male employees in decisions involving leaves of absence for family reasons. Apparently the effects of sex role stereotypes in work situations are fairly pervasive and represent a clear obstacle to managerial effectiveness.

Age stereotypes can also be found in organizations. A study by Rosen and Jerdee (1976) found that some business students have clear stereotypes of older employees. They are thought to be: 1) more resistant to organizational change; 2) less creative; 3) less likely to take calculated risks; 4) lower in physical capacity; 5) less interested in learning new techniques; and 6) less capable of learning new techniques. When asked to make personnel decisions concerning older people, the business students generally indicated that: 1) older people would receive lower consideration in promotion deci-

Box 6–1 Union-Management Stereotypes

A classic study of social perception in work organizations was carried out by Mason Haire* to examine the stereotypes business managers and union leaders had of each other. These stereotypes have obvious importance for such activities as contract negotiations and grievance handling.

Research Design   Haire presented photographs of two men to samples of 108 industrial relations managers and 76 union leaders. Half the members of each group were told that the first man was a plant manager and that the second man was a labor official. The other half of both groups were given the same photographs but the descriptions were reversed. Subjects were then asked to describe the people in both pictures using a standardized list of adjectives.

Findings   As expected, Haire found that regardless of which picture was identified as a manager, the actual managers consistently described the person as more honest, dependa-

ble, and interpersonally competent than the labor official. Union leaders responded in the opposite fashion. In addition, managers felt that the manager was better able to appreciate labor's viewpoint than was the labor official capable of appreciating management's viewpoint. Again, opposite results occurred for actual union leaders.

Implications   This study has clear implications in the area of union-management relations. As noted by Stagner (1956, p. 35), "It is plain that unionists perceiving company officials in a stereotyped way are less efficient than would be desirable. Similarly, company executives who see all labor unions as identical are not showing good judgment or discrimination. To the extent that such stereotypes can be reduced, both managers and union leaders are in a better position to understand the other's point of view, to see the facts of a situation clearly and to resolve differences with less stress, mistrust and turmoil."

Source: M. Haire, "Role perception in labor-management relations: An experimental approach." *Industrial and Labor Relations Review*, 1955, 8, 204–216.

sions; 2) older people would receive less attention and resources for training and development; and 3) older people would tend to be transferred to other departments instead of confronted by their superiors when a problem with their performance emerged.

As can be seen, stereotypes affect all segments of the working population; male and female, young and old, black and white, and union and management. The dysfunctional influence of stereotypes and the behaviors they prompt can only be imagined. Even so, their impact on organizational behavior cannot be minimized.

Box 6–2 Sex-Role Stereotypes

Given the increasing number of women entering managerial ranks, it is important to understand how both men and women view the manager's job. If managerial jobs are viewed as being primarily masculine in nature, then negative reactions to women in management may inhibit women from either choosing or being chosen for managerial positions. In order to discover more about the possible effects of sex role stereotypes on women in management, Virginia Schein carried out two related studies among male and female managers.*

Research Design A questionnaire survey was carried out among samples of 300 male and 167 female managers. Managers asked to identify those traits which characterized men in general, women in general, and successful middle managers. It was hypothesized that both men *and women* managers would describe successful middle managers as possessing characteristics, attitudes, and temperaments more commonly ascribed to men than to women.

Findings The results of the study clearly indicated that both men and women have strong male-oriented stereotypes of successful managers. That is, managers of both sexes described successful managers as exhibiting primarily masculine traits.

Implications Several important implications for management result from this study, particularly in the area of employee selection, placement, and promotion. First, if a woman's self image incorporates certain aspects of the stereotypical feminine role, she may be less inclined to pursue a managerial career because of an inconsistency between her (male-oriented) perceptions of the job and her own self image. Moreover, if other male managers also view a managerial career as primarily a masculine one, they may attempt to dissuade (or even block) a woman from attempting it. Finally, a male sex-role stereotype of a manager's job may cause a sink-or-swim attitude among a new female manager's male peers. Without co-worker support, her chances of survival in a predominantly male world would obviously be diminished.

Source: V. E. Schein, "The Relationship Between Sex- Role Stereotypes and Requisite Management Characteristics." *Journal of Applied Psychology,* 1973, *57,* 95–100; and V. E. Schein, "Relationships Between Sex-Role Stereotypes and Requisite Management Characteristics among Female Managers." *Journal of Applied Psychology,* 1975, *60,* 340–344.

Halo Effect

A second important barrier to accurate social perception is the *halo effect*. A halo effect is a tendency to allow knowledge of one trait to influence our impressions of an individual's other traits. Halo effects act as a screen inhibiting perceivers from actually seeing the trait being judged (Zalkind and Costello, 1962). Halo effects can be either positive or negative.

Several examples of halo effects in social situations can be identified. For instance, one study found that people who were shown a photograph of a person who was smiling generally judged the person to be more honest than a person pictured as frowning even though there is no reason to expect a strong connection between smiling and honesty. Moreover, in another study of halo effects, army officers who were well liked were also judged to be more intelligent than those who were disliked, in spite of equivalent intelligence test scores (Zalkind and Costello, 1962). Finally, a study by Asch (1946) found that when a stranger was described as warm, people described him as also being wise, imaginative, popular, and humorous. No such description was given of the *same* person when he was described as being cold.

These examples clearly demonstrate how one attribute can color people's impressions on other *unrelated* attributes of the same person. This finding has strong implications, particularly in the area of performance evaluation. Often, one positive attribute of an employee, like a consistent attendance record, can influence a supervisor's ratings of the employee's productivity or quality of work, regardless of the actual level of performance.

In addition to the area of performance evaluation, halo effects are also important in the way employees view the organization. Oftentimes, one negative attitude serves to nullify many positive aspects of the work situation. For instance, an early study by Grove and Kerr (1951) examined employee attitudes in a company that was in receivership. The company paid relatively high salaries, provided excellent working conditions, and had above average supervision. Even so, the insecurity brought about by the financial exigency of the company led to a generalized negative attitude toward the company in all areas.

Three other points need to be made concerning halo effects. First, it has been found that negative information about people more strongly influences impressions of others than positive information (Hollman, 1972). Second, it appears that people place greater weight on social perception and information which comes from respected, trusted, or favored sources (Filley, House and Kerr, 1976). Third, halo effects tend to be most severe under three conditions: 1) when the perceiver has little experience or knowledge in the area under evaluation; 2) when the evaluation concerns a person well known to the perceiver; and 3) when the traits have strong moral implications (Bruner and Tagiuri, 1954).

Implicit Personality Theory

Somewhat related to halo effects is the notion of *implicit personality theory*. Implicit personality theory is marked by a relatively fixed set of biases in judging others (Bruner and Tagiuri, 1954). Without knowing it, many people tend to have a theory about what others are like in general and this theory influences perceptions.

For example, a person who is overly trusting tends to view others as honest, sincere, and kind. We are all familiar with the perpetual grouch who seems to have negative attitudes about everybody and everything. Such people have a theory or model that ascribes a host of attributes to people even before actual encounters.

The clearest approach to implicit personality theory in work organizations has been postulated by McGregor (1960) in his Theory X–Theory Y distinction. McGregor postulated that managers tend to have one of two views of employees. Theory X managers assume that the average worker: 1) is lazy and dislikes work; 2) must be coerced and closely controlled on the job; 3) wants security instead of responsibility. Theory Y managers, on the other hand, assume that the average worker: 1) has the capacity to enjoy meaningful work; 2) is self-directed and needs little supervision; 3) actively seeks responsibility; and 4) is capable of being imaginative and creative at work. Both of these oversimplified views of people represent implicit personality theories managers possess. The acceptance of either one in its entirety as a consistent picture of employees guarantees perceptual inaccuracies which will interfere with managerial effectiveness.

Two problems exist with implicit personality theory in social perception. First, the tendency to regard people as the same clearly ignores important individual differences. People are not the same and a generalized impression of others only distorts our understanding. Second is the related tendency to group or cluster several attributes to form one's own unique theory of personality. This assumes incorrectly that such attributes are consistently found together in people. This is not the case.

Selective Perception

Selective perception is the process by which we systematically screen out information we don't wish to hear and focus instead on more salient information. Saliency here is obviously a function of our own experiences, needs, and orientations. The example of the Dearborn and Simon (1958) study of managers from various departments provides an excellent glimpse of selective perception. Production managers focused on production problems to the exclusion of other problems. Accountants, personnel specialists, and sales managers were similarly exclusive. Everyone saw their own specialty as more important in the company than other specialties.

Another example of selective perception in groups and organizations is provided by Miner (1973). Miner summarizes a series of experiments dealing with groups competing with one another on problem solving exercises. Consistently, the groups tended to evaluate their own solutions as better than the solutions proposed by others. Such findings resemble the not-invented-here syndrome found in many research organizations. There is a frequent tendency for scientists to view ideas or products originating outside their organization or department as inferior, and to judge other researchers as less competent and creative than themselves. Similar patterns of behavior can be found among managers, service workers, and secretaries.

Projection

Projection is a defense mechanism people use to protect their self-concept. In essence, people sometimes attribute or project onto others negative characteristics or feelings they have about themselves. Projection represents a barrier to accurate social perception because the perceiver sees certain self-related traits in ways that may not be accurate.

Several examples of projection in social perception can be cited. For instance, people who are fearful or anxious will often view others as being more aggressive and frightening than is warranted (Feshback and Singer, 1957). It has been demonstrated that people high in traits like stinginess, obstinancy, and disorderliness tend to rate others as being much higher on these traits than did the people who themselves were rated low on these same traits (Sears, 1936). The point here is that employees at all levels often ascribe to others characteristics they themselves possess, leading to misunderstanding, distrust, and decreased efficiency.

Temporal Extension

Temporal extension occurs when we observe a momentary characteristic of a person and consider it an enduring attribute (Secord and Backman, 1964). For instance, a smile often indicates that an individual is momentarily happy or is responding in a friendly way. Thus, if a person happens to smile when we first meet him, we may extend this attribute and continue to see the person as a happy or friendly person, long after the first encounter.

Temporal extensions are really first impressions in meeting people. Several studies point to the fact that people tend to give undue emphasis to their first impressions of people and these first impressions tend to be enduring. As such, it is quite possible for different people to get very different impressions of a single individual, depending upon the circumstances of their first meeting.

Perceptual Defense

A final barrier to social perception is *perceptual defense*. As described by Secord and Backman (1964, pp. 26–27), perceptual defense is comprised of three related processes:

1. Emotionally disturbing or threatening stimuli have a higher recognition threshold than neutral stimuli;

2. Such stimuli are likely to elicit substitute perceptions that are radically altered so as to prevent recognition of the presented stimuli;
3. These critical stimuli arouse emotional reactions even though the stimuli are not recognized.

In other words, through perceptual defense we tend to distort or ignore information which is either personally threatening or culturally unacceptable. Because emotionally disturbing stimuli have a higher recognition threshold (#1), people are less likely to fully confront or acknowledge the threat. Instead, they may see entirely different or even erroneous stimuli that are safer (#2). Even so, the presence of the critical stimuli often leads to heightened emotions despite its lack of recognition (#3). For instance, suppose that during a contract negotiation for an assembly plant, word leaked out that because of declining profits the plant may have to close down permanently. Anxious workers may ignore this message and instead choose to believe that company management is only starting false rumors to increase their leverage during wage negotiations. Even if the leverage claim is accepted by the workers as truth, strong emotional reactions against the company can be expected.

One result of perceptual defense is to save us from facing squarely events that we either do not wish to handle or may even be incapable of handling. Perceptual defense helps us ignore these events. We dissipate our emotions by directing our attention to other (substitute) objects and hope the original event that distressed us will eventually disappear.

Perceptual defense is especially pronounced when people are presented with a situation that contradicts their long-held beliefs and attitudes. In a classic study of perceptual defense among college students, Haire and Grunes (1950) presented the students with descriptions of factory workers. Included in these descriptions was the word intelligent. Since the word was contrary to the students' beliefs concerning factory workers, they chose to reject the description by using perceptual defenses. Haire and Grunes (1950, pp. 407–411) describe four such defense mechanisms:

1. *Denial*   A few of the subjects denied the existence of intelligence in factory workers.
2. *Modification and distortion*   This was one of the most frequent forms of defense. The pattern was to explain away the perceptual conflict by joining intelligence with some other characteristic, for instance, "He is intelligent but doesn't possess initiative to rise above his group."
3. *Change in perception*   Many students changed their perception of the worker because of the intelligence characteristic. Most of the change, however, was very subtle, e.g., "cracks jokes," became "witty."
4. *Recognition, but refusal to change*   A very few students explicitly recognized the conflict between their perception of the worker and the characteristic of intelligent that was confronting them. For example, one subject stated, "The trait seems to be conflicting . . . most factory workers I have heard about aren't too intelligent."

Perceptual defense makes any situation in which conflict is likely to be present more difficult. It creates blind spots and so we fail to hear and see events as they really are. The challenge for managers is to somehow reduce or minimize the perception of threat in a situation so these defenses are not immediately called into play. This can be done by reassuring people that those things which are important to them will not be tampered with or by accentuating the positive.

Summary

In this chapter, we have considered perceptual processes and how they relate to employee behavior at work. Perceptual selectivity is distinguished from perceptual organization. Major influences on perceptual processes in general were discussed as was the concept of social perception at work. A model of this process was presented. Next, attribution theory was introduced as one explanation of the relationship between behaviors and perception. Major differences were noted in the perceptions of managers and subordinates. Finally, major barriers to accurate perceptions of others were identified, including stereotyping, halo effects, and selective perception. Throughout, emphasis was placed on gaining an understanding of how perception can affect our attitudes and behavior in the workplace.

Managers face a variety of barriers to accurate perception of others in the work situation. These barriers may be directed at the manager or held by the manager. Whatever the origin of these biases, it is important to recognize the existence of barriers and work to reduce or eliminate them. This can be done in a variety of ways. Stereotyping can be reduced if the persons being stereotyped continually point out the problem. This is often seen in situations where women must often point out that all managers are not "he." Halo effects in evaluating employees can be minimized by changing the ways in which employees are rated; this is discussed in Chapter 17. Problems of selective perception and perceptual defense can be relieved through improved communications, as we discuss in Chapter 10. Other examples could be cited. The point is that by recognizing the existence of perceptual problems, managers can take measures to remedy situations. First, however, they must be convinced of the importance of the problem. If this can be accomplished, several avenues of approach are open to them.

Key Words

perception	organizational role
perceptual selectivity	attribution theory
perceptual organization	locus of control
absolute threshold of activation	stereotyping
sensory adaptation	halo effect

primacy effects	implicit personality theory
recency effects	selective perception
response salience	projection
response disposition	temporal extension
self concept	perceptual defense

Questions for Discussion

1. What is meant by perception?
2. Describe perceptual selectivity. How does it relate to absolute thresholds of activation and sensory adaptation?
3. Describe several major external influences on perceptual selectivity.
4. Describe the principle of ordering.
5. Discuss some major personal influences on perceptual selectivity as they relate to the workplace.
6. Contrast response salience and response disposition.
7. Describe the major influences on social perception at work.
8. How does attribution theory work?
9. Explain the concept of locus of control.
10. Explain how superiors and subordinates may interpret the same facts or events differently.
11. Identify several barriers to accurate perception of others.
12. How does the implicit personality theory work?
13. What is meant by temporal extension?
14. How can a manager guard against halo effects?
15. Explain the concept of perceptual defense. How does it work?
16. What actions can managers take to reduce the barriers to accurate social perception at work?

chapter 7

Learning Processes and Behavior Modification

The role of learning in organizational settings has received increased attention in recent years. Managers have come to realize that a basic understanding of learning can help improve employee motivation and performance. One technique of learning, namely, behavior modification, has become a popular motivation and reward strategy for more closely tying rewards to improved performance and attendance.

In view of this widespread attention, it is appropriate to examine in some detail the nature of learning and behavior modification in organizations. Our examination of the topic consists of four parts. First, a definition of learning and several basic models of learning are presented. Next, major influences on learning are reviewed. Third, the notion of reinforcement is introduced as it relates to motivation and performance in work settings. Finally, behavior modification techniques are considered. This later discussion includes both industrial applications of the technique, as well as criticisms that have been leveled against it.

Importance of Topic for Managers

Before launching into this discussion, we should briefly consider why learning processes are important to students of management. Several reasons can be suggested:

1. Learning is a prerequisite to most forms of behavior, both on the job and off. Managers, skilled craftspeople, and even janitors must learn certain skills that are necessary for good job performance. Hence, it is important to understand how learning takes place and how it influences subsequent behavior.

2. Most companies spend considerable sums on training and developing their employees. To the extent that such efforts are based on a sound understanding of the principles of learning, their chances for success are enhanced.

3. Just as personality and motivation are related, so too are learning and motivation. A knowledge of learning processes can improve our understanding of employee motivation at work. This connection is particularly evident in recent efforts to use behavior modification techniques in organizations.

4. Behavior modification, an application of learning theory, is gaining popularity among managers as a strategy for improving employee performance. It is useful to be familiar with the technique. Without a thorough understanding of the mechanisms which underlie behavior modification, managers run the risk of inappropriately applying the technique to the detriment of performance and organizational effectiveness.

5. A major responsibility of managers is to evaluate and reward their subordinates. Such reward practices rest on the principle of reinforcement. If managers are to maximize the impact of available (and often limited) rewards, a thorough knowledge of reinforcement techniques is essential.

Basic Models of Learning

Definition of Learning

Learning may be defined for our purposes here as a relatively permanent change in behavior which occurs as a result of practice. That is, someone is said to have learned something when he or she consistently exhibits a new behavior over time. Several aspects of this definition are noteworthy (Kimble and Garmezy, 1963):

- Learning involves a change in an attitude or behavior. This change does not necessarily have to be an improvement, however, and can include things like learning bad habits or forming prejudices.

- In order for learning to occur, the change that takes place must be relatively permanent. So, changes in behavior that result from fatigue or temporary adaptations to a unique situation would not be considered as examples of learning.

- Learning typically involves some form of practice or experience. Thus, the change that results from physical maturation, as when a baby develops the physical strength to walk, is in itself not considered learning.

- This practice or experience must be reinforced over time for learning to take place. Where such reinforcement does not follow practice or experience, the behavior would eventually diminish and disappear.

- Finally, learning is an inferred process; it is not possible to directly observe learning. Instead, we must infer the existence of learning from observing changes in overt behavior.

Scientific interest in learning dates from the early experiments of Pavlov at the turn of the century. Much of this early work and, indeed, much of the current research results from laboratory experiments using animals. While these techniques may help to enlighten our understanding of the most basic forms of human learning, it is necessary to study more complex learning processes in the field, as we shall see later in this chapter.

To date, three major theories of learning can be identified: 1) classical conditioning; 2) operant conditioning; and 3) cognitive learning theory. The first two models, classical and operant conditioning, both focus on the stimulus-response (S-R) connection as the basic unit of analysis in learning processes, although each suggests alternative explanations about how these bonds are established. The third model, cognitive learning theory, represents a significant departure from the other two models. We will briefly examine each of these models.

Classical Conditioning

Classical conditioning focuses on the process whereby a stimulus-response bond is developed between a conditioned stimulus and a conditioned response through the repeated linking of a conditioned stimulus with an *un*-conditioned stimulus. This process is shown in Exhibit 7–1.

The classic example of Pavlov's experiments performed around the turn of the century should serve to explain the process. Pavlov was interested in the question of whether animals could be trained to draw a causal relationship between previously unconnected factors. Specifically, using dogs as subjects, he wished to know whether they could *learn* to associate the ringing of a bell with the act of salivation. The experiment began with unlearned,

Exhibit 7–1   Classical vs. operant conditioning

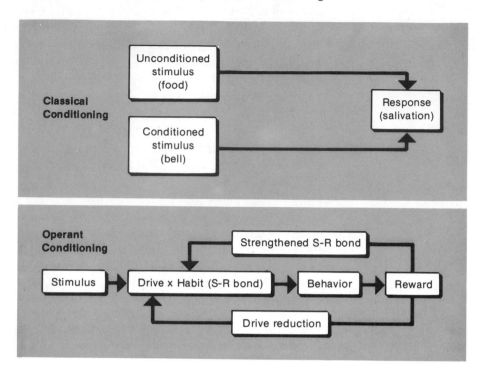

or *unconditioned,* stimulus-response relationships. When a dog was presented with meat (unconditioned stimulus), the dog salivated (unconditioned response). No learning was necessary here as this relationship represented a natural physiological process.

Next, Pavlov paired the unconditioned stimulus (meat) with a *conditioned* stimulus (the ringing of a bell). The ringing of the bell by itself would not be expected to elicit salivation. However, over time, a learned linkage developed for the dog between the bell and meat, ultimately resulting in an S-R bond between the conditioned stimulus (the bell) and the response (salivation) without the presence of the unconditioned stimulus (the meat). Evidence eerged that learning had occurred and that this learning resulted from conditioning the dogs to associate two normally unrelated objects, the bell and the salivation.

Although Pavlov's experiments are widely cited as evidence of the existence of classical conditioning, it is necessary from the perspective of organizational behavior to ask how this process relates (or can relate) to people at work. Ivancevich, Szilagyi, and Wallace (1977, p. 80) provide one such work-related example of classical conditioning:

An illustration of classical conditioning in a work setting would be an airplane pilot learning how to use a newly installed warning system. In this case the behavior to be learned is to respond to a warning light that indicates that the plane has dropped below a critical altitude on an assigned glide path. The proper response is to increase the plane's altitude. The pilot already knows how to appropriately respond to the trainer's warning to increase altitude (in this case we would say the trainer's warning is an unconditioned stimulus and the corrective action of increasing altitude is an unconditioned response). The training session consists of the trainer warning the pilot to increase altitude every time the warning light goes on. Through repeated pairings of the warning light with the trainer's warning, the pilot eventually learns to adjust the plane's altitude in response to the warning light even though the trainer is not present. Again, the unit of learning is a new S-R connection or habit.

Although classical conditioning clearly has applications to work situations particularly in the area of training and development, it has been criticized as explaining only a limited part of total human learning. Skinner (1963) argues that classical conditioning focuses on respondent, or reflexive, behaviors; that is, it concentrates on explaining largely involuntary responses that result from stimuli. More complex learning cannot be explained solely by classical conditioning. As an alternative explanation, Skinner and others have proposed the operant conditioning model of learning.

Operant Conditioning

The major focus of operant conditioning is on the effects of reinforcements or rewards on desired behaviors. One of the first psychologists to examine such processes was Watson (1914). Watson, a contemporary of Pavlov, argued that behavior was largely influenced by the rewards one received as a result of actions. This notion is best summarized in Thorndike's (1911) *Law of effect*. This law states that:

> of several responses made to the same situation, those which are accompanied or closely followed by satisfaction [reinforcement] . . . will be more likely to occur; those which are accompanied or closely followed by discomfort [punishment] . . . will be less likely to occur (Thorndike, 1911, p. 244).

In other words, Thorndike's law of effect posits that behavior which leads to positive or pleasurable outcomes tends to be repeated, while behavior which leads to negative outcomes or punishment tends to be avoided. In this manner, individuals learn appropriate, acceptable responses to their environment. For example, by repeatedly docking the pay of an employee who is habitually tardy, we would expect that employee to learn to arrive early enough to receive a full-day's pay.

A basic operant model of learning is presented in Exhibit 7–1. There are three important concepts of this model:

Drive   A *drive* is an internal state of disequilibrium; it is a felt need. It is generally believed that drive increases with the strength of deprivation. A drive or desire to learn must be present for learning to take place.

Habit   A *habit* is the experienced bond or connection between stimulus and response. For example, if a person learns over time that eating satisfies hunger, a strong stimulus-response (hunger-eating) bond would develop. Habits thus determine the behaviors or courses of action we choose.

Reinforcement or reward   This represents the feedback individuals receive as a result of action.

A stimulus activates an individual's motivation through its impact on drive and habit. The stronger the drive and habit (S-R bond), the stronger the motivation to behave in a certain way. As a result of this behavior, two things happen. First, the individual receives feedback (or rewards) that reduces the original drive. Second, the individual srengthens his or her belief in the veracity of the S-R bond to the extent that it proved successful. That is, if one's response to the stimulus satisfied one's drive or need, the individual would come to believe more strongly in the appropriateness of the particular S-R connection and would respond alike under similar circumstances.

An example will clarify this point. Several recent attempts to train chronically unemployed workers have used a daily pay system instead of weekly or monthly systems. The primary reason for this is that the workers, who do not have a history of working, can more quickly see the relationship between coming to work and receiving pay. An S-R bond develops more quickly because of the frequency of the reinforcement or reward.

Operant vs. classical conditioning.

Operant conditioning can be distinguished from classical conditioning in at least two ways (Luthans, 1977). First, the two approaches differ in what is believed to cause changes in behavior. In classical conditioning, changes in behavior are thought to arise through changes in stimuli, that is, a change from an unconditioned stimulus to a conditioned stimulus. In operant conditioning, on the other hand, changes in behavior are thought to result from the *consequences* of previous behavior. When behavior has been rewarded, we would expect it to be repeated; when behavior has not been rewarded, or has been punished, we would not expect it to be repeated.

Second, the two approaches differ about the role and frequency of rewards. In classical conditioning, the unconditioned stimulus, acting as a sort of reward, is administered during every trial. In contrast, in operant conditioning the reward results only when individuals choose the correct response. That is, in operant conditioning, individuals must correctly operate on their environment before a reward is received. Thus, the response is instrumental in obtaining the desired reward.

Rules for using operant conditioning.   In the use of operant conditioning to shape employee behavior, several important guidelines should be kept in mind (Hamner and Hamner, 1976, p. 6–7):

Rule 1. Don't give the same level of reward to all.
Rule 2. Failure to respond to behavior has reinforcing consequences: Superiors are bound to shape the behavior of the subordinates by the way in which they utilize the rewards at their disposal. Therefore, managers must be careful that they examine the consequences on performance of their nonactions as well as their actions.
Rule 3. Tell a person what behavior gets reinforced.
Rule 4. Tell a person what he or she is doing wrong.
Rule 5. Don't punish in front of others.
Rule 6. Make the consequences equal to the behavior. In other words, don't cheat the worker out of his just rewards.

Cognitive Learning Theory

Cognitive theories will be discussed more fully in Chapter 8. It should be noted here, however, that cognitive theorists have long been interested in learning processes. Without rejecting traditional stimulus-response approaches to the study of learning, cognitive theorists like Edward Tolman believe that much learning takes place outside of the S-R bond. That is, learning is viewed as a process which requires an individual's entire personality. As such, the learning process is seen as being far more complex than simple S-R connections.

Cognitive learning theorists believe that much learning results from simply thinking about a problem, from insight, and from piecing together known facts. Thus, "the significant process in learning is the acquisition of information (including abstract concepts and generalizations) rather than of specific responses" (Zimbardo and Ruch, 1975, p. 110). As a result, the cognitive approach to understanding learning processes emphasizes an individual's reasoning and analytical, perceptual, and problem solving abilities. This approach also places significance on an individual's purposiveness and goal-orientation, assuming that the individual is motivated and desires to learn. This approach stands in stark contrast to the two earlier conditioning models which rely on S-R bonds developed over time.

Major Influences on Learning

While classical or operant conditioning may be successful for learning simple or repetitive tasks, complex learning of more sophisticated material requires the proper learning environment if it is to be highly successful. Filley, House, and Kerr (1976) identify five major influences on learning effectiveness:

Motivation to learn   Drawing largely from cognitive theory, substantial research evidence indicates that learning effectiveness is increased considerably when individuals are highly motivated to learn. We often see examples of students who work day and night to complete a term paper that is of interest to them, while others postpone uninteresting term papers until the last possible minute. Maximum transfer of knowledge is achieved when a student or employee is motivated to learn by a high need to know.

Knowledge of results   Considerable evidence also demonstrates that learning is facilitated by providing individuals with feedback on their performance. Such feedback serves a gyroscopic function, showing individuals where they are correct or incorrect, furnishing them with the perspective to improve. Feedback also serves as an important positive reinforcer which can enhance an individual's willingness or desire to learn.

Prior learning   In many cases, prior learning can increase the ability to learn new materials by providing needed background or foundation materials. These beneficial effects of prior learning on present learning tend to be greatest when the prior tasks and the present tasks exhibit similar stimulus-response connections. For instance, most of the astronauts selected over the years have had years of previous experience flying airplanes. It is assumed that this prior experience will facilitate learning to fly the new, though related, vehicles.

Whole vs. part learning   Another influence on learning concerns whether the materials to be learned are presented in their entirety or in parts. Available evidence suggests (McCormick and Tiffin, 1974), that when a task consists of several distinct and unrelated duties, part learning is more effective. Each task should be learned separately. However, when a task consists of several *integrated* and related parts (like learning the components of a small machine), whole learning is more appropriate because it insures that major interrelationships between parts as well as proper sequencing of parts is not overlooked or underemphasized.

Distribution of practice   The final major influence on learning highlights the advantages and disadvantages of concentrated as opposed to distributed training sessions. Evidence reviewed in Bass and Vaughn (1966) indicates that *distributed* practice, or short learning periods at set intervals, are more effective for learning motor skills than for learning verbal or cognitive skills. Distributed practice also seems to facilitate learning of very difficult, voluminous, or tedious material. On the other hand, *concentrated* practice appears to work well where insight is required for task completion. Apparently, concentrated effort over short durations provides a more synergistic approach to problem solving.

While there is general agreement that these influences are important (and are under the control of management in many cases), they cannot substitute for the lack of an adequate reinforcement system. In fact, reinforcement is widely recognized as the key to effective learning. If managers are concerned with eliciting desired behaviors from their subordinates, a knowledge of reinforcement techniques is essential. It is to this that we now turn.

Reinforcement

Definition

A central feature of both operant learning theory and behavior modification is the concept of reinforcement. This concept dates from Thorndike's law of effect which, as mentioned earlier, states that behavior that is positively reinforced tends to be repeated while behavior that is negatively reinforced tends not to be repeated. Hence, *reinforcement* can be defined in terms of anything that causes a certain behavior to be repeated or inhibited.

Reinforcement vs. Motivation

It is important to differentiate reinforcement from the concept of employee motivation. Motivation, as described in an earlier chapter, represents a primary psychological process that is largely cognitive in nature. Thus, motivation is largely internal; it is *experienced* by the employee and we can only see subsequent manifestations of it in actual behavior. If a person is motivated to perform, we expect to see subsequent performance. Reinforcement, on the other hand, is both observable and most often externally administered. A supervisor may reinforce what he or she considers desirable behavior without knowing anything about the underlying motives that prompted it. This distinction should be kept in mind when examining the nature of behavior modification later in this chapter.

Types of Reinforcement

From a managerial standpoint, several methods, or types, of reinforcement are available to facilitate learning in organizational settings. Rachlin (1970) has identified four basic types: 1) positive reinforcement; 2) avoidance learning; 3) extinction; and 4) punishment. Each type plays a different role in both the manner and extent to which learning occurs. Each will be considered separately here.

Positive reinforcement. Positive reinforcement consists of presenting someone with an attractive outcome following a desired behavior. As noted by Skinner (1953, p. 73), "a positive reinforcer is a stimulus which, when added to a situation, strengthens the probability of an operant response." A simple example of positive reinforcement is when a supervisor praises subordinates when they perform well in a certain situation. For example, a supervisor may praise an employee for being consistently punctual in attendance, as shown in Exhibit 7–2. This behavior-praise pattern may encourage the subordinate to be on time in the future in the hope of receiving additional praise.

In order for a positive reinforcement to be effective in facilitating the repetition of desired behavior, several conditions must be met. First, the reinforcer itself (praise) must be valued by the employee. It would prove ineffective in shaping behavior if employees are indifferent to it. Second, the reinforcer must be strongly tied to the desired behavior. Receipt of the reinforcer by the employee must be directly contingent upon performing the desired behavior. "Rewards must result from performance, and the greater the degree of performance by an employee, the greater should be his reward" (Hamner, 1977, p. 98). It is important to keep in mind here that "desired behavior," represents behavior defined by the supevisor, not the

Exhibit 7–2 Examples of types of reinforcement

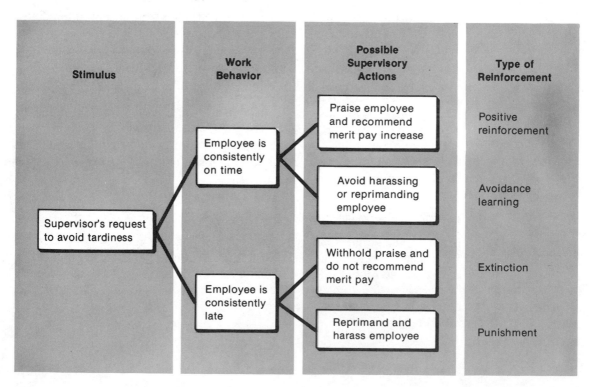

employee. Third, there must be ample occasion for the reinforcer to be administered following desired behavior. If the reinforcer is tied to certain behavior that seldom occurs, such as *very* high performance, then individuals will seldom be reinforced and will probably not associate this behavior with a reward. It is important that the performance-reward contingencies be structured so that they are easily attainable.

Avoidance learning. A second method of reinforcement is *avoidance learning,* or negative reinforcement. Avoidance learning is the seeking to avoid an unpleasant condition or outcome by following a desired behavior. Employees learn to avoid unpleasant situations by behaving in certain ways. If an employee correctly performs a task, or is continually prompt in coming to work (see Exhibit 7–2), the supervisor may refrain from harassing, reprimanding, or otherwise embarrassing the employee. Presumably, the employee learns over time that engaging in correct behavior diminishes distasteful admonishing from the supervisor. In order to maintain this condition the employee continues to behave as desired.

Extinction. The principle of extinction suggests that undesired behavior will decline as a result of a lack of positive reinforcement. If the perpetually tardy employee in the example in Exhibit 7–2 consistently fails to receive supervisory praise and is not recommended for a pay raise, we would expect this non-reinforcement to lead to an "extinction" of the tardiness. The employee may realize—albeit subtly—that being late is not leading to desired outcomes and may try being on time for work.

Punishment. Finally, a fourth type of reinforcement used by managers and supervisors is punishment. Punishment is the administration of unpleasant or adverse outcomes as a result of undesired behavior. An example of the application of punishment is for a supervisor to publicly reprimand or harass an employee who is habitually tardy (see Exhibit 7–2). Presumably, the employee would refrain from being tardy in the future in order to avoid such an undesirable outcome. The use of punishment is indeed one of the most controversial issues of behavior modification.

In summary, positive reinforcement and avoidance learning focus on bringing about the *desired* response from the employee. With positive reinforcement the employee behaves in a certain way in order to gain desired rewards, while with avoidance learning the employee behaves in order to avoid certain unpleasant outcomes. In both cases, however, the behavior desired by the supervisor is enhanced. In contrast, extinction and punishment focus on supervisory attempts to reduce the incidents of *undesired* behavior. That is, extinction and punishment are typically used to get someone to stop doing something. It does not necessarily follow that the individual will begin acting in the most desired, or correct, manner.

From a managerial perspective, questions arise about which types of reinforcement are most effective. Advocates of behavior modification, such as Skinner, answer that positive reinforcement combined with extinction is the most suitable way to bring about desired behavior. There are several reasons for this focus on the positive approach to reinforcement. First, although punishment can inhibit or eliminate undesired behavior, it often does not provide information to the individual about how or in which direction to change. Also, the application of punishment may cause the individual to become alienated from the work situation, thereby reducing the chances that useful change can be effected. Similarly, avoidance learning tends to emphasize the negative; that is, people are taught to stay clear of certain behaviors, like tardiness, for fear of the repercussions. In contrast, it is felt that combining positive reinforcement with the use of extinction has the least undesirable side effects and allows individuals to receive the rewards they desire. A positive approach to reinforcement is believed by some to be the most effective tool management has to bring about desired changes in organizations.

Schedules of Reinforcement

We have seen that there are four distinct types of reinforcement that can be used to elicit desired behavior. We shall now turn to an examination of the various ways, or *schedules,* of administering this reinforcement. As noted by Costello and Zalkind (1963, p. 193), ''The speed with which learning takes place and also how lasting its effects will be is determined by the timing of reinforcement.'' Thus, a knowledge of various schedules of reinforcement is essential to managers if they are to know how to choose rewards that will have maximum impact on employee performance.

Although there are a variety of ways in which rewards can be administered, most approaches can be categorized into two groups: continuous and partial reinforcement schedules. A *continuous* reinforcement schedule rewards desired behavior every time it occurs. For example, a manager could praise (or pay) employees every time they perform properly. With the time and resource constraints most managers work under, this is often difficult if not impossible. So, most managerial reward strategies operate on a partial schedule. A *partial* reinforcement schedule rewards desired behavior at specific intervals, not every time desired behavior is exhibited. Compared to continuous schedules, partial reinforcement schedules lead to slower learning but stronger retention. Thus, learning is generally more permanent. Four kinds of partial reinforcement schedules can be identified: 1) fixed interval; 2) fixed ratio; 3) variable interval; and 4) variable ratio (see Exhibit 7–3).

Fixed interval schedule. A *fixed interval* reinforcement schedule rewards individuals at pre-specified intervals for their performance. If

Exhibit 7–3   Schedules of partial reinforcement

Schedule of Reinforcement	Nature of Reinforcement	Effects on Behavior when Applied	Effects on Behavior when Perceived	Example
Fixed interval	Reward on fixed time basis	Leads to average and irregular performance	Quick extinction of behavior	Weekly paycheck
Fixed ratio	Reward consistently tied to output	Leads quickly to very high and stable performance	Quick extinction of behavior	Piece-rate pay system
Variable interval	Reward given at variable intervals around some average time	Leads to moderately high and stable performance	Slow extinction of behavior	Monthly performance appraisal and reward at random times each month
Variable ratio	Reward given at variable output levels around some average output	Leads to very high performance	Slow extinction of behavior	Sales bonus tied to selling X accounts, but X constantly changes around some mean

employees perform even minimally, they are paid. This technique generally does not lead to high or sustained levels of performance, since employees know that marginal performance usually leads to the same level of rewards as high performance. Thus, there is little incentive for high effort and performance. Also, when rewards are withheld or suspended, extinction of desired behavior occurs quickly. Many of the recent job redesign efforts in organizations were prompted by the recognition of the need for alternate strategies of motivation rather than pay on fixed interval schedules. It is hoped that redesigning employees' jobs will motivate people where weekly or monthly paychecks do not.

Fixed ratio schedule.   The second fixed schedule is the *fixed ratio* schedule. Here the reward is administered only upon the completion of a given number of desired responses. In other words, rewards are tied to performance in a ratio of rewards to results. For every so many results, employees receive a reward. A common example of the fixed ratio schedule is a piece-rate pay system, where employees are paid for each unit of output they produce. Under this system, performance rapidly reaches high levels. In fact, according to Hamner (1977, p. 105), "the response level here is significantly higher than that obtained under any of the interval (or time-based) shedules." On the negative side, however, performance declines sharply upon the cessation of the receipt of the reward, as with fixed interval schedules.

Variable interval schedule. Using variable reinforcement schedules both variable interval and variable ratio reinforcement is administered at random times that cannot be predicted by the employee. The employee is generally not aware of when the next evaluation and reward period will be. Under a *variable interval* schedule, rewards are administered at intervals of time which are based on an average. For example, an employee may know that *on the average* his performance is evaluated and rewarded about once a month, but he does not know when this event will occur. He does know, however, that it will occur sometime during the interval of a month. Under this schedule, effort and performance will generally be high and fairly stable over time. This is because employees never know when the evaluation will take place.

Variable ratio schedule. Finally, a *variable ratio* schedule is one in which rewards are administered only after an employee has performed the desired behavior a number of times, with the number changing from the administration of one reward to the next but averaging over time to a certain *ratio* of number of performances to rewards. For example, a manager may determine that a salesperson will receive a bonus for every fifteen new accounts sold. However, instead of administering the bonus every fifteenth sale (as in a fixed interval schedule), the manager may vary the number of sales that are necessary for the bonus, from perhaps ten sales for the first bonus to twenty for the second. On the average, however, the 15:1 ratio prevails. As with the variable interval, the variable ratio schedule typically leads to high and stable performance. Moreover, extinction of desired behavior is slow.

Which method of these four schedules of reinforcement is superior? In a review of several studies which compared the various techniques, Hamner (1977, p. 105) concluded:

> The necessity for arranging appropriate reinforcement contingencies is dramatically illustrated by several studies in which rewards were shifted from a response-contingent (ratio) to a time-contingent basis (interval). During the period in which rewards were made conditional upon occurrence of the desired behavior, the appropriate response patterns were exhibited at a consistently high level. When the same rewards were given based on time and independent of the worker's behavior, there was a marked drop in the desired behavior. The reinstatements of the performance-contingent reward schedule promptly restored the high level of responsiveness.

In other words, the performance-contingent (or ratio) reward schedules generally lead to better performance than the time-contingent (or interval) schedules, regardless of whether such schedules are fixed or variable. We will return to this point in a subsequent chapter on performance appraisal and reward systems.

Behavior Modification in Organizations

The application of learning theory and reinforcement principles to organizational situations is seen in *behavior modification* programs. Behavior modification is the use of operant conditioning principles to shape human behavior to conform to desired standards defined by superiors.

In recent years, behavior modification has been applied in a wide variety of organizations. In most cases, positive results are claimed. For example, at Emery Air Freight, the implementation of behavior modification purportedly led to a cut in operating costs of $2 million during its first three years of operation. The 3M Company estimated that the technique saved them $3.5 million in one year alone. In the accounting department of Collins Foods International, behavior modification led to a reduction in the error rate in accounts payable from 8% to 0.2% (*Business Week,* 1978). Examples such as these stimulate interest in the technique as a management tool to improve performance and reduce costs.

Because of its emphasis on shaping behavior, it is more appropriate to think of behavior modification as a *technique* for motivating employees, rather than as a *theory* of work motivation. It does not attempt to provide a comprehensive model of the various personal and job-related variables that contribute to motivation. Instead, its managerial thrust is on *how* to motivate and it is probably this emphasis that has led to its current popularity among managers. Even so, we should be cautioned against the unquestioned acceptance of any technique until or unless we understand the assumptions underlying the model. If the underlying assumptions of a model appear to be questionable or inappropriate in a particular situation or organization, its use is clearly questionable.

Assumptions of Behavior Modification

The foundation of behavior modification as a theory of management rests on three ideas (Skinner, 1971). First, advocates of behavior modification believe that individuals are basically passive and reactive (instead of proactive). They respond to stimuli in their environment rather than assuming personal responsibility in initiating behavior. This assertion is in direct contrast to cognitive theories of motivation (like expectancy theory) which hold that individuals make conscious decisions about their present and future behaviors and take an active role in shaping their environment.

Second, advocates of behavior modification focus on behavior itself; on observable and measurable behaviors, instead of non-observable needs, attitudes, goals, or motivational levels. In contrast, cognitive theories focus on both observable and unobservable factors as they relate to motivation.

Third, behavior modification stresses that permanent change can be brought about only as a result of reinforcement. Behaviors that are positively reinforced will be repeated (learned) while behaviors not so reinforced will diminish (law of effect).

Designing a Behavior Modification Program

If behavior modification techniques are to work, their application must be well thought out and systematically applied. Systematic attempts to implement these programs typically go through five phases:

First, management attempts to define and clearly specify the behavioral aspects of acceptable performance. Management must be able to clearly specify what constitutes acceptable behavior, and this specification must be in objective measurable terms. Examples of *behavioral criteria* are good attendance, promptness in arriving for work, and completing tasks on schedule. Sometimes it is difficult to determine suitable objective indicators of successful performance. For instance, as a training director of a major airline asks, "How do you quantify what a flight attendant does?"

Second, once behavioral criteria have been specified, a *performance audit* can be done. Because management is concerned about the extent to which employees are successfully meeting behavioral criteria, the audit is aimed at pinpointing trouble spots where desired behaviors are not being carried out. For instance, a review of attendance records of various departments may reveal a department where absenteeism is unusually high. Action can then be taken to focus on the problem area.

Third, *specific behavioral goals* must be set for each employee. As noted by Hamner and Hamner (1976), failure to specify concrete behavioral goals is a primary reason for the failure of many behavior modification programs. Examples of goals are to decrease absenteeism and meet production schedules. The goals should be both reasonably achievable by the employees and acceptable to them (Meyer, Kay, and French, 1965).

Fourth, employees are asked to *keep a record* of their own work. This record provides them with continuous feedback concerning the extent to which they are on target in meeting their goals.

Fifth, supervisors examine the employees' records, as well as other available performance indicators, and *praise* the positive aspects of their work performance. Such praise is designed to strengthen desired performance by the employee (positive reinforcement). The withholding of praise for less than adequate performance, below established goals, supposedly causes employees to change inappropriate behavior (extinction). It is this fifth step in the program (the use of praise and the absence of punishment) which advocates of behavior modification suggest differentiates it from other motivational strategies.

Examples of Behavior Modification in Organizations

While many of the principles of operant conditioning and behavior modification have been used by organizations for years, systematic attempts to apply behavior modification programs were rare prior to the last decade. In fact, as late as 1973, one researcher concluded: "There is little objective evidence available [that behavior modification works], and what evidence there is abounds in caveats—the technique will work under the proper circumstances, the parameters of which are usually not easily apparent" (Organizational Dynamics, Winter 1973, p. 49).

The earliest experiments in behavior modification (most notably Emery Air Freight, as shown in Box 7–1) were hailed by some as a clear demonstration of the usefulness of these techniques for motivating employee behavior and facilitating organizational effectiveness. Concern soon arose, however, over the long–term effects of the techniques. As a result of this concern, Hamner and Hamner (1976) surveyed companies which had used positive reinforcement and behavior modification to determine the effects which resulted from the programs. Several of these results are summarized in Exhibit 7–4.

Several interesting points can be seen in Exhibit 7–4. First, it should be noted that most behavior modification programs have been carried out among blue-collar workers, possibly because the tasks performed by these employees are usually somewhat routine and lend themselves to goal-setting techniques. Second, most of the goals set by the organizations deal with improving performance and attendance. Third, feedback provided on goal-directed effort is typically provided either on a daily or weekly basis; thus, employees receive a good deal of immediate feedback on performance. It appears that the frequency of feedback declines as higher-level employees become involved in the program. Fourth, the most typical reinforcers used are praise, recognition, and positive feedback. Monetary reinforcers were used in only two of the ten programs surveyed. Finally, the results of the programs were consistently described as successful (from the company's standpoint). Typical results included cost savings, increased production, and increased attendance. In only one of the ten cases was the program discontinued because of lack of success. In other words, this survey by Hamner and Hamner (1976) suggests that behavior modification techniques can be successfully used in organizational settings and can lead to specific desired outcomes at little cost to the organization.

Much of the success of these programs can be attributed to a combination of goal-setting, providing accurate, timely feedback, and adequate rewards for task accomplishment. As the general manager of Michigan Bell–Operator Services observed (quoted in Hamner and Organ, 1978, p. 253):

Box 7-1 The Case of Emery Air Freight

The program   Perhaps the most widely known example of the application of behavior modification in industry is that of Emery Air Freight. Under the direction of Edward J. Feeney, Emery selected behavior modification as a simple answer to the persistent problems of inefficiency and low productivity. In an air freight firm, rapid processing of parcels is important to corporate profitability.*

Emery Air Freight began with a performance audit, which attempted to identify the kind of job behaviors which had the greatest impact on profit and the extent to which these behaviors were shown in the company. One area of special concern was the use of containers. Emery loses money if shipping containers are not fully loaded when shipped. Hence, one goal was to ensure that empty container space was minimized. Before the program was implemented, workers reported that they believed they were filling the containers about 90% of the time. However, the performance audit revealed that this was really so only about 45% of the time. In other words, over half of the containers were shipped unfilled.

The results   Through the use of feedback (in the form of self-report checklists provided to each worker) and positive reinforcement (praise), the percentage of full containers rose swiftly from 45% to 95%. Cost reductions for the first year alone exceeded $500,000, and rose to $2 million during the first three years. In other words, when workers were given consistent feedback and kept informed of their performance, subsequent output increased rapidly. As a result of this initial success, similar programs were initiatied at Emery, including the setting of performance standards for handling customer problems on the telephone and for accurately estimating the container sizes needed for shipment of lightweight packages. Again, positive results were claimed.

The aftermath   While the use of praise as a reinforcer proved initially to be a successful and inexpensive reinforcer, its effects diminished over time as it became repetitious. As a result, Emery had to seek other reinforcers. These included invitations to business luncheons, formal recognition such as a public letter or a letter home, being given a more enjoyable task after completing a less desirable one, delegating responsibility and decision making, and allowing special time off from the job. Hence, the use of praise alone does not appear to have sustained effects and managers had to continually turn to new reinforcers to keep the program in operation.

*Source: W. C. Hamner and E. P. Hamner. "Behavior modification on the bottom line." *Organizational Dynamics*, 1976, *4*(4), 8-21.

We have found through experience that when standards and feedback are not provided, workers generally feel their performance is at about the 95 percent level. When the performance is then compared with clearly defined standards, it is usually found to meet only the 50th percentile in performance. It has been our experience, over the past ten years, that when standards are set and feedback provided in a positive manner, performance will reach very high levels—perhaps in the upper 90th percentile in a very short period of time. . . . We have also found that when positive reinforcement is discontinued, performance returns to levels that existed prior to the establishment of feedback.

Advocates of behavior modification can point to a series of successful applications of the technique. This success has emerged using objective indicators like attendance and increased output that clearly relate to organizational effectiveness. Even so, behavior modification has been criticized on several grounds. It is to these criticisms that we will now turn.

Criticisms of Behavior Modification

At least five criticisms have been leveled against behavior modification in work situations. None of these criticisms is clear-cut; for each point there is a counterpoint in the continuing controversy over reinforcement techniques. We shall examine each criticism as well as a possible response to each.

1. Behavior modification ignores individual differences. A consistent complaint against the use of operant techniques in work situations is that they ignore the fact that people are different and have differing needs, desires, values, abilities, and so forth (Locke, 1977). For instance, when we set up a positive reinforcement system that gives praise for desired behaviors, we assume that all individuals value praise and that all individuals have the requisite skills and abilities to carry out the desired behaviors. This is often not the case.

This problem of individual differences is recognized by advocates of behavior modification. For instance, Hamner and Organ (1978, p. 61) note, "What is reinforcing to one person may not be reinforcing to another person because of the latter's past history of satiation, deprivation, and conditioning operations." Even so, it is suggested that managers can account for these differences in their application of operant techniques in at least two ways. First, managers can attempt to select and hire employees who value the rewards offered by the organization. Efforts can be made to match employee values (insofar as rewards are concerned) with organizational values. To the extent that this approach is successful, it might lead to the hiring of employees with high needs for achievement, since these employees typically desire frequent feedback on performance. However, attempts by managers to adequately screen applicants for appropriate values is no easy task. Also, this solution does nothing for the majority of employees—those already employed.

Exhibit 7-4 Results of positive reinforcement and similar behavior modification programs in organizations

Organization Surveyed	Type of Employees	Specific Goals	Frequency of Feedback	Reinforcers Used	Results
Michigan Bell— Operator Services	Employees at all levels in operator services	(a) Decrease turnover and absenteeism (b) Increase productivity (c) Improve union-management relations	(a) Lower level—weekly and daily (b) Higher level—monthly and quarterly	(a) Praise and recognition (b) Opportunity to see oneself become better	(a) Attendance performance has improved by 50% (b) Productivity and efficiency has continued to be above standard in areas where positive reinforcement (PR) is used
City of Detroit Garbage Collectors	Garbage collectors	(a) Reduction in paid man-hour per ton (b) Reduction on overtime (c) 90% of routes completed by standard (d) Effectiveness (quality)	Daily and quarterly based on formula negotiated by city and sanitation union	Bonus (profit sharing) and praise	(a) Citizen complaints declined significantly (b) City saved $1,654,000 first year after bonus paid (c) Worker bonus = $307,000 first year or $350 annually per man (d) Union somewhat dissatisfied with productivity measure and is pushing for more bonus to employee
B. F. Goodrich Chemical Co.	Manufacturing employees at all levels	(a) Better meeting of schedules (b) Increase productivity	Weekly	Praise and recognition; freedom to choose one's own activity	Production has increased over 300%
ACDC Electronics Division of Emerson Electronics	All levels	(a) 96% attendance (b) 90% engineering specifications met (c) Daily production objectives met 95% of time (d) Cost reduced by 10%	Daily and weekly feedback from foreman to company president	Positive feedback	(a) Profit up 25% over forecast (b) $550,000 cost reduction on $10 M sales (c) Return of 1900% on investment including consultant fees (d) Turnaround time on repairs went from 30 to 10 days (e) Attendance is now 98.2% (from 93.5%)

Source: W. C. Hamner and E. P. Hamner. "Behavior modification on the bottom line." *Organizational Dynamics*, 1976, *4*(4), 12–14.

The second technique managers may use to attempt to overcome the problem of individual differences is to allow greater employee participation in the determination of rewards. Thus, if the present rewards or performance–reward contingencies are ineffective, employee advice may be sought about ways to improve the situation. This solution gives employees a greater voice in the design of their work environment and, as Vroom (1960) has noted, such actions should lead to greater employee ego involvement in seeing that the solution arrived at is successful. However, the success of such an approach assumes that managers have a genuine concern for the welfare of the employees. If behavior modification is used simply to exploit employees, employees will find suitable ways to nullify the impact of the technique on performance results.

2. Behavior modification ignores prevailing work group norms. It is often the case in work situations that employees feel that management has consistently tried to exploit them. Where these feelings exist, group norms often emerge which aim to control or restrict the degree of employee cooperation with management. This control typically takes the form of employee restriction of output. Where this situation prevails, the implementation of a behavior modification program (particularly one that relies on praise for increased performance) is likely to be met with stiff resistance from the work group. Group members feel there is little reason to cooperate with management since outcomes may have detrimental effects like an increase in output without a corresponding raise in pay.

The power of work group norms to reduce the effectiveness of reward systems is possible in all types of reward systems, not just behavior modification. Even so, these influences should not be overlooked by managers contemplating implementing such techniques. Where an organization has a history of distrust between managers and employees, behavior modification is not likely to improve performance. It is first necessary to develop suitable work climate and improve the degree of perceived organizational concern and dependability. Once accomplished, and the employees do not feel they are being exploited, operant techniques stand a better chance of success.

3. Behavior modification ignores the fact that employees can be intrinsically motivated. As a strategy of employee motivation, behavior modification relies on the use of *extrinsic* (that is, externally administered) rewards, such as praise, positive feedback, and money. Opponents of this technique point out that, in many cases, the nature of the job itself may represent an *intrinsic* source of motivation, making operant techniques often unnecessary. It is argued that behavior modification relies too heavily on satisfying lower-order needs while ignoring higher-order needs (see Chapter 4). Instead, opponents such as Deci (1972) suggest deemphasizing contingent reward systems like the piece-rate system and substituting noncontingent systems such as salaries. Such noncontingent systems will provide sufficient income to employees for their lower-order needs to be met. Then, managers can concentrate on redesigning jobs to be intrinsically motivating and appeal more to employees' higher-order needs.

This criticism of behavior modification may be misdirected since proponents of the technique are supportive of job redesign efforts (Skinner, 1969). As Skinner (p. 18) notes:

> It has often been pointed out that the attitude of the production-line worker toward his work differs conspicuously from that of the craftsman, who is envied by workers and industrial managers alike. One explanation is that the craftsman is reinforced by more than monetary consequences, but another important difference is that when a craftsman spends a week completing a given set object, each of the parts produced during the week is likely to be automatically reinforcing because of its place in the completed object.

So, there appears to be no disagreement over the advantages of enriched jobs, although there is some disagreement over why such jobs motivate as they do. Whereas Deci (1972) argues that enriched jobs motivate because of their intrinsic appeal to higher-order needs, Skinner suggests that they motivate because they offer a wide array of positive reinforcers.

Thus, while advocates of behavior modification and operant techniques may focus their attention on extrinsic reward systems and not as fully discuss intrinsic reward systems, it does not follow that they reject them. They do, however, reject the use of non-contingent reward systems (such as standardized salaries) where pay is not linked to performance. In this sense, they are in agreement with most theories of work motivation discussed in the next chapter.

4. Behavior modification assumes incorrectly that all behaviors must be externally reinforced in order to be learned. Advocates of operant techniques assume that most behavior can be controlled by reinforcements given individuals. This assumption ignores the fact that people can learn new responses by observing other people getting reinforced for the same response. This process is called *vicarious reinforcement* (Kanfer, 1965). In addition, people often learn something by imitating others who are *not* reinforced for their behavior; this is called *vicarious learning* (Marlatt, 1970). Finally, some people learn to behave in certain ways through *self-reinforcement;* that is, they evaluate their own behavior and decide to change some aspect of it without external interference (Kanfer and Karoly, 1972). Given the existence of such practices, it would seem that behavior modification and operant techniques have a limited range of application.

In cases where junior managers observe and imitate the behavior of their senior counterparts, learning can easily take place without the need of overt reinforcements from the organization. In fact, a major organizational benefit of the use of managerial assistants (for example, Assistant to the Controller) is that they learn by imitation to perform desired behaviors. Assuming that lower-level employees wish to rise through the ranks of an organization, it is only natural that they wish to prepare for this, and a major part of this preparation is imitating those who rank above them.

5. Behavior modification is not a new technique for motivating employees. Finally, several people have pointed out that the techniques advocated by behavior modification are not new. In discussing Feeney's widely-cited behavior modification effort at Emery Air Freight, Locke (1977, p. 549) notes:

> There is little difference between Feeney's ideas and some key elements of Scientific Management presented more than 60 years ago by Taylor. Taylor's central concept, the task, which consisted of an assigned work goal (with the work methods also specified), is virtually identical in meaning to Feeney's concept of a "performance standard," a term which also was used by advocates of Scientific Management. Similarly, Taylor argued that work should be measured continually and the results fed back to employees so that they could correct errors and improve or maintain their quantity of output. . . . Two additional concepts occasionally used by Feeney are praise and participation. Both are taken directly from the Human Relations school of management.

Locke (1977) goes on to argue that many so-called successful applications of behavior modification may not be attributed to the use of operant techniques but instead may have resulted simply through job redefinition. For example, in the Emery Air Freight experiment, it was claimed that behavior modification caused performance to leap from 30% of standard to 95% in a single day in the customer service offices. In the container departments, container use jumped from 45% to 95% in a single day. As Locke (1977, p. 548) points out, "Since genuine conditioning is asserted to be a gradual process, the very speed of these improvements mitigates against a conditioning explanation of the results. More likely what occurred was a conscious *redefinition of the job* resulting from the new standards and the more accurate feedback regarding performance in relation to those standards.

Perhaps the most serious criticism of behavior modification is that it is simply a return to closer supervision, tighter job specifications, and more frequent evaluation and feedback on performance. This is not to say that the technique is inappropriate, only that such techniques have been around since the emergence of scientific management. Recent studies clearly show that such techniques do improve performance. Whether credit for them goes to Skinner's theory and techniques or simply to closer supervision and increased task specification will be debated for some time. The techniques have generally proven successful in improving performance and attendance, if not job attitudes.

Summary

In this chapter, learning processes were shown to be an important facet of employee behavior. Basic models of learning were introduced and compared. Following this, we examined several influences on learning.

Next, the concept of reinforcement was discussed at length, including consideration of various types of reinforcement and schedules of reinforcement. Behavior modification was reviewed as it relates to work organizations. Examples f behavior modification programs were reviewed and the basic design of these programs was highlighted. Also included was a review of several major criticisms of behavior modification with rebuttals by advocates of the technique.

Key Words

learning	extinction
classical conditioning	punishment
operant conditioning	behavior modification
law of effect	vicarious reinforcement
drive	vicarious learning
habit	self-reinforcement
reinforcement	fixed interval schedule
cognitive learning theory	fixed ratio schedule
behavioral criteria	variable interval schedule
performance audit	variable ratio schedule
avoidance learning	

Questions for Discussion

1. Explain what is meant by learning.
2. Compare and contrast classical conditioning and operant conditioning. Compare both of these to cognitive learning theory.
3. According to Hamner and Hamner, what are some of the rules for using operant conditioning?
4. Discuss several major influences on learning.
5. What is the difference between reinforcement and motivation?
6. Identify the various types of reinforcement.
7. What are some schedules of reinforcement? Which ones are more effective in motivating performance?
8. Describe the various assumptions underlying behavior modification. Do you agree with these assumptions? Why or why not?
9. Review the design of a typical behavior modification program.
10. Discuss several criticisms that have been advanced against behavior modification. Do you agree or disagree with them?

chapter 8

Complex Models of Motivation and Performance

In previous chapters, we examined various influences on employee behavior in work organizations. We noted that factors such as employee needs, abilities, and traits, as well as perception and learning influence how we behave at work. Throughout, emphasis has been placed on the need not only to recognize these various influences but also to understand how they fit together to *jointly* determine human behavior. It is only through a systematic understanding of the major variables and how they affect one another that managers can take the necessary actions to facilitate a performance-oriented and satisfying work environment.

In this chapter, we will outline a systematic framework by examining complex cognitive models of employee motivation. We call these models complex because they incorporate individual characteristics, job characteristics, and organization-wide characteristics. They attempt to incorporate many of the factors discussed earlier that have been shown to influence behavior and show how these factors interact. They are cognitive in that the models attempt to reflect the decision making of individuals as they decide the extent of their involvement in work activities.

Importance of Topic for Managers

The topic of employee motivation is clearly one of the most important topics for managers. There are numerous reasons for this.

1. One of the most persuasive arguments for studying motivation is advanced by Katz and Kahn (1978). They note that organizations have three *behavioral requirements* of the people who work in them. First, people must be attracted to join the organization and remain with it. Second, people must dependably perform the tasks they were hired for. Third, people must transcend dependable role performance and engage in some form of creative, spontaneous, and innovative behavior at work. These three behavioral requirements deal squarely with the issue of motivation. Motivational techniques must be employed not only to encourage employees to join and remain with an organization, but also to perform in a dependable fashion and to think and take advantage of unique opportunities.

2. In addition, the ever-present nature of motivational processes in organizations should not be overlooked. Motivation affects and is affected by a multitude of factors in the work environment. A comprehensive understanding of the way in which organizations function and survive requires an in-depth knowledge of why people behave as they do on the job.

3. With respect to the ever-tightening constraints that are placed on organizations by unions, government agencies, and increased foriegn and domestic competition, companies must find ways to improve their efficiency and effectiveness in the work place. Much of the organizational slack that was relied on in the past has diminished, requiring that all resources—including human resources—are utilized to their maximum.

4. Increased attention has been devoted in recent years to developing employees as future resources—a sort of talent bank—from which organizations can draw in the future as they grow and develop. Examples of these efforts can be seen in the increase in management development programs, manpower planning, and job redesign. Motivation is the foundation upon which these efforts are built.

5. From the individual's standpoint, motivation is a key to a productive and useful life. Work consumes a sizeable portion of our waking hours. If this time is to be meaningful and contribute toward the development of a healthy personality, the individual must be willing to devote effort toward task accomplishment. Motivation plays a central role in this.

Motivational Factors in Low Productivity

To set the stage for our discussion of cognitive models of motivation and performance, it may be useful to first consider a major reason why such models have received so much attention in recent years. The reason is seen in the problem of low productivity and the motivational factors inherent in it. An awareness of several of the reasons for low productivity highlights the importance of understanding motivational processes in work organizations. In fact, a major aim of many contempory motivational models is to diagnose and alleviate these kinds of problems.

Managers often complain that employees don't put forth as much effort on the job as they would like to see. We hear that employees are lazy or that they conspire to reduce output. Although many of these complaints are heard, we seldom see managers attempt to identify the reasons behind such restriction of output. In fact, employees often feel, rightly or wrongly, that it is in their best interest to restrict productivity. At least five reasons for this behavior can be identified (Steers, 1977c).

Potential rewards unappealing   As will be discussed later in this chapter, employees place different values on different outcomes. Some employees prize added income while others want additional time off or an opportunity to enter a training program. In many instances, employees may simply not place a high enough value on the rewards available for increased performance to justify special effort. This difference can be seen in situations where some employees will continually take work home at night to maximize job performance and in hope of getting a raise or promotion, while others prefer to spend the evening hours with their families even if it slows their career progression.

Weak performance-reward linkage   Sometimes, employees fail to see a strong linkage between increased performance and receipt of additional rewards. The failure to see a linkage is often because there is none. It is difficult to measure performance accurately, especially at the managerial level. As a result, opportunities for inequity emerge in the reward system and good performance may not be rewarded to the extent it should be. When employees fail to see a clear relationship between performance and subsequent rewards, a major motivating force is lost. This point is demonstrated in Box 8–1.

Distrust of management   Employees often distrust management and feel that increased performance may only result in increases in the quotas or production rates required. Such distrust, which can be particularly strong among blue-collar workers, tends to neutralize the incentive system. In addition, workers at times feel that increased performance will lead to a reduction in the workforce (that is, they may work themselves out of a job). These fears lead to group pressures to maintain acceptable, moderate performance levels and to punish rate-busters as a threat to the well-being of the group.

Desire to have control over one's job   On an individual level, one cause of restricted output is the desire to maintain at least some control over one's behavior on the job. As jobs become increasingly automated, people lose autonomy and personal discretion on the job. In order to resist being a cog in the wheel, people often attempt to leave sufficient slack in their work

---

Box 8–1 Are Employees Concerned About Productivity?

Is employee apathy toward productivity or restriction of output a problem in contemporary work organizations? Available evidence seems to suggest this is the case. One poll of over 4,000 U.S. employees on various jobs carried out by the Opinion Research Corporation found that 57 percent of those surveyed felt they could easily produce more on their jobs if they wanted to.* The survey found that many people simply saw no reason to increase their output at work.

Or, take the recent example of a west coast plywood manufacturer. In the plywood industry, a typical spreader machine crew will produce from 65,000 to 90,000 core-line feet of plywood in an eight hour shift. In an effort to determine how much plywood could be produced at maximum pace, one crew (running a high average of 108,020 core-line feet) attempted to set a new record for plywood production. The result: 214,720 core-line feet—an increase of almost 100 percent over their own average and almost 300 percent over the industry average. Or,

from a qualitative standpoint, consider the plight of the U. S. automotive industry which in 1977 recalled more cars than they manufactured due to faulty design and workmanship.

In contrast, while many U. S. corporations are concerned about discovering ways to improve employee commitment to high productivity, many Japanese firms are concerned about workers pushing themselves too hard. A recent study found that a majority of Japanese workers take less than one-third of the time off they are entitled to and feel that utilizing all of their holiday time reflects disloyalty or lack of interest in their work. Things in Japan have reached such a state that the Japanese ministry of labor has begun a campaign aimed at encouraging workers to take full advantage of their vacation benefits. Moreover, some firms that have been unable to convince employees to take time off have been forced to shut down factories entirely so employees were unable to come to work.

*Sources: Opinion Research Corporation, America's growing anti-business mood. *Business Week,* June 17, 1972, p. 101; D. Wyant, Plywood crew claims production record. *Eugene Register-Guard,* December 6, 1978; Industry recalls more cars than it sold in worst year. *Eugene Register-Guard,* April 12, 1978; Workaholics, *Parade,* December 24, 1978.

---

schedule (by intentional underproduction) so they can vary their work methods. By doing so, they reassure themselves that they still have some degree of control over their own behavior and therefore count as people. It increases individuals' feelings of self-worth and independence by increasing their freedom of action.

Lack of job involvement   Another reason for output restriction may be a simple dislike of the job. If employees lack interest in the job and prefer to be doing something else, it is difficult to focus their energies on the tasks at hand. This lack of involvement can often lead to absenteeism or other forms of withdrawal (such as alcoholism), thereby reducing performance levels even further.

One way to better understand how these factors influence or inhibit productivity is to use a *force field analysis*. A force field analysis is a technique developed by Kurt Lewin to pictorially represent forces (or pressures) to do something (in this case, pressures for productivity), as compared to forces *not* to do something (in this case, restriction of output). We can develop a fairly simple force field analysis of influences on productivity by comparing various factors that promote production with factors that may inhibit production, as shown in Exhibit 8–1.

At least five forces against productivity can be identified, as noted above. These are shown in the right half of Exhibit 8–1. Opposing these are a series of positive performance forces. As we shall see such positive forces can include having valued rewards contingent upon performance, strong personal work values and goals, employee perceptions of equitable treatment by peers and management, role clarity, and employees who have the necessary abilities and traits to do the job. These are only examples of many of the forces in favor of productivity. These examples do illustrate how the employee weighs positive and negative forces to determine how much effort to devote to performance.

Problems resulting from poor motivation to work are commonplace in contemporary work organizations. If managers intend to remedy this situation, they must make an effort to understand the underlying influences on such behavior and how the nature of the job and the work environment affects it. One way is to develop more comprehensive models of employee

Exhibit 8–1   A force field analysis of pressures for and against productivity

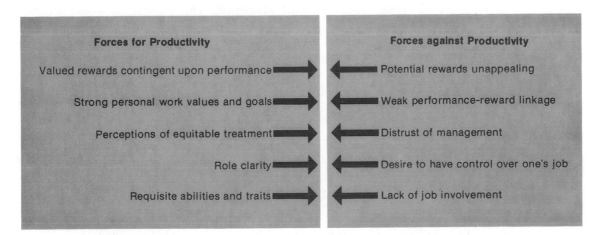

Forces for Productivity	Forces against Productivity
Valued rewards contingent upon performance	Potential rewards unappealing
Strong personal work values and goals	Weak performance-reward linkage
Perceptions of equitable treatment	Distrust of management
Role clarity	Desire to have control over one's job
Requisite abilities and traits	Lack of job involvement

motivation that focus on the way individuals react to the work situations. Some such complex models are discussed here. A review of three major cognitive models of motivation will shed light both on *why* employees do or do not produce and on *what* managers can do to facilitate employee performance and job satisfaction. First, let's look at the nature of cognitive models.

Cognitive vs. Acognitive Models of Motivation

There are now two basic schools of thought concerning the nature of employee motivation. They are the acognitive and the cognitive approaches. In the last chapter on reinforcement theory and behavior modification, a primarily acognitive point of view was expressed. *Acognitive* models of motivation assert that it is possible to predict behavior without an understanding of internal thought processes. Instead, they stress the relationship between external stimuli and behavior and do not explore the effects of internal mechanisms. People are seen as being largely reactive to environmental stimuli, and it is therefore viewed as not necessary to examine internal processes.

On the other hand, *cognitive* models of motivation, such as the models discussed in this chapter, rest on the assumption that individuals often make conscious decisions about their behavior, and that this decision process must be clearly understood if we are to understand human behavior. Cognitive theories emphasize the how and why of behavior by focusing on internal mechanisms. Individuals are seen as active organisms in their environment. They are proactive as well as reactive to environmental forces.

While these two basic approaches to understanding human behavior are not totally incompatible, they do represent distinct differences in emphasis and assumptions about the nature of people. This distinction should become clear as we examine three complex cognitive theories of employee motivation: equity theory, goal-setting theory, and expectancy/valence theory. Each theory rests on the assumption that people are reasoning (if not reasonable) creatures that often make conscious choices from among alternative forms of behavior. [See Steers and Porter (1979) for a more detailed discussion of the three models]. All three models emerge from—and are unified by—the role of cognitions in human behavior.

Equity Theory

Basic Premises of Equity Theory

One cognitive explanation of human behavior in work organizations is equity theory. Equity theory, as first advanced by Adams (1965) and Weick (1966), is the most popular in a series of *social comparison theories* of motivation (Goodman, 1977). Social comparison theories all focus on individuals' feelings or perceptions of how fair they are being treated as compared to others.

Equity theory rests on two basic assumptions about human behavior (Mowday, 1979). First, it is assumed that individuals engage in a process of evaluating their social relationships much like they would evaluate economic transactions in the marketplace. Social relationships are viewed as an exchange process in which individuals make contributions or investments and expect certain outcomes in return. March and Simon's (1958) inducements-contributions theory is one such early example. We expect individuals to have expectations (cognitions) about the outcomes they receive as a result of their contributions of time and effort.

Second, it is assumed that people do not assess the equity of an exchange in a vacuum. Instead, they compare their own situation or exchange balance with others to determine the relative balance. The determination of the extent to which an exchange is satisfactory is influenced by what happens to oneself compared to what happens to others.

In this section, we shall examine the basic ingredients of equity theory, and follow this with a discussion of the consequences of inequity. Next, a brief summary of the research on equity theory will be presented, followed by a discussion of the managerial implications of the model. Throughout, be aware of the central role played by cognitions in the process.

Antecedents of Inequity

Social comparison processes, like those involved in equity theory, are typically based on the relationship between two variables: inputs and outcomes. *Inputs,* or investments, represent those things an individual contributes to an exchange. In a work situation, inputs include items like previous work experience, education, and level of effort on the job. *Outcomes* are items that an individual receives from the exchange. Outcomes may include pay, fringe benefits, accrued status, seniority, and positive feedback.

In order for an input or outcome to be relevant in evaluating exchange relationships, two conditions must be met. First, the existence of an input or outcome must be recognized by one or both parties in the exchange. The major outcome from a particular job is irrelevant unless some of the parties involved consider it a major outcome. Second, an input or outcome must be considered relevant or have marginal utility to the exchange. Unless both conditions, recognition and relevancy, are met, potential inputs or outcomes will not be considered in determining the degree of equity in the exchange.

According to the theory, individuals assign weights to the various inputs and outcomes according to their perceived importance. This is not to say that people are highly precise in these weighting processes, but that they roughly differentiate between more important and less important inputs and outcomes. Intuitively, people arrive at a ratio of their outcomes to inputs *as compared to* the ratio of another individual's or group's outcomes to inputs. The other individual or groups may be people or groups with whom we engage in direct exchanges, other individuals engaged in exchanges with a common third party, or persons in a previous or hypothetical work situation. This referent other becomes the point of comparison for people in determining the degree to which they feel equitably treated.

From this, a state of equity exists whenever the ratio of a person's outcomes to inputs is equal to the ratio of other's outcomes to inputs. This state can be represented where *p* represents the ratio of the person and *o* represents the ratio of the comparison other:

$$\frac{O_p}{I_p} = \frac{O_o}{I_o}$$

A state of inequity exists whenever these two ratios are unequal:

$$\frac{O_p}{I_p} < \frac{O_o}{I_o} \quad \text{or} \quad \frac{O_p}{I_p} > \frac{O_o}{I_o}$$

In this approach to the concept of equity in social exchange, several specific aspects of the model must be emphasized. To begin, the conditions necessary to produce a state of equity or inequity are based on a person's *perceptions* of inputs and outcomes. If an individual has a highly distorted view of the major factors involved in an exchange (e.g., he thought his co-workers were earning far more than they actually were), these distortions will be incorporated into the person's calculations of equity or inequity. Second, inequity is a *relative* phenomenon. That is, inequity does not necessarily exist simply because a person has high inputs and low outcomes, so long as the comparison other also has a similar ratio. Employees may be fairly satisfied with a job demanding high effort and offering low rewards if their frame of reference is in a similar situation.

Third, it is important to note that inequity occurs when people are relatively underpaid *or overpaid.* Available research suggests that the threshold for underpayment is lower than it is for overpayment (Mowday, 1979). People are more willing to accept overpayment in an exchange relationship than underpayment. Even so, both theory and research observe that people who experience overpayment will sometimes be motivated to reduce the exchange imbalance by working harder. The ways people strive to reduce inequities in exchange are discussed below.

Consequences of Inequity

The implications of equity theory in motivation follow from the hypothesized consequences of perceived inequity. As formulated by Adams

(1965), the major postulates of the theory are as follows: 1) perceived inequity (underpayment or overpayment) creates tension within individuals; 2) the tension is proportionate to the magnitude of the inequity; 3) the tension experienced by individuals will motivate them to attempt to reduce it; and 4) the strength of the motivation or drive to reduce it is proportionate to the perceived inequity. This process is shown in Exhibit 8–2.

In this process, individuals are faced with the problem of *how* to reduce perceived inequity. Adams (1965) suggests six methods of resolution:

People may alter their inputs   People may increase or decrease their inputs depending upon whether the inequity is advantageous or disadvantageous. For instance, underpaid people may reduce their level of effort on the job or increase absenteeism, while overpaid people may increase effort.

People may alter their outcomes   Similarly, it is possible for individuals to increase or decrease outcomes received on the job. One clear example of increasing outcomes can be seen in union efforts to improve wages, hours, and working conditions without parallel increases in employee effort (or input).

People may distort their inputs or outcomes cognitively   For instance, people who feel inequitably treated may artificially increase the status outcomes attached to their job ("This is really an important job") or may decrease perceived effort ("I really don't work that hard on this job"). By doing so, the input-outcome ratios become more favorable by comparision and people are more content.

People may leave the field   Simply put, individuals who feel inequitably treated may decide to leave the situation by transferring to another job or department or by quitting. In doing so, they apparently hope to find a more favorable balance of inputs to outcomes. This behavior is demonstrated in a study reviewed in Box 8–2.

People may distort the inputs or outcomes of others   In the face of injustice, people may cognitively distort the ratio of the referent. For instance, people may come to believe that the referent other actually works harder

Exhibit 8–2   Motivational implications of perceived inequity

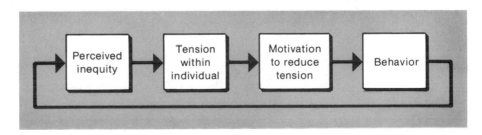

than they do, and thereby deserves greater rewards. Or, they may reduce the perceived salary that the referent other makes and thereby reduce the other's outcomes.

People may change objects of comparison   Finally, people may decide that their referent other is not the most suitable point of comparison and may select another who will yield a more favorable balance in the social exchange process. For instance, if the other receives a salary increase while the person does not, he may decide that the other now belongs to a different level in the organization hierarchy, thereby justifying the need to select a more relevant other.

Through these techniques, individuals attempt to cope with situations they believe are unfair. Their efforts and motivations are largely aimed at returning to a state of equity and reduced tension. Equity theory, like other cognitive theories of motivation, views individuals as existing in a constant state of flux. They continually try to understand their environment and to act on it in a way that satisfies their more pressing needs, desires, and expectations.

Box 8–2 Perceived Equity and Employee Turnover

One example of equity theory at work can be seen in a study of its impact on employee turnover.* In this study, it was hypothesized that perceptions of inequity would cause individuals to be more inclined to leave the organization. Among a sample of hourly employees in a manufacturing firm, the extent of perceived equity was measured with respect to pay, supervision, security, advancement, working conditions, intrinsic rewards, and co-worker relations. Responses were compared between a shop that traditionally had high turnover rates and one that traditionally had low turnover rates.

Results indicate that employees in the high turnover shop experienced greater perceived inequity with respect to supervision, working conditions, intrinsic rewards, and social aspects of the job than employees in a low turnover shop. These results suggest that perceived inequity can represent a potent factor in influencing employee behavior at work. Moreover, the study clearly demonstrates the utility of equity theory in examining individual behavior on the job. Where employees feel that they are being inequitably treated, these results (and equity theory) suggest that they will be motivated to take action aimed at restoring an equitable balance of inputs and outcomes. One clear way to accomplish this is to leave the field and seek employment elsewhere.

*Source: C. S. Telly, W. L. French, and W. G. Scott. "The relationship of inequity to turnover among hourly workers." *Administrative Science Quarterly*, 1971, *16*, 164–172.

Research on Equity Theory

A great deal of research generated over the past decade focuses on the validity and utility of equity theory (Goodman, 1977; Mowday, 1979; Pritchard, 1969). From the standpoint of work-related behaviors, the most relevant research has focused on equity theory predictions of employee reactions to pay. These predictions generally distinguish between two conditions of pay inequity (underpayment and overpayment) and two methods of compensation (hourly and piece rate). The specific predictions of each interaction are shown in Exhibit 8–3.

Available evidence tends to support many equity theory predictions, particularly concerning underpayment, as they relate to expected behaviors under various compensation and equity conditions. The findings are not unanimous. Following a recent review, Mowday (1979, p. 134) concluded:

> In summary, predictions from Adams' theory about employee reactions to wage inequities have received some support in the research literature. Research support for the theory appears to be strongest for predictions about underpayment inequity. Although there are fewer studies of underpayment than of overpayment, results of research on underpayment are relatively consistent and subject to fewer alternative explanations. There are both theoretical and empirical grounds for being cautious in generalizing the results of research on overpayment inequity to employee behavior in work organizations. Where such studies have manipulated perceived inequity by challenging subject's qualifications for the job, observed differences in performance can be explained in ways that have little to do with inequity. Where other methods of inducing overpayment inequity are used, considerably less support is often found for the theory. Predicted differences in productivity and satisfaction due to overpayment inequity are often in the predicted direction but fail to reach acceptable levels of statistical significance.

Exhibit 8–3 Equity theory predictions of employee reactions to inequitable payment (Mowday, 1979)

	Underpayment	Overpayment
Hourly payment	Subjects underpaid by the hour produce less or poorer-quality output than equitably paid subjects	Subjects overpaid by the hour produce more or higher-quality output than equitably paid subjects
Piece-rate payment	Subjects underpaid by piece rate will produce a large number of low-quality units in comparison with equitably paid subjects	Subjects overpaid by piece rate will produce fewer units of higher quality than equitably paid subjects

Equity theory does make a contribution toward a better understanding of work behavior in organizations. Perceived states of equity (or inequity) affect our responses to the work environment (in terms of experienced tension), as well as our intentions and behavior on the job. Although equity theory is not a complete statement of employee motivation, it does describe several important motivationally relevant processes that managers should understand. Now, let's consider some of the more salient managerial implications of the theory.

Managerial Implications of Equity Theory

From a managerial standpoint, equity theory suggests several useful techniques of employee motivation. In particular, equity theory emphasizes the points we'll turn our attention to now.

Perhaps the most obvious implication is the necessity for managers to be continually alert to social comparison processes in organizations and, as a consequence, to view motivation in dynamic and changing terms. For example, redesigning someone's job may not increase subsequent motivation and performance if the changes do not change the inputs-outcomes balance. If employees still think they are inequitably treated (perhaps they feel they are paid less than comparable others), there is little reason to expect increased effort. Hence, as much as possible, managers have a responsibility to insure that employees feel they are equitably treated.

Employers and managers must also recognize the importance of perception in employee motivation. If employees *perceive* that they are inequitably treated, they will act accordingly—even if they are in fact overcompensated for their level of effort. Managers, who view the workplace differently from workers, often fail to understand this critical point.

Equity theory attaches much importance to monetary rewards and the manner in which they are distributed. Money is one of the few rewards that people clearly see and measure. As a result, it often becomes a major focal point in employee assessments about their own equity.

Finally, equity theory requires managers to evaluate (and reevaluate) the bases on which they distribute available rewards. Leventhal (1976) identifies three general types of *distribution rules:* 1) distribution of rewards based on equity or contribution; 2) distribution of rewards based on feelings of social responsibility; and 3) distribution of rewards based on equality, with equal outcomes given to all participants. Managers tend to select one or more of these ways based on the nature of the situation and based on certain known factors at the time. It should be clear that the manager's choice of distribution rule in no small way affects employee's perceptions of their own state of equity and their willingness to respond and participate.

Goal-Setting Theory

A second cognitive theory of motivation is *goal-setting theory*. The chief proponent of this model is Edwin A. Locke (1968). We will examine several aspects of the model here. First, the basic premises are introduced. Next, the role of task-goal attributes in goal-setting success is examined, followed by a discussion of the effects of individual and situational factors on the model. Finally, we review managerial implications.

Basic Premises of Goal-Setting Theory

Locke's (1968) basic premise in support of goal-setting theory is that behavior is determined by two cognitions: values and intentions (or goals). As shown in Exhibit 8–4, values (or what one regards as conducive to welfare) are experienced by people in the form of emotions and desires. Our values cause us to want certain things that are consistent with our values. For instance, we may have a strong personal work ethic which causes us to have a desire to perform at high levels. As a result of these emotions and desires, we set intentions or goals concerning our behavior. We may decide to put in longer hours on the job, for instance. These goals then represent the primary determinant of actual behavior. In other words, Locke's model emphasizes the role of conscious intentions in actual behavior. If we set out to accomplish something, like either to work harder or less hard, these intentions guide our effort and performance.

Much research supports the basic premises of a goal-setting model of motivation. People set goals concerning their future behaviors and these goals influence actual behaviors. If we are to understand more about the goal-setting process, however, it is necessary to look beyond the basic premise of the model and understand many of the complexities involved. To do this, we begin with an examination of the role of task-goal attributes in goal-setting and performance.

Exhibit 8–4   The goal-setting model of motivation and performance

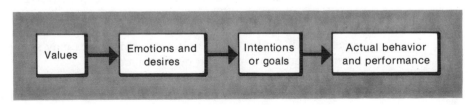

Task-Goal Attributes
and Performance

Although Locke's goal-setting model implies a fairly refined sequence of events leading up to behavior and performance, the research on the topic has not been as systematic. Instead, much of what we know of the effects of goal-setting on performance comes from studies of the effects of several task-goal attributes.

A *task-goal attribute* may be defined as a characteristic or dimension of an employee's task goals (Steers and Porter, 1974). It is possible to identify six relatively distinct task-goal attributes that facilitate task performance in a goal-setting environment: 1) goal specificity; 2) goal difficulty; 3) participation in goal-setting; 4) feedback on goal effort; 5) peer competition for goal attainment; and 6) goal acceptance. The relation of these to employee performance is summarized below and shown in Exhibit 8–5. See Latham and Yukl (1975) and Steers and Porter (1974) for extensive reviews of the literature.

Goal specificity.   It has been consistently found that goal specificity is directly related to increased performance. When employees are given specific goals they consistently perform at higher levels than when they are simply told to do their best or are given no instructions at all. The more specific the goals, the higher the performance (Locke, 1967). Such findings are not surprising. Increasing goal specificity on a task reduces role ambiguity and reduces the search for acceptable modes of behavior. The employee has a very clear idea of what is expected and can perform accordingly.

Goal difficulty.   A second tenet of goal-setting theory is that, up to a point, increasing the difficulty of employees' goals increases the perceived challenge of the task, and increases the amount of effort expended for goal attainment. This is particularly true for high need achievers. Strong support is shown for this position. More difficult goals tend to lead to increased effort and performance (at least to the point such goals are still seen as feasible). However, serious exceptions to this trend can be noted. It has been found that difficult goals may lose their motivating potential when they are not properly reinforced. Past failures on previous goals may negate the effects of setting difficult future goals (Zander & Newcomb, 1967). Goals apparently must not be set at such a level that they are seldom, if ever, achieved. Under these conditions, employees may simply stop trying, leading to reduced effort and performance.

Participation in goal-setting.   The virtues of participative decision making have long been described as a means not only of increasing organiza-

Exhibit 8–5   A general model of major influences on goal-setting and performance

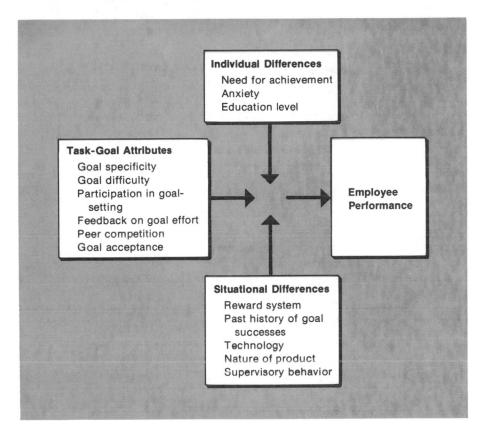

tional efficiency and effectiveness but also of increasing employee involvement and job satisfaction (Vroom, 1964). Unfortunately, available evidence suggests that, while increased participation in goal-setting may increase job satisfaction and attendance, its effects on job performance are mixed. While participation does not seem to detract from performance, it appears that the act of setting goals (goal specificity) is a far more powerful tool in influencing performance (Lawrence & Smith, 1955). This is made clear in Box 8–3. A possible explanation for this finding is suggested when we consider the effects of individual differences.

Feedback on goal effort.   Another influence on goal-setting effectiveness is the extent to which employees are given feedback on task-oriented behavior. Feedback serves at least two functions: 1) it acts as a directive,

Box 8-3 Goal-Setting and Performance among Typists

The problem Does goal-setting really work and, if so, which aspects of goal-setting are most pronounced in their influence on employee behavior? In order to answer this question, Gary Latham and Gary Yukl have carried out a series of studies relating different aspects of goal–setting programs to employee performance.* One study focused on typists.

The program In this experiment forty-one typists from the word processing center of a major corporation were assigned to two groups. In the first group, productivity goals were assigned by the supervisor, while in the second group goals were participatively set by the typists and their supervisors. Goals were established each week and the previous week's performance was used in setting goals for the next week. Performance was measured using an index of the weighted sum of the number of lines typed each week divided by the number of hours worked. The weights were determined based upon the difficulty level of the material typed.

The results After ten weeks, *both* groups experienced significantly higher performance rates than before the experiment. Productivity increased 18 percent in the participative group and 15 percent in the assigned group. So, while level of goal difficulty and goal specificity (that is, whether or not goals were set at all) were both found to be important influences on performance, participation in setting goals did not emerge as an important influence in this study. The utility of goal–setting processes in facilitating employee performance was clearly established.

*Source: G. P. Latham and G. A. Yukl. "Effects of assigned and participative goal–setting on performance and job satisfaction." *Journal of Applied Psychology,* 1976, *61,* 166–171.

keeping a goal-directed behavior on target, and 2) it serves as an incentive, stimulating employees to greater effort (Payne & Hauty, 1955). When available evidence is considered, it must be concluded that no simple feedback-performance relationship exists. While feedback is obviously important in facilitating performance for some people, other factors like individuals' needs, appear to moderate the relationship.

Peer competition for goal attainment.   Many managers feel that performance can be enhanced by placing employees in a competitive situation relative to their peers. Unfortunately, available evidence is again not too clear about the purported benefits of peer competition on performance. Several additional factors need to be taken into account in order to adequately explain this association. First, the relationship between peer competition and performance depends on how we define performance. We would expect competition to positively influence performance *only* when product quality either is not a consideration or is controlled by technology. This is because competition often leads i reased *quantity* of output at the expense of *quality*. If craftsmanship is a central concern, competition may be detrimental.

Second, the nature of job technology may influence the effects of competition. Under conditions of high task interdependence (such as those found on assemblylines where product manufacture depends on many people working together), we would not expect competition to lead to improved results. On the other hand, under conditions of task independence (where people are responsible for their own product or component), competition is often useful.

Finally, competition among peers for goal attainment is also influenced by the nature of the reward system. Competition would be expected to be strongly related to performance where a ''zero-sum game'' situation dictates rewards. There can be only one winner in a race, for example. Similarly, there can be only one best sales representative who wins a trip to Hawaii. On the other hand, where there can be many winners (that is, a non-zero-sum game), as would probably be the case in a majority of actual work situations, we would expect the effects of peer competition to be greatly diminished.

Goal acceptance.   Finally, Locke (1968) has noted that employee level of aspiration significantly affects motivation to perform. It is important to draw a clear distinction between externally assigned task goals (by a supervisor) and those goals that are set by employees. In fact, Locke's theory suggests that task goals will affect behavior only to the extent that they are accepted by employees in the form of personal aspiration levels:

> . . . it is not enough to know that an order or request was made; one has to know whether or not the individual heard it and understood it, how he appraised it, and what he decided to do about it before its effects on his behavior can be predicted and explained (Locke, 1968, p. 174).

In other words, goal acceptance, defined as a congruence of assigned task goals and the personal aspiration levels on such goals, apparently represents an important influence on the relation between goals and performance. This fact is often overlooked by managers when they attempt to implement a goal-setting or MBO program in organizations. The fact that the managers accept the goals is clearly no reason to believe the employees will accept them. First, employees must understand why they should accept the goals and what benefits accrue to them for doing so. The failure of managers to understand this simple fact probably explains many of the failures of many MBO programs in business today.

Additional Influences on
Goal-Setting Success

It was noted that several aspects of the goal-setting environment (task-goal attributes) influence the extent to which goals are actually achieved. It was also noted, that in many cases no direct relationship exists between these task-goal attributes and subsequent performance. Instead, two major moderators of the task-goal attribute-performance relationship can be identified (see Exhibit 8-5).

First, several *situational differences* must be taken into account. Variations in reward systems (zero-sum games vs. non-zero sum games), past history of goal successes, technology (independent vs. interdependent), and the nature of the product (quantity vs. quality) all can influence performance under goal-setting conditions. Added to this is the nature of supervisory behavior. We might expect that attempts to allow employees greater participation in goal setting would be facilitated by a considerate leadership style, rather than by a task-oriented one. Under these conditions, employees feel that their supervisor has a sincere interest in their opinions and inputs.

In addition, several *individual differences* can be identified. In particular, employee need for achievement moderates the extent to which attributes influence performance. For instance, it has been found that high need achievers perform better when given high levels of feedback and very specific goals, while low need achievers perform better when allowed to participate in goal setting (Steers, 1975; see also Ivancevich and McMahon, 1977). These findings are expected in view of the theory on the achievement motive. Recent evidence suggests that anxiety or apprehension about being evaluated by one's supervisor against specific criteria facilitates performance (White, Mitchell, & Bell, 1977). Finally, it has been found that goal-setting tchniques, particularly goal specificity, are more effective with less educated rather than highly educated employees (Latham & Yukl, 1975; Ivancevich and McMahon, 1977).

Clearly, the notion of goal-setting is more complex than was first believed. If goal-setting techniques are to be successfully implemented in organizations, managers must pay attention not only to the attributes of task goals but also to the personal characteristics of employees and the various situational characteristics.

The way managers do this—the way they translate their various findings into actual practice—is best characterized by the management-by-objectives programs that are now widely used in organizations. *Management-by-objectives* (MBO) is a process in which employees of complex organizations, working in conjunction with one another, identify common goals and coordinate their efforts toward achieving them (Tosi, Rizzo, and Carroll, 1970). It is future oriented and, as such, focuses employee attention and effort on "where are we going" instead of "where have we been." While MBO is clearly not a panacea for poorly managed organizations, managers can make use of the technique to provide greater structure, clarity, and focus in otherwise ambiguous situations. In doing so, however, concern should be demonstrated for the impact of variations in task-goal attributes and their modifiers. The naive assumption that MBO can solve management's problems, without proper attention to the nature of the goals and the people asked to work toward them, will hardly bring about success.

Managerial Implications of Goal-Setting Theory

The concept of goal-setting (and MBO) is very rich in terms of the implications for management. Some of these implications follow.

First, greater consideration can be given by managers to the precise nature of the task-goal attributes of each employee. Managers have a responsibility not simply to assign goals to their subordinates, but to see to it that these goals are specified in such a way that they have maximum motivational potential.

In addition, increased attention can be paid to how different types of employees react to their assigned goals. For instance, it has been found that high and low need achievers each perform better under different conditions. Such findings suggest that managers have a responsibility to tailor goals to individual needs as much as possible, and to create an optimal performance environment for each employee.

Increased attention can also be paid to how different situational variables influence performance effectiveness. Differences in leadership style, technology, and group structure often influence the impact of various task-goal atributes on performance.

Some awareness of the possible negative job attitudes that might result from certain aspects of MBO programs is necessary. Recent research has indicated that while goal-setting techniques often lead to improved performance, this performance is at times achieved at the expense of decreased job satisfaction. Where goals are seen be employees as being far too rigid, the credibility of the program itself may be jeopardized, leading to poor effort and performance. Care must be taken to insure that the general parameters of the program are widely accepted by program participants.

Where MBO programs are used, it is often useful to continuously monitor both performance and attitudes among employees as an early-warning system for possible trouble spots. Some research has indicated that MBO programs can lose their potency as a motivating force over time. Continuous monitoring systems can help identify trends and suggest remedies where needed.

Finally, consideration must be given to reinforcing contingencies, thereby improving the motivating potential of the program. Where employees can clearly see personal rewards to be gained from directing effort toward goal attainment, effort and performance should be enhanced.

In summary, available evidence on the effectiveness of goal-setting techniques clearly shows that the relative success of these techniques is largely a result of management's ability to assess their problems comprehensively. Consideration must be given not only to the feasibility of task goals and their applicability to the larger issue or organizational objectives, but also to the role played by individual and situational differences as they relate to performance. When all of these factors are jointly considered, program effectiveness is enhanced and the rate of goal failure diminished.

Expectancy/Valance Theory

Finally, we come to our third cognitive model of employee motivation, *expectancy/valence theory*. Expectancy/valence theory, or simply expectancy theory, of work motivation dates from the early work of Kurt Lewin and Edward Tolman during the 1930s and 40s. These early investigators rejected many of the notions of drive theory and instead argued that much of human behavior results from interaction between the characteristics of individuals (e.g. their personality traits, attitudes, needs, and values), and their perceived environment. This basic model was first applied to work settings by Georgopoulos, Mahoney, and Jones (1957) in their path-goal theory of motivation. It should be noted that expectancy theory is known by many titles, including path-goal theory, instrumentality theory, and valence-instrumentality-expectancy theory.

According to the basic model, individuals are seen as thinking, reasoning individuals who make conscious choices about present and future behavior. People are not seen as inherently motivated or unmotivated, as many earlier models suggest. Instead, motivational level is seen as depending on the particular work environment people find themselves in. To the extent that this environment is compatible with their needs, goals, and expectations, they are motivated. This point will become clearer as we examine the major parts of the theory.

The first systematic, comprehensive formulation of expectancy theory as it relates to work situations was presented by Victor Vroom in his classic book *Work and Motivation* (1964). This was followed closely by extensions and refinements on the model by Galbraith and Cummings (1967), Porter and Lawler (1968), Graen (1969), and Campbell et al. (1970). Instead of presenting several variations of models that exist, we shall review a general expectancy model as it relates to the work situation. Following this, available research evidence will be discussed as it concerns the validity of the model. Finally, some of the more important managerial implications of the model will be presented.

A useful way to review expectancy theory is to break it down into its various components. Expectancy theory attempts to answer two basic questions: 1) What causes motivation? and 2) What causes performance? Expectancy theory also has a third component—what causes job satisfaction?—discussed in Chapter 13. We shall deal with these first two questions here.

What Causes Motivation?

In expectancy theory, motivation is determined by expectancies and valences. An *expectancy* is a belief about the likelihood or probability that a particular behavioral act (such as working harder) will lead to a particular outcome (such as a pay raise). The degree of this belief can vary from 0 (where an individual sees no chance that the behavior will lead to the outcome), to 1.0 (where an individual is absolutely certain that the behavior will lead to the outcome). Of course, most expectancies fall somewhere in between these two extremes. *Valence* refers to the value an individual places on available outcomes or rewards. A valence can range from $+1.0$ to -1.0, depending upon whether the outcome is highly prized by the employee (money) or highly undesirable (being fired).

$E \rightarrow P$ *expectancies.* Expectancies can be divided into two types (Lawler 1973): 1) *effort-performance* (or $E \rightarrow P$) *expectancies* and 2) *performance-outcome* (or $P \rightarrow O$) *expectancies.* An $E \rightarrow P$ expectancy is an individual's belief that effort will, in fact, lead to performance. For example, an employee may feel that working overtime will lead to a higher level of output. Lawler (1973) has suggested several influences on the effort-performance expectancies we form about work. These include: 1) level of self-esteem; 2) past experiences in similar situations; and 3) perception of the actual situation.

$P \rightarrow O$ *expectancies.* A performance-outcome expectancy (or $P \rightarrow O$ expectancy), is the belief that if a person performs well in a given situation certain desired outcomes will follow. For instance, an employee may believe that a higher level of output will result in a pay raise. Conversely, the same employee may also believe that increased performance might lead to a layoff as he works himself out of a job.

Performance-outcome expectancies are influenced by a variety of factors, including: 1) past experience in similar situations; 2) attractiveness of the various outcomes; 3) extent of one's internal locus of control and belief in an ability to control the environment; 4) $E \rightarrow P$ expectancies; and 5) perception of the actual situation.

Valence. Valence is the value individuals place on the available outcomes or rewards. If employees truly do not value the rewards offered by an organization, we do not expect them to be motivated to perform. The valence attached to certain outcomes can vary widely. For instance, some employees do not want to be promoted into positions of increased responsibility and stress, while others welcome such opportunities. Hence, rewarding employees with a promotion is not always likely to be well received. (Consider the detrimental effects of the up-or-out promotional policies of many large companies.) On the other hand, some rewards like money are consistently valued in their own right or because of their instrumental value in leading to the acquisition of other outcomes.

Now that we have identified the major variables which influence motivation in expectancy theory, we can consider how they fit together. As shown in Exhibit 8–6, these three variables are believed to influence an employee's motivational level in a multiplicative fashion. According to expectancy theory, employee motivation (not to be confused with actual performance) is a result of an employee's $E \rightarrow P$ expectancies *times* the $P \rightarrow O$ expectancies *times* the valences for the outcomes.

A simple example will illustrate how this process works. If a salesperson believes that the chances are good (say 8 out of 10, or .8) that increased effort in selling leads to higher sales, we say the person has a high $E \rightarrow P$ expectancy. Moreover, if this individual further believes (also at a .8 level of probability) that such sales increases would lead to a bonus or a pay raise, we say that he or she has a high $P \rightarrow O$ expectancy. Finally, let's assume the salesperson places a high value on this bonus or pay raise (say .9 on a scale

Exhibit 8–6 A model of expectancy/valence theory of motivation and performance (adapted from Porter and Lawler, 1968)

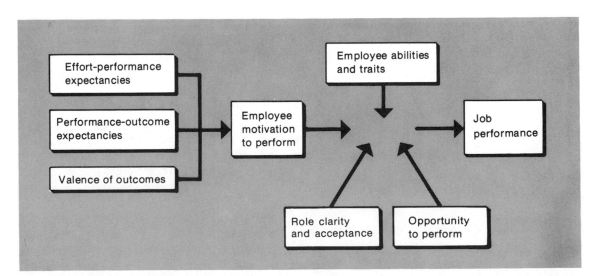

from -1.0 to $+1.0$). When these three factors are combined in a multiplicative fashion ($.8 \times .8 \times .9 = .58$), it becomes clear that the salesperson has a high motivational force. On the other hand, if expectancies were high (.8 and .8, respectively), but the salesperson genuinely had little desire for money (say a valence of .1 instead of .9), the motivational force would be considerably lower ($.8 \times .8 \times .1 = .06$). Hence, for an employee to be highly motivated, *all three* factors must be high. In the absence of one of the factors, we do not expect to see high motivational levels.

What Causes Performance?

Although an understanding of the determinants of employee motivation is obviously important, the concepts of motivation and performance are not synonymous. Motivation represents an employee's desire to perform, or level of effort, while *performance* is the extent to which an individual can successfully accomplish a task or achieve a goal. Performance as a concept includes not only the production of certain tangible units of output but also less tangible outputs like effectively supervising others, thinking in a creative way, inventing a new product, resolving a conflict between others, or selling a good or service. In many ways, effective employee performance is the ultimate criterion by which managers are judged.

As can be seen in Exhibit 8–6, performance is influenced by several factors. Clearly, motivation is a central influence. But *in addition to motivation*, at least three ingredients are also necessary: 1) abilities and traits; 2) role clarity and acceptance; and 3) opportunity to perform (Porter and Lawler 1968; Campbell and Pritchard 1976).

Abilities and traits. The abilities and traits which employees bring to the job largely determine their *capacity* to perform, as opposed to employee motivation, which is largely concerned with employees' *will* to perform. Abilities and traits are believed to be enduring and stable over time, although some changes are possible as a result of outside intervention, like employee training (see Chapters 4 and 5).

Job performance can be influenced by employee abilities and traits in several ways. For example, it has been shown that managerial effectiveness is modestly related to intellectual capabilities, (such as verbal comprehension, inductive reasoning, and memory. It has been suggested by Ghiselli (1966) that these capabilities increase in importance as individuals move up the managerial hierarchy into increasingly responsible positions. Abilities and skills, like typing or knowing a trade, are also obviously important for the successful performance of clerical or blue-collar employees. Finally, several personal traits (such as cognitive complexity) have been shown to influence performance.

These findings have clear implications in the recruitment, selection, and placement of new employees *as long as* management is willing to fit individuals to jobs which match their skills. Hiring employees who are highly intelligent or who have high needs for achievement and then placing them in jobs that lack challenge or interest would not only inhibit their level of motivation and performance but also probably hasten their leaving the organization altogether. A major responsibility for managers is to insure that they select employees who are suitable to the tasks to be done.

Role clarity and acceptance. Being motivated to perform and having the requisite abilities do not insure good job performance. In addition, employees must understand and accept the requirements of the job (Porter and Lawler 1968). Providing employees with increased role clarity increases the amount of energy that is directed specifically toward work goals and decreases the amount of energy that is wasted on other activities. For instance, if supervisors know that they bear primary responsibility for reducing shop floor accidents, they will be likely to devote effort to accomplishing this goal. On the other hand, if roles are unclarified, supervisors may take a "let the employee worry about it" attitude, leading to negative results. Role clarity has also been found to lead to increased goal commitment, work group cohesiveness, job involvement, and job satisfaction (Graen, 1976; Locke, 1976).

Opportunity to perform. Finally, a point that is often overlooked in a consideration of employee motivation is that employees must have an *opportunity* to perform in order to achieve job success (Campbell and Pritchard 1976). If a salesperson is asked to sell a product that nobody wants, like buggy whips, or if a production manager is given an unrealistic deadline to produce a quantity of a certain product, the chances of successful job performance are low—even if the employee is motivated, has the requisite abilities, and has a clear picture of the task.

The inhibiting effects placed on the opportunity to perform can be seen in the problems personnel managers face when asked to develop programs to improve employee motivation *without* affecting production levels or changing jobs substantially or changing the compensation and reward system. Under such circumstances, it is not surprising that managers are unable to improve motivational levels substantially; they simply do not have the opportunity to perform.

Another example of the lack of opportunity to perform can be seen in assemblyline jobs where the pace of production is determined by machines. Where technology controls production, improved motivation can do little to increase quantity of output, although it may influence quality of output in some cases.

In summary, the model outlined in Exhibit 8–6 suggests four primary influences on job performance: 1) employee motivation; 2) employee abilities and skills; 3) role clarity and acceptance; and 4) opportunity to perform. These four factors together suggest that successful job performance is indeed determined jointly by individuals and their environment, as suggested by Kurt Lewin. Individuals can contribute to job performance through their motivation to perform and the skills and abilities they bring to the workplace. Managers, on the other hand, can contribute to job performance by insuring that reward systems encourage motivation and that job requirements are clear and precise. In addition, managers can attempt to create work assignments in which employees have opportunities to really perform. The more control employees have over their performance environment, the greater is the impact of their motivation on subsequent job performance.

Research on Expectancy Theory

In recent years, over forty empirical studies have been done which examine various aspects of the expectancy model of employee motivation. Details of these findings are reviewed in Mitchell (1974) and Campbell and Pritchard (1976). While a detailed review of the various problems in research on this topic is beyond the scope of our discussion, it is possible to summarize the current status of research on the model.

Each of the three components of the expectancy model, $E \rightarrow P$ expectancy, $P \rightarrow O$ expectancy, and valence, has been found to be moderately and independently related to effort and performance (Campbell and Pritchard, 1976). This relationship is particularly strong in $P \rightarrow O$ expectancies. In a number of studies, it has been found that modifying performance-outcome contingencies (so employees see a clear relationship between performance and subsequent rewards) consistently leads to improved levels of performance. Nowhere is this relationship more clearly demonstrated than in pay incentive systems where pay is based on performance rather than seniority or some other criteria. Under these conditions, employees see that performance on their part leads to the receipt of desired rewards and so performance levels are generally higher.

The predictive powers of the expectancy model are improved somewhat when the three basic variables are combined in a multiplicative fashion, instead of in an additive one (Campbell and Pritchard, 1976). This finding supports the idea that all three components must be present for motivational force to be high. If individuals value a reward and feel they can perform the task but do not believe that performance will lead to the reward, they would probably not be highly motivated.

There is some disagreement about whether employee abilities are better predictors of performance than motivational force. Dunnette (1972) reviews several laboratory experiments which suggest that brief aptitude or general intelligence tests predict task performance better than does motivational level. Lawler and Suttle (1973) disagree, however, noting that it is very difficult to accurately measure motivational level. In fact, they suggest that "the theory has become so complex that it has exceeded the measures which exist to test it" (p. 502). In other words, available evidence, while oftentimes modest, suggests that "the heuristic value of the expectancy framework will remain as a powerful force in organizational psychology even though its empirical house is certainly not in order" (Campbell and Pritchard, 1976, p. 92).

Managerial Implications of Expectancy Theory

Given the somewhat complicated structure of expectancy theory, it might be thought that the model had little to say to managers concerned with real organizational problems. This is not the case, however. In fact, expectancy theory provides a rich conceptual framework for managers interested in understanding how motivation and performance can be improved. Included in these managerial implications are the following.

Clarify E → P expectancies. Employees' beliefs that effort will lead to performance can be enhanced in several ways, including the use of training programs, coaching, supervisory support, guidance, and participation in job-related decisions. Through such assistance, employees will feel that high levels of performance are actually within reach.

Clarify P → O expectancies. One of the most important functions of management is to design reward systems that are based on actual performance. Increasing performance-reward contingencies lets employees know exactly what they can expect in exchange for high levels of performance. Such contingencies add equity to the reward system.

Match rewards to employee desires. Different employees often want different rewards or outcomes from their jobs. While some employees may place a high valence on receiving additional income, others may prefer time off, either for vacation or for receiving additional training for a future promotion. Managers can improve motivational levels by offering a variety of rewards for employees. "Cafeteria" fringe benefit plans have been used successfully by organizations like TRW and the Educational Testing Service (see Chapter 17).

Recognize conscious behavior. A major tenet of expectancy theory is that individuals often make conscious decisions about their present and future behavior based on the outcomes they expect for the various behaviors. This is not to say that people make conscious decisions before every act. Instead, it suggests that people periodically evaluate and reevaluate what they are doing and why they are doing it. For example, when a job applicant is confronted with two job offers, the applicant typically weighs the positive and negative aspects of each job to arrive at a decision of which job to accept. Once on the job, employees often reassess the jobs they hold in comparison to alternative options. In short, managers should acknowledge that employees often do not accept the status quo for very long, thus forcing situations and managers to change and adapt over time.

Select people who are equipped for the job. The role of employee abilities and traits in performance should not be minimized. All too often, employees are hired, promoted, transferred, or fired based on personality rather than ability.

Clarify role expectations. Sometimes, people are hired into ambiguous jobs and given little guidance about what is expected of them. We hear the comment that "I want to see what he can *make* out of the job." Such attitudes can lead to wasted efforts while employees search for answers. If managers instead spend the necessary time to clarify job objectives (as in management-by-objectives programs), less search behavior and more task-related bhavior takes place.

Provide opportunities to perform. If employees are placed on impossible jobs or in situations where probability of success is small, they will see little reason to perform. An example of this problem can be seen in the frutstration experienced by local branch managers in banks. Although they are held accountable for improving such performance indicators as deposits on account, these indicators are often more a function of the location of the branch than of the manager's effort. An encyclopedia salesperson in a poor neighborhood experiences similar frustration from learning that no one there can afford the product. If we want people to perform, they must be placed in situations where high performance is possible.

The expectancy model of motivation points to several concrete guidelines for managers seeking to increase performance. The majority of these suggestions are not simply ways to manipulate employees. Instead, they often lead to improved situations for employees. In this sense, the implications suggested here represent a strategy for integrating employee needs, desires, and goals with those of the organization.

Comparison of Models of Motivation

We have now reviewed three contemporary models of employee motivation. It will be useful now to pause and consider how these models compare. Obvious differences can be seen in the various implications each model suggests for management. As noted in earlier discussions, the three models emphasize quite different aspects of persons and work situations as primary motivators.

In addition to differences in application, distinct differences can also be noted in theory. For instance, equity theory suggests that people make motivational decisions almost exclusively by comparing their own situations to others. Expectancy theory, on the other hand, recognizes the importance of peer influence but allows for situations where individuals make decisions irrespective of others. Expectancy theory is more of an individual-oriented theory.

While equity theory and expectancy theory both emphasize the role of future rewards in motivation and behavior, goal-setting theory focuses largely on the nature of task-goals (and whether they are accepted) and is relatively silent about the role of rewards. Even so, goal-setting theory possibly has clearer applications for managers than the other two models.

Several similarities across the three models should also be recognized. To begin with, all three recognize individual and situational differences, although this recognition is more pronounced in expectancy theory and goal-setting teory. All three models focus on the motivational *process;* the steps leading up to behavior. This is important if we are to better understand employee behavior at work. Finally, the models are in agreement in their predictions of human behavior. In fact, it has been argued by Campbell and Pritchard (1976) that equity considerations and goal-setting processes could be subsumed under the more general expectancy theory framework.

For those in management, there is a natural tendency here to ask which is the best theory of motivation. This question is basically unanswerable since each theory may at some time be most appropriate depending upon the situation and the people involved. Rather than attempting to select the one best model, it is probably far more useful to ask what managers can learn from a review of cognitive models of motivation in general. In this we can be much more specific. Several useful lessons can be learned from a review (Steers and Porter, 1979).

Perhaps most important, managers must understand that if they are truly concerned with improving performance and work attitudes, they must take an active role in *managing* motivational processes on the job. Managing motivation represents a conscious attempt by managers to actively participate in creating proper work environments and matching people to jobs. This approach contradicts those in which managers sit back and simply complain about unmotivated workers. It suggests that motivating employees requires work.

Efforts by managers to improve employee motivation and performance should be preceded by self-examination of their own strengths and weaknesses. Do they really understand thcir own needs, aspirations, and expectations? Are their self-perceptions consistent with the perceptions others have of them? Failure to understand oneself does not facilitate motivation in others.

The need to recognize and deal with individual differences in the work environment has emerged consistently throughout our discussion of motivational processes. Managers must recognize that employees possess different abilities, expectations, and valences. An awareness of these differences allows managers to utilize more effectively the diversity of talent among subordinates and, within policy limitations, reward good performance with rewards most valued by employees.

It is important for managers to establish clear performance-reward contingencies. This suggests a need for managers to know their subordinates well enough to recognize good performance when it occurs (and not be unduly influenced by stereotypes or halo effects). Once such performance occurs, rewards should be forthcoming in a way clearly recognized by employees as resulting from performance. This contention argues against compensation systems that fail to recognize individual merit.

Questions of motivation ultimately come to rest on the nature of the job or task that we ask employees to perform. While the issue of job design is reserved for Chapter 16, we can point out here the obvious need to design jobs when possible in a way that employees find meaningful and personally satisfying. When this cannot be done, greater management creativity is called for to compensate for less desirable jobs with other rewards.

Managers should give attention to improving the overall quality of the work environment. What effects do group processes, supervisory style, or working conditions have on employee morale and the desire to participate actively in organizational activities?

Efforts can be made to monitor employee attitudes periodically and discover gneral trends. When attitudes begin to decline, managers are alerted to potential problems that can be solved before they adversely affect employee performance or retention.

Finally, managers can recognize the simple fact that, without employee cooperation and support, a great deal of managerial energy can be wasted. It is important to involve employees as much as possible in decisions and problems affecting their jobs. Employees have a major stake in what happens to an organization and are often willing to contribute beyond what is asked (or allowed) of them. In short, managers can recognize that employees represent a human resource for which they are responsible. A major criterion for evaluating managerial effectiveness is the extent to which managers efficiently make use of these resources.

Summary

We have presented three widely accepted cognitive theories of work motivation. Cognitive and acognitive motivational models were distinguished. The cognitive models presented are based on the assumptions that much human behavior is planned and that people often make conscious decisions about their behavior. This is not to say that people always do so, only that much behavior is thought out in advance.

Throughout the discussion of the three models, managerial implications were stressed. These models should not be seen as abstract or irrelevant for managers. Indeed, each model provides insight to practicing managers about how to structure work situations and reward contingencies so employees and organizations benefit from increased performance. To do this, managers must clearly be interested in the welfare of employees and not in simply pursuing profit in a shortsighted manner. Managers must understand the needs, goals, and abilities of their subordinates and incorporate them into work design. Employees will then be more likely to respond by providing individual service in support of organizational performance. In this way, both benefit.

Key Words

behavioral requirements	management-by-objectives
equity theory	expectancy/valence theory
force field analysis	$E \rightarrow P$ expectancy
goal-setting theory	$P \rightarrow O$ expectancy
task-goal attributes	valence

Questions for Discussion

1. What do Katz and Kahn mean when they argue that every organization must meet three behavioral requirements?

2. Discuss several reasons for employee restriction of output.

3. In Box 8–1, major differences are noted between performance levels among U. S. and Japanese employees. What differences account for this diversity?

4. Contrast cognitive and acognitive theories of employee motivation.

5. What are the basic premises of equity theory? How do these premises differ from goal-setting theory and expectancy/valence theory?

6. Describe the process by which perceptions of equity or inequity result.

7. How can an employee resolve feelings of inequity on the job?

8. Does existing research support equity theory?

9. Describe how the various task-goal attributes influence performance under goal-setting conditions. Which task-goal attributes are most powerful in determining performance?

10. What individual and situational influences serve to moderate the influence of task-goal attributes on performance?

11. According to expectancy theory, what causes motivation? What causes performance?

12. Compare and contrast the various managerial implications of the three theories of motivation.

part three

Work Group Behavior

chapter 9

Groups in Organizations: Basic Considerations

Up to this point, we have focused on the nature of individuals and individual behavior. We examined personality, perception, learning, and motivation. Now we are ready to put individuals together in groups for purposes of study. After all, most work in organizations is performed by groups or is the result of group effort.

In this chapter, two general topics will be discussed. First, we will consider what is meant by the term group and how groups are structured. Based on this, we will be prepared in the next chapters to examine several group processes, including communication, conflict, decision-making, and leadership. Throughout, we will see how group dynamics influence behavior and attitudes in work settings and how managers can intervene in the process to facilitate greater individual need satisfaction and organizational effectiveness.

Importance of Topic for Managers

Why should managers know something about group dynamics? Several reasons demonstrate clearly the importance of this understanding for those interested in management:

1. Groups are a fact of organizational life. They are the building blocks of organizations. A knowledge of organizational behavior would be incomplete without a thorough understanding of basic group processes.

2. In every organization there are various groups, each pursuing different goals and composed of different employees. A knowledge of the various types of groups enables managers to recognize diversity of purpose and to deal with it.

3. People join groups for different reasons. Knowing the various reasons can be useful (e.g., why do some employees unionize while others do not?).

4. Groups structure themselves in a variety of ways. In designing a work group or assigning employees to various tasks in work groups, how does group size influence behavior and attitudes? How does managerial behavior influence the development of group norms and roles? How do these norms and roles, in turn, constrain behavior? The answers to these questions can help managers who are interested in facilitating task accomplishment.

5. Power relationships within and between groups influence who does what for whom. Status relationships determine one's standing in a particular group or organization. Again, an understanding of these relationships can help managers understand and deal with interpersonal dynamics in group situations.

6. Finally, group cohesiveness represents an important factor in determining level of group effort and performance. How can a manager work with group cohesiveness instead of against it? Under what conditions will cohesive groups facilitate organizational goal attainment?

Answers to these questions are considered in this chapter. A clear picture of work group dynamics will be presented. After this examination of group dynamics, which will take us over the next four chapters, we will consider (in Part IV) several more serious problems faced by individuals and groups at work, as well as a variety of possible solutions. First, however, let's take a close look at the anatomy of work groups.

Nature of Work Groups

Available research on group dynamics demonstrates rather conclusively that individual behavior is highly influenced by co-workers in a work group. For instance, we see many examples of individuals who when working in groups intentionally set limits on their own income so they earn less than they otherwise would if they were working alone. We see other situations where individuals choose to remain on undesirable jobs because of their friends in the plant, even though more preferable jobs are available elsewhere. In summarizing much research on the topic, Hackman and Morris (1975, p. 49) concluded that:

> there is substantial agreement among researchers and observers of small task groups that something important happens in group interaction which can affect performance outcomes. There is little agreement about just what that "something" is—whether it is more likely to enhance or depress group effectiveness, and how it can be monitored, analyzed, and altered.

In order to gain a clearer understanding of this something, we must first consider in detail what we mean by a group, how groups are formed, and how various groups differ.

In this section, we will consider several characteristics of groups. This discussion is a prelude to our later discussion focusing on work group characteristics. The literature on group dynamics is a very rich field of study, with a wide variety of important works (Shaw, 1976; Katz and Kahn, 1978; Cartwright and Zander, 1968). It is not possible to cover all this material in one or two chapters. We will attempt to highlight several important topics as they relate to the practice of management. Before we get started, however, let's consider what we mean by the term group.

Definition of a Group

Many definitions of work groups can be found in the literature. We might conceive of a group in terms of *perceptions;* that is, if individuals see themselves as a group, then a group exists (Bales 1950). Or, we can view a group in *structural* terms. For instance, McDavid and Harai (1968, p. 237) define a group as "an organized system of two or more individuals who are interrelated so that the system performs some function, has a standard set of role relationships among its members, and has a set of norms that regulate the function of the group and each of its members." Groups can also be defined in *motivational* terms as "a collection of individuals whose existence as a collection is rewarding to the individuals" (Bass, 1960, p. 39). Finally, a group can be viewed with regard to *interpersonal interaction,* the degree to which members communicate and interact with one another over time (Homans, 1950).

By integrating these various approaches to defining groups, we may conclude for our purposes here that a *group* is a collection of individuals who share a common set of norms, who generally have differentiated roles among themselves, and who interact with one another to jointly pursue common goals. This definition assumes a dynamic perspective and leads us to focus on two major aspects of groups: group structure and group processes. We must first learn something about how groups are put together and structure themselves for protection and task accomplishment. Next, we need to learn something about the dynamics of groups as they pursue task accomplishment. In this chapter, we will examine group structure.

Types of Groups

There are two primary types of groups: formal and informal. *Formal* groups are work units that are prescribed by the organization. Examples of formal groups include sections of departments (like the accounts receivable section of the accounting department), committees, or special project task forces. These groups are set up by management either on a temporary or permanent basis to accomplish prescribed tasks.

In addition, all organizations have a myriad of *informal* groups. These groups evolve naturally as a result of individual and collective self-interest among the members of an organization and are not the result of deliberate organizational design. People join informal groups because of common interest, social needs, or simply friendship. Informal groups typically develop their own norms and roles and establish unwritten rules for their members. Studies in social psychology have clearly documented the important role of these informal groups in facilitating (or inhibiting) performance and organizational effectiveness (Roethlisberger and Dickson, 1939; Shaw, 1976).

One of the more interesting aspects of group processes in organizations is the way in which informal groups work with—or against—formal groups. Both groups establish norms and roles, goals and objectives, and demand loyalty from their members. When an individual is a member of many groups—both formal and informal—a wide array of potentially conflicting situations emerge that have an impact upon behavior in organizations. We shall focus on this interplay throughout the next few chapters.

Reasons for Joining Groups

People join groups for many reasons (Kemp, 1970). The following reasons are common:

Security People have a basic need for protection from external threats, real or imagined. These threats include the possibility of being fired or intimidated by the boss, the possibility of being embarassed in a new situation, or simply the anxiety of being alone. Groups are a primary source of social support. We have often heard that there is ''security in numbers.''

Social needs Basic theories of personality and motivation emphasize that most individuals have relatively strong social needs. They need to interact with other people and develop meaningful relationships. People are clearly social creatures. Groups provide structured environments in which individuals can pursue friendships.

Self-esteem needs Similarly, membership in groups can assist individuals in developing self-esteem. People often take pride in being associated with prestigious groups, like professors elected to membership in the National Academy of Sciences or salespersons who qualify for a million dollar club as a reward for sales performance.

Economics People often associate with groups to pursue their own economic self-interest. Labor unions are a prime example as are various professional and accrediting agencies, like the American Bar Association. These organizations often attempt to limit the supply of tradespeople or professionals in order to maintain employment and salaries.

Group goals Many groups are formed to pursue goals that are of interest to group members. Included here are bridge clubs, company-sponsored baseball teams, and literary clubs. By joining together, individuals can pursue interests that are typically not feasible alone.

Proximity Finally, many groups form simply as a result of people being located near one another.

As can be seen, there are many reasons individuals join groups. Often, joining one group can simultaneously satisfy several of these reasons. That is, joining a company-sponsored baseball team can satisfy social needs, esteem needs, and group goals.

Stages in Group Development

Before we begin our rather comprehensive examination of the characteristics of groups, we should consider briefly the stages of group development. How do groups grow and develop over time? Tuckman (1965) has proposed one model of group development that consists of four stages. It is not claimed that every group proceeds through these four stages. Rather, the stages are simply illustrative. According to Tuckman, groups generally proceed through these four stages:

Testing and dependence (forming) In the first stage, group members attempt to discover which interpersonal behaviors are acceptable or unacceptable in the group. In this process of sensing out the environment, the new member is heavily dependent upon others for providing cues to acceptable behavior.

Intragroup conflict (storming) In the initial stages of group development, a high degree of conflict can be expected among group members as they attempt to develop a place for themselves and to influence the development of group norms and roles.

Development of group cohesion (norming) Over time, group members come to accept fellow members and develop a unity of purpose that unites them. (We shall say more about this later in the chapter.)

Functional role-relatedness (performing) Once group members agree on basic purposes they set about developing separate roles for the various members. This role differentiation takes advantage of task specialization in order to facilitate goal attainment.

Again, it should be recognized that all groups do not go through this sequence of events. Rather, this model provides a generalized conceptual scheme to help us understand the processes by which groups form and develop over time.

Framework for Analyzing Groups in Organizations

We have examined several aspects of work groups, including what constitutes a group, types of groups, reasons for joining groups, and, finally, stages in group development. Based on this knowledge, we will now take a more in-depth look at group structure and group processes. In order to accomplish this, we have proposed a general framework for analyzing groups in organizations (after Mitchell, 1978). This framework is shown in Exhibit 9–1. The framework consists of five parts.

Personal factors Group structure is seen as being influenced by two primary factors. The first is personal factors. Personal factors include the attitudes and abilities individuals bring to the work situation, as well as their individual motives. Personality and other background factors can also be included here. These variables were discussed in detail in Part II of this book. Simply put, it can be expected that the manner in which groups structure themselves is a function of these personal factors.

Situational factors In addition to personal factors, a variety of situational factors must also be taken into account. Situational factors include the type of group under consideration, the reasons why people chose to join the group, the motives or objectives of the group, and the stage of group development. These factors set the conditions under which many aspects of group structure can form, although other factors clearly influence group structure.

Group structure The remainder of this chapter will be devoted to a consideration of group structure. We will be concerned with the way in

Exhibit 9–1   A general framework for analyzing groups in organizations (Adapted from Mitchell, 1978).

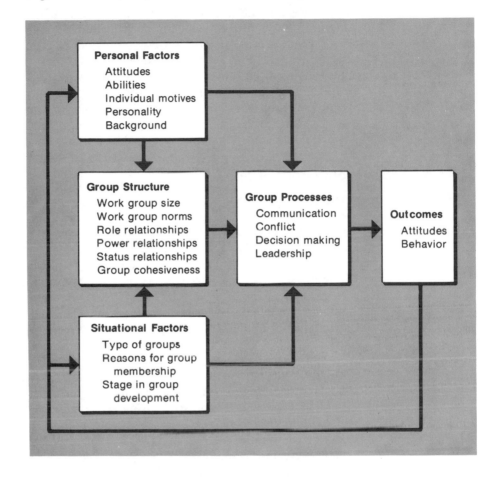

which group members organize themselves for task accomplishment and with groups' defining characteristics.

Group processes   The subject discussed in the next several chapters is group processes; that is, what groups actually do. Topics included will be communication, conflict, decision making, and leadership. According to our model, these group processes are influenced by at least three factors: personal factors, situational factors, and group structure.

Outcomes   Finally, most groups have tangible outcomes that result from the existence of the group. These outcomes may include individual attitudes resulting from group processes, as well as individual and group performance. These outcomes will be referred to throughout the next several chapters.

Work Group Structure

There are many different ways in which we could characterize work group structure. Our approach will be to simply examine several of those characteristics that are useful in describing and understanding what makes one group different from another. We shall attempt to describe a matrix of variables which, when taken together, will paint a portrait of work groups in terms of relatively enduring group properties.

For purposes of discussion, we will consider six aspects of group structure: 1) work group size; 2) work group norms; 3) role relationships; 4) power relationships; 5) status relationships; and 6) group cohesiveness.

Work Group Size

Obviously, work groups can be found in various sizes. Classical management theorists spent considerable time and effort to no avail attempting to identify the right size for the various types of work groups. There is simply no right number of people for most group activities. Even so, we can summarize the available research and indicate, roughly, what happens as group size increases. At least five size-outcome relationships are relevant. These involve the relation of group size to: 1) group interaction patterns; 2) satisfaction; 3) productivity; 4) absenteeism; and 5) turnover (see Porter and Lawler, 1965; Cummings and Berger, 1976). These results are summarized in Exhibit 9–2.

Group interaction patterns.   A series of classic studies begun by Bales and Borgatta (1956) examined the variations in group interaction patterns as a result of changes in group size. Using a technique called *interaction process analysis* which records who says what to whom, Bales and his colleagues found that smaller groups (2–4 persons) typically exhibited greater tension, agreement, and opinion seeking, while larger groups (5–7 persons) showed greater tension release and giving of suggestions and information. It was argued that in smaller groups, harmony was crucial, and that people had more time to develop their thoughts and opinions. On the other hand, individuals in larger groups must be more direct because of the increased competition for attention.

Satisfaction.   In a comprehensive review of the early research on the topic, Porter and Lawler (1965) found increases in work group size to be inversely related to satisfaction, although the relationship was not overly strong. That is, people working in smaller work units or departments report higher levels of satisfaction than those in larger units. This finding is not surprising in view of the greater attention one receives in smaller groups and the greater importance group members typically experience.

Exhibit 9–2   Effects of increases in work group size on various outcomes

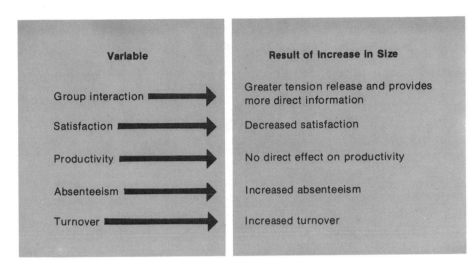

Variable	Result of Increase in Size
Group interaction	Greater tension release and provides more direct information
Satisfaction	Decreased satisfaction
Productivity	No direct effect on productivity
Absenteeism	Increased absenteeism
Turnover	Increased turnover

Productivity.   No clear relationship has been found between increases in group size and productivity (Porter and Lawler, 1965; Cummings and Berger, 1976). There is probably good reason for this. Unless we take into consideration the type of task that is being performed we really cannot expect a clear or direct relationship. Michell (1978, p. 188) explains it as follows:

> Think of a task where each new member adds a new independent amount of productivity (certain piece-rate jobs might fit here). If we add more people, we will add more productivity. . . . On the other hand, there are tasks where everyone works together and pools their resources. With each new person the added increment of new skills or knowledge decreases. After a while increases in size will fail to add much to the group except coordination and motivation problems. Large groups will perform less well than small groups. The relationship between group size and productivity will therefore depend on the type of task that needs to be done.

Absenteeism.   Available research indicates that increases in work group size and absenteeism are moderately related among blue collar workers, while no such relationship exists for white-collar workers (Steers and Rhodes, 1978). One explanation for these findings is that increased work group size leads to lower group cohesiveness, higher task specialization, and poorer communication (Porter and Lawler, 1965). As a result, it becomes more difficult to satisfy higher-order needs on the job and job attendance becomes less appealing. In view of the increased job autonomy and control of white-collar workers compared to blue-collar this explanation tends to be more relevant for the latter group. White-collar workers typically have more avenues available to them for need satisfaction.

Turnover. Similar findings exist for employee turnover. Turnover rates are higher in larger groups compared to smaller (Porter and Steers, 1973). Again, it can be hypothesized that since larger groups make need satisfaction more difficult, there is less reason for individuals to remain with the organization. The topics of turnover and absenteeism are considered in greater detail in Chapter 14.

Work Group Norms

The idea of work group norms is a complex one with a history of social psychological research dating back several decades. In this section we will highlight several of the essential aspects of norms and how they relate to people at work. We shall consider: 1) characteristics of work group norms; 2) pattern and intensity of group norms; 3) conformity and deviance from group norms; and 4) behavioral consequences of group norms.

Characteristics of work group norms. A *norm* may be defined as a standard that is shared by group members and which regulates member behavior. McGrath (1964) notes that group norms include: 1) a frame of reference for viewing relevant objects in the environment; 2) prescribed correct attitudes and behaviors toward those objects; 3) feelings about the correctness of these attitudes and about tolerance for violators of norms; and 4) positive and negative sanctions by which acceptable behavior is rewarded and unacceptable behavior is punished by group members.

An example of a norm can be seen in a typical classroom situation when students develop a norm against speaking up in class too often. It is believed that such highly visible students improve their grades at the expense of others. Hence, a norm is created that attempts to govern acceptable classroom behavior.

Why do norms develop in groups? Festinger (1950) has suggested two principal reasons. First, norms provide group members with an easy frame of reference for understanding the complicated world of work. They provide readily apparent cues to what is right and what is wrong. Union members are often cautioned not to cooperate with management, for example, because of questionable motives attributed to management. Secondly, norms provide uniformity of action necessary if the group is to survive and reach its goals. When all members behave in a like manner (toward a supervisor, for example), group cohesiveness is enhanced and group goals are facilitated.

After reviewing available research on group norms in work settings, Hackman (1976) suggested that norms were characterized by five major characteristics:

1. Norms are structural characteristics of groups, which summarize and simplify group influence processes. They denote the processes by which groups regulate and regularize member behavior.

2. Norms apply only to behavior, not to private thoughts and feelings. Although norms may be based on thoughts and feelings, the norms themselves do not govern them. That is, private acceptance of group norms is unnecessary, only public compliance.

3. Norms are generally developed only for behaviors which are viewed as important by most group members.

4. Norms usually develop gradually, but the process can be quickened if members wish. Norms usually are developed by group members when the occasion arises, like when a situation occurs that requires new ground rules for members in order to protect group integrity. Sometimes, however, these norms are prescribed by the group in an immediate fashion when the need arises.

5. All norms don't apply to all members. Some norms, for example, apply only to young initiates (like getting the coffee), while others are based on seniority, sex, race, or economic class.

Pattern and intensity of group norms. A clearer understanding of group norms in organizations can be achieved by considering two factors that distinguish various norms. These are pattern and intensity. *Pattern* refers to behaviors that are acceptable or unacceptable (speaking up in class) while *intensity* refers to the extent or degree to which these behaviors are approved or disapproved. Pattern and intensity are incorporated into Jackson's (1965) *Return Potential Model* (RPM) of group norms.

An example will clarify the RPM model. Consider the expectations that students may have about student participation in classroom discussions. There may exist a norm that all students should speak up in class once in a while but should not show off by talking incessantly. A schematic representation of this norm is shown in Exhibit 9–3. The number of times a student should speak in class according to the norm in our example is shown on the horizontal x-axis, ranging from 1 to 10 times. This is the pattern. The vertical y-axis shows the intensity, ranging from highly approve to highly disapprove. In this example it can be seen that the norm (the most highly approved behavior) for number of times a student should speak up in class is around 6 times (point a), with an approved range from 3 to 7 times (point b). Less than 3 times or more than 7 times is disapproved by group members.

Exhibit 9–3 Schematic representation of the Return Potential Model (RPM) of normative structure. The ordinate is an axis of evaluation; the abscissa is an axis of behavior.

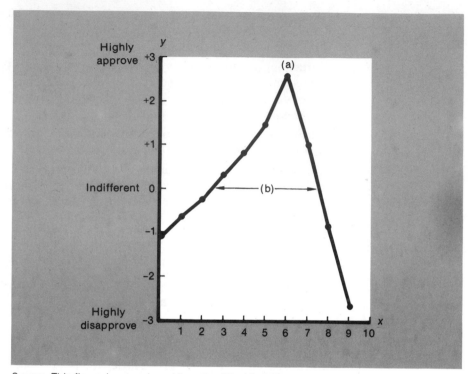

Source: This figure is reproduced from the *Fifty-Ninth Yearbook* of the National Society for the Study of Education, with permission of the Society.

Also note that overspeaking is more highly disapproved of than underspeaking.

The RPM model has many applications in organizational settings. Recently, Spencer (1979) used the model to measure the norms people have among their friends and co-workers about turnover. That is, to what extent would one's friends and co-workers approve or disapprove of one leaving the organization? Using the RPM model allows us not only to examine or measure a norm but also to consider its pattern and intensity. By doing so, a clearer understanding can be achieved about how norms affect member behavior in organizations.

Conformity and deviance. Managers often wonder why employees comply with the norms and dictates of their work group even when they seemingly work against their best interests. This concern is particularly strong when workers intentionally withhold productivity that could lead to higher incomes. What causes such conformity to group norms and under what conditions will an individual deviate from these norms?

Conformity to group norms is believed to be caused by at least four factors (Reitan and Shaw, 1964). First, personality plays a major role. For instance, negative correlations have been found between conformity and intelligence, tolerance, and ego-strength, while authoritarianism was found to be positively related (Crutchfield, 1955).

Second, the initial stimulus that evokes responses can influence conformity. The more ambiguous the stimulus (e.g., a new and confusing order from top management), the greater the propensity to conform to group norms (e.g., continue what you were doing prior to the new order). In this sense, conformity provides a sense of protection and security in a new and perhaps threatening situation.

Third, a variety of situational factors can affect the degree of conformity. As Asch found (see Box 9–1), conformity to false answers increased with group size up to size four and then leveled off. He found that conformity was higher when there was unanimity among group members.

Box 9–1 Asch's Experiment on Group Pressure and Individual Judgement

In a classic study of individual conformity to group pressures, Solomon Asch created a laboratory situation in which a naive subject was placed in a room with several confederates.* Each person in the room was asked to match the length of a given line (X) with one of three unequal lines, as shown below:

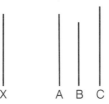

X   A B C

Confederates, who spoke first, were all instructed prior to the experiment to identify line C as the line closest to X in length, even though line A was in fact clearly the correct answer. In over one-third of the trials in this experiment, the naive subjects who accurately perceived the correct answer (A) denied the evidence of their own senses and agreed with the answers given by the unknown confederates (C). In other words, when confronted by a unanimous answer to a question by others in the group, a large percentage of individuals chose to go along with the group rather than express a conflicting opinion, even though the individuals were sure their own answer was correct.

*Source: S. Asch. "Studies of independence and conformity: A minority of one against a unanimous majority." *Psychological Monographs*, 1955, *20*, Whole No. 416.

Finally, group characteristics themselves can influence conformity to group norms. Factors like the extent of pressure exerted on group members to conform, the extent to which a member identifies with the group, and the extent to which the group has been successful in achieving previous goals can influence conformity.

What happens when someone deviates from group norms? Research indicates that groups often respond by increasing the amount of communication directed toward the deviant member (Schachter, 1951). This communication is aimed at bringing the deviant back into the acceptable bounds set by the group. A good example of this process can be seen in Janis' (1972) classic study of the group processes leading up to the abortive Bay of Pigs invasion in Cuba. At one meeting Arthur Schlesinger, an advisor to President Kennedy, expressed opposition to the plan even though no one else expressed similar doubts. After listening to his opposition for a while, Robert Kennedy took Schlesinger aside and said, "You may be right or you may be wrong, but the President has his mind made up. Don't push it any further. Now is the time for everyone to help him all they can." (Janis, 1972, Ch. 2).

When a deviant member refuses to heed the communications and persists in breaking group norms, group members often respond by rejecting or isolating the deviant. They tell the deviant, in essence, that they will no longer tolerate such behavior and prefer to reconstitute the group. If the deviant is not expelled, the group must continually confront behavior that conflicts with what it holds to be true. Rather than question or reexamine its beliefs, it is simpler—and safer—to rid the group of dangerous influence.

Effects of norms on behavior.   One aspect of the effects of group norms on individual behavior was already discussed in the experiment by Asch. In addition, however, we know that group norms affect employee behavior in a number of ways. For example, when a group establishes a norm concerning a reasonable level of output on a job, serious performance side effects can be felt by the organization. This is especially true when groups are highly cohesive and exert strong social pressures to conform. From the managerial perspective, group norms represent a force to be ackowledged when seeking to optimize motivation and performance at work.

Role Relationships

In order to accomplish its goals and maintain its norms, groups of necessity differentiate the work activities of their members. One or more members assume leadership positions, while others carry out the major work of the group and still others serve as "gofers." This specialization of activities is commonly referred to as role differentiation. More specifically, a *role* is an expected behavior pattern assigned or attributed to a particular position. It defines individuals' responsibilities on behalf of the group.

Perhaps the best way to understand the nature of roles is to examine a *role episode*. A role episode attempts to explain how a particular role is learned and acted upon (Katz and Kahn, 1978). As can be seen in Exhibit 9–4, a role episode begins with group members having expectations about what one person should be doing in a particular position (Stage 1). These expectations are then communicated to the individual (Stage 2), causing the individual to perceive the expectations about the expected role (Stage 3). Finally, the individual decides to act upon the role in terms of actual role-related behavior (Stage 4). In other words, Stages 1 and 2 deal with the *expected* role, while Stage 3 focuses on the *perceived* role, and Stage 4 focuses on the *enacted* role.

Consider the following simple example. A group may determine that its newest member is responsible for getting coffee for group members during breaks (Stage 1). This role is then explained to the incoming member (Stage 2), who becomes aware of his or her expected role (Stage 3). Based on these perceptions (and probably reinforced by group norms), the individual then would probably accept the assigned role (Stage 4).

Several aspects of this model of a role episode should be noted. First, Stages 1 and 2 are initiated by the group and are aimed at the individual. Stages 3 and 4, on the other hand, represent thoughts and actions of the individual receiving the stimuli. In addition, Stages 1 and 3 represent cognitive and perceptual evaluations, while Stages 2 and 4 represent actual behaviors. The sum total of all the roles assigned to one individual is called the *role set*.

Although the role episode presented here seems straightforward, in reality we know that it is far more complicated. For instance, individuals typically receive multiple messages from various groups all attempting to assign them a particular role. This can easily lead to *role conflict*. Messages sent to an individual may sometimes be unclear, leading to *role ambiguity*. Finally, individuals may simply receive too many role-related messages, contributing

Exhibit 9–4 A simplified model of a role episode (Adapted from Katz and Kahn, 1978)

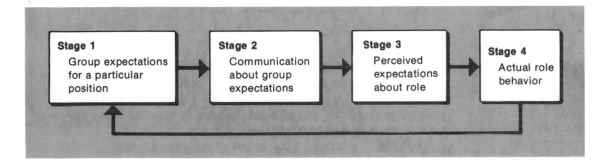

to *role overload*. Discussion of these topics is reserved for Chapter 15, where we will examine several important aspects of psychological adjustment to work.

Power Relationships

Within and between work groups there exists a series of power relationships that help determine the actual structure and functioning of the group. Role relationships and norms are reinforced through these power relationships. Although people often feel uncomfortable discussing or even acknowledging the existence of power and power relationships in organizations, power must be recognized as a fact of organizational life and dealt with by managers interested in facilitating organizational effectiveness.

Simply put, *power* may be defined as an interpersonal relationship in which one individual (Person A) has the ability to motivate another individual (Person B) to an action that would not be taken otherwise. In other words, power involves one person changing the behavior of another. It is important to note here that in most organizational situations we are talking about *implied* force to comply, not *actual* force. That is, Person A has power over Person B if Person B *believes* Person A can, in fact, force Person b to comply.

Bases of social power.   French and Raven (1968) and their colleagues have identified six primary ways in which power can be exerted in social situations. These are referred to as *bases of power:*

Reward power   Person A has power over B if A controls rewards (promotions, pay raises, desirable job assignments) that B wants.

Punishment power   Likewise, A has power over B if A can administer some form of punishment to B (reprimands, undesirable job assignments, terminations).

Information power   To the extent that A has information that B wants or needs, Person A has power over B.

Legitimacy power   In many cases, B submits to A because B feels that A has a right to exert power in a certain area. Legitimate power is really authority. A supervisor has a right, for instance, to assign work.

Expert power   Some people gain power because of their knowledge or ability (or presumed ability). Professors presumably have expert power because of their presumed level of expertise in an area.

Referent power   Finally, in some cases Person B looks up to or admires Person A. As a result, B submits to A largely because of A's personal qualities or characteristics. Referent power has also been referred to as charismatic power because submission is based on the interpersonal attraction of one individual for another.

Power dependencies.   As noted, there are least six bases of power that individuals can use to exert influence on others. The extent to which these influence attempts will be successful is determined by the *power dependencies* of the individuals receiving the influence attempts. People are not all subject to (or dependent upon) the same influence attempts.

What causes some people to be more submissive to power attempts? At least three factors have been identified (Mitchell, 1978). First, Person B's *values* can influence his or her readiness to be influenced. If the outcomes that A can influence are important to B, than B is more likely to be open to influence attempts than if the outcomes are unimportant. In addition, the nature of the *relationship* between A and B can be a factor. Are they peers, or a superior and subordinate? Is the job temporary or permanent? A person in a temporary job may feel less need to acquiesce since he or she won't be there long. The nature of the relationship often determines one's susceptibility to power attempts. Finally, a third factor to consider in power dependencies is the notion of *counterpower*. Does B have alternative sources of power to buffer the effects of A's power? For instance, if B is unionized, the union's power may serve to negate A's influence attempts.

In summary, Person A, who presumably can use one or more of the six bases of power to attempt to influence Person B, is more likely to be successful if B is heavily dependent upon A. These power dependencies include A's ability to control outcomes valued by B, A's relationship with B, and B's available counterpower.

Power in use.   The final question here deals with the extent to which power holders actually use the power they possess. Research indicates that those who hold power typically make use of it. A study by Kipnis (1972) found that when managers had power they: 1) sent more messages to subordinates; 2) rated their subordinates less highly on performance appraisals; 3) indicated a lower willingness to meet socially with subordinates; and 4) were more likely to attribute subordinate performance to managerial expertise than to subordinate ability.

From the subordinate's standpoint, the findings are also clear. People do not like power to be used on them and often resist the attempts. However, when the exercise of power is based on legitimate, expert, or referent aspects, resistence is less likely than when based on coercion or punishment. While the use of reward power may lead to greater performance, it often does so at the expense of job satisfaction. People often prefer to do something for someone else because they enjoy doing so rather than because they need to get rewarded. Contemporary managers—who typically hold considerable power themselves—must be sensitive to how their influence attempts are received. In this regard, the issue is not so much getting the job done but *how* one goes about trying to get the job done. Some strategies have fewer undesirable side effects than others.

Status Relationships

Another characteristic or structural property of work groups is the emergence of status systems. *Status systems* serve to differentiate individuals from each other based on some criterion or set of criteria. Parsons (1949) identifies five bases on which status differentiations are made: birth, personal characteristics, achievement, possessions, and formal authority.

All five bases can be seen in establishing status in work groups. An employee may achieve high status because he is the boss's son (birth), or the brightest or strongest member of the group (personal characteristics), the best performer (achievement), the richest or highest paid (possessions), or the foreman or supervisor (formal authority).

Status systems can be seen throughout organizations. We differentiate between blue-collar and white-collar employees, skilled tradespersons and unskilled workers, senior and junior employees, high achievers and low achievers, and popular and less popular. Why do we do this? Scott (1967) suggests that status differentiation (and concomitant status symbols) serve four purposes:

Motivation We ascribe status to persons as rewards or incentives for performance and achievement. If high achievement is recognized as positive behavior by an organization, individuals are more willing to exert effort.

Identification Status and status symbols provide useful cues to acceptable behavior in new situations. In the military, for example, badges of rank quickly tell members who has authority, and who is to be obeyed. Similarly, in business, titles serve the same purpose.

Dignification People are often ascribed status as a means of signifying respect that is due them. A clergyman's attire, for instance, identifies a representative of the church.

Stabilization Finally, status systems and symbols facilitate stabilization in an otherwise turbulent environment by providing a force for continuity. Authority patterns, role relationships, and interpersonal interactions are all affected and indeed defined by the status system in effect. As a result, much ambiguity in the work situation is reduced.

An interesting aspect of status systems in organizations is the notion of *status incongruence*. This situation exists when a person is high on certain valued dimensions but low on others or when a person's characteristics seem inappropriate for a particular job. Several examples of status incongruence can be identified, including a college student who takes a common laborer's job during the summer (the college kid), the president's son who works his way up through the organizational hierarchy (at an accelerated rate, needless to say), or a young fast-track manager who is promoted to a level typically held by older employees.

Status incongruence presents problems for everyone involved. For the individual, hostility and jealousy are often experienced by co-workers who feel the individual has risen above his or her station. For co-workers, their own lack of success or achievement must be clearly acknowledged. (Why has this "youngster" been promoted over me when I have more seniority?) As noted by Mitchell (1978), at least two remedies for this conflict appear: 1) an organization can select or promote only those individuals whose characteristics are congruent with the job and work group; 2) an organization can attempt to change the values of the group. Neither of these possibilities seem realistic or fair. Hence, dynamic organizations that truly reward high achievement (instead of seniority) must accept some level of conflict resulting from status incongruence.

Group Cohesiveness

We have all come in contact with groups whose members feel a high degree of camaraderie, group spirit, and sense of oneness. In these groups, individuals seem to be concerned about the welfare of other group members, as well as the group as a whole. There is a feeling of "us against them" that creates a closeness among them. This phenomenon is called group cohesiveness.

More specifically, *group cohesiveness* may be defined as the extent to which individual members of a group are motivated to remain in the group. According to Shaw (1976, p. 197), "members of highly cohesive groups are more energetic in group activities, they are less likely to be absent from group meetings, they are happy when the group succeeds and sad when it fails, etc., whereas members of less cohesive groups are less concerned about the group's activities."

Determinants of group cohesiveness. What causes people to join groups and develop a high degree of group cohesiveness? Cartwright and Zander (1968) have attempted to answer this question in their model of group cohesiveness (see Exhibit 9–5). It is suggested that at least four factors influence the extent to which this cohesiveness develops:

Motive base for attraction A primary influence on group cohesiveness is individual needs and motives. These motives include the needs for affiliation, recognition, security, and other needs that can be met by the group.

Incentive properties of the group This consists of the goals, programs, and characteristics of the group members, style of operation, prestige, and other significant properties of their motive base.

Expectancy about outcomes This concerns the extent to which employees feel that group membership and involvement will, in fact, be instrumental in achieving personal goals.

Exhibit 9–5 Determinants and consequences of group cohesiveness (after Cartwright and Zander, 1968, p. 92)

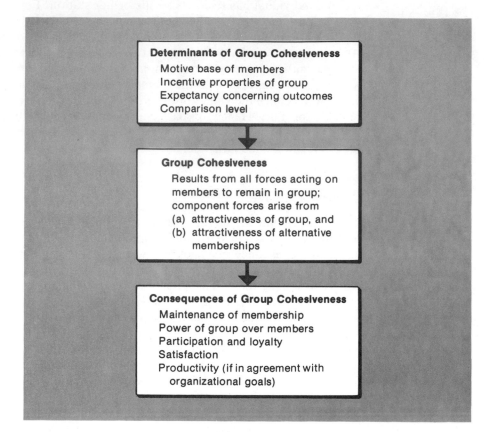

Comparison level Finally, employees are seen as comparing the cost–benefit ratio of membership and involvement in one group against alternative paths to goal attainment. This factor follows from equity theory.

Several interesting implications follow from this formulation. For instance, Cartwright and Zander (1968, p. 96) suggest the following:

If, for example, a person joins a group with the expectation of fulfilling certain personal needs but these change while he is a member, the attractiveness of the group will decrease for him unless the group is able to fulfill the new needs equally well or better. It is possible, of course, for an individual's needs to be modified through experience in the group. Indeed, some groups deliberately attempt to change the needs of their members. Sometimes such groups "lure" members into joining, by promising certain inducements, and then work on the members to develop other needs and interests that are considered more important to the group.

The precise manner in which these processes occur is not known. Even so, managers must recognize the existence of certain forces of group cohesiveness if they are to understand the nature of group dynamics in organizations. The second aspect of group cohesiveness that must be understood by managers relates to their consequences.

Consequences of group cohesiveness.

As shown in Exhibit 9–5, several consequences can be identified. The first and most obvious consequence is *maintenance of membership*. If the attractiveness of the group is sufficiently stronger than the attractiveness of alternative groups, then we would not expect the individual to want to voluntarily leave the group. Hence, turnover rates should be low.

In addition, high group cohesiveness typically provides the group with considerable *power over group members*. Several explanations for this finding exist. According to Thibaut and Kelley (1959), the power of a group over members depends upon the level of outcomes members expect to receive from the group compared to what they could receive through alternate means. When the group is seen as being highly instrumental to personal goals, individuals will typically submit to the will of the group.

Third, members of highly cohesive groups tend to exhibit greater *participation and loyalty* (Cartwright and Zander, 1968). A variety of studies has shown that as cohesiveness increases there is more frequent communication among members, a greater degree of participation in group activities and less absenteeism. Moreover, members of highly cohesive groups tend to be more cooperative and friendly, and generally behave in ways designed to promote integration among members (Shaw, 1976).

Fourth, members of highly cohesive groups generally report high levels of *satisfaction* (Shaw, 1976). In fact, the concept of group cohesiveness almost demands that this be the case since it is unlikely that members will feel like remaining with a group with which they are dissatisfied.

Finally, what is the effect of group cohesiveness on *productivity*? No clear relationship exists here. Instead, research shows that the extent to which cohesiveness and productivity are related is moderated by the extent to which group members accept organizational goals. Specifically, when cohesiveness is high and acceptance of organizational goals is high, performance will probably be high. Similar results would be expected for low cohesiveness and high goal acceptance, although results may not be as strong. On the other hand, performance would not be expected to be high when cohesiveness is high and goal acceptance is low. In this case, group effort will probably be directed away from organizational goals and toward goals valued by the group. Finally, when both cohesiveness and goal acceptance are low, effort will probably become dissipated, leading to low productivity.

The effects of group cohesiveness on performance and attitudes can be seen in two studies performed decades apart. The first, shown in Box 9–2, reviews the classic Trist and Bamforth (1951) study among British coal miners. The second study, shown in Box 9–3, reviews how simple participation by workers in a Swedish truck factory led to several desirable consequences. In both studies, it can be seen that the cohesiveness and oneness experienced by group members had a significant impact on performance outcomes. In the British coal mining study (Box 9–2), members reacted to threats to group solidarity by inhibiting company efforts to improve output through mechanization. It was only after modifications were made that allowed a sufficient degree of group interaction that the miners "allowed" the company to implement changes.

A similar phenomenon can be seen in the Saab-Scania experiment (Box 9–3). By allowing employees greater input in decision making—and hence greater responsibility for decision outcome—members of the group identified more strongly with group goals and demonstrated a greater willingness to work with company officials to improve productivity. The rather dramatic results emphasize the important role of teamwork and group cohesiveness in facilitating overall organizational effectiveness.

Managing Effective Work Groups

We have examined in detail the nature and structure of work groups. It has been noted that work groups differ along several dimensions like size, norms, and roles. Despite these differences, there are several actions managers can take in order to encourage groups to be more effective. Before beginning our discussion of major group processes we will consider some of these actions.

1. Managers can make themselves more aware of the nature of groups and the functions groups perform for individuals. By understanding why individuals join groups, for example, managers should be able to better understand the motivational implications of group dynamics. Is high group cohesiveness in a particular group a result of high commitment to the organization and its goals or is it a result of alienation from the organization?

2. Managers can be sensitive to group norms and the extent to which they facilitate or inhibit group and organizational performance. The potency of group norms has been clearly established. It has also been shown that company actions can increase the likelihood that norms will work to the benefit of the organization, as in the Saab-Scania example, or decrease this likeli-

Box 9–2 The British Coal Mining Study

A classic study of the effects of group cohesiveness on productivity has been carried out by Trist and Bamforth among British coal miners.*

The background   Prior to mechanization in the mines under study, coal was gathered by six-man teams who worked together and shared various coal gathering functions in the mines. With the mechanization that emerged shortly after World War II, increased task specialization was implemented and each worker was given specific required tasks. This new system, called the conventional long–wall method, was based on using a long face conveyor belt that allowed the company to fractionalize various tasks to increase efficiency and reduce training costs. Work teams were no longer needed since every miner now performed specialized tasks individually.

The conventional long-wall method of mining failed to yield desired economic returns. Social and technical problems became rampant, leading to increased inefficiency and labor strife. In an effort to discover the nature of the problem, a team of social scientists led by Eric Trist was called in to analyze the situation.

The results   In their investigation, the researchers found that for many mines, the fractionated jobs destroyed group cohesiveness, and productivity suffered because of a lack of clear performance norms among group members. In other mines, however, workers had evolved into a new work system, called the composite long-wall method. There the miners themselves rejected the conventional method and adapted it to suit their own needs. This new method combined the technological advantages of the conventional long-wall method with the social system benefits of the earlier method. In essence, work group cohesiveness was rekindled as teams of miners worked together and made the new technology work for them instead of working for it.

Group cohesiveness in the new composite method was enhanced by having the groups select their own members, allocating work responsibilities to individual miners, and receiving payment based on group performance instead of individual effort.

As a result of increased group cohesiveness, several results emerged in the composite groups: 1) members were more sensitive to the work needs of co-workers and helped each other more; 2) greater task variety; 3) roughly one-half the absenteeism than that experienced in the conventional groups; 4) an average productivity rating of 95% compared to 78% in the conventional groups; and 5) fewer conflicts and labor disputes than in the conventional groups.

Trist and Bamforth concluded that social systems manifested in group cohesiveness cannot be ignored in carrying out technological innovations in the work place. Instead, both social and technical aspects of the job must be considered and integrated if changes are to be successful. This conclusion, resulting from the Trist and Bamforth study, formed the basis for the sociotechnical movement prevalent today.

*Source: E. Trist and K. Bamforth. "Some social and psychological consequences of the longwall method of coal-getting." *Human Relations,* 1951, *4,* 1–38.

Box 9–3 Group Cohesiveness and Performance at Saab-Scania

The recent Swedish experiments in job redesign have received considerable publicity. One is often left with the impression that job redesign can work miracles for organizations. However, an often overlooked fact is that the most successful aspects of the Saab-Scania experiment occurred *before* the jobs were technologically redesigned.*

The experiment In 1969 when the engine plant of Saab-Scania (a truck manufacturer) initiated its Quality of Working Life experiments, phase one addressed itself to building highly cohesive, well-integrated work teams. (This was before changes in the assemblyline were begun). In two experimental groups, employees were brought into the decision-making process and asked to help the company solve its productivity and morale problems. Technical help was offered to group members when requested,

but work groups were largely responsible for solving their own problems.

The results The results of phase one—before any technical redesign of jobs—were significant. Between 1969 and 1972, unplanned work stoppages dropped from 6% to 2% of total time, extra work and adjustment needed to correct omissions and errors in the finished products dropped by one-third, and turnover dropped from an average of 55% to 20% per year.

Clearly, allowing employees greater involvement in problem–solving leads to increased cohesiveness among group members and greater commitment to group goals which, in this case, were largely compatible with those of the organization. The second phase at Saab-Scania, involving redesigning the assembly techniques themselves, has yet to produce such significant results.

*Source: R. Katz and D. Kahn, *The social psychology of organizations.* New York: Wiley, 1978.

hood, as in the British coal mining example. Much of the thrust of current organizational development efforts is to use process consultation techniques to develop group norms that are compatible with company goals.

3. Much has been said in the research literature about the effects of groups on individual conformity and deviance. Groups often place significant pressures on individuals to conform and punish deviants by means such as ostracism. From a managerial standpoint, conformity can represent a mixed blessing. On one hand, there are many work situations where managers typically want workers to conform to standard operating procedures. Katz and Kahn (1978) call this dependable role performance. On the other hand, employees must be sufficiently free to take advantage of what they believe to be unique or important opportunities on behalf of the organization. Katz and Kahn refer to this as innovative and spontaneous behavior. If pressures toward conformity are too strong, this sponaneity may be lost as well as unique opportunities for the organization.

4. Several aspects of power were discussed in this chapter. The point was made that power and power relationships are a fact of organizationl life. Managers have a responsibility to understand power dynamics. It was noted that there are at least six bases of power available to managers. Managers in different situations (or organizations) may employ different bases in order to influence behavior. Employees have different levels of power dependency. Managers should view the influence process as one of matching their own bases of power with the particular situation and group. Thus, a purchasing manager may have some expert power when discussing purchasing practices with engineers in need of supplies. This power may be nullified when the same purchasing manager meets with other purchasing managers and is no longer the sole expert.

5. The importance of group cohesiveness for group effectiveness was discussed. Where it is desirable to develop highly cohesive groups, managers attempt to influence this process through tactics like showing employees how groups can help each other by working together. It is important to note, however, that group cohesiveness by itself does not guarantee increased group effectiveness. Instead, managers must take the lead in showing group members why they benefit from working toward organizational goals. One way to accomplish this is through the reward systems used by the organization.

As can be seen, several recommendations for managerial action follow from a better knowledge of group structure. As we begin our consideration of group processes in the next chapter, additional implications for management will be seen.

Summary

Based on the preceding section on individual behavior, we turned in this section to a consideration of group processes and behavior. The nature of work groups was introduced. Consideration was given here to identifying various types of groups, reasons for joining groups, and stages in group development. A framework for analyzing group processes in organizations was reviewed.

Next, aspects of work group structure were examined. These included work group size, norms, roles, power, status, and group cohesiveness. To highlight these various aspects of work group structure, three studies were reviewed in some detail. The first, by Asch, examined the effects of group pressure for conformity on individual judgement. The second, by Trist and

Bamforth, reviewed a classic study of the influences of group cohesiveness on a major organizational change. Finally, the third study reviewed the impact of cohesiveness on performance in a major automobile manufacturer.

Based on this discussion, several implications in group management were suggested. The primary focus of these recommendations was the need for managers to first understand the nature of group dynamics and behavior and then take a proactive approach to facilitating group effectiveness. All groups look to leaders for guidance and support. Leaders can be either formally appointed by the organization or informally designated by the group. Proactive managers attempt to provide necessary support and direction. In this way, group goals and organizational goals become compatible and both are achieved.

Key Words

work groups	role set
interaction process analysis	power
norms	power dependencies
return potential model	status
conformity	status systems
role	status incongruence
role episode	group cohesiveness

Questions for Discussion

1. What are the various types of groups often found in work situations?
2. Why do people join groups?
3. Describe the four stages of group development.
4. Critically analyze the model of groups in organizations described in Exhibit 9–1.
5. How does work group size influence individual and group behavior?
6. Discuss the role of work group norms in the work situation.
7. Describe Jackson's return potential model of group norms in organizations.
8. Consider how groups influence conformity and deviance in work situations.
9. What is the major conclusion of Asch's experiment on group pressure and individual judgement?
10. Describe a role episode.

11. Why is a knowledge of role relationships important for managers?
12. What are the six bases of power?
13. Discuss the relationship between bases of power and power dependencies.
14. What purposes are served by status differentiations in work organizations? What problems emerge from these differentiations?
15. What determines group cohesiveness and what impact does it have on group behavior?
16. What are the major conclusions to be drawn from the British coal mining study and the Saab-Scania examples given in Boxes 9–2 and 9–3?

chapter 10

Communication and Conflict in Organizations

In the next three chapters, we will focus on an examination of four important group processes: communication, conflict, decision making, and leadership. Group processes combine with group structure to determine the nature and quality of group performance and behavior. In this chapter, the first two of these group processes will be considered.

Importance of Topic for Managers

Why should managers know something about communication and conflict in organizational settings? Several reasons can be mentioned:

1. Communication is one of the vital processes that make organizations run. It is obvious that in any endeavor requiring two or more persons, communication is necessary if individual efforts are to be coordinated for group action.

2. The quality of the decisions that managers make rests squarely on the amount and quality of information they receive from other employees and

from the external environment. The more accurate the information, the greater the likelihood that appropriate decisions will result.

3. A knowledge of barriers to effective communication can assist managers in skirting some of these problems, leading to improved organizational communications.

4. Like communication, conflict also permeates work organizations. Conflict may be large or small, negative or positive. Whatever the nature of the conflict, its existence must be recognized and dealt with by managers if organizational energies are to be concentrated on achieving the goals of the organization.

5. Conflict arises from many diverse causes. A knowledge of the antecedents of conflict can help managers seek remedies that have a high probability of success.

We will consider communication and conflict processes together in this chapter for several reasons. Although most group processes are related in various ways, it is felt that communication and conflict as social processes are strongly and uniquely related. Much of the conflict experienced in work organizations is instigated by inaccurate (and sometimes accurate) verbal cues employees send each other. For instance, annual performance appraisals often promote conflict and much of this conflict results not so much from the actual rating an employee receives but rather from the way the rating is described to the employee or written up for company files. Conversely, groups that experience high levels of conflict typically respond by modifying their communication patterns (e.g., conflict may stifle communication for some and accentuate it for others). Hence, we will treat both of these topics in this chapter.

Communication In Organizations

Nature of Communication

The first process to be examined in this chapter is organizational communication. In any organizational endeavor, communication is of utmost importance. In fact, as Barnard (1938, p. 91) noted long ago, "in any exhaustive theory of organization, communication would occupy a central place, because the structure, extensiveness, and scope of the organization are almost entirely determined by communication techniques." Other important organizational processes like decision-making and leadership rely heavily on communication for their implementation.

Although communication is important in any group or organizational situation, it is particularly important in business organizations: 1) that must deal with high levels of uncertainty; 2) that are highly complex; and 3) that employ technologies that do not easily lend themselves to routinization or automation (R. Hall, 1977). Communication processes may be somewhat more important in a research and development lab than on an assembly line. Even so, an understanding of communication processes is essential for all groups, departments, and organizations if efforts are to be coordinated for achieving common goals.

In the sections that follow, we will explore several aspects of communication in organizations. First, a basic model of the communication process is presented. This is followed by consideration of the major influences on communication, barriers to effective communication, and strategies for overcoming these barriers. Throughout, emphasis is placed on what managers can learn in order to facilitate effective communication in their own organizations.

A Basic Model of Communication

Any attempt to diagram a communication episode between two individuals must necessarily be an oversimplification of what really happens. Even so, it is possible to represent the process as shown in Exhibit 10–1.

A simple communication episode consists of a communicator who encodes and sends a message to a receiver who decodes it and responds in some way, either verbally or behaviorally (Shannon and Weaver, 1948).

Two important aspects of this model are encoding and decoding. *Encoding* is simply the process by which individuals initiating the communication

Exhibit 10–1   A basic model of communication (after Shannon and Weaver, 1948)

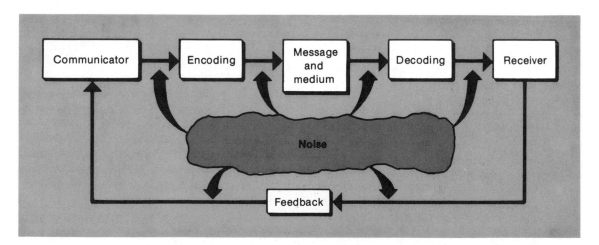

translate ideas into a systematic set of symbols (language). Encoding is influenced by the sender's previous experiences with the topic and people involved, his or her emotional state at the time, and the importance attached to the message (or part of the message). *Decoding,* on the other hand, is the process by which the recipient of the message interprets it. Decoding is influenced by factors like the receiver's previous experiences and frame of reference at the time of the message.

In any basic communication episode, there can be a variety of ways in which the intended message gets distorted. Factors that can distort message clarity are referred to as *noise*. Noise can occur at any point along the process shown in Exhibit 10–1. For example, a manager may be under considerable time pressure and issue a succinct message that lacks the needed clarity for employees to carry out a task correctly. The manager may tell his or her foreman "I want this job done today regardless of how much it costs," when in fact the manager does care how much it costs. Noise can also occur in the decoding process. As shown in Exhibit 10–2, there are many ways in which message transmission can be distorted.

Major Influences on Communication

In any organizational setting, the nature, direction, and quality of communication processes can be influenced by several factors (R. Hall, 1977; Porter and Roberts, 1976). To begin with, communication is clearly a *social* process. Obviously, it takes at least two persons to complete a communication episode. A variety of social influences exist that can affect the accuracy of the intended message. For example, status barriers between employees on different levels of the organizational hierarchy influence modes of address (Sir vs. Joe vs. waitress). Prevailing norms and roles may dictate who initiates which kinds of messages, who speaks to whom, and how one responds when spoken to. The social processes at work in a group or organization determine what is said, to whom it is said, and how it is said.

In addition, the communication process is heavily influenced by employees' *perceptual processes*. For example, the extent to which employees accurately receive job instructions from supervisors may be influenced by their opinions of the supervisors, the extent to which the instructions are controversial or conflicting, or interest in the job. If an employee has stereotyped the boss as an incompetent manager, chances are that little the boss says will be regarded seriously. On the other hand, if the boss is seen as influential in the company, everything he or she says may be interpreted as important, even when it is not.

Finally, the communication process is influenced by the *structure* of the organization itself. For instance, it has often been argued that a major reason

Exhibit 10–2 Examples of noise and distortion in the communicaton process (after Hodgetts and Altman, 1979, p. 305).

What the Manager Said	What the Manager Meant	What the Subordinate Heard
I'll look into hiring another person for your department as soon as I complete my budget review.	We'll start interviewing for that job in about three weeks.	I'm tied up with more important things. Let's forget about hiring for the indefinite future.
Your performance was below par last quarter. I really expected more out of you.	You're going to have to try harder, but I know you can do it.	If you screw up one more time, you're out.
I'd like that report as soon as you can get to it.	I need that report within the week.	Drop that rush order you're working on and fill out that report today.
I talked to the boss but at the present time, due to budget problems, we'll be unable to fully match your competitive salary offer.	We can give you 95 per cent of that offer and I know we'll be able to do even more for you next year.	If I were you, I'd take that competitive offer. We're certainly not going to pay that kind of salary to a person with your credentials.
We have a job opening in Los Angeles that we think would be just your cup of tea. We'd like you to go out there and look it over.	If you'd like that job, it's yours. If not, of course, you can stay here in Denver. You be the judge.	You don't have to go out to L.A. if you don't want to. However, if you don't, you can kiss good-bye to your career with this firm.
Your people seem to be having some problems getting their work out on time. I want you to look into this situation and straighten it out.	Talk to your people and find out what the problem is. Then get with them and jointly solve it.	I don't care how many heads you bust, just get me that output. I've got enough problems around here without you screwing things up too.

Source: *Organizational Behavior* by Richard M. Hodgetts and Steven Altman. Copyright © 1979 by W. B. Saunders Company. Reprinted by permission of Holt, Rinehart and Winston.

to decentralize an organization is that such structures are more participative and lead to improved communications between parties. When messages must travel through several levels in a hierarchy, opportunities for message distortion are greatly increased, leading to problems that possibly would not occur if face-to-face communication was possible.

Other factors could be mentioned that influence communication processes in organizations. However, social, perceptual, and structural influences should be recognized as placing major constraints on the manner and form of communication processes. With this in mind, we now turn to an examination of several major barriers to effective communication in organizational settings.

Barriers to Effective Communication

If, as Barnard said, communication forms the basis of organizations, then it is logical to consider several common problems associated with communication processes in organizations. A very lengthy list could easily be generated of various problems or barriers. For the sake of brevity, however, it is possible to identify five general categories of barriers to effective organizational communication (Guetzkow, 1965; R. Hall, 1977).

Distortion   Communication distortion occurs when an intended message becomes altered as it passes through the information channel from sender to receiver. There are several reasons why distortion can occur, including: 1) differing frames of reference of the sender and receiver; 2) imprecision of language; 3) interpretation errors in the receipt of the message; 4) necessity to condense information for purposes of transmission; and 5) social distance or status barriers between sender and receiver.

Omission   Omission occurs when only one part of an intended message is conveyed to the receiver. For example, a machine operator in a factory may tell his supervisor that his machine has broken down but fail to point out that he failed to properly maintain the machine, and caused the breakdown. Omission results either when the sender intentionally filters the intended message (perhaps because of fear of retribution) or when the sender is unable to grasp the entire message himself and therefore transmits incomplete information.

Overload   Oftentimes, a receiver is buried in an abundance of information and rational decision-making and management suffers. This is called communication overload. Managers often face this problem when their subordinates fail to adequately screen information presented to the manager. As a result, managers spend so much time sorting through the information that they may fail to identify the major issues.

Timeliness A major factor of the effectiveness of communication is timing. Since messages are intended to stimulate action, it is important that their transmission be timed so that they receive the necessary attention. Providing detailed instructions to employees on a task one month prior to the time the task is to be done, for example, may lead to problems of performance failure because of the lengthy time interval between task instruction and task performance. Conversely, we often see situations in which important memos are distributed to employees requesting actions but giving unrealistically short deadlines. If information is to be received properly and acted upon, it must arrive in a timely fashion.

Acceptance Finally, even if all four of the above barriers could be overcome, it is still necessary for the receiver to accept the message if it is to be acted upon. If employees refuse to accept a message, perhaps because they feel it is inappropriate or comes from a non-credible source (a supervisor asks the secretary of another supervisor to type a letter), there is little reason to believe the message will be acted upon.

Strategies for Improving Communication Effectiveness

None of the above barriers to communication effectiveness is insurmountable. The problem for managers is how to improve the accuracy, flow, and acceptance of relevant communication so that uncertainty and distortion are reduced and acceptance is enhanced. A variety of mechanisms exist to achieve this goal. These remedies can be grouped for convenience according to the direction of the intended instructions: downward, upward, or horizontal (see Exhibit 10–3).

Improving downward communication.
There are a variety of ways by which managers can facilitate improved communications with their subordinates. As shown in Exhibit 10–3, most of these techniques involve clarifying the nature of the job or task. The more employees understand about the nature of the job (including what they are to do and why), the less search behavior is required and the more goal-directed effort is available, assuming the employees accept the task and are motivated to perform.

In addition to clarifying job instructions and the rationale behind the instructions, managers can provide greater feedback to keep employees on target. Managers can also use multiple communication channels (written and verbal messages simultaneously) and repeat messages to reinforce the impact of the intended message. By doing so, the chances are increased that the message will be received and understood. Finally, it is desirable at times to bypass formal communication channels and go directly to the intended receiver with the message. By doing so, considerable noise and distortion in transmission is avoided.

Exhibit 10–3 Strategies for improving communication effectiveness (Steers, 1977c)

Downward Communications
1. Job instructions can be presented clearly to employees so they understand more precisely what is expected.
2. Efforts can be made to explain the rationale behind the required tasks to employees so they understand why they are being asked to do something.
3. Management can provide greater feedback concerning the nature and quality of performance, thereby keeping employees "on target."
4. Multiple communication channels can be used to increase the chances that the message is properly received.
5. Important messages can be repeated to insure penetration.
6. In some cases, it is desirable to bypass formal communication channels and go directly to the intended receiver with the message.

Upward Communications
1. Upward messages can be screened so only the more relevant aspects are received by top management.
2. Managers can attempt to change the organizational climate so subordinates feel freer to transmit negative as well as positive messages without fear of retribution.
3. Managers can sensitize themselves so they are better able to detect bias and distorted messages from their subordinates.
4. Sometimes it is possible to utilize "distortion-proof" messages (Downs, 1967), such as providing subordinates with report forms requiring quantified or standardized data.
5. Social distance and status barriers between employees on various levels can be reduced so messages will be more spontaneous.

Horizontal Communications
1. Efforts can be made to develop interpersonal skills between group members and departments so greater openness and trust exist.
2. Reward systems can be utilized which reward interdepartmental cooperation and minimize "zero-sum game" situations.
3. Interdepartmental meetings can be used to share information concerning what other departments are involved in.
4. In some cases, the actual design of the organization itself can be changed to provide greater opportunities for interdepartmental contacts (e.g., shifting from a traditional to a matrix organization design).

Improving upward communication. Clearly one of the more important problems in upward communication is information overload. Managers receive voluminous facts, opinions, suggestions, and complaints that can easily stifle managerial effectiveness by impeding the manager's ability to act quickly and decisively on pertinent information. An interesting example of this problem is provided by Allison (1971) in his analysis of the events leading up to the Cuban missile crisis of 1962. Allison found that the Central Intelligence Agency had sufficient information to assess accurately the deployment of missiles in Cuba and take quiet diplomatic steps to solve the problem long before events reached crisis proportion. Unfortunately, however, the CIA possessed so much information that it was months behind in its intelligence processing. By the time the information was properly analyzed, opportunities for quiet, diplomatic conflict resolution had long passed.

One popular way to reduce overload is *screening*. Screening occurs when only the important aspects of a message are transmitted through the hierarchy and the peripheral aspects are omitted. Screening has several formats. One consists of a *management by exception* procedure in which routine decisions and actions are handled through policy guidelines. Only exceptions, deviations, and emergencies are reported upward. A second approach is the *principle of sufficiency* (Dubin, 1959), where organizations intentionally regulate both the quantity and quality of upward information (e.g., where managers at each level in the hierarchy write summary reports for their superiors or where managers intentionally schedule meetings for less time than is thought to be needed so they can "get right to the point"). Finally, a third screening technique is *queuing*, where messages are handled sequentially by managers, usually in rank-order of importance.

A different way to improve upward communication involves attempting to improve the organizational climate so subordinates have less fear about reporting negative or positive outcomes to their superiors. A major problem in upward communication is that bad news often gets filtered out as it moves up the hierarchy and quick remedial action is inhibited. If employees had less fear of negative consequences for admitting mistakes, superiors would be more likely to receive rapid and accurate information on trouble spots for which they could then seek remedy.

In addition, other strategies can be employed, including the use of distortion-proof messages (Downs, 1967) where employees' messages are structured (perhaps using a standard form), the reduction of social and status barriers, and an increased awareness by managers of potential sources of bias in reporting. Another way is to recognize different individual communication roles in organizations (see Box 10–1). As a result, managers should receive more accurate and timely information from employees who feel secure about reporting information upward.

Improving horizontal communication. If managers are to be successful in coordinating and integrating the efforts of individuals and groups in all areas of an organization, it is crucial that a concerted effort be made to develop accurate, rapid lines of horizontal communication. Work groups and

Box 10–1 Individual Communication Roles in Organizations

A fact that is often overlooked by students of management is that all members of a group are not equivalent in their communication behavior. Instead, different individuals serve different purposes in the communication network. Rogers and Rogers identify four distinct roles played by various parties in the communication process:*

As would be expected, different roles carry varying amounts of power and influence within the groups of the organization. All roles carry some form of power, however. The problem for management is to identify who serves what roles and how to utilize the networks to best gather relevant information and disseminate it to the appropriate parties.

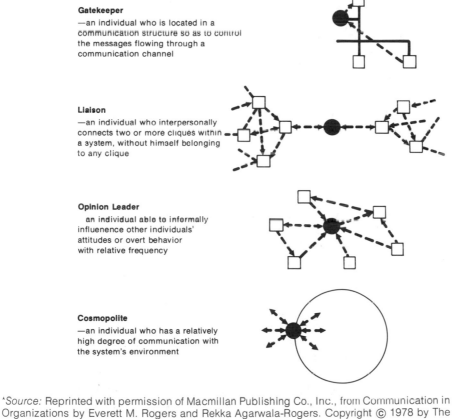

Gatekeeper
—an individual who is located in a communication structure so as to control the messages flowing through a communication channel

Liaison
—an individual who interpersonally connects two or more cliques within a system, without himself belonging to any clique

Opinion Leader
an individual able to informally influence other individuals' attitudes or overt behavior with relative frequency

Cosmopolite
—an individual who has a relatively high degree of communication with the system's environment

Source: Reprinted with permission of Macmillan Publishing Co., Inc., from Communication in Organizations by Everett M. Rogers and Rekka Agarwala-Rogers. Copyright © 1978 by The Free Press, a division of Macmillan Publishing Co., Inc.

departments must pool their efforts and coordinate their activities if organizational effectiveness is to be achieved. Questions must be raised concerning ways managers can facilitate horizontal communication between groups.

As shown in Exhibit 10–3, several mechanisms exist. One is to foster high levels of interpersonal trust and openness between work groups. To the extent that these efforts are successful, more spontaneous efforts can emerge and less energy will be devoted to promoting group or departmental territoriality. Reward systems can be implemented to reward cooperation between departments instead of competition. One example would be to include in a manager's performance appraisal a question about the extent to which the manager helped *other* departments reach their goals. By such techniques, the propensity to conceal information that could be helpful to other groups and departments might be reduced.

Another technique involves having inter-departmental meetings (instead of or in addition to departmental meetings) where all members of two or more departments or groups come together and share information, problems, and possible solutions. In this way, members of one department gain a better understanding of the problems of others and how to be of assistance. Using a matrix organization design is another way to accomplish the same end. There are many ways managers can facilitate improved communications at work so less effort is wasted and more energies are devoted toward goal attainment. However, in a very real sense, managers must make it happen; they must take an active part in developing a climate best suited for open and accurate interchange between employees at various levels.

Conflict in Organizations

Based on this discussion of communication processes in organizations, we are now ready to turn our attention to the study of conflict. The importance of conflict and conflict resolution in work settings can be seen in a variety of ways. One recent survey, for example, indicated that approximately 20% of top and middle managers' time was spent in dealing with some form of conflict (Thomas and Schmidt, 1976). Moreover, Graves (1978) found that managerial skills in handling conflict was a major predictor of managerial success and effectiveness. A knowledge of the nature of conflict processes and mechanisms to reduce conflict can be very helpful to managers interested in facilitating organizational effectiveness.

In the sections that follow, we will first consider the general nature of conflict processes in organizations. Next, various functions and dysfunctions are considered, followed by a review of the conflict process itself. Then we will consider the role of defense mechanisms in dealing with conflict. Finally, several strategies for resolving conflict are discussed.

Nature of Conflict

As one would expect, there are many ways to define conflict as it relates to work situations. Pondy (1967, p. 298) suggests four approaches, each dealing with one aspect of the conflict process:

(1) *Antecedent conditions* (for example, scarcity of resources, policy differences) of conflictful behavior; (2) *affective states* (e.g., stress, tension, hostility, anxiety); (3) *cognitive states* of individuals (i.e., their perception or awareness of conflictful situations); and (4) *conflictful behavior,* ranging from passive resistance to overt aggression.

Based on these approaches, Pondy and others have suggested that instead of arguing over which definition is more appropriate, it may be more functional to use the term conflict to refer to the entire process, including antecedent conditions, affective states, cognitive states, and actual conflictful behaviors. Using this approach, we can offer the following definition of *conflict.* "Conflict is the process which begins when one party perceives that the other has frustrated, or is about to frustrate, some concern of his" (Thomas, 1976, p. 891).

This frustration can involve at least four basic *types* of conflict:

- *Goal conflict,* where one person or group desires a different outcome than others.
- *Cognitive conflict,* where one person or group holds ideas or opinions that are inconsistent with others.
- *Affective conflict,* where one person's or group's feelings or emotions (attitudes) are incompatible with others.
- *Behavioral conflict,* where one person or group does something (behaves in a certain way) that is unacceptable to others.

Conflict can be found on several *levels.* Initially, there is intrapersonal conflict, or conflict within one individual. We often hear about someone who has an approach-avoidance conflict; that is, he or she is both attracted to and repelled by the same object. Similarly, a person can be attracted to two equally appealing alternatives, such as two good job offers (approach-approach conflict), or repelled by two equally unpleasant alternatives, like the threat of being fired if one fails to identify a co-worker guilty of breaking plant rules (avoidance-avoidance conflict).

Conflict can also take an *interpersonal* form, where two individuals disagree on some matter. Finally, disagreements can take the forms of *intragroup* and *intergroup* conflict. The possibility for conflict can be seen on all levels in an organization.

Functions and Dysfunctions of Conflict

It is often assumed that all conflict is necessarily bad and should be eliminated. On the contrary, there are some circumstances in which a moderate amount of conflict can indeed be helpful. For instance, conflict can lead to the search for new ideas and new mechanisms as a way out of conflict. Conflict can stimulate innovation and change. Conflict can also facilitate employee motivation in some cases where employees feel a need to come out ahead and, as a result, push hard on their performance objectives.

Conflict can at times help individuals and group members grow and develop self-identities. As noted by Coser (1956, p. 154):

> [C]onflict, which aims at a resolution of tension between antagonists, is likely to have stabilizing and integrative functions for the relationship. By permitting immediate and direct expression of rival claims, such social systems are able to readjust their structures by eliminating their sources of dissatisfaction. The multiple conflicts which they experience may serve to eliminate the causes for dissociation and to reestablish unity. These systems avail themselves, through the toleration and institutionalization of conflict, of an important stabilizing mechanism.

Even so, conflict can at the same time have negative consequences for both individuals and organizations. Conflict can cause people to divert energies away from performance and goal attainment while efforts to resolve the conflict continue. Continued conflict can take a heavy toll in terms of psychological well-being. As we shall see in Chapter 15, conflict represents an important factor in influencing stress as well as the psycho–physical consequences of stress. Finally, continued conflict can also affect the social climate of the group and inhibit group cohesiveness.

Thus, conflict in certain forms can be either functional or dysfunctional in work situations depending upon the nature of the conflict, its intensity, and its duration. Now we turn to an examination of the process by which conflicts come about.

The Conflict Process

How does conflict come about? A model has recently been proposed by Kenneth Thomas that attempts to answer this question by diagramming the basic conflict process. The model, shown in Exhibit 10–4, consists of four stages: 1) frustration; 2) conceptualization; 3) behavior, and 4) outcome.

Frustration.   Conflict situations originate when an individual or group is frustrated, or feels about to be frustrated, in the pursuit of important goals. This frustration may be caused by a wide variety of factors, including per-

Exhibit 10–4   A process model of conflict episodes (Thomas, 1976, p. 895).

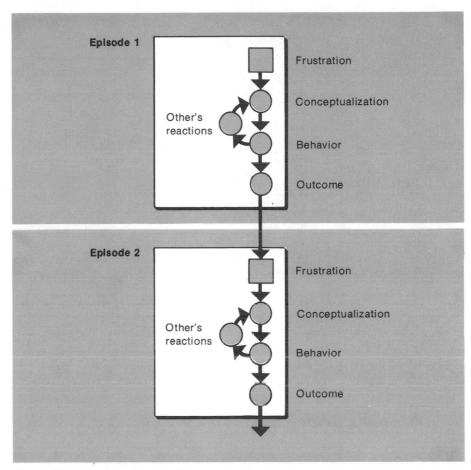

formance goals, promotion, pay raises, power, scarce economic resources, rules, and values. As Thomas (1976) notes, conflict can be traced to the frustration of anything a group or individual cares about.

Conceptualization.   In Stage 2, parties to the conflict attempt to understand the nature of the problem, what they themselves want as a resolution, what they think their opponents want as a resolution, and the various strategies they feel each side may employ in resolving the conflict. This stage is really the problem–solving and strategy phase, where individuals make attributions about the intent of their opponents and attempt to devise counter strategies aimed at solving the conflict in a fashion satisfactory to themselves. For instance, when management and union sit down to negotiate a labor contract, both sides attempt to decide what is most important and what can be bargained away in exchange for these more important needs.

A major part of this conceptualization stage consists of strategy decisions concerning how each party will attempt to resolve the conflict. Thomas (1977) identified five modes for conflict resolution (after Lawrence and Lorsch, 1967), as shown in Exhibit 10–5. These are competing, collaborating, compromising, avoiding, and accommodating. Also shown in the exhibit are situations that seem appropriate for each strategy.

The choice of an appropriate conflict resolution mode depends to a great extent on the situation and the goals of the party. This is shown graphically in Exhibit 10–6. Depending upon the relative importance of one's own concerns as opposed to the importance of the other party's concerns, the appropriate mode that a group or individual selects can vary significantly. Hence, if a union negotiator feels confident he or she can win on an issue that is of primary concern to union members (e.g., wages), a direct competition mode may be chosen. On the other hand, on issues on which the union is either indifferent or actually supports management's concerns (e.g., plant safety), we would expect an accommodating mode.

What is interesting in this process is the assumptions people make about their modes compared to their opponents. In a study of executives, Thomas and Pondy (1977) discovered that the executives typically described themselves as using collaboration or compromise to resolve conflict, while these same executives typically described their opponents as using a competitive mode almost exclusively. In other words, the executives by and large underestimated their opponents' concerns for satisfying both sides. Executives saw their opponents as uncompromising. Simultaneously, the executives had perhaps over-flattering self portraits of their own willingness to satisfy both sides in a dispute.

Exhibit 10–5 Five modes of resolving conflict

Conflict-handling Modes	Appropriate Situations
Competing	1. When quick, decisive action is vital—e.g., emergencies.
	2. On important issues where unpopular actions need implementing—e.g., cost cutting, enforcing unpopular rules, discipline.
	3. On issues vital to company welfare when you know you're right.

Exhibit 10–5 (Continued)

Conflict-handling Modes	Appropriate Situations
	4. Against people who take advantage of noncompetitive behavior.
Collaborating	1. To find an integrative solution when both sets of concerns are too important to be compromised. 2. When your objective is to learn. 3. To merge insights from people with different perspectives. 4. To gain commitment by incorporating concerns into a consensus. 5. To work through feelings which have interfered with a relationship.
Compromising	1. When goals are important, but not worth the effort or potential disruption of more assertive modes. 2. When opponents with equal power are committed to mutually exclusive goals. 3. To achieve temporary settlements to complex issues. 4. To arrive at expedient solutions under time pressure. 5. As a backup when collaboration or competition is unsuccessful.
Avoiding	1. When an issue is trivial, or more important issues are pressing. 2. When you perceive no chance of satisfying your concerns. 3. When potential disruption outweighs the benefits of resolution. 4. To let people cool down and regain perspective. 5. When gathering information supersedes immediate decision. 6. When others can resolve the conflict more effectively. 7. When issues seem tangential or symptomatic of other issues.
Accommodating	1. When you find you are wrong—to allow a better position to be heard, to learn, and to show your reasonableness. 2. When issues are more important to others than yourself—to satisfy others and maintain cooperation. 3. To build social credits for later issues. 4. To minimize loss when you are outmatched and losing. 5. When harmony and stability are especially important. 6. To allow subordinates to develop by learning from mistakes.

Source: K. W. Thomas "Toward Multidimensional Values in Teaching: The Example of Conflict Behaviors," Academy of Management Review, 1977, Vol. 2, Table 1, p. 487. Reprinted by permission.

Exhibit 10–6 A two-dimensional model of conflict behavior
(Thomas, 1976, p. 900).

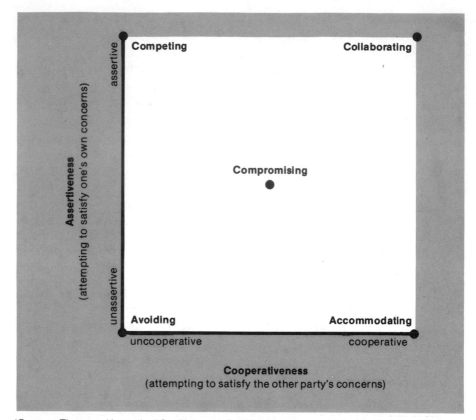

*Source: Thomas, Kenneth, "Conflict and Conflict Management," in M. D. Dunnette (ed.), *Handbook of Industrial and Organizational Behavior,* adapted from Figure 4, p. 900. Copyright © by Rand McNally College Publishing Company.

Behavior. The third stage in Thomas' model of the conflict process is actual behavior. As a result of the conceptualization process, parties to a conflict attempt to implement their resolution mode by competing or accommodating in the hopes of resolving problems.

Outcome. Finally, as a result of behavior, both sides determine the extent to which a satisfactory resolution of the conflict can be achieved. Where one party to the conflict does not feel satisfied, or feels only partially satisfied, the seeds of discontent are sown for a later conflict as shown in Exhibit 10–4. One unresolved conflict episode can easily set the stage for a second episode. The importance of managerial action aimed at achieving quick and satisfactory resolution is vital. Failure to do so leaves the possibility (more accurately, the probability) that new conflicts will soon emerge again.

Defense Mechanisms

As a result of conflict, individuals are often placed in situations in which they experience considerable anxiety but can find no satisfactory way to reduce it. In this circumstance, individuals attempt to reduce the conflict and anxiety through a variety of defense mechanisms.

At the heart of defense mechanisms is the concept of self-image. Conflict often represents a pronounced threat to self-image. Where threats to self-image occur, there are at least two ways an individual can dissipate the threats. First, the individual can change the self-image so it becomes congruent with whatever is causing the difficulty. This often involves accepting the fact that the individual is either wrong or a failure. Second, the individual can defend his or her self-image by denying, rejecting, or distorting that which is threatening, thus maintaining the integrity of the self-image. This distortion may be conscious or unconscious. This kind of behavior involves *defense mechanisms*.

Defense mechanisms may reduce one's awareness of a threat but they seldom affect that which is causing the threat. Argyris (1957, p. 37) provides an example:

> Let us say that supervisor A is threatened because he "knows" his boss does not think that he (supervisor A) is doing a good job. Let us assume that he defends himself by placing the blame on the boss. This will not in any way stop the boss from feeling the way he does about supervisor A. Soon the supervisor will have to justify his defensive reactions to himself. He may do this by saying the boss is "out to get him." Each of these defenses is a distortion which in turn will require further justification and further defense. After some time supervisor A has built up deep layers of defense, all of which will have to be uncovered if he is to understand the cause.

While there are many different kinds of defense mechanisms (see Exhibit 10–7) they may be classified into three general categories: 1) aggressive strategies; 2) compromise strategies; and 3) withdrawal strategies (Fitch, 1970).

Aggressive defense mechanisms include those reactions by which we directly or indirectly attack the source of the threat to our self-concept. Such mechanisms include displacement, negativism, and fixation. Examples of these defense mechanisms are provided in Exhibit 10–7. *Compromise* defense mechanisms allow individuals to make relatively satisfactory adjustments, or compromises to less than desirable situations. Compromise mechanisms include compensation, identification, projection, rationalization, and reaction formation.

Exhibit 10–7 Common defense mechanisms

Defense Mechanism	Psychological Process	Illustration
	Aggressive Strategies	
Fixation	Maintaining a persistent nonadjustive reaction even though all the cues indicate the behavior will not cope with the problems.	Persisting in carrying out an operational procedure long since declared by management to be uneconomical as a protest because the employee's opinion wasn't asked.
Displacement	Redirecting pent-up emotions toward persons, ideas, or objects other than the primary source of the emotion.	Roughly rejecting a simple request from a subordinate after receiving a rebuff from the boss.
Negativism	Active or passive resistance, operating unconsciously.	The manager who, having been unsuccessful in getting out of a committee assignment, picks apart every suggestion that anyone makes in the meetings.
	Compromise Strategies	
Compensation	Individual devotes himself to a pursuit with increased vigor to make up for some feeling of real or imagined inadequacy.	Zealous, hard-working president of the twenty-five year club who has never advanced very far in the company hierarchy.
Identification	Individual enhances his self-esteem by patterning his own behavior after another's, frequently also internalizing the values and beliefs of the other; also vicariously sharing the glories or suffering in the reversals of other individuals or groups.	The "assistant-to" who takes on the vocabulary, mannerisms, or even pomposity of his vice-presidential boss.
Projection	Individual protects himself from awareness of his own undesirable traits or unacceptable feelings by attributing them to others.	Unsuccessful person who, deep down, would like to block the rise of others in the organization and who continually feels that others are out to "get him."
Rationalization	Justifying inconsistent or undesirable behavior, beliefs, statements, and motivations by providing acceptable explanations for them.	Padding the expense account because "everybody does it."

Reaction formation	Urges not acceptable to consciousness are repressed, and in their stead opposite attitudes or modes of behavior are expressed with considerable force.	Employee who has not been promoted who overdoes the defense of his boss, vigorously upholding the company's policies.

Withdrawal Strategies

Conversion	Emotional conflicts are expressed in muscular, sensory, or bodily symptoms of disability, malfunctioning, or pain.	A disabling headache keeping a staff member off the job the day after a cherished project has been rejected.
Fantasy	Daydreaming or other forms of imaginative activity provides an escape from reality and imagined satisfactions.	An employee's daydream of the day in the staff meeting when he corrects the boss's mistakes and is publicly acknowledged as the real leader of the industry.
Regression	Individual returns to an earlier and less mature level of adjustment in the face of frustration.	A manager having been blocked in some administrative pursuit busies himself with clerical duties or technical details more appropriate for his subordinates.
Repression	Completely excluding from consciousness impulses, experiences, and feelings that are psychologically disturbing because they arouse a sense of guilt or anxiety.	A subordinate "forgetting" to tell his boss the circumstances of an embarrassing situation.
Resignation, apathy, and boredom	Breaking psychological contact with the environment, withholding any sense of emotional or personal involvement.	Employee who, receiving no reward, praise, or encouragement, no longer cares whether or not he does a good job.
Flight or withdrawal	Leaving the field in which frustration, anxiety, or conflict is experienced, either physically or psychologically.	The salesman's big order falls through, and he takes the rest of the day off; constant rebuff or rejection by superiors and colleagues pushes an older worker toward being a loner and ignoring what friendly gestures are made.

Source: Adapted from Timothy W. Costello and Sheldon S. Zalkind, *Psychology in Administration: A Research Orientation* © 1963, pp. 148–149. Reprinted by permission of Prentice Hall, Inc., Englewood Cliffs, New Jersey.

Withdrawal, the third category of defense mechanisms, includes a variety of ways in which individuals attempt to reduce the threat by removing themselves—physically or psychologically—from the situation in which the threat is perceived. Examples include conversion, fantasy, regression, repression, apathy, and flight.

All people use defense mechanisms in order to protect themselves from threat and maintain their self-image. It is difficult to label these mechanisms as being good or bad; they exist and must be recognized as powerful influences on people's perception, attitudes, and behavior.

Strategies for Resolving Conflict in Organizations

We have discovered that conflict is pervasive throughout organizations and that some conflict can be good for organizations. People often grow and learn from conflict as long as the conflict is not dysfunctional. The question for managers is how to select a resolution strategy that is appropriate to the situation and individuals involved (see Box 10–2). March and Simon (1958) have identified four general strategies for resolving conflict in organizations. They are: 1) problem solving; 2) persuasion; 3) politics; and 4) bargaining.

Problem-solving.   Perhaps the most straightforward approach to resolving conflict is to attempt to identify the exact nature of a problem, consider possible alternative solutions, and select the solution that is most appropriate when both parties are willing to work together and when the nature of the problem can be examined in objective or quantitative terms. For instance, when the sales department and the personnel department disagree over the most appropriate training procedures for new sales representatives, it can be assumed that both sides seek the same end (effective sales reps) and that various training procedures can be carefully and objectively compared to find the most appropriate one.

Persuasion.   Persuasion represents an attempt by one party to convince another to change an opinion about the nature of the conflict or the most appropriate resolution. The effectiveness of persuasion often depends on the personalities of the parties involved. For example, Hovland, Janis, and Kelley (1953) found that a person can more easily persuade others to change their opinions if that person has high credibility. Similarly, persons who are high in authoritarianism would probably be more subject to influence than others.

Politics.   Like power, politics is typically considered a dirty word. Even so, students of management must recognize that politics is a fact of organizational life that must be recognized and dealt with. Politics is the vehicle for getting many things done in work organizations, particularly if conflict is

Box 10–2 Sherif's Experiment on Inter-Group Conflict

One of the most illuminating experiments on group conflict processes and how conflict can be resolved was carried out in a classic study by Muzafer Sherif.*

Research design The study was carried out among boys attending a summer camp. In the experiment, Sherif created two cohesive groups and over time put the groups through a series of competitive exercises (win-lose situations) in which both group identity and inter-group conflict and hostility increased. Bitter resentment between groups surfaced and attitudes were adopted within each group to facilitate extreme criticism of members of the other group. The emergence of extreme hostility led Sherif to conclude early on in the experiment that when members of two groups are placed in a competitive situation where only one group can win, two situations occur: 1) the competitive activity soon engenders hostility between groups; and 2) the conflict between them facilitates solidarity within each group.

Based on these findings, Sherif set about to resolve the conflict. Several conflict resolution strategies were tried and failed. Among these were: 1) dispensing accurate and favorable in-

formation about the opposing groups; 2) appeals to moral values and brotherhood; and 3) the introduction of a common enemy to both groups.

Finally, Sherif placed both groups in a situation where both groups needed each other to solve a mutual problem. It was hypothesized that the conflict would be reduced by an appeal to a superordinate goal. Several mutual problems were presented to the groups (find a broken water pipe serving the camp, agree on one motion picture to be shown, work together to fix the camp truck so groceries could be secured).

Results In the experiment, it was found that the cumulative effect of having both groups pursue superordinate goals gradually reduced the conflict and hostility between them. The reinforced superordinate goals apparently led to the development of procedures for cooperating in specific activities. These activities, in turn, had transfer value to new situations, thus creating modes of intergroup cooperation. As the experiment drew to a close, members of previously opposing groups became overtly friendly.

*Source: M. Sherif. *In common predicament: Social psychology of intergroup conflict and cooperation.* Boston: Houghton Mifflin, 1966.

involved. Political resolution techniques rest on the distribution of power between parties. If a party can accumulate sufficient power (or acquire power through a coalition with others), that party can exert considerable influence over the outcome of the decision or solution to the problem.

Bargaining. Finally, where both parties have something to offer and are willing to give and take instead of forcing a decision, a bargaining mode can be employed. Here, concern is focused on arriving at a solution that offers something (if not everything) to all parties in the conflict. In this way, everyone sacrifices somewhat and everyone benefits, but no clear winner emerges. Numerous examples of bargaining can be identified, particularly in the realm of labor–management relations.

As can be seen, the responsibility for resolving conflict in organizations rests heavily upon the ability of a manager to initiate momentum for change. This change may involve solving a problem or convincing one group that the other group is right. This change may also involve causing power coalitions to shift through the political process or bargaining one resource for another. In any case, the processes by which change comes about and conflicts are solved rests squarely on communication. Without effective communication, many of the roots of conflict will remain. Without effective communication, managers may prove incapable of successful bargaining, solving problems, persuading, or engaging in political processes. An important key to reducing conflict in organizations is to improve the degree of effective communications.

Summary

Two different aspects of group processes were examined in this chapter. The first was communication in work organizations. The nature of communication processes was discussed and was accompanied with a model of the basic process. Major influences on communication were then examined, followed by a consideration of several barriers to effective communication. Finally, a variety of strategies were suggested for improving communication effectiveness. These strategies represent concrete actions managers can take to improve the dissemination and receipt of information in work situations.

The second part of the chapter dealt with conflict processes. The general notion of conflict was discussed, followed by an examination of the functional and dysfunctional aspects of conflict. A model of the conflict process was suggested. It was pointed out that one major way for individuals to respond to conflict was through a variety of defense mechanisms. Finally, major strategies for resolving conflict were discussed.

It has been said that communication and conflict represent two of the most serious problems facing contemporary organizations. Poor communication in a work situation can lead to wasted effort, lost opportunities, misunderstandings, and, invariably, conflict. Conflict, in turn, can lead to increased distrust among co-workers, less flexibility of action, and less desire by employees to get involved in a job. These two related problems therefore inhibit efforts to increase organizational effectiveness. Although some communication problems and conflict are inevitable, attempts can be made to minimize these problems where possible and to deal openly and effectively with them when they occur.

Key Words

communication
encoding
decoding
noise
screening

management by exception
principle of sufficiency
queuing
conflict
defense mechanism

Questions for Discussion

1. What is the importance of communication in organizations?
2. Describe several major influences on communication in organizations.
3. Identify the major barriers to effective communication. How can these barriers be overcome by managers?
4. According to Rogers and Rogers, what are the four individual communication roles in organizations?
5. Define conflict. Discuss a few types of conflicts in organizations.
6. What are some of the functions and dysfunctions of conflict in work situations?
7. Describe the conflict process.
8. Discuss how defense mechanisms work.
9. Identify various ways for resolving conflict.
10. What is the major conclusion of Sherif's experiment on inter-group conflict?

chapter 11

Decision Making in Organizations

We now come to the third group process to be discussed in this section of the book; namely, decision-making processes. As with communication and conflict discussed earlier, decision making represents a significant area of concern for managers interested in effectively managing people at work. Decision making is closely related to leadership processes, as will be seen in the next chapter. In fact, one theory of leadership has its foundations in the way managers allow (or do not allow) subordinates to participate in decisions affecting the group or department. In this chapter, we shall take an in-depth look at decision processes at work.

Importance of Topic for Managers

A knowledge of decision-making processes in organizations is important for several reasons:

1. Making decisions has been clearly identified as one of management's primary responsibilities. Decisions may involve allocating scarce resources, hiring employees, investing capital, or introducing new products. If resources were abundant, clearly few decisions would be necessary; however, such is typically not the case. Hence, managers should have an awareness of the basic processes by which decisions are made in organizations.

2. Several frameworks are available to help understand how decisions are made. However, each framework is based on different assumptions about the nature of people at work. So, an informed manager should be aware of the models and the different assumptions underlying each.

3. Another management concern is the extent to which subordinates should be included in decisions affecting their jobs. When are group decisions superior (or inferior) to individual ones? How much participation can be accommodated in work organizations where managers still assume responsibility for group actions?

4. The phenomenon of *groupthink* has emerged as an important consideration in understanding how decisions are made. How does this phenomenon affect decision quality?

5. Finally, what are some strategies that can be used by managers to improve decisions in organizations? A knowledge of these strategies can help managers make the most efficient use of their limited time and resources in their efforts to facilitate goal-attainment.

Nature of Decision Making

It has often been said that a common characteristic of effective leaders and effective work groups is their ability to make decisions that are appropriate, timely, and acceptable. If organizational effectiveness is defined as the ability to secure and utilize resources in the pursuit of organizational goals, the decision-making processes concerned with how these resources will be acquired and used emerges as a central topic in organizational analysis.

Because of the importance of this topic, we will consider several aspects. First, decision making will be defined. Next, three major models of decision-making processes will be compared, along with the assumptions underlying each model. Following this, individual and group decision making will be examined and compared. Included will be the concepts of participation in decision making and groupthink. Finally, several strategies for improving the quality and acceptability of decisions will be presented. Throughout, emphasis will focus on major lessons for management that will ease the responsibily of decision making.

For our purposes here, we define *decision making* as a process of selecting among available alternatives (Shull, Delbecq, and Cummings, 1970; MacCrimmon and Taylor, 1976). We look at how individuals and groups identify problem areas, consider potential solutions to problems, and select the most suitable solution (or solutions) in light of the particular situation.

If we take a close look at the decision-making process, it is possible to identify three relatively distinct stages (Simon, 1960). The first stage is represented by *intelligence activities*. Individuals and groups attempt to recognize and understand the nature of the problem, as well as search for the possible causes and potential solutions. In the second phase of the process, *design activities,* alternative courses of action are formulated and assessed in light of known constraints. The third phase is represented by *choice activities,* where the actual choice among possible alternative decisions is made. It is believed that the quality of the resulting decision is largely influenced by the thoroughness of the intelligence and design phases, combined with the rationality and goals of the decision makers themselves.

Models of the Decision-Making Process

Contrary to popular belief, it is no easy task to outline or diagram the general decision-making process. We actually know very little about how individuals and groups make decisions (Gerwin and Tuggle, 1978; Lang, Dittrich, and White, 1978). Even so, three different models of the decision-making process have been suggested. Each differs on the assumptions the model makes about the person or persons making the decision. These three models are: (1) the econologic model; (2) the bounded rationality model; and (3) the implicit favorite model. Each model is useful for understanding the nature of decision processes in organizations.

Econologic Model

The *econologic model* represents the earliest attempt to model decision processes (Miller and Starr, 1967; Von Neumann and Morgenstern, 1953). Briefly, this model rests on two assumptions: 1) it assumes people are economically rational; and 2) it assumes that people attempt to maximize outcomes in an orderly and sequential process. *Economic rationality,* a basic concept in many models of decision making, exists when people attempt to maximize objectively measured advantage, such as money or units of goods produced. That is, it is assumed that people will select the decision or course of action that has the greatest advantage or payoff from among the many alternatives. It is also assumed that they go about this search in a planned, orderly, and logical fashion. This model has also been referred to as the *economic man* model by Simon (1957).

A basic econologic decision model is shown in Exhibit 11–1. As can be seen, the model suggests the following orderly steps in the decision process based on the above two assumptions about the nature of people:

1. Discover the symptoms of the problem or difficulty.
2. Determine the goal to be achieved or define the problem to be solved.
3. Develop a criterion against which alternative solutions can be evaluated.
4. Identify all alternative courses of action.
5. Consider the consequences of each alternative, as well as the likelihood of occurrence of each.
6. Choose the best alternative by comparing the consequences of each alternative (step 5) with the decision criterion (step 3).
7. Act to implement the decision.

The simplicity of the econologic model is disarming. In fact, the model rests on two rather questionable foundations (Simon, 1957). First, the model portrays individuals or groups as having the capability to gather all necessary information for a decision. It assumes having complete information which is rarely achieved. As a result, rationality itself is rarely achieved. As Simon (1957, p. 81) notes:

> (1) Rationality requires a complete knowledge and anticipation of the consequences that will follow on each choice. In fact, knowledge of consequences is always fragmentary. (2) Since these consequences lie in the future, imagination must supply the lack of experienced feeling in attaching value to them. But values can be only imperfectly anticipated. (3) Rationality requires a choice among all possible alternative behaviors. In actual behavior, only a very few of all these possible alternatives ever come to mind.

In addition, the econologic model is based on the assumption that people can process the tremendous amount of information generated for one decision. It assumes that people can: 1) mentally store the information in some stable form; 2) manipulate the information in a series of complex calculations designed to provide expected values; and 3) rank all the consequences in a consistent fashion for purposes of identifying the preferred alternative. Unfortunately, a large body of research has shown that the human mind is simply incapable of executing such transactions at the level and magnitude that would be required for complex decisions. While the econologic model represents a useful representation of how decisions *should* be made (a *prescriptive* model), it seems to fall somewhat short concerning how decisions are actually made.

Exhibit 11–1 An econologic model of decision making (Behling and Schriesheim, 1976, p. 19)

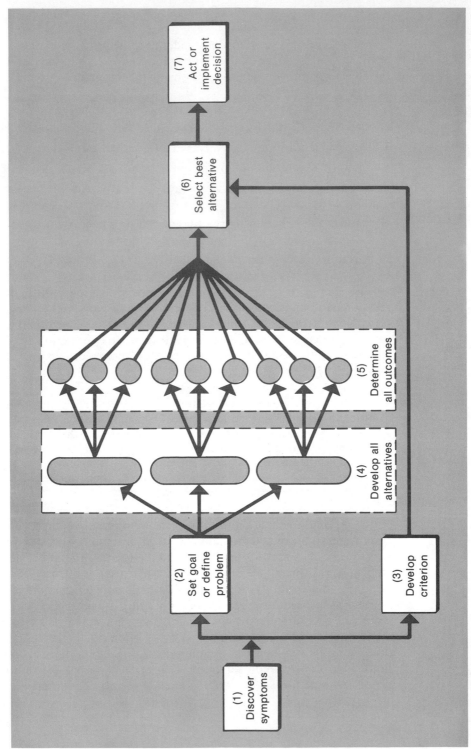

Source: Orlando Behling and Chester Schriesheim, *Organizational Behavior: Theory, Research and Application.* Copyright © 1976 by Allyn and Bacon, Inc., Boston. Reprinted with permission.

Bounded Rationality Model

An alternative model, one not bound by the above assumptions, has been presented by Simon (1957; March and Simon, 1958; Cyert and March, 1963). This is the *bounded rationality model,* also known as the *administrative man* model.

As the name implies, this model does not assume individual rationality in the decision process. Instead, it is assumed that people, while they may seek the best solution, usually settle for much less because the decisions they confront typically demand greater information processing capabilities than they possess. They seek a kind of bounded (or limited) rationality in decisions.

The concept of bounded rationality attempts to describe decision processes in terms of three mechanisms:

Sequential attention to alternative solutions People examine possible solutions to a problem sequentially. Instead of identifying all possible solutions and selecting the best (as suggested in the econologic model), the various alternatives are identified and evaluated one at a time. If the first solution fails to work it is discarded and another solution is considered. When an acceptable (though not necessarily the best) solution is found, search behavior is discontinued.

Use of heuristics A heuristic is a rule which guides the search for alternatives into areas that have a high probability for yielding satisfactory solutions. For instance, some companies continually hire MBAs from certain schools because in the past such graduates have performed well for the company. According to the bounded rationality model, decision makers use heuristics to reduce large problems to manageable propositions so decisions can be made rapidly. They look for obvious solutions or previous solutions that worked in similar situations.

Satisficing Whereas the econologic model focused on the decision maker as an optimizer, this model sees him or her as a satisficer. As described by March and Simon (1958, p. 140–141):

An alternative is *optimal* if: (1) there exists a set of criteria that permits all alternatives to be compared, and (2) the alternative in question is preferred, by these criteria, to all other alternatives. An alternative is *satisfactory* if: (1) there exists a set of criteria that describes minimally satisfactory alternatives, and (2) the alternative in question meets or exceeds all these criteria. . . . Finding that optimal alternative is a radically different problem from finding a satisfactory alternative . . . . To optimize requires processes several orders of magnitude more complex than those required to satisfice.

Based on these three assumptions about decision makers, it is possible to outline the decision process as seen from the standpoint of the bounded rationality model. As shown in Exhibit 11–2, the model consists of eight steps:

1. Set the goal to be pursued or define the problem to be solved.
2. Establish an appropriate level of aspiration or criterion level (that is, when do you know that a solution is sufficiently positive to be acceptable even if it is not perfect?).
3. Employ heuristics to narrow problem space to a *single* promising alternative.
4. If no feasible alternative is identified (a) lower the aspiration level, and (b) begin the search for a new alternative solution (repeat steps 2 and 3).
5. After identifying a feasible alternative (a), evaluate it to determine its acceptability (b).
6. If the identified alternative is unacceptable, initiate search for a new alternative solution (repeat steps 3–5).

Exhibit 11–2   A bounded rationality model of decision making (Behling and Schriesheim, 1976, p. 29).

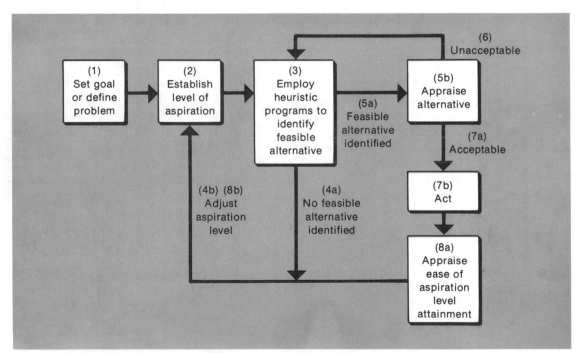

7. If the identified alternative is acceptable (a), implement the solution (b).

8. Following implementation, evaluate the ease with which goal was (or was not) attained (a), and raise or lower level of aspiration accordingly on future decisions of this type.

As can be seen, this decision process is quite different from the econologic model. In it we do not seek the best solution; instead, we look for a solution that is acceptable. The search behavior is sequential in nature (evaluating one or two solutions at once). Finally, in contrast to the prescriptive econologic model, it is claimed that the bounded rationality model is *descriptive;* that is, it describes how decision makers actually arrive at the identification of solutions to organizational problems.

Implicit Favorite Model

A third model deals primarily with nonprogrammed decisions. *Nonprogrammed* decisions are decisions that are novel or unstructured, like seeking one's first job. *Programmed* decisions, in contrast, are more routine or repetitious in nature, like the procedures for admitting new MBAs to graduate school. See Box 11-1 for further details.

The *implicit favorite model,* developed by Soelberg (1967), rests strongly on the theory of cognitive dissonance described in Chapter 13. It emerged when Soelberg observed the job choice processes of graduating business students and noted that, in many cases, the students identified implicit favorites very early in the recruiting and choice process. However, they continued their search for additional alternatives and quickly selected the best alternative candidate, known as the confirmation candidate. Next, the students atempted to develop decision rules that demonstrated unequivocally that the implicit favorite was superior to the alternative confirmation candidate. This was done through perceptual distortion of information about the two alternatives and through weighting systems designed to highlight the positive features of the implicit favorite. Finally, after a decision rule was derived that clearly favored the implicit favorite, the decision was announced. Ironically, Soelberg noted that the implicit favorite was typically superior to the confirmation candidate on only one or two dimensions. Even so, the decision makers generally characterized their decision rules as being multidimensional in nature.

The process is shown in Exhibit 11–3. As noted, the entire process is designed to justify to the individual through the guise of scientific rigor, a nonprogrammed decision that has already been made in an intuitive fashion. By doing so, the individual becomes convinced that he or she is acting in a rational fashion and making a logical, reasoned decision on an important topic.

Box 11–1 Gresham's Law of Planning and Management Decisions

Simon distinguishes between programmed (routine, repetitive) decisions and nonprogrammed (unique, one-shot) decisions.* While programmed decisions are typically handled through structured or bureaucratic techniques (standard operating procedures), nonprogrammed decisions must be made by managers using available information and their own judgement. As is often the case with managers, however, decisions are made under the pressures of time.

An important principle of organization design that relates to managerial decision making is Gresham's Law of Planning. This law states that there is a general tendency for programmed activities to overshadow nonprogrammed activities. Hence, if a manager has a series of decisions to make, those that are more routine and repetitive will tend to be made before those that are unique and require consider-

able thought. This happens presumably because managers attempt to clear their desks so they can get down to the really serious decisions. Unfortunately, the desks very often never get cleared.

The implications of Gresham's law for managerial decision making is clear. Provisions must be made for insuring that nonprogrammed decisions are completed in a timely fashion. This can be done, according to Simon, by creating specific organizational responsibilities and organizational units to assume the responsibility. Staff units in major organizations are examples. Where this is not possible, time management programs may be useful in training managers to better allocate their limited time. However it is accomplished, it is important for managers see that important nonprogrammed decisions receive the attention they deserve.

*Source: H. A. Simon. *The New Science of Management Decisions*. Revised edition. Englewood Cliffs, N. J.: Prentice-Hall, 1977.

Individual and Group Decision Making

The three models of the decision-making process can be used both for examining how individuals make decisions and how groups (and organizations) make decisions. The basic processes remain the same. For instance, using the econologic model, we observe that both individuals and groups often identify money as an objective to be sought. Both individuals and groups in some cases attempt to identify all possible outcomes before selecting one. Similarly, both individuals and groups are often observed engaging in satisficing behavior or using heuristics in the decision process. Finally, both individuals and groups develop implicit favorites and attempt to justify those favorites after the fact by procedures that appear to others to be rationalization. In fact, recent research indicates that people often stick with a prior decision even when they know it to be wrong (Staw and Ross, 1978).

Exhibit 11–3 An implicit favorite model of decision making
(Behling and Schriesheim, 1976, p. 32).

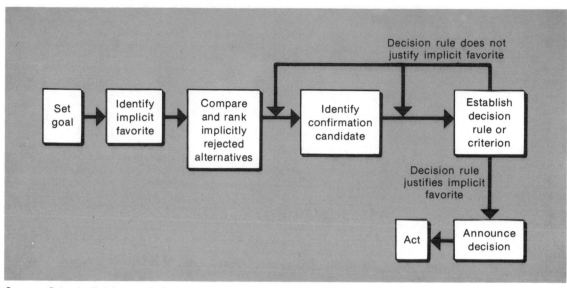

Source: Orlando Behling and Chester Schreisheim, *Organizational Behavior: Theory, Research and Application.* Copyright © 1976 by Allyn and Bacon, Inc., Boston. Reprinted with permission

Advantages and Disadvantages of Group Decision Making

However, while the general models of the decision process are similar, there are differences in the *outcomes* of individual and group decision making. There are situations where group decision making can be an asset and other times when it can be a liability. Several of these assets and liabilities are summarized in Exhibit 11–4 (Maier, 1967).

In summarizing what we know about the impact of groups on the decision-making process—particularly in *non*programmed decisions—Harrison (1975) concluded the following:

- In *establishing objectives,* groups are typically superior to individuals in that they possess greater cumulative knowledge to bring to bear on problems.

- In *identifying alternatives,* individual efforts are important to insure that different and perhaps unique solutions are identified from various functional areas that later can be considered by the group.

- In *evaluating alternatives,* group judgement is often superior to individual judgment because it brings into play a wider range of viewpoints.

Exhibit 11–4 Assets and liabilities of group decision making

Assets	Liabilities
• Groups can accumulate more knowledge and facts.	• Groups often work more slowly than individuals.
• Groups have a broader perspective and consider more alternative solutions.	• Group decisions involve considerable compromise which may lead to less than optimal decisions.
• Individuals who participate in decisions are more satisfied with the decision and are more likely to support it.	• Groups are often dominated by one individual or a small clique, thereby negating many of the virtues of group processes.
• Group decision processes serve an important communication function, as well as a useful political function.	• Overreliance on group decision making can inhibit management's ability to act quickly and decisively when necessary.

- In *choosing an alternative,* involving group members often leads to greater acceptance of the final outcome.
- In *implementing the choice,* individual responsibility is generally superior to group responsibility. Regardless of whether decisions are made individually or collectively, individuals perform better in carrying out the decision than groups do.

Hence, it is not possible to conclude that one form of decision making (individual or group) is superior. Rather, individual situations as well as the individuals involved must be considered before choosing a decision technique. The major variables affecting our choice are considered in the next section as we examine the details of participation in decision making.

Participation in Decision Making

A central issue facing managers in carrying out their responsibilities is the extent to which they should allow their subordinates in the work group to participate in decisions affecting their jobs. Participation represents one method of decentralizing authority and influence throughout an organization. It is believed that this action will in many cases lead to improved decision quality, increased commitment of members to decision outcomes, and increased satisfaction resulting from involvement. These results are often associated with effective organizations.

The subject of participation in decision making is closely related to the nature of supervisory style to be discussed in Chapter 12. While the nature of this relationship is reserved until later, it is possible to summarize much of what we know about what happens when managers allow greater group input into decisions and what the effects of this input are. (See Locke and Schweiger, 1979, for an in-depth review of the subject.)

Based on a series of studies on managerial decision-making behavior, Vroom and Yetton (1973) found evidence in support of the following propositions:

- Managers tend to be *more* participative when the quality of the decision is important.

- Managers tend to be *more* participative when subordinate acceptance of the decision is critical for its effective implementation.

- Managers tend to be *more* participative when they trust their subordinates to focus on organizational rather than personal goals and when conflict among subordinates is minimal.

- Managers tend to be *less* participative when they have all the necessary information to make a high quality decision.

- Managers tend to be *less* participative when the immediate problem is well-structured or where there is a common solution that has been applied in similar situations in the past.

- Managers tend to be *less* participative when time is limited and immediate action is required.

In addition to understanding the circumstances in which managers are more or less likely to allow group input in the decision process, it is also useful to know the effects of participation on subsequent behavior and attitudes. Available research indicates that members of supportive, participative groups experience greater satisfaction and cooperation on task activities and have less turnover, absenteeism, and job-related stress (Filley, House, and Kerr, 1976; Steers and Porter, 1974; Vroom, 1964). Job performance is sometimes higher in participative groups, although the results are certainly not consistent (Dubin, 1965).

One question about the effects of participation remains to be asked; that is, why does participation seem to work in many instances? A partial answer to this question has been offered by Ebert and Mitchell (1975). First, they suggest that participation clarifies organizational contingencies so employees understand more fully what is expected of them. Second, it increases the likelihood that employees will work for rewards and outcomes they value. Third, it increases the effects of social influence on behavior. Finally, it increases the amount of control employees have over their own behavior. Participation in decision making can represent a useful vehicle for facilitating both organizational goal attainment and personal need satisfaction in many cases. We shall return to this topic for examples of the role of management in participation in Chapter 12.

Groupthink

Increased attention has been focused on a phenomenon known as *groupthink*. This phenomenon, first discussed by Janis (1971), refers to a mode of thinking in a group in which the seeking of concurrence among members becomes so dominant that it overrides any realistic appraisal of alternative courses of action. The concept emerged from Janis' studies of high level policy decisions by government leaders. These decisions included decisions by the U. S. Government about Vietnam, the Bay of Pigs, and Korea. By analyzing the decision process leading up to each action, Janis fround numerous indications pointing to the development of group norms that improved morale at the expense of critical thinking. One of the most common norms was the tendency to remain loyal to the group by continuing to adhere to policies and decisions to which the group was already committed, even when the decisions proved to be in error (Staw and Ross, 1978).

Symptoms of groupthink. In studies of both government and business leaders, Janis identified eight primary symptoms of groupthink. These include:

Illusion of invulnerability Group members often reassure themselves about obvious dangers and become overly optimistic and willing to take extraordinary risks. Members often fail to respond to clear warning signals. For instance, in the disastrous Bay of Pigs invasion, the U.S. operated on the false assumption that they could keep the fact that the U.S. invaded Cuba secret. Even after news of the plan leaked out, government leaders remained convinced of their ability to keep it a secret.

Rationalization Victims of groupthink also tend to collectively construct rationalizations aimed at discounting warning signs and other types of negative feedback that could lead to a reconsideration of the course of action if taken seriously. When General Motors introduced its down-sized X-cars (e.g., Citation) in 1979, a leading competitor commented that it was "no big thing" since his company already had such cars.

Illusion of morality Group members often believe in the inherent morality of the group and, as a result, ignore the ethical or moral consequences of their decisions. Leading tobacco companies continue to run advertisements about free choice in decision making about smoking, completely ignoring all the medical evidence on the hazards involved.

Stereotyping the enemy In-group members often stereotype leaders of opposition groups in so harsh a fashion as to rule out any need to negotiate with them on differences of opinion.

Pressure to conform In-group members often place tremendous pressure to conform on members who temporarily express doubts about the group's shared illusions or who raise questions over the validity of the arguments supporting the decisions of the group.

Self-censorship Moreover, group members often censor themselves; they avoid deviating from what appears to be a group consensus. They often minimize to themselves the seriousness of their doubts.

Illusion of unanimity Partly because of self-censorship by group members, a feeling of unanimity is often created in which members assume everyone holds the same opinion. It is assumed that individuals who remain silent are in agreement with the spoken opinions of others.

Mindguards Victims of groupthink often appoint themselves as mindguards to protect the leader and other members of the group from adverse information that may cause conflict in the group over the correctness of a course of action. This can be done by telling the dissident that he or she is being disruptive or nonsupportive, or by simply insulating the dissident from other group members. For many years, FBI agents in the Washington headquarters who expressed views contrary to the party line found themselves transferred to less desirable locations.

Outcomes of groupthink. Groupthink can have several deleterious consequences on the quality of decision making. First, groups often limit their search for possible solutions to problems to one or two alternatives and avoid a comprehensive analysis of all possible alternatives. Second, groups often fail to reexamine their chosen course of action after new information or events suggest a change in course. Third, group members spend little time considering whether there are any nonobvious advantages to alternative courses of action that indicate alternatives may be preferable to the chosen course of action. Fourth, groups often make little or no attempt to seek out the advice of experts either inside or outside their own organization. Fifth, members show positive interest in facts that support their preferred decision alternative and either ignore or show negative interest in facts that fail to support it. Finally, groups often ignore any consideration of possible roadblocks to their chosen decision and, as a result, fail to develop contingency plans for potential setbacks.

Overcoming groupthink. In view of the potentially serious consequences that can result from the emergence of a groupthink mentality in groups and organizations, questions are logically raised about what can be done to minimize its effects. Several strategies can be identified (Janis, 1971):

- Group leaders can encourage each member to be a critical evaluator of various proposals.

- When groups are given a problem to solve, leaders can refrain from stating their own position and instead encourage open inquiry and impartial probing of a wide range of alternatives.
- The organization can give the same problem to two different independent groups and compare the resulting solutions.
- At intervals before the group reaches a final decision, members can be required to take a respite and seek advice from other parts of the organization before returning to make a decision.
- Outside experts can be invited to group meetings and encouraged to challenge the views of group members.
- At every group meeting, one member could be appointed as a devil's advocate to challenge the testimony of those advocating the majority position.
- When considering the feasibility and effectiveness of various alternatives, divide the group into two sections for independent discussions and compare results.
- After deciding on a preliminary consensus on the first choice for a course of action, schedule a second-chance meeting during which members of the group express their residual doubts and rethink the entire issue prior to finalizing the decision and initiating action.

In other words, if groups are aware of the problems of groupthink, several specific, and relatively simple, steps can be taken to minimize the likelihood of falling victim to this problem. As is usually the case, recognizing the problem represents half the battle in the effort to make more effective decisions in organizational settings.

Strategies for Improving Decision Making

Up to now, we have considered decision processes in a general way. We have noted different attempts to model the process, differences between individual and group decisions, participation in decision making, and the concept of groupthink. Throughout, various limitations to the process were noted. Several of these limitations are shown in Box 11-2. Based on this discussion, we are now in a position to consider ways of improving the decision-making process beyond those discussed above.

Much of what we have said so far has focused on what is called the *interacting* (or discussion) group. That is, the pertinent people in a decision meet together and discuss the problem and possible solutions. This is certainly the most common form of group decision making. Two alternative

---

Box 11–2: Roadblocks to Effective Decision Making

In the early stages of any decision process, there is the likelihood that a variety of perceptual biases may interfere with problem analysis or the identification of possible solutions. Elbing has identified several roadblocks that can impede managerial effectiveness in arriving at the most suitable decision:*

- The tendency to evaluate before one investigates. Early evaluation precludes inquiry into a fuller understanding of the situation.

- The tendency to equate new and old experiences. This often causes managers to look for what is similar rather than what is unique in a new problem.

- The tendency to use available solutions, rather than consider new or innovative ones.

- The tendency to deal with problems at face value, rather than ask questions that might illuminate reasons behind the more obvious aspects of the problem.

- The tendency to direct decisions toward a single goal. Most problems involve multiple goals that must be handled simultaneously.

- The tendency to confuse symptoms and problems.

- The tendency to overlook unsolvable problems and instead concentrate on simpler concerns.

- The tendency to respond automatically or to act before thinking.

Problems like these often cause managers to act in haste before the facts are known and often before the actual underlying problem is recognized or understood. A knowledge of these roadblocks will assist managers in their attempts to analyze problem situations and make reasoned decisions.

*Source: A. Elbing. *Behavioral Decisions in Organizations*. Second edition. Glenview, Ill.: Scott, Foresman, 1978.

---

methods of group decision making have been suggested that attempt to structure the decision environment in a way that reduces or overcomes many of the problems inherent in the interacting technique. These are the nominal group technique and the delphi technique.

Nominal Group Technique

This technique, typically referred to as NGT, consists of four phases in the group decision-making process (Delbecq, Van de Ven, and Gustafson, 1975). First, individual members meet as a group (like the interacting technique) but begin by sitting silently and independently generating their ideas on a problem in writing. Next, this silent period is followed by a round-robin procedure in which each member of the group presents an idea to the group.

No discussion of the idea is allowed at this time. The ideas are summarized and recorded (perhaps on a blackboard). Third, after all individuals have had an opportunity to present their ideas, each idea is discussed for the purpose of clarification and evaluation. Finally, the group members conclude the meeting by silently and independently recording their rank-ordering of the various ideas or solutions to the problem. The final decision is determined by the pooled outcome of the members' votes on the issue.

This technique allows the group to meet formally but does not allow them to engage in much discussion or interpersonal communication; hence, the term *nominal* group technique. A chief advantage of this procedure, then, is to insure that everyone independently considers the problem without influence from other group members. As we found, this influence represents one of the chief obstacles to open-minded discussion and decision making.

Delphi Technique

In contrast to NGT, the delphi technique never allows participants to a decision to meet face to face. Instead, a problem is identified and members are asked to provide potential solutions through a series of carefully designed questionnaires. Members complete these questionnaires independently. Results of the first questionnaire are then circulated to other group members (who are still physically separated). After viewing the feedback, members are again asked their opinions (to see if the opinions of others on the first questionnaire caused them to change their own opinion). This process may continue through several iterations until group members' opinions begin to show a consensus on a prospective solution to the problem. (Dalkey, 1969).

The two methods, NGT and delphi, are compared in Exhibit 11–5. Many structural differences can be noted, as well as differences in process. Whether one technique is superior, however, remains an open question. From a managerial perspective, perhaps the best advice is to consider the nature of the problem and the people involved in the problem before selecting one method over the other.

These two techniques of decision making, the nominal group technique and the delphi technique, are illustrative of the fact that poor decisions do not have to be tolerated in organizations. Clearly, there are a variety of problems in decision-making processes. Individuals and groups have various biases and personal goals that may lead to suboptimal decisions. Groups often censor themselves as noted earlier in the discussion on groupthink. Even so, techniques such as NGT and delphi aim to minimize many of these problems by insulating individual participants to a decision from the undue influences of others. In this way, greater individual freedom of expression is experienced and the group receives far less filtered or slanted information with which to make its decision. Thus, while not perfect, these techniques

Exhibit 11–5 Comparison of qualitative differences between three decision processes based upon evaluations of leaders and group participants

Dimension	Interacting groups	Nominal groups	Delphi technique
Overall methodology	Unstructured face-to-face group meeting High flexibility High variability in behavior of groups	Structured face-to-face group meeting Low flexibility Low variability in behavior of groups	Structured series of questionnaires and feedback reports Low-variability respondent behavior
Role orientation of groups	Socioemotional Group maintenance focus	Balanced focus on social maintenance and task role	Task-instrumental focus
Relative quantity of ideas	Low; focused "rut" effect,	Higher; independent writing and hitchhiking round robin	High; isolated writing ideas
Search behavior	Reactive search Short problem focus Task-avoidance tendency New social knowledge	Proactive search Extended problem focus High task centeredness New social and task knowledge	Proactive search Controlled problem focus High task centeredness New task knowledge
Normative behavior	Conformity pressures inherent in face-to-face discussions	Tolerance for non-conformity through independent search and choice activity	Freedom not to conform through isolated anonymity
Equality of participation	Member dominance in search, evaluation, and choice phases	Member equality in search and choice phases	Respondent equality in pooling of independent judgments
Method of problem solving	Person-centered Smoothing over and withdrawal	Problem-centered Confrontation and problem solving	Problem-centered Majority rule of pooled independent judgments
Closure decision process	High lack of closure Low felt accomplishment	Low lack of closure High felt accomplishment	Low lack of closure Medium felt accomplishment
Resources utilized	Low administrative time and cost High participant time and cost	Medium administrative time, cost, preparation High participant time and cost	High administrative time, cost, preparation
Time to obtain group ideas	1½ hours	1½ hours	Five calendar months

Source: From A. H. Van de Ven and A. L. Delbecq, Academy of Management Journal, 1974, 17, 618. Reprinted by permission.

can be of assistance to managers in need of mechanisms to improve both the quality and timeliness of decisions in work organizations.

Summary

The topic of decision making was discussed here as it relates to organizational behavior. It was noted that the decision process normally consists of three stages: intelligence activities, design activities, and choice activities.

Moreover, three rather distinct models of how decisions are made were reviewed, including the econologic, bounded rationality, and implicit favorite models. It was noted that each rests on different assumptions about the nature of people and that each predicts different outcomes. New concepts introduced here included the notion of heuristics, satisficing, and programmed vs. nonprogrammed decisions.

Following this, the relative merits of individual as opposed to group decision making were discussed and it was noted that each approach carries with it certain advantages and disadvantages. The notion of participation in decision making was also discussed.

In addition, the concept of groupthink was introduced as a major potential flaw in many group efforts to make decisions. The symptoms of groupthink were reviewed, as were its outcomes. Finally, ways of overcoming groupthink were reviewed.

At the close of the chapter, two relatively new techniques for improving group decisions were reviewed, nominal group technique and delphi technique, and compared to the more commonplace interacting method. Advantages and drawbacks of each were discussed.

Key Words

decision making	implicit favorite model
econologic model	Gresham's law of planning
economic rationality	groupthink
economic man	mindguards
bounded rationality model	nominal group technique
administrative man	delphi technique
satisficing	

Questions for Discussion

1. What are the three stages in decision making?
2. What is the basic premise of the econologic model of decision making? How does it differ from the bounded rationality model?

3. What are the primary advantages of the bounded rationality model of decision making?

4. What is satisficing?

5. How does the implicit favorite model of decision making work?

6. Describe Gresham's law of planning and management decision making.

7. Discuss the advantages and disadvantages of group decision making compared to individual decision making.

8. When is it more appropriate for a manager to be more participative in the making of decisions? Less participative?

9. Describe the phenomenon of groupthink. What are its symptoms? What are its outcomes?

10. How can we overcome groupthink?

11. Compare and contrast the nominal group technique and the delphi technique of decision making.

12. What are some of the more prominent roadblocks to effective managerial decision making?

chapter 12

Leadership and Group Effectiveness

The final aspect of group processes to be discussed is leadership. As we shall see, leadership represents an essential aspect of successful management. In fact, it can be argued that without leadership, successful management is not possible. Because of this, we will examine the topic in some detail.

This chapter is organized into several sections. First, we will consider the basic nature of leadership, including definitions, functions, and patterns. Next, we will examine various leader attributes and behaviors. Following this, three contemporary models of leadership will be discussed. Finally, several problems and prospects associated with leadership will be reviewed. These include constraints on leadership, substitutes for leadership, and ways of improving leadership effectiveness.

Importance of Topic for Managers

The concept of leadership in work organizations is important for a variety of reasons. They include the following:

1. Leaders can have a substantial impact on group performance. It is therefore important for managers to understand how the process occurs, as well as what inhibits its occurrence.

2. Several contemporary models of leadership exist and each suggests certain mechanisms by which leader effectiveness can be improved. A knowledge of these models can help managers better understand what they can do to increase their own leadership skills.

3. In addition to a knowledge of when and how leadership works, it is also useful to know several constraints on leadership—situations where leadership may not work. In such cases, it is useful to know several substitutes for leadership.

4. It is also useful to understand the various reasons why leadership is important to organizations. As we shall see presently, leadership serves several functions in work organizations.

Nature of Leadership

Leadership Defined

In general, at least three approaches to a definition of leadership can be identified. Leadership has been viewed as an attribute of position (e.g., president of a corporation), a characteristic of a person ("she's a natural born leader"), and a category of behavior. From the standpoint of understanding the nature of people at work, perhaps the most useful approach is to consider leadership as a category of behavior; as something one person does to influence others.

Following this approach we will employ Katz and Kahn's (1978, p. 528) definition of *leadership* as "the influential increment over and above mechanical compliance with routine directives of the organization." Leadership occurs when one person can influence others to do something of their own volition instead of doing something because it is required or because they fear the consequences of noncompliance. It is this voluntary aspect of leadership that sets it apart from other influence processes like power or authority.

Functions of Leadership

One may well ask why leadership is necessary in contemporary work organizations. Most organizations are highly structured, have relatively clear lines of authority, stated objectives, and momentum to carry them forward. Why, then, do we need leadership?

Four reasons, or functions of leadership, have been advanced by Katz and Kahn (1978):

Incompleteness of organization design   Because it is not possible to design the perfect organization and account for every member's activities at all times, something must insure that human behavior is coordinated and directed toward task accomplishment. This something is leadership.

Changing environmental conditions   Leadership helps maintain the stability of an organization in a turbulent environment by allowing for rapid adjustment and adaptation to changing environmental conditions.

Internal dynamics of organizations   Leadership can assist in the internal coordination of diverse organizational units, particularly during periods of growth and change. It can act as a buffer between conflicting parties.

Nature of human membership in organizations   Organizations consist of individuals who pursue various needs and who place difficult demands on an organization. Leadership can play a major role in maintaining a stable workforce by facilitating personal need satisfaction and personal goal attainment.

Leadership plays a crucial role in organizational dynamics. It fills in many of the voids left by conventional organization design, allows for greater organizational flexibility and responsiveness to environmental changes, provides a way to coordinate the efforts of diverse groups within the organization, and facilitates organizational membership and personal need satisfaction. In short, it is the quality of managerial leadership that differentiates effective from ineffective organizations.

Leadership Patterns

In addition to a knowledge of the reasons leadership is necessary in work organizations, it is useful to understand basic differences in leadership patterns. How does the leadership role of top administrators and executives differ from the role of middle-level or lower-level managers and supervisors? This question has been answered by Katz and Kahn (1978) who suggest three different leadership patterns for three levels in the managerial hierarchy (see Exhibit 12-1).

The three basic types of leadership patterns are:

- *Origination*, or the introduction of structural change or policy formulation.

- *Interpolation,* or piecing out the incompleteness of existing formal structure and attempting to supplement or develop structure.

- *Administration,* or the use of the structure that is formally provided to keep the organization in motion and in effective operation.

The exercise of each of these three patterns of leadership calls for different cognitive styles, as well as different affective (or attitudinal) characteris-

Exhibit 12–1   Leadership patterns, their locus in the organization, and their skill requirements (Katz and Kahn, 1978, p. 539)

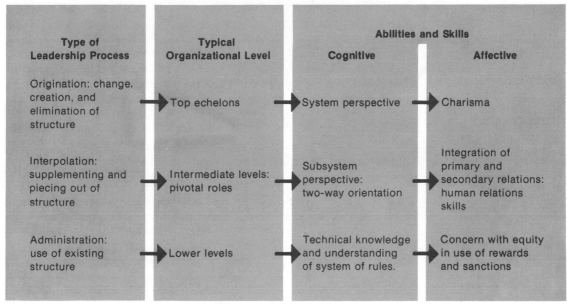

tics. Top level executives concerned with origination need a system-wide perspective when making policy decisions. They are primarily concerned with goal formulation, strategic decision making, and buffering the effects of the external environment. Their concern must be almost exclusively "macro." The type of leadership they exhibit, as seen by the rank and file employee, is charismatic; they symbolize the organization and what it stands for.

Middle-level managers, on the other hand, are largely concerned with sub-system decisions. They are responsible for a department or a division and the people and activities contained therein. Their focus is shorter term than executives, although typically not concerned with day-to-day activities on the shop floor. Humans relations skills are clearly necessary here, but many interpersonal relations are impersonal and distant.

Finally, the lower echelon managers or supervisors are primarily responsible for day-to-day operations in a single work group. Their technical knowledge of the operations is important, as is their understanding of rules and policies made higher up in the hierarchy. These managers deal continually with the rewards and punishments that accrue to individual employees and are responsible for insuring that the work is accomplished in a timely fashion.

Although this distinction between three levels of managers is somewhat arbitrary (and exceptions no doubt exist), the framework is useful in emphasizing the fact that all leaders do not do the same thing. Some leaders are almost the embodiment of the organization while others are simply people trying to work through people to get their group's performance goals accomplished. This distinction should be kept in mind as we examine the various contemporary models of leadership effectiveness.

Leader Attributes and Behavior

Leader-Follower Transactions

It has been suggested that a solid understanding of the basic nature of leadership processes can be achieved by examining the *transactions* between leaders and followers (Hollander, 1978). Following this approach, effective leaders are those individuals who ''give'' something and who ''get'' something in return. In other words, we view leadership as a social exchange process.

This social exchange, or transactional, approach involves three basic variables: the leader, the followers, and the situation (see Exhibit 12–2). Leaders bring to a situation their personality, motivations, competencies and legitimacy, while followers bring their personalities, motivations, competencies, and expectations. Each situation has its own unique characteristics, including the availability of resources and nature of the tasks, social structure and rules, physical setting, and history. Where these three areas overlap, there exists what Hollander calls the *locus of leadership*, or that realm where leader and followers are bound together in a relationship within a situation. Leader and followers each contribute something to the relationship and each receives something in return. Neither is self-sufficient.

In view of this model, it becomes clear that in a systematic study of leadership processes in organizations we must examine all three variables: leaders, followers, and situations. Much of the current work on the topic attempts to do this. In order to properly review this material, we will first review some of the basics; specifically, research that has been done on leader attributes and leader behavior. Following this, we will review several contemporary theories of leadership that attempt to account for the variables involved in the locus of leadership.

Leader Attributes

The earliest work on leadership, dating from the times of the ancient Greeks, assumed that great leaders were born to their greatness. This approach, later

Exhibit 12–2   Three elements involved in leadership—the situation, the leader, and the followers—with some of their relevant attributes. The crosshatched area represents their intersection, which is the *locus of leadership*. The arrows indicate the social exchange which occurs between the leader and the followers. (Hollander, 1978, p. 8)

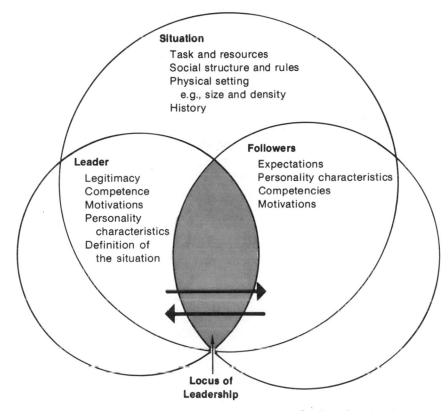

termed *the great man* theory of leadership, took an historical approach and concluded that in most instances leaders were destined for positions of influence as a result of birth. This position was popular throughout the 19th century. In 1869, for example, Sir Francis Galton wrote a widely read book entitled *Hereditary Genius* in which he argued that leadership qualities were based on heredity. As we entered the 20th century, belief in inherited leader traits diminished, although belief in the importance of the traits themselves remained popular.

Much of the research in the first half of the 20th century focused on attempts to identify the traits great leaders throughout history had in common. This research ignored the situation and followers, and assumed that a person who exhibited these traits would be successful in leading any group. This research on leader attributes was brought together in a classic work by Ralph Stogdill in 1948.

Stogdill reviewed 124 empirical studies of leader attributes covering 27 recurring characteristics. Among these studies, he discovered some consistent findings. Successful leaders generally exhibited the following characteristics: 1) *height*; leaders tended to be taller than the average height of the followers; 2) *intelligence*; leaders tended to be rated higher on IQ tests, verbal fluency, overall knowledge, originality, and insight; and 3) *initiative*; leaders tended to show high levels of energy, ambition, and persistence. Interestingly, no clear relationship was found between leader success and characteristics like emotional stability or extraversion.

In addition to the above attributes, Stogdill's review pointed to a conclusion that led the way to subsequent, more comprehensive research. He found that in many instances, the profile of a successful leader varied with the situation! Different groups and different group activities required different types of leaders. As a result of this finding, emphasis shifted in the early 1950s toward looking into how leaders interacted with groups under various conditions and how these interactions succeeded or failed. Much of this research focused on leader behavior as the basic unit of analysis.

Leader Behavior

Based on this early work, studies were begun in the 1950s to discover just what leaders did that caused others to follow. Two major research projects are noteworthy. The first was conducted at the University of Michigan under the direction of Rensis Likert and his associates, and the second was done at Ohio State University under the direction of Ralph Stogdill, Edwin Fleishman, John Hemphill, and others.

The results of both projects led to similar conclusions. Essentially, effective leader behavior was found to be multidimensional, implying that effective leaders exhibit different behavior in different situations. This multidimensional nature of leadership is clearly shown in the case of the Ohio State Leadership Studies, which began by identifying nine leader behaviors (see Exhibit 12–3). However, when these nine behaviors were examined more closely (through a procedure known as factor analysis), two relatively distinct behaviors emerged. These were:

- *Consideration*—including leader behaviors like helping subordinates, doing favors for them, looking out for their welfare, explaining things, and being friendly and available.

Exhibit 12–3 Nine dimensions of leader behavior (Shartle, 1956, p. 116)

Initiation—originates, facilitates, or resists new ideas and new practices.

Membership—mixes with the group, stresses informal interaction between self and members, or interchanges personal services with members.

Representation—defends the group against attack, advances the interests of the group, and acts in behalf of the group.

Integration—subordinates individual behavior, encourages pleasant group atmosphere, reduces conflicts between members, or promotes individual adjustment to the group.

Organization—defines or structures own work, the work of other members, or the relationships among members in the performance of their work.

Domination—restricts the behavior of individuals or the group in action, decision making, or expression of opinion.

Communication—provides information to members, seeks information from them, facilitates exchange of information, or shows awareness of affairs pertaining to the group.

Recognition—engages in behavior which expresses approval or disapproval of the behavior of group members.

Production—sets levels of effort or achievement or prods members for greater effort or achievement.

Source: Carroll L. Shartle, *Executive Performance and Leadership,* p. 116. Reprinted by permission of Prentice-Hall, Inc., Englewood Cliffs, New Jersey.

- *Initiating Structure*—including behaviors like getting subordinates to follow rules and procedures, maintaining performance standards, and making the leader and subordinate roles explicit.

Consideration has also been called by other terms, including socio-emotional activities and employee-centeredness, while initiating structure has also been called instrumental activities, production centeredness, and task-orientation.

In summarizing decades of research on consideration (socio-emotional orientation) and initiating structure (task-orientation), House and Baetz (1979, p. 359) concluded:

1. Task-oriented leadership is necessary for effective performance in all working groups.
2. Acceptance of task-oriented leadership requires that the task-oriented leader allows others to respond by giving feedback, making objections, and questioning the task-oriented leader.
3. Socio-emotionally oriented leadership is required in addition to task-oriented leadership when groups are not engaged in satisfying or ego-involving tasks.

4. Groups requiring both kinds of leadership behavior will be more effective when these leader behaviors are performed by one person rather than divided among two or more persons.

5. When the leadership roles are differentiated, groups will be most effective if those assuming the roles are mutually supportive and least effective when they are in conflict with each other.

6. When formally appointed leaders fail to perform the leader behaviors for group success, an informal leader will emerge and will perform the necessary leader behaviors, provided success is desired by the group members.

In other words, research on leader behaviors has demonstrated rather conclusively that *both* consideration and initiating structure are necessary (albeit at different times) for group effectiveness. If the manager cannot provide leadership in both these areas, the group will often find someone else who can and will develop a surrogate leader to accommodate group needs.

The major drawback to these findings was the limited attention given to situations. While leader-follower interactions were rather carefully considered, little effort was made to examine how situational differences might influence leader effectiveness. This important variable was considered, however, in subsequent leadership research commencing in the 1960s, and culminating with the publication of several contemporary theories of leadership. In contrast to earlier work on leader attributes or behaviors, these theories attempt to explain leadership dynamics within the context of the larger work situation.

While several of these theories can be identified, major attention has focused on three. These are: 1) Fiedler's Contingency Theory; 2) Vroom and Yetton's Normative Theory; and 3) House's Path-Goal Theory. We now turn our attention to an examination of each of these models.

Contingency Theory of Leadership

Certainly one of the most popular contemporary theories is the *contingency theory*, advanced by Fred Fiedler (1967). Fiedler's model argues that group performance or effectiveness is dependent upon the interaction of leadership style and the favorableness of the situation. We shall examine each of these two factors separately and then put them together to consider how the theory works.

Situational Factors

Fiedler's model suggests that the situation in which the leader operates can be characterized by three factors.

Leader-member relations—This refers to the degree of confidence, trust, and respect followers have for the leader. Is the leader accepted? Do leader and members get along well or poorly?

Task structure—How clear are the task-goals and role assignments? Does everyone know precisely what to do (e.g., an assemblyline worker) or is the job more ambiguous (e.g., a research scientist)? The more task structure, the easier it is for the leader to tell group members what to do.

Position power—Finally, who holds the power, the leader or the group? The more rewards and punishments leaders can use, the more influence they will have.

By dichotomizing these three dimensions it is possible to develop a list of eight leadership situations (called octants). These eight situations are shown in Exhibit 12–4. In other words, leader-member relations can be either good (octants 1-4) or bad (octants 5-8), task structure can be high (octants 1, 2, 5, 6) or low (octants 3, 4, 7, and 8), and leader position power can be strong (octants 1, 3, 5, and 7) or weak (octants 2, 4, 6, 8). These octants contain all possible permutations or combinations of the three major situational variables.

Once the situation is defined according to these three major situational variables, questions are raised about which octant or situation represents the most desirable from the leader's situation. Fiedler proposes that *situation favorableness* is highest (from the leader's viewpoint) in octant 1 and lowest in octant 8. A leader is in a far superior position when leader-member relations are good, when task structure is high, and when position power is strong (as in octant 1) than when the reverse is true (as in octant 8).

Exhibit 12–4 Fiedler's classification of situation favorableness

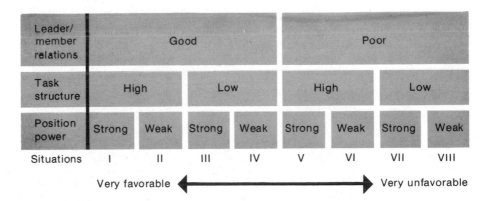

Source: F. Fiedler, *A Theory of Leadership Effectiveness.* New York: McGraw-Hill, 1967.

Leadership Orientation

The second key variable in this model is the leader. Fiedler suggests that two basic leader-orientations are useful, following earlier leadership research. These are relationship-oriented (a more lenient, people-oriented style) and task-oriented (where task accomplishment is a prominent concern).

These orientations are measured by the *least preferred co-worker* (LPC) scale. On this scale, the individual is asked to think of the person with whom he or she has worked who was least preferred as a co-worker, and to describe this person on several bi-polar scales (efficient–inefficient, tense–relaxed, frustrating–helpful). A favorable description of the least preferred co-worker (high LPC) suggests a relationship-oriented leader, while an unfavorable description (low LPC) suggests a task-oriented leader.

Finally, combining leader LPC scores with situation favorableness, Fiedler examined the statistical correlations between LPC scores and group performance for each situational octant. As shown in Exhibit 12–5, negative correlations emerged at both ends of the situational continuum, while positive correlations were found toward the middle of the continuum. It was concluded that high LPC (relationship-oriented) leaders were more effective in facilitating group performance when the situation was moderately favorable or moderately unfavorable (that is, toward the middle of the continuum). Here, the leader is moderately liked, has some power, and supervises jobs that are somewhat vague. A leader with high interpersonal skills can exert the necessary leadership in such situations to help clarify task ambiguity through discussions and participation.

On the other hand, when the situation is *either* highly unfavorable *or* highly favorable (that is, at either end of the continuum), Fiedler argues that a low LPC (task-oriented) leader is more effective in securing group performance (if not satisfaction). The logic of this argument is simple. If the situation is highly favorable (everyone gets along, the task is clear, and the leader has power), all that is needed is for someone to take charge and show direction (that is, a low LPC person). Similarly, if the situation is highly unfavorable (exhibiting the opposite characteristics), the leader is placed in a battle of wills with the group members. In this situation, Fiedler contends that a strong leader (low LPC) is necessary to counterbalance the power of the group and show direction in an ambiguous task environment. Since leader–member relations are already poor, being task-oriented in this situation does not run the risk of making the leader unpopular.

Research on the Contingency Model

During the past 25 years, Fiedler and his colleagues have carried out a series of studies on a variety of military and civilian samples. In general, consistent

Exhibit 12–5   Results from contingency theory research
(Fiedler and Chemers, 1974).

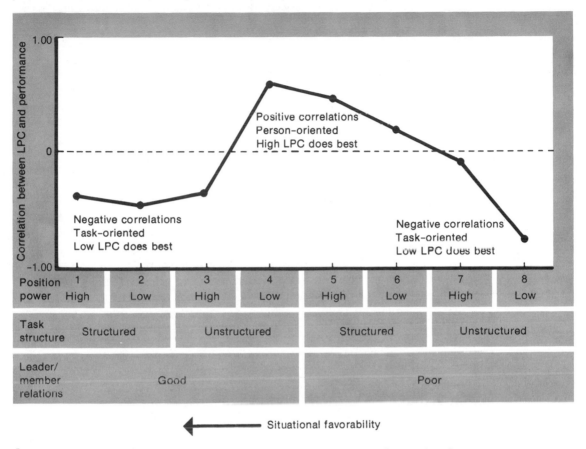

Source: Leadership by Fred E. Fiedler, p. 13. © 1971 General Learning Corporation. Reprinted by permission of Silver Burdett Company.

support has emerged for his hypothesis concerning the relationship between LPC and group performance for the various degrees of situation favorableness (see Exhibit 12–5). The results suggest that the model has some utility in helping managers understand leadership processes in organizations.

Even so, the model has also been criticized on several grounds (House and Baetz, 1979). In particular, critics have questioned the use of the LPC scale to measure leader orientation. It is argued that better and more reliable measures of leader orientation are needed. In addition, critics have suggested that Fiedler's classification system of situations is overly simplistic and that additional factors should be included in a more comprehensive description of situation favorableness or unfavorableness. While these criticisms may be justified, however, they do not diminish the utility of the basic model as a tool to help understand some of the variables that combine to influence leadership effectiveness in work organizations.

Normative Theory of Leadership

It is difficult to determine whether this next model is really a model of leadership or a model of decision making. In essence, the model focuses on the extent to which subordinates should be allowed to participate in decisions affecting their jobs. In addition, however, the model also considers how managers should behave in decision-making situations. Suffice it to say that the Vroom and Yetton (1973) model is a theory of how leaders should approach group-related decisions.

In contrast to Fiedler, Vroom and Yetton present a *normative theory of leadership*. It attempts to prescribe correct leader behavior by way of participation. The model rests on several assumptions. It assumes (like Fiedler) that there is no single leadership style that is appropriate for all situations. Instead, leaders must develop a repertoire of responses ranging from autocratic to consultative and employ the style that is most appropriate to the decision situation. Unlike Fiedler, however, this model assumes that leaders must adapt their style to the situation. Fiedler, in contrast, argues that situations should be altered to match what he considers a fairly unalterable leader style.

Decision Effectiveness: Quality, Acceptance, and Timeliness

Fiedler uses group performance as the evaluation criterion to determine whether or not a leader is effective, and Vroom and Yetton use decision effectiveness. Decision effectiveness is characterized by three factors:

Decision quality   This refers to the extent to which decisions under consideration are important for facilitating group performance. For instance, a decision on where to place a water cooler in a plant requires low decision quality since it has little impact on group performance, while a decision on performance goals or on work assignments requires high decision quality.

Decision acceptance   This refers to how important it is for group members to accept decisions in order for them to be successfully implemented. Some decisions do not require group acceptance to be successfully executed (what color to paint the walls in an office), while others must be accepted by group members in order to be successful (setting sales performance objectives).

Time required to reach decision   Finally, decisions must be made in a timely fashion. Some decisions can be made slowly (choice of color when repainting an office), while others may require immediate action (whether or not to invest in a particular stock).

This model suggests that a decision is effective to the extent that it satisfactorily accommodates these three factors. These criteria are in stark contrast to Fiedler, so much so that it has been suggested by some that two models really examine different areas of leader behavior. While Vroom and Yetton consider how leaders make decisions, Fiedler examines how they achieve a satisfactory performance level in light of power considerations and co-worker relations.

Leader Decision-Making Styles

Based on the above definition of what constitutes an effective decision, the normative model next turns its attention to how leaders might behave relative to group members in order to arrive at these decisions. The model suggests that leaders have five decision-making styles open to them and that these five styles can be placed on a continuum from highly autocratic to highly participative. The five styles are shown in Exhibit 12–6. As shown, *A* represents a more autocratic style of leadership, *C* represents a more consultative, and *G* represents a highly consultative, or group, decision.

Again, it should be remembered that one manager should be able to exhibit all five different styles, depending upon particular situations. The manager may be called upon to make an *A I* decision at one time, followed by a *G II* decision a short time later. Needless to say, this presumes the manager has the intuition to recognize the appropriate style for a given problem and the flexibility to implement that style.

Decision Rules of the
Normative Model

In order to select the appropriate decision strategy, Vroom and Yetton have suggested seven decision rules aimed at simplifying the process. By following these rules, it is argued that managers can easily discover the quickest and most acceptable way to arrive at a quality decision. The first three rules focus on assuring decision quality, while the remaining four deal with decision acceptance.

The leader information rule   If the quality of the decision is important and if the leader does not have sufficient information or expertise to solve the problem alone, *A I* style is eliminated from the feasible set, since using it risks a low quality decision.

Exhibit 12–6 Five decision styles (after Vroom and Yetton, 1973)

Decision Style	Definition
A I	Manager makes the decision alone.
A II	Manager asks for information from subordinates but makes the decision alone. Subordinates may or may not be informed about what the problem is.
C I	Manager shares the problems with subordinates and asks for information and evaluations. Meetings take place as dyads, not as a group, and the manager then goes off alone and makes the decision.
C II	Manager and subordinates meet as a group to discuss the problem, but the manager makes the decision.
G II	Manager and subordinates meet as a group to discuss the problem, and the group makes the decision.

Note: A = autocratic; *C* = consultation; *G* = group

Source: Reprinted from *Leadership and Decision-Making* by Victor H. Vroom and Phillip H. Yetton by permission of the University of Pittsburgh Press. © 1973 by the University of Pittsburgh Press.

The goal congruence rule   If the quality of the decision is important but the leader is not sure subordinates share the goals of the organization (that is, cannot be trusted to base their problem-solving efforts on these goals), then *G II* style is eliminated from the feasible set. In this case, the leader cannot afford to allow the group to make the decision alone.

The unstructured problem rule   If the quality of the decision is important but the leader lacks sufficient information and expertise *and* the problem is unstructured (that is, it is not clear exactly what information is needed or where it is located), then *A I, A II,* and *C I* are eliminated from the feasible set. In such cases, the ambiguity of the problem requires interaction between leader and subordinates to clarify the problem and possible solution.

The acceptance rule   If acceptance of the decision by subordinates is crucial to effective implementation, and if it is not certain that an autocratic decision made by the leader would receive acceptance, then *A I* and *A II* are eliminated from the feasible set.

The conflict role   If acceptance of the decision is crucial, an autocratic decision is not certain to be accepted, *and* subordinates are likely to be in conflict or disagreement over the appropriate solution, then *A I, A II,* and *C I* are eliminated from the feasible set. Conflict is probably best resolved here by allowing greater participation and interchange among group members.

The fairness rule   If the quality of the decision is *un*important but acceptance is critical and not certain to result from an autocratic decision, then *A I, A II, C I,* and *C II* are eliminated from the feasible set. Since group acceptance is the only relevant consideration, a *G II* style is likely to generate acceptance more effectively than less participative styles.

The acceptance priority rule   If acceptance is critical and not certain to result from an autocratic decision, and if subordinates are motivated to pursue organizational goals, then methods that provide equal partnership in the decision-making process will lead to greater acceptance without risking decision quality. Because of this, *A I, A II, C I,* and *C II* are eliminated from the feasible set.

Although these rules may seem imposing, careful reflection leads one to conclude that they are potentially of considerable heuristic value to managers. The rules serve to narrow the options open to managers and point to the most appropriate strategy; the right participation for a decision.

Vroom and Yetton (1973) have attempted to simplify the selection of an appropriate decision strategy for leaders and suggest a decision tree. This decision tree allows leaders to select a strategy by answering a series of questions relating to the decision rules. As shown in Exhibit 12–7, a manager begins at the left side of the flow chart with question A: does the problem possess a quality requirement? If the answer is yes, the manager then proceeds to question B. If the answer is no, the manager proceeds to question D, since questions B and C are irrelevant if quality is not a requirement. By working across the flow chart, the manager finally arrives at the strategies most appropriate for the particular situation. If a manager has a choice of acceptable strategies, it is recommended that the most autocratic within the feasible set be used, since this will save time without reducing decision-quality or acceptance. An example of this process is shown in Box 12–1.

Research on the Normative Model

Because the normative model has only been recently introduced, verification research is still light. Vroom and Yetton (1973) carried out a study involving 181 actual decision situations, using the model to predict which decisions would be effective; that is, those in which the leader actually chose an acceptable style according to the model. Results were in support of the model. In the situations where leader behavior agreed with the feasible set of acceptable styles, 68% were judged to have been successful. On the other hand, in those cases where leader behavior violated the feasible set of acceptable styles, only 22% were judged successful.

In other research, an attempt was made to consider how managers actually make decisions, instead of how they should make them according to the model. Several interesting results emerged. It was found that managers as a

Exhibit 12–7 Decision tree for determining appropriate decision strategy (Vroom and Yetton, 1973)

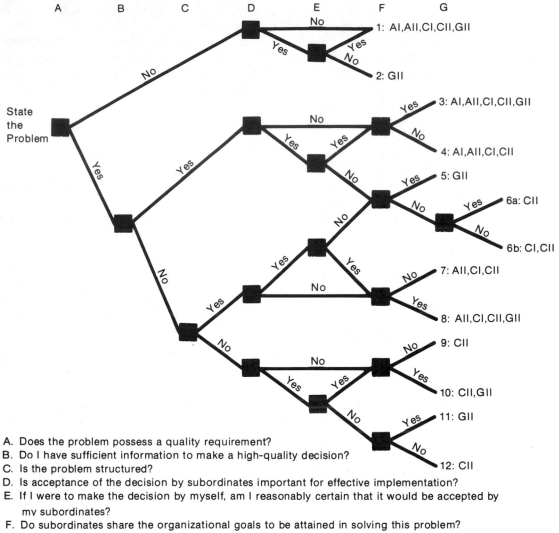

A. Does the problem possess a quality requirement?
B. Do I have sufficient information to make a high-quality decision?
C. Is the problem structured?
D. Is acceptance of the decision by subordinates important for effective implementation?
E. If I were to make the decision by myself, am I reasonably certain that it would be accepted by my subordinates?
F. Do subordinates share the organizational goals to be attained in solving this problem?
G. Is conflict among subordinates likely in preferred solutions?

Source: Reprinted from *Leadership and Decision-Making* by Victor H. Vroom and Phillip H. Yetton by permission of the University of Pittsburgh Press. © 1973 by the University of Pittsburgh Press.

group tend to be more participative than is required by the model (Vroom and Jago, 1974). It has also been found that females tend to be more participative managers than males (Steers, 1977b). Finally, business school stu-

Box 12–1 Example of Vroom and Yetton Model

The following example demonstrates how the Vroom and Yetton model works. Consider yourself the supervisor of a group of 12 engineers. Their formal training and work experience are very similar, permitting you to use them interchangeably on projects. Today you were informed that an overseas affiliate had requested that four of your engineers be sent abroad for a period of from six to eight months to assist the affiliate. Your supervisor concurred with this request, even though such overseas assignments are not generally regarded as desirable by company engineers. Your job is to select the four persons who will go. All of your people are capable of handling the assignment and there is no reason why any particular engineer should be retained over others.

How would you make this decision? Would you make it yourself, consult with the group, or let the group itself make the decision? Using Vroom and Yetton's framework (Exhibit 12–7), we would proceed as follows:

Question A (Quality requirement?): No

Question D (Subordinate acceptance critical?): Yes

Question E (Is acceptance likely without participation?): No

Feasible set of decision procedures: *G II* (only)

Source: Adapted from Victor H. Vroom and Phillip H. Yetton, *Leadership and Decision-Making*. Copyright © 1973, by the University of Pittsburgh Press.

dents were found to be more participative than actual managers (Jago and Vroom, 1978) and high level managers were more participative than were low level managers (Jago, 1977).

In summary, the normative model of leadership and decision making appears to represent a significant breakthrough both in terms of understanding how managers make decisions and in terms of training future managers to reach high quality decisions in a timely fashion. Now we turn to a third theory of leadership that will further expand our knowledge of leadership processes in work organizations.

Path-Goal Theory of Leadership

In the third leadership model to be discussed, we approach the topic from quite a different perspective than the first two. Fiedler's (1967) contingency theory focuses on how leaders can best facilitate performance by manipulating power, leader-member relations, and task clarity or structuring. Vroom and Yetton's (1973) normative model focuses on how much participation leaders should allow subordinates in decisions relating to their jobs. In contrast, the *path-goal* theory emphasizes how leaders can facilitate task performance by showing subordinates how performance can be instrumental in achieving desired rewards. The path-goal model builds heavily on the expectancy/valence theory of work motivation.

The path-goal model of leadership can be traced to the early work of Martin Evans (1970) and was developed more fully by Robert House (1971; House and Dessler, 1974; House and Baetz, 1979). Essentially, the model focuses on how managers influence subordinate perceptions of work, personal goals, and various paths to goal attainment. The basic emphasis is on the extent to which managerial behavior is motivating or satisfying for subordinates. It is argued that managerial behavior is motivating or satisfying to the extent that it increases goal attainment by subordinates and clarifies the paths to these goals.

Path-Goal Leader Behaviors

In the original model, Evans (1970, 1974) noted that leadership served two important functions. The first he called *path clarification*. This dealt with the extent to which the leader helps subordinates understand the kind of behavior necessary to accomplish goals and obtain valued rewards. The second function of the leader was to increase the *number of rewards* available to subordinates by being supportive and paying attention to their welfare, status, and comfort.

In expanding on Evans' original formulation, House (1971) argued that a comprehensive theory of leadership must recognize at least four distinctive types of leader behavior. They are:

Directive leadership Provides specific guidance, standards, and schedules of work, as well as rules and regulations; lets subordinates know what is expected of them.

Supportive leadership Shows concern for the status, well-being, and personal needs of subordinates; focuses on developing satisfactory interpersonal relations among group members.

Achievement-oriented leadership Sets challenging goals, emphasizes improvement in performance, and establishes high expectations of subordinate's ability to meet higher standards of excellence.

Participative leadership Consults with subordinates, solicits suggestions and advice in decision making.

In contrast to Fiedler, House (1971) asserts that these four styles can be practiced by the same manager at varying times and in varying situations. Fiedler, it will be remembered, argues that managers have great difficulty changing styles. House's model is similar to that of Vroom and Yetton, however, in that the latter also argue for changing leader behaviors.

Basic Propositions of Path-Goal Theory

The path-goal theory of leadership rests on two primary propositions:

- Leader behavior will be acceptable and satisfying when subordinates perceive it as an immediate source of satisfaction or as instrumental in future satisfaction.
- Leader behavior will be motivating to the extent that it makes subordinate satisfaction contingent upon effective performance *and* to the extent that is complements the subordinate's work environment by providing necessary guidance, clarity of direction, and rewards for effective performance.

Leaders have at their disposal a variety of mechanisms to facilitate increased subordinate motivation. Among these mechanisms are: 1) recognize and arouse subordinates' needs for outcomes over which leaders have some control; 2) increase personal payoffs to subordinates for effective performance or goal attainment; 3) clarify the path to those payoffs, either through coaching or additional direction; 4) help subordinates clarify expectancies; 5) reduce obstacles or frustrations that inhibit goal attainment; and 6) increase opportunities for personal satisfaction for effective performance. Leaders and managers have several available strategies for facilitating goal attainment by integrating employees' personal goals with organizational goals. When these two sets of goals are congruent, conflict is reduced and employees can pursue what they desire most by simultaneously pursuing managerial directives.

Contingency Factors

Like the two previous theories, the path-goal theory represents a situational model. It holds that effective leadership is a function of the interaction between leader behaviors and situational or contingency variables. In particular, House (see also House and Mitchell, 1974) identifies two basic contingency factors. These are shown in Exhibit 12–8 along with the other two factors, subordinate characteristics and environmental factors, involved in the theory.

Subordinate characteristics. The personal characteristics of subordinates determine how they will react to leader behavior. Several personality characteristics have been found to be related to the way in which subordinates respond to influence attempts. The first of these is an individual's *authoritarianism*. High authoritarian subordinates tend to be less receptive to a participative style of leadership and more responsive to directive leadership (House and Baetz, 1979).

Exhibit 12–8 Summary of path-goal relationships (House and Mitchell, 1974)

Leader Behavior	and	Contingency Factors	Cause	Subordinate Attitudes and Behavior
Directive		Subordinate characteristics:		Job satisfaction:
		Authoritarianism	Personal	Job → Rewards
Supportive		Locus of control	perceptions	Acceptance of leader:
		Ability		Leader → Rewards
Achievement-oriented		Environmental factors:	Motivational	Motivational behavior:
		The task	stimuli	Effort → Performance
Participative		Formal authority system	Constraints	Performance → Rewards
		Primary work group	Rewards	

Source: R. J. House and T. R. Mitchell "Path-goal theory of leadership," *Journal of Contemporary Business,* 1974. 5.

In addition, it has been discovered that an individual's *locus of control* also affects responses. Individuals who have an internal locus of control (they believe rewards are contingent upon their own efforts) are generally more satisfied with a participative leadership style, while individuals who have an external locus of control (they believe rewards are beyond their own control) are generally more satisfied with a directive style (Runyon, 1973; Mitchell, Smyser, and Weed, 1974).

Finally, individuals' own *abilities* can influence how they respond to different leadership styles. Where individuals feel they have high levels of task-related abilities, we do not expect them to be receptive to a close or directive leadership style (House and Baetz, 1979). Instead, these individuals may prefer a more challenging achievement-oriented style.

Environmental factors. In addition to subordinate characteristics, the path-goal model suggests that at least three environmental factors moderate the impact of leader style on outcomes (see Exhibit 12–8). These factors are: 1) the nature of the *task* performed by subordinates; 2) the *formal authority system* of the organization; and 3) the *primary work group.*

These factors can influence an individual's response to leader behavior in a variety of ways. They may *motivate* individuals, such as when a person performs an intrinsically satisfying job. Or, they may *constrain* variability on the job, such as on an assemblyline where behavior is prescribed by technology. Finally, they may clarify and provide *rewards* for satisfactory performance. For instance, group members may give praise to individuals who did most to help the group achieve its performance objectives. As House and Dessler (1974, p. 40) point out, "when goals, and paths to desired goals, are apparent because of the routine nature of the task, clear group norms, or objective controls of the formal authority system, attempts by the leader to clarify paths and goals would be redundant and would be seen by subordinates as an imposition of unnecessarily close control."

Subordinate Attitudes and Behavior

Finally, what is the outcome of this interaction between leader behavior and contingency factors? According to the model, three possible outcomes exist. First, individual perceptions, which are influenced by subordinate characteristics, can lead an employee to determine that the job itself can indeed lead to the receipt of rewards; hence, *job satisfaction* may be increased. Personal perceptions can also lead employees to conclude that the leader does, in fact, control many of the desired rewards; hence, *leader acceptance* may be increased. Finally, the motivational stimuli, constraints, and potential rewards can serve to heighten *motivational behavior*. It can increase an employee's expectations that effort will lead to rewards. The model leads to very specific outcomes that are useful if not imperative in the pursuit of organizational effectiveness.

Research on the Path-Goal Model

To date, little substantive work has been done to test the basic tenets of the path-goal theory of leadership. The research that is available is often clouded by methodological problems brought on by the complicated nature of the theory itself.

Even so, the studies that are available lend some credence to the model (Downey, Sheridan, and Slocum, 1976; Dessler and Valenzi, 1977). These studies have suggested that the model is probably more complex than first thought and that additional variables, like conflict and structure, should be incorporated into future versions of the model.

Comparing the Three Leadership Models

We have now examined three quite different ways of approaching the study of leadership dynamics in groups and organizations. How are these models similar and different and what can be learned from a comparative analysis of them?

The distinctiveness of orientations of the three models can be seen in Exhibit 12–9. Fiedler's model is based on leader style (high vs. low LPC) and how this style interacts with group power and the nature of the task. Vroom and Yetton focus on decision making processes and the role of leaders in facilitating participation in decisions. Finally, House clearly rests his model on the motivational bases of organizational behavior.

Exhibit 12–9 A comparison of elements in three situational theories of leadership

Model	Leader Behavior	Contingency Factors	Outcome Criteria
Fiedler's LPC	Task–oriented (Low LPC) Relationship–oriented (High LPC)	Leader–member relations Task structure Leader position power	Leader effectiveness
Vroom and Yetton's Decision Making	Autocratic, Consultative Group style	Importance of decision quality Degree needed information is available to leader and followers Problem structure Follower's probable acceptance and motivation regarding decision Disagreement among followers about preferred solutions	Quality of decision Acceptance of decision by followers Time required to reach decision
House's Path-Goal	Directive Supportive Achievement–oriented Participative style	Subordinate characteristics and personal perceptions Environmental factors: task, authority system, primary work group	Follower satisfaction Acceptance of leader And effort to gain rewards

Source: Reprinted with permission of Macmillan Publishing Co., Inc. from *Leadership Dynamics* by Edwin P. Hollander. Copyright © 1978 by The Free Press, a division of Macmillan Publishing Co., Inc.

All three models use somewhat different outcome criteria for evaluating the extent to which influence attempts are successful. Fiedler emphasizes group performance, Vroom and Yetton focus on decision quality, acceptance, and timeliness, and House focuses on follower satisfaction, leader acceptance, and motivational force aimed at achieving desired rewards.

Finally, each model differs with respect to the contingency factors that are thought to be at work in determining successful influence attempts. These differences are summarized in Exhibit 12–9. What this exhibit shows is not that one theory is superior to the others, but rather, that each model focuses on a different aspect of the leadership process. Managers can learn much from each theory.

This accumulation of knowledge about leadership processes should help managers to better understand leadership in broad terms and to employ the model that best suits the particular situation or problem. That is, if a decision must be made dealing with some aspect of group behavior, Vroom and Yetton's normative model may be most suitable. On the other hand, if the problem is one of facilitating performance, the other two models may be of more use. In any case, a thorough knowledge of the models can improve a manager's ability to understand the options open and to make an informed choice about the way in which a problem or situation is approached.

Problems and Prospects About Leadership at Work

Up to this point, we have assumed that leaders were relatively free to act on their environment and that they behaved according to theory with few constraints. Obviously, this is not always the case. There are many factors which inhibit leader behavior. We now turn to a review of many of these problems in the leadership process, as well as what managers can do to minimize them.

Constraints on Leadership

An important part of knowing how leadership processes work is recognizing occasions when they may not work or when they may have a diminished impact on employee behavior. If we view leadership as a central process in facilitating group performance and effectiveness, then constraints on the process must be clearly recognized. At least six constraints on leadership effectiveness have been suggested (Steers, 1977c):

- Extent to which managerial decisions and behavior are preprogrammed due to precedent, structure, technological specificity, or the absence of familiarity with available alternative solutions.

- Traits and skills (particularly leadership skills) of the manager. Research has indicated, for instance, that effective leaders tend to exhibit specific personal attributes. Good leaders demonstrate expertise in their own area of endeavor (such as the foreman who can perform any departmental job). A lack of skills may preclude effective leader behavior to some extent.

- Inability of leaders to vary their behavior to suit the particular situation. Rigid patterns of behavior may be inappropriate for many situations requiring certain styles of leadership.

- Extent to which a leader controls rewards desired by subordinates, such as pay raises and promotions.

- Characteristics of the situation, such as how much power a leader has, the importance of a given decision or action, and the quality of interpersonal relations between leader and subordinate.

- Openness of the organization to variations in leader behavior (e.g., a participative leadership style may be discouraged or prohibited in a military organization).

These constraints to a large extent set the stage on which influence attempts transpire. The greater the skills and abilities of the leader or manager, the more easily constraints can be dealt with. To the extent these constraints are recognized and accounted for, the leader can use available latitude to best advantage in securing the support of subordinates for task accomplishment.

Substitutes for Leadership

Partially because of the modest support that contemporary leadership theories have received, and because of the recognition of constraints on leader behavior, recent attention on influence processes has taken note of what has been called *substitutes for leadership*. As argued by Kerr and Jermier (1978, p. 375):

> While disagreeing with one another in important respects, these theories and models (of leadership) share an implicit assumption that while the style of leadership likely to be effective may vary according to the situation, *some* leadership style will be effective *regardless* of the situation. It has been found, however, that certain individual, task, and organizational variables act as "substitutes for leadership," negating the hierarchical superior's ability to exert either positive or negative influence over subordinate attitudes and effectiveness.

In other words, there are factors in the environment that act as a structure of support for subordinates, and leader behavior is at times irrelevant to subordinate performance or satisfaction. A list of possible substitutes is outlined in Exhibit 12–10. This exhibit differentiates between relationship-oriented and task-oriented leader behavior, since this distinction is common in the literature on leadership. For each leader behavior, Kerr and Jermier (1978) identify which substitutes (of the subordinate, the task, or the organization) serve to neutralize which behavior.

Exhibit 12–10   Substitutes for leadership (Kerr and Jermier, 1978, p. 378)

| | Substitutes for Leadership | |
| | Will tend to neutralize | |
Characteristic	Relationship–Oriented, Supportive, People-Centered Leadership: Consideration, Support, and Interaction Facilitation	Task-Oriented, Instrumental, Job-Centered Leadership: Initiating Structure, Goal Emphasis, and Work Facilitation
of the subordinate		
1. Ability, experience, training, knowledge		X
2. Need for independence	X	X
3. "Professional" orientation	X	X
4. Indifference toward organizational rewards	X	X
of the task		
5. Unambiguous and routine		X
6. Methodologically invariant		X
7. Provides its own feedback concerning accomplishment		X
8. Intrinsically satisfying	X	
of the organization		
9. Formatization (explicit plans, goals, and areas of responsibility)		X
10. Inflexibility (rigid, unbending rules and procedures)		X
11. Highly-specified and active advisory and staff functions		X
12. Closely-knit, cohesive work groups	X	X
13. Organizational rewards not within the leader's control	X	X
14. Spatial distance between superior and subordinates	X	X

Source: Kerr, S. and Jermier, J. Substitutes for leadership: Their meaning and measurement. *Organizational Behavior and Human Performance,* 1978, 22.

The point here is that there are many ways managers—and subordinates—can get something done. Only one of these is through the exercise of leadership. Other ways include making use of the personal characteristics of individuals (ability or experience), structuring tasks, or relying on the structure of the organization itself. The existence of these substitutes adds a note of realism to our study of influence processes and cautions against the naive belief that leader behavior alone will have a great impact on subordinate performance.

Improving Leadership Effectiveness

Although leader behavior may not be a panacea for performance ills of organizations, there are many instances in which leaders can make a real difference. It is important to understand how managers can develop leadership talent so that such talents can be put to use in facilitating organizational effectiveness. Many techniques could be suggested here. However, for the sake of brevity, we shall mention only five general strategies for improving leadership effectiveness (Steers, 1977c). These are: 1) managerial selection and placement; 2) leadership training; 3) rewarding leader behavior; 4) rewarding subordinate behavior; and 5) organizational engineering. As we shall see, many of these suggestions have their roots in the leadership theories discussed above.

Managerial selection and placement. Improved leadership effectiveness can be facilitated by increasing the likelihood that those in command possess the necessary skills to influence their subordinates on task-related activities. Following Fiedler's model, for example, we might wish to select a task-oriented (low LPC) person to supervise a work group characterized by high task structuring, centralized power, and distant leader-member relations. On the other hand, a relationship-oriented (high LPC) leader may be more appropriate when the task structuring is less concrete, power is diffused, and leader-member relations are cordial but not overly warm. The notion of matching people to leadership roles contradicts the current practice in many organizations of promoting employees to supervisory positions based on seniority or even based on good job performance. Although good job performance may be a desirable trait for supervisors to possess, it does not by itself insure good supervisory skills.

Leadership training. Attempts can also be made to develop individuals already in leadership positions to their fullest potential as managers through a variety of training techniques (Bass and Vaughn, 1966; Goldstein, 1975, 1980). Training can take many forms, including general management skills programs, human relations training, problem-solving and decision-making programs, and a variety of specialized programs.

Rewarding leader behavior.   A third method of improving leadership effectiveness involves designing reward systems so desired leader behavior is amply rewarded. If pay and promotions are based on a manager's ability to elicit successful subordinate efforts on goal-directed activities, then managers will see effective leader behavior as instrumental in obtaining desired rewards. A performance-reward contingency should serve to make managers more aware of the role of leadership in task accomplishment, making them more likely to attempt to improve their capacity for leadership activity.

Rewarding subordinate behavior.   In addition, it is also possible to structure reward systems to stimulate rather than inhibit desired subordinate behavior. By giving managers greater discretion in rewarding subordinates, the probability that subordinates will follow managerial directives is increased since this behavior would be instrumental to their own personal goal attainment. House's path-goal theory is essentially based on this relationship: to the extent that subordinates see following a manager's directives as instrumental to the accomplishment of their own goals, they will be more likely to follow them.

Organizational engineering.   Finally, in some instances, it is more suitable to adapt a structural (as opposed to a behavioral) approach to improving leader effectiveness. Here, one attempts to modify either the manager's job or the way jobs are clustered (reporting procedures, lines of authority, decentralization) and allow the structure itself to facilitate task accomplishment. In other words, as Fiedler (1965, p. 115) describes it, organizations may wish to "engineer the job to fit the manager." This approach is particularly useful when a particular individual (e.g., an R & D scientist) is necessary to the organization yet does not possess the requisite interpersonal skills for leadership. In these cases, the job can be engineered around the individual so many necessary leadership roles are fulfilled by other means.

Summary

Clearly one of the most popular and important topics in organizational behavior is leadership. This concept is also one of the least understood and most controversial. Despite several decades of serious attention, there is little agreement over what is meant by leadership or how it is brought about.

In this chapter, we considered this controversy, beginning with a discussion on the nature of leadership. The functions of leadership were examined, along with variations in leadership patterns. In addition, leader attributes and behaviors were discussed using the concept of leader-member transactions.

Next, three divergent theories of leadership were presented, along with their empirical support and their managerial implications. Finally, on a more general level, consideration was given to various constraints on leader behavior and to possible substitutes for leadership. This was followed by an examination of various techniques managers can use to improve leader effectiveness on the job.

Key Words

leadership
locus of leadership
consideration
initiating structure
contingency theory
situation favorableness

least preferred co-worker
normative theory
path-goal theory
path clarification
substitutes for leadership

Questions for Discussion

1. What do we mean by the term leadership? How does it differ from the term manager?

2. What functions do leaders serve?

3. Describe the leader-follower transactional process. What role is played in this process by the locus of leadership?

4. What are some rather generalizable leader traits?

5. What major conclusion can be drawn from the research on consideration and initiating structure?

6. What is the basic thesis of Fiedler's contingency theory of leadership? How does it differ from the other two theories of leadership discussed in this chapter? Compare and contrast.

7. What is meant by the least preferred co-worker?

8. Why is Vroom and Yetton's model called the normative theory of leadership? What is really new about this model?

9. Discuss the decision rules of the normative model.

10. What different implications for management follow from the three models of leadership? Similar implications for management?

11. Describe several constraints on leader behavior.

12. What is meant by substitutes for leadership?

13. How can managers improve their leadership effectiveness?

part four

Individuals and Groups at Work

chapter 13

Work-Related Attitudes and Behavior

One of the most widely discussed aspects of organizational life is work attitudes. We continually hear references to how satisfied—or dissatisfied—employees are on the job and most managers have their own pet theories on how to improve satisfaction. However, while the importance of work attitudes has been recognized for many years, it is only recently that we have begun serious study of the actual determinants of attitudes in organizational settings and their consequences for organizational well-being. In this chapter, we will examine the role of work attitudes in organizational behavior.

Importance of Topic for Managers

An understanding of attitudes, attitude formation, and attitude change is important for several reasons:

1. Attitudes can be found in every aspect of work life. We have attitudes about most things that happen to us, as well as about most people we

meet. In view of this universal characteristic of attitudes, an understanding of their nature is essential for managers.

2. Attitudes influence behavior. Much of how we behave at work is governed by how we feel about things. Therefore, an awareness of attitudes can assist managers in understanding human behavior at work. Changes in employee behavior can be expected to the extent that managers can change employee attitudes.

3. Bad attitudes on the job cost money. Poor job attitudes can be reflected in subsequent poor performance, turnover, and absenteeism, all of which result in direct costs to the organization.

In this chapter, we will examine several aspects of work attitudes. We begin with a discussion of the general nature of work attitudes, followed by a look at how attitudes are changed or not changed) over time. Next, job satisfaction, the most widely discussed job attitude, is examined. Finally, the influences and consequences of job satisfaction are reviewed.

Nature of Work Attitudes

Attitude Defined

Although there are various definitions for the concept of attitude (Allport, 1935), several common threads can be found. For our purposes here, an *attitude* may be defined as a predisposition to respond in a favorable or unfavorable way to objects or persons in one's environment. When we like or dislike something, we are, in effect, expressing our attitude toward the person or object. An attitude reflects our feelings toward other objects and people.

Three important assumptions underlie this definition of attitudes. First, an attitude is a hypothetical construct; that is, while the consequences of an attitude may be observed, the attitude itself cannot. We do not see attitudes; we only observe the resulting behavior. We only assume that attitudes exist inside of people.

Second, an attitude is a unidimensional variable. That is, an attitude towards a particular person or object ranges on a continuum from very favorable to very unfavorable. We like something or we dislike something. Something is pleasurable or unpleasurable. In all cases, the attitude can be measured along a continuum.

Third, attitudes are believed to be related to subsequent behavior. Our definition of attitude implies that people behave based on how they feel. For instance, research has consistently shown that low job dissatisfaction (a negative attitude) is moderately related to employee absenteeism and turnover (a behavior). As we shall see later, the relationship between attitudes and behavior is not a perfect one. Other factors like personality, external controls and conditions, etc., attenuate the impact of attitudes on behavior.

Components of Attitudes

One approach to gaining a clearer understanding of attitudes is to examine their various components. Most often, the attitude construct is divided into three components: 1) a *cognitive* component, dealing with beliefs and ideas a person has about a certain person or object; 2) an *affective* component dealing with a person's feelings toward the person or object; and 3) a *behavioral intention* component, dealing with the behavioral intentions a person has toward the person or object as a result of affective responses (Triandis, 1971).

More recently, Fishbein and Ajzen (1975) have argued that the notion of attitudes is easier to understand if we separate these three components and define attitudes simply as affective responses and treat the cognitive and behavioral intentions components as antecedents and outcomes of the attitude itself. This represents a more specific description of attitudes. While this model uses the same three basic components of earlier models, it clearly suggests how the components fit together and is helpful for measurement purposes.

This model, shown in Exhibit 13–1, has four basic components: beliefs (cognitions), attitudes (affects), behavioral intentions, and actual behavior. *Beliefs* represent the information a person holds about an object. For instance, an employee may describe his or her job as exciting or dull, dirty or clean, independent or dependent. These descriptions represent beliefs the individual has about the job. It is important to note that these beliefs may or may not be factual. An exciting job to one person may be dull to another. Regardless, beliefs are thought to be factual by the individual.

These beliefs, then, influence the *attitudes,* or affective responses, formed by employees. For instance, a person who believes his job is dull, dirty, and dependent may develop a negative attitude toward the job and be dissatisfied. This dissatisfaction with the job situation may, in turn, lead him to choose undesirable forms of behavior. For instance, he may decide to seek another job or to reduce his level of effort. This conscious decision to seek alternative employment is the *behavioral intention.* Finally, it is suggested by Fishbein and Ajzen (1975) that these behavioral intentions become translated into *actual job behavior* (such as high turnover, absenteeism, and lower performance).

This model clearly suggests that actual behavior is not determined by a person's attitudes. Instead, it is argued that behavioral intentions represent a primary influence on behavior. Thus, individuals dissatisfied with their jobs would only quit or reduce performance level after consciously deciding to do

Exhibit 13–1   A Conceptual Model of Job Attitudes (after Fishbein and Ajzen, 1975)

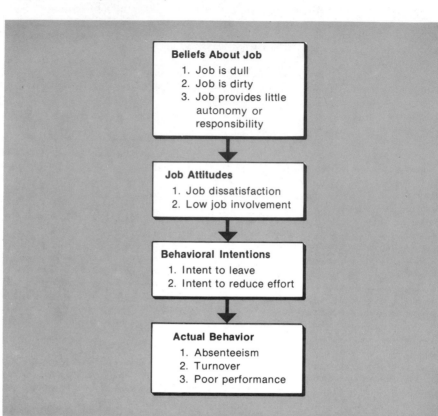

so (behavioral intention). This concept is closely related to Locke's (1968) theory of goal-setting.

Belief and Attitude Formation

It was suggested above that attitudes are influenced by the beliefs we hold about people, objects, and events. We are now in a position to take a closer look at how attitudes are formed. To do this, we will examine the notion of beliefs, the process by which beliefs are formed, and what types of factors influence beliefs and attitudes.

Beliefs.   A knowledge of the nature of beliefs is important in the study of attitudes for several reasons. To begin with, beliefs represent a major influence on attitudes. Changing beliefs can change attitudes. As noted by

Scheibe (1970, p. 26), "beliefs about future occurrences are often important determinants of those occurrences, for they influence the choices that are made, the chances that are taken, and the hypotheses that are adopted as working assumptions."

A *belief* may be defined as a perceived relationship between people, objects, and events. Beliefs are what individuals consider true about themselves and their environment. Beliefs differ from *values* in that beliefs are seen as having factual referents (Ebert and Mitchell, 1975). While beliefs may not actually be correct or accurate, the individual is convinced that they are true. Values, on the other hand, are closely-held normative standards that are chosen on the basis of personal preference among alternatives. Values carry with them the notion of "should." For example, one employee may place a high value on getting ahead in a company and may work overtime to demonstrate dedication. Another employee may place a high value on recreation and free time and may prefer a job that is less demanding. Neither value is right or wrong in the factual sense, although people may feel very strongly about the values they hold.

How are beliefs formed? This question is difficult to answer. Apparently, beliefs are formed as a result of at least four processes (Sarbin, Taft, and Bailey, 1960):

Induction   Beliefs are often based on past experiences. Over time, we observe events and draw inferences about an important issue. For instance, a manager may observe that one of his employees is constantly late for work, leaves early, and spends much of the day in idle gossip. Based on this observation, the manager may develop the belief that the employee is lazy or lacks dedication.

Construction   Beliefs may also be constructed by individuals based on available information about a particular issue. For example, since some women stay home with children or quit their jobs because of family responsibilities, we may develop the belief that many women really don't want to work. Such construction may or may not be based on actual fact.

Analogy   Oftentimes, beliefs are developed as a result of generalizing from similar situations, events, or objects. For instance, a manager who is transferred from one location to another may take with him his beliefs about line-staff relationships, union militancy, or status symbols, assuming that the new location will be identical to the previous one.

Authority   Finally, beliefs can be shaped by individuals in whom we have confidence. For instance, the first astronauts assumed that the engineers and scientists knew what they were doing when they built the spacecraft.

Thus, the beliefs we have are shaped by a variety of events, including our past experience, our trust in others, and our own imagination and inductive reasoning.

Influences on attitude formation. Perhaps the most important thing to note about the formation of attitudes is that they are *learned*. People learn from their environment and from prior experiences which beliefs and attitudes are acceptable.

At least four major influences on attitude learning can be identified. First, many of our general attitudes are learned as a result of *cultural influences*. For instance, our attitudes toward allowing lower-level employees to have a major voice in the operations and decisions of a business firm are generally culturally based (Rokeach, 1973). Second, attitudes are influenced by *group memberships*. The study by Haire (1955) cited earlier, demonstrated how managers and union members held different opinions of each other as a function of group membership. Third, the *family* can influence attitudes. Many attitudes toward members of other races and economic classes are formed here (Costello and Zalkind, 1963). Finally, *prior work experiences* influence our beliefs and attitudes about specific aspects of the job. For example, opinions of how much effort represents a fair day's work, what constitutes a fair day's pay and how employees should be treated can be influenced by prior experience.

Functions of Attitudes

Before examining the nature of work attitudes in any detail it is useful to know why attitudes are important for individuals. Katz (1960) has suggested that attitudes serve four important *functions* for individuals. (See Exhibit 13–2).

Exhibit 13–2 Functions of work attitudes

Functions	Definition	Example
Adjustment to work	To help individuals adjust to the necessity of work and to membership in an organization.	"This company is an okay place to work, since I have to have a job."
Ego-defense	To defend individuals from adverse truths about themselves.	"Why is management always acting so stuck up just because we workers don't have as much education or status?"
Value expression	To provide individuals with a vehicle for expressing values and opinions.	"What's good for General Motors is good for the country."
Knowledge	To help individuals explain and organize an otherwise chaotic world; to serve as a frame of reference.	"Workers should never trust management because, in the past, they have always tried to exploit us."

The adjustment function.   Attitudes often help people adjust to their work environment. They facilitate need satisfaction. We tend to develop favorable attitudes toward objects or people that are associated with providing positive rewards and benefits, and negative attitudes toward those that are associated with negative sanctions and penalties. In this way, our attitudes and experiences become relatively congruent. They provide a cognitive map of what is good and bad. This adjustment function can be seen in the attitudes employees have toward political parties. Blue-collar workers tend to have favorable attitudes toward more liberal politicians because they are seen as supportive of their causes, while executives and entrepreneurs tend to have favorable attitudes toward more conservative politicians for the same reason.

The adjustment function of attitudes is also clearly seen in Bem's (1972) *self perception theory.* According to this theory, people form attitudes as a result of their behaviors (instead of behaviors resulting from attitudes). These attitudes are formed as a defense or rationale for the behaviors. For example, an employee may say, ''I continue to work here (behavior) so I must enjoy the job (attitude).'' Here, the attitude helps the employee adjust to the work situation and, quite frankly, makes life easier for the employee.

Management often attempts to capitalize on this adjustment function as a vehicle for improving performance. In many instances, companies provide generous fringe benefits or recreational facilities in the hope of making workers become more committed to the organization (form more positive attitudes toward it) and desirous of performing at higher levels. However, as Katz (1960) notes, while these activities may serve to make the organization seem more attractive as a place to work, there is little reason to believe that performance itself will improve. The provision of universal rewards such as fringe benefits may make the work place more attractive, but the absence of a performance–reward contingency fails to create a motivating environment. While people may be motivated to join and remain with an organization, there is little reason to expect them to perform.

The ego-defensive function.   Attitudes can also protect individuals from acknowledging basic truths about themselves or the harsh realities of their external environments. In this way, they protect people's ego from internal or external threat. An employee who consistently has a negative attitude toward co-workers or who is persistently argumentative may, in fact, be acting out internal conflicts and thus may be relieving emotional tensions. This behavior does not, however, solve the problem of adjusting to the work situation.

Many attitudes in the work situation function in the defense of our self-image. For instance, at least part of the negative attitudes workers have of their supervisors can be traced to feelings of inferiority due to lack of education or lack of advancement. Similarly, the negative attitude managers often have toward workers can be explained in part by inner feelings of inferiority and an experienced need to feel superior. When people cannot admit to themselves that they have deep feelings of inferiority, these feelings can be easily projected onto a convenient group (managers, workers, minorities) to bolster their own attitude of superiority.

The value-expressive function. Although many attitudes prevent individuals from revealing their true nature to themselves or those around them, other attitudes provide a vehicle for positive expression of central values. They allow individuals to demonstrate to others the type of person they think they are, and thus establish or reinforce self-identity.

The value expressive function of attitudes can be readily seen in spontaneous political discussions at social gatherings. By clearly and forcefully stating political views, individuals are establishing a clear view of who they are and what they stand for. Similarly, many managers seem to be outspoken about ''my company, right or wrong'' in an effort to clearly portray their perceived role in the organization and society. Charlie Wilson, when he was president of General Motors, once stated that ''what is good for General Motors is good for the country.'' Such statements represent clear value-expressive attitudes in that they express strong feelings.

The knowledge function. Finally, attitudes help explain and organize an otherwise chaotic world. As Katz (1960) notes, people need standards or frames of reference for understanding and interpreting people and events around them. Attitudes help supply these standards. In Lippman's (1972) classic study of opinions and attitudes, it was pointed out that stereotypes (a form of attitude) provide order and clarity for a bewildering set of complexities that face individuals.

Attitude Change

One of the more difficult tasks of management is to create a work environment where employees have positive attitudes about their jobs and their place of work. If attitudes do, in fact, influence behavior, tten creating positive attitudes toward the job is of critical importance. Two aspects of attitude change are worthy of note. First, we should understand several prominent barriers to attitude change. Second, we should know a few widely recognized techniques used in attitude change.

Barriers to Attitude Change

There are at least two primary barriers that can inhibit the extent to which employees change their attitudes. These are: 1) insufficient justification and 2) prior commitments.

Insufficient justification. First, employees may see no reason to change their beliefs or attitudes. As Costello and Zalkind (1963, p. 275) note, just "because you [the manager] are dissatisfied with an individual's attitude is not a reason for him to want to change. His attitudes may be displeasing to you but satisfying to him." For example, a manager may want employees to trust management more and develop more favorable attitudes toward management. However, many employees may feel that in the past management had treated them unfairly and now see management's new overtures as somewhat hollow. In other words, such attitudes are serving an adjustment function. In the absence of a felt need to change, there is little reason to expect these employees to change their attitudes simply because management thinks it desirable.

Prior commitments. A second barrier to attitude change is prior commitments. This is the ego-defensive function of attitudes. As Staw (1976; Staw and Fox, 1977) found, people who feel personally responsible for a bad decision, one that led to negative consequences, tend to commit additional resources to the previously chosen course of action. Instead of admitting their mistake, individuals often cognitively distort the negative consequences into positive consequences in order to rationalize their previous decision, or to defend themselves psychologically against adverse consequences. One way to do this is to redouble the resolve to the previously chosen course of action, to "dig one's feet in," and selectively screen out, reject, or distort contradictory information. When we think about changing attitudes, it must be remembered that prior behavioral commitments made by others could represent significant barriers.

Mechanisms of Attitude Change

In view of these barriers, how then are attitudes changed? Several mechanisms for change can be identified: 1) providing new information; 2) fear arousal or reduction; 3) dissonance arousal; 4) position discrepancy; and 5) participation in decision making.

Providing new information. One of the most common methods of changing attitudes (and possibly subsequent behavior) is by providing individuals with new information which changes their set of beliefs. Fishbein (Fishbein and Ajzen, 1975), it will be recalled, argues that beliefs cause attitudes. Hence, if we can alter belief structures, subsequent attitude changes can be expected. For example, in a study of unionized manufacturing workers by Lieberman (1956), it was found that union workers held very strong beliefs regarding management on issues like management concern for workers and labor standards. Subsequently, however, a subsample from the original group was promoted into managerial ranks. This subsample was exposed to new (though not necessarily more accurate) information which changed their belief structures about the activities of management. As a result, the group receiving promotions altered their attitudes so they were substantially more pro-management and anti-union. In other words, being placed in a new situation with new information changed employee beliefs which, in turn, changed attitudes.

An important point relating to the provision of new information should be noted. In order for new information to affect beliefs and attitudes, it must come from what is perceived to be a credible or accurate source. If a supervisor announces that henceforth, instead of rewarding employees on a seniority basis, rewards (pay, promotion) will be closely tied to employee job performance, we would expect employees to try harder on the job if they believe the supervisor and value the rewards. Exhorting employees to work harder and promising unrealistic or nonexistent rewards should only lead to increased alienation, not increased effort. In the Lieberman study, it can be assumed that the employees who were promoted to managerial positions and who subsequently altered their attitudes toward management and union believed they were receiving new information which justified a modification in beliefs and attitudes.

Fear arousal and reduction.   Two related aspects of attitade change center around the notion of fear. It is somewhat ironic that attitude change can be facilitated, depending upon the circumstances, both by arousing fear and by reducing fear. Let us see how this works.

Several studies have shown that *arousing* an individual's fear of an object or event can cause the individual to modify his or her position regarding that object or event (Triandis, 1971). Efforts to arouse employee fear can be seen by both unions and management just prior to a strike, for instance. However, the fear arousal-attitude change relationship is somewhat more complex than this. Specifically, it appears that the relationship between fear and attitude change is characterized by an inverted U-curve. At very low levels of fear arousal, the message may not be rereived or paid much attention to; it may not be sufficiently threatening to stimulate change. At moderate levels of fear arousal, however, reception of the message is likely to increase and attitude change is expected. Finally, when extremely high fear levels are aroused, it has been found that reception of the message actually decreases, as individuals begin to defend themselves against highly objectionable stimuli. Under situations of extremely high fear arousal, attitudes do *not* tend to change because the message is rejected by individuals (McGuire, 1968).

An example will clarify this point. Consider a white, male manager working for a company that is under considerable affirmative action pressure from the government to hire minorities. Initially, this manager may not have strong opinions about minorities as managers. If a rumor is circulated throughout the organization that it is necessary to hire a few minority managers to "keep the government off our backs" (low fear arousal), there is little reason to believe that this manager would feel threatened or that he would modify his attitude toward the managerial capabilities of minorities. However, if a rumor is circulated that, given tremendous pressure, a disproportionate share of the new hires and promotions will be given to minorities (moderate fear arousal), it is highly conceivable that the white manager might feel threatened and develop negative (defensive) attitudes toward minorities. Finally, if a rumor is circulated that every new hire and every promotion must go to a minority and that perhaps many whites will be laid off to accommodate the minorities (high fear arousal), there is a good likelihood that the message will be rejected as either too extreme to be correct or too threatening to be acknowledged or responded to. In this circumstance, we would not expect much attitude change because the individual would either ignore or discount the message.

On the other hand, as noted by Katz (1960), there are times when fear *reduction* is more appropriate for changing attitudes than fear arousal. Specifically, when a particular attitude (e.g., a negative attitude toward management) protects the individual from internal conflicts or external threats (ego-defensive attitude), the use of threats to alter attitudes would only heighten fears, and thereby increase resistance to change. For instance, the installation of a new computer system is often met with stiff resistance by employees who fear such changes. In these situations, efforts by management to reduce fear (and hopefully reduce threats to self-image and self-esteem) may create an atmosphere where changes receive a fair chance and where employees may even be receptive to them.

Dissonance arousal. Much research has been conducted on the manner in which people accommodate discrepancies between behavior and attitudes. While several theories exist, the most widely received is Festinger's (1957) theory of *cognitive dissonance*. This theory states that when people find themselves behaving in a manner that is inconsistent with their attitudes, they experience tension and will attempt to reduce this tension.

For example, an employee may have negative attitudes toward her job but be required to work long hours. Here she is faced with a clear discrepancy between attitude and behavior and she will probably experience cognitive dissonance. In order to become *cognitively consistent,* the employee can do one of two things. First, she can change her behavior and work fewer hours. However, this may not be possible. Second, the employee can change her attitudes toward work so they are more consistent with her behavior. She may convince herself that the job really is not as bad as she envisioned and that the long hours may help her toward rapid promotion. In doing so, the employee achieves a state of cognitive consistency and the tension is reduced.

The potency of cognitive dissonance in attitude change can be seen in several studies of job choice behavior among business students (Lawler, Kuleck, Rhode, and Sorenson, 1975; Vroom and Deci, 1971). In these studies, graduating students were asked to rate the attractiveness (that is, favorableness of attitude) of several firms for which they could work. Students generally chose those firms which seemed to have greatest attractiveness. However, after the students actually began working for their selected firms, it was found that they lowered their attitudes toward the other firms (the firms they did *not* go to work for) and increased their attitudes toward the selected firms. In other words, the dissonance created by having to choose one firm was reduced by cognitively distorting (reducing) the attractiveness of the other firms. Thus, the students felt more secure that they had made the correct job choice decision.

Position discrepancy.   A fourth technique in which attitude change can be brought about concerns the difference between an individual's present position toward something and the position advocated by others. We are concerned here with the discrepancy between the two positions and their effects on change. Sometimes, an issue is not especially important to an individual or does not particularly involve him. When this is the case, research shows that the greater the discrepency between the individual's own position and the position advocated by others, the more the individual will move toward the position held by others. Hence, if someone told you that Fords were far superior to Chevrolets—and you did not drive—you would probably develop a more positive attitude toward Fords and less positive attitude toward Chevrolets.

However, when the issue involved is of personal importance to you, findings show that moderate position discrepancy produces more change than extreme discrepancy. So, if you were a traveling salesperson who used your car extensively, and you had just spent much time and money choosing a new Chevrolet (high personal involvement), you would probably consider the individual advocating the extreme position on Fords biased or uninformed. Hence, a moderate approach is more suitable for producing change.

Participation in decision-making.   A final way of effecting attitude change is to involve target individuals in the process by which decisions are made. Early experiments during World War II by Kurt Lewin showed that when housewives were involved in discussions over the value of buying less desirable meat, they were more inclined to make purchases than when simply asked to do so. Similar examples can be found in organizational settings. In fact, a primary rationale behind the participative management movement is that the act of involving lower-level employees in decisions affecting their jobs creates more positive job attitudes. As noted by Vroom (1960), when employees are allowed to participate in decisions, they become more ego-involved in the outcomes and tend to identify more with the actual issues involved and with the organization.

One mechanism of facilitating employee participation is the use of attitude surveys. As noted in Box 13–1, these surveys represent a potentially powerful mechanism for attitude change.

Box 13–1 Attitude Surveys in Organizations

For many years companies have taken annual attitude (or morale) surveys to assess the general level of satisfaction among employees. In recent years, however, these surveys have become more important for at least two reasons: 1) attitude surveys now focus on a wider range of organizational activities, and provide more information to management about possible trouble spots; and 2) companies have begun to take attitude surveys more seriously and actually implement changes based on results.

Here are three examples of successful applications of attitude surveys:*

General Electric Company In a survey of more than 20,000 employees, G.E. found that over one-half of the respondents were dissatisfied with the information and recognition they received and with their opportunities for advancement. As a result, management instituted regular monthly meetings, brought in experts to answer questions, and initiated a newsletter. One year later, a follow-up survey found that the number of employees dissatisfied with the information they received dropped from 50% to none, while the number dissatisfied with promotional opportunities fell from 50% to 20%.

Geosource, Incorporated This Houston-based company found that its welders were extremely dissatisfied with pay levels, despite the competitive wage paid there. In a survey feedback session, management discovered that welders were reading want ads for welders offering "up to $7.84 per hour" for welders. When it was pointed out that no company hires at the maximum wage the discontent subsided.

American Can Company A survey found employees concerned about a lack of career opportunities. As a result, the company initiated a job information center where employees could discuss their qualifications, ambitions, and training needs, and a weekly 30-minute job seminar where senior executives would talk about career opportunities in their areas.

Two factors seem to influence the success of these attitude surveys. First, it is important that results are fed back to all employees, not just to top management. There must be ready access to all information. Second, successful programs are marked by a commitment from top management to initiate changes where needed. Quick action by management, as noted in the three examples above, reassures employees that the company is concerned about creating a suitable work environment and about what employees' opinions are about such an environment.

Source: Business Week "A productive way to vent employee gripes." October 16, 1978, pp. 168–171.

In summary, there are several ways in which attitudes can be changed. Most of these techniques involve changing the beliefs held by individuals which, in turn, affect attitude formation (Fishbein and Ajzen, 1975). To the extent that beliefs and attitudes can be changed, we would expect some changes in subsequent behavior.

Job Satisfaction

When the concept of attitudes is applied to work settings, it is necessary to be specific about which attitude we are concerned with. While a variety of work-related job attitudes can be mentioned, it appears that attitudes relating to job satisfaction are particularly important from the standpoint of management. The notion of job satisfaction is one of the most widely studied variables in organizational behavior. We will examine this concept in detail as it relates to the management of people at work.

The Concept of Job Satisfaction

Job satisfaction may be defined as "a pleasurable or positive emotional state resulting from the appraisal of one's job or job experience" (Locke, 1976, p. 1300). It results from the perception that an employee's job actually provides what an employee values in the work situation.

Several characteristics of the concept of job satisfaction follow from this definition. First, satisfaction is an emotional response to a job situation. It can only be fully understood by introspection. As with any attitude, we cannot observe satisfaction; we must infer its existence and quality either from an employee's behavior or verbal statements.

Second, job satisfaction is perhaps best understood as a discrepancy. Several writers have pointed to the concept of job satisfaction as being a result of how much a person wants or expects from the job *compared to* how much he or she actually receives (Locke, 1969; Katzel, 1964; Porter and Steers, 1973). People come to work with varying levels of job expectations. These expectations may vary not only in quality (different people may value different things in a job), but also in intensity. Based on work experiences, people receive outcomes, or rewards, from the job. These outcomes include not only extrinsic rewards like pay and promotion, but also a variety of intrinsic rewards, such as satisfying co-worker relations and meaningful work. To the extent that the outcomes received by an employee meet or exceed expectations, we would expect the employee to be satisfied with the job and wish to remain. On those occasions when outcomes actually surpass expectations, we would expect employees to reevaluate their expectations and probably raise them to meet available outcomes. However, when outcomes do not meet expectations, employees are dissatisfied, and may prefer to seek alternative sources of satisfaction, either through changing jobs or by placing greater value on other life activities, like outside recreation.

Dimensions of Job Satisfaction

It has been argued oy several investigators (Smith, Kendall, and Hulin, 1969) that job satisfaction actually represents several related attitudes. So, when we speak of satisfaction, we must specify "satisfaction with what?" Smith et al. have suggested that five job dimensions represent the most salient characterstics of a job about which people have affective responses. These five are:

- *Work itself* The extent to which tasks performed by employees are interesting and provide opportunities for learning and for accepting responsibility.
- *Pay* The amount of pay received, the perceived equity of the pay, and the method of payment.
- *Promotional opportunities* The availability of realistic opportunities for advancement.
- *Supervision* The technical and managerial abilities of supervisors, the extent to which supervisors demonstrate consideration for and interest in employees.
- *Co-workers* The extent to which co-workers are friendly, technically competent, and supportive.

While other dimensions of job satisfaction have been identified (satisfaction with company policies, fringe benefits) these five dimensions are employed most often when examining aspects of job attitudes at work.

Measurement of Job Satisfaction

Probably the most common survey that managers carry out among employees is the measurement of job satisfaction. Satisfaction is felt by many managers to be an important indicator of organizational effectiveness and, as such, necessitates continuous monitoring of attitudes to assess employee feelings toward their jobs and the organization.

There are many ways in which job satisfaction can be measured (Locke, 1976). We will identify five: 1) rating scales; 2) critical incidents; 3) interviews; 4) overt behavior; and 5) action tendencies.

Rating scales. The most popular technique for assessing job satisfaction is the use of rating scales. Rating scales are direct verbal self-reports and have been used since the 1930s (Hoppock, 1935). Several job satisfaction scales exist (Smith et al., 1969; Lofquist and Davis, 1969). One scale that has been used in a variety of studies is the Minnesota Satisfaction Questionnaire (Lofquist and Davis, 1969). This instrument uses a Likert-response format to generate satisfaction scores on 26 scales. Examples of MSQ questions are shown in Exhibit 13–3.

Exhibit 13–3   Examples of two job satisfaction measures

A. Examples from the *Minnesota Satisfaction Questionnaire*

On my present job, this is how I feel about . . .	Not satisfied	Only slightly satisfied	Satisfied	Very satisfied	Extremely satisfied
1. the chance to be active much of the time	1	2	3	4	5
2. the variety in my work	1	2	3	4	5
3. the policies and practices toward employees of this company	1	2	3	4	5
4. the chance to be responsible for planning my work	1	2	3	4	5
5. the opportunities for advancement on this job	1	2	3	4	5

Source: Used by permission of the University of Minnesota Industrial Relations Center, Minneapolis, Minnesota.

B. On Scale from the *Job Descriptive Index*

The instructions for each scale ask the subject to put "Y" beside an item if the item described the particular aspect of his/her job (e.g., work, pay, etc.), "N" if the item did not describe that aspect, or "?" if he/she could not decide.

The response shown beside each item is the one scored in the "satisfied" direction for each scale.

Work		Work	
Y	Fascinating	Y	Useful
N	Routine	N	Tiresome
Y	Satisfying	Y	Healthful
N	Boring	Y	Challenging
Y	Good	N	On your feet
Y	Creative	N	Frustrating
Y	Respected	N	Simple
N	Hot	N	Endless
Y	Pleasant	Y	Gives sense of accomplishment

Source: Patricia Cain Smith, Lorne M. Kendall, and Charles L. Hulin, *The Measurement of Satisfaction in Work and Retirement.* (Chicago: Rand McNally and Company, 1969).

*Copyright © 1975, Bowling Green State University. Researchers wishing to use these scales in their own work are asked to purchase the scales from Bowling Green State University, Department of Psychology, Bowling Green, Ohio 43403.

Another widely used scale is the Job Descriptive Index (Smith et al., 1969). The JDI, also partially shown in Exhibit 13–3, presents employees with a series of adjectives which may or may not describe five aspects of their job (work itself, pay, promotion, supervision, and co-workers). Employees are asked to answer each item with yes (Y), no (N), or don't know (?) to indicate the extent each adjective applies to their job.

The MSQ, the JDI, and similar rating scales have several advantages for evaluating levels of job satisfaction. First, they are relatively short and simple and can be completed by large numbers of employees quickly. Second, because of the generalized wording of the various terms, the instruments can be administered to a wide range of employees in various jobs. It is not necessary to alter the questionnaire for each job classification. Finally, the JDI has extensive normative data (or norms) available. These norms include summaries of the scores of thousands of people who have completed the JDI (see Smith et al., 1969). Hence, it is possible for employers in other organizations to determine relative standings.

However, while rating scales have many virtues compared to other techniques, at least two drawbacks must be recognized (Locke, 1976). First, as with any self-report inventory, it is assumed that respondents are both willing to and capable of accurately describing their feelings. As noted by several researchers (Staw, 1976; Vroom, 1964), people often consciously or unconsciously distort information that they feel is damaging and enhance information that they feel is beneficial. For example, it is possible that employees who think their supervisors may see the results of their questionnaire may report overly favorable job attitudes.

A second problem with rating scales is the underlying assumption that questionnaire items mean the same thing to all people. There may, in fact, not be a common agreement of meaning across individuals. For instance, the JDI (see Exhibit 13–3) uses adjectives like fascinating and routine to describe the job. However, these adjectives may have different meanings for various employees based on their abilities, expectations, needs, and previous experiences. Even so, rating scales have proved to be helpful in assessing satisfaction in various aspects of the job situation.

Critical incidents. The use of the critical incident technique for assessing job satisfaction was first popularized by Herzberg (Herzberg et al., 1959). In their study of job attitudes, employees were asked to describe incidents on their jobs that were particularly satisfying and incidents that were particularly dissatisfying. These incidents were then content analyzed to determine which aspects of the work situation (work itself, supervision, pay and promotion, etc.) were most closely related to affective responses. In contrast to rating scales, this technique focuses on qualitative data rather than quantitative data.

A primary advantage of the critical incident technique is that it is typically non-directive. Employees are simply asked to describe a satisfying event. Thus, they are not biased by being given predetermined topics or categories. Even so, several drawbacks of this technique must be noted. First, it is time consuming, both to collect the data and then to content analyze them. It is also open to bias in that the researcher or manager may distort incidents during the process of analyzing the content of the responses. Finally, it is highly likely that the employees themselves may distort their responses (Vroom, 1964). Employees may attribute a negative event to some fault of the supervisor, while attributing a positive event to their own abilities or skills.

Interviews.   A third way to assess employee satisfaction is personal interviews. Interviews may be structured (where pre-determined and standardized questions are asked) or unstructured (open-ended). Interviews have several advantages in the assessment of job attitudes. First, interviews allow for in-depth explorations of those aspects of the job which are not possible to assess in rating scales. In addition, interviews are often useful when studying people with lower educational levels or language barriers who may not otherwise understand the terminology used on a printed questionnaire. Third, interviews allow a closer examination of the true meaning of the responses. What *exactly* did an employee like about the job?

On the other hand, at least three problems with the interview technique can be identified. First, there is a problem of objectivity; people may distort their responses. Second, there are often differences between interviewers which bias the results. The manner in which the interviewer asks questions, the types of information the interviewer chooses to record, all can affect the outcomes. Finally, there is a problem of time; interviews of large numbers of employees simply consume too many hours to be practical in many cases.

One strategy that has proven useful in the study of job attitudes is to combine rating scales with personal interviews. This strategy combines the highly quantitative data from rating scales with the important in-depth qualitative data from interviews. Often, a small subsample is selected for the interviews because of the time-consuming nature of this technique. By combining these two techniques, better cross-validated information is available for examination and decision making.

Overt behaviors.   A fourth technique often used by managers is to observe overt (or actual) employee behaviors (poor performance, absenteeism, turnover) as surrogate measures of dissatisfaction. As Locke (1976) notes, there are three reasons why this technique is questionable as a measure of job attitudes:

> This approach is clearly inadequate because there is no known behavior which would satisfy the minimal criteria needed to justify it, namely: (1) the behavior inevitably follows the experience of satisfaction; that is, satisfaction is always expressed in this particular way; (2) the behavior occurs with a frequency or intensity that is directly proportional to the intensity of the attitude experienced; and (3) no causal factors other than satisfaction influence the behavior, or if so, their influence can be precisely calculated (Locke, 1976, p. 1335).*

*Locke, Edwin A., "Nature and causes of job satisfaction," in Dunnette, M.D. (ed.) *Handbook of Industrial and Organizational Behavior*. Copyright © 1976 by Rand McNally College Publishing Company.

Action tendencies.   Closely related to the notion of behavioral intentions discussed earlier is the concept of *action tendencies*. Action tendencies are the inclinations people have to approach or avoid certain things. Given these tendencies, and their relationship to behavioral intentions, another way to assess job attitudes is to ask people which action tendencies they experience with respect to their jobs. Instead of asking employees how they *feel* about their job, we can ask them how they feel like *acting* (other things equal) with respect to their job. Examples of action tendencies are shown in Exhibit 13–4.

Several advantages can be noted about the use of action tendencies. First, while some self-insight by the individual is necessary, this technique apparently requires less self-insight than rating scales. Second, action tendency questions have more of an absolute frame of reference than do evaluative questions. So, fewer distortions are incurred. In fact, in a study of blue-collar workers by Kornhauser (1965), it was found that by asking employees action tendency questions ("If you could start all over again, would you choose the same type of work?"), substantially lower levels of satisfaction were noted than by using more traditional rating scales. To date, little use has been made of the action tendency technique. It is believed, however, that it will be used more often in the future.

Exhibit 13–4   Sample Items for an Action Tendency Schedule for Job Satisfaction

---

1. When you wake up in the morning, do you feel reluctant to go to work?
2. Do you ever feel reluctant to go home from work at night because of the enjoyment you are getting from the job?
3. Do you often feel like going to lunch at work sooner than you do?
4. Do you feel like taking a coffee break more often than you should?
5. Do you ever wish you could work at your job on evenings or weekends?
6. Are you sometimes reluctant to leave your job to go on a vacation?
7. When you are on vacation, do you ever look forward to getting back to work?
8. Do you ever wake up at night with the urge to go to work right then and there?
9. Do you ever wish holidays or weekends would get over with so that you could go back to work?
10. If you were starting over in your working career, would you lean toward taking the same type of job you have now?
11. Would you be tempted to recommend your present job to a friend with the same interests and education as yours?

Source: Locke, Edwin A., "Nature and Causes of Job Satisfaction," In Dunnette, M.D. (ed.) *Handbook of Industrial and Organizational Behavior,* Table 7, p. 1336. Copyright © 1976 by Rand McNally College Publishing Company.

How Satisfied are Employees?

Presumably, a major reason for studying the concept of job satisfaction is to learn ways to improve satisfaction levels in the work place. Given this goal, it is important to consider just how satisfied people are with their jobs. Many people think that most workers are very dissatisfied. The available evidence, however, contradicts that. In view of this contradiction, the reader must carefully study the evidence that is available and look behind the seemingly obvious conclusions.

First, consider the results of a series of job attitude surveys carried out by the University of Michigan, the University of California, and the National Opinion Research Center (Gallup). These results are summarized in a report released by the U.S. Department of Labor (1974), and clearly suggest that workers by and large are satisfied with their jobs based on self-report data. More specifically, between 80% and 90% of employees on various jobs and working in a wide range of organizations *consistently* report that they are satisfied with their jobs.

Based on these findings, one may conclude that employee job satisfaction does not need to be an area of management concern. However, several disturbing questions remain. If employees are so satisfied, why do many report that they wish to change jobs and occupations (Kahn, 1972)? Why are absenteeism, turnover, and work stoppages so prevalent? According to Kahn (1972), the results reported in these surveys may be greatly distorted. He criticizes the use of the direct question, "How satisfied are you with your job?", because the question threatens self-esteem. As Kahn (1972) notes, asking the question of employees in this way poses:

> a choice between no work connection (usually with severe attendant economic penalties and a conspicuous lack of meaningful alternative activities) and a work connection which is burdened with negative qualities (routine, compulsory scheduling, dependency, etc.). In these circumstances, the individual has no difficulty with choice; he chooses work, pronounces himself moderately satisfied, and tells us more only if the questions become more searching. Then we learn that he can order jobs clearly in terms of their status or desirability, wants his son to be employed differently from himself, and, if given a choice, would seek a different occupation.

Support for Kahn's argument can be found when we examine the results of an action tendency questionnaire, instead of a rating scale. (Remember that Locke (1976) argues that action tendency questionnaires are superior to evaluative rating scales). In a large survey of employees, respondents were asked "What type of work would you try to get into if you could start all over again?" Results are shown in Exhibit 13–5.

As can be seen, results are markedly lower than comparable results gathered through evaluative ratings. For instance, on the average, only 43%

Exhibit 13–5   Percentages in occupational groups who would choose similar work again (Kahn, 1972)

Professional and White-Collar Occupations	%	Working Class Occupations	%
Urban university professors	93	Skilled printers	52
Mathematicians	91	Paper workers	42
Physicists	89	Skilled autoworkers	41
Biologists	89	Skilled steelworkers	41
Chemists	86	Textile workers	31
Firm lawyers	85	Unskilled steelworkers	21
Lawyers	83	Unskilled autoworkers	21
Journalists (Washington correspondents)	82	*Blue-collar workers, cross section*	24
Church university professors	77		
Lawyers in private practice	75		
White-collar workers, cross section	41		

of white-collar workers (including professionals) would again choose the same occupation while only 24% of blue-collar workers would again choose the same occupation.

Similarly, in a separate study, when a sampling of employees was asked, "What would you do with the extra two hours if you had a 26-hour day?" 66% of the university professors and 25% of the lawyers responded that they would use the extra two hours in work-related activities. By contrast, only 5% of nonprofessionals gave the same response (Wilensky, 1966). In short, if we look at what people *want* to do as an index of how well they enjoy their jobs, it becomes clear that most people—particularly blue-collar workers—are largely dissatisfied with their jobs. Thus, job satisfaction is indeed an important area for management concern and action.

Influences on Job Satisfaction

Investigators have long sought to determine the major causes of job satisfaction in work organizations. To date, while we have been able to identify a variety of factors that are consistently related to satisfaction, we have yet to attain a comprehensive empirically validated model of satisfaction, although some useful attempts have been made (Lawler, 1973). We can, however, review briefly several of the more important factors found to be associated with it. It has been suggested by Porter and Steers (1973) that influences on employee attitudes and behavior can be grouped into four relatively discrete categories, representing four levels in the organization. These four levels are: 1) organization-wide factors, those variables widely available or applied to most employees; 2) immediate work environment factors, those variables which make up the work group; 3) job content factors, or the actual job activities; and 4) personal factors, those characteristics that differentiate one person from another. Influences on employee satisfaction can be found in all four levels (see Exhibit 13–6).

Organization-Wide Factors

With respect to job satisfaction, the *pay* and *promotional opportunities* used by organizations are prominent factors. Substantial evidence points to pay as a primary determinant of satisfaction, especially when the pay received is seen as equitable, that is, when it is viewed as fair compared to level of effort and what others receive (Lawler, 1971; Locke, 1976). To the extent that employees feel that pay meets their expectations and is fair given their level of effort, they will tend to be satisfied. Likewise, individuals' perceptions of the rate and equity of their promotions also tend to influence their satisfaction (Locke, 1976).

In addition, *company policies and procedures* play a role in the determination of overall job satisfaction. Policies often govern or restrict employee behavior and can generate either positive or negative feelings toward the organization. For instance, company practices like the use of time clocks, reserved parking spaces for managers, and titles (Mr. Smith versus Joe) can influence employee perceptions of personal freedom on the job as well as

Exhibit 13–6 Primary factors influencing overall job satisfaction

Organization-wide factors	*Job content factors*
pay system	job scope
promotional opportunities	role clarity and conflict
company policies and procedures	
organization structure	*Personal factors*
Immediate work environment factors	age
supervisory style	tenure
participation in decision making	personality
work group size	
co–worker relations	
working conditions	

status or place in the organization. Employees who feel unduly constrained or who feel like second-class citizens probably would not enjoy the work environment to the extent that others do.

Finally, a recent survey has found that *organization structure* often influences satisfaction (Cummings and Berger, 1976). In particular, available evidence suggests that increased job satisfaction is often associated with: 1) higher levels in the organizational hierarchy; and 2) increased decentralization in decision-making authority. Variations in organization size, span of control, or line vs. staff differences had no consistent or perceptible influence on satisfaction levels.

Immediate Work Environment Factors

The immediate work environment can also influence satisfaction in a variety of ways. One of these is *supervisory style*. Several studies have demonstrated that more considerate supervision leads to higher levels of satisfaction (Vroom, 1964; Stogdill, 1974). This is not to imply that considerate supervision leads necessarily to greater productivity, only satisfaction. Caution is in order in interpreting these results, however. Because of the correlational nature of the studies, direction of causality in the supervision–satisfaction relationship cannot be determined with any degree of certainty. It is possible that satisfied employees themselves create an environment that is more conducive to considerate supervisory behavior.

Related to supervisory consideration is the extent to which employees are allowed to participate in decisions affecting their jobs. *Participative decision making* has been found to lead to increased satisfaction, especially when the decisions involved are important to employees' jobs and when employee participation is authentic (Scott and Mitchell, 1976).

Several studies have also found a consistent relationship between *work group size* and satisfaction, where lager work groups lead to lower satisfaction levels (Porter and Lawler, 1965). It is believed that larger work groups lead to greater task specialization, poorer interpersonal communication, and reduced feelings of group cohesiveness. These factors, in turn, create conditions which reduce satisfaction.

The quality of *co-worker relations* has also been consistently found to be related to satisfaction (Smith et al., 1969). As noted by Locke (1976), people are generally attracted to and feel more comfortable with co-workers who exhibit characteristics, interests, and beliefs similar to their own. Where compatibility exists, we expect the affective response to the work environment to increase.

Finally, some evidence suggests that general *working conditions* can also have an impact on employer attitudes. People value having a clean and orderly workplace, adequate equipment for the job, and acceptable levels of environmental quality (temperature, humidity, noise). Most employees prefer a location close to their home (Barnowe, Mangione, and Quinn, 1972). However, as noted by Chadwick–Jones (1969), these working conditions apparently only become salient for job attitudes when they are present (or absent) in the extreme or when employees have clear standards for comparison (perhaps based on earlier jobs). Otherwise, these factors may be ignored or overlooked by employees.

Job Content Factors

Two aspects of the job itself have been found to represent especially strong influences on satisfaction: job scope and role clarity. *Job scope* refers to those attributes which characterize a job, like the amount of variety, autonomy, responsibility, and feedback provided (see Chapter 16 for a more detailed discussion of job design). The more these attributes are present, the higher the job scope. Much research has been done on the effects of job scope on employee attitudes. It has generally been found that increased job scope is related to increased satisfaction (Stone, 1975; Hackman and Lawler, 1971; Brief and Aldag, 1975). For a few employees, however, such as those who have low needs for achievement, providing a challenging job may lead not to satisfaction but to increased anxiety and frustration because of either an unwillingness or an inability to respond to the challenge (Steers, 1976; Hackman and Lawler, 1971; Hackman and Oldham, 1976). Even so, most evidence suggests that enriching employees' jobs typically increases their level of job satisfaction (if not their performance).

In addition, *role ambiguity* and *role conflict* have both been found to lead to increased stress and reduced job satisfaction for many people (Miles and Perreault, 1976; Morris, 1976). Apparently, employees feel more secure and prefer situations in which they know what is expected of them and where they have clear task goals.

Personal Factors

The fourth category of influences on job satisfaction is the attributes of individual employees. A good deal of research has shown that *age* and *tenure* are positively associated with favorable job attitudes (Herman, Dunham and Hulin, 1975; O'Reilly and Roberts, 1975; Porter and Steers, 1973). Several explanations might account for this relationship. As people get older and acquire seniority, they typically move into more responsible (and perhaps challenging) positions. These individuals often receive at least some organizational rewards just for remaining with the organization. Finally, it may be that older employees have simply adjusted their expectations to more realistic levels based on experience and are therefore more satisfied with available rewards (Wanous, 1973).

A final factor often associated with satisfaction—albeit very modestly—is *personality*. O'Reilly and Roberts (1975) found, for example, that several personality variables (self-assurance, decisiveness, and maturity) were related to increased job satisfaction. Steers and Braunstein (1976) found that individuals manifesting higher needs for achievement and dominance were more satisfied, while individuals with high needs for autonomy tended to be less satisfied. Finally, Korman (1977) has suggested that individuals with high self-esteem also tend to be more satisfied with the work situation and take more pleasure (and reinforcement) from a job well done.

Summary. In conclusion, it can be seen that a multitude of factors—both within organizations and within individuals—are capable of influencing job satisfaction. The question that remains focuses on *which* factors are more important for satisfaction? This question is difficult to answer. The available evidence to date suggests that personal factors are far *less* important in determining job satisfaction than are those factors which characterize the work place (O'Reilly and Roberts, 1975; Herman et al., 1975; Newman, 1975). In this regard, Locke (1976, p. 1328) has summarized what he feels are the most salient factors influencing satisfaction:

> Among the most important values or conditions conducive to job satisfaction are: (1) mentally challenging work with which the individual can cope successfully; (2) personal interest in the work itself; (3) work which is not too physically tiring; (4) rewards for performance which are just, informative, and in line with the individual's personal aspirations; (5) working conditions which are compatible with the individual's physical needs and which facilitate the accomplishment of his work goals; (6) high self-esteem on the part of the employee; (7) agents in the work place who help the employee attain job values such as interesting work, pay, and promotions, and whose basic values are similar to his own, and who minimize role conflict and ambiguity.

Consequences of Job Satisfaction

An awareness of the salient consequences of job satisfaction is equally as important as understanding what causes job satisfaction in the first place. Since most of these factors are discussed more fully later in the book, they will be mentioned only briefly here as they relate to employee job satisfaction or dissatisfaction.

Satisfaction and Turnover

Consistently, satisfaction and employee turnover have been found to be moderately related. In an early review of the literature, Vroom (1964) found that correlations between the two variables ranged from $r = -.13$ to

$r = -.42$ across various studies. More recently, Porter and Steers (1973) reviewed fifteen studies and found a median correlation of $r = -.25$ between satisfaction and turnover. Thus, while the modest magnitude of the relationships suggests that several other factors influence turnover, job satisfaction is clearly an important influence. In addition, this influence translates into a direct financial loss for the organization, as shown in Box 13–2. The nature and causes of employee turnover will be discussed in greater detail in Chapter 14.

Box 13–2 Measuring the Costs of Employee Attitudes

A major difficulty that has faced both managers and researchers in the study of job attitudes has been an inability to attach dollar amounts to changes in attitudes. Without hard data, it is difficult to convince managers of the need to monitor attitudes in work organizations. This lack of monetary association makes it difficult to assess the value to the organization of changes in job attitude levels.

Research Design A recent attempt to overcome this difficulty has been carried out by Mirvis, Macy, and Lawler.* The concept is called behavioral accounting. Simply put, they attempted to measure the financial impact of employee attitudes. Their study focused on a sample of 160 bank tellers. Attitudinal measures were collected for intrinsic job satisfaction, organizational involvement, and intrinsic motivation. In addition, behavioral measures were also collected, including absenteeism, voluntary turnover, and the number of shortages or overpayments to customers by the tellers.

Findings Based on these measures, attempts were made to attach dollar amounts to each attitude and behavior, based on financial and cost data supplied by the organization. For example, it was estimated that each incident of absenteeism cost the bank $66.45. The cost was estimated as follows:

Absent Employee:		
Salary	$	23.04
Benefits		6.40
Replacement Employee:		
Training & staff time		2.13
Unabsorbed burden		15.71
Lost profit contribution		19.17
Total cost	$	66.45

Similarly, the cost of one turnover was estimated as follows:

Replacement acquisition:		
Direct hiring costs	$	293.95
Other hiring costs		185.55
Replaement training:		
Preassignment		758.85
Learning curve		212.98
Unabsorbed burden		682.44
Lost profit contribution		388.27
Total cost		$2,522.03

*Source: B. A. Macy and P. H. Mirvis. Measuring the quality of work and organizational effectiveness in behavioral–economic terms. *Administrative Science Quarterly*, 1976, *21*, 212–226. P. H. Mirvis and E. E. Lawler. Measuring the financial impact of employee attitudes. *Journal of Applied Psychology*, 1977, *62*, 1–8.

By relating past attitude changes to changes in behavior, estimates were then calculated of the costs (in dollars) for a .5 change in the standard deviation in an attitude (e.g., satisfaction). (Details of this procedure are outlined in Mirvis and Lawler, 1977.) Based on these cost estimates, the investigators estimated that for the total sample of bank tellers (N)160) for a one-year period, an improvement in teller satisfaction of .5 standard deviations would result in a direct savings of $17,644. Combining the attitudinal and behavioral measures, the total cost savings for the bank for a one-year period of this change would be $125,160.

Implications While attempts to attach dollar amounts to employee attitudes and behavior have obvious limitations, several potential benefits accrue. Most notably, it provides a relatively practical approach to relating attitudes and behavior to costs. Efforts to change job attitudes could be evaluated and the costs of these efforts could be compared against estimated savings on the job. Behavioral accounting allows for a clear recognition of the role people play in facilitating organizational effectiveness. While we can easily evaluate investments in physical and financial resources, much less is known about evaluating investments in human resources. This approach, when more fully developed, offers one possibility at better recognizing how employee attitudes and behavior can affect organizational efficiency and goal attainment.

Satisfaction and Absenteeism

While much less has been done with respect to absenteeism, available evidence again suggests the existence of a moderate inverse relationship between satisfaction and employee absenteeism. Vroom's (1964) review of several studies found correlations that ranged from $r = -.14$ to $r = -.38$. Porter and Steers (1973), Muchinsky (1977), and Steers and Rhodes (1978) found similar results. Muchinsky notes that "of all the variables that have been related to absenteeism, the most consistent results have occurred with attitudinal predictors" (p. 322). Even so, as noted in Chapter 14, other important influences on satisfaction must also be acknowledged.

Satisfaction and Performance

One of the most controversial issues encountered in the study of job satisfaction is its relationship to job performance. Three competing theories have been advanced: 1) satisfaction causes performance; 2) performance causes satisfaction; 3) rewards intervene between performance and satisfaction (Porter and Lawler, 1968; Schwab and Cummings, 1970; Greene, 1972).

The first two theories find only weak support. For instance, Vroom (1964) reviewed 20 studies dealing with the performance-satisfaction relationship and found a median correlation of only $r = .14$. More recent studies arrived at similar conclusions (Greene, 1972). Both of the first two theories can be rejected on theoretical grounds. That is, the fact that workers are satisfied does not mean they will necessarily produce more, only that they are satisfied. There is no compelling argument that performance must necessarily cause satisfaction, particularly if performance goes unrewarded.

The third theory, that rewards mediate the performance–satisfaction relationship, receives considerable support in the literature. This model, shown in Exhibit 13–7 was first suggested by Porter and Lawler (1968) and has received fairly consistent support in subsequent studies (Schwab and Cummings, 1970; Greene, 1972).

As shown in the exhibit, past performance of an employee leads to the receipt of rewards. These rewards can be both intrinsic (a feeling of personal accomplishment) and extrinsic (pay, promotion). To the extent that these rewards are perceived by the individual to be equitable (fair when compared to level of effort and to what other employees receive), the individual is satisfied. The receipt of perceived equitable rewards should also tend to create strong performance-reward contingencies in the minds of employees, leading to future effort and performance.

In other words, performance is really not a consequence of satisfaction at all! Instead, the two variables *by themselves* are virtually unrelated. It is only when we consider the role of rewards and reward contingencies that a substantial relationship emerges. See Chapter 17.

Satisfaction and Organizational Effectiveness

The impact of job attitudes on organizational effectiveness, while admittedly an indirect one, is nonetheless important. It has been noted that one of the

Exhibit 13–7 Relationship of job performance to job satisfaction (adapted from Porter and Lawler, 1968).

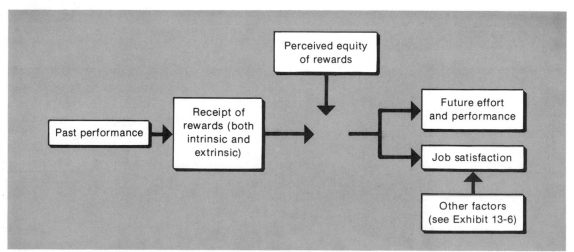

most popular indicators used by analysts and investigators to assess organizational effectiveness is job satisfaction (Steers, 1977c). Moreover, job attitudes affect organizational effectiveness to the extent that they influence turnover and absenteeism. Lawler (1973) notes that the cost of one turnover among lower-level jobs can easily surpass $2,000 while the cost of one turnover among the managerial ranks can be five to ten times this amount. From the standpoint of the effective functioning of the organization, managers have a responsibility to consider seriously the impact of job attitudes and to attempt to discover ways of improving them.

Additional Consequences of Job Satisfaction

In addition, job satisfaction has been found to be related to several other dysfunctional consequences. Highly satisfied employees tend to file fewer grievances (Fleishman and Harris, 1962), live longer (Palmore, 1969), exhibit better mental and physical health (Burke, 1969; Chadwick-Jones, 1969; Kornhauser, 1965), learn new job-related tasks more quickly (Wyatt et al., 1937) and have fewer on-the-job accidents (Vroom, 1964).

In short, job satisfaction brings with it a variety of positive consequences, both from the individual and organizational standpoints. It influences how an employee feels about the organization and contributes to the desire to maintain membership in it. It spills over to affect an employee's home life and general outlook toward living. Moreover, job satisfaction significantly influences how people approach their jobs, their levels of effort and commitment, and their contributions to organizational effectiveness.

Summary

In this section we began a discussion of individuals and groups at work. Based on our earlier discussions of individual and group characteristics, we are now in a position to consider how these various characteristics interact with workplace characteristics to determine attitudes and behavior.

In this chapter, the concept of work attitudes was introduced and a model of these attitudes was presented. It was noted that attitudes serve a variety of functions for individuals.

Next, the way in which attitudes change was discussed. Barriers to attitude change and mechanisms for overcoming barriers were discussed. Following this discussion, the specific attitude of the job satisfaction was considered, including its various dimensions and its measurement. Major influences on job satisfaction were discussed. Finally, the primary consequences of job satisfaction (or dissatisfaction) were considered. Included were the effects of job satisfaction on turnover, absenteeism, and organizational effectiveness.

When discussing job attitudes there is an inclination to assume that everything possible must be done to facilitate job satisfaction. Unfortunately, there are many situations in which managers must confront a basic conflict between improving job satisfaction and improving performance. For instance, job satisfaction may be increased by allowing employees more time off from the job, but this also has the effect of potentially reducing productive hours. Production may be increased if a manager presses vigorously for maximum output at almost any cost, but this may also reduce employee job satisfaction. Thus, the manager must make difficult tradeoffs at times, based on what appears to be a conflict in basic goals.

There is no easy resolution to this conflict. In some situations, it may be possible to pursue both goals by recognizing that improved job attitudes may lead to at least some increase in performance. Through employee participation, perhaps increased employee involvement in the task will also come about. On the other hand, managers also face situations where no compromise is possible and decisions must be made among equally attractive (or unattractive) outcomes. Then, managers are presented with the traditional conflict between concern for production and concern for people. Although compromises can sometimes be found, it would be misleading not to recognize that in some situations a clear choice must be made. In these cases, managers face a lose-lose situation but must nevertheless carry out their responsibilities.

Key Words

attitude	cognitive dissonance
belief	job satisfaction
value	critical incident
self-perception theory	action tendencies
cognitive consistency	

Questions for Discussion

1. What are the various components of an attitude? How are these components related?
2. How are beliefs formed? What is the relation between beliefs and attitudes?
3. What influences attitude formation?
4. What functions do attitudes serve?
5. Describe how self-perception theory works.
6. Identify some barriers to attitude change. How can these barriers be overcome?

7. What are the most commonly used dimensions of job satisfaction?

8. Discuss the various ways in which job satisfaction can be measured. What are the advantages and disadvantages of each?

9. Based on available evidence, how satisfied are most employees today?

10. Identify the major influences on job satisfaction.

11. Examine the utility of measuring the costs of employee attitudes, as suggested in Box 13–2.

12. Discuss the major consequences of job dissatisfaction.

chapter 14

Employee Attachment to Organizations

In their classic book, *Organizations,* March and Simon (1958) distinguish between the "decision to produce" and the "decision to participate." The decision to produce is basically the issue of motivation to perform on the job and has been dealt with extensively in this book. We now turn to the second issue: the decision to participate. Here we are concerned with factors that influence people to join organizations, to develop attachments to those organizations, and to want to come to work and remain with the organization. Facilitating these two decisions—to participate and to produce—represents the primary charge of management with respect to an organization's human resources.

Importance of Topic for Managers

The concept of employee participation in (or attachment to) organizations has received increased attention by managers in recent years. Several reasons account for this:

1. By better understanding the processes individuals go through in choosing and joining organizations, managers can be better prepared in the recruitment and selection process. For instance, providing employees with realistic job previews gives both sides a better opportunity to accurately assess the potential match between individual and organization.

2. Research has consistently demonstrated that activities such as the realistic job preview can lead not only to improvements in job performance and satisfaction levels, but also to reduced turnover.

3. By understanding the concept of careers and career stages, managers can improve employee counseling efforts and can recognize differing needs and wants of growing and maturing employees.

4. The related concepts of socialization and individualization represent primary vehicles by which individuals and organizations attempt to mold and shape each other to adapt and survive. This never-ending process has important implications for both employee behavior and attitudes and for managerial action.

5. The concept of organizational commitment has emerged in recent years as a primary concern of management. In the pursuit of organizational goals, committed employees play a major part. High organizational commitment has been fairly consistently shown to lead to increased employee effort and reduced turnover.

6. Finally, a better understanding of the primary factors leading up to withdrawal—both absenteeism and turnover—can help managers take steps to minimize withdrawal where possible.

In all, then an understanding of attachment processes—from entry to exit—helps managers comprehend and deal with employee participation decisions. In doing so, it is likely that increased effort will be generated toward facilitating organizational goals.

Career Stages and the Attachment Process

Employee career patterns vary considerably. Some employees join a particular organization at an early age and remain with the same organization through retirement. Others change jobs—and even vocations—almost at will. Despite these differences, it is possible to develop a portrait of what the average pattern looks like. We can do this by looking at the notion of career stages. Based on this concept, we will ask questions about the way employees become attached to or separated from their employers.

Hall (1976, p. 4) defines a *career* as an "individually perceived sequence of attitudes and behaviors associated with work-related experiences and activities over the span of the person's life." Underlying this definition are four rather important assumptions:

- The notion of career as such does not imply success or failure. A career is viewed as a life-long series of events rather than an evaluation of how successful someone has been over his or her life.
- Career success or failure is best judged by the person whose career is being considered, not by the normative opinions of others.
- A career consists of the events that happen to an individual over time. It consists of what an individual does and feels at work.
- A career is best viewed as a process of work-related experiences. These experiences may consist of a series of promotions within a single company or they may involve different jobs in varied organizations.

When viewed in this manner, it is possible to identify a series of relatively discrete *career stages*. (Of course, these stages must be presented in a generalized form and variations on this pattern must be recognized). Following Super (1957) and others, we can identify at least four stages: 1) exploration; 2) establishment; 3) maintenance; and 4) decline. These four stages are shown in Exhibit 14–1.

Exhibit 14–1 Stages in career development (adapted from D. T. Hall, 1976).

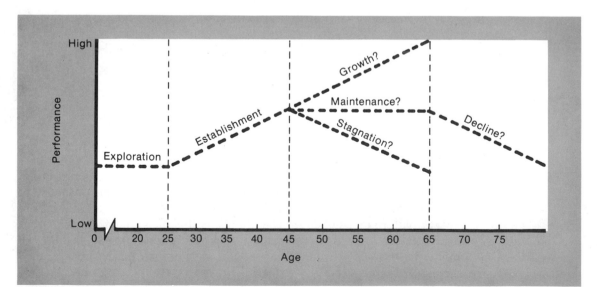

In general, the *exploration* stage consists of the time period when individuals are completing school and seeking initial employment. (This stage is closely related to the process of *organizational entry,* which is discussed in the next section.) Here, individuals try to match their needs, abilities, and skills with organizational requirements. This search usually continues during the early months on the job, during which individuals question whether the correct job choice was made.

In the *establishment* stage, individuals begin to better understand the work environment and organizational demands and strive to establish their worth in the organization. This is also a period when the organization is often carefully evaluating individuals to determine their long-term worth.

Next, in the *maintenance* stage, individuals have usually arrived and entrenched themselves in the organization. In this stage, they usually experience fairly strong linkages to the organization and often find it difficult if not impossible to leave and go elsewhere. Also, during this stage, individuals' performance levels can be expected to vary considerably. Some individuals continue to grow and develop, while others begin to stagnate and retreat. Certainly, in terms of wasted employee time and energy, this stage is where the greatest problem lies.

Finally, in the *decline* stage, individuals approach retirement. Often, however, physical age does not reflect mental age and individuals may be capable of contributing far more to the organization than the organization allows.

While a detailed review of the career development literature goes beyond the scope of this book (see Hall, 1976, and Van Maanen, 1977), we will examine several aspects of career and attachment processes. First, the concept of organizational entry is introduced. This concerns how people join organizations. Next, attention will be focused on what happens to people once they have joined an organization. Two aspects of employee adaptation and development will be discussed: 1) socialization and individualization processes; and 2) commitment processes. Finally, we will examine mechanisms by which people withdraw from organizations, both temporarily (absenteeism) and permanently (turnover).

Organizational Entry

For several decades, industrial psychologists have studied employee recruitment and selection processes from the organization's standpoint. These processes constitute a major part of any contemporary text on industrial psychology or human resources management. It is only recently, however, that psychologists have focused attention on recruitment and selection from the *employee's* standpoint. This study of the manner in which a newcomer moves from outside to inside the organization—from the individual standpoint—is an area of study known as *organizational entry* (Wanous, 1977).

Organizations are continually involved in matching processes between individuals and organizations. Prospective employees bring their skills and abilities to an organization and attempt to match these with an organization's job requirements. In addition, prospective employees also bring a variety of human needs, and attempt to find an organization climate in which many of these needs can be satisfied. In many respects, organizations focus their attention during the recruitment process on the first match (skills and abilities vs. job requirements), while individuals focus on the second match (needs vs. climate). The end result of these two matching processes determines how satisfied both individuals and organizations are with the choice and how likely each is to want to continue the relationship. It is this matching process leading up to organizational entry that we will discuss in this section.

The topic of organizational entry generally addresses four questions: (1) How do individuals choose new organizations? (2) How accurate and complete is the information that prospective employees have about new organizations? (3) What is the impact of organizational recruitment on matching individuals and organizations? (4) What are the consequences of matching or mismatching individuals and organizations?

Answers to these questions can help managers better understand the individual's point of view in the recruitment process and can in many cases help both managers and potential employees make more informed choices that benefit both.

Choosing an Organization

The most common approach to analyzing how people choose from among various organizations is based on expectancy theory. A simplified model of this choice process is shown in Exhibit 14–2, which is adapted from the work of Vroom (1966) and Lawler (1973). As can be seen in this model, it is important to distinguish between three stages in the choice process: 1) the relative attractiveness of an organization; 2) the amount of effort directed toward joining the organization; and 3) the actual choice of an organization from among the job offers the individual receives. Hence, attractiveness, effort, and choice refer to the entry process from an individual's point of view (Wanous, 1977).

In Stage 1, the relative attractiveness of an organization is determined by a combination of expectations about the characteristics of each organization and valences attached to each of those characteristics. In one classic study, Vroom (1966) studied a group of MBA students as they chose their first job. Job expectations and job valences were measured for each student for each organization being considered. As it turned out, the students' overall organi-

Exhibit 14–2   The organizational choice process (adapted from Vroom (1966) and Lawler (1973)).

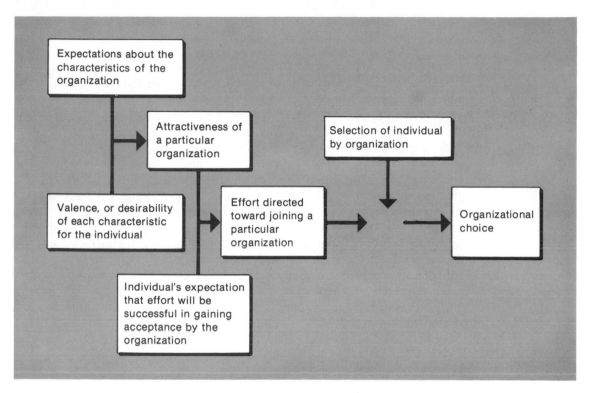

zational attractiveness score (expectations × valences) accurately predicted 76% of actual subsequent job choices. These findings offer strong confirmation of the role of expectancies and valences in choice behavior.

In Stage 2, individuals must determine the amount of energy to devote toward joining an organization. Here applicants "put their best foot forward." The decision to make this effort is influenced by both the attractiveness of the organization and the belief that the effort will in fact be successful in gaining acceptance (that is, a job offer). Many jobs (e.g., President of the United States) are quite attractive to some people, yet we realistically know that our chances of securing them are low.

As a result of this effort, organizations make *their* selections and offer positions to their favored candidates. Once offers are made, individuals select among alternative offers in Stage 3. Most individuals select the position that appears to offer the greatest attractiveness in either the short or long term.

The model of job choice suggested here is intentionally oversimplified to highlight many prominent aspects of the choice process. Obviously, other factors enter into actual job choice decisions. Some people do not follow anything like a rational or quasi-rational process in their decision but rather take positions almost by caprice. Even so, the model is helpful in identifying some of the factors that influence decisions.

Two additional aspects of the organizational choice process need to be mentioned. The first consists of the cognitive distortions that occur in the decision process. The act of choosing from among job alternatives often causes us to distort our perceptions of the characteristics (and desirability) of the various alternatives. Once we have chosen a particular job, (but before we report for work) we often *increase* our perceptions of the chosen job (increase organizational attractiveness) and *decrease* our perceptions of the alternative positions (Lawler et al., 1975; Vroom, 1966). This is done to justify our choice and to reduce possible dissonance about the decision.

However, studies have also shown that once individuals actually join an organization (that is, come to work), they become less satisfied with their decision than they were before, or immediately after, making it (Vroom and Deci, 1971). This reality shock occurs as a result of incomplete or inaccurate information people have about the future job. Once they arrive at work they are confronted with aspects of the job that they either failed to recognize or thought were less important. As a result, satisfaction with their decision diminishes and propensity to leave increases. In fact, in many industries, a major share of all turnover (often 70% or higher) occurs during the first year of employment as employees attempt to deal with their newly chosen job.

Accuracy of Information in Organizational Choice

Obviously, many people are led to expect a work environment quite different than what confronts them upon arrival at work. The existence of reality shock raises questions about the accuracy of the information people use in choosing from alternative organizations. How incomplete is this information, and what can be done to increase the accuracy of it?

Several studies indicate that company recruiters tend to give glowing descriptions of jobs to prospective employees rather than balanced descriptions (Dunnette, Arvey, and Banas, 1973; Ward, 1972). This is probably done in the hope of attracting desirable candidates in a competitive job market. As a result, however, the inflated expectations of many employees are not met, and the disappointed employees subsequently leave (Porter and Steers, 1973).

There are two important ways in which employee expectations can be met. The first is to increase the positive outcomes experienced by the employee (perhaps through pay increases, better supervision, job enrichment, new office furniture, or increased social activities). By doing so, the likelihood of meeting an employee's inflated expectations is enhanced. Unfortunately, this is often difficult to accomplish for a variety of reasons. The second approach is to reduce employee expectations so they more accurately reflect organizational reality. This is done through realistic job previews.

A *realistic job preview* (RJP) attempts to provide prospective employees with accurate job information. When they have been given such information, employees have more realistic (as opposed to inflated) initial expectations, and can therefore make more informed and appropriate choices. A realistic job preview can emphasize specific facts about the job and present both the positive and negative aspects. Based on these facts, employees are more likely to identify a suitable match between their own needs and those of the organization. In contrast, the traditional approach typically attempts to sell the job and present it in its most favorable light. (See Box 14–1.)

Several experiments have been done in industry in an attempt to compare the relative advantage of realistic job previews with the traditional approach. In the realistic job previews, job information was presented to candidates in either a film about the job, a booklet describing the job, a practice session, or interviews with actual job incumbents.

What effect did the previews have? Several benefits were noted (Wanous, 1977). First, contrary to expectations, RJPs did not impair the organization's ability to recruit and hire desired candidates. People were still willing to take the positions, despite less positive impressions. Second, several studies show that RJPs clearly lowered job expectations, and created more realistic perceptions of what the actual job would be like. Third, RJPs led to more positive job attitudes after the initial employment period, as well as fewer thoughts about leaving. Finally, RJPs consistently led to reduced turnover compared to traditional methods. Employees exposed to realistic job previews in a wide array of work organizations exhibited turnover rates between 10 to 20 percent lower than other employees. While realistic job previews should not be seen as a panacea for all organizational ills, they do appear to represent another factor contributing to the overall effectiveness of the organization and its management.

Employee Adaptation and Development

When individuals join a new organization they enter a new world filled with new experiences, challenges, and potential threats. This initial employment period is important for both the individual and the organization since so

Box 14–1 Realistic Job Previews

A major problem facing prospective employees is gathering sufficient, accurate information about an organization or job on which to base an intelligent decision about the desirability of joining the organization. During the recruitment process, many companies tend to be overly generous or optimistic in describing the job to job applicants in order to sell them on joining the firm. (Personnel managers get rewarded for how many people they hire, not for how many people they don't hire.) As a result, applicants are often misled and, once on the job, find that their job expectations are clearly not being met. As a result, many leave and the organization is faced with the task of selling the job to someone else.

Recently, major efforts have begun in many organizations to overcome this disruptive and costly cycle through the use of *realistic job previews* (RJP). In an RJP, in contrast to the traditional method, prospective employees are given a preview of what the job is really like—both positive *and negative* aspects. As a result, applicants develop a clearer portrait of the job and what they can expect from it. This process is shown as it compares to the traditional approach:*

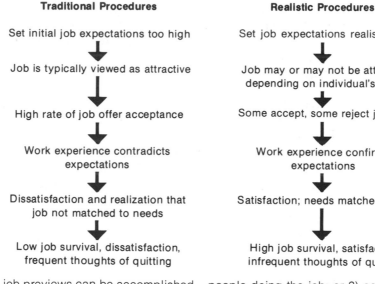

Traditional Procedures	Realistic Procedures
Set initial job expectations too high	Set job expectations realistically
Job is typically viewed as attractive	Job may or may not be attractive, depending on individual's needs
High rate of job offer acceptance	Some accept, some reject job offer
Work experience contradicts expectations	Work experience confirms expectations
Dissatisfaction and realization that job not matched to needs	Satisfaction; needs matched to job
Low job survival, dissatisfaction, frequent thoughts of quitting	High job survival, satisfaction, infrequent thoughts of quitting

Realistic job previews can be accomplished in a variety of ways, including exposing job applicants to: 1) interviews with employees doing the same job; 2) video-tape or films of people doing the job; or 3) actually letting the applicant do the job for a while. In any case, applicants learn first-hand what to expect.

*Chart is reprinted, by permission of the publisher, from "Tell it like it is at realistic job previews," J.P. Wanous, *Personnel,* July–August 1975, © 1975 by AMACOM, a division of American Management Associations, p. 54. All rights reserved.

What kind of results emerge from RJPs? A series of studies has been carried out that compared the attitudinal and behavioral consequences of the two approaches. As summarized by John Wanous,* several important conclusions can be drawn: 1) Newly hired employees who received RJPs have greater job survival rates than those hired by traditional recruiting methods. 2) Employees hired after RJPs indicate higher job satisfaction, ostensibly because their initial expectations were more easily met by the actual job situation. 3) RJPs do in fact set job expectations at more realistic levels. 4) RJPs do not reduce the flow of highly qualified applicants.

Results like these suggest that RJPs do have significant potential for managers interested in developing a stable workforce of qualified employees. They can reduce turnover and increase satisfaction in many cases with little additional time or effort on the part of management.

much turnover (voluntary and involuntary) occurs during this matching period. Many employees discover that they simply cannot handle—or do not wish to handle—their assigned job. For a variety of reasons they discover somewhat too late that a mistake has been made and choose to leave. Others learn to cope, adapt to, and even enjoy their new position, and decide to remain.

What causes differences in the reactions of employees? Several factors account for this. First, many employees are simply not equipped technically to handle the job. Perhaps they either cannot type, make decisions, deal with people, or make sales. Under these circumstances, people either seek additional training or leave. In addition to technical factors, several psychological factors account for success or failure in adaptation and development. Two points are relevant here. First, there are the related processes of socialization and individualization. Second is the concept of organizational commitment. We will consider each as it relates to employee ability to successfully adapt to an organization.

Socialization and Individualization

One way to view the employment relationship is a process of exchange between employees and organizations. Levinson and associates (1962) refer to this as a *psychological contract* in which both parties create mutual expectations of each other that govern their relationship. Ironically, both sides are often unaware of the expectations of the other party and assume that their own view of the exchange is shared by the other party. Included in this psychological contract is a series of legitimate demands (level of output, types of work activities) placed on the individual by the organization. The individual accepts these demands as part of the contract in exchange for receiving valued outcomes (salary, job security) from the organization.

In this process, organizations typically attempt to exert—overtly or covertly—subtle pressures on employees to shape them into the kinds of employees desired. This process is called *socialization*. Simultaneously, individuals continue to attempt to shape the work environment so it meets their own needs. This process is called *individualization*. The interaction of these two processes, operating continuously, creates the work place in which everyone works and lives. It is important to understand how these processes work.

Socialization is vital to the efficient operation of any work organization. As noted by Schein (1968, p. 2), ''the speed and effectiveness of socialization determine employee loyalty, commitment, productivity, and turnover. The basic stability and effectiveness of organizations therefore depends upon their ability to socialize new members.'' Without some degree of socialization, employees would diffuse their work efforts, often in conflicting directions, because of disagreements over the major purposes and values of the organization.

Stages in socialization.

The socialization process consists of three stages:

Prearrival Individuals typically enter organizations with preconceptions about the nature of the organization and job. These preconceptions are formed as a result of previous education, work experiences, and contacts with organization members. For instance, a dominant attitude taught in many business schools is the need for an efficient, dedicated workforce. Hence, many individuals who are exposed to this idea are already well on the way to socialization before actual organizational entry.

Encounter Once inside the organization, the individual encounters other members who exhibit accepted attitudes and behavior. These day-to-day interactions, combined with positive reinforcements for behaving in a similar fashion (and punishment for contrary behavior), condition the individual over time to accept the status of peers and superiors.

Change and acquisition These initial encounters, along with their conditioning and reinforcement attempts, ultimately lead to solidifying the new attitudes and behaviors individuals have learned. People develop new self-images more consistent with other members. They develop new social relationships, often with members of the same organization. Finally, they develop new values and new modes of behavior. At this point, the individual has been transformed from an outsider into a member.

The success of socialization attempts is influenced by two factors (Schein, 1968). First, attempts are more successful if individuals are highly motivated upon entry. If individuals are eager to join a firm, for instance, they are more likely to put up with initial discomforts, and to be more receptive to company-sanctioned norms and values. In addition, socialization attempts are usually more successful if the organization offers inducements to remain with the organization and comply with its dictates. Offering an employee perquisites not offered elsewhere (a private office, a company car) can often entice the individual to remain.

Techniques of socialization. How do organizations socialize their employees? Several common methods can be identified (Caplow, 1964):

Employee selection Employers and interviewers seek the ''right kind of person.'' This search often translates into a search for individuals who already share common values.

Training and development Once inside the organization, employees are often exposed to a series of training programs designed to instill in them certain beliefs and values that are desired by the organization. These programs may take the form of new employee orientation, management development workshops, and departmental meetings.

Apprenticeships Here a senior employee assumes responsibility for socializing a new employee. Under this ''buddy system'', the senior advisor is in an advantageous position to instill in the new employee both technical skills and workplace norms and values. Failure to comply with these efforts can lead to expulsion from the apprentice program, thereby adding significant reinforcing power to socialization attempts.

Debasement experiences This refers to a dramatic experience an employee undergoes which causes him to detach himself from earlier attitudes and to substitute a more humble self-perception that allows for easier socialization attempts. Periodically, an old hand or a supervisor will set up a new employee in a way that the employee fails on a task or is publicly embarrassed. As a result of the experience, the employee is more prone to look up to the supervisor for advice and knowledge.

Anticipatory socialization This process consists of an individual accepting the beliefs and values of a group he aspires to become a member of but does not already belong to. In essence, the person socializes himself in the hopes that it may facilitate membership and acceptance by the group or organization. Anticipatory socialization can be seen among students in many professional schools (business, law, medicine) as they prepare for their careers and develop belief systems that are compatible with the profession.

Trial and error Finally, socialization often occurs almost by chance. Organizations do not conrol the daily activities of all their employees. They must allow the employees to experience various aspects of the organization and, in the process, learn about the organization. While these non-programmed efforts may not be as systematic as other methods, they are nevertheless a necessary part of organizational life.

Individualization. The second half of the psychological contract consists of efforts by individuals to change the workplace to meet their needs (Porter, Lawler, and Hackman, 1975). While the organization attempts to socialize individuals to accept its beliefs and values, individuals often respond in several ways aimed at nullifying or reducing these attempts and maintaining a certain degree of control over their own work life. Efforts aimed at asserting individualization can be classified into three broad categories (Schein, 1968):

Rebellion   At one extreme, an individual may respond to socialization attempts with open rejection and hostility. This rejection, however, may lead to the individual being dismissed (perhaps as a nonconformist). Alternatively, it could lead to actual change in the organization. More probably, it would result in an attempt by the organization to "co-opt" the rebel and blunt the attack.

Creative individualism   Toward the middle of the individualization continuum is creative individualism. This is where individuals choose to accept the basic aspects of the organization's norms and values but reject the peripheral ones and substitute their own. In essence, this is a compromise position where both parties attempt to make peace: the individual will accept certain aspects of organizational life, while the organization allows room for dissent and unconventional behavior.

Conformity   At the other extreme, many individuals adapt to organizational life by simply giving up their individuality and conforming to corporate norms. The "organization man" (or woman) is a prime example. However, as noted in Chapter 15, the personal costs associated with such behavior can be high.

We have seen how individuals and organizations attempt to accommodate one another and create relatively stable situations in which both can survive and prosper. As individuals continue on the job, they come to think more about the nature of their relationship with the organization. Do they agree with the goals and values of the organization? Are they motivated to work hard to help the organization realize the goals? Do they wish to remain with the organization or go elsewhere? Answers to questions like these focus on the extent to which employees feel committed to the organization. Because of the relationship between socialization and organizational commitments—particularly during the initial employment period—we will now turn to an examination of the nature of commitments in organizations.

Organizational Commitment

Briefly defined, *organizational commitment* refers to the relative strength of an individual's identification with and involvement in an organization (Porter, Steers, Mowday, and Boulian, 1974; Steers, 1977a). It can be characterized by at least three factors: 1) a strong belief in and acceptance of the organization's goals and values; 2) a willingness to exert considerable effort on behalf of the organization; and 3) a strong desire to maintain membership in the organization.

When viewed in this way, commitment represents something beyond mere passive loyalty to an organization. Instead, it involves an active relationship with the organization in which individuals are willing to give something of themselves in order to help the organization succeed and prosper. As noted by March and Simon (1958), real commitment often evolves into an exchange relationship in which individuals attach themselves to the organization in return for certain rewards or outcomes from the organization.

As an attitude, commitment differs in several ways from the more widely studied attitude of job satisfaction. First, commitment involves a wider perspective reflecting an individual's feelings toward an organization as a whole. Job satisfaction, on the other hand, focuses on a person's responses either to the job or to certain aspects of the job. Job satisfaction levels can change rapidly over time in response to immediate changes in the work environment, while commitment attitudes develop more slowly but consistently over time (Porter et al., 1974).

Outcomes of commitment.   If commitment represents part of the adaptation process, how do high levels of commitment influence employee behavior? Specifically, at least four outcomes or consequences are apparent. To begin, employees truly committed to the goals and values of an organization are more likely to participate actively in organizational activities (March and Simon, 1958). High employee commitment is reflected in lower absenteeism.

In addition, highly committed employees generally have a stronger desire to remain with their employer and will continue to contribute toward the attainment of the organizational objectives with which they agree. Considerable empirical support exists for this position. Commitment has been consistently found to be inversely related to turnover (Mowday, Steers, and Porter 1979). In fact, although job satisfaction may represent a better predictor of employee turnover during the *initial* development period, commitment becomes a stronger predictor than satisfaction as time goes on and employees begin to identify more with the organization and its goals.

Third, as employees continue to identify themselves with the organization and to believe in its objectives, they may become more involved in their jobs, since their jobs represent the key mechanism by which they can contribute to the attainment of organizational goals. This relationship may not be overly strong, however. It is possible, for instance, that a nurse's aide could be highly committed to the public health goals of a hospital, but not become involved in the more distasteful aspects of caring for the sick. Here, an employee may continue to be committed to the organization—and faithfully perform the job—yet remain uninvolved in the actual task requirements of the job itself.

Fourth, we expect highly committed employees to be willing to expend a good deal of effort on behalf of the organization. This follows from the definition of commitment itself. While such effort may at times be translated into actual job performance (Mowday et al., 1974), this would not always be the case. Job performance is a function of several factors. While effort is certainly one of these factors, it is not in itself sufficient to determine actual performance level.

Building organizational commitment. Given the importance of employee commitment to the attachment process, what can managers do to facilitate or increase commitment? Several strategies are available. First, when employees are placed in situations where they have opportunities to achieve goals that are personally meaningful to them, employees may come to link personal outcomes with organizational outcomes instead of being in conflict with them (Argyris, 1957). Employees should be shown that management and other employees are truly concerned about their welfare. Many times managers are in fact concerned yet fail to indicate it. Third, it is possible under some circumstances to modify jobs so employees have greater autonomy and responsibility and can identify with the actual tasks they perform. Finally, managers can attempt to foster better employee understanding of organizational goals and objectives. Why are the goals meaningful and how can employees contribute toward goal attainment? Actions like these can help create an atmosphere of mutual trust and support between employee and employer, where both contribute something to the attainment of the other's goals, and where an exchange is made with adequate consideration for employee needs and goals.

Employee Absenteeism

Each year, approximately 400 million work days are lost in the U.S. as a result of employee absenteeism. This amounts to about 5.1 days lost per employee per year (Yolles, Carone, and Krinsky, 1975). In fact, many industries, particularly those characterized by highly stressful jobs, have proportionately higher absenteeism rates, often approaching 15–20% per day. It has been estimated by Mirvis and Lawler (1977—see Box 13–2) that the cost of non-managerial absenteeism is about $66 per day per employee, including salary, fringe benefits, costs associated with temporary replacement, and estimated profit loss. Combining this figure with the number of work days lost yields an estimated annual cost of absenteeism in this country of $26.4 billion! Clearly, absenteeism represents a significant problem for managers and organizations that must be understood and dealt with if effectiveness of operations is to be achieved.

Many managers assume that absenteeism and turnover represent similar behaviors and are caused by the same factors. This is not the case, however. Absenteeism differs from turnover in several ways that require special managerial attention (Porter and Steers, 1973). First, the negative consequences associated with absenteeism for the employee are usually much less than those associated with turnover. Second, absenteeism is more likely to be a spontaneous and relatively easy decision, while the act of termination is more carefully considered over time. Finally, absenteeism often represents a substitute form of behavior for turnover, particulary when alternative forms of employment are unavailable. Sufficient reason exists to justify the study of employee absenteeism as a separate category of behavior and not simply as a part of the turnover process.

In this section, we will consider a model of the major influences on employee absenteeism or attendance (after Steers and Rhodes, 1978). The model attempts to answer two basic questions: What causes *attendance motivation* (a desire or willingness to come to work) and what causes *actual attendance*? It is important to clearly recognize that the answers to these two questions are quite different. Both sets of factors are depicted in Exhibit 14–3.

Causes of Attendance Motivation

First, let's examine the major causes of attendance motivation. Based on available data, *attendance motivation* appears to be influenced by two primary factors: 1) satisfaction with the job situation, and 2) various pressures to attend. If employees enjoy the work situation and the tasks associated with the job, they are more likely to *want* to come to work, since the work experience is a pleasurable one. In addition, even if the job is not a pleasurable one, there are many conditions (pressures) under which it would be in employees' best interest to attend. We will consider both of these factors separately.

Satisfaction with the job situation.   With what we know about the nature of job attitudes, we can suggest that people are more satisfied when the characteristics of the job and the surrounding work environment meet their personal values and job expectations (Locke, 1976). The job situation may be characterized by many factors, including job scope, job level, and role stress. (box 1 in Exhibit 14–3). These factors are evaluated by employees in the light of their own values on job expectations (box 2) to determine the extent to which employees have positive or negative attitudes about the work situation (box 4).

Exhibit 14–3 Major influences on employee attendance (Steers and Rhodes, 1978).

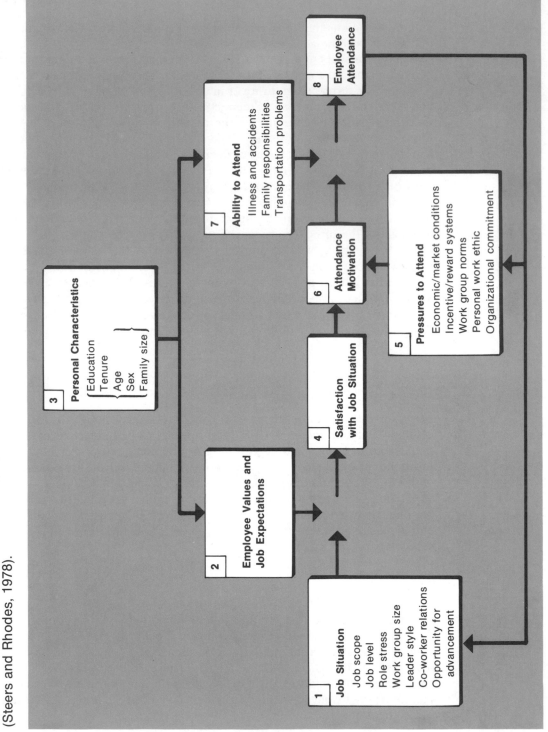

Job expectations, in turn, are influenced by several personal characteristics (box 3). For example, tenured employees or employees with more education often expect more from a job, making it harder for the job situation to satisfy their demands.

An example will help clarify this situation. An employee who has considerable seniority (a personal characteristic) comes to expect certain perquisites as a result of longevity on the job. These expectations may include higher-grade jobs, greater status, or being first in line for promotion. Under this circumstance, we expect the individual to be satisfied when these expectations are met by the job situation. When expectations are not met, satisfaction with the job situation diminishes.

Pressures to attend.   The second factor in attendance motivation consists of a series of what may be called pressures to attend. These pressures are conditions, characteristics, or incentives that make it desirable to attend—from an employee viewpoint—even if the job itself is not attractive or satisfying. As in box 5, these pressures may include: 1) economic and market conditions, including options in finding alternative employment; 2) incentive/reward systems, or the extent to which pay and other rewards are contingent upon good attendance; 3) work group norms about attendance behavior; 4) personal work ethic, or the belief that an individual has a moral obligation to attend; and 5) organizational commitment, or the extent to which an employee identifies with the organization and its goals and wants to help attain them.

These pressures, and one's relative satisfaction with the overall job situation are the primary causes of attendance motivation (box 6). In this process, we expect different factors to be more important to different employees. For instance, a traveling sales representative who works alone would probably not be significantly influenced by work group norms, particularly when compared to an assemblyline worker. Similarly financial incentives would probably not motivate someone who has more than sufficient income (or whose family has sufficient income) to come to work. Even so, we expect the sum total of these various pressures to combine with satisfaction levels to influence attendance motivation.

Causes of Employee Attendance

Now we come to the second question: how do we get from attendance motivation to actual attendance? As was pointed out above, an employee's *desire* to come to work is not the same as the *ability* to come to work. As shown in the model (Exhibit 14–3), actual attendance is a result of *both* factors: attendance motivation and ability to attend.

We can identify at least three limitations on people's ability to attend (box 7). These are: 1) illness and accidents; 2) family responsibilities; and 3) transportation problems. Probably the most significant problem here is illness and accidents. It has been estimated that nearly 60% of all absences are due to health-related causes. Over 40 million work days are lost every year as a result of work-related accidents (Hedges, 1973). Illness and accidents clearly represent a major factor in absenteeism.

Family responsibilities also place limitations on ability to attend. For instance, it has been found that women are absent from work more often than men and statistics bear this out. However, if we look for the reasons for this we discover that much of the difference in absence rates can be attributed both to differences in the kinds of jobs women typically hold and in the traditional roles and responsibilities assigned to them. It is generally the wife or mother who stays home and cares for sick children. As a result, as family size increases so does female absenteeism.

Transportation problems represent a third influence on one's ability to attend. Transportation problems involve travel distance, weather conditions, and the reliability of the mode of transportation.

In many ways, ability to attend serves as gatekeeper in the attendance process. Assuming the ability to come to work, attendance motivation fairly accurately predicts actual attendance. The higher the motivation the more regular the attendance. However, when an employee is sick or has car problems, attendance motivation alone will probably not suffice. Both factors must be present for us to expect high levels of attendance at work.

One final note should be emphasized. Exhibit 14–3 contains a feedback arrow indicating that the model is cyclical in nature. Superior attendance is often seen as an indicator of good performance and readiness for promotion. Poor attendance may adversely influence relationships with supervisors and co-workers and could even result in changes in these relationships. Widespread absenteeism may cause the company to alter its incentive or control programs. In short, absence or attendance behavior should not be seen solely as an end result. It causes other aspects of the work situation to change which, in turn, may also affect future attendance.

Managing Attendance Behavior

The purpose of any model like the one proposed here is to explain human behavior. What can managers learn from the model to aid them in reducing avoidable absenteeism from the workplace? The model described here leads to several recommendations.

1. First, before any action is taken, a *systematic* analysis of the problem can be made. The model suggested here provides a framework for diagnosis and points to several areas in which major problems may be found. By working through the model, major problem areas may become apparent. As a result, efforts aimed at eliminating the problem can be more focused.

2. If diagnosis reveals that a major problem exists with the satisfaction component of the model, efforts can be made in this area. Several strategies can be suggested, including:

- implement job enrichment
- reduce job stress
- build group cohesiveness and co-worker relations
- improve leadership training
- clarify job expectations
- provide employee career counseling

3. If the problem seems to be in the area of pressures or incentives to attend, other remedies may be attempted (see Box 14–2):

- clarify rewards for good attendance
- review sick leave policies
- encourage an attendance-oriented work-group norm
- foster a personal work ethic
- facilitate organizational commitment

4. Finally, if ability to attend is the problem, several remedies are:

- encourage sound physical health (perhaps through company-sponsored exercise programs and physical examinations)
- institute employee counseling programs to foster sound mental health
- be sensitive to problems of alcoholism and drug abuse and provide relevant programs where necessary
- consider company-sponsored or supported day care facilities
- consider shuttle busses for employees living in outlying areas

This list of possible remedies to problems of employee absenteeism is meant to be illustrative of the kinds of actions management can take. Through actions like these, serious efforts can be made to reduce the occurrence of absenteeism, thereby creating conditions more conducive to organizational effectiveness.

Employee Turnover

One of the most widely studied topics in the area of organizational behavior is employee turnover. In fact, well over 1,000 articles on the subject have

Box 14–2 Well Pay and Retro Pay

We have all heard of sick pay, but at least one firm is experimenting quite successfully with well pay.* The firm, Parsons Pine Products of Ashland, Oregon, views well pay as the opposite of sick pay. It is an extra eight hour's wages that the company gives employees who are neither absent nor late for a full month.

Well pay was begun as a response to chronic tardiness and absenteeism in the manufacturing plant. After its introduction, tardiness was reduced to "almost zero" and absenteeism dropped more than Parsons wanted, since employees started coming to work even when they were sick. This practice increased the possibility of illness-related accidents on the job. As a result, Parsons introduced retro pay.

Retro pay offers a bonus to employees based on any reductions in the premiums from the state industrial accident insurance fund. Before the retro plan, the company had an accident rate 86% above the state-wide base and paid into the fund accordingly. Under the retro pay plan, any savings that resulted from reduced accidents would be distributed to the employees. As a result, the accident bill in one year dropped from $28,500 to $2,500. After deducting for administrative expenses, the state returned over $89,000 of the $100,000 premium, or some $900 per employee.

By using simple techniques such as well pay and retro pay, employees saw a fairly direct benefit in coming to work and avoiding accidents. As a result, attendance (and performance) increased, accidents decreased, and employees benefited.

*Source: "How To Earn Well-Pay" *Business Week,* June 12, 1978, pp. 143–146.

been published in the last few decades (Mobley, Griffeth, Hand, and Meglino, 1979; Price, 1977; Porter and Steers, 1973; Steers and Mowday, 1980). As a result of these studies, several useful models of the turnover process have been proposed. We shall examine one model here, developed by William H. Mobley, followed by a consideration of what managers can learn from the model to help reduce turnover on the job.

The model presented here is basically a cognitive model in that it assumes employees typically make conscious decisions to leave their jobs. It is a process model in that it attempts to describe the processes leading up to actual termination. A schematic diagram of this model is shown in Exhibit 14–4 (Mobley, 1977).

The starting point in this model is an employee's evaluation of his or her existing job (shown in block A). As employees think about the positive and negative aspects of their jobs, they experience various levels of job satisfaction or dissatisfaction (block B). When dissatisfaction is experienced, at least two outcomes often result. First the employees may begin thinking

Exhibit 14–4   The employee turnover process (Mobley, 1977, p. 238).

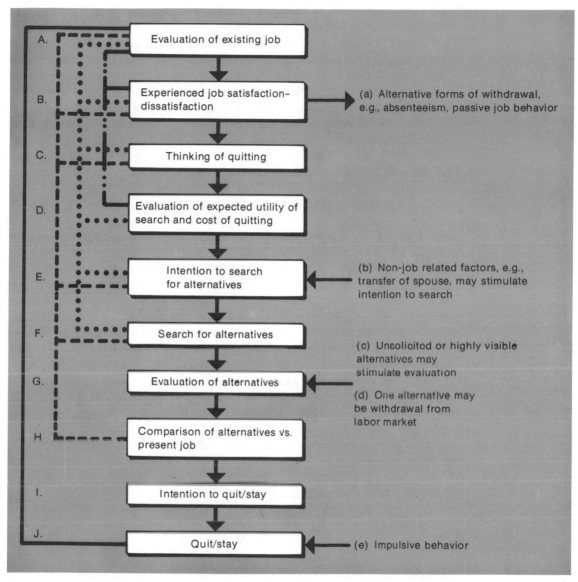

Source: Mobley, W.H. "Intermediate linkages in the relationship between job satisfaction and employee turnover," 1977:62. Copyright © 1977 by the American Psychological Association. Reprinted by permission of the author and the publisher.

about quitting (block C) and making alternate plans for employment. At the same time, however, employees may also begin engaging in several alternative forms of withdrawal (absenteeism, reduced job effort) as shown by arrow a.

Thoughts of quitting, in turn, often cause employees to consider the utility and costs associated with searching for (and possibly accepting) a new job (block D). The expected utility of search would include factors like the chances of finding another job, the desirability of alternative jobs, and the costs of search (travel costs, time away from the job). The evaluation of the costs of quitting might also include a consideration of loss of seniority and loss of vested benefits in retirement programs. In short, employees consider whether it is worth the trouble to look for a job elsewhere.

If employees determine that the costs of leaving are fairly high and/or that the expected utility of searching for a new job is low, they may decide to remain. In fact, employees may then reevaluate the existing job and begin to see it in a more positive light. ("This isn't such a bad job after all.") On the other hand, if the costs of search are reasonable and the expected utility of search is high, we predict that the employee will develop a behavioral inention to search for alternatives (block E). This intention would also be influenced by a series of non-work factors (arrow b), like a spouse's employment situation and geographic preferences. One may decide not to leave a dissatisfying job because one wishes to stay in the same geographic area or because one's spouse has a job nearby. Similarly, these non-work factors may stimulate search behavior even if an employee is satisfied with the job if one's spouse is about to be transferred. These intentions to search, however activated, generally lead to actual search behavior (block F).

If an individual is successful in identifying alternative job opportunities or if a unique opportunity is presented to the individual by others (arrow c), these opportunities must be evaluated (block G). In this process, the alternatives are compared to the present job (block H) to determine the relative merits of both staying and leaving. The end result of this decision process is an intent to either stay or leave (block I), followed by the actual behavior of staying or leaving (block J).

Finally, arrow e suggests that some individuals may bypass this somewhat rational decision process and act impulsively. They may simply quit because of an argument with a co-worker or supervisor. Whatever the reason, it is important to recognize here that the process is not entirely a rational one, as the model may suggest. Instead, exceptions to the process may occur at any stage in the model. Still, the model is helpful in highlighting some of the major influences leading up to the decision to stay or leave.

Managing Turnover Behavior

Using this model, several avenues are open to managers who are interested in reducing employee turnover.

1. Clarify job expectations for new and prospective employees. Realistic job previews have been shown to lead to reduced turnover since resulting expectations are more easily met by the actual job situation.

2. Make sure that expected rewards or outcomes are closely tied to desired behaviors. In this way, it is more likely that employee expectations will be met following suitable performance.

3. When examining turnover rates, differentiate between turnover among high performers and low performers. These two groups may leave for quite different reasons. While reducing turnover among high performers may be desirable, there are many reasons why a *high* turnover rate among poor performers may be desirable.

4. Recognize the importance of job attitudes (both job satisfaction and organizational commitment), since these attitudes can have important repercussions in terms of influencing both subsequent job performance and intent to leave.

5. As much as possible, recognize individual characteristics in the selection and placement process and match people to jobs. (An alternative approach—matching jobs to people—is discussed in Chapter 16). In matching, it is more likely that individuals will have the requisite skills to succeed on the job and, in doing so, may develop more positive attitudes toward staying with the organization.

6. Organizations can endeavor to increase commitment by convincing employees that management is truly concerned about their welfare. This can be done, among other ways, through career counseling programs (D. T. Hall, 1976), where employees are shown the various options available to them should they remain.

7. Recognize non-work factors as a potent influence on intent to leave. Many employees leave not by choice, but because of non-work-related reasons, as discussed earlier. In some situations, organizations may be able to help. Successful examples include subsidizing day-care centers, policies that allow the company to hire spouses, or policies that attempt to take family considerations into account in promotions and transfers.

8. Finally, as discussed earlier in the text, it may be desirable in some cases to monitor employee attitudes toward the job and organization at regular intervals (perhaps annually) as an early warning system for potential turnover. If attitudes drop substantially, management is alerted to the problem and can take remedial action aimed at solving the problem and reducing the probability of increased terminations.

Other management implications can be identified. The point here is that, based on the above model, there *are* things managers can do to reduce employee turnover and develop a more stable workforce for the pursuit of organizational effectiveness.

We have now come full circle in this chapter. We began by considering the attachment cycle, the process by which individuals join organizations, become socialized, and grow and develop with experience. We also considered absenteeism and turnover, the latter being the final stage in the attachment cycle. People tend to consider the earlier stages in this cycle as positive and the latter stages as negative. This view is overly simplistic for several reasons.

Where turnover is concerned, there are many situations in which some turnover is desirable. For instance, turnover among poor performers allows an organization to replace them with more skilled and motivated employees. Turnover can be beneficial to many of the leavers themselves when it facilitates their seeking other positions that may be more suitable to their own personal goals and needs. In this regard, it should be noted that some employees have to be pushed out of the nest before they will attempt something more rewarding. Turnover can serve this function. Turnover can also reduce entrenched conflict; long-standing situations where two individuals or groups oppose each other's actions to the point of being dysfunctional for the organization as a whole (Staw, 1980). Finally, turnover opens up avenues of promotion for those who aspire to make a career with the organization yet find upward mobility slow.

On the other hand, it should also be recognized that many adverse results accompany turnover that offset many of these benefits. Disadvantages include increased recruitment and selection costs, increased training and development costs, disruption of on-going group processes, and possible demoralization of remaining members. Managers should not automatically set out to reduce turnover without first assessing potential costs and benefits. Only then should a decision be made with respect to actions aimed at reducing turnover and stabilizing the workforce.

Summary

The major focus of the book so far has been on motivating employee performance. In this chapter, we shifted this focus to motivating participation; that is, we considered major influences on the psychological linkages that develop between individuals and organizations and how these linkages affect withdrawal behavior.

The concept of careers was introduced, followed by a consideration of the process by which employees enter or join organizations; this is called organizational entry. Next, we considered the developmental processes that occur as employees remain with an organization. Then, various influences on absenteeism were discussed and a model was presented that attempted to describe absence behavior. Implications of the model for management were also discussed.

Finally, employee turnover was considered. A model of turnover was discussed and, again, implications for management were suggested. In all, the point was made that reducing employee turnover and absenteeism required the active efforts of management.

Key Words

career

career stages

organizational entry

realistic job preview

psychological contract

socialization

individualization

anticipatory socialization

organizational commitment

absenteeism

attendance motivation

well pay

retro pay

turnover

debasement experiences

Questions for Discussion

1. Describe the typical career stages that many employees go through. How might exceptions to this typical pattern occur?
2. What major factors influence a person's choice of an organization? In general, how accurate is the information most people have in making this choice?
3. How does a realistic job preview differ from a traditional one? What are some advantages/drawbacks of RJPs?
4. What is a psychological contract? How does it work?
5. How do socialization processes work in organizations?
6. What are some techniques used to socialize employees?
7. Describe the process of individualization. How do employees attempt to individualize their jobs?
8. Define organizational commitment. How does an organization build organizational commitment?
9. Discuss several outcomes of organizational commitments.
10. What are the major causes of employee absenteeism?
11. Distinguish between attendance and attendance motivation.
12. What role do pressures to attend play in actual attendance? What role does ability to attend play?
13. Identify several major strategies that can be used by managers to reduce absenteeism.
14. How do the major causes of turnover differ from those of absenteeism? How are they similar?
15. What can managers do to reduce turnover?

chapter 15
Work and Stress

We have heard much recently about blue-collar blues, white-collar woes, and quality of work. We learn from surveys that workers of all age groups, occupations, and backgrounds are discontented and suffer from various maladies of the workplace (Seashore and Barnowe, 1972). At issue here are several important problems, including how the work people do is designed and implemented and how people adjust to the required activities of the job. The first issue, job design and its consequences, is the subject of the next chapter. In this chapter, we will examine the ways people adjust—or fail to adjust—to work.

Importance of Topic for Managers

An understanding of work adjustment and job-related stress is important to managers for several reasons:

1. Prolonged stress has been shown to have deleterious physical and psychological side effects on individuals. Thus, employee health, as well as employee contribution to the organization, is jeopardized. Studies show that these effects are particularly pronounced in managerial personnel.

2. Stress is a major cause of employee turnover and absenteeism, and it inhibits the effectiveness of an organization.

3. Stress experienced by one employee can jeopardize the safety of others. This is clearly seen in the air traffic controller's job (discussed later) and in machine operators.

4. Finally, in recent years we have gained sufficient knowledge concerning stress and work adjustment to see that much experienced stress is needless. Reducing stress can both improve an employee's contribution to an organization and increase satisfaction with the job itself.

Problems of Work Adjustment

Failure to adjust to work represents a major problem in industry today. It has been estimated that between 80% and 90% of industrial accidents are caused by personal factors (Yolles, 1967). Turnover, absenteeism, drug abuse, alcoholism, and sabotage remain relatively permanent fixtures of most contemporary work organizations. To the extent that individuals are unable to adjust to work, we would expect them to persist in counterproductive behavior.

In a study of why people have problems adjusting to work, Neff (1968) identified five major reasons. Following type theory of personality, he suggests that each of the five types represents a "clinical picture of different varieties of work psychopathology" (p. 208):

Type I: People who lack motivation to work. These individuals have a negative conception of the work role and choose to avoid it.

Type II: People whose predominating response to the demand to be productive is fear or anxiety.

Type III: People who are characterized predominantly by open hostility and aggression.

Type IV: People who are characterized by marked dependency. These people often exhibit the characteristic of helplessness, constantly seeking advice from others and are unable to initiate any action on their own.

Type V: People who display a marked degree of social naivete. These individuals lack perception when it comes to the needs and feelings of others and may not realize that their behavior elicits reactions from and has an effect on others. Typically, these individuals are socially inept and unaware of appropriate behavior in ordinary social situations.

Several important points follow from Neff's analysis. First, it should be noted that failure to adjust to a normal job or work schedule does not automatically imply that an individual is lazy or stupid. Several deeply ingrained psychological problems keep people from normal adjustment in many cases.

Second, it should be noted that only one of the five types (Type I) represents a motivational problem. We must look beyond motivation for answers to the psychopathology of work. Third, one type (Type V) represents a form of personality disorder, or at least social immaturity.

The remaining three types—anxiety, aggression, and dependency—relate not only to personality, but more importantly to how the nature of the job affects that personality. In fact, anxiety, aggression, and dependency are major factors inherent in the nature of stressful jobs in organizations. Hence, it seems that at least three of the five reasons for failure to adjust to work relate to the extent to which the job is experienced as stressful and causes the individual to want to withdraw. In view of the importance of stress as a major factor in an individual's adjustment to work, we will focus on it in this chapter.

It has been wisely observed that "If, under stress, a man goes all to pieces, he will probably be told to pull himself together. It would be more effective to help him identify the pieces and to understand why they have come apart" (Ruddock, 1972, p. 94). This is the role of the contemporary manager in dealing with stress. Managers cannot simply ignore the existence of stress on the job. Instead, they have a responsibility to understand the nature and causes of stress and to know how to deal with it on the job.

We will explore the somewhat ambiguous topic of work-related stress in several stages. First, we will consider what we mean by stress. Next, major organizational and personal influences on stress will be examined. Following this, consideration will be given to several outcomes of stress. Finally, we will focus on what employees and managers can do to help cope with stress on the job. Throughout, emphasis will be placed on how stress and its consequences affect people at work and what role managers can play in attempting to minimize the effects of stress on both the individual and the organization. (See Cooper and Payne (1978) for an in-depth discussion of research relating to stress at work.)

The Nature of Work-Related Stress

Definition of Stress

Stress refers to the reaction of individuals to characteristics of the environment which pose a threat. It points to a poor fit between individuals and their environment in which either excessive demands are being made or individuals are ill equipped to handle a given situation (French, 1976). Under stress, individuals are unable to respond to environmental stimuli without undue psychological and/or physiological damage like chronic fatigue, tension, or high blood pressure. This damage resulting from experienced stress is usually referred to as *strain*.

Before examining the concept of work-related stress in detail, several important points need to be made. First, stress is pervasive in the work environment (McGrath, 1976). Most of us must grapple with stress. For instance, a job may require too much from us or too little. In fact, almost any aspect of the work environment is capable of producing stress, including excessive noise, light, or heat, too much or too little responsibility, too much or too little work to accomplish, or too much or too little supervision.

Second, it is important to note that all people do not react in the same way to stressful situations even in the same occupation. One individual (a high need achiever) may thrive on a certain amount of job-related tension; this tension may serve to activate the achievement motive. A second individual may respond to this tension by worrying about his or her inability to cope with the situation. We must recognize the central role of individual differences in the determination of experienced stress.

Third, all stress is not necessarily bad. Although highly stressful situations invariably have dysfunctional consequences, moderate levels of stress often serve useful purposes. A moderate amount of job-related tension not only keeps us alert to environmental stimuli (possible dangers and opportunities), but in addition often provides a useful motivational function. Some experts argue that the best and most satisfying work that employees do is work performed under moderate stress. Some stress may be necessary for psychological growth, creative activities, and the acquisition of new skills. Learning to drive a car or play a piano or run a particular machine typically creates tension which is instrumental in skill development. It is only when the level of stress increases or when it is prolonged that physical or psychological problems emerge.

General Adaptation Syndrome

The general response to stressful events follows a fairly consistent pattern known as the *General Adaptation Syndrome* (Selye, 1956). This syndrome consists of three stages. The first stage, *alarm,* occurs at the first sign of stress. Here the body prepares to fight stress by releasing hormones from the endocrine glands. During this initial stage, heartbeat and respiration increase, blood-sugar level rises, muscles tense up, pupils dilate, and digestion slows. Following this initial shock, the body moves into the second stage, *resistance.* Here the body attempts to repair any damage and return to a condition of homeostasis. If successful, physical signs of stress will disappear. If the stress continues long enough, however, the body's capacity for adaptation becomes exhausted. In this third stage, *exhaustion,* defenses wear away and we experience a variety of stress-related illnesses, including headaches, ulcers, and high blood pressure. This third stage is the most severe and presents the greatest threat both to individuals and organizations.

Types of Stress:
Frustration and Anxiety

We have several different ways to categorize stress. However, from a managerial perspective, it is useful to focus on only two forms: frustration and anxiety. *Frustration* refers to an obstruction or impediment to goal-oriented behavior. Frustration occurs when an individual wishes to pursue a certain course of action but is prevented from doing so. This obstruction may be externally or internally caused. Examples of frustration include a salesperson who continually fails to make a sale, a machine operator who cannot keep pace with the machine, or even simply an inability to get back correct change from a coffee machine. The prevalence of frustration in work organizations should be obvious from this and other examples.

Whereas frustration is an obstruction in intrumental activities or behavior, *anxiety* is a feeling of inability to deal with anticipated harm. Anxiety occurs when people do not have appropriate responses or plans for coping with anticipated problems. It is characterized by a sense of dread, a foreboding, and a persistent apprehension of the future for reasons that are sometimes unknown to the individual.

What causes anxiety in work or organizations? Hamner and Organ (1978, p. 202) suggest several factors:

Differences in power in organizations which leave people with a feeling of vulnerability to administrative decisions adversely affecting them; frequent changes in organizations, which make existing behavior plans obsolete; competition, which creates the inevitability that some persons lose "face," esteem, and status; and job ambiguity (especially when it is coupled with pressure). To these may be added some related factors, such as lack of job feedback, volatility in the organization's economic environment, job insecurity, and big visibility of one's performance (successes as well as failures). Obviously, personal, nonorganizational factors come into play as well, such as physical illness, problems at home, unrealistically high personal goals, and estrangement from one's colleagues or one's peer group.

In the remainder of this chapter, we will consider in more detail various factors that have been found to influence both frustration and anxiety. We will do so by presenting a general model of stress, including its major causes and its outcomes. Following this, we will explore several mechanisms by which employees and their managers cope with or reduce experienced stress in organizations.

Major Influences on Work-Related Stress

The model of stress presented here draws heavily on the work of several social psychologists at the Institute for Social Research at the University of Michigan, including John French, Robert Caplan, Robert Kahn, and Daniel Katz. In essence, the proposed model identifies two major sources of stress: organizational sources and individual sources. In addition, the moderating effects of social support are considered. These influences are shown in Exhibit 15–1. First, we will consider organizational influences on stress.

Organizational Influences on Stress

Although many factors in the work environment have been found to influence the extent to which people experience stress on the job, six factors have been shown to be particularly strong. These are: 1) occupational differ-

Exhibit 15–1   Major influences on work-related stress

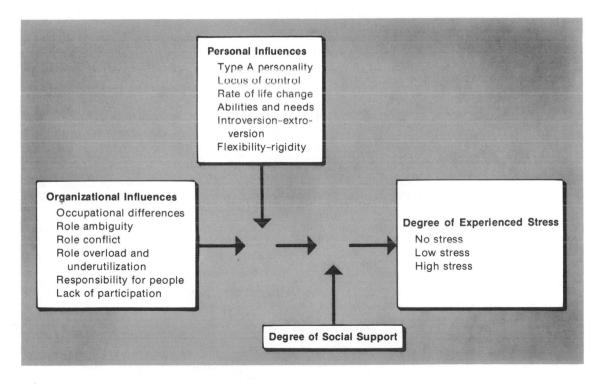

Personal Influences
Type A personality
Locus of control
Rate of life change
Abilities and needs
Introversion–extro-
version
Flexibility–rigidity

Organizational Influences
Occupational differences
Role ambiguity
Role conflict
Role overload and
underutilization
Responsibility for people
Lack of participation

Degree of Experienced Stress
No stress
Low stress
High stress

Degree of Social Support

ences; 2) role ambiguity; 3) role conflict; 4) role overload and underutilization; 5) responsibility for people; and 6) lack of participation. We will consider each of these factors in turn.

Occupational differences.   Tension and job stress are prevalent in our contemporary society and can be found in a wide variety of jobs. Consider, for example, the following quotes from interviews with working people (Terkel, 1972). The first is from a busdriver (p. 275):

> You have your tension. Sometimes you come close to having an accident, that upsets you. You just escape maybe by a hair or so. Sometimes maybe you get a disgruntled passenger on there, and starts a big argument. Traffic. You have someone who cuts you off or stops in front of the bus. There's a lot of tension behind that. . . . Most of the time you have to drive for the other drivers, to avoid hitting them. So you take the tension home with you. Most of the drivers, they'll suffer from hemorrhoids, kidney trouble, and such as that. I had a case of ulcers behind it.

Or, consider the plight of a bank teller (p. 348):

> Some days, when you're aggravated about something, you carry it after you leave the job. Certain people are bad days. (Laughs). The type of person who will walk in and says, "My car's double-parked outside. Would you hurry up, lady? . . . You want to say, "Hey, why did you double park your car? So now you're going to blame me if you get a ticket, 'cause you were dumb enough to leave it there?" But you can't. That's the one hassle. You can't say anything back. The customer's always right.*

Other examples could be cited: a secretary, assemblyline worker, foreman, waitress, even an executive. In fact, it is difficult to find many jobs that are without some degree of stress. We seldom talk about stress-less jobs; instead, we talk about the degree or magnitude of the stress.

The work roles (or occupations) which people fill have a substantial influence on the degree to which they experience stress (Cooper and Payne, 1978; French and Caplan, 1972). These occupational differences do *not* follow the traditional blue-collar/white-collar dichotomy, however. In general, available evidence suggests that high stress occupations are those in which incumbents have little control over their jobs, work under relentless time pressures, or threatening physical conditions, or have major responsibilities for either human or financial resources. Low stress occupations are not characterized by these features.

*From *Working: People Talk About What They Do All Day and How They Feel About What They Do,* © 1972, 1974 by Studs Terkel. Reprinted by permission of Pantheon Books, a division of Random House, Inc., and by permission of Wildwood House, Ltd., London.

A recent survey of 130 occupations by the National Institute for Occupational Safety and Health (NIOSH) attempted to identify those occupations that were most (and least) susceptible to occupational stress (*U.S. News and World Report,* March 13, 1978). By examining death rates and admission records to hospitals and mental health facilities, NIOSH was able to rank the various occupations by fairly objective measures of stress. The results are shown in Exhibit 15–2. As can be seen, high stress occupations (managers, secretaries, foremen) are typified by the stress producing characteristics noted above, while low stress occupations are not. It can be concluded that a major source of general stress emerges from the occupation one chooses or finds oneself in.

One of the most stressful occupations is that of air traffic controller. Although not included in the NIOSH study, controllers consistently confront tasks that not only tax their mental and physical capabilities, but also have serious personal risks to the passengers whose safety depends on their judgement and skill. The plight of these air traffic controllers is discussed in Box 15–1.

Role ambiguity.   Role ambiguity exists when individuals have inadequate information concerning their roles. It is the opposite of role clarity. This uncertainty over job definition takes many forms, including not knowing expectations for performance, not knowing how to meet those expectations, and not knowing the consequences of job behavior (Kahn et al., 1964). Role ambiguity is particularly strong among managerial (as opposed to non-managerial) jobs, where role definitions and task specification lack clarity. Role ambiguity can also occur among non-managerial employees (e.g., secretaries) where supervisors fail to take sufficient time to clarify role ex-

Exhibit 15–2   High and low stress jobs

High Stress Jobs	Low Stress Jobs
Manager	Farm laborer
Secretary	Maid
Foreman	Craft worker
Waitress/waiter	Stock handler
Office manager	Heavy equipment operator
Inspector	College professor
Clinical lab technician	Personnel worker

Source: Study conducted by the National Institute for Occupational Safety and Health, Department of Health, Education and Welfare. Cited in *U.S. News and World Report,* March 13, 1978, pp. 80–81.

Box 15–1 Job Stress in the Control Tower

Certainly one of the most stressful jobs in contemporary society is that of the air traffic controller, the person who monitors and guides airplanes in for a landing.* Nowhere is this stress more acute than in Chicago's O'Hare airport, the busiest airport in the world and called the "ulcer factory" by the controllers who work there. O'Hare airport handles 1,900 flights per day, and has one take-off or landing every 20 seconds during peak hours. Because of this pressure, controllers are only allowed to work 90 minutes at a stretch during peak hours, landing a plane every two minutes while simultaneously monitoring a half dozen more.

The problem. This pressure, combined with the ever-present fear of causing a crash or collision (known with studied casualness as creating an "aluminum shower") places controllers under tremendous stress on the job. Of the 94 controllers at O'Hare, only two have been there more than ten years; most controllers don't reach five years. Two-thirds of those remaining either have ulcers or ulcer symptoms. Most exhibit signs of prolonged stress: high blood pressure, arthritis, colitis, skin disorders, headaches, allergies, and upset stomachs. Other controllers struggle with more severe problems, like alcoholism, depression, persistent nightmares, and acute anxiety. In one year alone, seven men had to be carried from the O'Hare control tower on stretchers, victims of acute hypertension. And since 1970, more than 40 controllers have been permanently removed from their jobs for medical reasons.

Lack of remedies. Although the nature and extent of the problem is fully acknowledged, the prevailing work environment and Federal Aviation Administration (FAA) policies seem to conspire to thwart a workable solution. First, controllers contend that their supervisors and FAA policies place them in a no-win situation since FAA regulations require proper spacing of all aircraft yet the volume of traffic makes this spacing unrealistic. Supervisors encourage controllers to overlook these regulations and prevent delays, but if an error is made or a near-miss occurs, the controller is disciplined for not following regulations. Second, the controllers charge the FAA with understaffing, computer malfunctions, inadequate training programs, unrealistic transfer policies, and nerve-wracking conditions that jeopardize their health and public safety. However, a lawsuit filed by the controllers against the FAA to remedy these conditions was dismissed in court on the grounds that the controllers had not pursued other avenues of redress. Third, controllers who experience high stress are subject to a catch-22 transfer policy. Since O'Hare is understaffed, the FAA is reticent to transfer healthy controllers to smaller, less stressful airports. Yet when a controller becomes unable to cope with the pressure at O'Hare, the FAA prefers to terminate the controller rather than transfer him to a smaller airport, where he could use his skills in a less stressful environment. Finally, while FAA maintains a staff of qualified flight surgeons, controllers seldom visit them for fear that their stress-related disorders will be reported to the FAA. Hence, the controller's only way out is through some form of physical ailment.

*For details, see D. Martindale, "Sweaty Palms in the Control Tower," *Psychology Today,* February 1977, pp. 71–73, and "The Constant Quest for Safety," *Time Magazine,* April 11, 1977.

pectations for subordinates, thus leaving them unsure of how to best contribute to departmental—and organizational—goals. (It should be noted here that a major benefit ascribed to management-by-objectives programs is that they substantially reduce role ambiguity by specifying task goals.)

How prevalent is role ambiguity at work? In two independent surveys of employees, it was found that 35% of one sample (a national random sample of male employees) and 60% of the other sample (primarily scientists and engineers) reported some form of role ambiguity (Kahn et al., 1964; French and Caplan, 1972). Hence, ambiguity of job role is not an isolated event.

Role ambiguity has been found to lead to several negative stress-related outcomes. French and Caplan (1972) summarized their study findings as follows:

> In summary, role ambiguity, which appears to be widespread, (1) produces psychological strain and dissatisfaction: (2) leads to underutilization of human resources; and (3) leads to feelings of futility on how to cope with the organizational environment (p. 36).*

In other words, role ambiguity has far-reaching consequences beyond experienced stress, consequences which include employee turnover and absenteeism, poor coordination and utilization of human resources, and increased operating costs due to inefficiency.

It should be noted that not everyone responds in the same way to role ambiguity. Studies have shown that some people have a higher *tolerance for ambiguity* and are less affected (in terms of stress, reduced performance, or propensity to leave) than those with a low tolerance for ambiguity (Kahn et al., 1964).

Role conflict.   Role conflict may be defined as "the simultaneous occurrence of two (or more) sets of pressures such that compliance with one would make more difficult compliance with the other" (Kahn et al., 1964, p. 19). In other words, role conflict occurs when an employee is placed in a situation where contradictory demands are placed upon him. For instance, a factory worker may find himself in a situation where the supervisor is demanding greater output, yet the work group is demanding a restriction of output. Similarly, a secretary who reports to several supervisors may face a conflict over whose work to do first.

One of the best known studies of role conflict and stress was carried out by Robert Kahn and his colleagues at the University of Michigan. Kahn studied fifty-three managers plus their subordinates (a total of 381 people)

---

*French, J. R. P. and Caplan, R. D. "Organizational Stress and Individual Strain" Marrow, Alfred J., ed., *The Failure of Success* (New York: AMACOM, a division of American Management Associations, 1972.

and examined the nature of each person's role and how it affected subsequent behavior. As a result of the investigation, the following conclusions emerged:

> Contradictory role expectations give rise to opposing role pressures (role conflict), which generally have the following effects on the emotional experience of the focal person: intensified internal conflicts, increased tension associated with various aspects of the job, reduced satisfaction with the job and its various components, and decreased confidence in superiors and in the organization as a whole. The strain experienced by those in conflict situations leads to various coping responses—social and psychological withdrawal (reduction in communication and attributed influence) among them.
>
> Finally, the presence of conflict in one's role tends to undermine his reactions with his role senders, to produce weaker bonds of trust, respect, and attraction. It is quite clear that role conflicts are costly for the person in emotional and interpersonal terms. They may be costly to the organization, which depends on effective co-ordination and collaboration within and among its parts (1964, pp. 70–71).

Other studies have found similar results about the serious side effects of role conflict both for individuals and organizations (House and Rizzo, 1972; Miles and Perreault, 1976). It should be noted, however, that personality differences may serve to moderate the impact of role conflict on stress. In particular, it has been found that introverts and people who are more flexible respond more negatively to role conflict than others do (French and Caplan, 1972). Even so, role conflict should not be overlooked by managers as a primary source of stress and strain needing serious attention.

Role overload and underutilization. In addition to role ambiguity and conflict, a third aspect of role processes has also been found to represent an important influence on experienced stress, namely, the extent to which employees feel either overloaded or underutilized in their job responsibilities. *Role overload* is a condition in which individuals feel they are being asked to do more than time or ability permits. Individuals often experience role overload as a conflict between quantity and quality of performance. *Quantitative* overload consists of having more work than can be done in a given time period. It can be visualized as a continuum ranging from too little to do to too much to do. *Qualitative* role overload, on the other hand, consists of being taxed beyond one's skills, abilities, and knowledge. It can be seen as a continuum ranging from too easy work to too difficult work. It is important to note that *either* extreme represents a bad fit between the abilities of the employee and the demands of the work environment (French and Caplan, 1972). A good fit occurs at that point on both scales of workload where the abilities of the individual are relatively consistent with the demands of the job.

There is evidence that both quantitative and qualitative role overload are prevalent in our society. A review of findings suggests that between 44% and 73% of white-collar workers experience a form of role overload (French and Caplan, 1972). What induces this overload? As a result of a series of studies, French and Caplan (1972) concluded that a major factor influencing overload is the high achievement needs of many managers. Need for achievement correlated .42 with the number of hours worked per week and .25 with questionnaire measures of role overload. Much overload is apparently self-induced.

Similarly, the concept of *role underutilization* should also be acknowledged as a source of experienced stress. Role underutilization occurs when employees are allowed to use only a few of their skills and abilities, even though they are required to make heavy use of these. The most prevalent form of role underutilization is monotony, where the worker performs the same routine task (or set of tasks) over and over. Other examples of underutilization include total dependence on machines for determining work pace and sustained positional or postural constraint. Several studies have found that underutilization often leads to low self-esteem, low life satisfaction, and increased frequency of nervous complaints and symptoms (Gardell, 1976). Underutilization has also been found to lead to increased absenteeism and lower participation (even in union activities).

Both role overload and role underutilization have been shown to influence psychological and physiological reactions to the job. This U-function relationship between the extent of role utilization and stress is shown in Exhibit 15–3. Here it can be seen that the least stress is experienced at that point where an employee's abilities and skills are in balance with the requirements of the job. It should be noted in this respect that many of the current efforts to redesign jobs and improve the quality of work are aimed at minimizing overload or underutilization in the work place (see Chapter 16 for details), and achieving a more suitable balance between abilities and skills and using them on the job.

Responsibility for people. Some evidence suggests that managers and supervisors—people who are responsible for other people—experience considerable stress as a result of responsibility. Studies in the United States and abroad indicate that these individuals consistently have more ulcers and experience more hypertension than the people they supervise (Cooper and Payne, 1978; Katz and Kahn, 1978). Responsibility for people was found to represent a greater influence on stress than responsibility for non-personal factors like budgets, projects, equipment, and other property. As noted by French and Caplan (1972, p. 48):

> If there is any truth to the adage that "man's greatest enemy is himself," it can be found in these data—it is the responsibility which organizational members

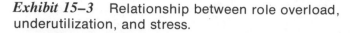

Exhibit 15–3 Relationship between role overload, underutilization, and stress.

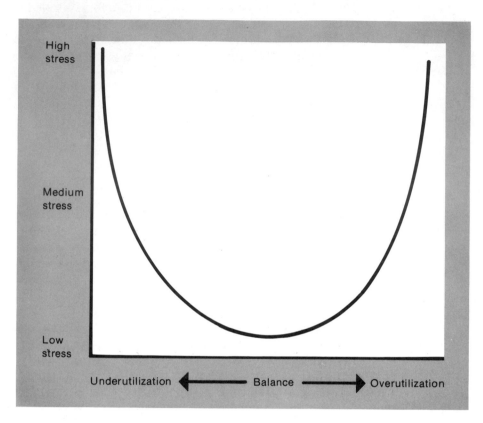

have for other organizational members, rather than the responsibility for impersonal aspects of the organization, which constitutes the more significant organizational stress.

Lack of participation. A final organizational influence on stress is the extent to which employees are allowed to participate in decisions affecting their work. To the extent that employees' opinions, knowledge, and wishes are excluded from organizational decision processes, the resulting lack of participation can lead not only to increased stress and strain, but also to reduced productivity (Coch and French, 1948; French, Isreal, and As, 1960).

The importance of employee participation in decision making (or PDM) in reducing stress is reflected in the French and Caplan (1972) study. After a major effort to uncover the antecedents of job-related stress, these investigators concluded (p. 51):

Since participation is also significantly correlated with low role ambiguity, good relations with others, and low overload, it is conceivable that its effects are widespread, and that all the relationships between these other stresses and psychological strain can be accounted for in terms of how much the person participates. This, in fact, appears to be the case. When we control or hold constant, through statistical analysis techniques, the amount of participation a person reports, then the correlations between all the above stresses and job satisfaction and job related threat drop quite noticeably. This suggests that low participation generates these related stresses, and that increasing participation is an efficient way of reducing many other stresses which also lead to psychological strain.

So convinced were French and Caplan of the centrality of participation in decision-making in reducing dysfunctional behavior and increasing organizational effectiveness that they have suggested a series of hypothetical consequences of PDM. These consequences, shown in Exhibit 15–4, are based on their review of a series of studies. As can be seen in the exhibit, PDM is hypothesized to lead to a wide variety of desirable consequences that not only improve the quality of work for individuals but also improve the level of effectiveness of the organization. Many of these outcomes (increased performance, commitment, innovation, and decreased turnover and absenteeism) have been repeatedly identified in the literature as indicators of organizational effectiveness. While the extent to which PDM actually determines or influences these outcomes may be questioned, it appears that increased employee participation in decisions affecting their jobs seems to be an important factor in reducing various dysfunctional psychological and behavioral reactions to the workplace.

Personal Influences on Stress

The second major category of stress-causing factors at work are the personal characteristics of individuals. It was noted at the beginning of this chapter that individual differences play a major role in determining the extent to which people experience stress. All people do not react the same way to potentially stressful events. Here we will consider five personal influences on stress: (1) Type A personality; (2) locus of control; (3) rate of life change; (4) abilities and needs; and (5) other personality traits, particularly introversion–extroversion and flexibility–rigidity.

Type A personality. Research over the past decade has focused on what is perhaps the single most dangerous personal influence on experienced stress and subsequent physical harm. This characteristic was first introduced by Friedman and Rosenman (1974) and is called *Type A personality* (as opposed to Type B personality). Type A and Type B personalities are felt to be relatively stable personal characteristics exhibited by individuals.

Exhibit 15–4 Characteristics of persons who participate in decisions which affect their work (French and Caplan, 1972, p. 52).

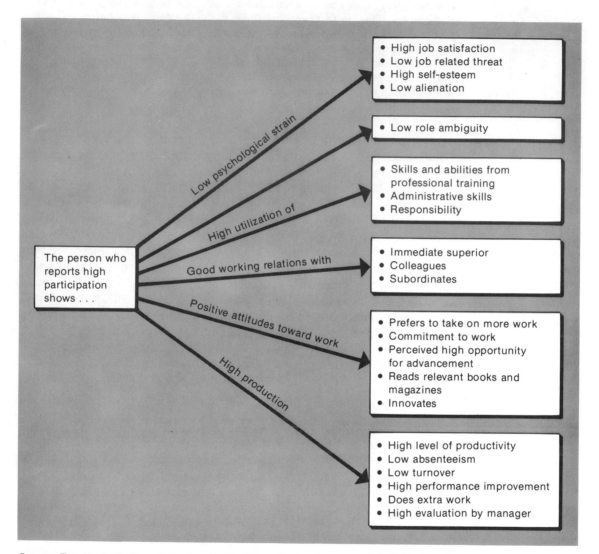

Source: French, J. R. P. and Caplan, R. D. "Organizational stress and individual strain," Marrow, Alfred J., ed., *The Failure of Success*. New York: AMACOM, a division of American Management Associations, 1972. Reprinted by permission of the publisher. All rights reserved.

Type A personality is frequently observed in managers. Indeed, one study found that 60% of managers were clearly identified as Type A, while only 12% were clearly identified as Type B (Howard, Cunningham, and Rechnitzer, 1976). It has been suggested that this type of personality is most helpful in rising through the ranks of an organization. Type A personality is characterized by impatience, restlessness, aggressiveness, competitiveness, polyphasic activities (having many "irons in the fire" at one time), and being under considerable time pressure. Work activities are particularly important to Type A individuals and they tend to freely invest long hours on the job to meet pressing (and recurring) deadlines. Type B people, on the other hand, experience no pressing deadlines or conflicts and are relatively free of any sense of time urgency or hostility.

The importance of Type A personality in producing stress is exemplified by the relationship between this behavior and heart disease. Rosenman and Friedman (1971) studied 3,500 men over an 8½ year period and found Type As to be twice as prone to heart disease, five times as prone to a second heart attack, and twice as prone to fatal heart attacks when compared to Type Bs. Similarly, Jenkins (1971) studied over 3,000 men and found that, of 133 coronary heart disease sufferers, 94 were clearly identified as Type As in early test scores. The rapid rise of women in managerial positions suggests that they too may be subject to this same problem. Hence, Type A behavior very clearly leads to one of the most severe outcomes of experienced stress.

One irony of Type A is that, although this behavior is helpful in securing rapid promotion to the top of an organization, it may be detrimental once the individual has arrived. That is, while Type As make successful managers (and salespeople), the most successful *top* executives tend to be Type Bs. They exhibit patience and a broad concern for the ramifications of decisions. As Dr. Elmer Green, a Menninger Foundation psychologist who works with executives, notes: "this fellow—the driving A—can't relax enough to do a really first-rate job, at the office or at home. He gets to a level that dogged work can achieve, but not often to the pinnacle of his business or profession, which requires sober, quiet, balanced reasoning" (*Business Week,* October 17, 1977, p. 137). The key is to know how to shift from Type A behavior to Type B.

How does a manager accomplish this? The obvious answer is to slow down and relax. However, many Type A managers refuse to acknowledge either the problem or the need for change since they feel it may be viewed as a sign of weakness. In these cases, several small steps can be taken, including scheduling specified times every day to exercise, delegating more significant work to subordinates, and eliminating optional activities from the daily calendar. Some companies have begun experimenting with retreats, where managers are removed from the work environment and engage in group psychotherapy over the problems associated with Type A personality. Initial results from these programs appear promising (*Business Week,* October 17,

1977). Even so, more needs to be done if we are to reduce job-related stress and its serious health implications.

Locus of control.   The concept of locus of control was discussed in some detail in Chapter 6. This concept has implications with respect to how persons respond to a potentially stressful environment. In essence, locus of control can influence experienced stress by affecting perceived ability to cope with (and possibly alter) a stressful environment. That is, internals (individuals who feel that surrounding events are largely under their own control) are more likely to be upset by threats to the control of surrounding events than are external (those who believe they are largely controlled by surrounding events). Recent evidence indicates that internals react to frustrating situations (like goal frustration over which they have little or no control) with aggressiveness, presumably in an attempt to reassert control over on-going events (Carver and Glass, 1978). On the other hand, externals tend to be more resolved to external control and are much less involved in or upset by a turbulent work environment and do not react as emotionally to organizational stress factors.

However, when internals face a potentially stressful situation over which they *do* have control (like the amount of time and effort spent studying for an examination), these individuals are likely to take charge of modifying the environment and reducing or eliminating stresses. The extent to which the environment can be changed has a significant impact on the reactions of internals and externals in potentially stressful situations.

Rate of life change.   A third personal influence on experienced stress is the extent to which the events in individuals' lives are stable or turbulent. A long term research project by Ruch and Holmes (1971) has attempted to document the extent to which *rate of life change* generates stress in individuals and leads to the onset of disease or illness.

As a result of their research, Ruch and Holmes identified a variety of life events and assigned points to each event to reflect its impact on stress and illness (see Exhibit 15–5).

Exhibit 15–5   Scaling the life-change units for various experiences

Life event	Scale value
Death of spouse	100
Divorce	73
Marital separation	65
Jail term	63

Exhibit 15–5 Scaling the life-change units for various experiences (continued)

Life event	Scale value
Death of a close family member	63
Major personal injury or illness	53
Marriage	50
Fired from work	47
Marital reconciliation	45
Retirement	45
Major change in health of family member	44
Pregnancy	40
Sex difficulties	39
Gain of a new family member	39
Business readjustment	39
Change in financial state	38
Death of a close friend	37
Change to a different line of work	36
Change in number of arguments with spouse	35
Mortgage over $10,000	31
Foreclosure of mortgage or loan	30
Change in responsibilities at work	29
Son or daughter leaving home	29
Trouble with in-laws	29
Outstanding personal achievement	28
Wife begins or stops work	26
Begin or end school	26
Change in living conditions	25
Revision of personal habits	24
Trouble with boss	23
Change in work hours or conditions	20
Change in residence	20
Change in schools	20
Change in recreation	19
Change in church activities	19
Change in social activities	18
Mortgage or loan less than $10,000	17
Change in sleeping habits	16
Change in number of family get-togethers	15
Change in eating habits	15
Vacation	13
Christmas	12
Minor violations of the law	11

Source: Reprinted with permission from Journal of Psychosomatic Research, Vol 15, L. O. Ruch and T. H. Holmes, "Scaling of life change: Comparison of direct and indirect methods, Copyright © 1971, Pergamon Press, Ltd.

The death of a spouse was seen as the most stressful change and was assigned 100 points. Other events were scaled proportionately in terms of their impact on stress and illness. It was found that the accumulation of more than 200 points in a single year led to a better than 50 percent chance that a person will encounter a serious illness the following year. Apparently, the influence of life changes on stress and illness is brought about by the endocrine system. This system provides the energy needed to cope with new or unusual situations. When the rate of change surpasses a given level, the system experiences overload and malfunctions. The result is a lowered defense against viruses and disease.

It is important to note here that potentially dysfunctional life changes may be positive changes (changing a job, shift in job responsibilities) as well as negative changes (being fired, trouble with boss).

Abilities and needs. Another influence on the extent to which stress is experienced is the closeness of fit between employee abilities and needs and the demands of the work environment (French and Caplan, 1972). To the extent that an individual's job-related abilities are commensurate with job demands *and* to the extent that an individual's needs are satisfied by the job, we predict less experienced stress. A clerk-typist's job would cause much less stress for someone with excellent typing skills than for a beginning typist. A person with a high need for affiliation would tend to experience much less anxiety or frustration when working in a group as opposed to working alone (Schachter, 1959). This view of the "goodness of fit" between the individual and the work environment as the central determinant of experienced stress forms the basis for one of the major theories of job-related stress (French and Caplan, 1972).

Other personality traits. Finally, several additional personality traits have also been found to influence the way people respond to potentially stressful situations. In particular, it has been found that role conflict produces much greater job-related tension in introverts than in extroverts. Introverts are generally less sociable and more independent than extroverts and have more difficulty coping with conflict because it occurs in social situations and threatens their independence. Similarly, flexible people also experience greater stress as a result of role conflict than rigid people. Since flexible people more often blame themselves when things go wrong and rigid people blame others (Kahn et al., 1964), it is reasonable to assume that flexible people turn the blame for conflict inward, resulting in greater job related tension. Rigid persons typically blame someone else for the conflict, thus removing themselves from the center of controversy and conflict.

Buffering Effects of Social Support

We have seen in the above discussion how a variety of organizational and personal factors influence the extent to which individuals experience stress on the job. While many factors, or stressors, have been identified, their effects on psychological and behavioral outcomes is not always as strong as we might expect. This lack of a direct stressor–outcome relationship suggests the existence of a moderator variable that buffers the effects of potential stressors on individuals. Recent research has identified *social support* as a major buffer in this relationship (Katz and Kahn, 1978). The effects of social support on stress is shown in Exhibit 15–1. Social support is simply the extent to which organization members feel their peers can be trusted, are interested in each other's welfare, respect one another, and have a genuine positive regard for one another. When social support is present, individuals feel that they are not alone as they face the more prevalent stressors. This "misery loves company" factor is well established, dating from a classic study by Stanley Schachter (Box 15–2). The feeling that those around you really care about what happens to you and are willing to help blunts the severity of potential stressors and leads to less painful side effects.

Box 15–2 Schachter's Experiment on Stress and Affiliation

Stanley Schachter and his colleagues carried out a series of laboratory experiments to better understand the effects of stress (particularly anxiety) on affiliative behavior.*

Research design. The study was carried out among a sample of female college students. Subjects were divided into an experimental group and a control group. None of the subjects knew each other.

The experimental group was brought into a room filled with scientific-looking equipment, replete with electric wires and switches. A sinister-looking "doctor" then entered the room and explained to the subjects that they were about to take part in a series of experiments examining the effects of electric shock on humans. While the shocks would be painful, the doctor explained, they would not cause permanent injury.

This procedure was used to create a strong sense of fear in the experimental group. (No such treatment was administered to the control group.) Subjects were then informed that there would be a short delay in the experiment and given the option of waiting either by themselves or in a group.

*Source: S. Schachter. *The Psychology of Affiliation.* Palo Alto, CA: Stanford University Press, 1959.

Results. In the experimental group (fear condition), the subjects overwhelmingly preferred to wait in a group. Not only did the subjects prefer to wait in a group, they further preferred to wait with others in the same condition (fear), rather than with others who were not in the same condition. In the control group (no fear condition), however, still uninformed about the nature of the experiment, subjects tended to prefer to wait alone. In other words, the creation of threatening conditions increased the affiliative need substantially.

Implications. The Schachter study points out how powerful anxiety and fear can be in their influence on the social behavior of individuals. For instance, we often observe that union solidarity is strongest prior to and during a strike. Solidarity results in part from fear of the unknown. (Will the company settle? How long will the strike last? Can we afford to hold out?) Having others around who are in the same condition can provide ego support and the reassurance needed to continue everyday activities.

Much of the rigorous work on the buffering effects of social support in stress comes from the field of medicine but has relevance for organizational behavior. In a series of medical studies, it was consistently found that high peer support reduced negative outcomes of potentially stressful events (surgery, job loss, hospitalization) and increased positive outcomes. These results clearly point to the importance for group relations and processes in individual well-being. These results also indicate that managers should be aware of the importance of building cohesive, supportive work groups, particularly on jobs (like on an assemblyline) that are most subject to stress. We will return to what managers can do to reduce employee stress later in this chapter. First, however, we will examine by way of summary, several of the more important outcomes of stress in organizational settings.

Consequences of Work-Related Stress

We have spent much time examining major influences of stress. It was pointed out that the intensity with which a person experiences stress is a function of organizational factors and personal fctors, moderated by the degree of social support in the work environment. We come now to an examination of the major *consequences* of work-related stress. Here we will attempt to answer the ''so what?'' question. Why should managers be interested in stress and resulting strain?

As a guide for our examination of the topic, we recognize three intensity levels of stress (no stress, low stress, and high stress) and will examine the outcomes of each level. These outcomes are shown schematically in Exhibit 15–6. Three major categories of outcomes will be considered: stress and health, stress and performance, and stress and counterproductive behavior.

Exhibit 15–6 Major consequences of various levels of work-related stress

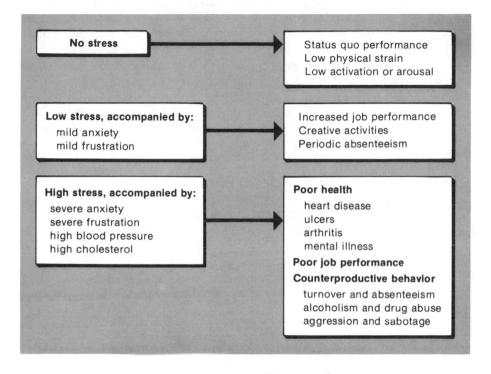

Stress and Health

High degrees of stress are typically accompanied by severe anxiety and/or frustration, high blood pressure, and high cholesterol levels. These psychological and physiological changes contribute to the impairment of health in several different ways. Most importantly, high stress contributes to heart disease (Cooper and Payne, 1978). The relationship between high job stress and heart disease is well established. In view of the fact that well over a half million people die of heart disease every year, the impact of stress is important (Glass, 1976).

High job stress also contributes to a variety of other ailments, including peptic ulcers (Susser, 1967), arthritis (Cobb, 1971), and several forms of mental illness. In a study by Cobb and Kasl (1970), for example, it was found that individuals with high educational achievement but low job status exhibited abnormally high levels of anger, irritation, anxiety, tiredness, depression, and low self-esteem. In another study, Slote (1977) examined the effects of a plant closing in Detroit on stress and stress outcomes. While factory closings are fairly common, the effects of these closings on individuals has seldom been examined. Slote found that the plant closing led to ''an alarming rise in anxiety and illness,'' with at least one-half the employees suffering from ulcers, arthritis, serious hypertension, alcoholism, depression requiring medical help, and even hair loss. Clearly, this life change event took its toll on the mental and physical well-being of the workforce.

Finally, in a classic study of mental health of industrial workers, Kornhauser (1965) studied a sample of automobile assemblyline workers, clearly a stressful job. Of the employees studied, he found that 40% had symptoms of mental health problems. His main findings may be summarized as follows:

- Job satisfaction varied consistently with employee skill levels. Blue-collar workers holding high-level jobs exhibited better mental health than those holding low-level jobs.

- Job dissatisfaction, stress, and absenteeism were all related directly to the characteristics of the job. Dull, repetitious, unchallenging jobs were associated with the poorest mental health.

- Feelings of helplessness, withdrawal, alienation, and pessimism were widespread throughout the plant. As an example, Kornhauser noted that 50% of the assembly line workers felt they had little influence over the future course of their lives; this compares to only 17% for non-factory workers.

- Employees with the lowest mental health also tended to be more passive in their non-work activities: typically, they did not vote or take part in community activities.

In conclusion, Kornhauser (1965) noted:

Poor mental health occurs whenever conditions of work and life lead to continuing frustration by failing to offer means for perceived progress toward attainment of strongly desired goals which have become indispensable elements of the individual's self-identity as a worthwhile person. Persistent failure and frustration bring lowered self-esteem and dissatisfaction with life, often accompanied by anxieties, social alienation and withdrawal, a narrowing of goals and curtailing of aspirations—in short . . . poor mental health.

Managers need to be concerned about the problems of physical and mental health because of their severe consequences both for the individual and for the organization. Health is often related to performance and to the extent that health suffers, so too does performance. Given the importance of performance for organizational effectiveness, we will now turn to this topic.

Stress and Job Performance

A major concern of management is the effects of stress on job performance. The relationship is not as simple as might be supposed. The stress-performance relationship resembles an inverted J-curve, as shown in Exhibit 15–7. At very low or *no stress* levels, individuals maintain their current level of performance. Under these conditions, individuals are not activated (Scott, 1966), do not experience any stress-related physical strain, and probably see no reason to change their performance level. Note that this performance level may be high or low. In any event, an absence of stress probably would not cause any change (Gowler and Legge, 1975).

On the other hand, under conditions of *low stress,* studies indicate that people are activated sufficiently to motivate them to increase performance. For instance, salespeople and many managers perform best when they are experiencing mild anxiety or frustration. Stress, in modest amounts, acts as a stimulus for the individual, as when a manager has a tough problem to solve. The toughness of the problem often pushes managers to their performance limits. Similarly, mild stress can also be responsible for creative activities in individuals as they try to solve difficult (stressful) problems.

Exhibit 15–7   Relationship between stress and job performance.

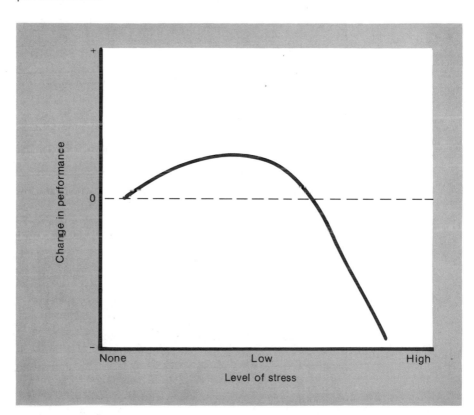

Finally, under conditions of *high stress,* individual performance drops markedly, as shown in Exhibit 15–7. Here, the severity of the stress consumes attention and energies and individuals focus considerable effort on attempting to reduce the stress (often employing a variety of counterproductive behaviors as noted below). Little energy is left to devote to job performance, with obvious results. (For a detailed discussion of the effects of high stress on job performance, see Chapter 2 in Cooper and Payne (1978).)

Stress and Counterproductive Behavior

Finally, it is useful from a managerial standpoint to consider several forms of counterproductive behavior that are known to result from prolonged stress. These counterproductive behaviors include turnover and absenteeism, alcoholism and drug abuse, and aggression and sabotage.

Turnover and absenteeism. Turnover and absenteeism represent convenient—if temporary—forms of withdrawal from a highly stressful job. Results of several studies have indicated a fairly consistent if modest relationship between stress and subsequent turnover and absenteeism (Porter and Steers, 1973; Steers and Rhodes, 1978; Mobley et al., 1978). In fact, one survey found that while there has been a 22% rise over the last fifteen years in the amount of absenteeism attributable to purely physical diseases, during the same period absenteeism associated with psychological ills increased 152% for men and 302% for women (Kearns, 1973). These forms of withdrawal may indeed represent two of the less undesirable consequences of stress, particularly when compared to alternative consequences like alcoholism, drug abuse, or aggression. While high turnover and absenteeism may inhibit productivity, at least they do little physical harm to the individual or co-workers. It must be remembered, however, that many other factors contribute to this type of withdrawal.

Alcoholism and drug abuse. It has long been known that stress is linked to alcoholism and drug abuse among employees at all levels in the organizational hierarchy. These two forms of withdrawal offer a temporary respite from severe anxiety and severe frustration. A recent study by the Department of Health, Education, and Welfare (1973, p. 85) reported that ''our interviews with blue-collar workers in heavy industry revealed a number who found it necessary to drink large quantities of alcohol during lunch to enable them to withstand the pressure or overwhelming boredom of their tasks.'' A similar study by the New York Narcotics Addiction Control Commission (1971) revealed a surprising amount of drug abuse by young employees on blue-collar jobs, especially among assemblyline employees and long-haul truck drivers. A third study of a UAW local involving 3,400 workers found 15% of the workforce addicted to heroin (Executive Office of the President, 1972).

In other words, both alcohol and drugs are used by a significant proportion of employees to escape from the rigors of a routine or stressful job. Although many companies have begun in-house programs aimed at rehabilitating chronic cases, these forms of withdrawal seem to continue to be on the increase, presenting yet another problem for modern managers. One answer to this dilemma lies in reducing stress on the job that creates the need for withdrawal from organzational activities.

Aggression and sabotage. Severe frustration can also lead to overt hostility in the form of aggression toward other people and toward inanimate objects. Aggression occurs when individuals feel frustrated and can find no acceptable, legitimate remedies for the frustration. For instance, a busy secretary may be asked to type a stack of letters, only to be told later that the boss changed his mind and no longer needs the letters typed. The frustrated secretary may react by covert verbal abuse, an intentional slow down on subsequent work, or by throwing a fit. A more extreme example of aggression can be seen in the periodic reports in newspapers about a worker who "goes beserk" (usually after a reprimand or punishment) and attacks fellow employees.

One common form of aggressive behavior on the job is sabotage. As a recent H.E.W. (1973, p. 88) study reported:

> The roots of sabotage, a frequent aspect of industrial violence, are illustrated by this comment of a steelworker: "Sometimes, out of pure meanness, when I make something, I put a little dent in it. I like to do something to make it really unique. Hit it with a hammer deliberately to see if it'll get by, just so I can say I did it." In a product world where everything is alike, sabotage may be a distortion of the guild craftsman's signature, a way of asserting individuality in a homogeneous world—the only way for a worker to say, "That's mine." It may also be a way of striking back against the hostile, inanimate objects that control the worker's time, muscles, and brain. Breaking a machine in order to get some rest may be a sane thing to do.

The extent to which frustration leads to aggressive behavior is influenced by several factors often under the control of managers (Hammer and Organ, 1978). Aggression tends to be subdued when: (1) employees anticipate that it will be punished; (2) the peer group disapproves; and (3) it has not been reinforced in the past (that is, when aggressive behavior failed to lead to positive outcomes). It is incumbent upon managers to avoid reinforcing undesired behavior and at the same time to provide constructive outlets for frustration. In this regard, Levinson (1959) has suggested that organizations provide official channels for the discharge of aggressive tendencies. Many companies have experimented with ombudsmen, whose task it is to be impartial mediators of employee disputes. Results have proved positive. These procedures or outlets are particularly important for non-union personnel who do not have contractural grievance procedures.

Coping With Work-Related Stress

We come now to a most important question from a managerial standpoint: What can we do to reduce job-related stress? Many suggestions for coping with stress are implicit in the above discussions. Even so, it is possible to summarize several important actions employees and managers can take in order to provide a more desirable work environment and improve employee adjustment to work.

Individual Strategies

There are many things people can do by themselves to help eliminate the level of experienced stress or, at the very least, to help cope with continuing high stress.

1. Individuals can increase their own *self-awareness* of how they behave on the job. They can learn to know their own limits and recognize signs of potential trouble. Employees should know when to withdraw from a situation (known to some as a "mental health day" instead of absenteeism) and when to seek help from others on the job in an attempt to relieve the situation.

2. Individuals can develop *outside interests* to take their minds off work. This solution is particularly important for Type A people, whose physical health depends on toning down their drive for success.

3. Individuals can insure that they get regular *physical exercise* to relieve pent-up stress. Many companies sponsor athletic activities and some have built athletic facilities right on company premises to encourage employee activity.

4. Individuals may in some situations find it necessary (i.e., healthful) simply to *leave the organization* and find alternative employment. While this is clearly a difficult decision to make, there are times when turnover is the only answer.

5. Finally, individuals may find a variety of *personal* or *unique solutions* to coping with stress. For instance, here is how one manager described his reaction to a stressful situation (*U.S. News & World Report,* March 13, 1978, p. 81): "If someone finally bugs me, I politely hang up the phone and then pound the hell out of my typewriter, saying all the things on paper I wanted to say to that person on the phone. It works every time. Then, I rip up the paper and throw it into the trash can."

Organizational Strategies

Since managers usually have more control over the working environment than subordinates, it seems only natural that they have more opportunity to contribute to a reduction of work-related stress. Among their activities, managers may include the following.

1. They can pay more attention in the *selection* and *placement* process to the fit between job applicants, the job, and the work environment. As French and Caplan (1972) point out, current selection and placement procedures are devoted almost exclusively to preventing qualitative role overload by insuring that people have the required education, ability, experience, and training for the job. Managers could extend these selection criteria to include, in addition, a consideration of the extent to which job applicants have a tolerance for ambiguity and can handle role conflict. In other words, managers could be alert in the job interview and subsequent placement process to potential stress-related problems and the ability of the applicant to deal successfully with them.

2. In some cases, stress can be reduced through better job-related *skills training* procedures, where employees are taught how to do their jobs more effectively with less stress and strain. For instance, an employee might be taught how to reduce overload by taking shortcuts or by being provided with new or expanded skills. These techniques would only be successful, however, if management did not follow this increased effectiveness by increasing work quotas. Along with this could be a greater effort by managers to specify and clarify job duties to reduce ambiguity and conflict. Employees could also be trained in human relations skills in order to improve their interpersonal skills so that they might encounter less interpersonal and intergroup conflict.

3. Managers can change certain aspects of jobs or the ways people perform those jobs. Much has been written about the benefits of *job enrichment.* Enriching a job may lead to improved task significance, autonomy, responsibility, and feedback. For many people, these jobs will present a welcome challenge, thus improving the job-person fit and reducing experienced stress. It should be noted, however, that all people do not necessarily want an enriched job. Enriching the job of a person with a very low need for achievement or external locus of control may only increase anxiety and fear of failure. Care must be taken in job enrichment to match these efforts to employee needs and desires. In addition to job enrichment, a related technique aimed at reducing stress is *job rotation.* Job rotation is basically a way of spreading stress among employees and providing a respite—albeit temporary—from particularly stressful jobs.

4. Several companies and universities have begun experimenting with *counseling programs.* For instance, Stanford University's executive program includes a module on coping with stress, and the Menninger Foundation conducts a one week anti-stress seminar in Topeka. A recent experiment by Sarason et al. (1978) among police officers examined the value of a stress management program. In the program, which consisted of six two-hour sessions, officers were told about the nature and causes of stress and were put through several simulated stressful situations (like role playing the handling of an arrest) and shown useful relaxation exercises. Throughout, emphasis was placed on reinforcing the officers' confidence that they could, in fact, successfully cope with on-the-job stress. The result of the program showed that those officers who went through the program performed better, exhibited greater self-control, and less stress than similar officers who did not go through the program. Similar findings have emerged in a variety of business organizations. Once again, much work-related stress can be reduced simply by encouraging managers to be more supportive and to provide the necessary tools for people to cope with stress.

5. Managers can allow employees greater *participation* in decisions affecting their work. As noted above, participation increases job involvement and simultaneously reduces stress by relieving ambiguity and conflict. However, while the benefits of increased participation are many, it should be noted that being more participative is no easy task for some supervisors. One recent study, for example, found significant differences in the extent to which different supervisors would allow their subordinates to participate in decision making (Steers, 1977b). Females were found to allow more participation than males. Supervisors with high achievement needs, high levels of confidence in the abilities of their subordinates, and low feelings of being threatened by others allowed more subordinate participation. The issue of participation does not appear to be whether subordinates desire it; instead, it appears to be whether superiors will allow it.

6. Managers can attempt to build work *group cohesiveness*. Team building efforts are common in industry today. These efforts focus on developing groups so they are both more productive and mutually supportive. A critical ingredient in the extent to which stress is experienced is the amount of social support employees receive. Team building represents one way to achieve this support.

7. Finally, as discussed in Chapter 10, managers can open *communication* channels so employees are more informed about what is happening in the organization. With greater knowledge, role ambiguity and conflict are reduced. Managers must be aware, however, that communication is a two-way street and should allow and be receptive to communication from subordinates. To the extent that subordinates feel their problems and complaints are being heard, they experience less stress and are less inclined to engage in counterproductive behavior.

Here, then, are seven specific techniques that have proven useful in work organizations in reducing the amount of experienced stress. None is particularly costly. However, all require an acknowledgement by management that stress is a significant problem on the job, and a commitment by management to take positive actions to change the work environment. The alleviation of work-related stress is mostly in the hands of management, not employees, and solutions to the problem seem well within the reach of those who are concerned.

Summary

This chapter examines the relationship between work and stress. First, the dimension of the problem was discussed, followed by a discussion of the basic processes involved in stress. The general adaptation syndrome was discussed, as were frustration and anxiety.

Next, major influences on stress were identified. This was done through a model of work-related stress. In addition, the consequences of experienced stress and strain were reviewed. It was noted that stress can influence health and job performance and can in many cases lead to counterproductive behavior.

Finally, a variety of individual and organizational strategies for coping with stress were suggested. Emphasis was placed on the need for managers to be sensitive to the emergence of stressful situations at work and act quickly to attempt a remedy. These actions benefit both the employees and the organization.

Key Words

stress	role conflict
strain	role overload
general adaptation syndrome	role underutilization
frustration	type A personality
anxiety	locus of control
role ambiguity	social support

Questions for Discussion

1. Discuss the five types of problems related to employee work adjustment.
2. Define stress. How does it differ from strain?
3. How does the general adaptation syndrome work?
4. Contrast frustration and anxiety.

5. Identify the major categories of variables that have been found to influence stress. What role does social support play in this process?

6. In Box 15–1, the plight of air traffic controllers was discussed. What realistic suggestions would you make to relieve the tension and stress of this job?

7. Compare and contrast role conflict and role ambiguity.

8. How does a manager achieve a useful balance in a person-job fit so neither role overload nor role underutilization occurs?

9. How should a manager deal with a subordinate who is clearly a Type A personality? How should a manager who is a Type A personality handle his or her own stress?

10. Of what utility is the rate of life change concept?

11. In organizations with which you are familiar, which of the many suggestions for coping with stress would be most applicable? Are the strategies you selected individual or organizational strategies?

chapter 16

Work Design

People are often overheard saying things like "I hate my job" or "My job is one of the worst in the world." Obviously, some jobs are, in fact, less rewarding than others. For example, Walters (cited in Dickson, 1975, p. 57) identifies what he claims are the "Ten Worst Jobs." These, in no specific order, are:

- assembly line worker
- highway toll collector
- car-watcher in a tunnel
- pool typist
- bank guard
- copy-machine operator
- bogus typesetter (those who set type that is not to be used)
- computer-tape librarian (a fancy title for a person whose job is rolling up spools of tape all day)
- housewife (not to be confused with mother)
- automatic-elevator operator

Although we could disagree with specific choices here, clearly these jobs lack the status, challenge, and rewards that are found in other jobs like airplane pilot, line manager, engineer, architect, systems analyst, or chemist. Jobs are different. Our concern in this chapter is with the nature of these differences and what managers can do to improve the integrity and quality of certain jobs.

The problems of employee discontent have been well documented throughout the previous chapters. In Chapter 1 we saw the various negative ways in which people describe their jobs. In Chapters 4, 7, and 8, we examined models of employee motivation and how many organizational environments fail to provide a motivating work environment. In Chapter 13, we found that job attitudes play an important part in job behavior. Finally, in Chapters 14 and 15, we considered several dysfunctional consequences (including turnover, absenteeism, and stress) that can result from unhealthy work environments. We now come to an examinaton of one of the major ways in which many of these problems can be reduced; namely, attempts to redesign the job and work environment.

First, we will examine early approaches to job design, followed by a consideration of a more contemporary approach. Following this, several examples of work redesign experiments will be recounted. Additional techniques of work redesign will then be considered, followed by a summary of the problems and prospects inherent in work redesign efforts.

Importance of Topic for Managers

The topic of work redesign in organizations is of concern to managers for several reasons:

1. Many studies have shown that recent experiments in work redesign have resulted in increased job performance and/or job attitudes. Work redesign represents an important tool in a manager's repertoire of skills for improving organizational effectiveness.

2. Work redesign experiments have become increasingly popular in recent years. Hence, it is important for managers to understand the reasons for this popularity. Is there anything behind the technique and does it relate to your organization? Answers to these questions should be of use in deciding whether to attempt a similar program in your own organization.

3. In any attempt to change the work place, it is important to know some of the problems that may arise that stifle managerial efforts. Before adopting work redesign techniques, a manager should know the possible drawbacks of the technique, as well as possible ways of overcoming them.

Early Approaches to Job Design

Serious efforts to efficiently structure jobs people perform date from the early 1800s and the rise of the industrial revolution. As factories grew in size and developed in sophistication, greater efforts were made to break down workers' jobs so they could be performed more quickly and with less training cost and time. It was reasoned that, since workers were mostly economically motivated, efforts at job fractionization would benefit both companies and workers. Companies would benefit because of increased efficiency and output. Workers would benefit, it was thought, because the piece-rate compensation system tied monetary rewards directly to output: the greater the production, the higher the wages.

Scientific Management

Attempts to simplify job design reached this zenith from a technological standpoint in the assemblyline production techniques that became popular in the early 1900s (see Exhibit 16–1). A study of assemblyline technology in automobile manufacturing (Walker and Guest, 1952) identified six predominant characteristics of job fractionization:

Machine pacing   The production rate is determined by the speed of the conveyor belt and not by the workers.

Repetitiveness   Tasks are performed over and over during a single work shift. On auto assemblylines, for example, typical *work cycles* (that is, the time allowed for an entire piece of work) range from between 30 seconds to 1½ minutes. This means the worker performs the same task up to 500 times per day.

Low skill requirements   Because of the simplified task requirements, jobs can be easily learned and workers are easily replaced.

Task specialization   Each job consists of only a few operations. Final product assembly is often done elsewhere in the factory so workers seldom see the complete product.

Limited social interaction   Because of the speed of the assemblyline, noise, and physical separation, it is difficult to develop meaningful social relationships on the job.

Tools and techniques specified   Staff specialists (usually industrial engineers) select the tools and techniques to be used by the workers to maximize efficiency of operations.

These principles are typical of the techniques suggested by advocates of *scientific management* (like Frederick Taylor). Although these techniques led to early successes on the shop floor, drawbacks also began to appear that

Exhibit 16–1 Evolution of job design. (Filley, House, and Kerr, 1975, p. 33).

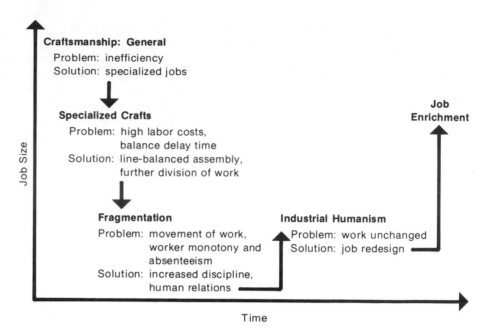

Source: From *Managerial Process and Organizational Behavior* by Alan C. Filley, Robert J. House and Stephen Kerr. Copyright © 1976 by Scott, Foresman and Company. Reprinted by permission.

nullified many of the advances made. First, job fractionization or fragmentation ignored human needs for growth and development. Taylor (1911, p. 59) noted that ''one of the very first requirements for a man who is fit to handle pig iron as a regular occupation is that he more nearly resembles in his mental makeup the ox than any other type.'' This view of employees hardly encouraged efforts to improve working conditions.

Second, it became apparent in the early 1920s that job fractionization led to boredom and unauthorized breaks (Vernon, 1924). People simply did not like the jobs and they reacted by not cooperating with the wishes of management. Sabotage and unionization efforts also became prevalent during this period.

Industrial Humanism

Partly as a result of these problems, concern began to be shown in the 1930s for improving the job attitudes at work. Behavioral scientists began seriously examining the plight of the worker and, under the rubric of *industrial humanism* (also known as the Human Relations movement), efforts were made to make employees happier on their jobs. Human relations training came into vogue, as did company newspapers, employee awards, and company social events. However, the basic nature of the job itself remained unchanged and the problems persisted. It was not until the late 1950s that the concept of job enrichment emerged as a potential solution to problems of worker aberration and poor performance.

Herzberg's Contribution to Job Enrichment

One of the most significant early contributors to job redesign was Frederick Herzberg (Herzberg, Mausner, and Snyderman, 1959). Based on a study of accountants and engineers, Herzberg discovered that employees tended to describe satisfying experiences in terms of factors that were intrinsic to the job itself. These factors were called *motivators* and included variables like achievement, recognition, responsibility, advancement, and personal growth. On the other hand, these same employees described dissatisfying experiences (called *hygiene* factors) in terms of non-job-related factors. These hygiene factors included salary, company policies, supervisory style, and co-worker relations; all of these were factors that surrounded but did not include the job activities themselves.

Based on these findings, Herzberg argued against the efforts toward industrial humanism that prevailed at the time. These efforts treated hygiene factors, while the roots of employee motivation lay in the job itself. The implication of this conclusion for managers is clear: employee motivation can be enhanced through changes in the nature of the job (job enrichment). Efforts to change or enrich the job could include the following:

- *Control over resources* Employees should have maximum control over the mechanisms of task performance.
- *Accountability* Employees should be held accountable for their performance.
- *Feedback* Supervisors have a responsibility to provide direct, clear, and frequent feedback.
- *Work pace* Within limits, employees should be able to set their own work pace.
- *Achievement opportunities* Jobs should allow employees to experience a feeling of accomplishment.
- *Personal growth and development* Employees should be able to learn new and different procedures on the job and should be able to experience some degree of personal growth.

A quick comparison of this list with the earlier list pertaining to attributes of scientific management will show a clear difference in management philosophies over the nature of tasks in the workplace. The philosophy underlying job enrichment takes a more optimistic view of the nature of workers and their needs, drives, and aspirations. It assumes that employees want to tackle problems at work and want to show their creative abilities. In this sense, it assumes that money, while important, is clearly not the only important motivator of good performance.

Herzberg's model has not escaped criticism. It has been sharply criticized on several points (Steers and Porter, 1979): (1) It ignores individual differences; it assumes *all* employees want an enriched job. (2) The existence of two independent factors (motivators and hygiene factors) has not been substantiated. (3) The theory itself is open to different interpretations and Herzberg failed to present an unambiguous statement of the model. (4) Finally, the model remains moot concerning *how* factors like achievement and recognition influence motivation; it does not describe the psychological processes underlying job design and motivation. Despite its limitations, however, Herzberg deserves considerable credit for ushering in the concept of job enrichment as a central topic in the study of people at work. In fact, much of the current work on job design can be traced directly to the early formulations proposed by Herzberg.

A Contemporary Approach to Work Redesign

Today there exist several contemporary and often overlapping approaches to changing the design of work.* These include job enlargement, job enrichment, socio-technical systems, and others (see Steers and Mowday (1977) for a discussion of different approaches). Recently, Richard Hackman (1976), a leading figure in job redesign theory, has suggested that instead of comparing the nuances or finer points of these models, we may make better progress by simply combining the various models into the study of work redesign. According to Hackman, *work redesign* refers to any activities that involve the alteration of specific jobs (or interdependent systems of jobs) with the intent of increasing both the quality of employees' work experience and their productivity.

Why Redesign Work?

Work redesign does not offer a panacea for organizational problems. Nor is it always appropriate in all situations. Rather, work redesign represents a

*This section relies heavily on the work of J. Richard Hackman (1976) and subsequent work in the area.

systematic technique that has been found to be useful for improving life at work in a number of situations. Why has work redesign proved successful as a change strategy? Hackman (1976) suggests four basic reasons:

Work redesign alters the basic relationship between people and their jobs. It is based on the premise that the work itself can be a powerful influence on motivation, performance, and satisfaction. By changing the job, intrinsic motivation can be increased.

Work redesign directly changes behavior. Instead of attempting to change attitudes and hope that attitude changes get translated into changed behavior, work redesign focuses directly on what employees do—their behavior. By changing the job, employees must change what they do. As a result of experiencing more rewarding work, it is thought that employees develop more favorable attitudes which then reinforce behavior. Hence, the behavior tends to remain changed.

Work redesign opens numerous opportunities for initiating other changes. Advocates of systems theory note the importance of recognizing that changes in one area often cause changes in other areas. So it is with work redesign. The very act of implementing such techniques points to other areas within the organization where changes could be made (like the need for supervisory training or skills training or a career development program). The ability to initiate one change in a work situation often makes it easier to initiate others.

Work redesign can ultimately result in organizations that rehumanize rather than dehumanize people at work. In contrast to the effects of assemblyline technology, work redesign can help individuals experience feelings of personal growth and development as a result of engaging in challenging work activities. People are rewarded for creative activities and for accepting responsibility for task accomplishment. As a result, people may find it easier to satisfy their higher-order needs at work.

In short, work redesign offers the promise that organizations can develop work environments that challenge employees and make better use of their human resources. If properly carried out, work redesign can help managers facilitate organizational effectiveness while at the same time improving the quality of working life.

The Job Characteristics Model

Several recent attempts have been made to develop a model of how work redesign influences employees and their behavior (Hackman and Oldham, 1976; Staw, 1976). To date, the model that has received the widest attention is that proposed by Hackman and Oldham (1976) and known as the *Job Characteristics Model*. This model summarizes and integrates much of the earlier work in the area (Turner and Lawrence, 1965; Trist, 1970; Hackman and Lawler, 1971).

The Job Characteristics Model, shown in Exhibit 16–2, consists of four parts. As shown, five core job dimensions influence three critical psychological states which, in turn, influence several desired personal and work outcomes. The links between job dimensions and psychological states and between psychological states and outcomes are moderated by employee growth-need strengths. We will briefly review this process.

Critical psychological states.   According to the model, an employee's motivation and satisfaction is influenced by the nature of three psychological states:

Experienced meaningfulness of the work Employees must feel that the work is important, worthwhile, and valuable.

Exhibit 16–2   The job characteristics model of work motivation (Hackman and Oldham, 1976).

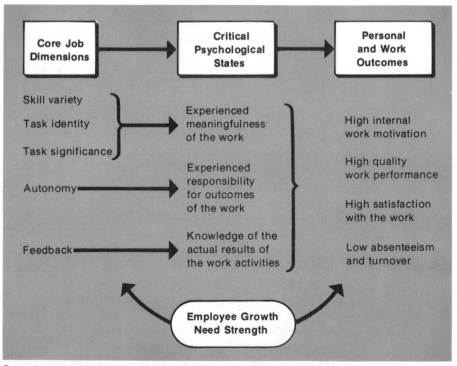

Source: Hackman, J. R. and Oldham, G. R. "Motivation through the design of work: Test of a theory," *Organizational Behavior and Human Performance,* 1976, *16.* Copyright © 1976 by Academic Press. Reprinted by permission of the authors and the publisher.

Experienced responsibility for work outcomes Employees must feel personally responsible and accountable for the results of the work they perform.

Knowledge of results Employees must receive regular feedback concerning the quality of their performance.

As Hackman (1976, p. 129) explains, "the model postulates that internal rewards are obtained by an individual when he *learns* (knowledge of results) that he *personally* (experienced responsibility) has performed well on a task that he *cares about* (experienced meaningfulness)." The more these three psychological states are present on a job, the more satisfied individuals will feel when they perform well. These internal rewards act as incentives for individuals to continue their efforts to perform in order to obtain additional intrinsic rewards. When individuals fail to perform well, positive reinforcement is not experienced and they may be motivated to try harder on subsequent tasks in order to regain the intrinsic rewards.

Core job dimensions.

What activates these psychological states? According to Exhibit 16–2, five core job dimensions combine to determine motivational level:

- *Skill variety* The degree to which a job requires a variety of different activities that involve the use of a number of different skills and talents.
- *Task identity* The degree to which the job requires completion of a whole and identifiable piece of work; that is, doing a job from beginning to end with a visible outcome.
- *Task significance* The degree to which a job has a substantial impact on the lives or work of other people, in the immediate organization or in the external environment.
- *Autonomy* The degree to which a job provides substantial freedom, independence, and discretion to an individual in scheduling work and in determining the procedures to be used in carrying it out.
- *Feedback* The degree to which carrying out work activities required by the job results in individuals obtaining direct and clear information about the effectiveness of their performance.

The first three job dimensions above are believed to influence the experienced meaningfulness of work, as shown in the exhibit. Autonomy influences experienced responsibility for work outcomes, while feedback influences knowledge of results. Any work redesign effort should, according to the model, attempt to develop jobs that are high in these core dimensions.

The job dimensions are often measured using a questionnaire developed by Hackman and Oldham (1976). Based on this questionnaire, it is possible to calculate a *motivating potential score* (MPS) which simply reflects the extent to which employees see their jobs as motivating. According to the model, a high motivating potential score is only possible if a job is high on at least one of the three dimensions that influence experienced meaningfulness, *and* high on autonomy *and* high on feedback. The existence of these three dimensions creates the necessary work environment for all three critical psychological states. Mathematically, then, the MPS can be calculated as follows:

$$\text{Motivating Potential Score} = \frac{\text{Skill variety} + \text{Task identity} + \text{Task significance}}{3} \times \text{Autonomy} \times \text{Feedback}$$

This formula shows that a near-zero score on any of the three factors will reduce the MPS score to near-zero. Again, it is important to note that all three factors are imperative in redesigning work.

Employee growth need strength. Hackman and Oldham use *growth need strength* to refer to a collection of higher-order needs (achievement, affiliation, autonomy) which are believed to moderate the way in which employees react to the work environment. This influence emerges at two points in the model (see Exhibit 16–2). First, employees with high growth need strengths (GNS) are more likely to experience the desired psychological states when their objective job has been enriched than those with low GNS. This occurs because, based on their needs, they are more sensitive to (have a greater demand for) these job characteristics.

Second, high GNS individuals tend to respond more favorably to the psychological states when they occur than do low GNS individuals, since these states are more likely to facilitate the satisfaction of these higher-order needs. For instance, a person who has a high need for achievement can satisfy that need by successfully performing challenging tasks (high MPS). On the other hand, a person with a low *n Ach* may experience frustration or anxiety by being placed on such a job. The role of individual differences must be recognized when designing work for people. It must be recognized that enriched jobs may have greater impact on some people (high GNS individuals) than on others.

Personal and work outcomes. Finally, the model indicates that several personal and work-related outcomes result from the combination of psychological states and GNS. Specifically, when people experience the psychological states described above, we expect them to exhibit high levels of internal work motivation, high quality of performance, high job satisfaction, and low turnover and absenteeism. While the psychological states are clearly not the only variables to affect these outcomes, they are believed to be an important influence.

Research on the job characteristics model.   As with any conceptual model of human behavior, it is difficult to provide an adequate test of the model. While much research on the model has emerged recently, most research takes the form of correlational designs instead of experimental designs. Hence, caution is in order in evaluating the results. Even so, it is possible to summarize the research to date as it bears on the validity of the model.

On the positive side, several studies have found that people who work on jobs high in the core job dimensions are more motivated and satisfied than people who work on jobs low in these dimensions. Similar (though weaker) findings exist for absenteeism. Second, the MPS-outcome relationship has been found to be stronger for employees with a high GNS than for those with a low GNS. Third, some inferential evidence is claimed that core job dimensions work *through* psychological states to influence outcomes (Hackman and Oldham 1976; Steers and Mowday, 1977).

On the negative side, however, several limitations should be noted. First, the predictive powers of the model are far less significant in predicting performance than job satisfaction. In fact, the model does rather poorly in predicting performance, although this may be caused by our inability to accurately measure the study variables. In addition, considerable trouble has been experienced in attempting to demonstrate conclusively that core job dimensions work through psychological states to influence outcomes (Wall, Clegg, and Jackson, 1978). In view of the fact that we are dealing with psychological (and non-observable) variables, this difficulty is understandable.

In summary, the Job Characteristics Model does appear to represent a useful conceptual framework for understanding how and why work redesign influences employee behavior and attitudes. While more work on the topic is clearly in order, the utility of the model for management practice should not be overlooked.

Principles for Redesigning Work

Based on the Job Characteristics Model (and earlier work on the topic), Hackman (1976) has suggested five principles, or guidelines, for enriching jobs and redesigning work. These principles suggest ways in which managers can make substantive work changes, as well as how such changes will affect the core job dimensions (see Exhibit 16–2). Together, they show very clearly how the model can be applied to work situations.

Forming natural work units   To the extent possible, workload should be divided into natural work units; pieces of work that logically fit together. For instance, a typist may be assigned all the typing responsibilities for a person or department instead of spreading the work around to various typists who never see completed projects. The creation of natural work units will encourage employees to increase their ownership of the work and to see its significance.

Combining tasks   Similarly, jobs can be enlarged by combining several of their related aspects. By combining tasks, skill variety and task identity are both increased.

Establishing client relationships   Jobs that are designed traditionally (assemblyline or fractionated jobs) provide little or no contact between the producer (employee) and the clients (whether these clients are inside or outside the organization). By getting producer and client closer together, several things occur. First, feedback increases since the ultimate user is now in a position to respond to the quality of the product or service. Second, skill variety may increase since the producer (employee) now needs to develop the interpersonal skills necessary to interact with clients. Third, autonomy may also increase since the producer now has the responsibility to decide how to manage the relationship with the clients.

Vertical loading   The principle of vertical loading aims at closing the gap between the doing and controlling aspects of work. Examples include letting employees select their own work methods, inspect their own work, choose their hours of work, or participate in decisions affecting their job or the organization. By doing so, employee autonomy is increased.

Opening feedback channels   Most employees receive supervisor-provided feedback about their job performance. However, using work redesign, another source of feedback emerges: job-provided feedback. When jobs are designed so they provide built-in feedback mechanisms (having employees check their own work), employees are continually reminded of their performance quality and these reminders come from the job without the interpersonal problems inherent in supervisor-provided feedback.

While these principles may sound fine in theory, how do they work in actual practice? How do we take a dull job and apply the principles to improve the quality of work? Hackman and associates (Hackman, Oldham, Janson and Purdy, 1975) provide one answer in the example shown in Box 16–1.

The principles suggested here are meant to be illustrative of the types of interventions that can be used in organizations. Through techniques like these, it may be possible to build core job dimensions that sufficiently cue psychological states and lead to employee motivation and satisfaction. As we shall see in the examples below, this is easier said than done.

Examples of Work Redesign Experiments

The recent literature on organizational behavior and management is filled with examples of successful (and sometimes unsuccessful) work redesign

Box 16–1 Redesigning a Keypunch Operator's Job

The problem. Perhaps one of the clearest examples of the application of the Job Characteristics Model can be seen in one effort to redesign the job of keypunch operators at Traveler's Insurance Company. Using the core job dimensions described in the model, the job of keypunch operator prior to enrichment can be described as follows:

- *Skill variety* None. Only a single skill was needed: the ability to accurately punch data on cards.

- *Task identity* Little. Batches were assembled to provide an even work load, but not whole identifiable jobs.

- *Task significance* Not apparent. While keypunching is a necessary step in providing service to company customers, the individual operators were isolated by an assignment clerk and a supervisor from any knowledge of what the operation meant to the receiving department, let alone to the ultimate consumer.

- *Autonomy* Little. The operators had no freedom to arrange their daily tasks to meet schedules, to resolve problems with receiving departments, or even to correct information that was obviously wrong.

- *Feedback* None. Once a batch was completed, the operators received no feedback on performance quality.

Work redesign. The investigators, using the Job Characteristic Model, made the following simple changes:

- *Natural work units* Instead of randomly assigning batches of work, each operator was assigned continuing responsibility for certain accounts (particular departments or recurring jobs). All work for an account was given to the same operator.

- *Task combination* Some planning and controlling functions were integrated with the main task of keypunching.

- *Client relationships* Each operator was given several channels of direct contact with clients. Operators, not assignment clerks, could now examine documents for legibility and autonomy. When a problem arises, the operator, not the supervisor, contacts the client.

- *Feedback* In addition to client feedback, the operators also receive feedback from the job itself. For example, all incorrect cards are returned to the operator for correction. Weekly computer printouts are provided listing error rates and productivity. These are sent directly to the operator, not the supervisor.

- *Vertical loading* Operators were given authority to correct obvious errors on their own. They could also set their own schedules and plan their daily work.

Results. As a result of the work redesign experiment, several desired outcomes emerged: (1) While the control group (where no changes were made) showed an increase in productivity of 8.1% during the trial period, the work redesign group showed an increase of 39.6%. (2) Prior to the study the experimental group had an error rate of 1.53%; following the intervention, the average error rate fell to 0.99%. (3) During the study period, absenteeism in the experimental group declined 24.1%, while it in-

Source: J. R. Hackman, G. Oldham, R. Janson and K. Purdy. A new strategy for job enrichment. *California Management Review,* 1975, *17,* (4), 57–71.

creased 29% in the control group. (4) While no attitude changes occurred in the control group, overall job satisfaction increased 16.5% in the experimental group after intervention. (5) Because of the improved operator proficiency, fewer controls were necessary, reducing supervisory needs. (6) Since the operators took over many of the mundane supervisory responsibilities, supervisors were now able to devote more time to developing feedback systems, setting up work modules, overseeing the enrichment effort, and planning. In short, supervisors were now able to manage instead of dealing with day-to-day problems.

efforts (Gyllenhammer, 1977; Cummings, Molloy, and Glen, 1977). We continually see vignettes of simple ways in which work can be made both more satisfying and more productive. Consider the following examples:

- At Southern Central Bell Telephone Company, employees who were responsible for compiling telephone directories were given the right to establish their own cut-off dates for the sale of Yellow Page advertisements. On their own, the employees consistently set later deadlines than management had previously allowed. As a result, in one year, this practice gave the company a total of three extra weeks of sales time and led to an increase of $100,000 in additional advertising sold.

- At Möet & Chandon, the famous French champagne producer, each portion of the production process is broken down into small profit centers which ''buy'' the produce in process from the group before it and ''sell'' it to the next. The ''profit'' (that is, the value added to the product) in excess of the norm—a standard negotiated between management and labor—is returned to the workers as a bonus.

- Taking a simple approach to increased employee participation, the 3M Company, in an effort to reduce manufacturing costs, simply asked employees to set up their own cost-cutting programs. Within one year, costs had been reduced by $10 million.

- In Denmark, Sadolin and Holmblad, manufacturers of printing ink, asked workers to design the new plant the company intended to build. The company supplied the architects and technical help and agreed within reason to abide by the outcomes. The finished product was ''perhaps 80% like the factory which the bosses would have created on their own.'' In addition to subtle design changes, the workers installed a swimming pool which doubled as a water reservoir that was required for fire protection. As a result of the changes, the absenteeism rate dropped from 10% to 5% per day, turnover dropped to zero for the first two years of operation, and productivity increased 15% (with no changes in production technology or machinery).

- At the Communications Division of Motorola, Inc., a single person is now responsible for the assembling, testing, and packaging of Pageboy

II pocket radio-paging devices. Previously, these devices were made using assemblyline technology that consisted of 100 steps (and people). As a result, both the quantity and quality of production have increased, while turnover and absenteeism have decreased.

Examples like these are often cited as proof that work redesign represents a useful technique for simultaneously improving the quality of work and organizational effectiveness. However, these vignettes often fail to document the developmental work that preceded the changes and the possible problems or side-effects that resulted. To understand the whole picture, it is necessary to examine case histories of work redesign in some detail. We will do so here by reviewing three work redesign experiments that have been carried out among different types of employees performing different jobs. All too often, we are given one case history that may be industry specific and may be difficult to apply to other types of workers in various industries. The following examples demonstrate the widespread application of the technique. As you read each case, consider the principles of the Job Characteristics Model for guidance.

Xerox Corporation: Service Representatives

In October, 1970, Xerox Corporation initiated a trial project in work redesign focusing on a sample of field technical representative (Jacobs, 1975). Xerox employs 7,000 representatives to service their copying machines at customer locations. The representatives provide maintenance at regular intervals and emergency maintenance for breakdowns. In the experiment, a sample of ninety representatives in one branch was selected for the experimental group, while several other branches served as control groups.

The program.   The primary emphasis in the program was to increase the authority and reponsibility of the representatives. Prior to work redesign, representatives could not order parts or tools for maintenance; these were ordered by the field service managers. Under the new program (see Exhibit 16–3), representatives were given full responsibility for ordering parts and tools to maintain their own inventory. When they needed technical assistance, they were allowed to call branch, region, or headquarters for advice (instead of going through the field service manager). Representatives were allowed to determine their own schedules for maintenance and installation as well as their own work hours as long as the hours conformed to customer needs. They were authorized to work overtime and approve repairs without prior approval. Finally, some representatives helped interview and train new representatives. These changes were instituted a few at a time over a period of three months.

Exhibit 16–3 Comparison of technical representatives' job, pre- and post-job enrichment.

Preenrichment	Postenrichment
Technical representatives lack authority to order parts or tools necessary for maintenance; field service manager must order all non-routine parts and tools, within set dollar limits.	Technical representatives have full responsibility for ordering and maintaining parts inventory and tool supply.
Only field service managers or branch managers allowed to arrange for technical assistance from branch technical specialties, field engineers, or technical trainers or to make long-distance calls to contact specialists.	Technical representatives given authority to utilize branch technical specialists, field engineers, and technical trainers in the management of the representatives' territories. Technical representatives make all necessary telephone calls to summon aid.
Technical representatives must follow fixed monthly or weekly schedules for preventive maintenance.	Technical representative given responsibility to determine the preventive maintenance schedule on each assigned machine.
Fixed work hours for all technical representatives in branch.	Technical representatives given authority to determine their own work hours, as customer needs require.
Technical representatives' territories and workloads planned and assigned by management.	Technical representatives have responsibility of determining their own geographic territories and workload size.
Overtime determined by management.	Technical representatives have full responsibility for determining the need for overtime and accompanying expenditure.
Prior approval from manager required before repairs could be made to company cars used by technical representatives.	Technical representative has full responsibility for upkeep expenditure for assigned company car.
New installations of machines determined by salespersons and branch managers; proper installation requirements not always met, necessitating frequent service by technical representatives.	Technical representatives have authority to refuse installations that did not meet company standards (where wiring and space did not meet company requirements).
Field service manager reviews technical representatives' performance and decides merit increases.	Technical representatives are present and involved in writing their own performance appraisals.

Exhibit 16–3 (continued)

Preenrichment	Postenrichment
	Technical representatives provide input for determining their own merit increases when performance appraisal is written.
	Technical representatives are responsible for portions of service meeting presentations.
	Technical representatives involved in screening and interviewing applicants for the job of technical representative.
	Technical representatives have a portion of the responsibility for training new representatives.
	Technical representatives have discretion to schedule the rate at which they receive retrofits.

Source: Reprinted with permission of Macmillan Publishing Co., Inc., from Chapter 18 "Job enrichment of field technical representatives: Xerox Corporation," by C. D. Jacobs. In *The Quality of Life, Volume 2,* edited by Louis E. Davis and Albert B. Chems. Copyright © 1975 by Louis E. Davis and Albert B. Chems.

Results.   As a result of the changes, several outcomes were noted:

- Employee attitudes (particularly with respect to responsibility, recognition, and challenge) increased significantly in the experimental group while no changes were noted in the control groups.
- Absenteeism decreased by 40% in the experimental group.
- Performance also improved somewhat during the project. Before the experiment, the branch under study ranked next to last among sixteen branches in the region. After the initial 14–month trial period, the experimental group had achieved a median ranking.

As a result of the early success, field service managers (the representatives' immediate superiors) began to show concern as to the abilities of the representatives to exercise good judgment in carrying out their new responsibilities. After discussions about the utility of the experiment, the managers developed a wait-and-see attitude. As time went on and they began to see that work redesign was successful in improving performance and attitudes, the commitment of the senior managers increased and their uneasiness and hostility subsided. Hence, the experiment made some contribution toward developing greater confidence and trust between levels within the organization. Based on these results, efforts continue at Xerox to expand the parameters of employees' jobs in various areas of the company.

General Foods—Topeka: Production Workers

Whereas the Xerox work redesign efforts described above focused on field representatives, a program using the same basic principles was attempted among production workers at the Gaines Pet Food Plant of General Foods in Topeka, Kansas. This case history is noteworthy both for its far-reaching change efforts and for the chronology of events that followed program implementation (Glaser, 1976).

The program. In 1968, General Foods decided to construct a new plant to manufacture pet foods. As a result of several serious labor problems at an existing plant in Kankakee, Illinois, including sabotage, shutdowns, product waste, and low morale, management determined to build the new plant (in a separate geographic region) following basic principles of work redesign. Every effort was made to design both the factory and the work to provide challenging, meaningful jobs.

Although many new innovations were introduced, several important changes include:

Autonomous work groups Production processes were built around 7 to 14 member work teams. Teams were created for: 1) processing; 2) packaging and shipping; and 3) office duties. Each member was assigned to a team but not to fixed job duties within the team. Each team had the responsibility for work assignments, screening and selecting new members, and other major decisions affecting group function.

Self-governance Teams were responsible for determining policies and procedures as they saw fit, instead of abiding by formal plant rules. As a result, fewer rules were issued and freedom of action increased.

Job enrichment Each job was designed to maximize variety, autonomy, significance, and feedback. The boring or repetitive aspects of work were eliminated where possible.

Job mobility and rewards for learning As a result of having enriched jobs, it was possible to have a single job classification for all workers. Pay raises were then based on ability to learn new skills or master new jobs. Workers were paid for what they were capable of doing instead of what they actually were allowed to do.

Freedom of access to information All information pertinent to the operation of the plant—production output, quality control data, economic forecasts—was made available to the work teams.

Elimination of status symbols   Efforts were made in plant design to reduce needless status differentiation between managers and workers. The plant contained only one dining facility (no executive dining room), one parking lot (no reserve spaces), and one office decor.

Continuous monitoring of attitudes and output   Plant productivity and worker morale were continually evaluated and changes were made only after their impact on these outcomes was considered.

During the implementation stage, several problems had to be recognized and overcome. The first problem was compensation rates. Pay rates were based on attained skill level and were determined by the team leader. Everyone began at the same rate but soon some workers received raises because they demonstrated new skills. As a result, other workers complained about both the equity of the decisions and the availability of opportunities to learn new skills and qualify for raises.

Second, from the start, the management at corporate headquarters was lukewarm about the project. This lack of enthusiasm possibly resulted from traditional resistance to innovation (Walton, 1975).

Finally, several rather minor problems arose among the team members themselves. Some individuals felt uneasy in group meetings or in participating in spontaneous mutual-help patterns of behavior. Some team leaders had difficulty overcoming an inclination to act like a traditional authority figure. Excessive group pressure was often applied to workers who failed to meet the output norms set by the group. Even so, the initial program was allowed to continue to provide a fair test of the program.

Results.   What happened as a result of these changes in work design? A summary of the findings to-date was presented by Dulworth (1976), the original Topeka plant manager:

- Cost savings were between 20% and 40% greater at Topeka than at other plants. The savings amounted to about $2 million per year.
- Quality control improved. Rejects were about 80% less than is normal for the industry.
- No sabotage or worker-caused shutdowns were experienced.
- Absenteeism ran about 1½% and 80% of that was with the knowledge and approval of management.
- Turnover was about 10%, compared to 15% for the company as a whole. About one-half the turnover was company initiated.
- Compared to other plants, about three times as many employees have taken advantage of outside educational programs.
- Job attitudes and organizational commitment were higher than at similar plants.

With results like these, it is difficult not to become an advocate of work redesign efforts. Even so, caution is in order in interpreting these results. Mitchell Fein (1974), an industrial engineer, summarizes many of the problems as follows:

> General Foods—Topeka is a controlled experiment; a small plant with conditions set up to achieve desired results. The employees are not a cross section of the larger employee population; or even of Topeka. The plant and its operations are not typical of those in industry today. The results obtained are valid only for this one plant. What are other managers to do? Should they screen out nine of ten possible candidates and hire only from the select group that remains [like Topeka]. . .
>
> If the investigators had shown how they converted a plant bursting with labor problems into one where management and employees told glowingly of their accomplishments, the study would truly merit the praise it has received. Instead, they turned their backs on the company's parent plant in Kankakee, which has many of the problems of big city plants. Even worse, they tantalize management with the prospect that, in building a new plant with new equipment, carefully selected employees, and no union, productivity will be higher (pp. 71–72).

Clearly, while the prospects for a Topeka-like work redesign project should not be discounted, we should not be oblivious to the potential spurious effects often found in such experiments.

Aftermath. By 1976, the project had been operating for some time and serious problems began to emerge, not with the work design techniques, but with the political environment surrounding it. As described by *Business Week* (1977, p. 78):

> The problem has been not so much that the workers could not manage their own affairs as that some management and staff personnel saw their own positions threatened because the workers performed almost too well. One former employee says the system—built around a team concept—came squarely up against the company's bureaucracy. Lawyers, fearing reaction from the National Labor Relations Board, opposed the idea of allowing team members to vote on pay raises. Personnel managers objected because team members made hiring decisions. Engineers resented workers doing engineering work.

As one former employee noted:

> Creating a system is different from maintaining it. There were pressures almost from the inception, and not because the system didn't work. The basic reason was power. We flew in the face of corporate policy. People like stable states. This system has to be changing or it will die.

As a result of this power struggle, many managers who instituted the program left the company. As a result of concerns expressed by various professional groups, several changes were made. These included more job classifications, less participation, more supervision, and the addition of seven management positions to the plant, including controller, plant engineering manager, and manufacturing services manager. Despite these setbacks, General Foods describes the experiment as a success and has implemented similar—though scaled-down—programs at several other sites. As one of the ex-managers notes, "every time you make a mistake, you wonder if White Plains (corporate headquarters) thinks that maybe if we had a traditional system there wouldn't have been a mistake . . . Still, it's the best place I ever worked."*

Federal Government: Clerical Workers

This work redesign experiment differs from the earlier ones in at least two respects: it focuses on clerical workers and it was carried out in a federal agency, not in a private corporation. In contrast to the General Foods experiment, this program was implemented in an ongoing organization exhibiting severe morale problems. Finally, it represents one of the more rigorous studies of workers on the job. It provides additional evidence of the wide range of applications of work redesign techniques.

The program. This experiment focused on a large sample of clerical workers (mostly at the GS-3 level) in one federal bureaucracy (Locke, Sirota, and Wolfson, 1976). The jobs generally consisted of sorting incoming mail, searching for lost or misplaced files, and filing. The site was selected because of its widely known morale problems and history of labor-management conflict. Attitudes toward all aspects of the work environment as measured by standardized questionnaires were particularly negative prior to the intervention.

Three experimental work units were identified and were matched with three control units. In the experimental units, the following changes were made:

- Employees in the mail posting department were divided into four 6-person teams instead of working independently. Three teams worked on sorting and one worked on miscellaneous mail room jobs on a rotating basis. The teams could decide for themselves how to divide the various operations rather than being assigned specific tasks. Daily productivity was recorded and posted.

*Reprinted from the October 17, 1977 issue of Business Week by special permission. Copyright © 1977 by McGraw-Hill, Inc. All rights reserved.

- For those responsible for searching for misplaced files, the experimental unit was allowed to decide for themselves what needed to be done. If materials could not be found, they decided on the next step rather than referring it to their supervisor. Clerks allotted time to various tasks based on what needed to be done rather than on what was assigned them. They kept their own records. A team captain was selected on a rotating basis to screen incoming work, complete unit time cards, dispatch outgoing work and telephone other units regarding file problems. Meetings were also held to discuss common problems.

- For those employees charged with filing, fixed production standards were eliminated. Employees could switch back and forth between tasks at will instead of being told what to do each hour. All clerks were trained to do the advanced tasks rather than being assigned to carry out only one small task. Employees kept track of their own production and these records were posted daily.

Results.   Pre and post-measures on attitudes and behaviors were taken. Results are shown in Exhibit 16–4.

As can be seen, productivity in the experimental units increased substantially while turnover, absenteeism and complaints decreased. Job attitudes remained unchanged in both groups, however.

While these results are impressive, the authors caution against interpreting them as highly supportive of job enrichment efforts (Locke et al., 1976).

Exhibit 16–4   Summary of results of job enrichment experiment

| | Group | |
Measure	Experimental units	Control units
Productivity	+23%	+2%
Absenteeism	−5%	+7%
Turnover	−6%	+20%
Complaints and disciplinary actions	0	4
Attitudes	No change	No change

Source: Locke, Sirota, and Wolfson (1976, p. 708).

For instance, they attribute productivity increases to the following factors (p. 708):

(a) more efficient use of manpower as a result of enrichment, since after enrichment, employees could work where they were needed rather than where they were assigned;
(b) elimination of some unnecessary work procedures;
(c) more precise and/or frequent feedback regarding performance, and
(d) competition among employees.

Similarly, reduced absenteeism and turnover may have resulted in part from the enrichment efforts but also in part from *initial* changes in attitudes resulting from program implementation. The implementation of the program served to heighten workers' expectations and, when all of these expectations were not met, attitudes returned to their previous (low) levels. Locke et al. (1976, pp. 709–710) continue:

Another group that complained about not having enough enrichment was reminded that they were being given substantially new responsibilities, which were formerly held by GS-4 employees in another unit, even as the experiment ended. Their reply was, "How come they are giving us their work? Don't they want it?" When pressed for why they viewed the new work in this way, they indicated that since they were not getting any practical rewards for their higher level work, their unit must be considered, in effect, a repository for unwanted tasks.

It was clear from the interviews that these employees viewed their jobs *instrumentally,* that is, as a means to an end. Their comments . . . indicated that the concept of intrinsically satisfying work was not psychologically real to them. Their greatest concern was to get good ratings so that they could get promoted and get more pay. When these outcomes did not follow the enrichment program, the employees were angry and bitter.*

Hence, while this study found that the work redesign program was a partial success (particularly in terms of improving productivity), the findings may have resulted as much from improved efficiency and job engineering as from job enrichment. This study clearly shows that major changes in the work situation often create new employee expectations which, if unmet, lead to additional problems for management.

As a postscript, it should be noted that upon receiving the report from the investigators summarizing the results of the study, the agency lost interest in

*Locke, E. A., Sirota, D. and Wolfson, A. D. "An experimental case study of the successes and failures of job enrichment in a government agency." *Journal of Applied Psychology,* 1976, *61.*

the job enrichment idea. While two of the three experimental units were allowed to remain as they were, the enrichment idea failed to spread to other units in the agency.

Additional Techniques of Work Redesign

From reading the above cases, one forms the impression that most work redesign efforts are built principally upon job enrichment. However, several other changes in the work place have also been tried with varying success. In many cases, these additional techniques are possible when job enrichment is not. Included among these other techniques of work redesign are: 1) job rotation; 2) four-day work week; 3) flexitime; and 4) job sharing. Each will be briefly described.

Job Rotation

When an organization has a series of routine jobs that cannot be combined or enriched, it is possible to rotate workers from one job to the next over time. The aim of this *job rotation* is to minimize the routine and boredom to the extent possible through a change in activities. The employee learns different jobs and the company develops a more flexible workforce. Even so, job rotation does not solve the basic problem of unenriched and unchallenging jobs and should be used only as a temporary or last resort technique.

Four-Day Workweek

Beginning in the early 1970s, the *4/40* (four days/forty hours) *work week* emerged as a popular experiment in work redesign. It is estimated that close to two thousand companies employing over one million people now use the 4/40 plan (Dickson, 1975). The major push behind the 4/40 plan came from companies who hoped to gain greater productivity and efficiency and workers who wanted more leisure time. The 4/40 aims at accomplishing both without changing the job technology.

In a 1972 survey by the American Management Association, 143 companies using the 4/40 plan were asked to evaluate the plan. Results showed that the plan increased production in 62% of the companies, increased efficiency in 66%, and boosted profits for 51%. Similarly, a Bureau of Labor Statistics study showed that companies that had installed the plan generally met their objectives, whether they were to reduce costs, improve efficiency, reduce absenteeism, or improve job satisfaction (Dickson, 1975).

On the negative side, the AMA study revealed that 4/40 plans often presented problems for working mothers, as well as shipping and receiving problems, customer confusion about new hours, and occasionally cost increases. Clearly, an organization must consider the characteristics of the workforce and whether the product or service performed lends itself to a four-day week before committing to the strategy.

Flexitime

One approach to change in the workplace that has received increasing attention in recent years is *flexitime*. It is currently being used in over 5,000 firms of varying sizes. Flexitime is a technique that allows employees more latitude and freedom in determining their own work schedules. It differs from plans like the 4-day work week in that, while the employees have a certain degree of choice over starting and quitting time, they are all required to be present during certain daily core hours, so that necessary interpersonal and interdepartmental communication can take place.

Perhaps an example will clarify the technique. A New Jersey company, Sandoz-Wander, introduced a flexitime program that contained the following parameters (Dickson, 1975):

Earliest starting time:	7:30 AM
Latest starting time:	9:30 AM
Earliest leaving time:	4:00 PM
Latest leaving time:	6:00 PM
Lunch period:	12:00–2:00 PM
Maximum lunch period	2 hours
Minimum lunch period	1 hour
Core hours (when everyone must be present):	9:30–12:00 noon 2:00–4:00 PM
Average work week:	37.5 hours
Maximum work week:	40 hours
Minimum work week:	22.5 hours
Average workday:	7.5 hours
Maximum workday:	9.5 hours
Minimum workday:	4.5 hours

Within these guidelines, employees are free to select the working hours that best fit their own needs and desires. Following this plan, then, does not alter the basic nature of the job but does provide employees with some discretion as to when to perform. Results of a series of experiments (summarized in Golembiewski and Proehl (1978) reveal fairly consistent positive results. Both attitudes and behaviors (particularly in the form of reduced absenteeism and turnover) are generally improved.

Job Sharing

Finally, another strategy for relieving job fatigue while at the same time accommodating the needs of part-time workers is *job sharing*. Job sharing consists of two or more persons who jointly cover one job over a normal forty-hour week. For instance, two manuscript typists may share one job, with one working in the morning and one in the afternoon. The typing gets done and both employees have ample time for outside activities. While job sharing does not change the basic nature of the work, it does allow an organization to tap previously unavailable labor markets.

Work Redesign:
Problems and Prospects

Problems with Work Redesign

Although work redesign holds much promise for improving both employee performance and the quality of working life, it is by no means a panacea. In fact, several rather serious problems have been identified by various researchers that suggest caution in work redesign attempts (Fein, 1974; Hackman, 1975; Walton, 1975).

Failure to recognize individual differences   Several recent studies have shown that some employees respond more positively to enriched jobs than others. For instance, for an employee with a high need for achievement, an enriched job may serve to cue the achievement motive, facilitating increased effort (Steers and Spencer, 1977). However, putting employees with *low* need for achievement on an enriched job may only heighten their anxiety, frustration, and dissatisfaction.

Technological constraints   In many cases, the nature of the job does not lend itself to enrichment or redesign. This is particularly true on continuous-process jobs, where the jobs are paced by machines. In these circumstances, job rotation or flexitime may perhaps offer a partial solution.

Costs   In many cases, work redesign efforts are simply very costly. These increased costs include additional expenditures for training, tools, construction, start up, and sometimes wages. The problem is whether the consumers are willing to pay the additional costs associated with work redesign passed along in the form of higher prices.

Lack of proper diagnosis prior to introduction   Oftentimes, in their haste to be the first in innovation, companies fail to carefully consider the nature of the problems they are facing, as well as what constitutes the best approach to solving them.

Failure to actually change the work   Many failures in job redesign have been traced to the fact that no substantive changes were made in the job itself. Instead, lip service was paid by indifferent or hostile managers. Since the jobs were not changed, no changes were recorded in attitudes or behavior.

Managerial resistance   Occasionally, managers feel threatened by the increased autonomy given to workers under work redesign (see General Foods example). They fear loss of both power and status. As a result, they drag their feet and sabotage such efforts in numerous ways.

Union resistance   Similarly, unions often resist work redesign efforts, surprisingly for many of the same reasons as managers. Unions develop power bases as a result of their ability to represent workers to management. Work redesign often allows a more direct interchange between workers and management and bypasses the union. Unions often feel that these efforts are simply another attempt to increase productivity. One union official described work redesign as a "speed-up in sheep's clothing." Traditional unions tend to have traditional demands (wage, hours, job security) and, as a result, are oftentimes less innovative than management when it comes to improving the quality of working life.

Overcoming Problems with Work Redesign

The seriousness of the above problems must not be overlooked. Even so, there are several steps that managers can take to help reduce the impact of these problems and enhance the chances for program success. Among these are (Hackman, 1976):

Diagnose work system prior to change   Know what the problems are (union resistance, individual differences, etco) before beginning to seriously consider changing the workplace. To the extent possible, get the union involved in the diagnosis.

Keep the focus on the work itself   Keep personal differences outside the discussion. Suspend, at least for the moment, the "it can't be done" syndrome. Assume it can be done.

Prepare ahead of time for unexpected problems   Develop contingency plans ahead of time and be ready for possible problems that could side-track redesign efforts.

Evaluate continuously   Whether evaluation is done by outside consultants or by union-management teams, continuous feedback can assist in pinpointing potential trouble spots so remedial action can be taken.

Confront difficult problems early   Don't bury important issues or potential problems in the hope they will disappear. Confront them. If management is not committed to change, consider ways of increasing (not bypassing) their commitment.

Design change processes that facilitate change objectives Utilize implementation procedures that are congruent with change objectives. For instance, if you want to develop work teams that exhibit high levels of participation and autonomy, use a participative change strategy. Get workers involved in designing job changes. By using techniques in the design and planning phases that you wish continued in the actual program, employees become introduced to the techniques gradually and have an opportunity to test management's sincerity and commitment to the proposed changes.

By following these guidelines, managers can provide a work environment conducive to experimentation in redesigning work. While these changes by themselves certainly do not guarantee that the quality of working life will be significantly improved, they will at least make a useful contribution in that direction.

Summary

In this chapter, we have examined the concept of work design. Initially, consideration was given to early approaches to work design. Next, a contemporary model of work design was presented. Based on the model, other principles for redesigning jobs were discussed.

In an effort to move from the theoretical to the practical, specific examples of work redesign experiments were reviewed. These examples came from both public and private organizations and covered several different types of employees.

Next, additional techniques of work redesign were discussed, including job rotation, the four-day workweek, flexitime, and job sharing. Finally, several problems with work redesign were discussed, as were techniques for overcoming these problems. It was emphasized that although work redesign can be a valuable management test in many situations, it should not be seen as a panacea for all organizational ills.

Key Words

scientific management
industrial humanism
work redesign
job characteristics model
critical psychological states
core job dimensions
motivating potential score
work cycle
motivators

hygiene factors
growth need strength
vertical loading
autonomous work groups
job rotation
four-day workweek
flexitime
job sharing

Questions for Discussion

1. In view of the history of job redesign efforts, how far have we actually come in improving productivity and the quality of working life?

2. What are the main characteristics of scientific management?

3. Herzberg has been given credit for making substantial contributions to the field of work redesign. Describe the nature of these contributions.

4. Provide reasons why a manager would want (or would not want) to implement work redesign.

5. What implications for management follow from the Job Characteristic Model?

6. In Box 16–1, a work redesign experiment among keypunch operators was described. What techniques other than work redesign might managers have attempted in order to increase productivity and satisfaction?

7. What general lessons for management emerge from reviewing the various work redesign experiments discussed in this chapter?

8. How useful do you think techniques like job rotation or the four-day workweek are for improving performance and satisfaction? What limitations exist for these techniques?

9. Identify several important problems with work redesign. How might these problems be overcome?

chapter 17

Performance Appraisal and Reward Systems

One of the most important responsibilities managers have is to evaluate and reward the performance of their subordinates and devise mechanisms for improving performance where it fails to meet acceptable standards. This evaluation process is done through the performance appraisal system. Most organizations have these programs. In fact, a recent survey by Locher and Teel (1977) found that 90% of organizations contacted had some form of performance appraisal system.

Because of the importance of performance appraisal and reward systems for employee development and organizational development, we will examine various aspects of them here. First, we will consider the general characteristics of appraisal systems, including their associated problems. Next, specific appraisal techniques will be examined. Then, the nature and purpose of reward systems in organizations is considered, followed by a discussion of various incentive plans. Finally, we will take a look at several new developments in reward systems.

Importance of Topic for Managers

Why are appraisal and reward systems so important to managers?

1. Performance appraisal systems provide a means of systematically evaluating employees across various performance dimensions to insure that organizations are getting what they pay for.

2. Performance appraisal systems provide valuable feedback to employees and managers, and may assist in identifying promotable people as well as problem areas.

3. Since different approaches to appraisal exist, managers should be aware of the advantages and disadvantages of each. In this way, the most appropriate system can be selected for an organization.

4. Reward systems represent a powerful motivational force in organizations, but for this to occur the system must be fair and tied to performance. An understanding of reward systems will help managers select the system best suited to the needs and goals of the organization.

5. Managers should keep abreast of recent developments in compensation and reward systems so they can modify existing systems when more appropriate alternatives become available.

Performance Appraisal Systems

Three aspects of performance appraisal systems are considered here. First, we will consider the various functions of appraisal systems. Next, several of the problems associated with these systems are examined, followed by a discussion of ways to reduce them. We will provide an overview of performance appraisals. More detailed information is available in most books on personnel administration or compensation.

Functions of Performance Appraisals

In most work organizations, there are many reasons why performance appraisals are used. These reasons range from improving various aspects of employees' output to developing the employees themselves. This diversity of uses is well documented in a recent survey of 216 organizations which sought to determine the uses for appraisals (Locker and Teel, 1977). As shown in Exhibit 17–1, compensation and performance improvement were the most prominent reasons organizations used performance appraisals.

Exhibit 17–1 Primary uses of appraisals (Locher and Teel, 1977)

Use	Small Organizations (Percent)	Large Organizations (Percent)	All (Percent)
Compensation	80.6	62.2	71.3
Performance improvement	49.7	60.6	55.2
Feedback	20.6	37.8	29.3
Promotion	29.1	21.1	25.1
Documentation	11.4	10.0	10.7
Training	8.0	9.4	8.7
Transfer	7.4	8.3	7.9
Manpower planning	6.3	6.1	6.2
Discharge	2.3	2.2	2.3
Research	2.9	0.0	1.4
Layoff	0.6	0.0	0.3

Source: "Performance appraisal—A survey of current practices," Alan H. Locher and Kenneth S. Teel. Reprinted with permission *Personnel Journal,* Costa Mesa, CA, copyright © May, 1977.

Summarizing this information, it is possible to identify the major reasons, or functions, of performance appraisals as follows:

- Performance appraisals provide *feedback* to employees in terms of the quantity and quality of job performance. Without this information, employees have less knowledge of how well they are doing on the job and how they might improve.

- Performance appraisals are useful in making *personnel decisions,* like promotion, transfer, and termination. Based on appraisal information, more informed decisions can be made with regard to individuals' strengths and weaknesses.

- In addition, appraisals form the basis of organizational *reward systems,* particularly merit-based compensation plans.

- Appraisal systems also suggest areas in which employee *training and development* are most needed. If employee appraisals consistently point to a problem area (interpersonal competence, required skills), programs can be developed to remedy the situation.

- Performance appraisals can be a *self-development* indicator, too, where individuals learn about their strengths and weaknesses as seen by other people.

- Finally, performance appraisal systems help the organization evaluate the effectiveness of its *selection and placement* decisions. If newly hired employees consistently perform poorly, managers must consider whether or not the right kind of people are being hired in the first place.

As can be seen, performance appraisal systems serve a variety of functions in organizations. In light of the importance of these functions, it is imperative that methods of evaluation be selected that attempt to maximize the accuracy and fairness of the appraisal. Many such methods of performance appraisal exist. The job for the manager, as we shall soon see, is to select that technique or combination of techniques that best serves the particular needs (and constraints) of the organization. Before considering these various techniques, however, we should examine several of the more prominent sources of error, or problems, in performance appraisals.

Problems with Performance Appraisals

A number of problems can be identified that pose a threat to the usefulness of performance appraisal techniques. Most of these problems deal with the related issues of validity and reliability. *Validity* is the extent to which a measure or instrument actually measures what it intends to measure, while *reliability* is the extent to which the instrument consistently yields the same results each time it is used. Ideally, a good performance appraisal system will exhibit high levels of both validity and reliability. If not, serious questions must be raised concerning the utility (and possibly the legality) of the system (Glueck, 1979).

It is possible to identify several of the more common sources of error, or problems, found in performance appraisal systems that can jeopardize validity and reliability. These include: 1) central tendency error; 2) strictness or leniency error; 3) halo effect; 4) recency error; and 5) personal biases.

Central tendency error.   It has often been found that supervisors rate most of their employees within a narrow range (Glueck, 1979). Regardless of how people actually perform, the rater fails to distinguish significant differences between group members and lumps everyone together in an average or above average category. This central tendency error is shown in Exhibit 17–2. This action fails to recognize both very good and very poor performers.

Strictness or leniency error.   A related rating problem exists when a supervisor is overly strict or overly lenient in evaluations (see Exhibit 17–2). In college classrooms, we hear of professors who are "tough graders" or, conversely, "easy A's." Similar situations exist in the workplace where

Exhibit 17–2 Examples of strictness, central tendency, and leniency errors

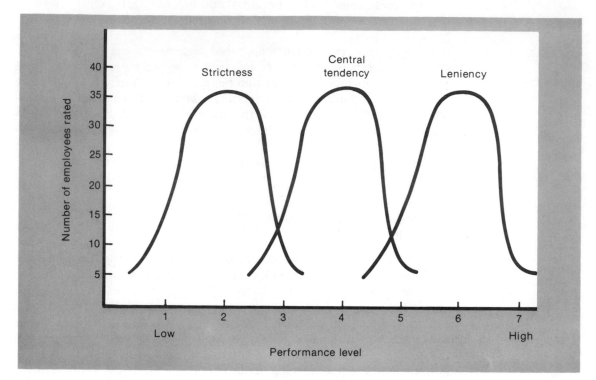

some supervisors see most subordinates as not measuring up to their high standards, while others see most subordinates as deserving of a high rating. As with central tendency error, strictness and leniency errors fail to adequately distinguish between good and bad performers and, instead, relegate most everyone to the same category.

Halo effect. The halo effect was discussed earlier in Chapter 5 on perceptual biases. Halo effect exists where a rater assigns the same rating to each factor being evaluated for an individual. An employee rated "above average" on quantity of performance may also be rated "above average" on quality of performance, interpersonal competence, attendance, and promotion readiness. Such a practice fails to differentiate strong points from weak and tells the employee that the supervisor cannot differentiate across presumably distinct categories of behavior.

Recency error.   Oftentimes, evaluators focus on an employee's most recent behavior in the evaluation process. That is, in an annual evaluation, a supervisor may give undue emphasis to performance during the past two or three months and ignore performance levels prior to this. This practice, if known to employees, leads to a situation where employees float for the initial months of the evaluation period and then overexert themselves in the last few months prior to evaluation. This practice leads to uneven performance, as well as contributing to the attitude of "playing the game."

Personal biases.   Finally, several studies have revealed that supervisors often allow their own personal biases to influence their appraisals (Jones, 1973). Biases include like or dislike for someone, as well as racial and sexual biases. Personal biases can interfere with the fairness and accuracy of an evaluation.

Reducing Errors in Performance Appraisals

A number of suggestions have been advanced recently to minimize the effects of various biases and errors on the performance appraisal process (Bernardin and Walter, 1977; Burnaska and Hollman, 1974). When errors are reduced, more accurate information is available for personnel decisions and personal development. These methods for reducing error include:

- Insure that each dimension or factor on a performance appraisal form represents a single job activity instead of a group of job activities.
- Avoid terms like average, since different evaluators react differently to the term.
- Insure that raters observe subordinates on a regular basis throughout the evaluation period. It is even helpful if the rater takes notes for future reference.
- Keep the number of persons evaluated by one rater to a reasonable number. When one person must evaluate many subordinates, it becomes difficult to discriminate. Rating fatigue increases with the number of ratees.
- Insure that the dimensions used are clearly stated, meaningful, and relevant to good job performance.
- Train raters so they can recognize various sources of error and understand the rationale underlying the evaluation process.

Using mechanisms like these, improved rating should result that have greater meaning both for the individual and the organization.

Techniques of Performance Appraisal

Numerous methods have been used in organizations to evaluate personnel. We will summarize several popular techniques. While countless variations on these themes can be found, the basic methods presented should provide a good summary of the commonly available techniques. Following this review, we will consider the various strengths and weaknesses of each technique. Six techniques are reviewed here: 1) graphic rating scales; 2) ranking methods; 3) critical incident technique; 4) behaviorally-anchored rating scales; 5) management-by-objectives; and 6) assessment centers.

Graphic Rating Scales

Certainly the most popular method of evaluation used in organizations today is the graphic rating scale. Locher and Teel (1977) found that 57% of the organizations they surveyed used rating scales. While this method appears in many formats, the rater is typically presented with a printed form which contains both the employee's name and several evaluation dimensions (quantity of work, quality of work, knowledge of job). The rater is then asked to rate the employee by assigning a number, or rating, on each of the dimensions. An example of the graphic rating scale is shown in Exhibit 17–3.

Exhibit 17–3 Typical graphic rating scale (Glueck, 1979, p. 302).

Name _____	Dept. _____			Date _____	
	Out-standing	Good	Satis-factory	Fair	Unsatis-factory
Quantity of work Volume of acceptable work under normal conditions Comments:	☐	☐	☐	☐	☐
Quality of work Thoroughness, neatness and accuracy of work Comments:	☐	☐	☐	☐	☐
Knowledge of job Clear understanding of the facts or factors pertinent to the job Comments:	☐	☐	☐	☐	☐

Exhibit 17–3 (continued)

	Out-standing	Good	Satis-factory	Fair	Unsatis-factory
Personal qualities Personality, appear-ance, sociability, leadership, integrity Comments:	☐	☐	☐	☐	☐
Cooperation Ability and willing-ness to work with associates, super-visors, and sub-ordinates toward common goals Comments:	☐	☐	☐	☐	☐
Dependability Conscientious, thorough, accurate, reliable with respect to attendance, lunch periods, reliefs, etc. Comments:	☐	☐	☐	☐	☐
Initiative Earnestness in seeking increased responsibilities. Self-starting, unafraid to proceed alone? Comments:	☐	☐	☐	☐	☐

Source: William Glueck, *Personnel: A Diagnostic Approach,* rev. ed. (Dallas, Texas: Business Publications, 1978), p. 302. Copyright © 1978 by Business Publications, Inc.

By using this method—and assuming that evaluator biases can be minimized—it is possible to compare employees among themselves in terms of who received the best and poorest ratings. It is also possible to examine the relative strengths and weaknesses of a single employee by comparing scores on the various dimensions.

However, one of the most serious drawbacks of this technique is its openness to central tendency, strictness, and leniency error. It is possible to rate most everyone in the middle of the scale or, conversely, at one end of the scale. In order to control for this, some companies have assigned required percentage distributions to the various scale points. Supervisors may be allowed to rate only 10% of their people outstanding and must rate 10% unsatisfactory, perhaps assigning 20%, 40%, and 20% to the remaining middle categories. By doing this, a distribution is forced within each department. However, this procedure may penalize a group of truly outstanding performers or reward a group of poor ones.

Ranking Methods

Less popular among managers is the *ranking method*. This procedure develops a ranking of employees in one department or work unit ranging from the best to the worst performer based on overall contribution to the organization.

Typically, a ranking is achieved by first selecting the best and worst performers, followed by a selection of the second best and second worst performers, and so on until all employees are placed in the ranking.

Several major problems are associated with this technique. While it may be fairly easy to distinguish the best and worst employees, it is often difficult to distinguish or rank those in the middle. Hence, a source of error is introduced into the system. Ranking requires the use of a single global performance dimension and often hides other useful information on various aspects of performance. Finally, ranking becomes increasingly difficult as the number of ratees increases.

Critical Incidents

With the *critical incident* method of performance appraisal, supervisors record incidents in each subordinate's behavior that led to either unusual success or unusual failure on some aspect of the job. These incidents are recorded in a daily or weekly log under predesignated categories (planning, decision making, interpersonal relations, report-writing). The final rating consists of a series of descriptive paragraphs about various aspects of an employee's performance.

The critical incident method provides useful information for appraisal interviews, and managers and subordinates can discuss specific incidents. Good qualitative data are generated. However, since no quantitative data emerge, it is difficult to use this technique for promotion or salary decisions. The qualitative output here has led some companies to combine the critical incident technique with one of the quantitative techniques, such as rating scales, to provide different kinds of feedback to the employees.

Behaviorally Anchored Rating Scales

An appraisal system that has received increasing attention in recent years is the *behaviorally anchored rating scale* (or BARS). This system requires considerable work prior to evaluation but, if the work is carefully done, can lead to highly accurate ratings with high inter-rater reliability. Specifically, the BARS technique begins by selecting a job which can be described in observable behaviors. Managers and personnel specialists then identify these behaviors as they relate to superior or inferior performance.

An example of this is shown in Exhibit 17–4, where the BARS technique has been applied to the job of grocery clerk. As can be seen, as one moves

Exhibit 17–4   Behaviorally anchored rating scale for evaluating judgment and knowledge of grocery clerks

Extremely good performance	7	–
	–	–By knowing the price of items, this checker would be expected to look for mismarked and unmarked items.
Good performance	6	–
	–	–You can expect this checker to be aware of items that constantly fluctuate in price.
		–You can expect this checker to know the various sizes of cans—No. 303, No. 2½.
Slightly good performance	5	–
	–	–When in doubt, this checker would ask the other clerk if the item is taxable.
	–	–This checker can be expected to verify with another checker a discrepancy between the shelf and the marked price before ringing up that item.
Neither poor nor good performance	4	–
	–	–When operating the quick check, the lights are flashing, this checker can be expected to check out a customer with 15 items.
Slightly poor performance	3	–
	–	–You could expect this checker to ask the customer the price of an item that he does not know.
	–	–In the daily course of personal relationships, may be expected to linger in long conversations with a customer or another checker.
Poor performance	2	–
	–	–In order to take a break, this checker can be expected to block off the checkstand with people in line.
Extremely poor performance	1	–

Source: L. Fogli, C. L. Hulin, and M. R. Blood, "Development of first-level behavioral job criteria," *Journal of Applied Psychology* 55 (1971), pp. 3–8. Copyright © 1971 by the American Psychological Association. Reprinted by permission.

from extremely poor performance to extremely good performance, the performance descriptions, or behavioral anchors, increase. Oftentimes, six to ten scales are used to describe performance on the job. Exhibit 17–4 concerns judgement and knowledge on the job. Other scales could relate to customer relations, promptness, attendance, and innovation. Once these scales are determined, managers have only to check the category that describes what they observe on the job and the employee's rating is simultaneously determined.

The BARS technique has several purported advantages. In particular, many of the sources of error discussed earlier (central tendency, leniency, halo) should be significantly reduced since raters are considering verbal descriptions of specific behaviors instead of general categories of behaviors like those used in graphic rating scales. The technique focuses on job-related behavior and does not consider less relevant issues like a subordinate's personality. Also, in the performance appraisal interview, emphasis is placed on these actual behaviors, not the person; hence, employees should be less defensive in the review process. Finally, BARS can aid in employee training and development by identifying those performance domains needing most attention.

On the negative side, as noted above, BARSs require considerable time and effort in designing the forms before the actual rating. A separate BARS is required for each job. Hence, it is only cost efficient on common jobs. Finally, since the technique relies on observable behavior, it may have little applicability on such jobs as a research scientist, where much of the job is mental and relevant observable behaviors are hard to obtain.

Management-By-Objectives

Another popular technique for appraising employees is *management-by-objectives* (MBO). Although the concept of MBO is really broader than the appraisal itself (incorporating an organization-wide motivation, performance, and control system), we will focus here on its narrower role in the evaluation process (see Tosi and Carroll, 1973). MBO is closely related to goal-setting theory of motivation, as discussed in Chapter 8.

Under MBO, individual employees or groups work with their supervisor to establish goals and objectives for the coming year. These goals are stated in clear language and relate to tasks that are within the domain of the employee. An example of these goals for a salesperson is shown in Exhibit 17–5. Following a period of time (usually one year) employees are evaluated against the goals to determine the extent to which the goals have been met or exceeded.

Several advantages of MBO have been noted. As noted by Gibson et al. (1979, p. 367), ''the assumed benefits include better planning, improved motivation because of knowledge of results, basing evaluation decisions on

Exhibit 17–5 MBO evaluation report for salesperson (Glueck, 1979, p. 307)

Objectives set	Period objective	Accomplishments	Variance
1. Number of sales calls	100	104	104%
2. Number of new customers contacted	20	18	90
3. Number of wholesalers stocking new product 117	30	30	100
4. Sales of product 12	10,000	9,750	92.5
5. Sales of product 17	17,000	18,700	110
6. Customer complaints/service calls	35	11	66.6
7. Number of sales correspondence courses successfully completed	4	2	50
8. Number of sales reports in home office within 1 day of end of month	12	10	80

Source: William Glueck, *Personnel: A Diagnostic Approach, rev. ed.* (Dallas, Texas: Business Publications, 1978), p. 307. Copyright © 1978 by Business Publications, Inc.

results instead of on personality or personal traits, improving commitment through participation, and improving supervisory skills in such areas as listening, counseling, and evaluating.''

On the negative side, MBO has been criticized because it emphasizes quantitative goals at the expense of qualitative goals and often creates too much paperwork. It is difficult to compare performance levels among employees, since most are responsible for different goals. Finally, in order to succeed, MBO must have constant care and support from management; it does not run itself. In the absence of this support, the technique loses legitimacy and often falls into disrepair.

Assessment Centers

A relatively new method of evaluation is the *assessment center*. Assessment centers are unique among appraisal techniques in that they focus more on evaluating employee long-range potential to an organization instead of on performance over the past year. They are also unique in that they are used almost exclusively among managerial personnel.

An assessment center consists of a series of standardized evaluations of behavior based on multiple inputs (Bray and Moss, 1972). Over a two or three day period (away from the job) trained observers make judgements on managers' behavior as a result of specially developed exercises. These exercises may consist of in-basket exercises, role playing, and case analyses, as well as personal interviews and psychological tests. An example of an assessment center program is shown in Exhibit 17–6.

Exhibit 17–6   Example of two-day assessment center

Day #1		Day #2	
8:00– 9:00 AM	Orientation session	8:00–10:30 AM	In-basket exercise
9:00–10:30 AM	Psychological testing	10:30–10:45 AM	Coffee break
10:30–10:45 AM	Coffee break	10:45–12:30 PM	Role playing exercise
10:45–12:30 PM	Management simulation game	12:30– 1:30 PM	Lunch
12:30– 1:30 PM	Lunch	1:30– 3:15 PM	Group problem-solving exercise
1:30– 3:15 PM	Individual decision making exercise	3:15– 3:30 PM	Coffee break
3:15– 3:30 PM	Coffee break	3:30– 4:30 PM	Debriefing by raters
3:30– 4:30 PM	Interview with raters		

As a result of these exercises, the trained observers make judgements on employees' potential for future managerial assignments in the organization. More specifically, information is obtained concerning employees' interpersonal skills, communication ability, creativity, problem-solving skills, tolerance for stress and ambiguity, and planning ability. This technique has been used successfully by some of the largest corporations in the U.S., including AT&T, Sears, Roebuck, and Company, J. C. Penney, IBM, and General Electric.

Results from a series of assessment center programs appear promising and the technique is growing in popularity as a means of identifying future managerial potential. Even so, some problems with the technique have been noted (Klimoski and Strickland, 1977; Norton, 1977). In particular, due to the highly stressful environment created in assessment centers, many otherwise good managers may simply not perform up to their potential. The results of a poor evaluation in an assessment center may be far-reaching; individuals may receive a "loser" image that will follow them for a long time. Finally, there is some question concerning exactly how valid and reliable assessment centers really are in predicting future managerial success. While some initial successes have been noted, more research is needed here to evaluate the true potential of the technique.

Comparison of Appraisal Techniques

From a managerial standpoint, questions are raised about which technique or set of techniques is most appropriate for a given situation. Although there is no simple answer to this question, we can consider the various strengths and weaknesses of each technique. This is done in Exhibit 17–7.

As can be seen—and as would be expected—the easiest and least expensive techniques are also the least accurate. They are also the least useful for purposes of personnel decisions and employee development. Once again, it

Exhibit 17–7 Major strengths and weaknesses of various appraisal techniques

	Ratings	Rankings	Critical Incidents	BARS	MBO	Assess-ment Centers
Meaningful dimensions	Sometimes	Seldom	Sometimes	Usually	Usually	Usually
Amount of time required	Low	Low	Medium	High	High	High
Developmental costs	Low	Low	Low	High	Medium	High
Potential for rating errors	High	High	Medium	Low	Low	Low
Acceptability to subordinates	Low	Low	Medium	High	High	High
Acceptability to superiors	Low	Low	Medium	High	High	High
Usefulness for allocating rewards	Poor	Poor	Fair	Good	Good	Fair
Usefulness for employee counseling	Poor	Poor	Fair	Good	Good	Good
Usefulness for identifying promotion potential	Poor	Poor	Fair	Fair	Fair	Good

appears that managers and organizations get what they pay for. If performance appraisals represent an important aspect of organizational life, clearly the more sophisticated—and more time consuming—techniques offer more useful information. If, on the other hand, it is necessary to evaluate employees quickly and with few resources, techniques like the graphic rating scale may be more appropriate. Managers must make cost-benefit decisions about the price (of time and money) they are willing to pay for a quality performance appraisal system.

Reward Systems in Organizations

After an organization has implemented and conducted a systematic performance appraisal, the next step is to consider how to tie rewards to the outcomes of the appraisal. Behavioral research consistently demonstrates that performance levels are highest when rewards are contingent upon performance. So, in this section, we will examine various aspects of reward systems in organizations. Four aspects of reward systems are considered: 1) types of rewards; 2) functions of reward systems; 3) bases for reward distribution; and 4) money and motivation.

Types of Rewards:
Extrinsic and Intrinsic

The variety of rewards that employees can receive in exchange for their contribution of time and effort can be classified into extrinsic and intrinsic rewards. *Extrinsic rewards* are those rewards external to the work itself. They are administered externally; that is, by someone else. Examples of extrinsic rewards include wages and salary, fringe benefits, promotions, and recognition and praise from others.

On the other hand, *intrinsic rewards* represent those rewards that are related directly to performing the job. In this sense, they are often described as self-administered rewards since engaging in the task itself leads to their receipt. Examples of intrinsic rewards include feelings of task accomplishment, autonomy, and personal growth.

Functions of Reward Systems

Reward systems in organizations are used for a variety of reasons. It is generally agreed that reward systems influence the following:

Performance   Both intrinsic and extrinsic rewards can be used to motivate performance. Following expectancy theory, employees' effort and performance would be expected to increase when they felt that rewards were contingent upon good performance. Hence, reward systems serve a very basic motivational function (Porter and Lawler, 1968).

Turnover and absenteeism   Reward systems have also been shown to influence an employee's decision to come to work or to remain with the organization (Steers and Rhodes, 1978; Porter and Steers, 1973; Price, 1977; Mobley, 1977).

Organizational commitment   Organizational commitment was discussed in Chapter 14. In brief, it has been found that reward systems in no small way influence commitment to the organization, primarily through the exchange process (Steers, 1977a; Salancik, 1977).

Job satisfaction   Job satisfaction has also been shown to be related to rewards. Lawler (1976) has summarized available evidence on satisfaction as follows: 1) Satisfaction with a reward is a function of both how much is received and how much the individual feels should be received; 2) Satisfaction is influenced by comparisons with what happens to others; 3) People differ with respect to the rewards they value; and 4) Some extrinsic rewards are satisfying because they lead to other rewards.

Occupational and organizational choice   Finally, the very occupation an individual selects, as well as the particular organization he or she joins within that occupation, is influenced by the rewards that are thought to be available in the occupation or organization (D. T. Hall, 1976).

Reward systems in organizations have far reaching consequences for both individual satisfaction and organizational effectiveness. Unfortunately, cases can easily be found where reward systems have been distorted to punish good performance or inhibit creativity. Particularly noteworthy here is a series of examples where U. S. Government bureaucracies have punished whistle blowers in their own agencies, as described in Box 17–1. These efforts hardly encourage employees to focus on efforts to perform well.

Box 17–1 Punishing Good Performance in Government

In theory, rewards should be tied to performance. In this way, employees who are highly committed to the organization and who exhibit exceptional peformance receive compensation to justify their efforts. In reality, however, there are many situations in which employees are actually *penalized* for high performance— particularly when their supervisors consider this high performance "rocking the boat."*

Consider the case of Ernest Fitzgerald. Fitzgerald was a civilian employee in the U. S. Air Force in charge of cost controls. In the course of carrying out his job, he discovered and reported to the Joint Congressional Economic Committee in 1968 that the Air Force was incurring a $2.5 billion cost overrun on the C-5A transport plane. Shortly after this whistle blowing, the Air Force laid off Fitzgerald in an "economy move."

Or, consider the case of Oscar Hoffman, a government inspector of pipe welds on combat ships being built for the U.S. Navy. In the course of his inspections, he discovered many defects in welds which he reported to his superiors. His superiors ignored the reports and threatened him with reprimand if he persisted in reporting the defects. When Hoffman filed a grievance against this threat, he was reprimanded and transferred from Seattle to Tacoma, Washington. Soon after his transfer, the Navy laid him off (in 1970) because his services were "no longer needed." Ironically, a series of accidents involving faulty welds have occurred on many of the ships identified by Hoffman. What has since happened to Hoffman? Although his superior has been promoted, Hoffman has been unable to secure another job as a government inspector.

Numerous other examples could be cited. The point here is that at least in two major government bureaucracies, effective means have been found to stifle or eliminate those who take their jobs too seriously. One can easily imagine the effects of these layoffs on other employees concerned with facilitating organizational effectiveness.

*Source: R. Vaughn. *The spoiled system.* New York: Charterhouse Books, 1975.

Bases for Reward Distribution

A common reality in many contemporary work organizations is the inequity that exists in the distribution of available rewards. One often sees little correlation between those who perform well and those who receive the greatest rewards. At the extreme, it is hard to understand how one company could pay its president over $1 million per year (as many large corporations do) while it pays its secretaries or clerks less than $10,000. Both work approximately 40 hours per week; both are important for organizational performance. Is it really possible that the president is 100 times as important as the secretary, as the salary differential suggests?

The issue we are concerned with is how organizations decide on the distribution of available rewards. At least four mechanisms can be identified:

Power In more cases than we chose to admit, rewards go to those with the greatest power. In many of the corporations whose presidents earn seven-figure incomes, we find that these same people are major shareholders in the company. Indeed, the threat to resign by an important or high performing manager often leads to increased rewards.

Equality Here all individuals within one job classification receive the same rewards. The most common example can be seen in many labor union contracts, where pay rates are established and standardized with no reference to performance level. These systems often recognize seniority, however.

Need The basis for the social welfare reward system in this country is need. In large part, the greater the need, the greater the level of support. It is not uncommon to see situations in business firms where need is taken into account in lay-off situations, where an employee is not laid off because he or she is the sole basis for the support of a family.

Distributive justice Under this system, employees receive (at least a portion) of their rewards as a function of their level of contribution. The greater·the contribution, the greater the rewards. This mechanism is most prominent in merit-based incentive programs where pay and perhaps bonuses are determined by performance levels.

Money and Motivation

A recurring debate among managers focuses on the issue of whether or not money is a primary motivator. Opsahl and Dunnette (1966) suggest that money serves several functions in work settings. These include: 1) money as a goal or incentive; 2) money as a source of satisfaction; 3) money as an instrument for gaining other desired outcomes; 4) money as a standard of comparison for determining relative standing or worth; and 5) money as a conditional reinforcer where its receipt is contingent upon a certain level of performance.

Even so, experience tells us that the effectiveness of pay as a motivator varies considerably. At times we see almost a direct relationship between pay and effort, while at other times no such relationship is found. Why? Lawler (1971) suggests that certain conditions must be present in order for pay to act as a strong motivator. These conditions include:

- Trust level between managers and subordinates is high.
- Individual performance can be accurately measured.
- Pay rewards to high performers are substantially higher than those to poor performers.
- Few perceived negative consequences of good performance exist.

Under these conditions, a climate is created where employees have reason to believe that significant performance-reward contingencies truly exist. Under this perception (and assuming the reward is valued), we would expect performance to be increased (see Hamner, 1975).

We turn now to an examination of various employee incentive programs used by organizations. Managers have choices among various alternative plans and must make decisions about which plan is most effective for the particular organization and workforce.

Individual and Group Incentive Plans

Incentive systems in organizations are usually divided into two categories, based on whether the unit of analysis—and the recipient of the reward—is the individual or the group (or organization).

Individual Incentives

Several individual incentive plans can be identified. Each assumes that the most effective method of motivating employee performance is by tying rewards to individual initiative and effort. These plans include the following:

Merit-based compensation plan   When a major portion of employee salary is determined by performance level, individuals have increased control over their output. In most organizations using these plans, all employees receive a base (cost-of-living) pay raise and then merit pay is added to this as a function of rated performance.

Piece-rate plan   On many blue-collar production jobs, employees are paid based on each unit of output they produce. The most common variation on this plan is when employees are guaranteed an hourly rate for performing at a minimum level of output (the standard). Production over and above this standard is then rewarded based on pay for each unit of output.

Bonus plans   A variety of bonus plans can be found in organizations, particularly among upper managers in private firms (not public organizations). Under this plan, individuals receive a bonus that is usually a percentage of some figure. Senior auto executives, for example, receive a bonus based on car sales volume above certain levels.

Commissions   Commissions are typically found among sales personnel where part or all of their salary is tied to their level of sales.

Although individual incentive systems in many cases lead to improved performance, some reservations have been noted. In particular, these programs may at times lead to employees competing with one another with undesirable results. For instance, paying sales people in a department store on commission may lead to fighting over customers. Second, these plans typically are resisted by unions, who prefer compensation to be based on seniority or job classification. Third, where quality control systems are lax, individual incentives like piece-rates may lead employees to maximize units of output, sacrificing quality. Finally, in order for these programs to be successful, an atmosphere of trust and cooperation between employees and managers is necessary. In order to overcome some of these shortcomings, many organizations have turned to group or organizational incentive plans.

Group and Organizational Incentives

Several incentive systems can be identified in which employees as a group benefit from improved performance, reduced costs, or increased profits. Three of the major plans are:

Profit-sharing plans   Basically, profit sharing plans pay company employees a certain percentage of profits each year. (See Glueck, 1979, for details). At least 100,000 corporations currently have these plans. The basic rationale is that by contributing to company profitability, all employees benefit.

Employee stock option plans   This plan, known as ESOP, is designed to give employees some ownership in the organization. Typically, a block of stock is set aside each year for distribution to employees based on tenure, performance level, or salary. Employees usually pay for the stocks at reduced rates. ESOPs are probably more useful in developing commitments among employees and reducing turnover than in improving performance.

Company incentive plans   A wide variety of organization-wide incentive plans are currently in use. Two of the most widely publicized plans are the Lincoln Electric Plan and the Scanlon Plan. While a detailed description of these plans goes beyond the scope of this chapter (see Glueck, 1979), these plans typically reward employees based on cost-savings or production increases that have been achieved during the past year or quarter.

Guidelines for Effective
Incentive Programs

Whatever incentive plan is selected, care must be taken to insure that the plan is appropriate for the particular organization and workforce. Mathis and Jackson (1979) note five guidelines for effective incentive programs. First, they point out that the plan should be tied as closely as possible to performance. This point has been discussed earlier in the chapter.

Second, if possible, incentive programs should allow for individual differences. They should recognize that different people want different outcomes from a job. Cafeteria-style plans, discussed below, do this.

Third, incentive programs should reflect the type of work that is done and the structure of the organization. This simply means that the program should be tailored to the particular needs, goals, and structures of a given organization. Individual incentive programs, for example, would probably be less successful among unionized personnel than would group programs like the Scanlon plan.

Fourth, the incentive program should be consistent with the climate and constraints of the organization. Where trust levels are low, for example, it may take considerable effort to get any program to work. In an industry already characterized by high levels of efficiency, basing an incentive system on increasing efficiency even further may have little effect since employees may see the task as nearly impossible.

Finally, incentive programs should be carefully monitored over time to insure that they are being fairly administered and accurately reflect current technological and organizational conditions. For instance, it may be more appropriate to offer sales clerks in a department store an incentive to sell outdated merchandise than to offer an incentive to sell current fashion items that sell themselves.

Responsibility falls on managers not to select the incentive program that is in vogue or used "next door", but rather to consider the unique situation and needs of their own organization. Then, with this understanding, a program can be developed and implemented that will facilitate goal-oriented performance.

New Developments in
Reward Systems

Recently, we have seen organizations become increasingly willing to experiment with new methods of compensation and reward systems. This development accompanies the quality of working life movement and represents one aspect of managerial efforts to improve the work situation to the benefit of both individuals and organizations. At least five new developments in reward systems can be identified (Lawler, 1976). Exhibit 17–8 summarizes these new developments.

Cafeteria-Style Fringe Benefits

A typical fringe-benefit package provides the same benefits—and the same *amount* of benefits—to all employees. As a result, individual differences or preferences are largely ignored. Studies by Lawler (1976) indicate that different employees prefer variations in the benefits they receive. For instance, young unmarried men prefer more vacation time, while young married men prefer to give up vacation time for higher pay. Older employees want more retirement benefits, while younger employees prefer greater income.

Through a cafeteria-style compensation program, employees are allowed some discretion in the determination of their own package and can make

Exhibit 17–8   Summary of new pay practices (Lawler, 1976)

	Major advantages	Major disadvantages	Favorable situational factors
Cafeteria-style fringe benefits	Increased satisfaction with pay and benefits	Cost of administration	Well-educated, heterogeneous work force
Lump-sum salary increases	Increased satisfaction with pay; greater visibility of pay increases	Cost of administration	Fair pay rates
Skill-based evaluation	More flexible and skilled work force; increased satisfaction	Cost of training and higher salaries	Employees who want to develop themselves; jobs that are interdependent
Open salary information	Increased satisfaction with pay; greater trust, and motivation; better salary administration	Pressure to pay all employees the same; complaints about pay rates	Open climate, fair pay rates, pay based on performance
Participative pay decisions	Better pay decisions; increased satisfaction, motivation, and trust	Time consumed	Democratic management climate; work force that wants to participate and that is concerned about organizational goals

Source: Reprinted, by permission of the publisher, from "New approaches to pay: Innovations that work," E. E. Lawler, *Personnel,* September–October 1976, © by AMACOM, a division of American Management Associations. All rights reserved.

trade–offs up to certain limits. Organizations like TRW and the Educational Testing Service already use such programs. While certain problems of administration exist with the programs, efforts in this direction can lead to increased need satisfaction among employees.

Lump Sum Salary Increases

Another technique that has received some attention is to allow employees to decide how (that is, in what amounts) they wish to receive their pay raise for the coming year. Under the traditional program, pay raises are paid in equal amounts in each paycheck over the year. Under this plan, employees can elect to receive equal amounts during the year or they can elect to take the entire raise in one lump sum.

This plan allows employees greater discretion over their own financial matters. If an employee wants to use the entire pay raise for a vacation, it can be paid in a lump sum in June. Then, if the employee quits before the end of the year, the unearned part of the pay raise is subtracted from the final paycheck.

This plan increases the visibility of the reward to the employee. That is, the employee receives a $600 pay raise (a rather sizeable amount) instead of twelve $50 monthly pay raises. As with the cafeteria-style plan, however, the administration costs of the lump sum plan are greater than those of the traditional method.

Skills-Based Evaluation

Typically, compensation programs are tied to job evaluations in which jobs are first analyzed to assess their characteristics and then salary levels are assigned to each job based on factors like job difficulty and labor market scarcity. In other words, pay levels are assigned based on the job, not the individual. This approach fails to encourage employees to continue learning new skills on the job since there is no reward for the learning. This approach also keeps everyone in their places and minimizes the possibility of inter-job transfers.

Under the skills-based evaluation program, employees are paid according to their skills level (that is, the number of jobs they can perform) regardless of the actual tasks they are allowed to perform. This approach has proven successful in organizations like Proctor and Gamble and General Foods. Employees are encouraged to learn additional skills and are appropriately rewarded. The organization is provided with a more highly trained and more flexible workforce. By the same token, however, training and compensation costs are necessarily increased. So, the program is only appropriate in some situations. The technique is most often seen as part of a larger quality of working life program where it is associated with job redesign efforts.

Open Salary Information

Secrecy about pay rates seems to be a widely accepted practice in work organizations, particularly among managerial personnel. It is argued that salary is a personal matter and we should not invade another's privacy. Evidence compiled during the past decade, however, suggests that pay secrecy may have several negative side-effects.

To begin, it has been consistently found that in an absence of actual knowledge people have a tendency to overestimate the pay of co-workers and those above in the hierarchy. As a result, much of the motivational potential of a differential reward system is eliminated (Lawler, 1971). Even if an employee receives a relatively sizeable salary increase, the individual may still perceive that he or she is receiving less than is due.

This problem is highlighted in the results of a study by Lawler (1971, p. 174). In considering the effects of pay secrecy on motivation, Lawler noted:

> Almost regardless of how well the individual manager was performing, he felt he was getting less than the average raise. This problem was particularly severe among high performers, since they believed that they were doing well yet received minimal reward. They did not believe that pay was in fact based upon merit. This was ironical, since their pay did reflect performance. . . . Thus, even though pay was tied to performance, these managers were not motivated because they could not see the connection.

Pay secrecy also affects motivation via feedback. Several studies have shown the value of feedback in motivating performance. The problem is that, for managers, money represents one of the most meaningful forms of feedback. Pay secrecy eliminates the feedback.

When salary information is open, employees are generally provided with more recognition for satisfactory performance and are often more motivated to perform on subsequent tasks. It is easier to establish feelings of pay equity and trust in the salary administration system. On the other hand, publicizing pay rates and pay raises can cause jealousy among employees and create pressures on managers to reduce perceived inequities in the system. There is no correct position concerning whether pay rates should be secret or open. The point is that managers should not assume *a priori* that pay secrecy—or pay openness—is a good thing. Instead, careful consideration should be given to the possible consequences of either approach in view of the particular situation in the organization at the time.

Participative Pay Decisions

Finally, a question of concern to many managers deals with the extent to which employees should be involved in decisions over pay raises. Recently several organizations have been experimenting with involving employees in raise decisions and the results seem to be quite positive. By allowing employees to participate either in the design of the reward system or in actual pay raise decisions (perhaps through a committee), it is argued that decisions of higher quality are made based on greater information. Also, employees then have greater reason to place confidence in the fairness of the decisions. On the negative side, this approach requires considerably more time for both the manager and for the participating subordinates. Costs must be weighed against the benefits to determine which approach is most suitable for the particular organization and its goals.

In deciding which, if any, of these new approaches to implement, Lawler (1976) suggests that two principal issues are of concern: the management style of the organization and the condition of the present day system (see Exhibit 17–9). If a participative style is preferred, a different approach may be in order than if an authoritative or top-down style is desired.

Beyond this, concern must be raised about the degree of fairness in the present system. As will be noted in Exhibit 17–9, most of the newer techniques require fairness in order to succeed. While this diagram is only meant

Exhibit 17–9 Guide to choosing among the new approaches to pay administration (Lawler, 1976).

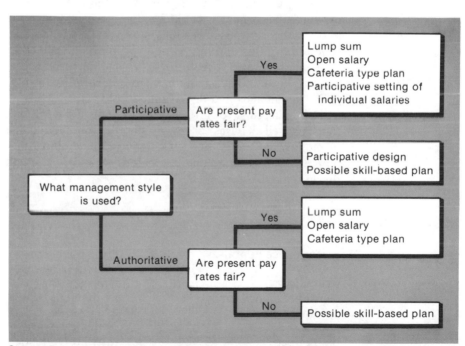

to be illustrative, it does suggest some of the more relevant management concerns when deciding on changes in compensation and reward systems.

It must be remembered that allowing employees to participate in pay decisions, as well as the other techniques described above, is relatively new and in many cases largely untested. This is not to suggest that these new developments are without merit. On the contrary, many of these procedures hold considerable promise for improving the equity and fairness of pay decisions and pay practices. Rather, we suggest that caution is in order as managers consider the suitability of the techniques in their own unique work environments. Clearly, many of these techniques are more appropriate for some organizations than for others. Thus, the important role of management is to decide how (or if) the compensation and reward systems should be modified. Whatever solution is chosen, it should be consistent with the larger purpose and goals of the organization and facilitate organizational objectives.

Summary

Based on our earlier discussions of employee motivation and performance in various work environments, we attempted in this chapter to consider ways in which performance could be appraised and rewarded. The concept of performance appraisal was introduced and it was noted that appraisals have several purposes and that various problems are inherent in the appraisals.

Next, several of the commonly used performance appraisal techniques were reviewed. The methods were compared with one another to identify major advantages and disadvantages of each.

Following this, reward systems were discussed. Functions of reward systems, as well as bases for reward distribution, were considered. The relation of money and motivation was also examined. Finally, various reward systems were introduced and compared. New developments in this field were discussed.

Key Words

performance appraisal	critical incident
validity	behaviorally anchored scale
reliability	management-by-objectives
central tendency error	assessment center
strictness error	extrinsic rewards
leniency error	intrinsic rewards
halo effect	distributive justice
recency error	cafeteria-style fringe benefits
graphic rating scale	skills-based evaluation

Questions for Discussion

1. Identify the various functions of performance appraisal. How are appraisals used in most work organizations?
2. What are some of the problems associated with performance appraisals?
3. What is meant by validity and reliability? Why are these two concepts important from a managerial standpoint?
4. Suggest several ways in which errors in appraisal systems can be reduced.
5. Critically evaluate the advantages and disadvantages of the various techniques of performance appraisal.
6. Differentiate between intrinsic and extrinsic rewards.
7. What are the main functions of reward systems?
8. Identify the major bases for reward distribution.
9. How does money influence employee motivation?
10. Discuss the relative merits of individual vs. group incentive plans.
11. What are some potential problems and benefits of many of the new developments in reward systems?

part five
Conclusion

chapter 18

Managing People at Work:
A Review

We now come to a close in our examination of the nature of people at work. As noted in Chapter 1, our intent has been to introduce the subject of organizational behavior by focusing on individuals and groups at work, and by considering what managers can learn that will facilitate managerial and organizational effectiveness. Our analysis has used individuals and groups as the basic unit of analysis instead of organizations.

We have proceeded through four different, though related, topics (see Exhibit 18–1). The first focused on the problems of people at work and considered how organizational research is done, and how organizational effectiveness can be facilitated. This introductory material was aimed at providing the necessary background for a more detailed consideration of people at work. Second, we examined the nature of individual differences in the workplace. Third, we took a look at group processes in work organizations and how these processes influence behavior and attitudes. Finally, we put people into the work situation and reviewed a variety of work-related outcomes and processes. Throughout, emphasis was placed on integrating theory and research with practical applications for managers. Throughout the book, numerous practical implications were identified as they followed

Exhibit 18–1   A framework for analyzing people at work

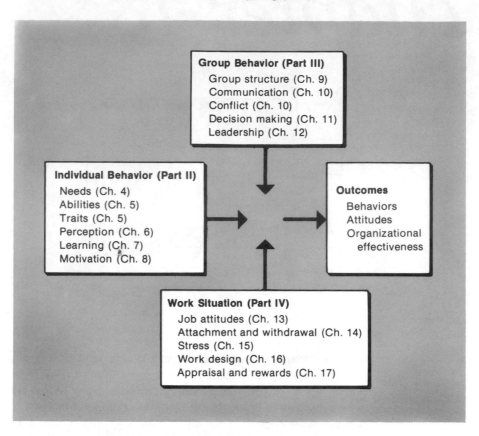

from the materials covered. We would now like in this concluding chapter to provide a review of what we have learned about managing people at work.

Problems of People in Organizations

In Part I, we were introduced to the nature of work (see Chapter 1). It was pointed out that work can be defined as an activity that produces something of value for others. It was noted that work serves several functions for individuals, including economic, social, status, and self-esteem functions. Hence, work provides something of value, not only to society at large, but also to the individuals performing the work.

Even so, there appears to be a crisis of productivity brought on by employees increasingly questioning traditional work values in today's society. Closer analysis suggests that workers today are not rejecting the work ethic but are instead demanding more challenging and meaningful jobs. The crisis, then, is not declining work values but management's inability to design suitable jobs that adequately utilize an organization's human resources.

As a result of this inability, a variety of social problems at work have become prevalent. These problems include alienation and low job satisfaction, a lack of employee motivation, communication problems, increased conflict, and problems associated with technological change. The challenge for management is to grapple with these problems in a way that satisfies employee needs while pursuing organizational goals.

The nature of scientific inquiry was also introduced in Part I in order to exemplify how we know what we know about people at work (Chapter 2). It was argued that this knowledge of methods of research can help managers not only to be intelligent consumers of behavioral data, but also to carry out their own studies in order to solve real-life problems at work.

To truly understand the nature of people at work, it is necessary to consider on a broader scale the workplace where job activities occur. This was done in Chapter 3 in our discussion of organizations. We were introduced to the concept of organization. Various definitions of organizations were discussed, as well as several organizational requirements for survival. Next various aspects of organizations were reviewed. These included the concepts of organization structure, technology, and external environment. We noted that these three variables interact to create a dynamic system of people working with people pursuing goals.

The important concept of organizational effectiveness was also introduced here. Effectiveness was defined as an organization's ability to acquire and efficiently use available resources to achieve its goals. Effectiveness was contrasted with efficiency, which is the cost–benefit ratio incurred by an organization in the pursuit of its goals. It was noted that a variety of factors influence effectiveness. In particular, organizational effectiveness seems to be influenced by organizational characteristics, environmental characteristics, employee characteristics, and the way management uses its own policies and practices to coordinate them. Clearly, the extent to which an organization is effective rests very heavily upon its people and the extent to which they have the desire and the ability to work toward organizatonal goals.

Role of Individual Behavior

In Part II, we considered in some detail the nature of individuals at work. We saw how different employees exhibit differing needs, abilities, and traits (Chapters 4 and 5). Some employees have high needs for achievement, while others do not. Some have strong mental abilities, while others have mechanical abilities. Some have high levels of emotional maturity or cognitive complexity, while others do not. The point is that managers must recognize these differences and account for them in designing work environments and reward systems. The assumption that all people are alike only guarantees failure by managers who are looking for a shortcut to effectiveness of operations.

The concept of motivation was introduced and it was argued that much of our understanding of the nature of human behavior can be traced to motivational processes (Chapter 4). In addition to a review of basic motivational processes, we also examined two opposing approaches to employee motivation. The first, an acognitive approach, suggests that employee motivation is largely influenced by a manager's ability to shape an employee's work environment and reinforcement contingencies. This approach is based on learning theory and is best expressed in behavior modification (Chapter 7). The second approach is represented by a series of cognitive theories (Chapter 8). These theories attempt to model human behavior as it relates to decisions to produce. Included here are the three related cognitive models of equity theory, goal-setting theory, and expectancy/valence theory. Implications for management of the two approaches are discussed.

Closely related to motivation is perception, since how we see events around us clearly influences how we respond to them (Chapter 6). The notion of perceptual selectivity was discussed, as well as major influences on it. The nature of social perception at work was covered. A model of perceptual processes at work was presented that attempted to identify major influences. The relation of perception to behavior was addressed by introducing attribution theory. Finally, major barriers to accurate perception of others were identified and discussed as they relate to managing people at work. These barriers include stereotyping, halo effects, and selective perception.

Role of Group Behavior

Next, we shifted the focus of our examination from individual processes to group processes in Part III. First, the nature and characteristics of work groups were reviewed (Chapter 9). It was noted that work organizations consist of a variety of formal and informal groups. People join groups for different reasons, including security, social needs, self-esteem needs, economics, the pursuit of group goals, and simple proximity. It was also noted that many groups proceed through a fairly predictable sequence of stages as they develop. These stages have been described as forming, storming, norming, and performing.

Work groups were also considered in terms of basic group characteristics. Six structural characteristics of groups were considered. These include group size, norms, roles, power, status, and group cohesiveness. It was noted that these characteristics can influence significantly the behavior and attitudes of group members. For instance, large groups tend to exhibit less satisfaction and greater turnover and absenteeism. Group norms facilitate group conformity and punish disruptive behavior by group members. A model of group cohesiveness was introduced that identified major determinants of cohesiveness, as well as major consequences.

Four group processes were discussed. These are communication, conflict, decision making, and leadership. All represent important influences on the extent to which an organization becomes effective. In the discussion on communication in organizations, a model of the basic communication process was presented (Chapter 10). Major influences on this process were reviewed. Based on this discussion, major barriers to effective communication were noted, as were several strategies that managers can use to improve communication effectiveness.

The nature of conflict was also discussed (Chapter 10). It was noted that conflict served several functions and dysfunctions and that conflict must be recognized as a fact of organizational life. A basic model of the conflict process was presented. Then, the concept of defense mechanisms was introduced to show how some individuals react to conflict. Finally, several strategies for resolving conflict were discussed.

Next, we considered decision-making processes in organizations (Chapter 11). It was noted that most decisions pass through three relatively distinct phases: intelligence activities, design activities, and choice activities. Three competing models of decision making were presented and discussed. These were the traditional econologic model, the bounded rationality model, and the implicit favorite model. Individual and group decision making were compared and the advantages and disadvantages of each highlighted. Next, the concept of groupthink was introduced. Here we focused on the processes by which group members set up barriers to effective decision making in which critical or perhaps threatening information is silenced. Strategies for improving decision making were discussed, particularly the delphi technique and the nominal group technique.

The last group process dealt with in this part was leadership (Chapter 12). While important to group effectiveness, it was pointed out that leadership is perhaps one of the least understood processes in contemporary organizations. Leadership was defined as the ability to influence the behavior of others over and above mechanical compliance (based on power or authority). In other words, leadership carries with it the concept of voluntary compliance on the part of followers. The attributes of leaders and leader behaviors were discussed. Three divergent theories of leadership were introduced and compared. These are Fiedler's contingency theory, Vroom and Yetton's normative theory, and House's path–goal theory. Each rests on different assumptions and each carries with it different implications for management.

to be illustrative, it does suggest some of the more relevant management concerns when deciding on changes in compensation and reward systems.

Based on these theories, a series of constraints on leadership was discussed. These constraints include occasions when managerial actions or decisions are preprogrammed due to precedent or policy, the traits and skills of the manager, and the extent to which the manager controls valued rewards. Where leadership fails, the concept of substitutes for leadership was introduced, and it was pointed out that a manager has a variety of structural approaches to task accomplishment that do not rely on a manager's leadership qualities. Finally, several strategies for improving leader effectiveness were discussed. These include managerial selection and placement, leadership training, rewarding leader behavior, rewarding follower behavior, and organizational engineering.

Improving Productivity and the Quality of Working Life

In the final section, we considered in some detail how people respond to the work place. Several important topics were discussed. First, we examined work-related attitudes, including a definition of attitudes and the functions they serve (Chapter 13). Next, barriers to attitude change and mechanisms to effect attitude change were discussed.

On a more specific level, job satisfaction was reviewed. We considered various dimensions of job satisfaction and various ways it can be measured. The general question of how satisfied employees are was discussed. Influences on satisfaction were reviewed. Finally, several consequences of satisfaction were mentioned, including turnover, absenteeism, performance, and organizational effectiveness. It was noted that, while a direct relationship between satisfaction and these outcomes could not be established, satisfaction was nevertheless an important variable for managers to consider.

We were then introduced to the attachment process (Chapter 14). The manner in which employees choose organizations was discussed under the concept of organizational entry. Specifically, the notion of realistic job previews was considered as a technique to reduce employee turnover by presenting prospective employees with a balanced description of their jobs. Employee adaptation and development were also discussed through the related concepts of socialization and individualization.

Two forms of employee withdrawal were also discussed: absenteeism and turnover. It was noted that different factors influence each behavior. Absenteeism is largely influenced by attendance motivation plus an ability to come to work. Turnover, on the other hand, is largely influenced by an intent to stay or leave combined with the availability of alternative opportunities. Management implications for controlling or reducing both absenteeism and turnover were discussed.

The effects of work on employee stress and strain were considered (Chapter 15). A distinction was made between frustration and anxiety. Major organizational and personal influences on stress were considered in a general model. The model recognized the potential buffering effects that groups may have on stress. Consequences of work-related stress were shown to be serious, leading to health problems, low job performance, and counterproductive behavior. Finally, various individual and organizational mechanisms for coping with stress were suggested.

In Chapter 16, we considered various aspects of work design. Early approaches to work design were reviewed as a prelude to the introduction of a relatively new model, the job characteristics model. Based on the model, principles for redesigning work were suggested. Next, case histories of several organizations that implemented work redesign programs were reviewed. These programs were applied in both public and private organizations among employees in widely different jobs. The positive and negative results were discussed, along with other techniques for work redesign, such as job rotation, four-day workweeks, flexitime, and job sharing. The problems and prospects of work design were also discussed. Several problems were noted and ways of possibly overcoming such problems were reviewed.

In the final chapter (Chapter 17), the related issues of performance appraisals and reward systems were discussed. Functions of performance appraisals as well as problems were reviewed. Methods of reducing errors in performance appraisals were also considered. Next, several specific techniques of rating emiloyee performance were presented. These include graphic rating scales, ranking methods, critical incidents, behaviorally anchored rating scales, management-by-objectives, and assessment centers. The various methods were compared to identify relative strengths and weaknesses.

Reward systems were also discussed in Chapter 17. A distinction was made between intrinsic and extrinsic rewards and functions of such rewards were mentioned. Money and motivation were also discussed. Next, the relative merits of individual and group incentive plans were considered and guidelines were discussed for implementing an effective incentive program. Finally, several new developments in reward systems were discussed. These include cafeteria-style fringe benefits, lump-sum salary increases, skills-based evaluations, open salary information, and participative pay decisions. In all, it was noted that appraisal and reward systems were a primary means of insuring that rewards were contingent upon satisfactory performance. Through the use of these reward systems, employees can see mechanisms by which their support of organizational goals can lead to the receipt of desired rewards. Hence, where the systems are properly designed, it is possible to see situations where personal and organizational goals are truly integrated.

Throughout this book, an attempt has been made to develop an appreciation of the problems of individuals and groups at work and what managers can do to help solve some of these problems and at the same time facilitate organizational effectiveness. With an understanding of the nature of people at work and the problems they face, managers should be in a position to take intelligent actions aimed at improving both productivity and the quality of work. This is the basic charge of management and it is hoped that the material presented here will help managers carry out this charge. This hope rests on the assumption that the informed manager is better able to make reasonable decisions in the design of work activities. In this regard, we are reminded of J. M. Clark's quotation, ''Knowledge is the only instrument of production that is not subject to diminishing returns.'' It is hoped that this book has contributed to this knowledge.

appendix A
Cases

437

case 1

Universal
Insurance Company

At the Universal Insurance Company, in November, 1970, managers in the field agency department (with 90 to 100 employees) decided to create the position of coordinator (job grade 6) in the field agency department. The coordinator's function would be to ensure that the work load among secretaries was more evenly divided than it had been. Up to that time, some secretaries had been consistently overworked while others frequently had much less work than they could do.

Obviously the qualifications for such a position would include intelligence, reliability, knowledge of the work, and insight into motivational and personality differences among agency personnel, as well as ability to establish and maintain good working relationships with secretaries and supervisors. Promotion from within was company policy, and job posting was a regular procedure.

To understand the importance of effective coordination among secretaries, and the difficulties to be expected in achieving it, the reader needs a minimum of information about functions of the field agency department as well as responsibilities of agency supervisors and their secretaries.

The overall function of the field agency department (in the home office) was to provide continuous contact with district managers in the field. Each of the 10 to 12 agency supervisors served a marketing group in a specific geographical area. Major objectives of all agency supervisors were to help district managers increase the number of policyholders and to prevent policy lapses. For both purposes it was necessary to keep company representatives in the field fully informed as to all current developments in the insurance business and any changes in home office procedures.

Meeting these liaison responsibilities required prompt and reliable response to all correspondence and telephone inquiries. To help supervisors in this part of their job, each was assigned a personal secretary. However, the amount of activity, and therefore of correspondence, differed considerably among the various geographical areas covered by the agency supervisors. And this fact accounted for the unequal work load that had to be carried by the personal secretaries.

These secretaries had no understudies (though their work was supplemented by clerical employees in *information and service centers* who, supervised by unit heads, could be drawn upon as needed). As is customary, the personal secretaries enjoyed a special status. In this division, the vacation of each was timed to coincide with that of her boss (though normally the secretary's vacation was shorter). And she left for lunch at the same time as he did. (During her absence from the office, telephone calls were answered by any qualified clerical employee who happened to be in the office at the time.)

In 1971, two secretaries in the division were outstanding: Marilyn Wiener and Hope Tetzeli.

Marilyn started working for Universal in 1967, as

Source: Adapted from *Personnel Administration: A Point of View and a Method, 7th Edition,* by P. Pigors and C. A. Myers. Copyright © 1973 by McGraw-Hill. Used with the permission of McGraw-Hill Book Company.

a part-time clerk, during her last 2 years in high school. Immediately after her graduation (at eighteen, in June, 1969), she began full-time employment as a secretary (job grade 4) in Agency C of the field agency division. Her work was consistently outstanding, and she had received both of the annual merit increases that were open to employees at her level. In addition to her technical proficiency and reliability (she had never been tardy and rarely absent) she was well liked because of her pleasant way with people. And, despite her quiet manner, her supervisor and associates were aware that she was ambitious. Some of her friends, but not her supervisor, also knew that by June, 1971, Marilyn had reached the conclusion that secretaries in the field agency department had little chance for promotion.[1] She was, therefore, tentatively planning to leave Universal during the next few months and to continue her education. In this way she hoped to qualify herself for a better position, if not at Universal, then in some other company.

Hope Tetzeli was another outstanding secretary in the field agency division at that time. She was secretary to Phil James (supervisor of Agency D). She first came to Universal in June, 1970, immediately after graduating from high school (at eighteen years of age). She prided herself on having been an honor student throughout her high school career, having graduated in the top 10 percent in her class of 550 students.

Her employment interviewer described her as "neat and well dressed, petite, vivacious, with a markedly Latin temperament, deeply committed to equal rights for women, and with a keen sense of social justice." In her first performance appraisal, her supervisor (Phil James) rated the quality and quantity of her work as outstanding and commended her willingness to assume extra responsibilities when necessary. Like Marilyn, Hope had never been tardy and very rarely absent.

However, Hope's office conduct had occasionally been such as to elicit from John Lord (division manager) the comment "Hope is a self-elected moralist. She has an opinion on everything that happens, inside the department and out, and no hesitation about expressing her opinion however unfavorable it may be." In fact, Mr. Lord had

gradually become convinced that Hope's outspokenness tended to create unrest in the office. That opinion had been formed on the basis of Hope's behavior in the following incidents.

Hope's "keen sense of social justice," as well as her outspokenness, first came to John Lord's attention in January, 1971, as a result of a misunderstanding that had occurred 6 months earlier. In July, 1970, Lord was orienting a group of relatively new women—including Hope. He told them that after 6 months they would receive an automatic salary increase. However, at the end of the 6 months several of the women, including Hope, did not receive the increase. Thereupon, Hope appeared in John Lord's office (with three other women whom she had apparently egged on to join her in making a protest). Serving as spokeswoman for the group, she demanded to know why they had not been given the promised increase. The division manager expressed regret for the misunderstanding, explaining that he must have forgotten to mention that the automatic increase applied only to low-level entry jobs (grades 1 through 3). He added that after this first automatic increase, pay raises were considered annually for all employees. The other women appeared to be satisfied with this explanation. But not long afterwards news reached Mr. Lord (through the grapevine) that Hope was harping on the "unjust treatment" that some of them had received in regard to the promised salary increase. When developing this theme in conversation with her friends, she reportedly cited the incident as proof that Mr. Lord "doesn't know what he's talking about when it comes to company policies."

When John Lord heard about these comments from Hope, he requested Phil James (her supervisor) to counsel her, explaining that her remarks were inappropriate in view of his apology and explanation—which should have ended the matter. James was reluctant to criticize the office conduct of an upstanding woman with whose technical performance he was more than satisfied. It seemed to him that her social shortcomings had nothing to do with her job performance. Therefore, his "counseling" of Hope consisted merely in saying: "You can't be a spokeswomen for all the women. Just keep on doing the excellent job you have been doing, and you're sure to get ahead."

A week later, another incident occurred which was reported differently by Hope and the other woman immediately involved. After an encounter in the ladies room, one of the women returned to the office in tears, complaining that Hope had humiliated her by talking in public about a "very personal matter." When asked about this incident, Hope replied that she had merely tried to console the woman (who was pregnant though unmarried), "and other women gathered around while I was talking."

When Mr. Lord heard about this encounter he sent for Hope and reproved her for "disturbing other employees and creating unrest in the office." According to Hope, he told her that in the future she should mind her own business and ended by saying, "If you keep on like this, I shan't be able to recommend you for promotion."

Shortly after this reprimand, Hope had her first progress review with the field agency department personnel assistant, Miss Page.[2] During this interview, Hope was full of complaints—ranging from the caliber of the company's medical clinic to the "injustice" she had suffered with regard to the "promised" salary increase. Miss Page suggested that Hope discuss her dissatisfactions with the division manager. But Hope refused. She said there would be no point in doing so because Mr. Lord was obviously prejudiced against her. To substantiate this statement, Hope asserted that ever since the difficulty about the pay raise, Mr. Lord had "consistently picked on" her. She went on to say that Mr. Lord's prejudice extended to some of the other women also; that he had a few favorites; and that, owing to his "ignorance of company policy, he was a very ineffective manager." Miss Page then suggested that Hope should speak with the department manager, Mr. O'Hara. Hope dismissed that suggestion also, saying that "everyone" knew Mr. O'Hara took no interest in personnel matters.[3] She insisted instead on having a confidential interview with Mr. Ryan (department director). Miss Page, knowing that Mr. Ryan was a firm believer in the "open-door policy," acceded to Hope's request. The interview took place shortly thereafter.

During Hope's talk with the director, she apparently expressed the same critical views and strongly negative opinions about Mr. Lord as in the interview with Miss Page, though she stated that the supervisors were "fine."

Shortly after this interview, Mr. Lord's record as a manager was discreetly investigated. The results completely exonerated him (including charges of favoritism and inadequate information as to company policies).

During the early spring of 1971, Hope became convinced that she would never get ahead in the field agency department. She therefore kept track of posted job opportunities in other departments. In May she found one that appealed to her because it would entail a promotion. She therefore told Mr. James that she would like to apply for it. James, extremely anxious to keep his competent secretary, tried to dissuade her. Hope then went to Mr. Lord, who acceded to her request. [Such a request and permission were standard operating procedure (S.O.P.) at Universal, a prepared form being signed by the management representative receiving the request.]

During the interview in the other department, Hope was told (according to her own later statement): "Don't get your hopes up, because this job requires a mature person." When the transfer failed to materialize, Hope jumped to the conclusion that Mr. Lord had stood in her way, because of his prejudice against her. Moreover, she was deeply offended by the implication that she was regarded as an immature person. On several later occasions, when criticizing behavior by other employees, she ended in a dramatic tone, "do you call *that* mature?" To cite one example: She told her friends that in the elevator one day she overheard an elderly man say to an associate: "There sure are lots of good-looking broads in this company." She added that although she regarded such a remark as evidence of extreme immaturity, she had made no official complaint because the man had a large family and could ill afford to lose his job.

On June 16, Hope had an encounter with Marilyn which brought about immediate and serious consequences. That afternoon (a Thursday), just before the end of the working day, Marilyn had been told that she was to be promoted to the position of coordinator as of the following Monday. She expressed delight at the prospect. The word spread like wildfire. Immediately after work, Hope waylaid Marilyn in the hallway. According to another woman who witnessed the encounter, Hope accused Marilyn of being unscrupulous in accepting the promotion since, by her own admission, she intended to leave Universal and "go back to school." Hope added that such behavior on Marilyn's part was not only exceedingly immature, under the circumstances, but also selfish, and "unfair to us three women who want to make a career at Universal." According to another report that reached Miss Page, Hope's remarks were even more bitter. "She accused Marilyn of taking the bread out of other people's mouths, told her she was greedy and ruthless and also that it is typical of your race to think only of yourselves."

After being the victim of this tirade, Marilyn burst into tears and rushed home.

News of the incident reached Mr. Lord the next morning, by telephone. Marilyn's mother called him to say that Marilyn would not be returning to Universal. She blamed Hope for this development. Mrs. Wiener was so angry that she almost hung up at this point. But when Mr. Lord urged her to tell him what had happened, she said that Hope had done "a complete job of character assassination"

on Marilyn who was "emotionally destroyed" and might require medical attention. She ended by saying that if this proved to be necessary, she would "hold the company morally and financially responsible."

Notes

1. Usually the only way a secretary got ahead—except by a promotional transfer—was when her immediate supervisor was promoted. However, in the field agency department, even the director was only in his early forties.
2. At Universal, a departmental personnel assistant was responsible for scheduling and conducting progress reviews and for reporting her findings to the manager. But she was not expected to initiate any other action with personnel or to make suggestions to representatives of line management.
3. This opinion of Hope's was probably based on the fact that the department manager's responsibilities related entirely to the company representatives in the field, though this information had never been relayed to nonsupervisory employees.

case 2

Hovey and Beard Company

The Hovey and Beard Company manufactured wooden toys of various kinds: wooden animals, pull toys, and the like. One part of the manufacturing process involved spraying paint on the partially assembled toys. This operation was staffed entirely by women.

The toys were cut, sanded, and partially assembled in the wood room. Then they were dipped into shellac, following which they were painted. The toys were predominantly two-colored; a few were made in more than two colors. Each color required an additional trip through the paint room.

For a number of years, production of these toys had been entirely handwork. However, to meet tremendously increased demand, the painting operation had recently been re-engineered so that the eight operators (all women) who did the painting sat in a line by an endless chain of hooks. These hooks were in continuous motion, past the line of operators and into a long horizontal oven. Each woman sat at her own painting booth so designed as to carry away fumes and to backstop excess paint. The operator would take a toy from the tray beside her, position it in a jig inside the painting cubicle, spray on the color according to a pattern, then release the toy and hang it on the hook passing by. The rate at which the hooks moved had been calculated by the engineers so that each woman, when fully trained, would be able to hang a painted toy on each hook before it passed beyond her reach.

The operators working in the paint room were on a group bonus plan. Since the operation was new to them, they were receiving a learning bonus which decreased by regular amounts each month. The learning bonus was scheduled to vanish in six months, by which time it was expected that they would be on their own—that is, able to meet the standard and to earn a group bonus when they exceeded it.

By the second month of the training period trouble had developed. The employees learned more slowly than had been anticipated, and it began to look as though their production would stabilize far below what was planned for. Many of the hooks were going by empty. The women complained that they were going by too fast, and that the time study man had set the rates wrong. A few women quit and had to be replaced with new operators, which further aggravated the learning problem. The team spirit that the management had expected to develop automatically through the group bonus was not in evidence except as an expression of what the engineers called "resistance." One woman whom the group regarded as its leader (and the management regarded as the ringleader) was outspoken in making the various complaints of the group to the foreman: the job was a messy one, the hooks moved too fast, the incentive pay was not being correctly calculated, and it was too hot working so close to the drying oven.

A consultant who was brought into this picture

Source: Abridgement of "Group Dynamics and Intergroup Relations" by George Strauss and Alex Bavelas (under the title "The Hovey and Beard Case") from *Money and Motivation,* edited by William F. White. Copyright © 1955 Harper & Row, Publishers, Inc. Reprinted by permission of the publishers.

worked entirely with and through the foreman. After many conversations with him, the foreman felt that the first step should be to get the employees together for a general discussion of the working conditions. He took this step with some hesitation, but he took it on his own volition.

The first meeting, held immediately after the shift was over at four o'clock in the afternoon, was attended by all eight operators. They voiced the same complaints again: the hooks went by too fast, the job was too dirty, the room was hot and poorly ventilated. For some reason, it was this last item that they complained of most. The foreman promised to discuss the problem of ventilation and temperature with the engineers, and he scheduled a second meeting to report back to the employees. In the next few days the foreman had several talks with the engineers. They and the superintendent felt that this was really a trumped-up complaint, and that the expense of any effective corrective measure would be prohibitively high.

The foreman came to the second meeting with some apprehensions. The operators, however, did not seem to be much put out, perhaps because they had a proposal of their own to make. They felt that if several large fans were set up so as to circulate the air around their feet, they would be much more comfortable. After some discussion, the foreman agreed that the idea might be tried out. The foreman and the consultant discussed the question of the fans with the superintendent, and three large propeller-type fans were purchased.

The fans were brought in. The women were jubilant. For several days the fans were moved about in various positions until they were placed to the satisfaction of the group. The operators seemed completely satisfied with the results, and the relations between them and the foreman improved visibly.

The foreman, after this encouraging episode, decided that further meetings might also be profitable. He asked the operators if they would like to meet and discuss other aspects of the work situation. They were eager to do this. The meeting was held, and the discussion quickly centered on the speed of the hooks. The operators maintained that the time study man had set them at an unreasonably fast speed and that they would never be

able to reach the goal of filling enough of them to make a bonus.

The turning point of the discussion came when the group's leader frankly explained that the point wasn't that they couldn't work fast enough to keep up with the hooks, but that they couldn't work at that pace all day long. The foreman explored the point. The employees were unanimous in their opinion that they could keep up with the belt for short periods if they wanted to. But they didn't want to because if they showed they could do this for short periods they would be expected to do it all day long. The meeting ended with an unprecedented request: "Let us adjust the speed of the belt faster or slower depending on how we feel." The foreman agreed to discuss this with the superintendent and the engineers.

The reaction of the engineers to the suggestion was negative. However, after several meetings it was granted that there was some latitude within which variations in the speed of the hooks would not affect the finished product. After considerable argument with the engineers, it was agreed to try out the operators' idea.

With misgivings, the foreman had a control with a dial marked "low, medium, fast" installed at the booth of the group leader; she could now adjust the speed of the belt anywhere between the lower and upper limits that the engineers had set.

The operators were delighted, and spent many lunch hours deciding how the speed of the belt should be varied from hour to hour throughout the day. Within a week the pattern had settled down to one in which the first half hour of the shift was run on what the operators called a medium speed (a dial setting slightly above the point marked "medium"). The next two and one-half hours were run at high speed; the half hour before lunch and the half hour after lunch were run at low speed. The rest of the afternoon was run at high speed with the exception of the last 45 minutes of the shift, which was run at medium.

In view of the operators' reports of satisfaction and ease in work, it is interesting to note that the constant speed at which the engineers had originally set the belt was slightly below medium on the dial of the control that had been given the women. The average speed at which they were running the belt was on the high side of the dial. Few, if any, empty hooks entered the oven, and inspection showed no increase of rejects from the paint room.

Production increased, and within 3 weeks (some 2 months before the scheduled ending of the learning bonus) the operators were operating at 30 to 50 percent above the level that had been expected under the original arrangement. Natu-rally their earnings were correspondingly higher than anticipated. They were collecting their base pay, a considerable piece rate bonus, and the learning bonus which, it will be remembered, had been set to decrease with time and not as a func-tion of current productivity. The operators were earning more now than many skilled workers in other parts of the plant.

case 3

The Ratebuster

Of the six people in the boys' department only the head was male, and he made sales only occasionally. Two of the women were high sellers—Mrs. White and Mrs. Brown. Mrs. White was fifty-nine years old, large physically and somewhat taciturn. She had worked at Lassiters* for fourteen years. Mrs. Brown was a small active person, thirty-two and had been with the store for eight years. Masters told me that when she started in the store she was much taken with Mrs. White and copied and improved upon Mrs. White's selling techniques. Then, too, Mrs. Brown had the insights that came from close personal experience in outfitting her son. Over a period of several months they developed a rivalry. For the last six years or so, according to Masters [Mike Masters, head of the boys' department], they were coldly polite to each other when it was necessary to speak. Masters regarded existence of this hostility as one of his major problems. His professed ideal was that the women should be circulating among the customers, busy all the time and cordial to each other.

The other three saleswomen were Mrs. Bonomo, thirty-five, a quiet amenable person, in the department for four years; Mrs. Selby, forty-eight, an employee for five years, who took things as they came without being much disturbed—though judging from her behavior and remarks she made, she disliked Mrs. White much more than she did Mrs. Brown. Mrs. Dawson, at twenty-two, was the youngest member of the department. She had dubbed Mrs. Brown and Mrs. White "saleshogs." She had worked there less than two years. She liked Mrs. Brown despite the epithet she had given her. Mrs. Dawson had two years of college, the most schooling in the department.

The saleswomen received from $1.75 to $2.25 per hour, depending on how long they had been in the department. Records of sales (dollar-volume) for the department were kept for the past year and varied from month to month. These records established the quota for the current year. Once this was

*The names of the individuals in this case and the department store (Lassiters) are fictional. The incidents described took place in the boys' department of Lassiters. The saleswomen in the department were all on commission.

It is common for members of work groups who are on a commission or other system of incentive payments to avoid showing each other up. In other words, there are informal standards about what members of the group perceive to be a reasonable amount of work. Individuals who produce significantly above this level are often called "ratebusters" or "grabbers" by social scientists. Members of the work group often apply less complimentary labels and even sanctions to individuals who violate the output norms. At Lassiters, ratebusters were called "saleshogs" by their peers.

Source: Melville Dalton, "The Ratebuster: The Case of the Saleswoman," in *Varieties of Work Experience: The Social Control of Occupational Groups and Roles,* by P. L. Stewart and M. G. Cantor, eds., pp. 206–214. Copyright 1974 by Schenkman Publishing Co., Inc. Reprinted by permission.

equaled, the women started drawing commission pay at the rate of five percent. Commission was paid separately once a month.

Before describing the selling tactics of Mrs. Brown and Mrs. White, the ratebuster types, it is instructive to note the average daily sales established over a six month period[1] by the five saleswomen. Mrs. Brown with $227 average daily sales is over twice as much as Mrs. Dawson and Mrs. Selby, nearly twice as much as Mrs. Bonomo, and $74 more than the second ratebuster, Mrs. White. Masters assured me that Mrs. White has slowed up noticeably in her selling over the last two years, but in terms of dollar sales and her constant challenge to Mrs. Brown she should still be classified as a ratebuster, or a ratebuster in decline.

Saleswomen	Average Daily Dollar Sales
Mrs. Brown	227
Mrs. White	153
Mrs. Bonomo	119
Mrs. Selby	110
Mrs. Dawson	101

Lassiters had an employee credit union. Masters had access to the complete membership which was seventy-six. He gave me *rank only* of the five saleswomen based on the individual amounts deposited in the credit union. (He was so shocked when I requested the total savings of each of the saleswomen that I gladly accepted the partial data.) Mrs. White stood third in the store, and Mrs. Brown was fourth. Mrs. Selby ranked forty-ninth and Mrs. Bonomo was sixty-sixth. Mrs. Dawson was not a member. These data alone do not tell much, but they do indicate that Mrs. White and Mrs. Brown were among the top investors, and that commission was important in their behavior.

Mrs. Brown apparently had more personal relations with customers than anyone in the boys' department. She learned from Masters when specially-priced merchandise was coming in. She telephoned customers she knew well and made arrangements to lay away items of given size and style that were scheduled to go on sale. When she had filled these private orders there was little of the merchandise left for the general public when the official sale day arrived. These sales by telephone constituted about fifteen percent of her total sales. Relatively new customers who bought heavily a time or two she filed in her retentive memory and took steps to acquaint them with her special services.

Among her repeat buyers was a working woman with four sons who treated their clothing roughly. Every six weeks this woman came in to buy nearly complete outfits for the boys. This included shirts, underwear, socks and blue jeans, which amounted to what the sales force called a "big ticket" of about $120.

Mrs. Brown had another woman customer who did not believe in having the younger boys of her five sons wear the older boys' outgrown clothing. She did not come in much oftener than once a year to buy complete outfits, usually just before Easter, which could run to two hundred dollars or more. Mrs. Brown acted as though she had an exclusive right[2] to these customers, and several others that she knew who had only two sons. When Mrs. Brown expected these people she would skip her lunch hour for fear she might miss them, or ask Masters to make the sale and ring it up on her cash drawer in case the woman came when she was out to lunch. He was glad to do this. When business was very good, whether she expected specific customers or not, she ignored the coffee breaks (ten minutes each morning and afternoon) and the lunch hour, leaving the selling floor only long enough to eat a sandwich in the dressing room.

She also had a practical monopoly on sales for boys on welfare. These boys had to be presented by an agent in the welfare organization the first time they did business with the store. Masters turned the welfare customer over to Mrs. Brown and forever afterwards[3] she made the sales. In some cases the welfare officer brought the boy, or boys, with their only clothes on their backs, to buy a complete outfit with extra socks, handkerchiefs and underwear. (Shoes were not sold in the boys' department.) In any case, Mrs. Brown took care of the sales then and afterwards.

Mrs. Brown's housekeeping area was just inside the entrance from the parking lot. She watched this approach closely. When she was not busy, or was talking to the other members of the department, she could break off instantly—even when she was telling a joke—and move toward the door. If she did not recognize the person she formed some judgment on him based on the affluence of his dress and bearing. If the customer had a boy along, she judged whether he would be hard to fit. In her own words, she had a theory that "the kids who are tall and skinny or short and fat are hard to fit."[4] Thus she made quick appraisals of everybody who moved toward the department. If she approached a customer and learned that he was not as promising as he looked, she often brought the person to one of the other saleswomen and presented him with a statement of what he wanted as though—according to the women—she was giving them an assured sale. She made no revealing comment on the matter, but she seemed at the same time to be putting a restraint on her rivals.

Mrs. Brown's most galling behavior to the group was her practice of getting sale claims on as many prospective buyers as possible. She thus deprived the other saleswomen of a chance at the buyers. For instance, as she was serving one person, she would see another coming through the door—which she nearly always faced even when busiest. Quickly she would lay a number of items before the first person with the promise to be back in a moment, then hurry to capture the second customer. If the situation were right, she might get her claim on three or four buyers while two or more of the saleswomen were reduced to maintaining the show cases, and setting things in order so as not to appear idle. Mrs. Brown was able to do this because her own housekeeping and stocking area (assigned by Masters) lay between the entrance to the store and the other sections of the boys' department. Only Mrs. White would challenge her by intercepting a patron. The rivalry between them never came to a visible break. As noted earlier some of the other saleswomen resented Mrs. Brown's behavior and privately called her a "sales hog." She was not called that by Mrs. Bonomo and Mrs. Selby who thought—as they said—that Mrs. Brown in action was a "show in itself."

A standard device was used by Mrs. Brown, for ends not intended, with the understanding and collaboration of Masters. On very slack days she frequently left the store shortly after one or two o'clock to do "comparative shopping," that is, to compare the selling prices of items that Lassiters sold with the prices that other local stores charged for the same or similar items. Sometimes Mrs. Brown actually did this, but often she would attend a matinee, or go home to catch up with her housework, or just take a nap. (Her time card was punched out by Masters at the official quitting time.) In any case, to the favorable implications of "comparative shopping," the further obvious inference was made that her absence from the store allowed the other salesgirls to make more commission. (Actually, business was so slow on some days, because of weather, etc., that it was not possible for any of the saleswomen to earn bonus pay.)

Mrs. Brown's conduct may suggest total indifference to the group. But possibly because she was a female in our society, she was not as nonconformist as the grim ratebusters in industry. Some of these could work for years without exchange of words with people, only a few feet away, that they knew hated them. To a degree Mrs. Brown was concerned about her group. Every week or so she would buy a two pound box of choice chocolates from a candy store near Lassiters and bring it in to share with the group. She could have bought a less expensive grade of candy at Lassiters. Sharing of the candy was almost certainly calculated (she ate little of it herself) but it appeared spontaneous and was received without hesitation. The saleswomen could not direct an unqualified hostility toward her.

She had another uncommon practice which made her stand apart from all of Lassiters' employees. Despite her determined assault on the commission system she did not use her right to a discount on items that she might buy for herself or members of her family. She took her fifteen-year-old son to a local independent department store to buy his clothes. She vigorously declared that "I don't want anything that [Lassiters] has." She was emphatic to the group—and implicitly condemned them—that she did not want to participate in the common practice of getting legal price reductions in addition to the regular employee discount by buying items at the end of a season. For example, an assortment of women's purses would be delivered to the selling floor. This was the "beginning of the season" for that batch of purses. The saleswomen with friends in the purse department would look at the display and select ones that appealed to them. These were laid away until the "end of the season" when they could be bought at the sale price which was further reduced by the regular discount. Mrs. Brown would have nothing to do with such items. She clearly did not want it said that she was taking advantage of her job.

A likely interpretation is that she sensed she was rejected and widely criticized for her methods and high bonus pay. She feared that some envious salesperson would report any borderline activity on her part to top management. Her own explanation implied that her esthetic taste could not be satisfied by the merchandise at Lassiters. In effect she downgraded the status of the store. As part of this complex she also implied that she was morally somewhat above the group. Also she may have been posing to hide her possible guilt feelings about her treatment of the group.

Although the aim of this paper is not to deal with morale problems, it was glaringly clear that Masters damaged group feeling by routing welfare customers to Mrs. Brown, and by ringing up some of his sales on her cash drawer. His tacit approval of her behavior discouraged the other saleswomen from attempting to control her.

Notes

1. Masters gave me these figures based on an average of 44 hours a week and including the back-to-school buying months of August and September 1969.
2. Probably she was encouraged by the customers to think that way; certainly some customers waited for her to be free to serve them.
3. The other saleswomen knew about this and resented it. Grateful to Masters for allowing me to observe and talk with the saleswomen, I naturally did not ask him why there was not sharing of such sales among his force. I inquired, but there was no voiced conception of a "day's work" among the saleswomen. This general practice of informal rewarding is not uncommon in industry where it is sometimes done even with the knowledge and cooperation of individual officers of the union. (Lassiters was not unionized.)
4. Alteration of coats and trousers was done free by the store's tailor. But measuring and marking and the extra trying on were time-consuming. In the extreme cases this was futile. In any case Mrs. Brown avoided customers with "odd size" boys unless she knew them to be liberal buyers and worth her time.

case 4

Petersen Electronics

"Grow old along with me, the best is yet to be." When Robert Browning expressed this sentiment, he was not writing as a spokesman for business to promising young executives. Yet in the nineteenth century, while such poetry may have been out of place in business, the thought was very fitting.

In fact, until quite recently corporations have been able to reward capable employees with increased responsibilities and opportunities. Based on our recently completed research into nine companies, however, the more prevalent corporate sentiment might be, "Stay young along with me, or gone you well may be."

We found a large number of managers who, in the judgment of their organization, have "plateaued." That is, there is little or no likelihood that they will be promoted or receive substantial increases in duties and responsibilities. These long-service employees are being regarded with growing concern because plateauing is taking place more markedly, and frequently earlier, than in years past. Further, executives feel that plateauing is frequently accompanied by noticeable declines in both motivation and quality of performance.

While plateauing, like aging, is inevitable, in years past it was a more gradual process. For the most part, those who sought advancement in their managerial careers had ample opportunity to get it, within broad limits of ability, while those who did not desire advancement (including competent individuals content with more modest levels of achievement and success) could be bypassed by colleagues still on the way up.

Today the situation has changed. Declining rates of corporate growth and an ever-increasing number of candidates have heightened the competition for managerial positions. The top of the pyramid is expanding much more slowly than the middle, and the managers who advanced rapidly during the growth boom of the 1960s are now at or just below the top. Their rate of career progress has necessarily slowed, and yet they are still many years from normal retirement and with many productive years to go. As these managers continue in their positions, the queue of younger, aggressive aspirants just below them is likely to grow longer, with spillover effects on opportunities and mobility rates throughout the organization.

This is precisely the dilemma confronting Benjamin Petersen, president and chairman of the board of Petersen Electronics.

Petersen founded the company in 1944, and it grew rapidly during the 1950s and 1960s, reaching sales of $200 million in 1968. Growth since then, though, has been uneven and at an average of less than 5% per year. However, 1974 was a good year, with sales and profits showing leaps of 12% and 18%, respectively.

Despite the good year, Benjamin Petersen, now 61 years old, is concerned about the company as he nears retirement. His major problem involves

Source: Reprinted by permission of the Harvard Business Review. Case from "Case of the Plateaued Performer" by E. Kirby Warren, Thomas P. Ference and James A. F. Stoner (January–February 1975). Copyright © 1975 by the President and Fellows of Harvard College; all rights reserved.

George Briggs, 53, vice president of marketing, and Thomas Evans, national sales manager, who is 34 years old and one of Briggs's four subordinates. Nor have the implications of the situation between Briggs and Evans been lost on Victor Perkins, 39, vice president of personnel.

Petersen's View of the Predicament

"When we started, a handful of people worked very hard and very closely to build something bigger than any of us. One of these people was George Briggs. George has been with me from the start, as have almost all of my vice presidents and many of my key department heads.

"For the first five years, I did almost all the inventing and engineering work. Tom Carroll ran the plant and George Briggs knocked on doors and sold dreams as well as products for the company.

"As the company grew, we added people, and Briggs slowly worked his way up the sales organization. Eight years ago, when our vice president of marketing retired, I put George in the job. He has market research, product management, sales service, and the field sales force [reporting through a national sales manager] under him, and he has really done a first-rate job all around.

"About ten years ago we began bringing in more bright young engineers and MBAs and moved them along as fast as we could. Turnover has been high and we have had some friction between our young Turks and the old guard.

"When business slowed in the early seventies, we also had a lot of competition among the newcomers. Those who stayed have continued to move up, and a few are now in or ready for top jobs. One of the best of this group is Tom Evans. He started with us nine years ago in the sales service area. Later, he spent three years in product management.

"George Briggs got him to move from head of the sales service department to assistant product manager. After one year, George Briggs named him manager of the product management group, and two years later, when the national sales manager retired, George named Evans to the post.

"That move both surprised and pleased me. I felt that Evans would make a good sales manager despite the fact that he had had little direct sales experience. I was afraid, however, that George would not want someone in that job who hadn't had years of field experience.

"I was even more surprised, though, when six months later (a month ago) George told me he was afraid Evans wasn't working out, and asked if I might be able to find a spot for him in the corporate personnel department. While I'm sure our recent upturn in sales is not solely Evans's doing, he certainly seems to be one of the keys. Despite his inexperience, he seems to have the field sales organization behind him. He spends much of his time traveling with them, and from what I hear he has built a great team spirit.

"Despite this, George Briggs claims that he is in over his head and that it is just a matter of time before his inexperience gets him in trouble. I can't understand why George is so adamant. It's clearly not a personality clash, since they have always gotten along well in the past. In many ways, Briggs has been Evans's greatest booster until recently.

"Since George is going to need a replacement someday, I was hoping it would be Evans. If George doesn't retire before we have to move Evans again or lose him, I'd consider moving Evans to another area.

"When we were growing faster, I didn't worry about a new challenge opening up for our aggressive young managers—there were always new divisions, new lines—something to keep them stimulated and satisfied with their progress. Now I have less flexibility—my top people are several years from retirement. And yet I have some younger ones—like Evans, whom I would hate to lose—always pushing and expecting promotion.

"Evans is a good example of this; I could move him, but there are not that many *real* opportunities. He could go to personnel or engineering or even finance. Evans has the makings of a really fine general manager. But I'd hate to move him now. He really isn't ready for another shift—although he will be in a few years—and despite what George claims, I think he is stimulating team work and commitment in the sales organization as a result of his style.

"Finally, while I don't want to appear unduly critical of Briggs, I'm not sure he could get the job done in these competitive times without a bright young person like Evans to help him."

Briggs's Account of the Situation

"Before I say anything else, let me assure you there is nothing personal in my criticism of Evans.

"I like him. I have always liked him. I've done more for him than anyone else in the company. I've tried to coach him and bring him along just like a son.

"But the simple truth is that he's in way over his head and showing a side of his personality I've never seen before. I brought him along through sales service and product management and he was always eager to learn. While I couldn't give him a lot of help in those areas (frankly, there are aspects of them I don't yet fully understand), I still tried, and he paid attention and learned from others as well.

"The job of national sales manager, however, is a different story. In the other jobs Evans had—staff jobs—there was always time to consult, to consider, to get more data. In sales, however, all this participative stuff he uses takes too long. The national sales manager has to be able to make quick, intuitive decisions. What's more, like the captain of a ship, he has to inspire confidence in those below him. If the going gets rough, the only thing that keeps the sailors and junior officers from panicking is confidence in the skipper. I've been there and I know.

"Right now, with orders coming in strong, he can get away with all of his meetings and indecisiveness. The people in the field really like him and are trying to keep him out of trouble. In addition, I have been putting in 60 to 70 hours a week trying to do my job and also make sure he doesn't make any serious mistakes.

"I know he is feeling the pressure, too. Despite the fact that he has been his usual cheery self with others, when I call him in to question a decision he has made or is about to make, he gets very defensive. He was never that way with me before.

"I may have lost a little feel for what's going on in the field over the years, but I suspect I still know more about the customers and our sales people than Tom Evans will ever know. I've tried for the past seven months to get him to relax and let the old man help him, but it's no use. I'm convinced he's just not cut out for the job, and before we ruin him I want to transfer him somewhere else. He would probably make a fine personnel director someday. He's a very popular guy who seems genuinely interested in people and in helping them.

"I have talked with Ben Petersen about the move, and he has been stalling me. I understand his position. We have a lot of young comers like Evans in the company, and Ben has to worry about all of them. He told me that if anyone can bring Evans along I can, and he asked me to give it another try. I have, and things are getting worse.

"I hate to admit I made a mistake with Evans, but I plan on seeing Ben about this again tomorrow. We just can't keep putting if off. I'm sure he'll see it my way, and as soon as he approves the transfer, I'll have a heart-to-heart talk with Tom."

Evans's Side of the Story

"This has been a very hectic but rewarding period for me. I've never worked as hard in may life as I have during the last six months, but it's paying off. I'm learning more about sales each day, and more important, I'm building a first-rate sales team. My people are really enjoying the chance to share ideas and support each other.

"At first, particularly with our markets improving, it was hard to convince them to take time to meet with me and their subordinates. Gradually they have come to accept these sessions as an investment in team building. According to them, we've come up with more good ideas and ways to help each other than ever before.

"Fortunately, I also have experience in product management and sales service. Someday I hope to bring representatives from this department and market research into the meetings with regional and branch people, but that will take time. This kind of direct coordination and interaction doesn't fit with the thinking of some of the old-timers. I ran into objections when I tried this while I was working in the other departments.

"But I'm certain that in a year or so I'll be able to show, by results, that we should have more direct contact across department levels.

"My boss, George Briggs, will be one of the ones I will have to convince. He comes from the old school and is slow to give up what he knows used to work well.

"George likes me, though, and has given me a tremendous amount of help in the past. I was amazed when he told me he was giving me this job. Frankly, I didn't think I was ready yet, but he assured me I could handle it. I've gotten a big promotion every few years and I really like that—being challenged to learn new skills and getting more responsibility. I guess I have a real future here, although George won't be retiring for some years and I've gone as high as I can go until then.

"George is a very demanding person, but extremely fair, and he is always trying to help. I only hope I can justify the confidence he has shown in me. He stuck his neck out by giving me this chance, and I'm going to do all I can to succeed.

"Recently we have had a few run-ins. George Briggs works harder than anyone else around here, and perhaps the pressure of the last few years is getting to him. I wish he'd take a vacation this year and get away for a month or more and just relax. He hasn't taken more than a week off in the nine years I've been here, and for the last two years he hasn't taken any vacation.

"I can see the strain is taking its toll. Recently he has been on my back for all kinds of little things. He always was a worrier, but lately he has been testing me on numerous small issues. He keeps throwing out suggestions or second-guessing me on things that I've spent weeks working on with the field people.

"I try to assure him I'll be all right, and to please help me where I need it with the finance and production people who've had a tough time keeping up with our sales organization. It has been rough lately, but I'm sure it will work out. Sooner or later George will accept the fact that while I will never be able to run things the way he did, I can still get the job done for him."

Perkins's Opinions

"I feel that George Briggs is threatened by Evans's seeming success with the field sales people. I don't think he realizes it, but he is probably jealous of the speed with which Tom has taken charge. In all likelihood, he didn't expect Tom to be able to handle the field people as well as he has, as fast as he has.

"When George put Tom in the job, I have a feeling that he was looking forward to having him need much more help and advice from the old skipper. Tom does need help and advice, but he is getting most of what George would offer from his own subordinates and his peers. As a result, he has created a real team spirit below and around him, but he has upset George in the process.

"George not only has trouble seeing Tom depend so much on his subordinates but I feel that he resents Tom's unwillingness to let him show him how he used to run the sales force.

"I may be wrong about this, of course. I am sure that George honestly believes that Tom's style will get him in trouble sooner or later. George is no doddering old fool who has to relive his past success in lower-level jobs. In the past, I'm told, he has shown real insight and interest in the big-picture aspects of the company.

"The trouble is he knows he was an outstanding sales manager, but I am not sure he has the same confidence in his ability as vice president. I have seen this time and again, particularly in recent years. When a person begins to doubt his future, he sometimes drops back and begins to protect his past. With more competition from younger subordinates and the new methods that they often bring in, many of our experienced people find that doing their job the way they used to just isn't good enough anymore.

"Some reach out and seek new responsibilities to prove their worth. Others, however, return to the things they used to excel in and try to show that theirs is still the best way to do things. They don't even seem to realize that this puts them in direct competition with their subordinates.

"What do we do about this? I wish I knew! At lower levels, where you have more room to shift people around, you have more options. When the company is growing rapidly, the problem often takes care of itself.

"In this case, I am not sure what I will recommend if Ben Petersen asks my advice. Moving Tom to personnel at this time not only won't help me (I really don't have a spot for him), but it won't help Briggs or Evans either. Moving Evans now would be wasteful of the time and effort we've invested in his development. It may also reverse some important trends Tom has begun in team building within the sales force.

"If Briggs were seven or eight years older, we could wait it out. If the company were growing faster, we might be able to shift people. As things stand, however, I see only one approach as a possibility. And I'm not entirely sure it will work.

"I would recommend that we get busy refocusing Briggs's attention on the vice president's job and get him to see that there is where he has to put his time and efforts. Perhaps the best thing would be to send him to one of the longer programs for senior executives. Don't forget he is a very bright and experienced person who still has a great deal to offer the company if we can figure out how to help him."

What Would You Suggest?

Petersen has agreed to talk with Briggs about Evans tomorrow afternoon. As he thinks about the situation, he wonders what he can do that would be best for the company and everyone concerned. Should he go along with Briggs's recommendation that Evans be transferred to personnel? Or would it be preferable to do as Perkins has suggested and send Briggs to an executive program? As you consider the various perspectives, why do you think the impasse came to be and what do you think could be done to resolve it?

case 5

General Motors Assembly Division

The General Motors Assembly Division is a tough, no-nonsense outfit charged with the responsibility "of being able to meet foreign competition." GMAD "adopted 'get tough' tactics to cope with increased worker absenteeism and boost productivity." According to *Business Week,* the new division was set up in 1965 to tighten and revamp assembly operations. "The need for GMAD's belt-tightening role was underscored during the late 1960s when GM's profit margin dropped from 10 percent to 7 percent."

At Lordstown, efficiency became the watchword. At 60 cars an hour, the pace of work had not been exactly leisurely, but after GMAD came in the number of cars produced almost doubled. Making one car a minute had been no picnic, especially on a constantly moving line. Assembly work fits the worker to the pace of the machine. Each work station is no more than 6 to 8 feet long. For example, within a minute on the line, a worker in the trim department had to walk about 20 feet to a conveyor belt transporting parts to the line, pick up a front seat weighing 30 pounds, carry it back to his work station, place the seat on the chassis, and put in four bolts to fasten it down by first hand-starting the bolts and then using an air gun to tighten them according to standard. It was steady work when the line moved at 60 cars an hour. When it increased to more than 100 cars an hour, the number of operations on this job were not reduced and the pace became almost maddening. In 36 seconds the worker had to perform at least eight different operations, including walking, lifting, hauling, lifting the

carpet, bending to fasten the bolts by hand, fastening them by air gun, replacing the carpet, and putting a sticker on the hood. Sometimes the bolts fail to fit into the holes; the gun refuses to function at the required torque; the seats are defective or the threads are bare on the bolt. But the line does not stop. Under these circumstances the workers often find themselves "in the hole," which means that they have fallen behind the line.

"You really have to run like hell to catch up, if you're gonna do the whole job right," one operator named Jerry told me when I interviewed him in the summer of 1972. "They had the wrong-sized bolt on the job for a whole year. A lot of times we just miss a bolt to keep us with the line."

In all plants workers try to make the work a little easier for themselves. At Lordstown, as in other automobile plants, there are many methods for making the work tolerable. Despite the already accelerated pace, workers still attempt to use the traditional relief mechanism of "doubling up." This method consists of two workers deciding that they will learn each other's operation. One worker performs both jobs while the other worker is spelled. At Lordstown, a half-hour "on" and a half-hour "off" is fairly normal pattern. The worker who is on is obliged to do both jobs by superhuman effort. But workers would rather race to keep up with the line than work steadily—in anticipation of a half-hour off to read, lie down, go to the toilet, or roam the plant to talk to a buddy. Not all jobs lend themselves to this arrangement, especially those where a specific part like a front seat must be placed on

Source: *False Promises* by Stanley Aronowitz. Copyright © 1973 by Stanley Aronowitz. Used with permission of McGraw-Hill Book Company.

all models; here the work is time consuming, and full of hassles. But there are many operations where doubling up is feasible, particularly light jobs which have few different movements. Fastening seat belts and putting on windshield wipers are examples.

"The only chance to keep from goin' nuts," said one worker, "is to double up on the job. It's the only way to survive in the plant. . . ."

The company claims that doubling up reduces quality. The method engenders a tendency for workers to miss operations, especially when they fall behind, according to one general foreman. Some workers believe that the company blames workers for doubling up as an excuse to explain its own quality control failures. There is a widespread feeling among the line workers that the doubling-up "issue" has more to do with the company's program of harrassment than with the problem of quality control.

The tenure of the previous management at the Chevrolet division of GM was characterized by a plethora of shop floor agreements between foremen and line workers on work rules. These agreements were not written down, but were passed from worker to worker as part of the lore of the job. As in many workplaces, a new line supervisor meant that these deals had to be "renegotiated."

When GMAD took over at Lordstown, management imposed new, universally applicable rules which, in fact, were applied selectively. On Mondays, "when there are not many people on the line," the company tolerates lateness. On Tuesdays, when young workers come back from their long weekends, "they throw you out the door" for the rest of the shift for coming in fifteen minutes or a half-hour late. "When the company gets a bug up its ass to improve quality, they come down on you for every little mistake. But then things start goin' good on the cars, so they start to work on other areas. Then you are not allowed to lay down—not allowed to read on the job; no talkin' (you can't talk anyway the noise is so terrific); no doubling up."

Efficiency meant imposing on workers the absolute power of management to control production. GMAD instituted a policy of compulsory overtime at the time of the model changeover. The "normal" shift became ten hours a day and there were no

exceptions to the rule. Absenteeism and lateness became the objects of veritable holy crusades for the new management. Nurses refused to grant permission for workers to go home sick. The company began to consider a worker a voluntary quit if he stayed off for three days and failed to bring a doctor's note certifying his illness. Doctors were actually sent to workers' homes to check up on "phony" illnesses in an effort to curb absenteeism.

The average hourly rate for production line workers was $4.56 an hour in mid-1972. In addition, annual cost of living increases geared to the consumer price index had been incorporated into the contract. Gross base weekly earnings for ten hours a day were more than $195. With overtime, some workers had made more than $13,000 a year. Besides, GM workers have among the best pension, health insurance, and unemployment benefits programs in American industry. Certainly, there is no job in the Warren area whose terms compare with high wages and benefits enjoyed by the GM workers. Equally significant, GM is among the few places in the area still hiring a large number of employees. The steel mills, electrical plants, and retail trades offer lower wages to unskilled workers and less steady employment to low-seniority people. For some, General Motors is "big mother." Many workers echo the sentiment of Joe, a forty-five-year-old assembly line worker who said that GM offered better wages and working conditions than he had ever enjoyed in his life—"I don't know how anybody who works for a living can do better than GM." Compared to the steel mill where he did heavy dirty jobs, GM was "not near as hard."

Of course Joe has had differences with company policies. The job was "too confining." He didn't like to do the same thing every day. He objected to the company harrassment of the men and had actually voted for a strike to correct some of the injustices in the plant. But, like many others, Joe had "married the job" because he didn't know where else he could get a retirement plan which would give him substantial benefits after thirty years of service, full hospital benefits, and real job security.

GMAD likes workers like Joe too. They know Joe isn't going anywhere. They believe him when he says he is sick and, if he misses installing parts on a car he can "chalk it up." In such cases, he simply tells the foreman about the missing operation and the "repairmen will take care of it."

Yet high wages and substantial fringe benefits have not been sufficient to allay discontent among the young people working on the line. If other area employers paid wages competitive with GM wages, GM would have serious difficulty attracting a labor force. The wages are a tremendous initial attraction for workers and explain why many are reluctant to leave the shop. But even the substantial unemployment in the Warren and Youngstown areas has not succeeded in tempering the spirit of rebellion among young workers or preventing the persistence of turnover among them. The promise of high earnings has not reduced the absentee rate in the plant. One young worker, married with a child, earned a gross income of $10,900 in 1971, a year when overtime was offered regularly to employees. This was a gross pay at least $2,000 below his possible earnings. He had taken at least one day off a week and refused several offers of Saturday work.

GM acknowledges that absenteeism, particularly on Mondays and Fridays, constitutes its most distressing discipline problem. Workers report line shutdown "for as much as a half hour" on Mondays because there are simply not enough people to perform the operations. But many young people are prepared to sacrifice higher earnings for a respite from the hassles of assembly line work, even for one day.

At Lordstown and other plants where youth constitute either a majority or significant minority of the work force there is concrete evidence that the inducements to hard work have weakened. Older workers in the plant as well as a minority of the youth admit that they have never seen this kind of money in their lives. But the young people are seeking something more from their labor than high wages, pensions, and job security. At Lordstown, they are looking for "a chance to use my brain" and a job "where my high school education counts for something." Even though workers resent the demanding pace of the line, no line job takes more than a half-hour to learn. Most workers achieve sufficient speed in their operation to keep up with the line in about a half a shift. The minute rationalization of assembly line operations to a few simple movements has been perfected by GMAD. One

operator whose job was to put two clips on a hose all day long said, "I never think about my job. In fact, I try to do everything I can to forget it. If I concentrated on thinking about it, I'd go crazy. The trouble is I have to look at what I'm doing or else I'd mess up every time." This worker spent some of his time figuring out ways to get off the line, especially ways to take days off. "I always try to get doctor's slips to take three days if I can." Another worker reported provoking a foreman to give him a disciplinary layoff (DLO) just to avoid the monotony of his tasks.

The drama of Lordstown is the conflict between the old goals of decent income and job security, which have lost their force but are by no means dead, and the new needs voiced by young people for more than mindless labor. The company and the union represent the promise that the old needs can be met on a scale never before imagined for many of the people on the line. The youth are saying that these benefits are not enough.

The picture is complicated by the fact that not all young people share the same attitudes. Even though the overwhelming majority of workers in the shop are between twenty and thirty years old, they are not all cut from the same cloth. The most disaffected group in the plant are the youth who were raised in the Warren-Youngstown area. Their fathers and mothers were industrial workers, or at least had been part of an urban environment for most of their lives. Since the area has had a long industrial tradition (it lies in the heart of the Ohio valley), high wages and traditional union protections and benefits are part of the taken-for-granted world of a generation brought up in the shadows of the steel mills and rubber factories. These workers share the same upbringing, went to the same schools, frequented the same neighborhood social centers, and speak the same symbolic languages. When they came to General Motors, they brought with them a set of unspoken expectations about their work and their future. Many were high school graduates; a smaller, but significant number were attending college. Although it cannot be denied that the "good money" paid by GM was an important inducement for these young people to choose to work there, few of them considered steady work and good wages sufficient to satisfy a life's ambition.

case 6

St. Luke's Hospital

Two days after she assumed her duties as director of nurses and of the nursing school of St. Luke's Hospital, Jenny Stewart started on the first of her "get acquainted" rounds. As she turned the knob of the door to the operating room, she heard her name called. The supervisor of the Pediatrics Department approached.

"Won't you let me show you around my department?" Miss Robbins asked. "An operation is in progress, and I think they would prefer that you wouldn't go into the operating room now."

"I know there's an operation going on," the director answered. "That's why I'm going in. You, see, I want to observe the methods being used."

Miss Robbins looked uncomfortable to Miss Stewart. "I know that's a very natural desire on your part, but I do hope you will put it off until you are better acquainted. *Please* come with me today and see my department."

Miss Stewart thought the nurse's request rather strange; nevertheless, she looked over the Pediatrics Department and did not return to the operating room. The same afternoon Lois Richards, supervisor of nurses in general surgery, appeared in the doorway of the director's office.

"I understand that you intended to call on us in the operating room this morning," she said.

Miss Stewart looked up from her desk and saw a trim, wide-awake looking woman. "Ah, then you're Miss Richards," Miss Stewart said. "Won't you come in. As a matter of fact, I should like to have dropped in on you this morning but I was side-tracked; so I had to postpone my first visit."

Miss Richards remained in the doorway. "Well, I thought I'd better tell you that you will not need to call on us. When any discussion comes up between the operating room and the nursing office, I come here to settle it."

Miss Stewart was surprised by the flatness of Miss Richards' remark, but she said, "I'm glad to hear that. This is certainly the place for any discussions between department heads to take place. But I shall want to visit you to acquaint myself with the technique used in surgery and with the students in your department."

"Well, I suppose you can come if you want to, but our surgeons won't like it very much. You see, we feel that our technique isn't open to question; so we hardly need any advice. I see that the students do their work well. You needn't have any worries about work in my department."

Miss Stewart smiled. "I can assure you that I'm not worried about the work or the technique used in your department. I just want to get acquainted."

"All right, come ahead, but remember that I told you it would be better if you didn't," Miss Richards said over her shoulder as she disappeared from the doorway.

Miss Stewart felt bewildered. She could not recall anything in her long experience as a nursing instructor and as a director of nursing schools which would have prepared her for what she believed was an antagonistic attitude on the part of the operating room supervisor.

Source: *The Personnel Management Process: Cases in Human Resources Administration* by Wendell French, John E. Dittrich and Robert A. Zawacki. Copyright © 1978 by Houghton Mifflin Company. Reprinted by permission.

457

Jenny Stewart's career included graduation from a large midwestern college, graduation from a school of nursing, ten years as teacher in schools of nursing, and seven years as director of schools of nursing. In addition she had spent one summer at the University of Wisconsin, taking courses in anatomy and bacteriology. Before accepting her first position as director of a nursing school, she had taken a course in nursing school administration at the University of Chicago.

As director of nurses and the nursing school at St. Luke's, Miss Stewart was directly responsible to the board of directors, although the superintendent of the hospital was nominally her superior. She planned to carry her serious problems to the superintendent, however, because she believed that her work would be easier and more pleasant. The superintendent of the hospital was Carleton B. Fischer, ex-city editor of the local *Centreville Press.* He had no training in hospital administration, but Miss Stewart considered him cooperative and intelligent. He was 50 years of age, a college graduate, and had been appointed to his position the previous July.

As director of nurses, Miss Stewart was responsible for the proper care and treatment of all patients in the 250-bed hospital.

Her responsibilities as nursing school director included the education of student nurses, the selection and employment of graduate assistants, and the overseeing of nurse instructors. A Nursing School Committee helped her formulate educational policies and advised her on disciplinary matters concerning student nurses.

The director of nurses, Miss Stewart had learned, was expected to take the advice of the Nursing School Committee on vitally important policies. When the committee was of the opinion that any drastic action needed to be taken in the nursing school, it notified the board of directors of its decision. Miss Stewart was an ex officio member of both the Nursing School Committee and the board of directors.

As she sat in her office contemplating what the operating room supervisor had said, Miss Stewart wondered if she had said anything to make Miss Richards angry. She concluded that she had not.

Three days later Miss Stewart visited the operating room while surgery was being performed. She observed carefully the work of the surgeons and was satisfied that what Miss Richards had said about their technique was correct. The surgeons appeared to Miss Stewart not to notice that she was present. She remembered that in former positions the doctors had seemed pleased when she watched them work.

About two weeks later two student nurses from the operating room, Clarice Maltz and June Bader, appeared in Miss Stewart's office. Miss Bader was in tears. Between sobs she blurted out, "Miss Richards kicked me. I used a forceps to take a soiled sponge off the table, but before I reached the sponge rack to hang it up, she kicked me so hard I dropped it. Then she struck my arm with an instrument and screamed in my ear. She said I was a little fool and if I knew anything I would have had the sponge on the rack. When I bent over to pick it up, she kicked me so hard I fell over. Oh, I hurt all over!"

"That's right, Miss Stewart," said Miss Maltz. "I was there when she did it. She kicked her and she hit her."

Miss Stewart, believing that both women were immature and emotionally upset, thought that imagination and exaggeration must have played a great part in their account of the incident. She thought Miss Maltz's, "That's right, Miss Stewart," rather childish.

She asked both women to sit down. They talked over the importance of operating room work. She told them that tensions in the operating room developed easily and that the life-and-death responsibility of persons in the room often led them to be irritable at times.

"We understand that," Miss Bader said. "Dr. Tompkins can be very snappy during surgery, but I think he forgets it afterwards."

"We don't like to have our clothing torn by the supervisor, though," Miss Maltz added.

After a 15-minute talk the student nurses left the nursing director's office. Miss Stewart decided to check on the condition of the operating room gowns to ascertain if they would tear easily. Her investigation showed that enough gowns were in good condition. A few which might have torn easily Miss Stewart ordered put to another use.

Exhibit 1. St. Luke's Hospital organization chart.

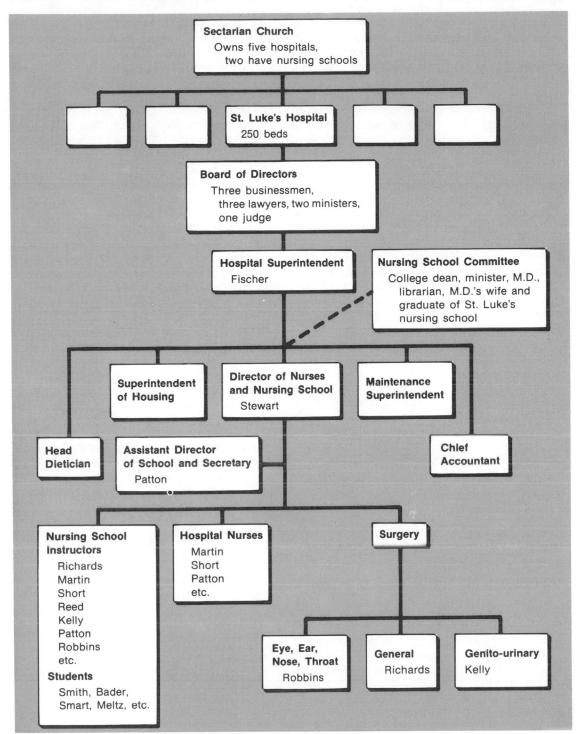

459

Miss Martin, a graduate assistant teacher, accosted Miss Stewart in the hall some ten days later. "I hate to confront you with a problem so soon," she said. "You undoubtedly know that for the past four years our directors of nursing have stayed only about one year each. But what you probably don't know is that each one has tried to do something about the way Miss Richards mistreats student nurses. What happens is that the director leaves in a few months and Miss Richards stays on. I think the situation is getting worse. One of the students—Bernice Smith—came to my room last night and showed me bruises on her legs. Miss Richards had kicked her while they were in the operating room. Bernice said that she was going to tell her parents but the other girls talked her out of it. They're afraid to let any outsiders know about the situation for fear that Miss Richards will find out about it and have her "gentleman friend," Dr. Schwartz, make life miserable for them for the rest of their training period. Bernice told me about Virginia Smeck who has scratches from her shoulders to her wrists—the result of Miss Richards' fingernails when something went wrong in the operating room. Bernice asked me not to take her word for it but to see for myself, but I told her that the best thing for me to do, since I knew about all this already, was to tell you about it. You are, after all, the only one whose position gives you the right to do anything about it."

"Yes, you're quite right," Miss Stewart answered.

"I heard that Clarice Maltz and June Bader tried to tell you but that you didn't quite believe them. I realize that you haven't been here long enough to know everything that's going on, so I thought I'd tell you about this myself," said Miss Martin.

"Miss Bader and Miss Maltz did come to see me," Miss Stewart admitted. "But, you see, they were so emotional at the time. . . . Besides, the story they told me just didn't fit into our way of life today—not the American way of life, anyway. I thought that the girls might not understand the intensity of the operating room situation. . . . I still think their story is most unusual to say the least. How about you? Are you convinced that all you've told me is true?"

"You don't live in the nurses' home, Miss Stewart; so you don't know how thin the walls are. For years I've heard that same sort of thing discussed. Since Miss Richards hasn't lived in the nurses' home for years, the students discuss her rather freely. I don't know whether or not they realize that anyone else can hear them. You know, your predecessors knew about this situation, but they found themselves in pretty hot water when they inquired into it. I want to tell you how badly I feel about it, though, because I know if you attempt to do anything about it, you will have to leave, too. And you've been here such a short time."

"You can stop worrying about my leaving," said Miss Stewart. "I'm asking you now to tell me anything that you know to be true and are willing to declare to the board of directors."

Miss Martin said, "Oh, I don't want to get mixed up in it at all. But for your own information I'll tell you this: the doctors are back of Miss Richards one hundred percent. They will probably like you in direct proportion to the completeness with which you let Miss Richards alone." She hurried away.

The next day Miss Stewart made it a point to look up Virginia Smeck. The director noticed the scratches. "Why, Miss Smeck, what happened to your arm?" she asked.

"Oh nothing—just a little accident. Excuse me. I've got to hurry to the laundry. Miss Richards sent me for some linen."

Miss Stewart asked Miss Richards to come to her office later that day. The operating room supervisor arrived two hours after the director's request. Miss Richards sat down near Miss Stewart's desk.

"I'm wondering, Miss Richards, if it is difficult here to get students to carry out procedures as taught or if, on the whole, they are quite sincere in their efforts," she began.

"The modern girl is just plain dumb, very careless, and often insubordinate. But don't worry. I don't let them get the best of me."

Said Miss Stewart, "Those are rather harsh words, Miss Richards. What do you mean—insubordinate?"

"Oh you know very well what it means," Miss Richards replied.

"If there's a question of insubordination, don't you think I should know about it?" asked Miss Stewart.

"I haven't come up against anything yet that I couldn't handle. The students all act the same, but I take care of them."

"But, Miss Richards, if I am to cooperate with you in the handling of students, it seems to me I ought to know a little more about their foibles. What do you mean they all act the same way?"

"Is this kind of talk all you called me down here for?" Miss Richards asked abruptly.

"Something like that," Miss Stewart answered. "You said that you don't let the students get the best of you. Just what do you mean?"

"You take care of the nursing office business and I'll take care of operating room business. See!" Miss Richards replied.

"Are you implying that I should not be interested in what goes on in the operating room?"

"I'm telling you frankly to keep out of what goes on there. Otherwise you'll be sorry. Now I'm busy, and I think I'll go." Miss Richards rose to leave.

Miss Stewart quickly walked to the door and held her hand on the knob. "It's not time for you to go just yet," she said. "I insist upon answers to my questions. As two grown women we should be able to lay our cards on the table and keep levelheaded while we do it."

"Well, just what do you want?" asked the operating room supervisor.

Miss Stewart said, "I'll come directly to the point then. Some very unpleasant stories concerning your treatment of students have been told to me. They are very hard to believe, yet at the present time there is no one but you who can prove whether or not they are true. Did you ever shake, scratch, or kick student nurses in the operating room?"

"Certainly not. I'm warning you to keep out of my business. If you don't, you'll be sorry I can promise you."

Miss Stewart continued, "If I ever attended to my own business, I'm doing it now. I still hope that you can prove that you do not do that sort of thing."

Miss Richards pushed the director aside and left the office.

Other matters of importance came to the attention of Miss Stewart in the next few days, and she did not have time to think about the affair with Miss Richards.

A week later the nursing director asked Miss Richards to step into a room where they could be alone to talk for a few minutes.

Miss Richards answered, "Our schedule has been heavy today, and our cleaning will take all afternoon. I cannot talk to you today."

Although Miss Stewart tried to find opportunity for another interview, she was never able to find the operating supervisor alone. One of her two graduate assistants was invariably nearby. The nursing director asked her secretary, Miss Patton, about the assistants. Miss Patton, who was also assistant director of the nursing school, told Miss Stewart that Miss Short, the first assistant, was the best graduate assistant on the staff in the school of nursing. Miss Reed, the other assistant, Miss Stewart learned, was also an efficient nurse. Both nurses got along well with Miss Richards.

When the nursing director finally found Miss Richards alone, she asked the supervisor to come into her office. Miss Richards replied: "I do not intend to have time to talk to you."

Two days after Miss Richards, the supervisor of nurses in general surgery, had told Miss Stewart that she did not intend to find time to talk with her, Helen Sommers, an alumna of St. Luke's, visited the nursing director at her apartment. In the course of their evening's conversation together, Miss Sommers confirmed what Miss Stewart had learned about Miss Richards.

"I still have some scratch marks on my arm, thanks to Miss Richards," she told Miss Stewart.

The nursing director went to see the superintendent of the hospital the following day. She told him of her concern about the mistreatment of student nurses and waited for his reply.

"I don't doubt that what you say is true, Miss Stewart," he said. "As a matter of fact, I've heard something about this myself from two or three members of the community. I don't mind telling you that the situation has me worried, but frankly I don't know what to do about it. What would you suggest?"

"Well, first of all, I feel directly responsible for all the nurses in the entire Nursing Department. Miss Richards' treatment of student nurses reflects as much on me as it does on the school of nursing. I was thinking that it might be best to take the matter to the Nursing School Committee first. Then . . . well, then perhaps I'll have a better idea of what to do about it."

"I think that would be the thing to do," Mr. Fischer said. "Please keep me posted on what the outcome is. I'm deeply concerned."

Miss Stewart promised to do so and left. That evening she wrote a list of grievances against Miss Richards. In it she included statements made by nursing students, Maltz, Bader, Smith (to Miss Martin), Miss Martin, Miss Sommers, and Superintendent Fischer. Three days later she took the statements, signed by herself, to the bimonthly meeting of the Nursing School Committee which was composed of a retired doctor, a minister, a college dean, a librarian, a graduate of St. Luke's nursing school, and a doctor's wife who was also a registered nurse.

At the meeting Miss Stewart laid before the committee the statements which she had prepared. Although some members of the committee expressed surprise at the disclosure of maltreatment of nursing students by Miss Richards, some committee members, it seemed to Miss Stewart, seemed to know about the state of affairs.

The college dean asked why the situation had not been reported before.

Said Miss Stewart, "I think my short tenure of office and the fact that the last four directors of nursing have occupied the position for a relatively short period of time make the answer to that question rather obvious."

"Something certainly ought to be done if this is true," said the minister, "and from the evidence Miss Stewart has cited, it certainly appears to be true. I think Miss Richards should be made to resign."

The doctor said, "Let's not be hasty in our judgment, ladies and gentlemen. Our surgeons are very proud of their record of no infections. It seems to me that they would be extremely averse to anything which might lead to Miss Richards' resignation and the possibility of incompetent nursing in general surgery."

"Are our nurses of no consequence as young women, sir?" the minister asked.

"Certainly no one wants to see them mistreated," the doctor rejoined, "but it seems to me that we must not lose sight of the fact that Miss Richards has a reputation as an efficient nurse in surgery."

"Or the fact that nurses are not easily hired these days," rejoined the college dean. "It seems to me . . ."

The nursing school graduate interrupted him. "I wonder if the fact that one of our surgeons, Dr. Schwartz, dates Miss Richards could explain her being allowed to mistreat students without reprimand. I know of certain instances in which nursing students have been mistreated, and I think—in reply to Dean Harmon's question before—that each student has been somewhat hesitant about reporting Miss Richards for fear that certain surgeons might make their lives miserable during the rest of the training."

"But that's foolish," said the doctor.

"Foolish, but possible. I've worked in operating rooms and I've seen that sort of thing; so I know it can happen," she answered.

The doctor's wife finally moved that the Nursing School Committee recommend to the board of directors that the director of nurses be given complete support in any measure to stop physical violence in the operating room. The motion was carried unanimously.

Miss Stewart, as an ex officio member of the board of directors, decided to take the recommendation to the next board meeting, the following Monday, but she first talked to Mr. Fischer. He advised her to consult the board. In the meantime Miss Stewart again attempted to talk to Miss Richards. The operating room supervisor told her that she was far too busy to be bothered with trivialities. Miss Stewart waited another day before she tried to interview Miss Richards again. They met in the hall outside the operating room. Miss Stewart said, "I'd like you to drop into my office this afternoon."

Miss Richards' reply was: "Stop bothering me."

On Monday evening Miss Stewart arrived at the directors' conference room early. She watched the various directors as they entered and made mental notes of what she remembered about them from their previous meetings. She nodded to the Reverend William Blakesly when he entered. (He had been chiefly responsible for informing the board of Miss Stewart's qualifications for the position of supervisor.) He had introduced her to Dr. Stephen R. Rauch, an elderly, retired minister, and James B. Davison, a lawyer, two more members of the board. Miss Stewart knew well the chairman of the board, Judge Selwyn C. Roberts of the State Supreme Court, and Thomas L. Alberts, a businessman, whom she had met because of his daily visits to the hospital to see his daughter who was recovering from an operation. Miss Stewart knew the other members were either lawyers or businessmen who were prominent in the community.

After the usual order of business, Miss Stewart asked for and was granted the floor.

"Gentlemen," she began, "I'm sorry that so soon after our first meeting together I must place a problem before you; nevertheless, a situation has come up with which I am unable to cope, so I've come for some advice. First, I would like to read to you a resolution of recommendation from the Nursing School Committee." She read from a paper: "The Nursing School Committee of St. Luke's Hospital hereby recommends to the board of directors that Miss Jenny Stewart, director of nurses of the hospital, be given complete, unwavering support in any measure to prevent physical violence under the guise of teaching in the operating room."

Miss Stewart awaited comments; when none were forthcoming, she continued:

"I had intended to seek the board's permission to ask Miss Lois Richards, supervisor of nurses in general surgery, to resign her position, but just before I came to this meeting I received her resignation sent through the mail—special delivery. So now you see that Miss Richards has perhaps solved the problem which I am posing for you. Of course, there is one possibility of difficulty: Miss Richards states that her two assistants will leave with her, but I do not accept her statement as final for them."

The members of the board expressed surprise.

"What's this all about?" asked one of the businessmen. "What prompted this resignation?"

In answer Miss Stewart read the report which she had presented to the Nursing School Committee.

"And now you'd like permission to accept Miss Richards' resignation?" Davison, the lawyer, asked.

"That's correct," Miss Stewart answered. "There is no other course open in view of the evidence, is there?" she asked in surprise.

Davison looked at Judge Roberts, who recognized Alberts.

"Now, Miss Stewart, don't you think that you're being a little hasty? I believe we can easily have one of the doctors explain to Miss Richards that she must not continue to mistreat student nurses," said Alberts.

"I'd like to ask you a question, Mr. Alberts," Miss Stewart said. "Do you think that she will listen to a doctor and suddenly mend the ways in which she has been conducting herself for so long? And suppose she decided not to change her attitude, what then?"

The judge answered for Alberts. "It seems to me that we would then know that we had the wrong doctor speak to her. We could easily arrange to have the right man speak to her."

"And in the meantime the students would continue to be kicked and scratched?"

"That is your responsibility," one of the businessmen interjected.

"No, it isn't. For my part I won't be responsible for what goes on in the operating room—I can't be—if Miss Richards is not responsible to me, and right now she's not."

"But, you can't avoid your responsibility to the entire hospital. After all, you haven't yet found a way to influence Miss Richards," said elderly Dr. Rauch. "You wouldn't want to remember that you failed in your job because you were unable to make Miss Richards responsible to you."

"Believe me, Dr. Rauch, I would much rather that Miss Richards and I could have settled this. I had not given up really trying until last Friday. I attempted to see Miss Richards twice to talk the matter out—even after my meeting with the Nursing School Committee, but she rebuffed me on both occasions. As a matter of fact, since I began to show interest in the matter of physical violence in the operating room, it seems to have increased. I have no reason to believe that a truce will be called while we wait for doctors to find time to talk this matter over with her. I want to accept her resignation. Of course, I realize that I must have the sanction of this board before I can."

"Have you talked to Mr. Fischer about this?" Davison asked.

"Yes, I have, and he recommended that I bring the problem before the board."

The judge said, "Miss Stewart, you know that Dr.

Tompkins, our leading surgeon, is out of town for a few days. Would you not rather we just hold Miss Richards' resignation until you have a chance to talk this situation over with him?"

"No, I wouldn't. Dr. Tompkins does not share any of the responsibility over student nurses with me," Miss Stewart answered.

"But, Miss Stewart, you must remember that Miss Richards has been with us for four years. During that time we have never had any complaints about her techniques in the operating room," one of the lawyers said.

"And after all, the primary purpose of a school of nursing is to teach students to do accurate work," Alberts added. "The results have been excellent for four years; so Miss Richards must have carried out the responsibility of teaching the students an accurate technique. I would hate to think what might have happened to my daughter while she was in the operating room if the nurses, as well as the surgeons, were not doing competent work. Miss Richards must be teaching them something of a very definite value in the operating room."

"I have to agree with Mr. Alberts," said the Reverend Mr. Blakesly. "Miss Stewart, you certainly realize that the lives of patients who go into the operating room must be safeguarded at all costs."

"And I agree with you that every patient must be safeguarded at all costs," said Miss Stewart. "But it seems to be that the real question is: Is physical violence to nursing students a necessary cost?"

A brief silence ensued, then the judge spoke:

"You realize, Miss Stewart, that you are not only asking the board to decide whether the hospital can get along without a trusted employee or not but that—well, you see—you are so new in your position. . . . It is hard for the board to decide by such an action as you now ask us to take—that you have already proved yourself, er—equal to the situation which confronts us. I say that with no sense of recrimination. As far as I know, the board is completely satisfied with your work . . . and your interest in the hospital is undoubtedly founded upon a sincere desire to do your job well."

Davison said: "No one has mentioned yet the scarcity of nurses today. It might be some time before we can get a capable successor for Miss Richards. In the meantime, Miss Stewart, can we expect that the lives of patients will be safeguarded in the operating room? There is such a shortage of nurses that it might be dangerous to lose Miss Richards at this time."

"I'd like to remind the board that there are two capable nurses who are Miss Richards' assistants in the operating room: Miss Short and Miss Reed. Although both of them are only graduate assistants, I believe that at least one of them should be capable of taking over the responsibilities of operating room supervisor in general surgery. From what I've seen of Miss Short and from what I've heard of her previous record, it seems to me that we would not be inviting trouble if the board would appoint her to the position of supervisor."

"But you said yourself that Miss Richards promised that the two assistants would leave with her," said one of the lawyers.

"And I added that I didn't accept her statement as final for them. . . ."

"But both those women are only graduate assistants," said Alberts.

"From the tenor of the conversation which I've been hearing around the table," the judge said, "I would surmise that the board is not yet ready to approve the resignation of Miss Richards. . . ."

"I move that we lay on the table this matter of accepting Miss Richards' resignation," said Alberts.

Davison seconded the motion, and it was carried unanimously.

The judge said, "Suppose, Miss Stewart, that you attempt to interview Miss Richards again between now and the next time the board meets. I'd like you to come into the next meeting and report any progress that you've been able to make toward securing her cooperation in this matter. I think I am expressing the feelings of the entire board when I say that we are assured of your deep-rooted interest in the case, and I also want to assure you that the board is completely in sympathy with your attitude toward the—the conduct—in the operating room. You can count on the board to cooperate with you in any further decisions that are made."

The meeting was adjourned, and Miss Stewart left. She walked slowly back to her office, repeating to herself: "And now what can I do?"

appendix B

Exercises

exercise 1

Determinants of Job Attitudes and Motivation

Purpose

To consider which factors motivate U.S. workers to perform on the job, and to compare the opinions of union leaders and executives with respect to the relative importance of such motivating factors.

Instructions

1. On the sheet below, rank the ten factors that relate to job attitudes and motivation in terms of how important each factor would be: 1) to union leaders; and 2) to business executives.

2. Next, get into a group of from four to six students, compare your individual rankings, and attempt to reach a group consensus as to the two rankings.

3. When you have finished, you instructor will distribute the results of a national survey of union leaders and business executives so you can compare your results against those of the national survey.

"In your organization at this time, how useful would each of the following be in improving employee attitudes and motivation?"

Rank Order (1 = most important)	Union Leaders			Business Executives		
	My Ranking	Group Ranking	National Survey	My Ranking	Group Ranking	National Survey
Better communication from management	_____	_____	_____	_____	_____	_____
Giving employees greater job security	_____	_____	_____	_____	_____	_____
Better treatment by supervisors	_____	_____	_____	_____	_____	_____
Sharing of profits or productivity gains	_____	_____	_____	_____	_____	_____
Higher pay	_____	_____	_____	_____	_____	_____
Improved work conditions	_____	_____	_____	_____	_____	_____
More feedback to employees	_____	_____	_____	_____	_____	_____
More opportunities for advancement	_____	_____	_____	_____	_____	_____
Better training programs	_____	_____	_____	_____	_____	_____
Building loyalty to the organization	_____	_____	_____	_____	_____	_____

exercise 2

Attendance and Performance: An Interview Exercise

Purpose

To study attendance behavior and work motivation firsthand by interviewing employees in various work organizations.

Instructions

Each student either individually or in pairs should contact and interview up to twenty employees who hold various kinds of jobs in different types of organizations. It would be helpful if this sample includes both males and females, minorities, managers and workers, and public and private employees. For each employee, note his or her occupation and place of work and ask the following three questions:

1. What determines whether or not you will come to work on a particular day?

2. On the job, what determines how much effort you will put forth on a given day?

3. Think back to a time in the past few months when you felt really motivated to perform on the job. What caused this high motivation to occur?

Note the answers during each interview and summarize the results for presentation in class. When summarizing, pay attention not only to differences in answers but also to possible differences across sex, race, occupation, and type of organization.

exercise 3

Managing Organizational Careers: Some Problems

Purpose

To practice your skills in making organizational decisions and planning programs to facilitate employees' career development.

Introduction

Many of the conditions necessary for better career development seem disarmingly straightforward —e.g., provide more initial job challenge, more realistic job previews, more opportunities for women and minorities. However, when put into practice, some of the unintentioned consequences and system effects (such as uncooperative supervisors or co-workers) come into play, indicating that we are dealing with organization development as well as career development. In the following problems you will be given a chance to try your hand at finding organizational solutions to some thorny career issues.

Procedure

Step 1. Formation. (5 minutes)   The class is first divided into groups of four to six people. Each group is assigned one of the problems at the end of the exercise.

Step 2. Preparation. (20 minutes)   Each group will meet separately to develop a solution to its problem and to prepare a five minute presentation to the rest of the class. In this presentation, the group will identify the problem and develop a persuasive case for the group's solution, while the rest of the class acts as a "board of directors."

Step 3. Presentations. (5 minutes per group) Each group will have five minutes to present their solutions.

Step 4. Discussion. (varying time)   During the free discussion, the various solutions might be compared. What are the costs and benefits of each? What resistance would each encounter? How could this resistance be reduced?

CAREER PROBLEMS

The "Dead-End" Employee

Jim Duncan is a 52-year-old department manager in your large manufacturing organization. He has been in this job for eight years. His performance has been very good, but lately has dropped off. He has had more sick days this year than ever before in his career.

Jim is not seen by top management or by personnel experts as having the ability to progress to a higher management position. He seems ideally placed in his present job.

You are Jim's boss, the plant manager. What action would you take to improve his performance and morale?

Source: From *Careers in Organizations* by D. T. Hall. Copyright © 1976 by Goodyear Publishing Company, Inc. Reprinted by permission.

The ''Deadwood'' Employee

Ralph Hamner is seen by most employees as ''deadwood.'' He was hired when the organization was much smaller, when you only had a few engineers, who had to be generalists. Now you have an engineering department of fifty people, most with advanced degrees and specialized backgrounds to deal with the increased complexity of your products—calculators and photographic equipment.

Ralph is now a senior engineer and just does not have the new knowledge necessary for most of your products. It has been hard to find projects on which he can use his present knowledge. At the same time, he is blocking the advancement of several promising junior engineers. Ralph is a well-liked guy, but he seems a bit defensive about his technical competence.

You are the personnel manager. What action would you recommend regarding Ralph Hamner?

Loss of Talented Young Employees

Your organization has traditionally been very attractive to college graduates as a place to work. The turnover among new employees has been about average for your industry. However, a recent study has just revealed a critical piece of information: the turnover is now occurring among your highest performing new employees. The people you'd like to lose are staying, and those you want to keep are leaving.

Exit interviews indicate that young people are frustrated by low challenge and low advancement opportunities. You have a lot of people in their fifties in middle management who are blocking promotions now and who are threatened by sharp young employees. But you won't have any good middle managers in ten years (when the present managers retire) if all your best young people leave now. Business has been rather slow lately, and no new positions through growth seem likely for several years.

What should be done to retain more of your promising young employees?

exercise 4
Lay-off Exercise

Purpose

To examine how to weigh a set of facts and make a difficult personnel decision about laying off valued employees during a time of financial hardship. To examine your own values and criteria used in the decision-making process.

The Problem

Walker Space (WSI) is a medium-sized firm, located in Connecticut. The firm essentially has been a subcontractor on many large space contracts which have been acquired by firms such as North American Rockwell and others.

With the cutback in many of the National Aeronautics and Space Administration programs, Walker has an excess of employees. Stuart Tartaro, the head of one of the sections, has been told by his superior that he must reduce his section of engineers from nine to six. He is looking at the following summaries of their vitaes and pondering how he will make this decision.

1. Roger Allison, age 26, married, two children. Allison has been with WSI for a year and a half. He is a very good engineer, with a degree from Rensselaer Polytech. He's held two prior jobs and lost both of them because of cutbacks in the space program. He moved to Connecticut from California to take this job. Allison is well liked by his co-workers.

2. LeRoy Jones, age 24, single. Jones is black and the company looked hard to get Jones because of affirmative action pressure. He is not very popular with his co-workers. Since he has been employed less than a year, not too much is known about his work. On his one evaluation (which was average) Jones accused his supervisor of bias against blacks. He is a graduate of Detroit Institute of Technology.

3. William Foster, age 53, married, three children. Foster is a graduate of "the school of hard knocks." After getting out of World War II, he started to go to school. But his family expenses were too much, so he dropped out. Foster has worked at the company for 20 years. His ratings were excellent for 15 years. The last five years they have been average. Foster feels his supervisor grades him down because he doesn't "have sheepskins covering his office walls."

4. Donald Boyer, age 32, married, no children. Boyer is well liked by his co-workers. He has been at WSI five years, and he has a B.S. and M.S. in engineering from Purdue University. Boyer's ratings have been mixed. Some supervisors rated him high, some average. Boyer's wife is an M.D.

5. Mel Shuster, age 29, single. Shuster is a real worker, but a loner. He has a B.S. in engineering from University of California. He is working on his M.S. at night; always trying to improve his technical skills. His performance ratings were above average for the three years he has been employed at WSI.

6. Sherman Soltis, age 37, divorced, two children. He has a B.S. in engineering from Ohio State University. Soltis is very active in community

Source: William F. Glueck, *Cases and Exercises in Personnel* (Dallas, Texas: Business Publications, 1978) pp. 24–26. © 1978 by Business Publications, Inc.

affairs: Scouts, Little League, United Appeal. He is a friend of the vice president through church work. His ratings have been average, although some recent ones indicate that he is out of date. He is well liked and has been employed at WSI for 14 years.

7. Warren Fortuna, age 44, married, five children. He has a B.S. in engineering from Georgia Tech. Fortuna headed this section at one time. He worked so hard that he had a heart attack. Under doctor's orders, he resigned from the supervisory position. Since then he has done good work, though because of his health, he is a bit slower than the others. Now and then, he must spend extra time on a project because he did get out of date during the eight years he headed the section. His performance evaluations for the last two years have been above average. He has been employed at WSI for 14 years.

8. Robert Treharne, age 47, single. He began an engineering degree at M.I.T. but had to drop out for financial reasons. He tries hard to stay current by regular reading of engineering journals and taking all the short courses the company and nearby colleges offer. His performance evaluations have varied, but they tend to be average to slightly above average. He is a loner and Tartaro thinks this has negatively affected his performance evaluations. He has been employed at WSI 16 years.

9. Sandra Rosen, age 22, single. She has a B.S. in engineering technology from Rochester Institute of Technology. Rosen has been employed less than a year. She is enthusiastic, a very good worker and is well liked by her co-workers. She is well regarded by Tartaro.

Tartaro doesn't quite know what to do. He sees the good points of each of his section members. Most have been good employees. They all can pretty much do each other's work. No one has special training.

He is fearful that the section will hear about this and morale will drop. Work would fall off. He doesn't even want to talk to his wife about it, in case she'd let something slip. Tartaro has come to you, Edmund Graves, personnel manager at WSI, for some guidelines on this decision—legal, moral, and best personnel practice.

Assignment You are Edmund Graves. Write a report with your recommendations for termination and a careful analysis of the criteria for the decision. You should also carefully explain to Tartaro how you would go about the terminations and reasonable termination pay. You should also advise him about the pension implications of this decision. Generally 15 years' service entitles you at least to partial pension.

exercise 5

Least Preferred Coworker (LPC) Scale

Purpose

This instrument was designed by Fred Fiedler to measure your LPC score as described in the contingency theory of leadership (Chapter 12).

Instructions

Think of the person with whom you work *least well*. He or she may be someone you work with now, or may be someone you knew in the past. He or she does not have to be the person you like least well, but should be the person with whom you *have* or *have had* the *most difficulty* in *getting a job done.* Describe this person as he or she appears to you by circling the number between each pair of adjectives that you believe best describes that person. Do this for each pair of adjectives that you believe best describes that person. Do this for each pair of adjectives. Then transfer the numbers to the spaces provided at the right. Add up the numbers in this column and write the value in the box marked "LPC Score." Your instructor will then explain the meaning of your score.

	LPC Scale (Circle one number for each line)		Transfer the numbers to these spaces
Pleasant	: 8 : 7 : 6 : 5 : 4 : 3 : 2 : 1 :	Unpleasant	_____
Friendly	: 8 : 7 : 6 : 5 : 4 : 3 : 2 : 1 :	Unfriendly	_____
Rejecting	: 1 : 2 : 3 : 4 : 5 : 6 : 7 : 8 :	Accepting	_____
Helpful	: 8 : 7 : 6 : 5 : 4 : 3 : 2 : 1 :	Frustrating	_____
Unenthusiastic	: 1 : 2 : 3 : 4 : 5 : 6 : 7 : 8 :	Enthusiastic	_____
Tense	: 1 : 2 : 3 : 4 : 5 : 6 : 7 : 8 :	Relaxed	_____
Distant	: 1 : 2 : 3 : 4 : 5 : 6 : 7 : 8 :	Close	_____
Cold	: 1 : 2 : 3 : 4 : 5 : 6 : 7 : 8 :	Warm	_____
Cooperative	: 8 : 7 : 6 : 5 : 4 : 3 : 2 : 1 :	Uncooperative	_____
Supportive	: 8 : 7 : 6 : 5 : 4 : 3 : 2 : 1 :	Hostile	_____
Boring	: 1 : 2 : 3 : 4 : 5 : 6 : 7 : 8 :	Interesting	_____
Quarrelsome	: 1 : 2 : 3 : 4 : 5 : 6 : 7 : 8 :	Harmonious	_____
Self–assured	: 8 : 7 : 6 : 5 : 4 : 3 : 2 : 1 :	Hesitant	_____
Efficient	: 8 : 7 : 6 : 5 : 4 : 3 : 2 : 1 :	Inefficient	_____
Gloomy	: 1 : 2 : 3 : 4 : 5 : 6 : 7 : 8 :	Cheerful	_____
Open	: 8 : 7 : 6 : 5 : 4 : 3 : 2 : 1 :	Guarded	_____
		Total LPC Score =	_____

Source: *A Theory of Leadership Effectiveness* by F. Fiedler. Copyright © 1967. Used with permission of McGraw-Hill Book Company.

exercise 6

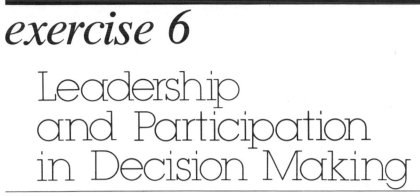

Leadership and Participation in Decision Making

Purpose

This exercise allows you to examine in some detail how Vroom and Yetton's normative theory of leadership works (see Chapter 12). Actual practice is provided using the basic framework of the model.

Instructions

Below are four short cases in which a manager must make a decision. Based on these four cases, you should make two sets of decisions. First, on your own, read each case and state whether you would make the decision by yourself, consult with your subordinates and then make the decision, or let the group of subordinates make the decision. Remember you are the supervisor and your job is to state *how* you would arrive at the decision. You are not asked to actually make the decision.

Second, after reading Chapter 12 concerning Vroom and Yetton's normative theory of leadership, read through the cases again. This time, however, you are asked to use the decision tree in Exhibit 12–7 to assist you in identifying a decision style. Following this, compare the results of your first decisions with those of your second. What do you think accounts for the difference?

CASE I You are a manufacturing manager in a large electronics plant. The company's management has recently installed new machines and put in a new simplified work system, but to the surprise of everyone, yourself included, the expected increase in productivity was not realized. In fact, production has begun to drop, quality has fallen off, and the number of employee separations has risen.

You do not believe that there is anything wrong with the machines. You have had reports from other companies that are using them and they confirm this opinion. You have also had representatives from the firm that built the machines go over them and they report that they are operating at peak efficiency.

You suspect that some parts of the new work system may be responsible for the change, but this view is not widely shared among your immediate subordinates who are four first-line supervisors, each in charge of a section, and your supply manager. The drop in production has been variously attributed to poor training of the operators, lack of an adequate system of financial incentives, and poor morale. Clearly, this is an issue about which there is considerable depth of feeling within individuals and potential disagreement among your subordinates.

This morning you received a phone call from your division manager. He has just received your production figures for the last six months and was calling to express his concern. He indicated that the problem was yours to solve in any way that you think best, but that he would like to know within a week what steps you plan to take.

You share your division manager's concern with the falling productivity and know that your workers are also concerned. The problem is to decide what steps to take to rectify the situation.

Source: Excerpted, by permission of the publisher, from "A New Look at Managerial Decision Making," V. H. Vroom, *Organizational Dynamics,* Spring, 1973, © 1973 by AMACOM, a division of American Management Associations, pp. 66–80. All rights reserved.

CASE II You are general foreman in charge of a large gang laying an oil pipeline and have to estimate your expected rate of progress in order to schedule material deliveries to the next field site.

You know the nature of the terrain you will be working across and have the historical data needed to compute the mean and variance in the rate of speed over that type of terrain. Given these two variables, it is a simple matter to calculate the earliest and latest times at which materials and support facilities will be needed at the next site. It is important that your estimate be reasonably accurate. Underestimates result in idle foremen and workers, and an overestimate results in tying up materials for a period of time before they are to be used.

Progress has been good and your five foremen and other members of the gang stand to receive substantial bonuses if the project is completed ahead of schedule.

CASE III You are supervising the work of 12 engineers. Their formal training and work experience are very similar, permitting you to use them interchangeably on projects. Yesterday, your manager informed you that a request had been received from an overseas affiliate for four engineers to go abroad on extended loan for a period of six to eight months. For a number of reasons, he argued and you agreed that this request should be met from your group.

All your engineers are capable of handling this assignment and, from the standpoint of present and future projects, there is no particular reason why anyone should be retained over any other. The problem is somewhat complicated by the fact that the overseas assignment is in what is generally regarded as an undesirable location.

CASE IV You are on the division manager's staff and work on a wide variety of problems of both an administrative and technical nature. You have been given the assignment of developing a standard method to be used in each of the five plants in the division for manually reading equipment registers, recording the readings, and transmitting the scorings to a centralized information system.

Until now there has been a high error rate in the reading and/or reporting the data. Some locations have considerably higher error rates than others, and the methods used to record and transmit the data vary among plants. It is probable, therefore, that part of the error variance is a function of specific local conditions rather than anything else, and this will complicate the establishment of any system common to all plants. You have the information on error rates but no information on the local practices that generate these errors or on the local conditions that necessitate the different practices.

Everyone would benefit from an improvement in the quality of the data; it is used in a number of important decisions. Your contacts with the plants are through the quality–control supervisors who are responsible for collecting the data. They are a conscientious group committed to doing their jobs well, but are highly sensitive to interference on the part of higher management in their own operations. Any solution that does not receive the active support of the various plant supervisors is unlikely to reduce the error rate significantly.

exercise 7

Stress Patterns and Behavior

Purpose

To provide the student with information concerning his or her own level of experienced stress (see Chapter 15).

Instructions

Below are listed fourteen questions relating to you and your life. For each question, please check yes, sometimes, or no to the left of the question in the appropriate boxes. Then, score each answer at the far left by assigning the number 3 to each yes answer, a 2 to each sometimes answer, and a 1 to each no answer. Your instructor will then show you how to tally the results.

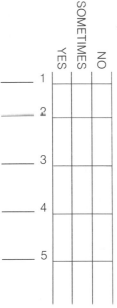

1. When working on a task, do you move rapidly?

2. Do you strive to do everything in the most efficient manner?

3. Can you enjoy doing nothing productive for several hours or days?

4. Do you wait in line patiently, as in a grocery store, bank, etc.?

5. Do you do two things at one time, such as read and eat, talk on the telephone and do something with your hands?

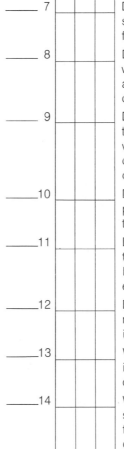

6. Do you stay relaxed when you have a deadline to meet?

7. Do you get impatient when someone else is slow or inefficient in doing a job?

8. Do you act spontaneously, without planning carefully ahead or weighing all the consequences?

9. Do you hurry through routine, repetitive acts, such as washing dishes, making out deposit slips, writing checks?

10. Do you try to hurry other people or tell them how to do things?

11. Do you live pretty much in the present, enjoying the beauty and excitement of everyday life?

12. Do you listen to others talk more than you talk about own interests?

13. When in a car, do you get impatient or angry with slow or erratic drivers?

14. When you think about your situation in life, are you satisfied with what you have accomplished?

exercise 8

Motivation Through Merit Pay Increases

Purpose

To examine the application of motivation theories to the problem of merit pay increases. To understand the relationship between motivation and performance. To consider the impact of multiple performance criteria in managerial decision making.

Instructions

Set up groups of four to eight students for the forty-five to sixty minute exercise. The groups should be separated from each other and asked to converse only with members of their own group. The participants should then read the following:

The Gordon Manufacturing Corporation is a small manufacturing company located in San Diego, California. The company is nonunionized and manufactures laboratory analysis equipment for hospitals.

Approximately one year ago, the manager of the Component Assembly Department established three manufacturing goals for the department. The goals were: (1) reduce raw material storage costs by 10 percent; (2) reduce variable labor costs (i.e., overtime) by 12 percent; and (3) decrease the number of quality rejects by 15 percent. The department manager stated to the six unit supervisors that the degree to which each supervisor met, or exceeded, these goals would be one of the major inputs into their merit pay increases for the year. In previous years, merit increases were based on seniority and an informal evaluation by the department manager.

The six department supervisors worked on separate but similar production lines. A profile of each supervisor is as follows:

Freddie McNutt: white; twenty-four; married with no children; one year with the company after graduating from a local college. First full-time job since graduation from college. He is well-liked by all employees and has exhibited a high level of enthusiasm for his work.

Sara Morton: white; twenty-eight; single; three years with the company after receiving her degree from the state university. Has a job offer from another company for a similar job that provides a substantial pay increase over her present salary (15 percent). Gordon does not want to lose Sara because her overall performance has been excellent. The job offer would require her to move to another state, which she views unfavorably; Gordon can keep her if it can come close to matching her salary offer.

Jackson Smith: black; thirty-two; married with three children; three years with the company; high-school education. One of our most stable and steady supervisors. However, he supervises a group of workers who are known to be unfriendly and uncooperative with him and other employees.

Lazlo Nagy: white; thirty-four; married with four children; high-school equivalent learning; one

Source: From *Organizational Behavior and Performance, 2nd Edition* by A. D. Szilagyi and M. J. Wallace. Copyright © 1980 by Goodyear Publishing Company, Inc. Reprinted by permission.

Exhibit 1: Individual performance for the six supervisors during the past year

Supervisor	Current Salary (000's Omitted)	Goal Attainment[a]				Manager's Evaluation[b]			
		Storage Costs (10%)	Labor Costs (12%)	Quality Rejects (15%)	Effort	Cooperativeness	Ability to Work Independently	Knowledge of Job
Freddie McNutt	$11.5	12%	12%	17%	Excellent	Excellent	Good	Good
Sara Morton	$12.5	12%	13%	16%	Excellent	Excellent	Excellent	Excellent
Jackson Smith	$12.5	6%	2%	3%	Good	Excellent	Good	Good
Lazlo Nagy	$11.5	4%	4%	12%	Excellent	Good	Fair	Fair
Karen Doolittle	$12.0	11%	10%	10%	Fair	Fair	Fair	Good
Vinnie Sareno	$12.0	8%	10%	3%	Fair	Fair	Fair	Fair

[a]Numbers designate actual cost and quality-reject reduction.
[b]The possible ratings are poor, fair, good, and excellent.

477

year with the company. Immigrated to this country six years ago and has recently become a U.S. citizen. A steady worker, well-liked by his coworkers, but has had difficulty learning English. As a result, certain problems of communication within his group and with other groups have developed in the past.

Karen Doolittle: white; twenty-nine; divorcee with three children; two years with the company; high-school education. Since her divorce one year ago, her performance has begun to improve. Prior to that, her performance was very erratic, with frequent absences. She is the sole support for her three children.

Vinnie Sareno: white; twenty-seven, single; two years with the company; college graduate. One of the best-liked employees at Gordon. However, has shown a lack of initiative and ambition on the job. Appears to be preoccupied with his social life, particularly around his recently purchased beach home.

Exhibit 1 presents summary data on the performance of the six supervisors during the past year. The presented data includes the current annual salary, the performance level on the three goals, and an overall evaluation by the department manager.

The new budget for the upcoming year has allocated a total of $79,200 for supervisory salaries in the Component Assembly Department, a $7,200 increase from last year. Top management has indicated that salary increases should range from 5 percent to 12 percent of the supervisors' current salaries and should be tied as closely as possible to their performance.

In making the merit pay increase decisions, the following points should be considered:

1. The decisions will likely set a precedent for future salary and merit increase considerations.

2. Salary increases should not be excessive, but should be representative of the supervisor's performance during the past year. It is hoped that the supervisors develop a clear perception that performance will lead to monetary rewards and that this will serve to motivate them to even better performance.

3. The decisions should be concerned with equity; that is, they ought to be consistent with each other.

4. The company does not want to lose these experienced supervisors to other firms. Management of this company not only wants the supervisors to be satisfied with their salary increases, but also to further develop the feeling that Gordon Manufacturing is a good company for advancement, growth, and career development.

Assignment:

1. Each person in the class should *individually* determine the *dollar amount* and *percentage increase* in salary for each of the six supervisors. Individual decisions should be justified by a rationale or decision rule.

2. After each individual has reached a decision, the group will convene and make the same decision as noted in (1) above.

3. After each group has reached a decision, a spokesperson for each group will present the following information to the full class:
   (a) The group's decision concerning merit pay increase for each supervisor (dollar and percentage).
   (b) The high, low, and average individual decisions in the group.
   (c) A rationale for the group's decision.

references

ABEGGLEN, J.C. Personality factors in social mobility: A study of occupationally mobile businessmen. *Genetic Psychology Monographs,* August, 1958, 101–159.

ADAMS, J.S. Injustice in social exchange. In L. Berkowitz (ed.), *Advances in experimental social psychology.* Vol. 2, New York: Academic Press, 1965.

ADLER, A. Individual psychology. Translated by S. Langer, in C. Murchison (ed.), *Psychologies of 1930.* Worcester, Mass.: Clark University Press, 1930, 398–399.

ADORNO, T.W., FRENKEL-BRUNSWIK, E., LEVINSON, D.J., and SANFORD, R.N. *The authoritarian personality.* New York: Harper, 1950.

ALDERFER, C.P. *Existence, relatedness, and growth.* New York: Free Press, 1972.

ALDERFER, C.P. A new theory of human needs. *Organizational Behavior and Human Performance,* 1969, *4,* 142–175.

ALLISON, G.T. *Essence of decision.* Boston: Little, Brown, 1971.

ALLPORT, G.W. *Pattern and growth in personality.* New York: Holt, Rinehart & Winston, 1961.

ALLPORT, G.W., and ODBERT, H.S. Trait names: A psycho-lexical study. *Psychological Monographs,* 1936, *47,* No. 211.

ALLPORT, G.W. Attitudes. In C. Murchison (ed.), *Handbook of social psychology.* Worcester, Mass.: Clark University Press, 1935, 798–844.

AMERICAN INSTITUTES FOR RESEARCH. *Project talent: Progress in education, a sample survey.* Washington, D.C., 1971.

ANDREWS, J.D.W. The achievement motive and advancement in two types of organizations. *Journal of Personality and Social Psychology,* 1967, *6,* 163–168.

ARGYLE, M. *The social psychology of work.* Harmondsworth, Middlesex: Penguin, 1972.

ARGYRIS, C. *Personality and organization.* New York: Harper, 1957.

ARGYRIS, C. Personality and organization theory revisited. *Administrative Science Quarterly,* 1973, *18,* 141–167.

ASCH, S. Forming impressions of personality. *Journal of Abnormal and Social Psychology,* 1946, *41,* 258–290.

ASCH, S. Studies of independence and conformity: A minority of one against a unanimous majority. *Psychological Monographs,* 1955, *20,* (Whole No. 416).

ATKINSON, J.W. *An introduction to motivation.* Princeton, N.J.: Van Nostrand, 1964.

ATKINSON, J.W., and RAPHELSON, A.C. Individual differences in motivation and behavior in particular situations. *Journal of Personality,* 1956, *24,* 349–363.

BALES, R.F. *Interaction process analysis: A method for the study of small groups.* Cambridge, Mass.: Addison–Wesley, 1950.

BALES, R.F., and BORGATTA, E.F. Size of group as a factor in the interaction profile. In A.P. Hare, E.F. Borgatta, and R.F. Bales (Eds.), *Small groups.* New York: Knopf, 1956.

BARNARD, C. *The functions of the executive.* Cambridge, Mass.: Harvard University Press, 1938.

BARNOWE, J.T., MANGIONE, T.W., and QUINN, R.P. The relative importance of job facets as indicated by an empirically derived model of job satisfaction. Unpublished paper, Survey Research Center, University of Michigan, 1972.

BARTOL, K.M., and BUTTERFIELD, D.A. Sex effects in evaluating leaders. *Journal of Applied Psychology,* 1976, *61,* 446–454.

BASS, B.M. *Leadership, psychology and organizational behavior*. New York: Harper & Row, 1960.

BASS, B.M. and VAUGHN, J.A. *Training in industry: The management of learning*. Belmont, Ca.: Wadsworth, 1966.

BEHLING, O., and SCHRIESHEIM, C. *Organizational behavior: Theory, research, and application*. Boston: Allyn and Bacon, 1976.

BEM, D.J. Self-perception theory. In L. Berkowitz (Ed.), *Advances in experimental social psychology*. New York: Academic Press, (1972), 1–62.

BERNARDIN, J.J., and WALTER, C.S. The effects of rater training and diary keeping on psychometric error in ratings. *Journal of Applied Psychology*, 1977, *61*, 64–69.

BERTALANFFY, L. VON. The history and status of general systems theory. *Academy of Management Journal*, 1972, *15*, 407–426.

BIRCH, D., and VEROFF, J. *Motivation: A study of action*. Monterey, Ca.: Brooks/Cole, 1966.

BLUM, P.M. *The dynamics of bureaucracy*, Chicago: University of Chicago Press, 1955.

BOSSOM, J., and MASLOW, A.H. Security of judges as a factor in impressions of warmth in others. *Journal of Abnormal and Social Psychology*, 1957, *55*, 147–148.

BRAY, D., and MOSS, J. Personnel selection. *Annual Review of Psychology*, Palo Alto, Ca.: Annual Reviews, 1972, 545–576.

BRIEF, A.P., and ALDAG, R.J. Employee reactions to job characteristics: A constructive replication. *Journal of Applied Psychology*, 1975, *60*, 182–186.

BRODY, N. *Personality: Research and theory*. New York: Academic Press, 1972.

BRUNER, J.S., and POSTMAN, L. On the perception of incongruity: A paradigm. *Journal of Personality*, 1949, *18*, 206–223.

BRUNER, J.S., and TAGIURI, R. The perception of people. In G. Lindzey (Ed.), *Handbook of social psychology*. Vol. 2 Reading, Mass.: Addison–Wesley, (1954) 601–633.

BURKE, R.J. Occupational and life strains, satisfaction, and mental health. *Journal of Business Administration*, 1969, *1*, 35–41.

BURNASKA, R.G., and HALLMAN, T.D. An empirical comparison of the relative effects of rater response bias on three rating scale formats. *Journal of Applied Psychology*, 1974, *59*, 307–312.

BURNS, T., and STALKER, G.M. *The management of innovation*. London: Tavistock, 1961.

BUSINESS WEEK, Productivity gains from a pat on the back. January 23, 1978, 56–62.

BUSINESS WEEK, Stonewalling plant democracy. March 28, 1977, 78–79.

CAMPBELL, J.P., DUNNETTE, M.D., LAWLER, E.E., and WEICK, K.E. *Managerial behavior, performance, and effectiveness*. New York: McGraw–Hill, 1970.

CAMPBELL, J.P., and PRITCHARD, R.D. Motivation theory in industrial and organizational psychology. In M.D. Dunnette (Ed.), *Handbook of industrial and organizational psychology*. Chicago: Rand McNally, 1976, 63–130.

CAPLOW, T. *Principles of organization*. New York: Harcourt, Brace, and World, 1964.

CARTWRIGHT, D., and ZANDER, A. *Group dynamics: Research and theory*. 3rd Edition. New York: Harper & Row, 1968.

CARVER, C.S., and GLASS, D.C. Coronary-prone behavior pattern and interpersonal aggression. *Journal of Personality and Social Psychology*, 1978, *36*, 361–366.

CATTELL, R.B. *The scientific analysis of personality*. Chicago: Aldine, 1965.

CHADWICK–JONES, J.K. *Automation and behavior*. New York: Wiley, 1969.

CHANDLER, A. *Strategy and structure*. Cambridge, Mass.: MIT Press, 1962.

CHAPPLE, E.D., and SAYLES, L.R. *The measure of management*. New York: Macmillan, 1961.

CHERRINGTON, D.J. Satisfaction in competitive conditions, *Organization Behavior and Human Performance*, 1973, *10*, 47–71.

COBB, S. *The frequency of the rheumatic diseases*. Cambridge, Mass.: Harvard University Press, 1971.

COBB, S. and KASL, S. Blood pressure changes in men undergoing job loss: A preliminary report. *Psychosomatic Medicine*, January/February, 1970.

COCH, L., and FRENCH, J.R.P. Overcoming resistance to change. *Human Relations*, 1948, *1*, 512–533.

COHEN, M., and NAGEL, E. *An introduction to logic and scientific method*. New York: Harcourt, Brace and Co., 1934.

COHEN, S.L., and BUNKER, K.A. Subtle effects of sex role stereotypes on recruiters' hiring decisions. *Journal of Applied Psychology*, 1975, *60*, 566–572.

COOPER, C., and PAYNE, R. *Stress at work*. London: Wiley, 1978.

COSER, L. *The functions of social conflict*. New York: Free Press, 1956.

COSTELLO, T.W., and ZALKIND, S.S. *Psychology in administration: A research orientation*. Englewood Cliffs, N.J.: Prentice–Hall, 1963.

CRUTCHFIELD, R.S. Conformity and Character. *American Psychologist*, 1955, *10*, 191–198.

CUMMINGS, L.L., and BERGER, C.J. Organization structure: How does it influence attitudes and performance? *Organizational Dynamics*. 1976, *5*, (2), 34–49.

CUMMINGS, T.G., MOLLOY, E.S., and GLEN R. A methodological critique of fifty-eight selected work experiments. *Human Relations*, 1977, *30*, 675–708.

CYERT, R., and MARCH, J.G. *A behavioral theory of the firm*. Englewood Cliffs, N.J.: Prentice–Hall, 1963.

DALKEY, N. *The delphi method: An experimental study of group opinion*. Santa Monica, Ca.: The Rand Corporation, 1969.

DEARBORN, D.C., and SIMON, H.A. Selective perception: A note on departmental identification of executives. *Sociometry*, 1958, *21*, 142.

DeCHARMS, R.C. Affiliation motivation and productivity in small groups. *Journal of Abnormal and Social Psychology*, 1957, *55*, 222–276.

DECI, E.L. The effects of contingent and noncontingent rewards and controls on intrinsic motivation. *Organizational Behavior and Human Performance*, 1972, *8*, 217–229.

DELBECQ, A., VAN DE VEN, A., and GUSTAFSON, D. *Group techniques for program planning*. Glenview, Ill.: Scott, Foresman, 1975.

DEPARTMENT OF HEALTH, EDUCATION, AND WELFARE. *Work in America*. Cambridge, Mass.: MIT Press, 1973.

DESSLER, G., and VALENZI, E.R. Initiation of structure and subordinate satisfaction: A path analysis test of path–goal theory. *Academy of Management Journal*, 1977, *20*, 251–259.

DICKSON, P. *The future of the workplace*. New York: Wybright and Talley, 1975.

DOWNEY, H.K., SHERIDAN, J.E., and SLOCUM, J.W. The path–goal theory of leadership: A longitudinal analysis, *Organization Behavior and Human Performance*, 1976, *16*, 156–176.

DOWNS, A. *Inside bureaucracy*. Boston: Little, Brown, 1967.

DUBIN, R. Stability of human organizations. In M. Haire (Ed.), *Modern organization theory*. New York: Wiley, 1959.

DUBIN, R. Supervision and productivity: Empirical findings and theoretical considerations. In R. Dubin, G. Homans, F. Mann, and D. Miller (Eds.), *Leadership and productivity*. San Francisco: Chandler, 1965.

DUBIN, R. *Theory building*. New York: The Free Press, 1969.

DUBIN, R. *World of work*. Englewood Cliffs, N.J.: Prentice–Hall, 1958.

DULWORTH, E.R. The changing world of work. Cited in E.M. Glaser, *Productivity gains through worklife improvements*. New York: Harcourt, Brace, Jovanovich, 1976, 61–62.

DUNCAN, R.B. The characteristics of organizational environments and perceived environmental uncertainity. *Administrative Science Quarterly*, 1972, *17*, 313–327.

DUNNETTE, M.D. *Performance equals ability and what?* Working paper. University of Minnesota, Minneapolis, 1972.

DUNNETTE, M.D., ARVERY, R.D., and BANAS, P.A. Why do they leave? *Personnel*, 1973, *3*, 25–39.

DUNNETTE, M.D., and KIRCHNER, W.K. *Psychology applied to industry*. New York: Appleton–Century–Crofts, 1965.

EBERT, R.J., and MITCHELL, T.R. *Organizational decision processes: Concepts and analysis*. New York: Crance, Russak, and Co., 1975.

ESPOSITO, J.P., and RICHARDS, H.C. Dogmatism and the congruence between self-reported job preference and performance among school supervisors. *Journal of Applied Psychology*, 1974, *59*, 389–391.

ETZIONI, A. *Modern organizations*, Englewood Cliffs, N.J.: Prentice–Hall, 1964.

ETZIONI, A. *A comparative analysis of comparative organizations* (Rev. ed.). New York: The Free Press, 1975.

EVANS, M. The effects of supervisory behavior on the path–goal relationship. *Organizational Behavior and Human Performance*, 1970, *5*, 277–298.

EVANS, M. Effects of supervisory behavior: Extensions of path–goal theory of motivation. *Journal of Applied Psychology*, 1974, *59*, 172–178.

EXLINE, R.V. Interrelations among two dimensions of sociometric status, group congeniality and accuracy of social perception. *Sociometry*, 1960, *23*, 85–101.

FEIN, M. Job enrichment: A reevaluation. *Sloan Management Review*, Winter 1974, 69–88.

FESHBACK, S., and SINGER, R. The effects of personal and shared threat upon social prejudice. *Journal of Abnormal and Social Psychology*, 1957, *54*, 411–416.

FESTINGER, L. Informal social communication. *Psychological Review*, 1950, *57*, 271–282.

FESTINGER, L. *A theory of cognitive dissonance*, Palo Alto, Ca.: Stanford University Press, 1957.

FIEDLER, F. Engineer the job to fit the manager. *Harvard Business Review*, 1965, *43*, 115–122.

FIEDLER, F. *A theory of leadership effectiveness.* New York: McGraw–Hill, 1967.

FIEDLER, F., and CHEMERS, M. *Leadership and effective management.* Glenview, Ill.: Scott, Foresman, 1974.

FILLEY, A., HOUSE, R.J., and KERR, S. *Managerial process and organizational behavior.* Glenview, Ill.: Scott, Foresman, 1975.

FISHBEIN, M., and AJZEN, I. *Belief, attitude, intention and behavior: An introduction to theory and research.* Reading, Mass.: Addison–Wesley, 1975.

FITCH, S.K. *Insights into human behavior.* Boston: Holbrook Press, 1970.

FLEISHMAN, E.A., and HARRIS, E.F. Patterns of leadership behavior related to employee grievances and turnover. *Personnel Psychology*, 1962, *15*, 43–56.

FRAUENFELDER, K.J. A cognitive determinant of favorability of impression. *Journal of Social Psychology*, 1974, *94*, 71–81.

FRENCH. E. Some characteristics of achievement motivation. *Journal of Experimental Psychology*, 1955, *50*, 232–236.

FRENCH, E. Effects of the interaction of motivation and feedback on task performance. In J.W. Atkinson (Ed.), *Motives in fantasy, action, and society.* Princeton, N.J.: Van Nostrand, 1958, 400–408.

FRENCH, J.R.P: Job demands and worker health. Paper presented at the 84th Annual Convention of the American Psychological Association; September 1976.

FRENCH, J.R.P., and CAPLAN, R.D. Organizational stress and individual strain. In A.J. Morrow (Ed.), *The failure of success.* New York: Amacom, 1972.

FRENCH, J.R.P., ISREAL, J., and AS, D. An experiment on participation in a Norwegian factory. *Human Relations*, 1960, *13*, 3–19.

FRENCH, J., and RAVEN, B. The bases of social power. In D. Cartwright and A. Zander (Eds.), *Group Dynamics.* New York: Harper & Row, 1968.

FREUD, S. Lecture XXXIII.*2 New introductory lectures on psychoanalysis.* New York: Norton, 1933, 153–186.

FREUD, S. *Das unbehagen in der kultur.* Vienna, 1929 (Eng. trans. Jvan Riviere, *Civilization and its discontents,* Hogarth Press, 1930).

FRIEDMAN, M., and ROSENMAN, R. *Type A behavior and your heart.* New York: Knopf, 1974.

GALBRAITH, J., and CUMMINGS, L.L. An empirical investigation of the motivational determinants of task performance: Interactive effects between valence-instrumentality and motivation–ability. *Organizational Behavior and Human Performance*, 1967, *2*, 237–258.

GARDELL, G. *Arbetsinnehall och livskvalitet.* Stockholm: Prisma, 1976.

GEORGOPOULOS, B.S., MAHONEY, G.M., and JONES, N. A path–goal approach to productivity. *Journal of Applied Psychology*, 1957, *41*, 345–353.

GERWIN, D., and TUGGLE, F. Modeling organizational decisions using the human problem solving paradigm. *Academy of Management Review*, 1978, *3*, 762–773.

GHISELLI, E.E. *Explorations in managerial talent.* Pacific Palisades, Ca: Goodyear, 1966.

GHISELLI, E.E. *The validity of occupational aptitude tests.* New York: Wiley, 1966.

GLASER, E.M. *Productivity gains through worklife improvements.* New York: Harcourt, Brace, Jovanovich, 1976.

GLASS, D.C. Stress, competition, and heart attacks. *Psychology Today,* 1976, *10*(7), 55–57, 134.

GLUECK, W.F. *Personnel: A diagnostic approach.* Dallas: BPI, 1979.

GOLDSTEIN, I.L. *Training: Program development and evaluation.* Monterey, Ca.: Brooks/Cole Publishing Co., 1975.

GOLDSTEIN, I.L. Training in work organizations. In M. Rosengweig and L. Porter (Eds). *Annual review of psychology.* Palo Alto, Ca.: Annual Reviews, 1980.

GOLEMBIEWSKI, R.T., and PROEHL, C.W. A survey of the empirical literature on flexible workhours: Character and consequences of a major innovation. *Academy of Management Review,* 1978, *3,* 837–855.

GOODMAN, P., and PENNINGS, J. *New perspectives on organizational effectiveness.* San Francisco: Jossey–Bass, 1977.

GOODMAN, P.S. Social comparison processes in organizations. In B.M. Staw and G.R. Salancik (Eds.) *New directions in organizational behavior.* Chicago: St. Clair, 1977, 97–131.

GOWLER, D., and LEGGE, K. (Eds.) *Managerial stress.* London: Wiley, 1975.

GRAEN, G. Instrumentality theory of work motivation: Some experimental results and suggested modifications. *Journal of Applied Psychology,* 1969, *53,* (2, Part 2).

GRAVES, J.P. Successful management and organizational mugging. In J. Paap (Ed.), *New directions in human resource management.* Englewood Cliffs, N.J.: Prentice–Hall, 1978.

GREENE, C.N. The satisfaction–performance controversy. *Business Horizons,* 1972, *15,* (5), 31–41.

GREER, F.L. *Small groups effectiveness.* Institute Report No. 6, Institute for Research in Human Relations, Philadelphia, 1955.

GROSS, B.M. What are your organization's objectives? A general systems approach to planning. *Human Relations,* 1965, *18,* 195–215.

GROVE, B.A., and KERR, W.A. Specific evidence on origin of halo effect in measurement of employee morale. *Journal of Social Psychology,* 1951, *34,* 165–170.

GUETZKOW, H. Communications in organizations. In J.G. March (Ed.). *Handbook of organizations.* Chicago: Rand McNally, 1965, 534–573.

GYLLENHAMMER, P.G. How Volvo adapts work to people. *Harvard Business Review,* July–August 1977, 102–113.

HACKMAN, J.R. Is job enrichment just a fad? *Harvard Business Review,* September–October 1975, 129–139.

HACKMAN, J.R. Work design. In J.R. Hackman and J.L. Suttle, *Improving life at work.* Santa Monica, Ca.: Goodyear, 1976, 96–162.

HACKMAN, J.R. Group influence on individuals. In M.D. Dunnette (Ed.), *Handbook of industrial and organizational psychology.* Chicago: Rand McNally, 1976.

HACKMAN, J.R., and LAWLER, E.E. Employee reactions to job characteristics. *Journal of Applied Psychology,* 1971, *55,* 259–286.

HACKMAN, J.R., and MORRIS, C.G. Group tasks, group interaction process, and group performance effectiveness: A review and proposed integration. In Berkowitz (Ed.), *Advances in Experimental Social Psychology.* Vol. 8, New York: Academic Press, 1975, 45–99.

HACKMAN, J.R., and OLDHAM, G.R. Motivation through the design of work: Test of a theory. *Organizational Behavior and Human Performance,* 1976, *16,* 250–279.

HACKMAN, J.R., OLDHAM, G., JANSON, R., and PURDY, K. A new strategy for job enrichment. *California Management Review,* 1975, *17*(4), 57–71.

HAIRE, M. Role-perception in labor-management relations: An experimental approach. *Industrial and Labor Relations Review,* 1955, *8,* 204–216.

HAIRE, M., and GRUNES, W.F. Perceptual defenses: Processes protecting an organized perception of another personality. *Human Relations,* 1950, *3,* 403–412.

HALL, D.T. *Careers in organizations.* Santa Monica, Ca.: Goodyear, 1976.

HALL, R.H. *Organizations: Structure and process.* Englewood Cliffs, N.J.: Prentice–Hall, 1977.

HAMNER, W.C. How to ruin motivation with pay. *Compensation Review,* 1975, 7(3), 17–27.

HAMNER, W.C. Reinforcement theory. In H.L. Tosi and W.C. Hamner (Eds.), *Organizational behavior and management: A contingency approach.* Chicago: St Clair, 1977, 93–112.

HAMNER, W.C., and HAMNER, E.P. Behavior modification on the bottom line. *Organizational Dynamics,* 1976, 4(4), 3–21.

HAMNER, W.C., and ORGAN, D. *Organizational behavior: An applied psychological approach.* Dallas: BPI, 1978.

HARE, A.P. *Handbook of small group research,* New York: The Free Press, 1976.

HARRISON, E.F. *The managerial decision-making process,* Boston: Houghton Mifflin, 1975.

HEDGES, J.N. Absence from work: A look at some national data. *Monthly Labor Review,* 1973, 96, 24–31.

HEIDER, F. *The psychology of interpersonal relations.* New York: Wiley, 1958.

HEMPEL, C.G. *Aspects of scientific explanation.* New York: The Free Press, 1965.

HERMAN, J.B., DUNHAM, R.B., and HULIN, C.L. Organizational structure, demographic characteristics, and employee responses. *Organizational Behavior and Human Performance,* 1975, 13, 206–232.

HERZBERG, F., MAUSNER, B., and SNYALERMAN, B. *The motivation to work.* New York: Wiley, 1959.

HICKSON, D.J., PUGH, D.S., and PHEYSEY, D.C. Operations technology and organizational structure: An empirical reappraisal. *Administrative Science Quarterly,* 1969, 14, 378–397.

HILGARD, E., and ATKINSON, R.C. *Introduction to psychology.* New York: Harcourt, Brace, and World, 1967.

HODGETTS, R., and ALTMAN, S. *Organizational behavior.* Philadelphia: Saunders, 1979.

HOLLANDER, E.P. *Leadership dynamics.* New York: Free Press, 1978.

HOLLMAN, T.D. Employment interviewer's errors in processing positive and negative information. *Journal of Applied Psychology,* 1972, 56, 130–134.

HOMANS, G.G. *The human group.* New York: Harcourt, Brace, and World, 1950.

HOPPOCK, R. *Job satisfaction.* New York: Harper, 1935.

HOUSE, R.J. A path–goal theory of leader effectiveness. *Administrative Science Quarterly,* 1971, 16, 321–338.

HOUSE, R.J., and BAETZ, M.L. Leadership: Some generalizations and new research directions. In B.M. Staw (Ed.), *Research in organizational behavior.* Greenwich, Conn.: JAI Press, 1979.

HOUSE, R.J., and DESSLER, G. The path–goal theory of leadership: Some *post hoc* and *a priori* tests. In J.G. Hunt and L.L. Larson (Eds.), *Contingency approaches to leadership.* Carbondale, Ill.: Southern Illinois University Press, 1974.

HOUSE, R.J., and MITCHELL, T.R. Path–goal theory of leadership. *Journal of Contemporary Business,* 1974, 5, 81–94.

HOUSE, R.J., and RIZZO, J.R. Role conflict and ambiguity as critical variables in a model of organizational behavior. *Organizational Behavior and Human Performance,* 1972, 7, 467–505.

HOVLAND, C., JANIS, I., and KELLEY, H. *Communication and persuasion.* New Haven: Yale University Press, 1953.

HOWARD, J.H., CUNNINGHAM, D.A., and RECHNITZER, P.A. Health patterns associated with Type A behavior: A managerial population: *Journal of Human Stress,* 1976, 2(1), 24–31.

IVANCEVICH, J.M., and McMAHON, J.T. A study of task–goal attributes, higher-order need strength, and performance. *Academy of Management Journal,* 1977, 20, 552–563.

IVANCEVICH, J.M., SZILAGYI, A.D., and WALLACE, M.J. *Organizational behavior and performance.* Santa Monica, Ca.: Goodyear, 1977.

JACKSON, J. Structural characteristics of norms. In I.D. Steiner and M. Fishbein (Eds.), *Current studies in social psychology.* New York: Holt, Rinehart, & Winston, 1965.

JACOBS, C.D. Job enrichment of field technical representatives—Xerox Corporation. In L.E. Davis and A.B. Cherns (Eds.), *The quality of working life.* Volume II. New York: The Free Press, 1975. 285–299.

JAGO, A. *Hierarchical level determinants of participative leader behavior*. Ph.D. dissertation, Yale University, 1977.

JAGO, A., and VROOM V.H. Predicting leader behavior from a measure of behavioral intent. *Academy of Management Journal*, 1978, *21*, 715–721.

JANIS, I.L. Groupthink. *Psychology Today*, November 1971.

JANIS, I.L. *Victims of groupthink: A psychological study of foreign–policy decisions and fiascos*. Boston: Houghton Mifflin, 1972.

JENKINS, C.D. Psychologic and social precursors of coronary disease. *New England Journal of Medicine*, 1971, *284*, 244–255 and 307–317.

JONES, S. Self and interpersonal evaluations, *Psychological Bulletin*, 1973, *80*, 185–199.

KAHN, R.L. The meaning of work: Interpretations and proposals for measurement. In A.A. Campbell and P.E. Converse (Eds.), *The human meaning of social change*. New York: Basic Books, 1972.

KAHN, R.L., WOLFE, D.M., QUINN, R.P., SNOEK, J.D., and ROSENTHAL, R.A. *Organizational stress: Studies in role conflict and ambiguity*. New York: Wiley, 1964.

KANFER, F.H. Vicarious human reinforcement: A glimpse into the black box. In L. Kresner and L.P. Ullman (Eds.), *Research in behavior modification*. New York: Holt, Rinehart & Winston, 1965, 244–267.

KANFER, F.H., and KAROLY, P. Self–control: A behavioristic excursion into the lion's den. *Behavior Therapy*, 1972, *3*, 398–416.

KAPLAN, A. *The conduct of inquiry*. San Francisco: Chandler, 1964.

KASL, S.V., SAMPSON, E.E., and FRENCH, J.R.P. The development of a projective measure of the needs for independence: A theoretical statement and some preliminary evidence. *Journal of Personality*, 1964, *32*, 566–586.

KATZ, D. Determinants of attitude arousal and attitude change. *Public Opinion Quarterly*, 1960, *24*, 1976–192.

KATZ, D., and KAHN, R. *The social psychology of organizations*. 2nd edition. New York: Wiley, 1978.

KATZELL, R.A. Personal values, job satisfaction, and job behavior. In H. Borow (Ed.), *Man in a world of work*. Boston: Houghton Mifflin, 1964, 341–363.

KEARNS, J.D. *Stress in industry*. London: Priory Press, 1973.

KELLEY, H.H. Attribution theory in social psychology. In D. Levine (Ed.), *Nebraska Symposium on Motivation*. Lincoln, Neb.: University of Nebraska, 1967.

KEMP, C.G. *Perspectives on group processes*. Boston: Houghton Mifflin, 1970.

KERR, S., and JERMIER, J. Substitutes for leadership: Their meaning and measurement. *Organizational Behavior and Human Performance*, 1978, *22*, 375–403.

KIMBLE, G.A., and GARMEZY, N. *Principles of general psychology*. New York: Ronald Press, 1963.

KIPNIS, D. Does power corrupt? *Journal of Personality and Social Psychology*, 1972, *24*, 33–41.

KLIMOSKI, R.J., and STRICTLAND, W.J. Assessment centers: Valid or merely prescient. *Personnel Psychology*, 1977, *30*, 353–361.

KLUCKHOHN, C., and MURRAY, H.A. *Personality in nature, society, and culture*. Second edition, revised and enlarged, New York: Alfred A. Knopf, 1953.

KOGAN, N., and WALLACH, M.A. Group risk taking as a function of members' anxiety and defensiveness. *Journal of Personality*, 1967, *35*, 50–63.

KORMAN, A.K. *Organizational behavior*. Englewood Cliffs, N.J.: Prentice-Hall, 1977.

KORNHAUSER, A. *Mental health of the industrial worker*. New York: Wiley, 1965.

KRETCH, D., CRUTCHFIELD, R.S., and BALLACHEY, E.L. *Individual in society*. New York: McGraw–Hill, 1962.

LANG, J., DITTRICH, J., and WHITE, S. Managerial problem solving models: A review and a proposal. *Academy of Management Review*, 1978, *3*, 854–866.

LATHAM, G.P., and YUKL, G. A review of research on the application of goal-setting in organizations. *Academy of Management Journal*, 1975, *18*, 824–845.

LAWLER, E.E., *Pay and organizational effectiveness*. New York: McGraw–Hill, 1971.

LAWLER, E.E. *Motivation in work organizations*. Monterey, Ca.: Brooks/Cole, 1973.

LAWLER E.E. New approaches to pay administration: *Personnel,* 1976, *53*(5), 11–23.

LAWLER, E.E., KULECK, W.J., JR., RHODE, J.G., and SORENSEN, J.E. Job choice and post decision dissonance. *Organizational Behavior and Human Performance,* 1975, *13,* 133–145.

LAWLER, E.E., and SUTTLE, J.L. Expectancy theory and job behavior. *Organizational Behavior and Human Performance,* 1973, *9,* 482–503.

LAWRENCE, L.C., and SMITH, P.C. Group decision and employers participation. *Journal of Applied Psychology,* 1955, *39,* 334–337.

LAWRENCE, P.R., and LORSCH, J.W. *Organization and environment.* Boston: Harvard University, Division of Research, Graduate School of Business Administration, 1967.

LEVENTHAL, G.S. Fairness in social relationships. In J. Thibaut, J. Spence, and R. Carson (Eds.) *Contemporary topics in social psychology,* Morristown, N.J.: General Learning Press, 1976.

LEVINSON, H. The psychologist in industry. *Harvard Business Review,* 1959, *37,*93–99.

LEVINSON, H., PRICE, C.R., MUNDEN, H.J., and SALLEY, C.M. *Men, management, and mental health.* Cambridge, Ma.: Harvard University Press, 1962.

LEWIN, K. Forces behind food habits and methods of change. *Bulletin of the National Research Council,* 1943, *108,* 35–65.

LEWIN, K. *A dynamic theory of personality.* New York: McGraw–Hill, 1935.

LEWIN, K. *The conceptual representation and the measurement of psychological forces.* Durham, N.C.: Duke University Press, 1938.

LIEBERMAN, S. The effects of changes in roles on the attitudes of role occupants. *Human Relations,* 1956, *9,* 385–402.

LIKERT, R. *New patterns in management.* New York: McGraw–Hill, 1961.

LITWIN, G.H., and STRINGER, R.A., JR. *Motivation and organizational climate.* Boston: Division of Research, Graduate School of Business Administration, Harvard University, 1968.

LOCKE, E.A. The motivational effects of knowledge of results: Knowledge or goal-setting? *Journal of Applied Psychology,* 1967, *51,* 324–329.

LOCKE, E.A. Toward a theory of task performance and incentives. *Organizational Behavior and Human Performance,* 1968, *3,* 157–189.

LOCKE, E.A. What is job satisfaction? *Organizational Behavior or Human Performance,* 1969, *4,* 309–336.

LOCKE, E.A. The nature and causes of job satisfaction. In M.D. Dunnette (Ed), *Handbook of industrial and organizational psychology.* Chicago: Rand McNally, 1976.

LOCKE, E.A. The myths of behavior mod in organizations. *Academy of Management Review,* 1977, *2,* 543–553.

LOCKE, E.A., and SCHWEIGER, D.M. Participation in decision-making: One more look. In B.M. Staw (Ed.), *Research in organizational behavior.* Greenwich, Conn.: JAI Press, 1979, 265–340.

LOCKE, E.A., SIROTA, D., and WOLFSON, A.D. An experimental case study of the successes and failures of job enrichment in a government agency. *Journal of Applied Psychology,* 1976, *61,* 701–711.

LOCHER, A.H., and TEEL, K.S. Performance appraisal: A survey of current practices. *Personnel Journal,* May 1977.

LOFQUIST, L., and DAWIS, R. *Adjustment to work: A psychological view of man's problems in a work–oriented society.* New York: Appleton–Century–Crofts, 1969.

LUTHANS, R. *Organizational behavior.* New York: McGraw–Hill, 1977.

LYNCH, B.P. An empirical assessment of Perrow's technology construct. *Administrative Science Quarterly,* 1974, *19,* 338–356.

MacCRIMMON, K., and TAYLOR, R. Decision–making and problem–solving. In M.D. Dunnette (Ed.), *Handbook of industrial and organizational psychology.* Chicago: Rand McNally, 1976, 1397–1453.

MACCOBY, M. *The Gamesman.* New York: Simon & Schuster, 1976.

MACY, B.A., and MIRVIS, P.H. Measuring the quality of work and organizational effectiveness in behavioral–economic terms. *Administrative Science Quarterly*, 1976, *21*, 212–226.

MAIER, N.R.F. Assets and liabilities in group problem solving: The need for an integrative function. *Psychological Review*, 1967, *47*, 239–249.

MAIER, N.R.F. *Psychology in industrial organizations*. Boston: Houghton Mifflin, 1973.

MARCH, J.G., and SIMON, H.A. *Organizations*. New York: Wiley, 1958.

MARLATT, G.A. A comparison of vicarious and direct reinforcement control of verbal behavior in an interview setting. *Journal of Personality and Social Psychology*, 1970, *16*, 695–703.

MASLOW, A.H. *Motivation and personality*. New York: Harper, 1954.

MASLOW, A.H. *Toward a psychology of being*. (Second edition). New York: Van Nostrand, 1968.

MASON, D.J. Judgements of leadership based upon physiognomic cues. *Journal of Abnormal and Social Psychology*, 1957, *54*, 273–274.

MATHIS, R.L., and JACKSON, J.H. *Personnel: Contemporary perspectives and applications*. Second edition: St. Paul: West Publishing Co., 1979.

McCLELLAND, D.C. Power is the great motivation. *Harvard Business Review*, 1976, *54*(2), 100–110.

McCLELLAND, D.C. *Power: The inner experience*. New York: Irvington, 1975.

McCLELLAND, D.C. *Assessing human motivation*. New York: General Learning Press, 1971.

McCLELLAND, D.C. Toward a theory of motive acquisition. *American Psychologist*, 1965, *20*, 321–333.

McCLELLAND, D.C. *The achieving society*. Princeton, N.J.: Van Nostrand, 1961.

McCLELLAND, D.C., ATKINSON, J.W., CLARK, R.A., and LOWELL, E.L. *The achievement motive*. New York: Appleton–Century–Crofts, 1953.

McCORMICK, E.J., and TIFFIN, J. *Industrial psychology*. Sixth edition. Englewood Cliffs, N.J.: Prentice–Hall, 1976.

McDAVID, J., and HARARI, M. *Social psychology: Individuals, groups, societies*. New York: Harper & Row, 1968.

McDOUGALL, W. *An introduction to social psychology*. London: Methuen, 1908.

McGRATH, J.E. *Social psychology: A brief introduction*. New York: Holt, Rinehart, & Winston, 1964.

McGRATH, J.E. Stress and behavior in organizations. In M.D. Dunnette (Ed.), *Handbook of industrial and organizational psychology*. Chicago: Rand McNally, 1976.

McGREGOR, D. *The human side of enterprise*. New York: McGraw–Hill, 1960.

McGUIRE, W.J. Personality and attitude change: An information-processing theory. In A.G. Greenwald, T.C. Brock, and T.M. Ostrom (Eds.), *Psychological foundations of attitudes*. New York: Academic Press, 1968, 171–196.

MEYER, H., KAY, E., and FRENCH, J.R. Split roles in performance appraisal. *Harvard Business Review*, 1965, *43*, 123–129.

MILES, R.E., PORTER, L.W., and CRAFT, J.A. Leadership attitudes among public health officials. *American Journal of Public Health*, 1966, *56*, 1990–2005.

MILES, R.H., and PERREAULT, W.D. Organizational role conflict: Its antecedents and consequences. *Organizational Behavior and Human Performance*, 1976, *17*, 19–44.

MILGRAM, S. Behavioral study of obedience. *Journal of Abnormal and Social Psychology*, 1963, *67*, 371–378.

MILGRAM, S. *Obedience to authority*. New York: Harper & Row, 1973.

MILLER, D., and STARR, M. *The structure of human decisions*. Englewood Cliffs, N.J.: Prentice–Hall, 1967.

MINER, J.B. *The management process: Theory, research, and practice*. New York: Macmillan, 1973

MINER, J.B., and DACHLER, H.P. Personnel attitudes and motivation. *Annual review of psychology*, Palo Alto, Ca.: Annual Reviews, 1973, 379–402.

MIRVIS, P.H., and LAWLER, E.E. Measuring the financial impact of employee attitudes. *Journal of Applied Psychology*, 1977, *62*, 1–8.

MITCHELL, T.R. Cognitive complexity and leadership style. *Journal of Personality and Social Psychology*, 1970, *16*, 166–174.

MITCHELL, T.R. Expectancy models of job satisfaction, occupational preference and effort: A theoretical, methodological and empirical appraisal. *Psychological Bulletin*, 1974, *81*, 1096–1112.

MITCHELL, T.R. *People in organizations*. New York: McGraw–Hill, 1978.

MITCHELL, T.R., SMYSER, C.M., and WEED, S.E. Locus of control: Supervision and work satisfaction. *Academy of Management Journal*, 1975, *18*, 263–630.

MOBLEY, W.H. Intermediate linkages in the relationship between job satisfaction and employee turnover. *Journal of Applied Psychology*, 1977, *62*, 237–240.

MOBLEY, W.H., GRIFFETH, R.W., HAND, H.H., and MEGLINO, B.M. Review and conceptual analysis of the employee turnover process. *Psychological Bulletin;* 1979, *86*, 493–522.

MORGAN, C.T., and KING, R.A. *Introduction to psychology*. Third Edition. New York: McGraw–Hill, 1966.

MORRIS, J.H. *Organizational antecedents and employee responses to role ambiguity and role conflict*. Unpublished doctoral dissertation; Graduate School of Management, University of Oregon, 1976.

MOWDAY, R.T. Equity theory predictions of behavior in organizations. In R.M. Steers and L.W. Porter (Eds.) *Motivation and work behavior*. (2nd ed). New York: McGraw–Hill, 1979.

MOWDAY, R.T., PORTER, L.W., and DUBIN, R. Unit performance, situational factors, and employee attitudes in spatially separated work units. *Organizational Behavior and Human Performance*, 1974, *12*, 231–248.

MOWDAY, R.T., and STEERS, R.M. *Research in organizations: Issues and controversies*. Santa Monica, Ca.: Goodyear, 1979.

MOWDAY, R.T., STEERS, R.M., and PORTER, L.W. The measurement of organizational commitment. *Journal of Vocational Behavior*, 1979, *14*, 224–247.

MUCHINSKY, P.M. Employee absenteeism: A review of the literature. *Journal of Vocational Behavior*, 1977, *10*, 316–340.

MURRAY, H.A. *Explorations in personality*. New York: Oxford University Press, 1938.

MUSSEN, P.H. *The psychological development of the child*. Englewood Cliffs, N.J.: Prentice–Hall, 1963.

NEFF, W.S. *Work and human behavior*. New York: Atherton, 1968.

NEWMAN, J.E. Understanding the organizationa structure–job attitude relationship through perceptions of the work environment. *Organizational Behavior and Human Performance*, 1975, *14*, 371–397.

NEW YORK NARCOTICS ADDICTION CONTROL COMMISSION. *Differential drug use within the New York State labor force*. July, 1971.

NORMAN, R.D. The interrelationships among acceptance–rejection, self–other, insight into self, and realistic perception of others. *Journal of Social Psychology*, 1953, *37*, 205–235.

NORTON, S. The empirical and content validity of assessment centers vs. traditional methods of predicting managerial success. *Academy of Management Review*, 1977, *2*, 442–453.

OMWAKE, K.T. The relation between acceptance of self and awareness of others shown by three personality inventories. *Journal of Consulting Psychology*, 1954, *18*, 443–446.

OPSAHL R.L., and DUNNETTE, M.D. The role of financial compensation in industrial motivation. *Psychological Bulletin*, 1966, *66*, 94–96.

O'REILLY, C.A., and ROBERTS, K.H. Individual differences in personality, position in the organization, and job satisfaction. *Organizational Behavior and Human Performance*, 1975, *14*, 144–150.

ORGANIZATIONAL DYNAMICS, ''At Emery Air Freight: Positive reinforcement boosts performance.'' 1973, Vol. 1, No. 3, Winter, 41–50.

PALMORE, E. Predicting longevity: A follow–up controlling for age. *The Gerontologist*, 1969, *9*, 247–250.

PARSONS, T. *Essays in sociological theory: Pure and applied*. New York: The Free Press of Glencoe, 1949.

PAYNE, R.B., and HANTY, G.T. Effect of psychological feedback upon work decrement. *Journal of Experimental Psychology*, 1955, *50*, 343–351.

PONDY, L.R. Organizational conflict: Concepts and models. *Administrative Science Quarterly*, 1967, *12*, 296–320.

PORTER, L.W. A study of perceived need satisfaction in bottom and middle management jobs. *Journal of Applied Psychology*, 1961, *45*, 1–10.

PORTER, L.W., and LAWLER, E.E. Properties of organization structure in relation to job attitudes and job behavior. *Psychological Bulletin,* 1965, *64*, 23–51.

PORTER, L.W., and LAWLER, E.E. *Managerial attitudes and performance.* Homewood, Ill.: Irwin, 1968.

PORTER, L.W., LAWLER, E.E., and HACKMAN, J.R. *Behavior in organizations.* New York: McGraw–Hill, 1975.

PORTER, L.W., and ROBERTS, K.H. Communication in organizations. In M.D. Dunnette (Ed.), *Handbook of industrial and organizational psychology.* Chicago: Rand McNally, 1976.

PORTER, L.W., and STEERS, R.M. Organizational, work, and personal factors in employee turnover and absenteeism. *Psychological Bulletin,* 1973, *80*, 151–176.

PORTER, L.W., STEERS, R.M., MOWDAY, R.T., and BOULIAN, P.V. Organizational commitment, job satisfaction, and turnover among psychiatric technicians. *Journal of Applied Psychology,* 1974, *59*, 603–609.

PRICE, J. *The study of turnover.* Ames: Iowa State University Press, 1977.

PRITCHARD, R.D. Equity theory: A review and critique. *Organizational Behavior and Human Performance,* 1969, *4*, 176–211.

RACHLIN, H. *Modern behaviorism.* San Francisco: W.H. Freeman, 1970.

REITAN, H.T., and SHAW, M.E. Group membership, sex composition of the group, and conformity behavior. *Journal of Social Psychology,* 1964, *64*, 45–51.

ROETHLISBERGER, F., and DICKSON, W.J. *Management and the worker.* Cambridge, Mass.: Harvard University Press, 1939.

ROKEACH, M. *The open and closed mind.* New York: Basic Books, 1960.

ROKEACH, M. *The nature of human values.* New York: The Free Press, 1973.

ROSEN, B., and JERDEE, T.H. Influence of sex–role stereotypes on personnel decisions. *Journal of Applied Psychology,* 1974, *59*, 9–14.

ROSEN, B., and JERDEE, T.H. The influence of age stereotypes on managerial decisions. *Journal of Applied Psychology,* 1976, *61*, 428–432.

ROSENBAUM, M.E. Social perception and the motivational structure of interpersonal relations.

Journal of Abnormal and Social Psychology, 1959, *59*, 130–133.

ROSENMAN, R., and FRIEDMAN, M. The central nervous system and coronary heart disease. *Hospital Practice.* 1971, *6*, 87–97.

ROTTER, J.B. Generalized expectancies for internal vs. external control of reinforcement. *Psychological Monographs,* 1966, *80*, 1–28.

RUCH, F.L. *Psychology and life.* Seventh Edition. Glenview, Ill.: Scott, Foresman, 1967.

RUCY, L.O., and HOLMES, T.H. Scaling of life change: Comparison of direct and indirect methods. *Journal of Psychosomatic Research,* 1971, *15*, 221–227.

RUDDOCK, R. (d.) *Six approaches to the person.* London: Routledge and Kegan Paul, 1972.

RUNYON, K.E. Some interactions between personality variables and management style. *Journal of Applied Psychology,* 1973, *57*, 288–294.

SALANCIK, G. Commitment and the control of organizational behavior and belief. In B.M. Staw and G.R. Salancik (Eds.), *New directions in organizational behavior,* Chicago: St. Clair Press, 1977, 1–21.

SANFORD, F.H., and WRIGHTSMAN, L.S., JR. *Psychology,* Third edition. Monterey, Ca.: Brooks/Cole, 1970.

SARASON, I.G., JOHNSON, J.H., BERBERICH, J.P., and SIEGEL, J.M. *Helping police officers cope with stress: A cognitive–behavioral approach.* Technical Report, Department of Psychology, University of Washington, February, 1978.

SARBIN, T.R., TAFT, R., and BAILEY, D.E. *Clinical inference and cognitive theory.* New York: Holt, Rinehart & Winston, 1960.

SCHACHTER, S. *The psychology of affiliation.* Stanford, Ca.: Stanford University Press, 1959.

SCHACHTER, S. Deviation, rejection, and communication. *Journal of Abnormal and Social Psychology,* 1951, *46*, 190–207.

SCHEIBE, K.E. *Beliefs and values.* New York: Holt, Rinehart, & Winston, 1970.

SCHEIN, E.H. Organizational socialization and the profession of management. *Industrial Management Review,* 1968, *9*, 1–16.

SCHEIN, V.E. Relationships between sex role stereotypes and requisite management characteristics among female managers. *Journal of*

Applied Psychology, 1975, *60*, 340–344.

SCHRODER, H.M., DRIVER, M.H., and STREUFERT, S. *Human information processing*. New York: Holt, Rinehart, & Winston, 1967.

SCHWAB, D.P., and CUMMINGS, L.L. Theories of performance and satisfaction: A review. *Industrial Relations*, 1970, *7*, 408–430.

SCOTT, W.E. Activation theory and task design. *Organizational Behavior and Human Performance*, 1966, *1*, 3–30.

SCOTT, W.G. *Organization theory*. Homewood, Ill.: Irwin, 1967.

SCOTT, W.G., and MITCHELL, T.R. *Organization theory: A structural and behavioral analysis*. Homewood, Ill.: Irwin, 1976.

SEARS, R.R. Experimental studies of perception: I. Attribution of traits. *Journal of Social Psychology*, 1936, *7*, 151–163.

SEASHORE, S.E., and BARNOWE, J.T. *Demographic and job factors associated with the "blue collar blues."* Working paper, University of Michigan, 1972.

SECORD, P.F. The role of facial features in interpersonal perception. In R. Tagiuri and L. Petrullo (Eds.), *Person perception and interpersonal behavior*. Stanford, Ca.: Stanford University Press, 1958, 300–315.

SECORD, P.F., and BACKMAN, C.W. *Social psychology*. New York: McGraw–Hill, 1964.

SELYE, H. *The stress of life*. New York: McGraw–Hill, 1956.

SHANNON, C., and WEAVER, W. *The mathematical theory of communication*. Urbana: University of Illinois Press, 1948.

SHARTLE, C.L. *Executive performance and leadership*. Englewood Cliffs, N.J.: Prentice–Hall, 1956.

SHAW, M.E. *Group dynamics: The psychology of small group behavior*. New York: McGraw–Hill, 1976.

SHAW, M.E., and COSTANZO, P.R. *Theories of social psychology*. New York: McGraw–Hill, 1970.

SHULL, F.A., DELBECQ, A.L., and CUMMINGS, L.L. *Organizational decision–making*. New York: McGraw–Hill, 1970.

SIMON, H.A., *Administrative behavior*. 2nd ed. New York: The Free Press, 1957.

SIMON, H.A. *The new science of management decision*. New York: Harper & Row, 1960.

SKINNER, B.F. *Science and human behavior*. New York: Macmillan, 1953.

SKINNER, B.F. Operant behavior. *American Psychologist*, 1963, *18*, 503–515.

SKINNER, B.F. *Contingencies of reinforcement: A theoretical analysis*. Englewood Cliffs, N.J.: Prentice–Hall, 1969.

SKINNER, *Beyond freedom and dignity*. New York: Alfred A. Knopf, 1971.

SLOTE, A. *Termination: The closing at Baker plant*. Ann Arbor: Institute for Social Research, University of Michigan, 1977.

SMITH, P.C., KENDALL, L.M., and HULIN, C.L. *The measurement of satisfaction in work and retirement*. Chicago: Rand McNally, 1969.

SOELBERG, P.O. Unprogrammed decision making. *Industrial Management Review*, 1967, *8*, 19–29.

SPENCER, D.G. *The influence of intrasubjective normative expectations on turnover intent*. Unpublished doctoral dissertation, Graduate School of Management, University of Oregon, 1979.

STAGNER, R. *Psychology of industrial conflict*. New York: McGraw–Hill, 1956.

STAW, B.M. Knee-deep in the big muddy: A study of escalating commitment to a chosen course of action. *Organizational Behavior and Human Performance*, 1976, *16*, 27–45.

STAW, B.M. *Intrinsic and extrinsic motivation*. Morristown, N.J.: General Learning Press, 1976.

STAW, B.M. The consequences of turnover. *Journal of Occupational Behavior*, 1980, in press.

STAW, B.M.. and FOX, F.V. Escalation: The determinants of commitment to a chosen course of action. *Human Relations*, 1977, *30*, 431–450.

STAW, B.M., and ROSS, J. Commitment to a policy decision: A multitheoretical perspective. *Administrative Science Quarterly*, 1978, *23*, 40–64.

STEERS, R.M. Task–goal attributes, n achievement, and supervisory performance. *Organizational Behavior and Human Performance*, 1975, *13*, 392–403.

STEERS. R.M. Problems in the measurement of organizational effectiveness. *Administrative Science Quarterly*, 1975, *20*, 546–558.

STEERS, R.M. Factors affecting job attitudes in a goal-setting environment. *Academy of Management Journal*, 1976, *19*, 6–16.

STEERS, R.M. When is an organization effective? A process approach to understanding effectiveness. *Organizational Dynamics*, 1976, *5*(2), 50–63.

STEERS, R.M. Antecedents and outcomes of organizational commitment. *Administrative Science Quarterly*, 1977, *22*, 46–56. (a)

STEERS, R.M. Individual differences in participative decision-making. *Human Relations*, 1977, *30*, 837–847. (b).

STEERS, R.M. *Organizational effectiveness: A behavioral view*. Santa Monica, Ca.: Goodyear, 1977. (c)

STEERS, R.M., and BRAUNSTEIN, D.N. A behaviorally based measure of manifest needs in work settings. *Journal of Vocational Behavior*, 1976, *9*, 251–266.

STEERS, R.M., and MOWDAY, R.T. The motivational properties of tasks. *Academy of Management Review*, 1977, *2*, 645–658.

STEERS, R.M., and MOWDAY, R.T. Employee turnover and post-decision accommodation processes. In L.L. Cummings and B.M. Staw (Eds.), *Research in Organizational Behavior*. Greenwich, Conn.: JAI Press, 1981.

STEERS, R.M., and PORTER, L.W. The role of task goal attributes in employee performance. *Psychological Bulletin*, 1974, *81*, 434–451.

STEERS, R.M., and PORTER, L.W. *Motivation and work behavior*. Second edition. New York: McGraw–Hill, 1979.

STEERS, R.M., and RHODES, S.R. Major influences on employee attendance: A process model. *Journal of Applied Psychology*, 1978, *63*, 391–407.

STEERS, R.M., and SPENCER, D.G. The role of achievement motivation in job design. *Journal of Applied Psychology*, 1977, *4*, 472–479.

STOGDILL, R. Personal factors associated with leadership: A survey of the literature. *Journal of Psychology*, 1948, *25*, 35–71.

STOGDILL, R. *Handbook of leadership*. New York: The Free Press, 1974.

STONE, E.F. *Research methods in organizational behavior*. Santa Monica, Ca.: Goodyear, 1978.

STRICKLAND, L.H. Surveillance and trust. *Journal of Personality*, 1958, *26*, 200–215.

SUPER, D. *The psychology of careers*. New York: Harper, 1957.

SUSSER, M. Causes of peptic ulcer: A selective epidemiologic review. *Journal of Chronic Diseases*, 1967, *20*.

TAYLOR, F.W. *The principles of scientific management*. New York: Harper, 1911.

TAYLOR, R.N., and DUNNETTE, M.D. Influence of dogmatism, risk-taking propensity, and intelligence on decision-making strategies for a sample of industrial managers. *Journal of Applied Psychology*, 1974, *59*, 420–423.

TAYLOR, R.N., and THOMPSON, M. Work value systems of young workers. *Academy of Management Journal*, 1976, *19*, 522–536.

TERKEL, S. *Working*. New York: Avon, 1972.

THIBAUT, J.W., and KELLEY, H.H. *The social psychology of groups*. New York: Wiley, 1959.

THIBAUT, J.W., and RIECKEN, H.W. Authoritarianism, status, and the communication of aggression. *Human Relations*, 1955, *8*, 95–120.

THOMAS, K.W. Conflict and conflict management. In M.D. Dunnette (Ed.), *Handbook of industrial and organizational psychology*. Chicago: Rand McNally, 1976.

THOMAS, K.W. Toward multi-dimensional values in teaching: The example of conflict behaviors. *Academy of Management Review*, 1977, *2*, 484–490.

THOMAS, K.W., and PONDY, L.R. Toward an intent model of conflict management among principal parties. *Human Relations*, 1977, *30*, 1089–1102.

THOMAS, K.W., and SCHMIDT, W.H. A survey of managerial interests with respect to conflict. *Academy of Management Journal*, 1976, 315 318.

THOMPSON, J.D. *Organizations in action*. New York: McGraw–Hill, 1967.

THORNDIKE, E.L. *Animal intelligence*. New York: Macmillan, 1911.

TOLMAN, E.C. Principles of purposive behavior. In S. Koch (Ed.), *Psychology: A study of a science*. Vol. 2. New York: McGraw–Hill, 1959.

TOSI, H., and CAROLL, S. *Management–by–objectives*. New York: Macmillan, 1973.

TOSI, H., RIZZO, J.R., and CARROLL, S. Setting goals in management by objectives. *California Management Review*, 1970, *12*(4), 70–78.

TRIANDIS, H.C. *Attitude and attitude change.* New York: Wiley, 1971.

TRIST, E. *A socio–technical critique of scientific management.* Paper presented at the Edinburgh Conference on the Impact of Science and Technology. University of Edinburgh, May 1970.

TRIST, E., and BAMFORTH, K. Some social and psychological consequences of the longwall method of goal–getting. *Human Relations*, 1951, *4*, 1–38.

TROTTER, W. *Instincts of the herd in peace and war.* New York: Macmillan, 1916.

TUCKMAN, B.W. Developmental sequence in small groups. *Psychological Bulletin*, 1965, *64*, 384–399.

TURNER, A.N., and LAWRENCE, P.R. *Industrial jobs and the worker.* Boston: Harvard University Press, 1965.

U.S. DEPARTMENT OF LABOR. *Job satisfaction: Is there a trend?* Manpower Research Monograph No. 30, 1974.

VALECHA, G.K. Construct-validation of internal–external locus of reinforcement related to work-related variables. *Proceedings,* 80th Annual Convention of the American Psychological Association, 1972, 455–456.

VAN MAANEN, J. *Organizational careers: Some new perspectives.* New York: Wiley, 1977.

VERNON, H.M. *On the extent and effects of variety in repetitive work.* Industrial Fatigue Research Board, Report No. 26. London: Her Majesty's Stationary Office, 1924.

VON NEUMANN, J., and MORGENSTERN, O. *Theory of games and economic behavior.* Princeton: Princeton University Press, 1953.

VROOM, V.H. Some personality determinants of the effects of participation. *Journal of Abnormal and Social Psychology*, 1959, *59*, 322–327.

VROOM, V.H. *Some personality determinants of the effects of participation.* Englewood Cliffs, N.J.: Prentice–Hall, 1960.

VROOM, V.H. *Work and motivation.* New York: Wiley, 1964.

VROOM, V.H. Organizational choice: A study of pre–and post–decision processes. *Organizational Behavior and Human Performance,* 1966, *1*, 212–225.

VROOM, V.H., and DECI, E.L. The stability of post decisional dissonance: A follow-up study of the job attitudes of business school graduates. *Organizational Behavior and Human Performance,* 1971, *6*, 36–49.

VROOM, V.H., and JAGO, A. Decision making as a social process: Normative and descriptive models of leader behavior. *Decision Sciences,* 1974, *5*, 743–769.

VROOM, V.H., and YETTON, P. *Leadership and decision making.* Pittsburgh: University of Pittsburgh Press, 1973.

WAHBA, M.A., and BRIDWELL, L.G. Maslow reconsidered: A review of research on the need hierarchy theory. *Organizational Behavior and Human Performance,* 1976, *15*, 212–240.

WALKER, C.R., and GUEST, R.H. *The man on the assembly line.* Cambridge, Mass: Harvard University Press, 1952.

WALL, T.D., CLEGG, C.W., and JACKSON, P.R. An evaluation of the job characteristics model. *Journal of Occupational Psychology.* 1978, *51*, 183–196.

WALTON, R.E. The diffusion of new work structures: Explaining why success didn't take. *Organizational Dynamics,* Winter 1975, 3–22.

WANOUS, J.P. Effects of a realistic job preview on job acceptance, job attitudes, and job survival. *Journal of Applied Psychology,* 1973, *58*, 327–332.

WANOUS, J. Organizational entry: Newcomers moving from outside to inside. *Psychological Bulletin*, 1977, *84*, 601–618.

WARD, L.B., and ATHOS, A.G. *Student expectations of corporate life.* Boston: Division of Research, Graduate School of Business Administration, Harvard University, 1972.

WATSON, J.B. *Behavior: An introduction to comparative psychology.* New York: Holt, Rinehart & Winston, 1914.

WEBBER, R.A. Perceptions of interactions between superiors and subordinates. *Human Relations,* 1970, Vol. 23, No. 3, 235–248.

WEICK, K.E. The concept of equity in the perception of pay. *Administrative Science Quarterly,* 1966, *11,* 414–439.

WEINER, B. *Achievement motivation and attribution theory.* Morristown, N.J.: General Learning Press, 1974.

WHITE, R.W. Motivation reconsidered: The concept of competence. *Psychological Review,* 1959, Vol. 66, No. 5, 297–333.

WHITE, S.E., MITCHELL, T.R., and BELL, C.H. Goal-setting, evaluation apprehension, and social cues as determinants of job performance and job satisfaction in a simulated organization. *Journal of Applied Psychology,* 1977, *62,* 665–673.

WILENSKY, H. Work as a social problem. In H.S. Becker (Ed.), *Social Problems: A modern approach.* New York: Wiley, 1966.

WOODWARD, J. *Management and technology.* London: Her Majesty's Stationary Office, 1958.

WORTHY, J.C. Organizational structure and employee morale. *American Sociological Review,* 1950, *15,* 169–179.

WYATT, S., LANGDON, J.N., and STOCK, F.G. Fatigue and boredom in repetitive work. Industrial Health Research Board, Report No. 37, Great Britain, 1937.

YOLLES, S.A. Mental health at work. In A. McLean (Ed.), *To work is human: Mental health and the business community.* New York: Macmillan, 1967.

YOLLES, S.F., CARONE, P.A., and KRINSKY, L.W. *Absenteeism in industry.* Springfield, Ill.: Charles, C. Thomas, 1975.

YANKELOVICH, D. We need new motivational tools. *Industry Week,* August 6, 1979.

ZALEZNIK, A. Power and politics in organizational life. *Harvard Business Review,* 1970, May–June, 47–60.

ZALKIND, S.S., and COSTELLO, T.W. Perception: Some recent research and implications for administration. *Administrative Science Quarterly,* 1962, *9,* 218–235.

ZANDER, A., and NEWCOMB, T. Group levels of aspiration in United Fund campaigns. *Journal of Personality and Social Psychology,* 1967, *6,* 157–162.

ZIMBARDO, P.G., and RUCH, F.L. *Psychology and life.* Glenview, Ill.: Scott, Foresman, 1975.

name index

subject index